PSYCHOLOGY

PSYCH

HARRY F. HARLOW

UNIVERSITY OF WISCONSIN

ALBION PUBLISHING COMPANY

SAN FRANCISCO

OLOGY

JAMES L. McGAUGH
UNIVERSITY OF CALIFORNIA, IRVINE

RICHARD F. THOMPSON
UNIVERSITY OF CALIFORNIA, IRVINE

ALBION PUBLISHING COMPANY
1736 STOCKTON STREET
SAN FRANCISCO, CALIFORNIA 94133

DESIGNER, NANCY CLARK
ILLUSTRATOR, DAVID A. STRASSMAN

Library of Congress Catalog Card Number 74-146249
ISBN 0 87843 601 4

TO PEGGY, BECKY, AND JUDITH

PREFACE

This is a book about psychology, one of the most fascinating of all subjects. We say "about" because psychology is a vast area. The American Psychological Association, which began with about 30 members, now has about 30,000. It would perhaps be more accurate to say that the field of psychology encompasses a vast number of disciplines, each concerned with the nature and causes of behavior. We have made no attempt to produce an encyclopedia. We have focused on what we regard as some of the most intriguing and important problems. Each of us is primarily responsible for approximately one-third of the chapters. You will undoubtedly recognize different approaches to the subject matter, as well as different styles of writing. You will also, no doubt, see some of our own biases in bold relief from time to time. Since the book was written by mortals, we think that this is only fitting.

This book contains many facts. We hope you will savor them, not cherish them. After all, science is very much the exchange of new facts for old ones. The book also contains many ideas, which are sometimes called hypotheses or theories. We hope you will cherish some of these, without sanctifying them. Above all, we hope you will share our deep interest in the mystifying and marvelous machinery of the mind.

We have enjoyed writing this book. We hope you will enjoy reading it.

Our deepest thanks to Helen Lauersdorf, Karen Dodd, Nancy M.

Kyle, and Brenda Longacre for their tireless and painstaking work in typing the several drafts of each chapter and handling the countless details of preparation. Although we bear full responsibility for the final manuscript, we are grateful to our colleagues for their consultation and comments on early drafts of the chapters: Herbert P. Alpern, Louis Breger, Ronald G. Dawson, Allyn C. Deets, Wilberta Donovan, Margaret Clifford, Amerigo Farina, Philip M. Groves, Philip W. Landfield, Gary S. Lynch, Gerald McClearn, Monte G. Senko, Randy M. Stothard, Stephen J. Suomi, Norman M. Weinberger, James F. Voss, and Steven F. Zornetzer.

We also wish to thank those who permitted us to quote or reproduce material from their works. Citations appear in the text, with full publication data in the bibliography. We are, of course, deeply, if not completely, indebted to all those whose work has influenced our thinking about psychology. Many of these influences are mentioned. Unfortunately greater numbers are not.

We thank our wives and children who tolerated, consoled, and helped during the period over which we worked on this book.

HARRY F. HARLOW

JAMES L. McGAUGH

RICHARD F. THOMPSON

vii

CONTENTS

PSYCHOLOGY

CHAPTER ONE

PSYCHOLOGY: THE STUDY OF BEHAVIOR

The definition of psychology has had a long and changing history. Psychology was first considered to be the study of the soul, then the study of the mind, next the study of consciousness, and lastly, the study of behavior. It has been said that psychology first lost its soul, then lost its mind, and finally lost consciousness. Psychology now is commonly defined as the study of the behavior of living organisms; depending on the methods employed and the problems attacked, it sometimes is described as the science of behavior.

All behavioral acts of human beings, normal or abnormal, appear to result from a bewildering array of intertwined and interwoven variables. There is never a single cause of any important human act. Behind every behavioral occurrence there is a series of hopelessly tangled behavioral backlashes, and no scientist or scientific technique can unravel them all.

It is a time-honored custom to use nonhuman animals as research subjects to obtain data under controlled situations as a basis for building models of behavior. As a starting point, these often are simplified models of human behavior. The first precise and accurate anatomical models

INTRODUCTION

were developed by Galen [Alexander and Selesnick, 1966], who dissected not man, but the Barbary ape, which is not an ape but a baboon. For centuries medical students had difficulty in exactly duplicating his drawings from dissection of human cadavers.

One of the first U.S. astronauts sent to secure the secrets and science of outer space was not a man, but a monkey from the Wisconsin Primate Laboratories. Through the fumbling of a lieutenant, the monkey named Able was almost able to escape from the laboratory, but he was captured by a private. The monkey entered the atmosphere safely and was ready, willing, and eager when he returned. Subsequently Able died and was buried with full military honors. His body still lies in state, but it is an unfortunate state; the Army disabled Able.

The conquest of most human diseases attests to the advantages of studying simpler nonhuman forms; the data obtained in such studies usually generalize to man. It is possible, for example, to study the source and course of a disease much more closely in a laboratory animal whose life is constantly regimented than in a human whose life is relatively unregimentable.

In behavioral research there are four fundamental reasons for using subhuman animals in specific kinds of experiments. Behavioral

3

α = 25 DEGREES
θ = 15 DEGREES

α = 90 DEGREES
θ = 45 DEGREES

FIGURE 1-1   *Geotropism in fetal rats.*

simplicity is one. All animal behaviors are the result of a vast number of variables, but in some animals a single variable, or even a single stimulus, is so dominant that it will override all others, and this dominant variable can be manipulated at will to illustrate the fact that animals are merely complex machines, whose behavior can be demonstrated to be completely lucid and lawful.

A simple form of behavior is called a *tropism*. *Heliotropism*, for example, characterizes an animal that orients and moves toward light; the more intense the light, the stronger the movement. *Geotropism* is a response to gravity. Fetal rats, prematurely delivered at fourteen days, are negatively geotropic—that is, they climb upward against the pull of gravity. At fourteen fetal days the rats cannot see, cannot hear, and cannot think [Crozier and Hoagland, 1934], and therefore distractions are held to a minimum. If they are placed on a wire-covered wooden surface, they climb upward, and the steeper the angle of the surface, the steeper their angle of climbing. The relationship between surface angle θ and climbing angle α can be expressed by a mathematical equation akin to $\theta = \log \sin \alpha$ where α is the climbing angle and θ is the angle of the surface to be climbed, as shown in Fig. 1-1. Theoretically all our behaviors could be expressed by mathematical equations if there were some way to unravel the complexity of variables.

A second reason for studying the behavior of nonhuman animals lies in the degree of control that can be exercised over their daily or even lifelong schedules of living. There have been only two human studies on the effects of prolonged partial food deprivation, and these were conducted on conscientious objectors during World Wars I and II. The overall weight of the incarcerated "volunteers" was reduced by 15 percent, and during this time their learning performance was excellent and their living acceptable; however, their love life deteriorated from the symbolic to the totally indifferent. At first they pasted pinup pictures over the walls of cubicles, but as their weight declined they lost interest in buttocks and breasts [Keys et al., 1950].

The behavioral scientist can easily control diet in rats and monkeys and test the effects of any and all dietary components on all categories of behavior. He can study protein deficiencies, vitamin deficiencies, or total starvation as they affect living, loving, and learning. Beyond these

4

three Ls there is little in life that matters. To some human beings learning does not matter; for those there are only two Ls. To a faint few human beings loving does not matter. They have only one L. Of course, when living no longer matters you are nothing but a statistic.

A third reason for using nonhuman animals as experimental subjects is that many psychological studies, like most physiological, pathological, and medical researches, are detrimental, dangerous, or even potentially lethal. The multiple incredible cruelties that society neglectfully inflicts on countless human children are unacceptable even as laboratory endeavors. No one in his right mind would plan deliberately to achieve the human "battered baby" syndrome [Helfer and Kempe, 1968].

A study of the effects of total social isolation inflicted on 20 boys and 20 girls from birth to age two would produce interesting data and extremely uninteresting children. Decades ago, a well-meaning scientist actually submitted a research proposal of this type to the National Institutes of Health, where it was, of course, summarily rejected. The disheartened scientist later became a doctor, and was very successful. He did not become a pediatrician. Since that time nonhuman experiments have told us what results this inhuman experiment would have produced [Harlow and Harlow, 1962].

Some important psychophysiological studies involve stimulation, or removal of precise areas of the brain. For obvious reasons, human mothers refuse to provide their own babies as subjects for such studies. Human adults are reluctant to offer up their brains, and many human brains would not be acceptable anyway. Hard-hearted human adolescents have never been known to volunteer. It is true that adolescents who ride high-powered motorcycles often accidentally provide neurological materials, but the brain damage is usually extensive and diffuse. (Of course there are some who may think that adolescents who ride high-powered motorcycles have little brain to lose in the first place.)

Finally, animals attain maturity relatively early, permitting a fairly rapid accumulation of data over several generations. As the population explosion roars and reverberates in the distance and we fall over each other's feet instead of into each other's arms, the problems of behavioral genetics achieve ever-increasing importance. Animal geneticists speak of improving the breed. Psychologically it would be desirable to breed the improved. There is real danger that the last thinker will be Rodin's. If so, he will have a heart of stone.

In this respect the problems of human behavioral genetics are staggering. In nonhuman animals it takes 7 to 10 generations to breed in or breed out a psychological trait, such as a specific kind of learning ability, high or low activity level, or any emotional trait including aggression or timidity [Tryon, 1940]. Human beings would make poor subjects for behavioral genetics studies of this type. Since each human generation is 30 years in length, the required 7 to 10 generations to attain a

5

genetic alteration would span 210 to 300 years. This would be the perfect way to win the Nobel Prize—posthumously. No one has ever bred creative intelligence into any animal, nonhuman or human, with the possible exception of the Huxleys in England and the Adamses in America.

Behavioral genetics experiments require rigid control in the breeding of animals. Human beings breed in a very haphazard, lackadaisical, and uncooperative way. They object to drawing their partners out of a Latin-square design; indeed, many human beings have only a single simple design in mind. If we bred for genius, many aberrant males would confuse wavy blonde hair for intellectual elegance, or their minds would be on curves other than those of normal distribution. It is pointless to criticize the females in this mythical experiment since all of these females would be women—some of them hell-bent on proving that it does not take 30 years to produce a new generation. The problems of regimenting the behavior of a control or comparative group deliberately bred to achieve stupidity is frightening. This might well be the only phase of the experiment that would succeed.

An impressive exploratory pilot study could be achieved by erecting a 30-foot wall around a corner of the Middle East. The inhabitants would be removed and the oil wells capped, thus delaying the pollution problem. Two appropriately selected sex-balanced populations would then be introduced to the area for comparative purposes—a group of bright men and women collected in Upper Slobbovia, an area whose inhabitants are known for their superior intelligence, and a group of dull men and women, collected from Lower Slobbovia, a region generally recognized for the outstanding stupidity of its populace. Seven years later the budget would be cut and the experiment would be stopped by an act of Congress. There are advantages in using nonhuman subjects.

THE ROLE OF RESEARCH IN PSYCHOLOGY

It has been stated that citation of a single authority is plagiarism, but that citation from two or more authorities is scholarship. Actually this statement gives basic information about real research. Research is designed to produce laws that have generality within all members of a species and even among members of different species.

Laymen may regard research as some esoteric, and even evil, technique that is basically incomprehensible. However, little children often automatically engage in research even though its meaning is unknown to them; also, their research techniques are slightly crude.

If you pull one hind leg off a grasshopper and observe the animal's behavior, this is probably sadism. If you pull the right hind leg off four grasshoppers, the left hind leg from another four, leave four grasshoppers intact, and observe the behavior of all of them, this could be called re-

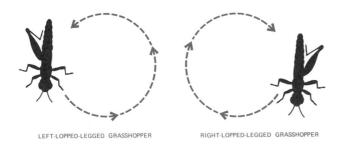

LEFT-LOPPED-LEGGED GRASSHOPPER   RIGHT-LOPPED-LEGGED GRASSHOPPER

FIGURE 1–2   *Circus movements in lopped-legged grasshoppers.*

search, since a biological experiment might reveal circus, or circular, movements in the lopped-legged grasshoppers.

You would find, as shown in Fig. 1-2, that the left-lopped-legged grasshoppers circled to the left, the right-lopped-legged grasshoppers circled to the right, and the intact grasshoppers jumped straight ahead. Experiments of this type were done by biologists 50 years ago.

For millions of years men lost in the woods have circled to the left if right-handed and circled to the right if left-handed. If an equally strong left-handed man and right-handed man hold hands and walk, they will probably go straight. If a left-handed man and a right-handed girl hold hands and go walking in the woods, the chance of their going straight is not very good, but they may have some exciting tales to tell when they return.

The most ingenious researchers are careful and methodological in planning research operations and thus in finding solutions to problems that are beyond the pale of speculation. Some years ago Edmund Jacobson, an American physiologist, developed a technique for muscle relaxation which he termed *progressive relaxation*. He trained his subjects to relax completely by directing them to exert maximal tension in a particular muscle, such as a flexor or extensor of the arm, and then to pay close attention to the sensations as the muscle was completely relaxing. Muscle after muscle was trained to relax—even the facial muscles [Jacobson, 1938].

Several decades later progressive relaxation became a basic component of a three-step behavior-therapy technique evolved by Wolpe [Wolpe and Lazarus, 1968] called *systematic desensitization*. This technique was based on the assumption not only that neurosis stems from emotional habits, but that this emotional behavior *is* the neurosis. Thus desensitization seeks to overcome anxiety by having the patient unlearn the emotional behavior associated with a specific fear-arousing situation.

The subjects were first trained in deep-muscle relaxation. Concurrent with this training they were questioned about their fears in order to construct an "anxiety hierarchy." For example, a person upset by large crowds of people would be asked to recall 10 situations or experi-

7

ences related to this fear and to arrange them in ascending order according to the degree to which they disturbed him.

Desensitization was initiated by asking the subject to imagine the least-feared situation first. While thinking of this minimal-anxiety situation the subject was instructed to relax completely. Soon he found that he was no longer anxious, even while imagining the situation. He was then asked to imagine the remaining situations in ascending order of fear arousal, relaxing completely for each one. Anxiety was inhibited through relaxation, and eventually the subject was able to reconstruct mentally the most fear-producing situation without experiencing the accompanying anxiety. In a follow-up study of many patients treated by systematic desensitization it was reported that 2 to 15 years after treatment an overwhelming majority had no recurring symptoms and that only 4 of the 249 patients had acquired new symptoms. The data were encouraging and suggested that progressive desensitization may sometimes be an effective way to treat some neuroses—particularly minor ones.

In a somewhat related vein, a series of exciting studies conducted by Miller et al. [Miller and Banuazizi, 1968; Miller and DiCara, 1968] cast some doubt on the age-old notion of scientists (as opposed to mystics) that the behavior of visceral organs, which are controlled by the autonomic nervous system, cannot be modified by learning. By definition, such physiological responses as heart rate, blood pressure, sweating, and brain waves are involuntary, and thus animals, human or otherwise, seldom learn to control them voluntarily. Trial-and-error learning—or *instrumental learning*, as it is usually called—refers to a procedure in which an animal produces the required response prior to receiving a reward.

It had been commonly assumed that responses to instrumental learning could be exhibited only in terms of the skeletal muscles, as when a rat responds by pressing a lever with its foreleg. The first problem was to convince a skeptical scientific audience of the feasibility of distinguishing between skeletal and visceral learning. By injecting rats with curare, a drug that paralyzes the skeletal muscles but does not affect the visceral muscles, Miller was able to show that changes in heart rate could be caused by direct control of the cardiac muscle rather than by the indirect control of some skeletal muscle. Even after the problem of skeletal muscle interference was resolved the researchers faced another serious problem. Physiological functions occur so rapidly that feedback must be almost instantaneous to reward the appropriate response. Take heart rate, for instance. Even with the normal heartbeat of 70 beats per minute there are constant fluctuations—minute increases or decreases in heart rate around the average. If we are interested in a decrease in an animal's heart rate, the reward must be given almost immediately after the decrease occurs, because any undue delay would reward not the decrease in heart rate, but some other event, perhaps even an increase in heart rate.

8

With the increased efficiency of modern instrumentation, feedback can be provided almost instantaneously. In an experimental situation various physiological functions can be continuously and independently monitored and a reward delivered immediately after the desired response. A reward often used for rats is electrical stimulation of pleasure centers in the brain. For humans the reward is the gratification of having made the right response, as indicated by a beep or flash of light. Obviously the rat cannot be told what response is required; this must be learned by trial and error. Miller's evidence that the involuntary visceral functions can be modified through instrumental learning astonished everyone—except perhaps Miller, who was gratified and rewarded by their astonishment.

Why do we care about controlling visceral responses? Many of us will undoubtedly care if the results found so far are substantiated by further research. Someone who has had a series of seizures or a couple of coronaries would be more than happy to learn to voluntarily reduce his heart rate from 100 beats per minute to an average of 70 beats per minute. Research on human heart patients is in fact now being conducted by Miller's research group at Rockefeller University, and it is entirely possible that by the time you would normally become susceptible to such physical malfunctions as heart attacks the means may be available for you to monitor your own cardiovascular system and correct the defects through visceral control.

Achievements of this kind do not happen overnight, but are the result of many years of investigation. Through research which entails the manipulation of many carefully controlled variables, a total picture of some manageable aspect of behavior eventually emerges.

METHODS IN BEHAVIORAL RESEARCH

All of science relies on the ability of men to observe carefully, and all scientists employ some kind of observation. However, the conditions and methods of observation vary. The techniques differ chiefly in the extent to which the experimenter makes manipulations in the environment while he observes, not in the observing *per se*. However, there are also some finer distinctions. As with all classification, the following divisions are arbitrary, but they will serve to indicate the basic techniques.

THE NATURALISTIC METHOD

A preliminary, if not always primary, technique used in all sciences and by all scientists is the naturalistic method, sometimes called the observational method. In this situation the experimenter merely observes and records data. The fact that he makes no environmental

9

manipulations while observing, not the observing *per se*, distinguishes this method from others. Astronomy, which is both the queen and mother of all other sciences, uses the naturalistic technique almost to the exclusion of other methods. Scientists cannot make suns and planets go one direction Monday, Wednesday, and Friday, and reverse directions Tuesday, Thursday, and Saturday. Sunday is no problem.

In behavioral research this naturalistic method is used in a variety of situations. In some studies, many of which are called *field studies*, direct observations are made of organisms in their natural settings. Since nearly an infinite number of responses and relationships could be recorded, the experimenter usually has a definite set of questions, exploratory or specific, which serves as a guide to the observations he will make. Subjects may range from baboons in their savanna setting in the wild of deepest Africa to a group of "wild" human five-year-olds in a preschool laboratory. The laboratory is a constructed environment, but if manipulations are not contrived by the experimenter, an investigation can be classified as a naturalistic study.

Although no manipulations are made, the experimenter may wish to control certain factors. For instance, the play activity of the preschoolers may vary greatly from the first to the second hour because of such conditions as fatigue or the length of absence from the mother. Depending on his interests, an observer might wish to record only the types of play and relationships established during either the first or second hour over a specified period of time, perhaps a few days or a few weeks. However, if the research is in the early exploratory phase, the experimenter may wish to keep fairly continuous behavioral records, such as the kind of information obtained about animals in the wilderness. Observation may be around the clock, but since experimenters are not as tireless as five-year-olds, there must be more than one experimenter if the data are to be trusted.

Although much valuable information is gained through the naturalistic method, the development and subsequent verification of psychological laws often requires the systematic manipulation of a particular variable or variables in order to determine their effects on other variables. The experimental method, to be discussed shortly, follows such a procedure. While this procedure is often a slow and tortuous one, the reward of determining causal relationships among the variables being observed more than justifies the effort.

THE RECORD-KEEPING METHOD

Another method that entails no manipulation of variables is record keeping, or record construction. In this case observation is not specifically related to environmental factors, real or constructed, as it was in the naturalistic method. A biography is an example of a record constructed to present certain limited data. From a scientist's point of view there are many pitfalls in this method of presenting data and then drawing conclusions. In general it is difficult to get a true or valid record. Specifically, most of the information is gathered "after the fact" and relies on the observer's memory. Although the writing is often fascinating, such records are almost invariably incomplete, inaccurate, biased, or all three.

Darwin [1877] and Preyer [1882] observed and recorded the daily progress of a child's sensory, motor, and intellectual development. These records are called a day-book, diary, or baby biography, and usually include a timetable of baby's firsts, such as his first smile and his first step.

The *clinical method* entails keeping records on the individual as he changes across time on some dimension, or group of dimensions, physical, mental, or emotional. Such records are, of course, often retrospective. However, from the ingenuity of many persons using this approach, various theories of personality development and intellectual growth have emerged. Total theories or aspects of theories are often verified, while new data obtained subsequently may modify or amend the original theory. The best way to tear down a theory is to replace it with a better one.

THE ASSESSMENT METHOD

In the assessment method the experimenter exerts considerable control, since he actually designs a situation, or environment, in order to assess particular characteristics of an individual or groups of individuals. An example would be the political-opinion polls in which the situation is limited to an oral interview or questionnaire designed by some interested individual. Responses from many persons are tallied, and some attempt at prediction usually follows. The perils and problems of political-opinion polls were clearly illustrated during the 1936 election campaign, when the *Literary Digest* proudly predicted that Alf Landon would defeat Franklin D. Roosevelt by a landslide. The surveyors had selected their sample population from the telephone directory and automobile-registration records. Those who were fortunate enough to own telephones and automobiles in 1936—during the very depths of the depression—represented an elite segment of the population that was hardly representative of the voting population as a whole.

Psychological testing is another example of this technique. Responses are obtained from some stimulus array, usually a series of questions, verbal or written, or a visual display. For instance, in the individualized IQ test the subject is required to respond verbally to a series of questions and to execute certain performance items indicative of nonverbal intellectual ability. From the quality and sometimes the quantity of the individual's responses a total score is obtained, but it has meaning only in relation to some preestablished norm based on the performance of others in a similar situation. The experimenter also may want to know whether the subject scores the same at a later time with a similar or identical form of the test. In this case he is determining the *correlation* between the subject's scores on the first and second tests. Let us assume that this subject and all the others tested maintained the same identical order on the second test as they exhibited on the first. Unfortunately a perfect correlation such as this seldom occurs with psychological data, but the hypothetical situation serves to make the point, which applies to other, less than perfect, correlations. Even though our experimenter has made particular manipulations in terms of setting up the situation, he cannot conclude that the score on test 1 caused the score on test 2. More than likely, some additional third factor, or multiple other factors—such as intelligence, motivation, or components of both—would have determined how individuals scored on successive tests.

THE EXPERIMENTAL METHOD

Ultimately all sciences are designed to determine causal relationships, because such relationships provide the foundation for laws and theories. Observation alone is often the first step in the development of theories either famous or forgotten. For instance, a critical creation in physics was based on simple observation and use of the observational method. It is alleged that Newton was lying on his back when he observed an apple fall, and from this casual, uncontrolled observation, the law of gravity was created. There was an important antecedent variable—the creation of Newton. From the law of gravity came the three laws of motion, and if they are read carefully, it will be seen that all apply just as well to human behavior as to falling apples. Newton's laws of motion state that (1) a material particle or body, if left to itself, will maintain its condition, either of rest or of motion, unchanged; (2) a change in the motion indicates a force due to the presence and effect of another body, and the change due to one force is the same even if there are other forces acting; and (3) to every force there is an equal and opposite reaction. They could be renamed virtue, seduction, and remorse. Someone once suggested a fourth law of motion—that buttered bread always falls butter-side down—but no physicist ever observed and quantified this law.

Remember Galileo, who simultaneously dropped a 5-pound and a 10-pound ball from the top of the leaning tower of Pisa? This act can be regarded as a controlled observational study or as an experiment, since the weight of the balls was systematically varied. Furthermore, Galileo made repetitive observations and each time obtained identical results.

12

In 1937 Lorenz, studying behavior instead of unromantic inanimate objects, observed that greylag goslings normally compulsively followed the mother goose and none other. This is a behavioral example of the observational method. Lorenz then raised goslings from birth in his company only, and the goslings compulsively followed Lorenz. Lorenz referred to this phenomenon as *imprinting*, a simple kind of learning.

The imprinting study was an experiment because the variable of motherhood, real or surrogate, was systematically varied. Like Galileo's weights, it made no difference to the goslings. (It made a significant difference to Lorenz's reputation, however.) Remember that all data are obtained from observation. The great scientist notices the most subtle and unexpected differences, the average scientist observes the large and expected differences but overlooks the subtle ones, while the poor scientist cannot even detect the large differences.

Systematic variation under controlled conditions distinguishes the experimental method from other methods. What is observed, what is held constant, and what is varied? Behavioral scientists like to talk and write about dependent variables and independent variables. In almost all cases the *dependent variable* is some motor, verbal, or physiological response. In the grasshopper experiment the dependent variable was leg movement, which was strong in the intact legs and totally absent in those legs removed. Very often behavioral scientists do not measure the muscle response, but what the muscle movements achieve. In the grasshopper experiment the experimenter did not measure the response in the legs removed. In mental tests psychologists do not measure the mind; rather, they make inferences about mental processes by measuring the spoken or written responses to questions of countless and curious kinds. In memory tests, the experimenter does not measure the movements of your tongue, lips, or larynx, but your ability to reproduce sentences, words, or jargon previously parrotted to you.

The *independent variables* are usually stimulus variables or time variables. It is the independent variables that are systematically varied in a research experiment. For example, in an experiment to measure the differential hugging responses made by baby monkeys to good cloth mothers and to evil wire mothers the dependent variable was the arm and body cling responses of the babies [Harlow, 1958; Harlow and Zimmerman, 1959]. However, instead of making direct measurements of muscular movement, the investigators measured the number of hours each day that the baby clung to each type of surrogate mother. In this case there were two independent variables. One was the age of the monkey—a measure of how clinging changes as the monkey grows older—and the other was the type of mother—cloth or wire. In graphing experimental data it is customary to plot dependent variables on the ordinate and independent variables on the abscissa. As shown in Fig. 1-3, the baby monkeys clung desperately for over 20 hours a day to the cloth mothers, but

13

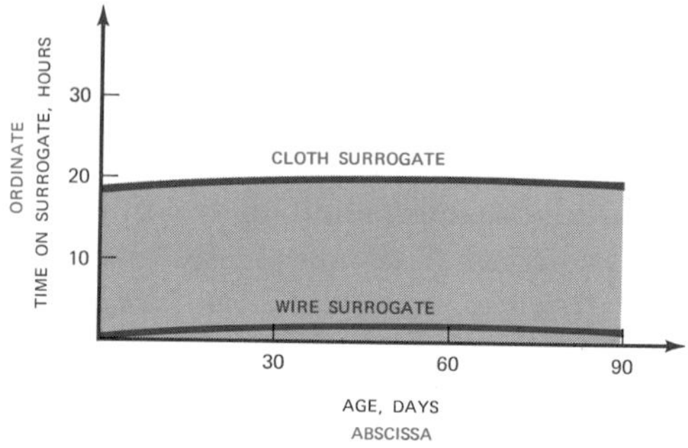

FIGURE 1–3 *Independent and dependent variables in a representative experiment.*

they clung indifferently for only 2 hours a day to the wire mothers. Aging had no effect on the differential amount of time the monkeys spent on the two types of mothers. Evidently, although wire may make fine fencing, it makes bad mothers.

NORMAL AND ABNORMAL BEHAVIOR

Although it might be argued that our ultimate goal is to make psychology the science of normal human behavior, there is both an interest in and a necessity for studying abnormal human behavior. Much of our present knowledge of normal behavior has been obtained from the investigation of disturbed, deranged, and demented people. Before Freud noted the neurotic needs of forgotten females, a large body of what is now everyday common-sense psychology and thought did not exist. Sex was a suppression, or at best a stigma, the unconscious was a lapse of momentary memory, infantile sexuality was a seething sea of sin, and the libido was unthinkable in little loved ones. Before Freud, the defense mechanisms were broken barricades hastily raised to restrain Wellington at Waterloo, Santa Ana at the Alamo, and the brutal brigands at the Bastille. Thousands of years of human analysis had never revealed the role played by the defense mechanism in normal behavior.

Probably the initial problem involved in trying to study and understand abnormal behavior is a definitional one. What is *abnormal behavior*? First, it should be emphasized that we are not talking about personal idiosyncrasies, which are the individual differences that make people and personal interactions interesting. Without them, life would indeed be dull.

Primarily, abnormality must be viewed in terms of a statistical definition. The term *abnormality* is relative and has meaning only in relation to what we accept as normal behavior. Thus normal and abnormal together form a basis for our understanding of all aspects of behavior. One must also keep in mind that abnormality is culturally defined. For many behaviors, such as sexual normality or abnormality,

14

what is abnormal in one culture is considered perfectly proper in another. The same principle holds for the many differences found between a predominant culture and its subcultures. However, in many cases a deviation from normal, such as a total break with reality, is so catastrophic that there seems to be universal agreement as to the apparently qualitative difference between them. Thus manic-depressive insanity and hysteria have been recognized as psychological entities from the time of Hippocrates to the present.

Presumably the individual displaying abnormal behavior cannot cope satisfactorily with life's stress and turmoil, and a condition we call *anxiety* typically follows. Anxiety is painful and must be managed in some manner. Each individual, through his own peculiar behavior, adapts to the situation, but often not in constructive ways. The muscle twitches or tics of a neurotic person may momentarily reduce his anxiety, but this is the only purpose the response serves; although he has found a way to partially control his ongoing anxiety, he may accomplish little else. Most of the personal methods of curbing anxiety, such as the twitches of a neurotic or the complete withdrawal of the psychotic, are crippling in an overall sense. However, the individual continues the behavior since it has momentarily reduced his anxiety in the past. Unfortunately the very behavior intended to reduce anxiety becomes in itself a source of anxiety. Thus anxiety increases still further, requiring more management, and a vicious cycle is set into motion.

In spite of an earlier comment about the seemingly qualitative difference between normal and abnormal behavior, we generally conceptualize the normality-abnormality dimension as being continuous. Drawing a sharp line between the two would be impossible, especially when we ourselves exhibit many behavioral characteristics of the neurotic individual at various times. For instance, under stress we may employ certain behavioral patterns that are more regimented and perhaps more superstitious than our ordinary behaviors. Although operating at a lesser degree, these mechanisms are similar to the obsessive-compulsive behavior of some neurotics. Furthermore, an experiment showed that before their final exams a group of psychology graduate students exhibited more characteristics similar to those of paranoid people than they did under usual circumstances. The paranoid characteristics were not lasting, however, and disappeared after the examination. Perhaps you feel the same way at test time.

In this context, the abnormal mirror is an extremely interesting psychological device in that it reflects not for us but against us. We do not see our idealized image in this mirror. There is a behavioral mirror which all of us constantly carry.

MOTHER MIRROR
Oh would some power the gift gie others
To see ourselves as did our mothers.

We now make our final decisions about definition, realizing that all definitions are arbitrary and that they are always man-made, never God-made. *Psychology* is the scientific study of animal behavior, normal and abnormal, human and nonhuman.

SUMMARY

Psychology has had many definitions through the years; it is now commonly defined as the study of behavior. Because all human behavior is so complex, it is traditional to use nonhuman subjects in psychological research in order to obtain data under controlled laboratory conditions. These data are useful in constructing simplified models as a basis for studying more complex behaviors.

Nonhuman subjects afford four fundamental advantages in behavioral simplicity. In some animals a single variable or stimulus may override the influences of all others, so that it can be systematically manipulated and observed. The simplest form of behavior is a tropism. A second advantage is the degree of control that can be exercised over laboratory animals, such as manipulation of living conditions, diet, and physiological state. A third factor is that many useful research experiments are detrimental, or even fatal, to an organism, and human subjects cannot be used in such research. Finally, many laboratory animals mature at a rapid rate, allowing for the rapid accumulation of data.

The purpose of research is to produce laws that have generality within a species and even from one species to another. The results of carefully and methodically planned research can often be applied later by others. For example, the development of progressive relaxation was later applied as the behavior-therapy technique of systematic desensitization, and instrumental learning has been shown also to be possible with such "involuntary" responses as heartbeat.

All science is based on observation, and the methods of observation vary chiefly in the extent to which the experimenter manipulates the environment as he observes. The naturalistic method, in which the experimenter makes no environmental manipulations, is often used in field studies. Record keeping and the clinical method entail recording observations across some dimension such as time. Examples of the assessment method are polls and questionnaires, in which many people are surveyed on some one characteristic, and psychological testing, in which an individual's performance at one time may be assessed against his performance at some other time. The experimental method is distinguished by systematic variation under controlled conditions in order to determine causal relationships. In a controlled observational study a dependent variable, usually some physiological or behavioral response, is measured against an independent variable, which is systematically varied.

Although the ultimate goal of psychology is an understanding of normal behavior, much of our present knowledge has been obtained from the study of abnormal behavior. In terms of human behavior no sharp line can be drawn between normality and abnormality. What we consider abnormal often varies from one culture and subculture to another, and all people exhibit some type of abnormal behavior at one time or another. Hence we generally conceptualize normality and abnormality as a continuous dimension, with the difference one of degree rather than kind. In this context abnormality provides us with an interesting reflection of all behavior.

CHAPTER TWO

BASIC CONCEPTS
OF DEVELOPMENT

All living things develop, each according to its kind. All have in common the aspect of physical growth, but motor development is limited to animate beings. Within the animal kingdom many species, especially those higher on the phylogenetic scale, are gregarious and hence social-emotional relationships develop among individuals. From this developmental process emerge the true affectional systems experienced by many mammals, especially primates, with man probably the most prominent example. Man stands alone, however, in the ability to represent his experiences symbolically and thus to create and convey to others new, abstract experiences which are not limited to direct interaction with the environment.

For human beings, as for all animals, the development of an individual begins at conception, which is defined as the moment the male sperm fertilizes the female egg. With this union two tiny entities are transformed into the creation of a new superentity, which develops through growth, maturation, and learning into the adult form of the species. *Growth* is usually limited to those aspects which increase in

DEVELOPMENT

size; *maturation* refers to those changes which appear to be genetically determined, are characterized by a fixed order of progression, are primarily irreversible, and are altered little by learning; *learning* includes those relatively permanent changes in behavior that result from practice or actively attending to the environment. The total qualitative change or the emerging and expanding capacities of the individual are termed the *developmental process*. It is an orderly and sequential process which accounts for changes in an individual from conception to death.

Like all other aspects of nature, the process of development appears to follow certain laws or principles.

CONTINUITY   From conception to death development is continuous and is interspersed with certain plateaus and spurts. We often refer for the sake of convenience to "stages of development," but any such stopping point is in the discussion, not in the process. There are, however, some aspects of growth that are more properly termed *negative* growth. For instance, the thymus gland, which is part of the lymphoid system, decreases greatly in size after puberty. Height decreases slowly but steadily after the age of twenty or thirty. Bones become less elastic with

19

age, as does the skin, and the deterioration of teeth and hair is often all too conspicuous.

EPIGENESIS   Development proceeds by epigenesis—that is, structures and systems develop in an orderly sequence—and all development takes place by building on antecedent foundations. Thus epigenesis is a process involving the emergence of new systems. This contrasts with the earlier idea that the fertilized egg was a small man and simply grew larger until reaching adult size.

DIRECTION   Physical growth occurs in two basic directions. The *anterior-posterior*, or *cephalocaudal*, gradient refers to the fact that initial growth is at the head region and progresses downward. The same principle is demonstrated in the sequence of postural and locomotor development. An infant is able to raise his chin off the floor fairly early; by two months he can also raise his chest. By six months he has more control over the whole trunk portion and can sit up, often without support.

At the same time development takes place in a *proximal-distal* direction, that is, from the midline to the periphery. This gradient is often referred to as *individuation* or *differentiation*, that is, a progression from gross or general to fine or specific control. Development proceeds from the trunk to the shoulders, out through the arms, wrists, and hands, and finally to the fingers and phalanges (fingertips)—and similarly, out through the legs to the feet and toes. From the standpoint of control, differentiation progresses from mastery of large-muscle arm movements, to the ability to grasp objects, and finally to finger manipulation of the object. The response itself is more global and undifferentiated at the outset and progresses to finer degrees of discrimination.

CRITICAL PERIOD   An organism develops in orderly sequence if it has the proper environment. However, throughout fetal life and early infancy there are apparently certain critical periods during which particular types of stimuli have some profound effect on development which they do not have at any other time. For example, German measles contracted during the third or fourth month of pregnancy may sometimes be damaging or fatal to the unborn child, but there is no evidence of this effect when the illness occurs at some other point in pregnancy. Development is also disrupted, however, by the *absence* of certain stimuli during critical periods. If an organism is deprived of light during the period when sight is developing, it may not develop normal vision no matter how much light is presented later.

Critical periods also apply in the formation of social bonds. For instance, the critical period for establishing such bonds between puppies and people seems to be from about the third to the sixth or seventh week of the puppy's life. If a puppy has absolutely no contact with

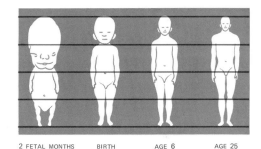

FIGURE 2-1   *Changes in body proportions during development.*

2 FETAL MONTHS   BIRTH   AGE 6   AGE 25

human beings during this period, when he is later confronted with one his reaction is extreme fear and refusal of any opportunity for inter-action [Scott, 1962]. The chances of his becoming man's best friend after the critical period has passed are pretty slim.

The existence in human infants of a critical period for establishing social bonds—represented by attachment to the mother—is more difficult to determine. Data from studies of institutionalized infants, who do not have normal mother-infant environment, offer material for speculation, but reports vary about the latest age at which a normal bond can be established. Some difficulties are reported if there has been no attachment by the end of the third month [Yarrow and Goodwin, 1960]. Although the difficulty increases with age, effective bonds have been initiated in one-year-olds [Bowlby, 1952], and some reports sug-gest that the critical period may last even as long as the age of three [Goldfarb, 1955].

One major problem is finding some objective measure of social attachment in the human infant. Caldwell [1962] suggests that the infant's ability at about six months to discriminate between his mother and other people coincides with the onset of "stranger anxiety." Thus the formation of the mother-infant bond may be related to visual dis-crimination which can be measured objectively by a visual-tracking re-sponse. The fact that institutionalized infants can still establish bonds after this age may be because exposure to several caretakers creates a more difficult discrimination problem and thus extends the critical period for establishing an effective attachment bond.

VARIATION IN BODY GROWTH   The various parts and systems of the body do not develop at a constant rate. As a result there are dramatic changes in proportion throughout the growing years (see Fig. 2-1). The head is one-half the total length at two fetal months, but from birth to maturity it does not even double in size, while during the same period the trunk portion triples and the legs increase fivefold. From birth to maturity weight increases approximately twentyfold, whereas in the brief period from fertilization to birth it increases by a factor of about 6 billion. Even during fetal life the rate of change is drastic. During the first four weeks of fetal life weight increases 40,000 times, while during the month before birth it increases by less than half.

21

Before we discuss specific areas of development let us take a look at the overall history
of a human organism from conception on.
About seven or eight days after conception
the fertilized ovum implants itself in the
thick, richly prepared decidua of the uterus.
At this point the single cell divides and becomes two complete cells,
each of which also divides so that the cell mass proliferates at a rapid
pace. As the cell mass grows, it folds in upon itself and begins to undergo
a qualitative differentiation into three germinal layers, the *endoderm*,
the *ectoderm*, and the *mesoderm*, which then develop into the organs,
tissues, and systems of the body. Until the end of the second month this
newly formed creation is called an *embryo*; from that point until birth it
is referred to as a *fetus*. At birth, about 266 days after conception, the
fetus becomes an *infant*.

At the end of the third month *in utero* the fetus develops some resemblance to a human being. By this time the internal organs are operating to some extent, in preparation for functioning independently at
birth. The heart starts to beat after the first month, and the kidneys
secrete urine by the middle of the third month. The lungs develop, although they are filled with fluid until birth, at which time the fluid is
expelled and true respiratory movement begins. Around the middle of
the fifth month the fetus is sufficiently vigorous that the mother becomes
aware of periods of activity interspersed with periods of rest. Activity
ranges from kicking and squirming to convulsive movements, often referred to as hiccups, and varies greatly for different fetuses.

A minimum of seven months *in utero* seems to be essential for vi-
ability and proper functioning after birth. A prematurely born infant
often requires special provision for warmth, nutrition, and oxygen, and
even then the rate of survival is lower than for mature or full-term babies.
Although there is a wide range, the average newborn is generally 19 to
21 inches long and weighs somewhere between 5½ and 9½ pounds. On
the average, boys are slightly longer and heavier at birth than girls. The
growth pattern of each individual, however, is fairly consistent, as indicated by the correlations of .77 for boys and .81 for girls between height
at age five and height at maturity [Tanner et al., 1956].

During the first year growth is rapid; the average infant grows 8 or
9 inches and gains 14 to 15 pounds. The pace gradually decelerates, and
during the second year there is an average gain of about 4 inches and 4
to 5 pounds. Development is then fairly even until the very rapid prepuberty growth spurt. At this point there is an exception to the cephalocaudal principle of development; the feet grow first, and then there is
an increase in leg length, while change in head size is negligible.

As shown in Fig. 2-2, the pattern of growth varies for different
body systems. The neural curve, which represents the brain, spinal cord,
and eye, shows rapid growth during the first few years, then slows down
during early childhood and reaches asymptote even before puberty. The
genital curve, which indicates growth of the reproduction organs, shows

little or no development until the prepuberty period, when there is a sudden spurt of growth. The lymphoid curve, which indicates such glands as the tonsils and lymph nodes, shows rapid growth, a peak at around age twelve, and then a decrease. Finally, the general growth curve, which includes growth of the musculature and skeleton, starts out with a rapid increase, followed by a slower but steady increase until maturity.

At birth about 25 percent of the total body weight can be attributed to muscle, 16 percent to visceral organs, and 15 percent to the central nervous system, whereas at maturity they constitute about 43, 11, and 3 percent, respectively. However, there is also some variation with sex, particularly in the amount of subcutaneous tissue, which is largely fat. Differences are negligible at birth and increase only slightly during the first year, but from the ages of one to six girls lose fat less rapidly than boys, and after six they gain it more rapidly [Tanner, 1962]. Although there are great individual variations, on the average, females reach puberty and attain maximal growth at about thirteen, approximately two years before males. However, by maturity the average male in the United States is approximately 5 feet 9 inches tall and the average female about 5 feet 4 inches. On the average this maximal height is reached by males at about nineteen or twenty and by females at about seventeen or eighteen.

It is interesting to observe that over the last several generations the rate of growth has increased and maximal growth has been attained progressively earlier [Tanner, 1962]. Data from military records indicate that males now reach their maximum height as much as two years earlier than they did 50 years ago. Moreover, average height at maturity has increased. Harvard men of the 1930s averaged 1¾ inches taller than their fathers and as much as 3 inches taller than college men in 1830 [Bowles, 1932]. The height of Norwegian soldiers has increased approximately 1½ inches over the last 100 years. Better nutrition and medical treatment are undoubtedly major factors in this change, but there is evidence that emotional stress also plays some role. Children suffer a general decline in development during wartime, and in nonwar periods stressful situations such as death in the family, divorce, or the arrival of a sibling appear to retard development temporarily.

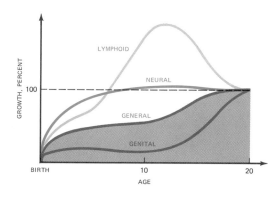

FIGURE 2-2 *Differential growth rates for various body parts.*

DEVELOPMENT

MOTOR DEVELOPMENT

During the first few years of life an individual makes astronomical strides in interacting with his environment. Mental and physical development are inseparable in this process. The general motor development and increased control over voluntary movement during the first few years of life depend both on the sequential maturation of certain behaviors and on learning of specific skills. Both these processes precede what is generally referred to as intellectual development. Two basic methods have been used to assess motor development. In the *cross-sectional method* data are collected on some specific dimension, the range of individual differences for each age group is recorded, and an average or normative value for each age is determined. Without reference to the range of values, normative figures alone may be misleading. However, normative tables such as the Gesell Developmental Schedules and Bayley's Scales of Infant Development have been used extensively to measure sensory-motor development. Ratings on such motor achievements as raising the head, crawling, and walking and such sensory-motor achievements as the ability to construct a two-cube tower are based on the age at which 50 percent of the children tested exhibit the skill in question.

In the *longitudinal method* data on the same individual are recorded over an extended period of time. For example, the Wetzel Grid shows the continuing of height-to-weight ratio for a single individual, and his development is evaluated in terms of his own particular growth pattern, without reference to his chronological age. The Iowa Growth Chart relates height and weight to chronological age, but again in terms of the individual's own pattern of growth.

The movements of a newborn infant are general and primarily reflex in nature. Many of these reflexes, such as the eye blink, have protective functions. Some, such as sneezing, coughing, sucking, and eliminating, are necessary for survival. However, the human newborn also has reflexes which have no apparent function, although their counterparts in various primates do appear to serve a definite purpose. One example is the grasp reflex, in which stimulation of the palm causes the hand to close tightly, with a grip that is brief but strong enough to support the infant's entire weight. This reflex is considerably weakened by the first month and has disappeared by the fourth month. A similar grasping response may have survival value for the baby monkey, since its sole means for remaining with the moving colony is to cling to its mother, who must have her hands free for other uses. Although it is initially a reflex, grasping behavior is voluntary in the infant monkey by the age of twenty days.

In the Moro reflex, elicited by tapping the infant's abdomen or by initiating any action which indicates that his support is not secure, the arms spread apart and come together again in a bow; the legs follow a similar action. This pattern, which disappears at about three months,

24

resembles the embracing or clinging responses of the infant monkey, whose safety depends on not becoming separated from its mother's body. In the Babinski reflex the toes extend when the sole of the foot is stimulated. This reflex gives way, sometimes as early as the fourth month, to the plantar reflex, in which the toes contract with stimulation of the sole. The persistence of any such reflex pattern long beyond the point at which it normally drops out of the infant's repertoire is usually a sign of some neurological malfunctioning.

THE BONES AND MUSCLES

As the infant matures his movements become more integrated and specialized. Maturation follows a universal progression, although the rate of development varies from infant to infant. All human babies sit before they can crawl, and they usually crawl before they walk. By the eighth or ninth month the infant is able to work his fingers and thumb in apposition. This skill, along with the freedom gained through locomotion, greatly increases his ability to interact with his environment. Further competence depends in part on the development of eye-hand coordination. In learning to grasp an object, for example, the infant starts by sweeping at it; next he raises first one hand and then the other toward the object and then turns his torso toward it. Finally, after several grasping motions in the right direction, he makes contact. This development of visually directed reaching is somewhat plastic, since the rate of development may be modified by specific experiences. The various steps in the sequence occur earlier when the infant is provided with a rich visual environment [White and Held, 1966].

The infant's neural, skeletal, and muscular systems all play a role in both motor and mental development. The skeletal framework not only supports the body, but is also constructed in such a way as to provide protection. For example, the skull encases and protects the brain, and the heart and lungs are surrounded by the ribs. In addition, the skeletal material stores minerals needed by other portions of the body, and the bone marrow manufactures certain blood cells. The marrow area is fairly diffuse at birth, and as the child grows it decreases in amount and becomes localized in specific sections of the bones. The process of ossification, the formation of bone from cartilage, begins early in embryonic life but is not fully completed until maturity.

Many differences between the infant and the adult skeleton are revealed by x ray. The infant's bones are much softer and farther apart, and the ligaments are not so firmly attached. As a result the child's skeletal structure is quite limber and flexible. There are also differences not only in the shape, but in the number of bones. Many of the 28 adult hand and wrist bones are completely lacking in the infant, and some structures that are single bones in the adult, such as the pelvis, result from the fusion of three separate bones in the infant.

25

Bones grow through the formation of new bone at the outer edges rather than by expansion of the entire structure. As they increase in length they grow toward each other until at maturity the ends meet. The rate of skeletal development, easily assessed by x rays, is often used as a single indicator of general physical growth because it is continuous from infancy to maturity, and except for a slight lag at the start, it seems to coincide with the general growth curve shown in Fig. 2-2.

In contrast to the skeletal framework, all muscle fibers are present at birth, and growth increases the length and thickness of the original fibers. The cephalocaudal principle is again demonstrated in muscular development; the earliest muscles to develop are those of the head and neck, followed by the arm, back, and leg muscles, in that order. Although the muscles of females develop at a faster rate during the fetal period, males have larger muscle fibers at birth.

THE CENTRAL NERVOUS SYSTEM

Development of the immensely important central nervous system begins in the third week after conception, and by birth essentially all the nerve cells have been formed. Later advancement consists in the development of these cells and their various processes. Behavior in the newborn is controlled primarily by subcortical brain areas, which are fairly well myelinated at birth. *Myelin*, the white substance that sheathes certain nerve fibers, results in more rapid conduction of activity along nerve fibers. The cerebral cortex is not so fully myelinated at birth.

The skull must grow rapidly to accommodate the growth of the brain. The cranial cavity increases from a capacity of 350 cubic centimeters at birth to 750 cubic centimeters at one year. By age six, and sometimes even earlier, the brain has reached its adult size of approximately 1300 cubic centimeters.

PERCEPTUAL DEVELOPMENT

Infants seem to be unable to discriminate their mothers from other people until they are several months old. In contrast, adults are able to recognize friends from a distance, step off a curb without breaking stride, and even judge the speed of an approaching automobile. This ability of the adult organism puzzled philosophers for years, antedating the more recent empirical attack on the problem by psychologists. In the past there were both philosophers and psychologists who claimed that infants were born with the ability to see the world essentially as the adult views it. They argued that during countless eons, as members of the species adjusted to the environment, only those sensory structures, neural connections, and response patterns which gave a close correspondence to the physical environment were retained, and all maladaptive structures and connections disappeared. In contrast to this "nativist" position, the "empiricists" argued that the ability to perceive form and move about in space is learned and results from the postnatal development of each individual as he interacts with the environment. In the words of William James, the infant perceives only a "blooming, buzzing confusion" upon entering the world. The crux of this early controversy was the extent to which spatial perception is learned. However, interest has since shifted to the process of perceptual development. Three basic methods have been used to obtain information about the origin and development of perceptual ability—testing after withholding visual stimulation, rearrangement of an organism's visual world for testing, and tests of the visual ability of newborns.

TESTING AFTER
WITHHOLDING VISUAL STIMULATION

Early studies of the effects of visual deprivation appeared to support the empiricist position that perceptual ability is influenced by learning. Riesen [1950] reared a chimpanzee named Debi without normal visual stimulation for seven months and then tested her for visually guided behavior. She was grossly inferior to chimps of the same age which had been reared with normal visual stimulation; she consistently bumped into things and was unable to track moving objects. From this and similar studies Riesen concluded that the deprived chimpanzees had not learned to perceive. However, since early and prolonged visual deprivation often produces ocular abnormalities and neural deterioration [Chow et al., 1957], it cannot be assumed that lack of the opportunity to learn was the sole cause of the observed deficiencies in behavior. Moreover, faulty visually guided behavior need not even indicate faulty perceptual ability. The deficiency may just as well lie in the ability to coordinate perception with the proper motor response. There is evidence, for example, that prolonged visual deprivation can also affect the functioning of neurons in the part of the cerebral cortex where pattern vision is coded.

REARRANGEMENT OF
THE VISUAL ENVIRONMENT

The second approach to determining the course of perceptual development entails a systematic displacement or rearrangement of visual input to study either innate tendencies in a newborn animal or the process of adaptation in an adult, which some investigators believe may have similar mechanisms.

Hess [1956] investigated the effect of altered vision on the pecking response of newborn chicks. After keeping chicks in the dark for the first day after they hatched, he adorned half the chicks with hoods containing prisms which displaced their visual field 7 degrees to the left or 7 degrees to the right; the visual field for the other half of the chicks was not displaced. All the chicks were then tested for pecking accuracy. Accurate pecking depends on locating the piece of grain in space and then coordinating this visual input with the pecking response. If the ability to locate in space is learned, then initial pecks should be randomly distributed around the piece of grain until a learned sensory-motor coordination enables the chick to aim directly. Moreover, if the integration of the response is completely learned, the visual displacement should have no effect, and both groups of chicks should perform similarly. If spatial location is an innate ability, however, the chicks without prisms should be able to center on target immediately, and the chicks with prisms should peck where they "saw" the grain—either 7 degrees to the left or 7 degrees to the right.

The chicks with prisms were unsuccessful in their attempts to find grain. Their pecks were consistently off target. The results indicated that a chick's ability to locate and peck grain appears to be largely innate, and also very resistant to change. Since the chicks with prisms persisted in pecking where they "saw" the grain, they were kept from starving only by being fed on a mash which did not require accurate pecking. Related studies have shown that if chicks are kept in total darkness for several weeks after they hatch, the original pecking response disappears entirely.

The sensory-motor system appears to be much more plastic in higher animals, including man. If a human's visual world is displaced by means of prism glasses, after a short period of interaction with the environment he adapts to the prisms and has no difficulty in reaching accurately for objects. Before the turn of the century it was found that adults are able to adapt after several days to a pair of glasses which inverts their visual world. This discovery generated considerable speculation that the same mechanism or mechanisms that underlie this type of adaptation may be responsible for the initial development of sensory-motor coordination. Held and Hein [1963] contend that in both cases effective adaptation depends on the correlation of self-produced movements with visual input. Thus, according to this view, proper sensory-motor coordination in the infant and effective adaptation to visual rearrangement in the adult take place only when the individual has the opportunity to make appropriate adjustments in his own movements.

To demonstrate the importance of self-produced movement for the development of sensory-motor control Held and Hein [1963] harnessed two kittens in such a way that the movements of one were completely governed by the movements of the other, which had relative freedom of activity. Thus both kittens received identical visual stimulation, consisting of alternating black and white stripes which lined the wall of the apparatus (Fig. 2-3). Both kittens were kept in the dark from birth until the experimental session began (8 to 12 weeks later), as well as during the period of the experiments when they were not in the apparatus. Thus the only difference in visual experiences of the kittens was that the active kitten had the opportunity to correlate its movements with the visual input while the passive kitten did not. After exposure to these conditions for 3 hours a day for 10 days the kittens were tested for visually guided paw placement and avoidance of a visual cliff, a device in which two depths appear beneath a sheet of glass. The passive kitten performed less well on both tasks. However, it developed appropriate visually guided behavior after it was given several days of free activity in a normal environment.

Held [1965] also demonstrated that the opportunity to correlate self-produced movement with visual input is necessary for adaptation to visual displacement in the human adult. Subjects were placed in rotating chairs in a dimly lit room and asked to adjust their chairs so that a visual target, a bright light, appeared directly in front. After training they were fitted with prisms which displaced their vision to one side. All subjects wore the prisms for the same length of time, but one group was free to move around and the other was moved around in wheelchairs. Immediately after the prisms were removed both groups were tested for ability to locate the visual target. Any error in target finding was taken as a measure of the subject's adaptation to the prisms. As with the kittens, only those subjects who had freedom of movement, and hence the opportunity to correlate their self-produced movement with visual input, showed any adjustment to correct for the effect of the prisms.

It appears from these studies that the development of accurate visually guided behavior requires the correlation of visual sensory experiences with experiences provided by self-produced movements.

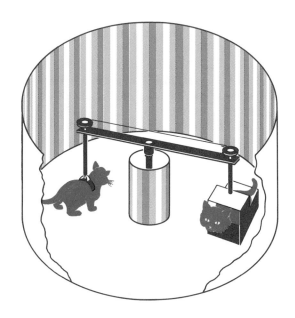

FIGURE 2-3 *Passive kitten transported by active kitten in experimental apparatus [Held and Hein, 1963].*

29

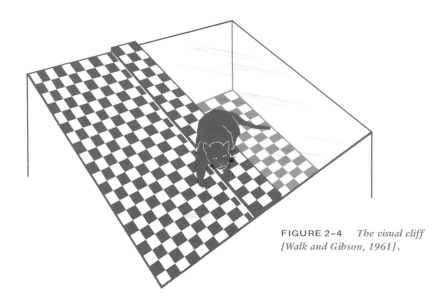

FIGURE 2-4   *The visual cliff*
[Walk and Gibson, 1961].

TESTS WITH THE NEWBORN

What does the world look like to a newborn? Our view of the perception of infants has been modified by recent experimental findings. Apparently his world is *not* entirely a "blooming, buzzing confusion." Rather, the infant discerns the same visual variables as the adult but is unable to attend to as many of them at one time.

Parents often assume that an infant falls off a couch or bed because he cannot perceive depth and misreaches for toys because of an inability to perceive distance. However, it is more likely that the infant makes such errors simply because he has not yet developed sufficient motor ability to coordinate his actions with his perception. If you were hanging on the edge of a cliff and could no longer hold on, you would not conclude that you had fallen because you were unable to perceive the depth. Nevertheless, the only way we can judge what the infant perceives is by observing his behavior. Perception is an internal process which we infer from some behavioral, verbal, or physiological response. Infants cannot talk to investigators (or parents). Hence investigators are limited to the investigation of responses which are either present at birth or develop shortly after birth. Moreover, the infant must be able to indicate this response to the investigator. Too often it is concluded that there is no response simply because the investigator is not clever enough to find a way of measuring it.

Two especially useful techniques have been developed to test the newborn's ability to perceive depth. The response most extensively studied is the *visual cliff*, devised by Walk and Gibson [1961]. As illustrated in Fig. 2-4, a centerboard is placed on a sheet of glass which is strong enough to hold the animal being tested. On the right side of the device a checkerboard pattern is placed immediately beneath the glass surface, and on the left side it is placed at floor level. Newborn animals can be tested on the visual cliff as soon as they are capable of loco-motion. Chicks, lambs, and kids, for example, can be tested when they are one day old. The animal is placed on the centerboard, and the choice of the deep or shallow side is recorded. Although the tactile stimulation provided by the surface is the same for both sides of the apparatus, all species show a consistent tendency to avoid the deep side.

Many species cannot be tested immediately after birth because they lack the necessary locomotor responses. Since it is six or seven months before human infants can crawl, it has been argued that they may learn to perceive depth during this time. A more recent technique enables us to investigate depth perception in infants as young as six weeks [Bower, 1966]. Infants were taught to turn their heads slightly when they were shown a 12-inch cube at a distance of 3 feet. In this case they could be responding to any of three variables—the retinal image of the cube shape, the 3-foot distance, or the size of the 12-inch cube. After the original training the experimenter determined which variable or combination of variables was eliciting the head turn by re-cording the responses to three other stimulus conditions. Stimulus A was a 36-inch cube placed at a distance of 9 feet, so that the retinal image was identical to the one used during training. If the retinal image had been a factor in eliciting the head-turn response, the infants would have responded in the same way. However, they responded very little to this stimulus, indicating that they could distinguish between a 12-inch cube at 3 feet and a 36-inch cube at 9 feet, even though both produced identical retinal images. Stimulus B was a 36-inch cube placed at the original training distance of 3 feet, and stimulus C was the original 12-inch cube at a distance of 9 feet. Infants consistently responded to stimuli B and C, although to a lesser extent than in the original training condition. The response to stimulus B indicates that depth or distance was a factor in eliciting the head-turn response; similarly the response to stimulus C indicates a response to the true size of an object, independent of its distance.

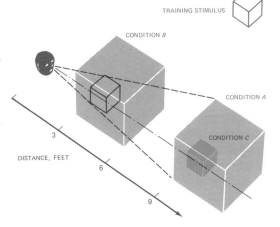

FIGURE 2-5   *Size and depth discrimination in the young infant [after Bower, 1965].*

There is increasing interest in discovering whether particular stimulus dimensions are preferred by newborns of various species. For instance, chicks start pecking as soon as they are hatched, but do they peck at any object, or are they selective? Fantz [1961] placed two- and three-dimensional round and triangular objects of various sizes behind a glass plate, presented the plate to newborn chicks, and recorded the number of pecks for each object. The responses revealed a definite preference for round three-dimensional objects, regardless of size, and given two such objects, a preference for the smaller one. Since the chick must secure its own grain and seed immediately after hatching, this preference for small, spherical objects is not surprising. Chicks preferring other objects did not become ancestors.

Fantz also investigated the visual preferences of newborn human infants by the fairly recent technique of recording eye fixations. If two different forms are presented, and the infant fixates on them for unequal periods of time, we can reasonably infer that it perceives some difference between them. Human infants only a few weeks old, or even a few days old, show distinct preferences for any patterned field, such as a face, a sheet of newspaper, or a checkerboard design. Patterns are evidently powerful stimuli; they are overwhelmingly preferred over stimuli differing only in size, brightness, and color.

The consistent preference for pattern over a homogeneous or solid field provides us with a means of testing an infant's visual acuity [Fantz, 1961]. The infant is shown a solid gray form and black-and-white striped forms with successively narrower stripes. The last point at which he expresses a preference for the stripes over the solid field is taken as a measure of his visual acuity at that age. Infants less than one month old can discriminate 1/8-inch stripes, and by six months they can discriminate 1/64-inch stripes. As resolution of visual detail increases with age, there is also an increasing preference for greater complexity of detail. For instance, the preference for an evenly spaced checkerboard gradually gives way to interest in a checkerboard with some of the squares scrambled.

A similar preference for patterned over plain forms is exhibited by infant monkeys. However, visual deprivation after birth has an interesting effect. Fantz [1965] found that after approximately eight weeks of visual deprivation infant monkeys still expressed a preference, but their preference was reversed; the deprived monkeys preferred size, brightness, and color over pattern. Evidently if infant monkeys do not experience patterned stimuli before they are three months old, their early preference for pattern disappears.

The importance of this original preference for patterned stimuli is apparent, since we rely on pattern—lines, contour, and texture—for object identification under diverse conditions. For instance, color is completely irrelevant to the task of identifying and locating a table in order to place an object on it. Similarly, except for total darkness, the condition of light, or brightness, has little or no effect on the performance of this task. Lines and contours or changes in texture give us vital information about the nature and the spatial position of all objects in our surroundings. It is little wonder that organisms have evolved in such a way that these all-important dimensions can be registered by the newborn.

Within the last few years Jean Piaget [1967] of Switzerland has provided a revolutionary and comprehensive theory of intellectual development which integrates many concepts of physics, philosophy, psychology, and biology. This impressive new approach to the question

INTELLECTUAL DEVELOPMENT

of how we acquire knowledge has been termed *genetic epistemology*. Piaget views intelligence as the individual's ability to adapt to and cope with the environment. On this basis intellectual development entails the constant organization and reorganization of thought and action and is a process which begins at birth. According to Piaget, since the structures necessary for the acquisition of knowledge are genetically influenced, the maturation stages through which all human organisms progress are the same, regardless of the rate of this progress. Intellectual development, like other aspects of development, proceeds by epigensis. Each new stage, with its own characteristics, unfolds and emerges from the stage which preceded it. This concept of emergent qualities contradicts the idea that a child's intellectual functioning differs from an adult's primarily in terms of the number of abilities. Piaget has convincingly demonstrated that the child's world is constructed very differently from that of the adult.

STAGES OF INTELLECTUAL DEVELOPMENT

Piaget has formulated four major stages of intellectual development— the sensory-motor period, the preoperational stage, the stage of concrete operations, and finally the stage of formal operations. The ages at which these stages are reached vary widely with the individual, but the succession of stages is the same for all.

THE SENSORY-MOTOR PERIOD   The preverbal behavior of the sensory-motor period, which begins at birth, is as much a part of intellectual development as the behavior accompanying verbalization, since it entails the organization of experience as the infant adapts to and copes with his environment (see Table 2-1). By systematic observation of his own infants Piaget noted six phases of this important period. Initial development centers on the newborn's innate equipment, that is, his reflexes. During the first month such reflexes as sucking become more effective and lead to the second phase, repeated simple actions such as opening and closing of the fist or kicking. These actions are apparently for their

33

TABLE 2–1   *Developmental milestones in motor and language development [Lenneberg, 1967].*

AGE	MOTOR DEVELOPMENT	VOCALIZATION AND LANGUAGE
12 weeks	Supports head when in prone position; weight is on elbows; hands mostly open; no grasp reflex	Markedly less crying than at 8 weeks; when talked to and nodded at, smiles, followed by squealing-gurgling sounds usually called cooing, which is vowel-like in character and pitch modulated; sustains cooing for 15 to 20 seconds
16 weeks	Plays with a rattle placed in his hands (by shaking it and staring at it), head self-supported; tonic neck reflex subsiding	Responds to human sounds more definitely; turns head; eyes seem to search for speaker; occasionally some chuckling sounds
20 weeks	Sits with props	Vowellike sounds begin to be interspersed with more consonant sounds; labial fricatives, spirants and nasals common; all vocalizations acoustically different from sounds of mature language
6 months	Sits: bending forward and uses hands for support; can bear weight when put into standing position, but cannot yet stand with support; reaching unilateral; no thumb apposition yet; releases cube when given another	Cooing changes to babbling resembling one-syllable utterances; neither vowels nor consonants have very fixed recurrences; most common utterances sound somewhat like ma, mu, da, or di
8 months	Stands with support; grasps with thumb apposition; picks up pellet with thumb and fingertips	Reduplication (or more continuous repetitions) becomes frequent; intonation patterns become distinct; utterances can signal emphasis and emotions
10 months	Creeps efficiently; takes side steps with support; pulls to standing position	Vocalizations mixed with sound play such as gurgling or bubble blowing; appears to wish to imitate sounds, but the imitations never quite successful; begins to differentiate between words heard by making differential adjustment
12 months	Walks when held by one hand; walks on feet and hands, knees in air; mouthing of objects almost stopped; seats self on floor	Identical sound sequences replicated with more frequency and words (mamma or dadda) emerging; definite signs of understanding some words and simple commands (show me your eyes)

DEVELOPMENT

AGE	MOTOR DEVELOPMENT	VOCALIZATION AND LANGUAGE
18 months	Grasp, prehension, and release fully developed; gait stiff, propulsive and precipitated; sits on child's chair with only fair aim; creeps; builds tower of three cubes	Has a definite repertoire of words—about 3 to 50; still much babbling, but now of several syllables with intricate intonation pattern; no attempt to communicate information and no frustration at not being understood; words may include expressions such as thank you or come here, but little ability to join any of the lexical items into spontaneous two-item phrases; understanding progressing rapidly
24 months	Runs, but falls in sudden turns; can alternate between sitting and stance; walks stairs up or down, one foot forward only	Vocabulary of more than fifty items (some children seem to be able to name everything in environment); begins spontaneously to join vocabulary items into two-word phrases; all phrases appear to be own creations; definite increase in communicative behavior and interest in language
30 months	Jumps into air with both feet; stands on one foot for about 2 seconds; takes few steps on tiptoe; jumps from chair; good hand and finger coordination, can move digits independently, manipulation of objects much improved; builds tower of six cubes	Fastest increase in vocabulary, with many new additions daily; no babbling at all; utterances have communicative intent; frustrated if not understood by adults; utterances consist of at least two words, many have three or even five words; sentences and phrases have characteristic child grammar, (rarely verbatim repetitions of an adult utterance); intelligibility not very good yet, though there is great variation among children; seems to understand everything said
3 years	Tiptoes 3 yards; runs smoothly with acceleration and deceleration; negotiates sharp and fast turns without difficulty; walks stairs by alternating feet; jumps 12 inches; can operate tricycle	Vocabulary of some 100 words; about 80% of utterances intelligible even to strangers; grammatical complexity roughly that of colloquial adult language, although mistakes still occur
4 years	Jumps over rope; hops on right foot; catches ball in arms; walks line	Language well established; deviations from the adult norm tend to be more in style than in grammar

own sake and have no specific goal. In the next phase, at about four to six months, the infant attempts to affect the environment by his actions, as in kicking a suspended toy to make it move. At seven to ten months he shows more purpose; he may kick aside one toy to obtain another. In the final phases of this first period he evidences more complex responses to a single stimulus or situation. Active exploration of the environment and the invention of new responses are characteristic.

One extremely important accomplishment during the latter part of the sensory-motor period is the concept of object permanency. At first an infant readily follows an object in his line of vision but shows no regret at its disappearance or any anticipation of its reappearance. He behaves as though objects that are out of sight do not exist. After about the ninth month he will reach for an object hidden from view provided he has watched it being hidden. During the last part of the second year, however, he will search for an object he has not seen being hidden, indicating a knowledge that the object exists independently of his own involvement with it.

THE PREOPERATIONAL STAGE   During the preoperational stage, which begins around the age of two, the acquisition of language profoundly affects the child's development. This tool enables him to visualize parts of his environment in symbolic form, so that he is no longer limited to direct responses to perception. The ability to symbolize events allows him to think of past events and thus to anticipate their recurrence in the future. The most rudimentary abstract concepts, however, do not emerge until age four or five. During the first half of the preoperational stage the child can deal with events by means of symbols, but he cannot yet manipulate the symbols—that is, he cannot reason.

During this period the child is the center of his own universe. He cannot visualize things from any viewpoint other than his own, nor is he even aware that there are other viewpoints. If he has one brother, he does not understand that his parents have two children. Since he cannot see others when he closes his eyes, he thinks that if he closes his eyes no one can see him. As a result of this egocentricity, his understanding of events is quite phenomenalistic; from his viewpoint the moon follows him as he walks down the street.

The most significant characteristic of the preoperational stage is the inability to visualize operations on form—hence Piaget's designation of this period as preoperational. The concept that a change in form is not a change in amount is not yet available at this stage, as illustrated by Piaget's classical conservation experiments. For example, two tall, thin glasses filled equally with water are placed before a child. After acknowledging that the amounts of water are the same, the child watches as one glass is emptied directly into a shorter, wider glass; he will now deny that the two amounts of water are the same. Presumably such a decision is based on some simple perceptual feature such as height, so that regardless of a corresponding increase in width, the child reasons that the shorter glass must hold less water.

THE STAGE OF CONCRETE OPERATIONS   Several new and important abilities emerge at the age of six or seven, as the child enters the stage of concrete operations. One is attainment of the concept of conservation of quantity. The child now understands that liquids and solids can change in shape without changing in amount. Similarly, before the age of six or seven a child cannot handle the concept of length. If sticks of the same length are laid parallel to each other with the ends aligned, he will judge them to be of equal length. If one stick is then moved forward a short distance, he will insist that the one which was moved forward is now longer. Presumably he cannot attend to the front and back ends of the sticks simultaneously, and again it appears to be the perceptual aspect of the single edge that guides his decision. By the age of six or seven the concept of length enables him to judge the lengths of the sticks as equal in length despite the superficial change of moving one of them.

The concept of weight is attained a few years later, during the ninth or tenth year. A child is said to have attained this concept when one of two identical clay balls is cut into several pieces and he responds that the pieces still total the same weight.

Another important step is the concept of number. This concept does not coincide with the ability to count. A child is able to count before he can reason that the number of objects is constant regardless of their arrangement. If two identical rows of pennies are presented to a child at the preoperational stage, he will say that each row contains the same number of pennies, and if the pennies in one row are then spread apart, he will maintain that the longer row now contains more pennies. Not until the stage of concrete operations is he able to see that the number of pennies in both rows is still the same.

In addition to acquiring the flexibility which allows him to comprehend transformation on events, the child makes other important advances during this period. He is now able to visualize a series of actions. Although he has already learned to *perform* a series of actions, such as walking several blocks to school, until this point he is unable to draw even a simple map of his route because he cannot reproduce the walk in his mind. As he emerges from his strong egocentricity he starts to differentiate between himself and his environment. He begins to realize that for the moon to follow him it would also have to follow other people, and since it cannot follow everyone at the same time, he eventually deduces that it only appears to follow him. Up to this point he has seen others only in terms of their relationship to him. He now begins to visualize his own relationship to someone else and realizes for the first time that his brother also has a brother. As he becomes aware that his viewpoint is only one of many the capacity for true cooperation with others finally emerges.

37

THE STAGE OF FORMAL OPERATIONS   It is only during the stage of formal operations, which begins around the age of twelve, that a child attains the ability to think in abstract terms. From this point on he becomes able not only to isolate the relevant factors in a problem and systematically manipulate the possible solutions in his mind, but also to draw conclusions from purely abstract hypotheses which have no reference to concrete observations.

RATE OF INTELLECTUAL DEVELOPMENT

Piaget's formulations have contributed substantially to our understanding of the intellectual development of the young child. Although there has been little formal research on either the sensory-motor stage or the first part of the preoperational stage to confirm Piaget's observations on his own infants, his views on formation of the concept of conservation have generated an abundance of research. There is general agreement on the successive steps in which this concept is attained. However, the studies show great variation in the ages at which they are reached, including reports that Middle-Eastern children frequently lag behind Western children [Hyde, in Flavell, 1963] and that children from the French West Indian island of Martinique are as much as four years behind children in Montreal, Canada [Laurendeau and Pinnard, 1963]. Some observations also seem to be at variance with Piaget's contention that once the concept of conservation of substance has been attained it is generalized to all situations involving conservation of substance. Studies by Lovell [1961] show that children who have attained this concept in one situation cannot necessarily apply it in another.

Bayley [1968] has investigated the rate at which infants and children reach the various stages of development. Bayley's Scales of Psychomotor Development, which measure many motor and perceptual abilities of the very young child, were recently standardized on a large national sample, and the average or median age for various items was recorded. The items range from the ability to say two words, at an average age of 14.2 months; to the ability to mend a broken doll, at an average age of 23.6 months; to the ability to name three objects, at an average age of 24.9 months. A child's score is based on his performance on all items. It is thus possible to assess his rate of progress in terms of some standard.

The extent to which future intellectual performance can be predicted from performance on these tests in infancy is of particular interest. The data show that infant tests are entirely unreliable indicators because performance on later tests of intelligence is based on different abilities. Infant tests are based on sensory-motor achievement, while the later tests rely heavily on language, abstract thinking, reasoning, and memory ability. Studies by Honzik [1938] and Bayley [1943] suggest that a child must be at least two, and perhaps older, for minimum reliability in predicting future ability from these scales.

38

A different approach was taken by Kagan et al. [1964], who demonstrated that some consistent individual differences in cognitive ability arise from personality factors. One such dimension, called *reflection-impulsivity*, refers to an individual's tendency to reflect on alternatives in a given situation. Because a reflective child spends more time considering his response, he makes fewer errors than the impulsive child. However, the tendency to make considered decisions does not necessarily indicate greater intelligence than the ability to make quick decisions. This general trait seems to hold across a variety of tasks, suggesting that measured differences in cognitive performance may in part reflect different styles of conceptualization rather than differences in intellectual ability.

Bruner [1964] accounts for intellectual development in terms of various means of representing reality at different stages. This concept is similar but not directly parallel to Piaget's formulation. According to Bruner, an infant first represents events through action. This stage of *inactive representation* encompasses aspects of Piaget's sensory-motor and preoperational stages. For example, a child cannot map his way to school because at this stage he can represent his reality only through actions. The next stage is representation through imagery or *iconic representation*, which is similar to Piaget's stage of formal operations. This achievement greatly increases the child's cognitive power, since the use of symbols enables him to rearrange events in combinations never experienced directly, thus freeing him from the need to respond solely in terms of immediate perceptual aspects of the environment. Bruner seems to differ from Piaget chiefly in his emphasis on the role of culturally transmitted skills in intellectual development. He stresses that cognitive growth depends on the "unlocking of capacity by techniques that come from exposure to specialized environments of culture."

Language is a prime example of a cultural technique which affects cognitive growth. Hess and Shipman [1965] investigated the influence of language on cognitive functioning in three groups of urban black mothers and their four-year-old children. The three groups were defined as upper middle class, represented by college-educated persons in the professions; upper lower class, represented by persons from skilled blue-collar occupations; and lower lower class, represented by persons with elementary school education employed in unskilled occupations. All interviews and tests were conducted in the homes, and mother-child interactions were observed. There appeared to be little difference in the emotional attitudes of mothers in the various groups, but the verbal and cognitive environments they provided were quite different. Middle-class mothers provided their children with a greater verbal output—they spoke more words to their children. Moreover, their verbal expression exhibited greater complexity of thought and detail. In other words, there was not just a quantitative difference, but also a qualitative difference in cognitive environments to which these children were exposed. These environmental differences were reflected in the children's performance on such cognitive tasks as sorting cards into classes or categories, which presumably measures the level of abstract thinking needed to perceive and order environmental objects. Evidently exposure to more effective linguistic representation of the environment equips the child to speculate on more alternate approaches to a problem and thus to deal with more complex problems.

We still have little understanding of the actual process by which a child learns language. Theories of language development fall into two basic categories. One is the simple imitation-learning approach, where it is assumed that the infant's random babbling is shaped through appropriate rewards until it resembles adult sounds [Mowrer, 1960; Skinner, 1957]. The other view is that children come to know the structure of language—grammar and syntax—rather than simply learning words [Brown and Fraser, 1964]. There is also a third, more extreme position that the basic universal aspects of language are innate and "wired into the brain" [Chomsky, 1965]. Imitation is evidently not a necessary condition, since children who can hear but cannot speak learn language perfectly well [Lenneberg, 1962]. However, one condition on which all theorists agree is that a child must *hear* the language. This corresponds with the findings of Hess and Shipman that the quantity and quality of language a child hears is directly related to his cognitive functioning.

Whether the effects of inadequate verbal interaction are reversible or not is a question of great importance to society. If the effects are permanent, at what age do they become irreversible? The Bereiter and Engelman Head Start program and the Early Training Project are both based on the hope that deprived children can be reached before the critical point.

Because of man's slow rate of maturation and great dependence on learning, the human infant, more than any other, needs and relies on members of his species for the creation of an environment in which he can express his potentialities. This dependency does not cease at maturity. Human beings continue to rely on each other for social and emotional relationships. In the following chapters we shall explore the nature and development of these relationships, as well as some of the ways in which their breakdown can interrupt, retard, and even destroy the physical, mental, or social development of the individual.

SUMMARY

The development of any organism begins at conception, and through the processes of growth, maturation, and learning it continues until death. Each new structure and system emerges by epigenesis from antecedent foundations. There appear to be certain critical periods during which the developing individual is maximally sensitive to certain classes of stimuli. Physical and motor development progress in a cephalocaudal direction, from the head toward the feet, and in a proximal-distal direction, from the center of the body out to the extremities. Different body structures develop at different rates, and the rate of growth is not constant. An individual's development may be assessed by both cross-sectional and longitudinal techniques.

The movements of a newborn are generalized and reflex in nature. Some reflexes of the human newborn are clearly functional. Others which disappear soon after birth appear to have no function, although their counterparts in lower animals do have survival value. As the infant matures and reflexes give way to integrated movements, motor development follows a universal sequence, although the rate varies considerably from one individual to another. The infant's skeleton differs markedly from that of the adult. Whereas ossification of bone continues until maturity, all muscle fibers are present at birth, and growth consists of an increase in size. Maximal physical development and the time of maturity vary with sex. However, over the last several generations average maximal growth has increased and is reached at an earlier age.

There was considerable early controversy over the extent to which spatial perception is learned. Visual deprivation apparently affects visually guided behavior, but it may also cause some physical deterioration. Visual displacement by means of prism glasses indicates that visual-motor coordination is innate in newly hatched chicks and is little affected by learning. In contrast, human adults are able to adapt within several days to a completely inverted visual field. An important factor in both the development and the adaptation of visually guided behavior seems to be the opportunity to correlate visual experience with self-produced movement. Perceptual ability of the newborn has been assessed by means of the visual cliff and the method of recording eye fixations. Both human and monkey infants show a distinct preference for the dimension of pattern, which is probably the basis of object perception.

Intellectual development has been characterized by Piaget in terms of genetic epistemology. During the sensory-motor stage the infant proceeds from reflexes to complex responses to a single stimulus. The preoperational stage is characterized by the acquisition of language, which enables the child to represent his environment symbolically. During the stage of concrete operations he acquires the important concept of conservation of substance or quantity. At the stage of formal operations he can think in abstract terms and apply operations to hypothetical situations. There are wide variations in the rate of intellectual development, and there has been some investigation of the extent to which rate of development may indicate future intellectual ability. Personality factors may also affect measured intellectual achievement. Cognitive development may be affected by the language environment to which the child is exposed.

CHAPTER THREE

THE AFFECTIONAL SYSTEMS

Whatever love may be, even the aloof scientist finds it difficult to approach the study of the phenomenon with total objectivity. Nevertheless, if we are to enter into the ordeal of affectional objectivism, we must recognize that love is not a single, invariant state, but that there are at least five basic kinds of interactive, interpersonal love. Let us define *love* as affectional feelings for others, thus ruling out self-love, or narcissism. Narcissism will be discussed later in terms of its function as an ego-protective mechanism.

The first of the affectional systems is maternal love, the love of the mother for her child. The second is infant love, the love of the infant for the mother, which can also be termed infant-mother love. The third is peer, or age-mate, love, the love of child for child, preadolescent for preadolescent, and adolescent for adolescent. This love system may, with good fortune, last throughout a first marriage, and with unusually good fortune it may even survive a second marriage. The fourth love system, heterosexual love, is one in which age-mate passion is augmented by gonadal gain. In deference to the two sexes, it is the period in which androgenic anxieties are quieted by estrogenic ecstasies. Even though adequate heterosexual acts may be, and have been, achieved unamelio-

LOVE

rated by love, the fact remains that adequate antecedent age-mate love is a prerequisite for heterosexuality, certainly in primates, probably in dogs [Beach, 1969], and possibly in male guinea pigs [Louttet, 1927]. Thus we must clearly concede the existence and remarkable motivational power of romantic love, the hallucinatory network that surrounds the image or form of the loved one. Heterosexuality as a complete love system appears to require memory as well as mating.

The fifth love system is that of paternal or father love, the love of the adult male for his family or members of his social group. Paternal love is expressed primarily in terms of protective functions, but it may also appear in more subtle forms, such as play with children. Paternal love may be lavished on a specific female and her offspring, as in the case of the titi monkey, the gibbon, and some ninteenth-century human males, or it may be very diffuse, as in rhesus and howler monkeys, chimpanzees, and the heroes of the Hollywood heyday.

Our description of five separate and discrete love systems is not meant to imply that each system is physically and temporally separate. Actually, there is always an overlap, so that affectional motives are continuous as the different forms and facets of love evolve. As with other aspects of development, each love system prepares the individual for the one that follows, and the failure of any system to develop normally

43

deprives him of the proper foundations for subsequent increasingly complex affectional adjustments. Thus the maternal and infant affectional systems prepare the child for the perplexing problems of peer adjustment by providing him with basic feelings of security and trust. Playmates determine social and sexual destiny, but without the certain knowledge of a safe haven, a potential playmate can at first sight be a frightening thing. By the same token, age-mate experience is fundamental to the development of normal and natural heterosexual love, whether this passion is deep and enduring as in most men or trivial and transient as in most monkeys. In all primates the heterosexual affectional system is hopelessly inept and inadequate unless it has been preceded by effective peer partnerships and age-mate activities.

The ties formed during each of the affectional systems are so strong and binding that they may sometimes impede transition to the appropriate new system when it eventually matures. Freud and others have described this difficulty as *fixation* at some infantile or early level. Thus an inability to break the maternal bond may hinder the development of peer affection, or some same-sex peer tie may block later heterosexual acceptance. Fortunately the very process of affectional maturation serves to offset affectional fixations. When maturation fails we may have to resort to learning—and when learning fails we may have to resort to psychiatry.

Although love has been an almost exclusive preoccupation of literature and legend, objective reports on human love are conspicuously scarce. Perhaps psychologists can live without love, and if so, this is doubtless the destiny they deserve. Fortunately for the rest of us, our meager data on man are supplemented by a wealth of data from other sources. The most relevant material, not just for the study of sex, but also for the study of love in all its manifestations, has been cooperatively provided by the monkey. Of course monkey data do not give a total picture of human devotion. Monkeys are much simpler than people. However, for this very reason they give us a clearer picture of the basic love systems, the nature of the variables underlying each, and the problems and perils of transition from one system to another. Furthermore, the scanty human experimental data, as well as the relatively rich human clinical data, can be seen in best perspective within the factual framework of primate affection.

MATERNAL LOVE

Mother love is one of the two love systems which has not remained unwept, unhonored, or unsung. Mother love has attracted the radiant raptures of poets and painters. Poets since Solomon have composed sensuous sonnets on the blessed beauties of the maternal face, form, and functions. Artists since time immemorial have immortalized the madonna, generally in a manner that in no way left her anatomical capabilities to the imagination. Scientists have also written about mother love. Some of their theses are true, and some are not.

44

The first scientific essay on mother love was strictly Freud [1949]; many subsequent essays have been strictly fraud. In tracing psychiatric case histories as far back as possible Freud eventually discovered motherhood, a discovery as important as that made by Columbus, and equally inevitable. Since neither he nor any other man really succeeded in going back farther than birth, Freud concluded that motherhood was his long-sought love and the ultimate and only source of all affection. One analyst did believe he could go back to the womb, but this was Rank [1952] folly. Freud conceived of the mother-child relationship as encompassing all the forces that shape the adult personality, with maladjustments at this level the sole cause of any later emotional catastrophes.

Although we would never discount the importance of mothers, it now appears that mother-child attachments are actually less critical to adult social and sexual relationships than the interactions arising from age-mate or peer attachments. Be that as it may, it is meaningless, and even misleading, to judge the importance of the various affectional systems in terms of the end result. Each system evolves from the one that precedes it, and the faulty development of any system, or the faulty transition from one system to another, may arise from any number of variables.

Since the affectional systems develop in sequence, let us examine the mechanisms and their interactions in the same sequence. The chief factor in maternal capabilities is a variable which is innate and genetically determined—being born a girl. Females have an enormous advantage in becoming effective mothers, since they will eventually possess the physical and physiological characteristics needed for effective motherhood—the happy triumvirate of hope, health, and hormones. However, there are more subtle factors than those built into the body and borne by the blood that give females an enormous advantage in mastering the meaning of motherhood. There may actually be inherent differences in the central nervous system.

Recent research efforts have been directed toward examining sex differences in human newborns, differences that occur so early they cannot be attributed to learning. On one hand, newborn females seem to be more responsive to skin exposure. They react more strenuously than newborn males to a covering blanket, are more disturbed when their skin is stimulated by an air jet, and are higher in basal skin conductance. On the other hand, newborn males raise their heads higher than newborn females [Hamburg and Lunde, 1966]. Behavioral differences between the sexes have often been attributed entirely to learning and culture. Learning is no doubt a factor of considerable significance, particularly in human beings, but there are also far more subtle, secretive, inborn variables. By the time children are four or five years old they show awareness of sex-appropriate behavior which appears to be determined by a combination of genetic factors and experience [Gari and Scheinfeld, 1968].

As we shall see in Chapter 4, sex differences in nonhuman primates cannot be explained simply in terms of learned variables. There is

45

FIGURE 3–1   *Elicitor of female ecstasy response.*

reason to believe that genetic variables condition similar differences in human primates. The gentle and relatively passive behavior characteristic of most little girls is a useful maternal attribute, and the more aggressive behavior of most little boys is useful preparation for the paternal function of protection.

In addition to differences in general personality traits, there are sex differences more directly related to motherhood. Girls will respond to babies—all babies—long before they approach adolescence. Attitude differences that are apparently inherent were demonstrated in the responses of preadolescent female and male macaque monkeys to rhesus monkey babies [Chamove et al., 1967]. Since the preadolescent macaques had never seen infants younger than themselves and had not been raised by real monkey mothers who could have imparted their own attitudes toward babies, we may assume that the differences in response pattern were primarily innately determined. When they were confronted with a baby monkey, almost all the responses made by the female monkeys were positive and pleasant, including contact, caressing, and cuddling. These maternal-type baby responses were conspicuously absent in the males. Instead the male monkeys exhibited threatening and aggressive behavior toward the babies, although fortunately this behavior never progressed to the point of real physical abuse or injury.

Some years ago the photograph shown in Fig. 3-1 was projected on a screen at a women's college in Virginia. All 500 girls in the audience gave simultaneous gasps of ecstasy. The same test has since been conducted with many college audiences. Not only are all-male audiences completely unresponsive, but the presence of males in coeducational audiences inhibits the feminine ecstasy response. Evidently nature has not only constructed women to produce babies, but has also prepared them from the outset to be mothers.

Maternal love differs from the other love systems in that the full sequence is normally recurrent. The love of the infant for the mother is normally nonrecurring. Peer companionships may come and go, but the total developmental cycle is never reinstituted. Heterosexual love may be fixated or fleeting—and with each new generation it seems to have become progressively more fleeting and less fixated—but the long-term developmental stages of heterosexual love are nonrecurring. With mater-

46

nal love, however, the advent of each infant initiates the entire sequence anew. In its early stages maternal behavior is based almost entirely on the mother's responses to the infant. As the infant matures and develops his own responses, these maternal responses are modified by the interaction between mother and child. Thus the mother's expression of love for her infant changes and in fact appears to follow some type of development pattern. Human mothers feed, fondle, and dress their infants for the first year. After patiently retrieving dropped toys, and even deliberately thrown toys, and placing spoons in fumbling fists, they gradually wean their infants from total dependence and start them on the road to independence.

In the monkey mother the appearance of each and every infant initiates the first of three stages of mother love—a stage of care and comfort, a stage of maternal ambivalence, and a stage of relative separation [Harlow et al., 1963]. These stages are not discrete or all-or-none in character; rather, each merges into the next. It is impossible to define exact temporal periods for any maternal affectional stage in either monkey or man, since there are large individual differences and variables of experience play an increasing role in the later stages. In general, however, the stage of care and comfort in monkeys evolves into the stage of maternal ambivalence when the monkey infant is about five months old, and the stage of maternal ambivalence evolves into the stage of maternal separation four months to a year later.

THE STAGE OF CARE AND COMFORT

The response of a human mother to her newborn depends on many personality and cultural variables and reveals a complexity of concerns. If the infant is one that she wanted, she may view it with love and affection and even consider it beautiful—truly a triumph of mind over matter. However, if she has any doubts or conflicts about her anguished achievement, her response may be one of complete indifference. Many human mothers typically have little maternal feeling until their infants have matured to the point that they can interact with their mothers by means of vocal and facial responses. When the infant begins to coo and smile in response to maternal vocalizations or manipulations, the mother responds with maternal love.

During the stage of care and comfort a primary function or obligation of the monkey mother is to provide her infant with intimate bodily contact, which is the basic mechanism in eliciting love from the neonate and infant. For almost all monkey mothers the initial appearance of the infant releases love, as evidenced by positive and spontaneous approach and cradling responses. During the first month of life the mother maintains her baby either in a close ventral-ventral position (Fig. 3-2) or in a looser and more relaxed cradling posture in which the infant's body is held gently within the confines of the mother's arms and legs. This position provides the maximum amount of bodily contact

47

FIGURE 3–3 *Maternal respon-siveness to twins.*

FIGURE 3–2 *Maternal ventral-ventral cradling of infant.*

between mother and infant. Such physical attachments seem to be comforting for both mother and infant, an observation that has given rise to the concept of *contact comfort*. The monkey mother both gives and receives contact comfort, and it may be assumed that contact is an important mechanism in eliciting maternal love from the mother.

The role of infant body contact, clinging, and nursing in eliciting maternal love was demonstrated some years ago at the Wisconsin Primate Laboratories. One monkey mother was separated from her infant and allowed to adopt a young kitten. Initially the monkey mother made every effort to mother the kitten, even to the point of initiating nursing. However, the kitten exhibited one enormous behavioral flaw; it could not cling to the mother's body. When the kitten failed to reciprocate the mother's contact-clinging efforts, monkey maternal love waned, and after 12 days the kitten was totally abandoned.

Another monkey mother that had been separated from her own infant was introduced to a month-old infant that had developed an autistic pattern of behavior in which it clutched and clung to itself while rocking and mouthing its penis. Whenever the potential foster mother approached and contacted this infant, it screeched violently and intensified its autistic actions. After several days the mother failed to show normal maternal responsiveness. When this mother was later offered a second infant, which was congenitally blind but would cling normally and nurse, her adoption of it was immediate and complete.

In a recent experiment [Deets, 1969] four monkey mothers were given the opportunity to adopt "twins," two newborns, neither of which was the mother's own infant (Fig. 3-3). All four mothers at first attempted to initiate ventral contact and suckling with their infants. However, the twin infants, clinging in a haphazard way to themselves as well as to the mother, did not provide the kind of clinging and suckling feedback that is maximally reinforcing for the mother monkey. The mothers experienced great difficulty in establishing a satisfactory contact-clinging relationship, and three of the four mothers became

48

ambivalent toward their twin infants and began to alternately accept and reject each. While the mothers eventually did accept the twins totally and permanently, affectional ambivalence continued for as long as a month in one case. Similar ambivalence was demonstrated by a monkey who gave birth to a pair of natural twins in our laboratory. These and many other observations lead us to conclude that an infant that does not feed back will not be fed.

Actually, during the infant monkey's first week of life maternal love is indiscriminate, and during this period a monkey mother will respond with equal intensity to her own or to a strange infant of similar age. Earlier research had indicated that mothers are very upset by separation from their infants, but that their distress is somewhat allayed when they can see the infants. However, a more recent experiment [Jensen, 1965] demonstrates that they are relieved by the sight of *any* infant until their own offspring are a week to ten days old. After that point only the sight of their own infants will satisfy them. Evidently a monkey mother develops feelings specific to her own infant only after she has interacted with it for a period of time.

A similar developmental process appears to take place in human mothers, at least with their first infants. Until the infant is four to six weeks old the mother perceives it as an anonymous asocial object and reports only impersonal feelings of affection. In the infant's second month of life, when it begins to exhibit visual fixation and following, smiling responses, and eye contacts, her maternal feelings intensify. She now begins to view the infant as a person with unique characteristics and believes that it recognizes her. By the end of the third month the maternal attachment is sufficiently strong that the infant's absence is experienced as unpleasant, and the imagined loss of the infant becomes an intolerable prospect [Robson and Moss].

A second primary obligation of mothers during the stage of care and comfort is that of satisfying the infant's biological homeostatic needs, particularly those of hunger and thirst, and some monkey mothers are admirably endowed along these lines (Fig. 3-4). Infantile satisfaction of hunger and thirst is essentially guaranteed from the monkey mother by the pattern of body-to-body and breast-to-breast ventral-ventral

FIGURE 3–4   *Madonna and child.*

49

positioning. The neonatal monkey is held tightly by the monkey mother, with its mouth at or near the level of the mother's breasts. Infantile attachments to the breast in both human and monkey infants are also facilitated by rooting reflexes, which are head-turning responses to cheek stimulation, and subsequent nipple attachment and suckling. Each monkey infant has an almost exclusive preference for one breast over the other; however, half the infants prefer the left breast and half prefer the right, demonstrating complete statistical impartiality.

Nursing is often achieved less flawlessly and faultlessly by the human mother, probably because of the intervention in the human of learned cultural factors. Possibly a little learning is a dangerous thing, and many people have trouble learning more. It is estimated that only about 25 percent of the mothers in the upper socioeconomic strata in this country nurse their babies. Some apparently do not choose to nurse their babies because they regard nursing as a crude, belittling, bovine act. Some human mothers have great difficulty in nursing or cannot nurse their babies because of abnormal nipple or breast structures [Gunther, 1961]. Nevertheless, the many studies comparing the fates of breast-fed and bottle-fed babies suggest that breast feeding in human infants is a variable of relatively little importance. While it appears to lead to no negative outcomes, at the same time few clearly positive effects can be attributed to the experience [Caldwell, 1964]. Breast feeding does provide occasions for intimate interaction between mother and baby, but it is probably the intimate interaction, not the source of milk, that is the critical factor. Many human mothers may be relieved to know that it is possible for them to elicit and maintain infant love when they are bearing nothing but a bottle. As long as the bottle at each feeding session is supplemented by tender loving care, the bottle-fed baby will achieve the same pervading love for the mother.

A final care-and-comfort task of tribulation, a test of maternal love and patience, is that of the control of the infant's eliminative functions. Countless monkeys have been raised on inanimate cloth surrogate mothers. The infants render these mothers a soggy mess in only a matter of hours. In amazing contrast, however, infant monkeys do not soil their real mothers. The techniques by which monkey mothers achieve this laudable goal remain a mystery, possibly to them as well as to us.

Toilet training of human babies, in contrast, entails a minimum of mystery and a maximum of agony. There are many techniques for early toilet training of human infants, and all have one thing in common—they do not work. Most studies show that eliminative functions cannot be trained reliably and effectively until the child has reached a certain level of maturation. Masochistic mothers are, of course, welcome to enter the ordeal as early as they wish. Some years ago, eleven months was the average age for the beginning of bowel training in the United States. Typically it takes about seven months to complete training, although some babies develop control within a few weeks, while others require a year and a half or more. Over the last three decades mothers have gradually postponed initiation of bowel training [Caldwell, 1964].

The more severe the training procedure and the earlier it is initiated, the more the child is upset by the training, with severity being the more important variable. A very substantial proportion of children with bowel and bladder malfunctions are found to have experienced very early or very severe training regimens, although no broad personality consequences have been convincingly demonstrated [Caldwell, 1964]. Nonetheless there is reason to believe that compulsive and impetuous maternal toilet training and its consequent storm and strife may be the primary factor in what Freud termed the anal-erotic stage of development. This period is probably entirely a product of culture and conditioning, with no truly unlearned biological base. Indeed Erikson [1950] contends that the underlying cause is a general conflict between the child's developing desire to gain some control over his own activities, as opposed to being controlled by others. In Western societies, where bowel and sphincter control are assigned great importance, they become the focus for this general conflict between self-regulation and regulation by others. In societies where eliminative control is not so highly valued, of course, this general conflict may become focused on some other area of behavior. Nevertheless, written references to the anal stage are so frequent that we must at least accord it lip service in passing.

The third obvious essential function of the mother at the maternal stage of care and comfort is that of protection, and this is dispensed by good mothers at a level of vigor and violence appropriate or more than appropriate to the situation (Fig. 3-5). Eventually every human mother sees her young son embroiled in more or less mortal combat with the neighbor's boy. Automatically maternal instincts provide her the obvious knowledge that it was the neighbor's boy who started the fight, and assuming the external and internal bodily patterns of the rhesus monkey mother, the human mother rushes out to ensure her child's salvation. Aggression matures less rapidly in females than in males, but aggression in both sexes reaches a similar frequency and ferocity of expression when the females become mature. This would make good evolutionary sense, since mature maternal females must

FIGURE 3-5   *Maternal protectiveness.*

exhibit aggressive responses to external animate objects that threaten their young.

The maternal protective function appears early in the initial maternal stage and continues long after this stage has passed. The protective function is commonly elicited during the stage of transition and ambivalence, with little or no decrease in belligerence. Actually maternal protective responses exist long after the infant has reached a state of relative physical and psychological separation from the mother. In their natural habitat monkey mothers are often observed to come to the aid and defense of their fully adult sons.

The protection of the infant, and to a lesser degree the juvenile and adolescent, is not an exclusive maternal function. In many primate species protection is in fact a prime obligation of the adult males, and it is a basic component of the paternal affectional system. Actually, the male primate is better endowed by form and fang to serve this function than is the female. In primate groups studied in natural or semi-natural settings the adult males are observed to defend infants and juveniles against social dangers arising from outside the troop. Moreover, in some groups of some species the adult males help keep the infant out of harm's way within the troop, as in breaking up vigorous bouts of rough-and-tumble play that threaten to injure some of the younger and weaker participants [DeVore, 1963].

THE STAGE OF TRANSITION

The love of the infant for the mother is so strong and so enduring that the very survival of the species is dependent on multiple separational factors or forces. Many mothers sever the strings with apparent ambivalence, and this feat is not commenced with ease. The early independence training which encourages the child to reach, retrieve, and replace his own toys quickly disappears when a cry of pain is emitted. The mother rushes to the child and swoops him up with hands which are otherwise only extended for finger contact at street crossings. This is indeed a period when the mother plays the ambivalent role of sending her infants forth to fend for themselves while also darting forth to defend her darlings.

As we noted earlier, Lorenz [1952] observed that immediately after birth goslings followed the heavy-hipped waddling of their mothers automatically and compulsively, and later would not approach and follow any other animal. Furthermore, when he removed the mother from newly hatched goslings, the goslings followed Lorenz in the same compulsive manner. This attachment was so strong that when the geese were grown they would not respond positively to members of their own species.

Imprinting in the goose has been endowed with many mystical or mythical characteristics. How any greylag gosling ever escaped from the maternal bonds to subsequently procreate the species was never explained by Lorenz. A possible explanation is that the greylag goose became extinct millions of years before Lorenz observed them, but this is contradicted by the facts.

IMPRINTING

Imprinted on a greylag goose
Is trapped within a hangman's noose.
How does an infant break away
To be a goose himself some day?

There are, of course, documented cases of human children who never break away from overly strong maternal ties. The typical "sissy" is one more closely bound to his mother than to his peers. Occasionally we read of the mother-trapped man who becomes engaged to the girl of his choice at age twenty and then waits until his mother passes away 50 years later before he marries. There are psychiatrists who believe that some subtle something may be lost in these intervening years. Most "mamma's boys" eventually escape. However, Portnoy is not the only one to have complained [Roth, 1969] of the difficulty of doing so, and even in such pretended patriarchies as ancient Sicilian society, it is mamma who is the source of final appeal in prayer as well as practice.

In view of the obvious strength of maternal ties, there must be even more superordinate mechanisms that unshackle the child from maternal bondage at an appropriate age or stage, so that he can become an independently functioning individual. In primates there are at least three processes that operate to gradually weaken mother-infant ties—changes in the mother's responses to her infant, changes in the infant's responses to his mother, and changes in the infant's responsiveness to the stimuli of the outside world. We shall treat these three processes as components of a single mother-infant separation mechanism. Certainly all of them operate toward a common goal—to free the child from the mother.

During the peak of the care-and-comfort stage almost all the normal monkey mothers' responses are positive, including such acts as intense maternal ventral contact, infant cradling, nipple contact, and restraining and retrieving the infant as it gains mobility and tentatively begins to explore the outside world. After this point maternal warmth wanes and separation supervenes and succeeds. Undoubtedly this stating of maternal affection is in part a function of acts by the infant designed to achieve maternal liberation. By sixty to ninety days of age the monkey infant has developed competent locomotor skills and has become an animal that can and needs to explore all aspects of the world about him. However, the decreasing frequency of maternal affectional responses is predominantly a function of fading maternal feelings and functions (see Fig. 3-6).

The development of the transitional or ambivalent stage is indicated by changes in the nature and number of maternal responses, particularly restraining and retrieving. For example, during the early months the mother is responsible for most of the physical separations of mother and infant, but the transitional or ambivalent stage is best

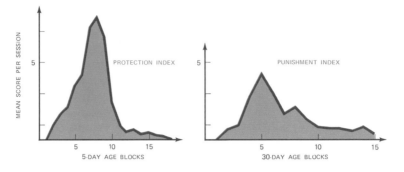

FIGURE 3-6 *Development of maternal protection and punishment.*

illustrated by the form and frequency with which the mother actively rejects her infant. Maternal punishment is almost nonexistent during the monkey infant's first three months of life. The frequency of negative maternal behavior—rejections, threats, and punishing—reaches a peak near the fifth month and then gradually declines to a low at about the ninth month. By that time either the monkey mother has faith in her infant or she has become terribly tired, while the infant has learned how to avoid maternal chastisement. Obviously the frequency of active maternal rejection is a joint function of both infant and maternal variables.

Rejection by the monkey mother begins as very gentle punishment, but increases in frequency and force as the infant matures. It eventually reaches the point at which the mother occasionally will deliberately dislodge the infant from her breast and body, or strike or stiff-arm the baby as it rushes impulsively to her in an attempt to gain maternal contact. As the transitional stage reaches a peak, maternal punishment is sometimes made without regard to any observable aggravation of the mother by the baby. However, the mother is ambivalent during this period. For example, if the infant appears to wander or stray beyond the maternal fold too quickly or too much, maternal responses appropriate to the stage of care and comfort reappear. Infantile independence during this transitional stage can be a source of frustration for the mother. She attempts simultaneously to protect and to emancipate. Human mothers no doubt experience similar ambivalence during this formative stage. Nevertheless, on all occasions in which the cherished infant is exposed to dangers, real or only imagined, the mother provides defense and protection with no hesitation or delay (Fig. 3-5).

Active rejection and punishment by the mother play an important role in helping the infant to break the overwhelmingly strong maternal ties and freeing him to make his own place in the world. Maternal rejection during this period is truly one of many forms of mother love; a mother who loves her infant will emancipate him.

Of course, in not all primate species do mothers rely on physical punishment to emancipate their infants. For example, chimpanzee mothers seldom punish their offspring. In the process of weaning their infants from the breast they use various techniques, such as tickling and play, to distract the baby that attempts to gain access to the nipple [Van Lawick-Goodall, 1967]. Human mothers display an even greater variety of constructive techniques in seeking to aid the development of independence in their offspring. Frequently a toddler will be enrolled in a nursery school not solely for the mother's benefit, but to wean him from parental comforts and to expose him to new socially significant stimuli. Another approach is to provide toys that require the cooperation of peers, such as a teeter-totter, which can be teetered only by two.

It is obvious that the affectional ties between mother and child are eventually dissolved—at least physically. In the case of both humans and monkeys the advent of a new baby is a variable of great importance, perhaps even primary importance, in establishing the stage of maternal separation. There are many mothers who have time for only one man at a time. However, the new baby only augments this natural process, and the older infant's own exploration and curiosity responses continue to function as a highly important force leading to separation.

The degree to which mothers and infants become physically and psychologically separated as the offspring mature varies greatly both within and among the different primate species. The rhesus monkey infants subjected to permanent physical separation from the mother eventually lose all affectional ties with the mother, and within one to two years ties with new associates replace the old bonds. In the original study on mother-infant separation [Hansen, 1966] the living quarters of the four mother-infant pairs tested were relatively small, and in these circumscribed surroundings mother and infant remained physically and psychologically close through the second year of life.

In large family-style living cages built to house nuclear family units (see Fig. 3-7) the first sibling may struggle successfully for many months

FIGURE 3-7   *The nuclear family unit.*

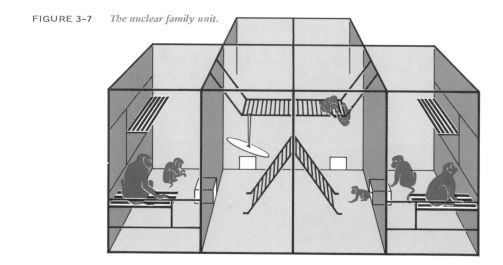

after the advent of a new sibling to maintain intermittent maternal contact, particularly at night. Maternal preoccupation with a new infant commonly augmented the detachment between the mother and the older infant. This was of little concern to the older infant during the day, when he spent his time in play with his age mates. However, as his interest in play and age mates departed with the daylight he commonly turned to prolonged and intensive efforts to regain maternal contact. On those occasions when even his most subtle and skillful efforts failed the rebuffed infant often tried to achieve close bodily attachment with some other mother and her offspring, and if even these desperate devices failed, he might as a last resort seek solace through ventral contact with his father, or even some other monkey's father. Although fathers are not totally adequate mother substitutes, apparently any body is better than no body at all.

Studies of two different species of macaque monkeys, bonnet and pigtail, have revealed striking differences in the extent of orientation toward the mother as the offspring matures. Adolescent and mature animals of both species spend approximately 80 percent of their time in friendly, positive interaction with other animals. However, in pigtail macaques this social interaction is directed almost exclusively toward the mother and close family members, whereas bonnets spend no more time interacting with kin than with nonkin [Kaufman and Rosenblum, 1969]. Cultural differences with respect to the extent of mother-infant separation are also apparent. For example, in the wild, in some groups of langur monkeys, after the second year of life the offspring interact with their mothers no more than with other adult females. In other groups of the very same species the offspring continue to direct their social interactions almost exclusively toward their mothers and close relatives well into adulthood. Similar cultural differences are evident within several other species of monkeys.

The human mother fortunately has both love to share and love to spare, for if she quickly separated physically and emotionally from her first infant upon the advent of the next, the problem of overpopulation would automatically be solved by the mortality rate among helpless first-born infants. Instead the human mother nestles and nurtures both, or even all, her offspring for a necessarily protracted time, thereby guaranteeing their survival—and along with it the full expression of sibling rivalry. Maternal separation in man is far more socially complex than it is in monkeys. It may be intermittent, semipermanent, or permanent throughout childhood as a result of baby-sitters, scholastic requirements, the miracle of remarriage, and in some instances deliberate choice. Maternal separation may be either physical or psychological, and it may be achieved by either maternal choice or offspring choice. Moreover, in man maternal contact is often maintained by written or spoken words long after physical separation has become a fact.

Physical separation between mother and child represents the final phase of each maternal-infant interaction sequence, and it is seldom, if ever, a simple process. Separation is commonly a period of stress, fear, and frustration, and the older infant must often be led to the top of the hill. Fortunately he almost always finds peers and playmates on the other side.

Infant love, which is the love of the neonate, baby, and young child for the mother, has often been confused with maternal love. These two affectional systems, the mother's love for the infant and the infant's love for the mother, operate simultaneously and are difficult to separate and unravel under normal physical and developmental circumstances. The intimate physical proximity and the close reciprocal relationship between mothers and infants make it difficult to distinguish the variables producing maternal affection for the baby from those producing baby affection for the mother. For example, nursing is an important variable in both affectional systems, but it is impossible under normal circumstances to determine its relative contribution to each. However, this does not mean that the mechanisms underlying each kind of love cannot be analyzed separately.

The mother has been physically aware of her infant's existence for some months while it was bundled in the pleasant paradise of the womb. Hence by the time of birth some form of maternal love, particularly in the human mother, is already in existence and is quickly affixed to the particular precious form which has made its appearance. Infant love, in contrast, is entirely indiscriminate at birth, and the neonate eagerly and equally attaches to any maternal object, animate or inanimate, that is endowed with adequate physical properties.

Inanimate stimulus models have been used for analyzing the variables underlying specific behavior patterns in fish and birds. The major advantage of using such models in research is the facility with which one or more variables can systematically be varied while all others are held constant. For example, models of the stickleback fish allowed Thompson [1963] to determine that the basic stimulus evoking aggression in the male stickleback was the belly color on another male stickleback.

Hess [1959], following the imprinting thesis of Lorenz, imprinted ducklings and chicks to inanimate wooden models and demonstrated the role of both visual and auditory variables in this limited learning process. He showed that the imprinting process depended in part on the amount of work or effort extended by the infant duckling. This differentiates imprinting from love; in love it is not the infant's effort, but the mother's that cements the affectional bond.

Similarly, the use of inanimate surrogate monkey mothers has allowed us to investigate important questions arising from several theories about the development of love and to analyze the individual stimulus properties of real mothers. For example, psychologists and psychoanalysts have long assumed that the infant's love for the mother developed

57

FIGURE 3–8   *Infant's religious conversion to diaper.*

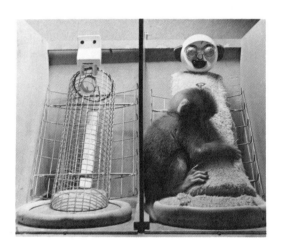

FIGURE 3-9   *Cloth and wire surrogate mothers.*

through association of the mother with organic pleasures resulting from the ingestion of milk and the alleviation of hunger. According to this "cupboard theory" of infant love, as Bowlby [1969] has termed it, the fundamental mechanisms are those related to functions of the breast.

Psychologists and their social science allies had long thought that mother love was a derived drive which developed from the association of the mother image with the alleviation of the primary drive of hunger. Motivation theory was dominated by the thesis that the only important unlearned motives were such homeostatic biological drives as hunger, thirst, elimination, and organic sex. All other motives were considered derived, learned, or secondary. Observations of monkeys suggest, however, that contact is actually the primary factor in the infant-mother relationship. Van Wagenen [1950], who raised newborn monkeys separated from their mothers, noted that unless their baskets were lined with soft cloth "even their feeding reflexes would become confused." The attachment of monkeys to their cheesecloth pads or diapers was so apparent that it looked as though they had joined a religious order (Fig. 3-8).

To determine whether infant love is learned or whether certain inherent properties of the mother elicit infant attachment Harlow [1958]

58

FIGURE 3–10   *Time spent on cloth and wire surrogate.*

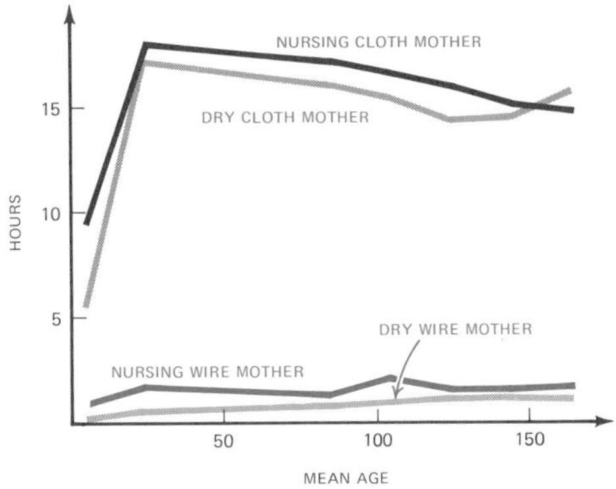

constructed sets of nursing and nonnursing cloth and wire surrogate mothers. One primary variable differentiating the two types of surrogate mothers was that of body surface. The wire surrogates had bare bodies of welded wire and the cloth surrogates were covered by soft, resilient terrycloth sheaths. The two surrogates, shown in Fig. 3-9, had long, tapered bodies which could be easily clasped by the infant rhesus monkey. Some of the surrogates were endowed with a single breast, and some had none (the nursing surrogate mothers did not need two breasts, since none ever gave birth to twins).

In Harlow's classical dual mother-surrogate study a cloth mother and a wire mother were set up in a cubicle attached to the baby's living cage. For four newborn monkeys the cloth mothers lactated and the wire mothers did not; for four other monkey infants this condition was reversed. In both situations the infant received all its milk from the appropriate surrogate breast as soon as it was able to sustain itself in this manner. Total time spent in contact with the cloth and wire surrogate mothers under the two conditions of feeding is shown in Fig. 3-10. As the infants developed, those who had been provided with a lactating wire mother showed decreasing responsiveness to her and increasing responsiveness to the nonlactating cloth mother—a finding completely contrary to the interpretation that infant love is a derived drive in which the mother's face or form becomes a condition for hunger or thirst reduction. It is clearly the incentive of contact comfort that binds the infant affectionately to the mother. If derived drive is to be invoked as an explanation, this drive must be fashioned from whole cloth rather than whole milk.

There is seldom, if ever, any single cause for any behavioral act by any animal, particularly animals as complex as monkeys, apes, and men. Multiple stimulus variables operate to elicit each and every response, and there are commonly multiple antecedent variables, both maturational and learned. Hence, although these data show contact comfort to be the primary factor in the formation of infant-mother affectional bonds, it is by no means the only variable. To test the role of the breast as an affection-forming force infants were reared with two cloth surrogates, one with a functioning breast and the other with none. Under these circumstances all baby monkeys showed a significant preference

59

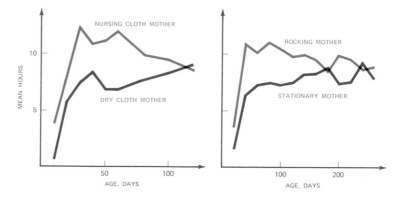

FIGURE 3-11   *Time spent on various cloth surrogates.*

for the mother with the bountiful breast (Fig. 3-11). In other words, activity associated with the breast and nursing is a significant variable when the more powerful variable of contact comfort is held constant. It has long been known that human babies are soothed by rocking motion, whether it is provided by the parent's nocturnal pacing with the baby in his or her arms or by a cradle. Studies also show (Fig. 3-11) that infant monkeys also have a preference for rocking surrogate mothers over stationary surrogate mothers [Harlow and Zimmermann, 1959].

In a series of small experiments designed to test the importance of temperature, since there is reason to believe that temperature is a variable of measurable merriment in the attachment of infant to mother, four infant macaques were given the choice of warm wire surrogates or cool cloth surrogates. The infants demonstrated a significant preference for the warm mother during the early days of life. This preference continued to be a significant variable until twenty days of age, when contact comfort became prepotent over temperature.

These follow-up studies illustrate the importance of history or experience as a factor in determining the role and importance of many affectional variables. It is difficult enough to determine the importance of the variables underlying infant love at any point, and since these variables change as a function of maturity and experience, the total task of variable analysis is heroic.

A similar multifactor theory concerned the human infant's love for and attachment to the mother. According to Bowlby [1969], the first attachment shown by the human infant to his mother is based on a number of primary, unlearned species-specific behavior patterns which he calls "instinctual response systems." These response systems mature and develop at different times and rates during the first year. Bowlby has described three such instinctual response systems in detail—suckling, clinging, and following—as mechanisms through which the infant actively maintains contact with his mother.

Two other instinctual response systems, ones in which the mother plays an active role, were mentioned in connection with the mother's

60

love for her infant. These response systems involve the infant's crying and smiling, which Bowlby suggests elicit maternal caretaking and strengthen the mother's attachment to her infant. At first the various instinctual response systems operate independently and lead the baby to attach himself to any mother figure; later, with development, these response systems become integrated and focused on a single mother figure. Although Bowlby's approach treats all infant love systems as merely component parts of one large, functioning love mechanism, his data add complexities rather than contradictions to the basic primate models we have discussed.

Recent research has shown that a number of stimuli and behaviors normally associated with the mother or maternal caretaking tie the infant to its mother. For example, Kessen and Mandler [1961] have demonstrated that the pure act of sucking, such as nonnutritive sucking on a pacifier, can in and of itself quiet an upset infant or prevent a content infant from becoming upset. Since these effects are observed in newborns before they are fed by breast or bottle, it is evidently determined by innate factors that are not learned as a result of hunger reduction following nursing. In monkeys bodily contact appears to be the primary variable determining attachment of the infant to the mother. However, certain forms of stimulation involving the distance receptors, particularly auditory and visual stimulation, apparently play a more important role in man than in monkey. For example, Salk [1960] demonstrated that the sound of the normal maternal heartbeat, as compared against other sounds, exerts a distress-relieving effect on the infant and even facilitates physical development. Other observations also point up the significance of distance-receptor stimulation in determining infant love in humans. However, studies of human infants exposed to intensive maternal handling and other forms of physical contact and infants whose maternal interaction was based primarily on auditory and visual stimulation, such as talking and smiling, indicate no significant difference in the infant-mother attachment [Schaffer and Emerson, 1964b].

Just as there is a progression in the stages of maternal love, so the infant love system proceeds through at least five stages—a stage of organic affection and reflexive love, a stage of comfort and attachment, a stage of security and solace, a stage of disattachment and environmental exploration, and a stage of relative independence.

THE STAGE OF ORGANIC AFFECTION

There has been prolonged and sometimes profound speculation by psychoanalysts, psychiatrists, anthropologists, and psychologists concerning the origin and nature of the baby's love for the mother and the stimulus or stimuli that call forth or evoke this attachment and emotional warmth. A common psychoanalytic position concerning the nature of the baby's original love is that the initial affectional force is not a love for the mother, since the neonate probably does not distinguish between his

61

own body and the body of any outsider, not even his mother's. Thus the original infant love is an egoistic love—not of himself or the body image of himself, but simply of organic sensations and satisfactions, initiated by the reflex act of nursing and maintained by the pleasures of food assimilation and the relief of organic tensions. This thesis seems reasonable, since approximately a half year elapses before the human infant differentiates between his own bodily self and the outside world of objects, animate or inanimate.

This period of lack of differentiation between internal sensations and precise external animate objects is probably greatly shortened in rhesus monkeys, because they are more mature at birth than human babies and develop about four times faster. Even so, a stage of organic affection probably exists. Since it is impossible to measure the introspective feelings of the neonate in either monkey or man, any early love or mere organic satisfaction must be based on inference rather than objectively measured fact. Almost by definition, however, a reflex stage of infant affection overlaps extensively, and probably completely, with an organic infant-mother affectional phase. Unlike the vague visceral feelings of a presumed organic stage, reflexes can be observed and objectively measured, and a reflex stage merits further consideration.

As we saw in Chapter 2, a basic law of growth and development is that both form and function begin at the head and sweep downward toward the posterior parts of the body. This cephalocaudal law of development holds for all species, but each species has its own characteristic pattern of growth. Opossums are born almost as soon as they are conceived and guinea pigs are nearly fully formed and functional at birth. In fact guinea pigs are approaching senility at birth; they are born strong of body and weak of mind.

The monkey is much more mature at birth than the human. Anatomically the monkey neonate is roughly equivalent to the human one-year-old, and its physiology and behavior are correspondingly advanced. Thus when the reflex stage of infant-mother love begins the human infant's reflexes are limited to the head and eyes, whereas the monkey infant has considerable reflex control over the trunk and legs as well.

In keeping with the cephalocaudal principle, human as well as monkey neonates possess some relatively efficient head and face reflexes. Sucking responses are adequately developed when and if the nipple is effectively attained. An allied reflex is the rooting reflex, which enables the neonate to search for the nipple by way of exploratory head movements. The normal adequate stimulus for the rooting reflex is stimulation of the neonate's cheek by the nipple. However, the rooting reflex may be elicited by stimulation of the monkey baby's cheeks with the human fingertip, preferably above and to one side of the oral cavity; the baby's head moves toward the direction of stimulation, and the lips clasp and try to engulf the stimulating object. The function of the rooting reflex is obvious; it aids both mother and neonate to achieve nipple placement and initiate nursing.

62

FIGURE 3-12 *Upward-climbing response.*

Another early response observed in human and monkey babies is vertical climbing, a response which appears to be meaningless, or even dangerous, but which must serve or have served some useful evolutionary purpose (see Fig. 3-12). Upward-climbing responses are observed in rhesus monkeys at a few days of age, since climbing responses in both men and monkeys mature in advance of walking and even more primitive locomotor patterns. If a neonatal monkey is placed head up at the base of an inclined plane which gradually rises to 2 or 3 feet above a tabletop or floor, the infant typically climbs slowly upward and, unless restrained or caught, crawls compulsively over the end of the plane and drops to whatever surface lies beneath—in all hope, the experimenter's hand. It is possible that this upward-climbing response serves to help position the infant monkey at or near the mother's breast. If he climbs forward and upward along the mother's belly wall, his movements will no doubt be restrained by the mother's arms at or near the level of the breasts.

Whatever the explanation, similar and equally malfunctional upward-climbing responses are frequently seen in human babies, who will try to climb stairs, chairs, sofas, and tables—and are saved only by adult intervention from steadfastly continuing right over the top and onto the floor. Even the painful experiences associated with falling from furniture usually fail to extinguish this innate response. As the human baby develops he sometimes finds new worlds to conquer, such as climbing onto and out of first-, second-, and even third-story windows, almost in direct refutation of his behavior in visual-cliff experiments. At this point the upward-climbing response becomes a response of limited survival value for the human.

The human and monkey babies differ very markedly in the development of the hands, arms, and trunk, which control the responses enabling the neonate or child to attach and maintain contact with the mother, primarily through groping, grasping, and clinging responses. The monkey possesses these reflexes at birth, and even before they become voluntary responses, he is able to obtain contact comfort from his mother largely by his own devices. Since it is five or six months before the human infant can grope for, grasp, and cling to his mother, for the first half

63

year he is completely at her mercy for contact comfort, the primary variable in the formation of deep and enduring infant-mother love.

Setting deadlines for primate maturational stages is mischievous and possibly meaningless. As we have already seen, infant organic love and reflex affection begin at the same time and may even wane and terminate at approximately the same time. The stage of comfort and attachment certainly overlaps them, but without question it continues after they have passed.

THE STAGE OF COMFORT AND ATTACHMENT

The stage of comfort and attachment of the infant-mother affectional system begins as soon as the infant is able to attach to the maternal body and breast. The infant macaque commonly achieves this on the first day of life, and comfort and attachment is usually maintained into the second year. For the first six months of life or longer the human infant is totally dependent on the mother for contact and attachment, and human mothers vary greatly in the degree and amount of bodily contact given during nursing or through cuddling or simple play. Studies with monkeys indicate that with relatively limited affection, if it is given readily and consistently, an infant adjusts successfully within each period of affectional development and proceeds to the next. Minimal comfort and attachment are not recommended, but human mothers beset with other problems may find it comforting to know that limited affection is better than none.

During this stage contact comfort is clearly a primary variable in infant monkeys, and nursing factors, temperature, and proprioceptive variables are significant. It is unlikely that these variables differ in nature and importance in the human infant. However, as we have seen, exteroceptive variables are probably more important in man than in monkeys.

Another important behavior at this stage of infant development is primary object following. Bowlby suggests that primary object following is a powerful mechanism in attaching the infant to the mother, and possibly in producing security responses. Unfortunately there are very limited data on primary object following by either human or monkey children. From casual observation it appears that the rhesus infant follows maternal behavior and, within the limits of its capabilities, matches her actions. When the mother mouths and ingests a food substance, so does the infant; when the mother is startled or frightened, the infant clings to the mother's body for security and safety, while perhaps still continuing to observe. These behaviors enable infants to profit from maternal experience, so that their own exploratory behavior is not blind and the dangers inherent in untutored exploration are minimized. Furthermore, such maternal association, reinforced by maternal bodily contact during moments of doubt, and probably by other maternal variables as well, undoubtedly abet the development of the infant

64

solace and security stage. Such responses are essentially nonexistent during the first 60 days of monkey life and then increase in frequency during the next five months.

The stage of solace and security in infant-mother affection develops at the time, or probably some time before, human or monkey infants develop affection for their specific mothers. Security at this stage is expressed by the willingness of the infant to wander beyond the mother's physical and functional confines to explore the strange new world of objects, playthings, and playmates. Early in the security stage the exploration is minimal and is always under watchful maternal eyes, with the infant frequently returning to the mother for care, comfort, and solace. As time passes the infant's expeditions are longer, with less frequent returns to the mother, and maternal reassurance may change from profound contact clinging to token maternal assurances expressed by a bare flick of the fingers or casual contact with the toes.

Some years ago, in an experiment planned to induce psychopathological behavior in infant monkeys, four surrogate monster mothers were constructed. One was a shaking mother which rocked so violently that the teeth and bones of the infant chattered in unison. The second was an air-blast mother which blew compressed air against the infant's face and body with such violence that the infant looked as if it would be denuded. The third had an embedded steel frame which, on schedule or demand, would fling forward and knock the infant monkey off the mother's body. The fourth monster mother, on schedule or demand, ejected brass spikes from her ventral surface, an abominable form of maternal tenderness and succor. All the monster mothers, however, had a comfort-giving cloth surface.

As disturbing as these monster mothers were, the infant monkeys did not even leave the bodies of the air-blast and rocking mothers, since the mother is an infant's only source of solace or succor, and the only response of an infant in distress is to cling more tightly to the mother. The infants had no choice about their departures from the throwing-frame mother and the brass-spiked mother. Nevertheless, crying and complaining, they waited for the frame to return to resting position and the spikes to retract into the mother's body and then returned to the ventral surrogate surface, expressing faith and love as if all were forgiven.

The infant monkeys apparently showed no apprehension between these trials of torture, and no cumulative terror effects. Although the experiment failed to achieve its original ghoulish goal, no experiment could have better demonstrated the power of any contact-comfort-giving mother to provide solace and security to her infant. These mechanisms clearly superseded any discomfort, disturbance, and distress, despite the fact that nociceptive stimulation is presumably prepotent.

65

Love, all kinds of love, is a mechanism or variable of almost unbelievable power.

Since all kinds of monkey mothers can instill solace and security in their babies' hearts and heads, it is no surprise that baby monkeys clasp and cling to soft cloth surrogates many hours a day. Moreover, they achieve security from the cloth surrogates at about the same age that they would achieve a sense of succor from their own real monkey mothers. However, a study by Hansen [1966] reveals that the security imparted by inanimate cloth mothers is less than that imparted by real mothers, at least during the first two months of life. Of course real mothers would be more efficient protective sources than cloth mothers if the baby monkey were being threatened by living predators. However, the laboratory is designed to keep predators, other than human ones, out.

The original study of the relative affection of infant monkeys for cloth and wire mothers, lactating and nonlactating, measured not only responsiveness to these four kinds of mothers in terms of total contact time, but also choice responses to each maternal type when the infant monkeys were frightened by the sudden appearance of a malevolent mechanical monster (see Fig. 3-13). Their responses to this awesome sight were measured in terms of surrogate contact time. The initial haven was a cloth surrogate for about 70 percent of the one-month-old-monkeys and 80 percent of the two-month-old monkeys. Many of the responses to wire surrogates were momentary and were quickly reversed, as if the terror-stricken baby had dashed blindly to any object in the immediacy of need, and finding the wire surrogate comfortless, quickly reversed its choice and sought the security of any cloth surrogate, lactating or nonlactating.

In other studies monkey infants had to circle around a vertical Plexiglas barrier guarded by a horrible mechanical monster to reach a cloth surrogate mother. Although they were greatly disturbed by this situation, all eventually braved passage around the monster to reach the mother, where they would snuggle against her and quickly become emotionally composed. After a number of these sessions the infants would rush to the mother, and once they had achieved sufficient maternal comfort and security, they would explore the previously fearful experimental chamber. Indeed, within a few more days, several brave infants actually approached and manipulated the monster that had previously left them prostrate. Finally one of them dismembered a monster and tore it to shreds, a perfect illustration of the achievement of solace and security.

The nature and function of the stage of security and solace is clearly demonstrated by the infant's bravery when the mother is present and his terror when the mother is removed. Various infant monkeys raised on cloth surrogates were placed in a strange test room, bare except for a few playthings and their cloth surrogate mothers. As soon as an infant spied his mother he rushed over and clung tightly; only then would he explore the chamber and play with the toys (see Fig. 3-14). When the same infant monkey was placed in the same room with the

LOVE: MATERNAL AND INFANT

FIGURE 3–13   *Response to mechanical monster.*

FIGURE 3–14   *Baby exploring chamber and manipulating toy.*

FIGURE 3–15   *Infant frozen in terror in absence of surrogate.*

cloth surrogate absent, he froze in terror (Fig. 3-15) and failed to show any emotional recovery throughout the entire experimental session.

Even more striking results were obtained with infants raised on lactating wire mothers. When the wire-weaned monkey babies surveyed the chamber they made little or no effort to go to their wire mothers, but instead threw themselves prone on the chamber floor, crying and grimacing all the time, or huddled against a chamber wall, rocking back and forth with their hands over their heads or faces. Evidently even infant monkeys can find no comfort in wire women.

Essentially identical data have been amassed on human children tested in the presence and absence of their mothers. Spitz [1946*a*] first noted the desperate fear of human children in a strange room when their mothers were absent; he termed this *eight-month anxiety* to call attention to the maturational age variable involved. This mother-loss anxiety appears two or three months earlier in some babies and several months later in others [Spitz, 1950].

Since all mothers of any one species are more alike than different, the formation of highly specific personal bonds for a particular mother is of necessity learned. Infant responsiveness that is specific to a specific mother does not reach fruition in the macaque infant until about the fourth month. By this time the macaque baby is able to discriminate his own mother from other mothers, and this discrimination is aided and abetted by fear responses in the presence of strange inanimate and animate objects. Both phenomena are dependent on the maturation of underlying neuroanatomical mechanisms. The newborn macaque shows no fear of any object, animate or inanimate, regardless of how strange, and he would without question expose himself to fatal dangers were it

67

not for the protective restriction of a real monkey mother or the laboratory environment. This fear of the strange or different develops gradually during the first three months of life.

A recent study has dramatically demonstrated the maturation of fear. Infants were reared from birth under conditions that isolated them from social stimuli, and pictures of monkeys engaged in various forms of behavior were then projected to them in their isolation chambers. One set of pictures depicted adult animals exhibiting facial threat grimaces. The infants in their isolation chambers showed little or no responsiveness to these threat-grimace pictures until they were about ninety days old, when the full fear pattern emerged suddenly and at peak strength [Sackett, 1966]. In a detailed study of this phenomenon in human children Schaffer and Emerson [1964b] found that under completely controlled experimental conditions the results were highly similar to those reported by Spitz. Pathological fear in the mother's absence appeared as early as six months and as late as fourteen months, and a few recalcitrant children showed no fear with the mother removed. Man is a strange animal and human data are intrinsically variable.

STAGE OF DISATTACHMENT AND ENVIRONMENTAL EXPLORATION

As the infant human and macaque mature, many factors arise that tend strongly toward maternal disattachment. One variable is maternal punishment, which, absent during the early months, peaks between the fourth and eighth month in the monkey, and drops to a low, stable baseline by about the tenth month. Monkey maternal punishment is usually gentle and restrained, but even when it is harsh and vigorous no mother has ever been seen to injure her own baby, or even attempt to do so.

Although maternal punishment is an important development at this stage, the infants are also lured by natural forces from maternal charms. There is general agreement that the primary mechanism in disattachment from the mother is maturation in the infant of freedom of activity, curiosity, and manipulatory needs concerning the external physical environment, and later, social drives for interaction with age mates and other members of the species. The primary maternal contribution is neither maternal restraint nor punishment, but rather the positive factor of establishing the personal and social security which the infant must have to be able to leave the mother and the mother's domain.

Disattachment in the human infant has been reported by Rheingold and Eckerman [1970], who studied human babies, some less than a year old and so young that they locomoted by wriggling or crawling. After the infants were placed in a room with their mothers, who doubtless provided them with effective maternal security, incentives ranging from no toys to three toys were placed in a large adjacent room whose entrance shut off visual contact with the mother. The distance that the infant traveled away from the mother was positively related to the infant's age, a fact not entirely surprising. No apparent differences between sexes were disclosed, but there was a positive relationship between number of toys in the open field and the time spent away from the maternal security figure. Moreover, the infants went from the starting room to the open field and back, probably for maternal support, even when no toy was present.

In this study the mothers apparently remained totally passive and behaved more like our inanimate cloth surrogate mothers than like normal mothers. Thus, despite its merits, the study does not reveal the development of maternal changes during the stage of mother disattachment; disattachment and distance traveled would certainly be maximized, since maternal restraining variables were eliminated. Actually, such a stage does not normally occur in human infants until they are much older than one year. The investigators' conclusions, however, are equally apt as an interpretation of the maternal disattachment phase in both monkey and human infants [Rheingold and Eckerman, 1970, p. 78]:

> The infant's separating himself from his mother is also of psychological importance, for it enormously increases his opportunities to interact with the environment and thus to learn its nature. . . . Similarly, what can be learned about the physical environment parallels [what] can be drawn for the social environment.

STAGE OF RELATIVE INDEPENDENCE

The important variables relating to the infant's separation from the mother are similar to those discussed in terms of the mother's separation from the infant. However, there are apparently important differences between the infant-mother disattachment phase and the infant-mother separation stage. There are, moreover, important activities in this stage which are initiated by the infant, and it is probable that these activities are more important than those of the mother. Disattachment is an almost totally infant-guided process, with the mother's role remaining passive unless disturbance or danger develops, whereas separation appears to be primarily mother-determined, and even the most resolute infant struggles against it in moments of apprehension and whenever daylight fades into dusk.

In the next chapter we shall consider the development of the age-mate or peer affectional system. Probably the most important function of the maternal and infant love systems is to prepare the infant, human or monkey, to indulge in the wonders of age-mate acceptance and interaction.

69

SUMMARY

Love, or affectional feeling for others, may be described in terms of five basic systems, each of which provides a foundation for the increasing requirements of the next. The first affectional system is maternal love, the love of the mother for her child. The second is infant love, or infant-mother love. This is followed by peer, or age-mate love, which is fundamental to the development of normal heterosexual love. The fifth system is paternal love, the love of the adult male for his family or social group.

Mother love is the first affectional system experienced by the newborn. Maternal characteristics appear to some extent to be genetically determined, since behavioral differences between the sexes are apparent even in newborn infants. These differences increase with age, but not all of them can be attributed to learning. The maternal affectional system is the only one of the love systems in which the full developmental sequence is repeated; it is initiated anew with each successive infant. Mother love is indiscriminate, and in human mothers often absent, at the outset. It appears to be elicited by the infant's response to contact comfort provided by the mother.

The first phase of maternal love, the stage of care and comfort, is characterized by the infant's dependence on the mother for satisfaction of physical and emotional needs. The stage of transition is marked by intermittent and ambivalent rejection, as evidenced by a decrease in the nature and number of maternal responses to the infant. The final stage, of relative separation, varies greatly in different primate species and even among individuals. The advent of a new baby often augments separation of the mother and the older infant. However, the primary force leading to separation is normal maternal rejection during this stage and the growing infant's own motivation to explore his growing world.

Infant love is indiscriminate for a much longer period than mother love. In monkey infants this attachment appears to be related primarily to contact comfort rather than to result directly from association of the mother with satisfaction of the organic need for food. Of course other variables, such as the source of food, warmth, and rhythmic rocking motions, also play a role in this attachment. Certain types of stimulation, particularly stimuli involving distance receptors, may play a more important role in human infant attachment for the mother than they do in nonhuman primates.

The infant affectional system is characterized by five major stages. The stage of organic affection and reflexive love, presumed to be related to organic satisfaction from nursing, is indicated by the various reflexes in the infant monkey which ensure its clinging to the mother and finding the nipple. The stage of comfort and attachment begins as soon as the infant is able to attach itself to the mother; the most important variable in this stage is clearly contact comfort. The stage of solace and security develops around the time that infants form a specific attachment to a specific mother. This stage is marked by curiosity and exploration, but with a constant return to contact with the mother for solace and in many cases by gentle punishment, and in human mothers by distraction and other creative means. However, the primary mechanism in the infant's disattachment from the mother is the maturation of freedom of activity, curiosity, and manipulative needs in connection with the external physical environment.

The final stage in the infant love system is the stage of relative independence. In its most important phases the dissattachment of infant from mother is an almost totally infant-guided process, while separation is determined primarily by the behavior of the mother. By the time of separation the mother-love and infant-love systems have served their important function of preparing the infant for later age-mate interaction.

CHAPTER FOUR

AGE-MATE OR
PEER LOVE

Probably the most pervading and important of all the affectional systems in terms of long-range personal-social adjustments is the age-mate or peer affectional system. This system develops through the transient social interactions among babies, crystallizes with the formation of social relationships among children, and then progressively expands during childhood, preadolescence, adolescence, and adulthood. Individual age-mate or peer affectional relationships may exist between members of the same sex or opposite sexes. There are, however, certain basic physical, biological, and behavioral differences conducive to sexual separation in infancy, and subsequently, to the development of intensified heterosexual interests and choices which begin in late adolescence.

The primary positive variable pervading peer love is that of play, which progresses from the asocial exploratory play characterizing early infancy to parallel play, and subsequently to the multifaceted forms of social, interactive play achieved by the child, the adolescent, and the adult. There have been many theories, and even some overinterpretations, of the social importance of play, but all have failed to see play as the

72

LOVE

primary factor in integrating the earlier forms of love, in fulfilling the inexhaustible social needs of the peer affectional or love system, and in organizing the experiences of the individual in preparation for the requirements of heterosexual or adult attachment.

Quaint and curious are some of the theories of early authors concerning the forms and functions of play. These speculations were based for the most part on anecdotal evidence of children's play, forgotten physiological theories, or an awakened interest in an evolutionary hypothesis long since put to rest. Spencer [1873] conceived of play as simply a release of surplus energy, as play must look to any aging man. The only relationship, of course, is that vigorous play and available animal energy are maximal at approximately the same age or developmental period. A theory of historical interest is that of Hall [1920], who, imbued with Haeckel's theory of evolutionary recapitulation, believed that each child reenacted the activities of his primitive ancestors and that ontogeny paralleled the phylogenetic evolution of man in all regards. Hall would be delighted to know that infants can swim before they can crawl, crawl before they can walk, and walk before they can speak [McGraw, 1935]. However, these fascinating facts have no importance in the development of human or monkey play. As we shall see, even the

73

development of play in infants of such closely allied species as macaque monkeys and men does not fit any such pattern as that of following the phyletic leader. There are basic qualitative differences in the play of men and monkeys at every stage and every age.

Groos [1901], on the basis of extensive personal observations of human and animal children, discovered and described the fact that the play of children had an essential functional value, and was not simply a diversion for the release of energy. Unfortunately he did not recognize the orderly progression of various developmental stages of play and failed to point out the effect of each stage on each subsequent stage. Instead, he saw infant play as direct training for future adult activity.

The child does learn and master such traits as affectional expression, friendship formation, social ordering, and even aggression in relations with age-mate friends and foes. However, these traits do not transfer to adulthood unaltered or unchanged. What is proper with peers is improper with parents. These basic behaviors may inherently influence the social development of all later stages, and the traits named are admittedly basic to the subsequent mastery of adult goals, games, and gambits. However, the infant plays for play itself, unaware and unconcerned about its adult significance. Indeed, as emphasized by Dewey [1922], play is freed from "the fixed responsibilities attaching to the special calling of the adult."

The data on human play are almost without exception limited, lonely, cross-sectional studies, observational rather than experimental in design, and conducted in homes and nursery schools, where control and management of salient variables is nearly impossible. All homes hope for happiness, and all nurseries need neatness and nicety. By the time the peer pattern has approached perfection or importance, nursery schools are only memories, and homes are temporary havens where vigorous play is strictly forbidden. In contrast, much can be learned in the laboratory, where an animal can be born, reared, and studied for years on end under scientifically controlled surroundings. In no other way can adequate information be obtained concerning the fundamental nature of play, the developmental interactions among the systematically sequencing play systems, the effects of enriching play development, and the heartrending catastrophes that transpire when normal play development is denied or distorted.

Although peer love and play have an important role in socialization, and possibly in some aspects of intellectual growth, neither peer love nor play arises from a vacuum or terminates in vacuity. Peer love is preceded by two antecedent love systems, mother love and infant love, which transmit their own heritage. It is also preceded by the two transitional mechanisms of contact acceptability and basic trust. Actually the transitional mechanisms may be of more social importance than the specific learnings acquired in the antecedent love system. It is possible that the love the infant has acquired for his mother, including the physical properties of her form and face, is transposed by simple stimulus generalization to the physical properties of peers. Such a theory is implicit in Freud's famous, and possibly fatuous, formulation of the power of the mother image in fashioning the wishes and wills, wondrous but not wanton, in each human adult male. Attempts by experimental psychologists to test such a theory have had doubtful results. Of course man may not be the best subject for such a test, but for some mysterious reason tests on other animals are rare. In casual observation the data on monkeys raised with surrogate mothers do not appear to support Freudian dogma. The first objects they found and loved in the world outside the maternal domain were inanimate rather than animate objects. Surely no real mother ever looked like a broken brickbat, a celluloid ball, or a multicolored painted piece of plywood.]

Whether or not specific affectional attachments are passed on by way of stimulus generalization from mothers to peers, there are at least two very important transitional mechanisms for which we must account. The first of these transitional or developing mechanisms is the mutual acceptance of physical or bodily contact with members of the same species. We believe, in the absence of specific experimental data, that the intimate mother-infant contact comfort does transfer from the maternal figure to age mates or peers. Play in all its complex forms is impossible if bodily contact is looked upon as undesirable or loathsome. Just as there is seldom fun without feeling, there is seldom feeling without fun. A second overwhelmingly important positive transitional mechanism is the gift of basic trust and security, as described by Erikson [1950]. We have already discussed the formation of trust and security in connection with maternal and infant affectional systems. Here we simply accept reasonable basic security as an essential social antecedent to the formation of peer love. Without basic security, neither the human nor the monkey infant would be free to express physical contact and to explore the playthings and playmates that are essential for the formation of age-mate love.

The age-mate affectional system begins when the intimate physical bonds between mother and child weaken and the infant wanders beyond the range of the maternal body and the reach of the maternal arms. This detachment process is primarily a function of the infant's developing powers of curiosity and wanderlust, the only lust the buoyant baby really has. The act of detachment may be supported by maternal rejection and punishment or by maternal apathy and fatigue. Even human mothers become tired and troubled.

As we have seen, mother love is usually prolonged and persisting, although in some societies and some mothers it may be relatively brief. Moreover, its duration is frequently a function of normal or abnormal interaction on the part of mother or child. Infant love, which depends on specific mother recognition and attachment, is established at six to nine months. It wanes as dependency ties decrease, although its persistence depends on numerous social and situational variables.

The age-mate or peer system is less standard, in both its origin and duration, partly because of the increase in number and complexity of learned or cultural variables. It is theoretical folly to assign rigid age ranges for the affectional systems. Nevertheless, age boundaries have convenience value in planning and producing developmental research, normal or abnormal, and interpreting such data. With this injunction in mind let us say that the peer affectional system begins at about three years in humans, peaks between the ages of nine and eleven, and wanes with the onset of adolescence, when peer relations become hopelessly entangled with heterosexual affection. Similar developmental periods exist for the monkey, but they make their appearance much earlier because of the monkey's greater physical and physiological maturity at birth. Subsequent monkey developmental periods tend to be about one-quarter the duration of the analogous human stages. Thus monkey infant love is probably specific at one month, vigorous age-mate play is present at four months, and childhood ends at three years.

We have defined the affectional systems in terms of broad social developmental mechanisms, with suggested age ranges [Harlow and Harlow, 1965; 1966]. As a matter of convenience we shall relate these to several of the well-established age classifications as well as to some occasional nontechnically defined terms. The human *neonatal*, or *newborn*, period is defined as the first two weeks of life. The term *baby* refers to the first year of human life, which is by definition the first part of infancy. *Infancy* is commonly described as that time between the neonatal and the *childhood* period, which begins at approximately three years of age and lasts until the beginning of adolescence. It is during childhood that the truly social forms of play develop and become organized, and begin to operate as creative socializing forces.

PRESOCIAL PLAY

The age-mate affectional system is of superordinate importance for normal social and sexual development. In fact it now appears that the increasingly complex processes of play provide the means and motives for the development of the peer system. However, play does not spring spontaneously like an Athena from the head of Zeus, even though it is indeed a godlike gift. Developmentally and functionally, it progresses according to a definite maturational pattern. Play with inanimate objects precedes play with animate objects, so that presocial play by definition precedes social play of comparable complexity. For example, the tiny tot plays with his dangling mobile and musical bells before he is six months old, whereas the social-partner games of peek-a-boo and patty-cake develop some months later. The detailed development and interaction between presocial and social play in the rhesus monkey has been outlined by Harlow [1969]. The presocial play of the boisterous baby mixing his pudding and his cereal, rolling his peas across the tray, and pounding the spoons in clanging cacophony precedes any activity approximating social play. Months pass before these simple acts are transmuted into social behaviors, at which time children might be

76

found exchanging sand trucks, rolling balls back and forth, or concomitantly pounding rhythmic patterns with kitchen lids and ladles.

We will briefly discuss three types of nonsocial or presocial play, the first of which is *exploration*. Simple examples of this are the child's playful exploration of his own body—touching toes, flapping ears, picking nose, and the inevitably disapproved act of masturbation. The second form is that of *parallel play*, in which two or more individuals play simultaneously and in close proximity, but without any apparent interaction. The final presocial play form is *instigative play*. In this case the activity initiated by one child serves as a model to another, who immediately accepts the challenge and attempts the chosen chore. The basic importance of presocial play and its effect on the child lies in the fulfillment of three functions: It trains the child in exploration of the environment; it weans him from the maternal figure as the sole security agent; it progressively prepares him to respond socially to the activities of peers. This progression is evidenced in the very nature of the three presocial play forms—exploration, parallel, and instigative.

EXPLORATION PLAY   Human children have presocial play capabilities unmatched by any other animal. The child drops his spoon on the floor and the mother replaces it religiously and relentlessly, again and again. Ultimately she may attach it to the highchair with a string and leave the retrieval to the infant's own devices. As mischievous behavior is reinforced, it gains in gaiety. From the child's point of view this is not social play, but asocial play. The mother is merely an inanimate object with marvelous cooperative capabilities. Other solitary play is that with a hobby horse or blocks, or looking at picturebooks and coloring with crayons. Solitaire may later represent a very nonsocial game of cards played on a table.

PARALLEL PLAY   Parallel play is playing beside others rather than with them. This type of play is commonly seen when two pretoddlers share the same play area but share absolutely nothing else. Each is fully content with himself and his toy and perhaps even the presence of his partner, but there is no desire to interplay. Thus the children engage in the manipulation of one or more objects without resorting to any social goal or social interactions, as shown in Fig. 4-1.

FIGURE 4-1   *Parallel play in human infants.*

FIGURE 4-2   *Monkey infants in close physical proximity.*

FIGURE 4-3   *Parallel play in macaque infants.*

INSTIGATIVE PLAY   Antecedent to the stage of true social play, but subsequent to the stage of parallel play, are the activities of a child which serve as initiators or motivators for other children but do not lead to social interaction *per se*. Such evoked activities may be conceived of as social sequential responses. They are socially motivated but are not necessarily socially achieved. Examples of such behavior include follow-the-leader, imitation, mimicking, the copy-cat routine, or monkey-see monkey-do.

MACAQUE PRESOCIAL PLAY   Play ranging from solitary to sequential appears in monkeys early in the first month. The members of a group of infant monkeys, as shown in Fig. 4-2, tend to remain in close physical proximity to one another, and when one member physically detaches himself, the others may visually orient to him and follow in sequence. Transient and relatively aimless oral, manual, and total bodily contact may take place without any social feedback being expected or received.

A crude type of parallel play is shown in Fig. 4-3, with early infant monkeys exhibiting parallel activities toward a single object. Whether or not monkeys engage in human baby-type parallel play is an open question. As the monkeys' motor capabilities mature during the first month, patterns of sequential play are commonly seen. A monkey climbs a wire-mesh ramp, and a second monkey follows; a monkey walks across a rod high above the floor, and one, two, or three monkeys may follow in sequence. One monkey finally swings free from a ramp to a flying ring, and other observing monkeys then approach the flying ring in sequence.

SOCIAL PLAY

As presocial play wanes, more complex and more socially demanding forms of play appear, and these comprise the multitudinous categories of social play. There has been a spate of studies on social play, but most

78

of the studies of human children have been observational studies in the home or nursery school or questionnaire researches on parents. Nursery school studies usually stop when the child is five, when play is literally in its early infancy. Homes and nursery schools greatly restrict many forms of play, particularly those judged by homemakers to be antisocial or inimical to orderly operation of clean kitchens or pretty parlors. As for the play questionnaires, most of the items appear to have been formulated by men whose memories of childhood play suffered severely from critical degeneration, retrospective falsification, or Freudian inhibition.

Social play may properly be divided into three major forms—free play, creative play, and formal play. Free play can be conducted without recourse to formal rules and may be physically vigorous and even violent, or sedately satiating. Rough-and-tumble play, cops and robbers, and chase, as well as playing house, school, and store exemplify free-play activities. Either physical or cognitive factors may predominate, but the outcome of the activity is not predetermined, and there is no prescribed process. Formal play, as the name implies, is conducted within the limits of prescribed or proscribed rules. In games such as hide-and-go-seek, London Bridge, and drop the hankie, the rules and regulations have been almost identical for hundreds of years. Formal play is doubtless limited to man, since language is almost an essential adjunct. Most other animals would inevitably find formal play a dull and deadly drag. Creative play differs from free play and formal play in many ways. One of these is that creative play is not unique to any fixed ontogenetic phase, but can be found throughout a series of ontogenetic stages. Creative play may be constructive and as simple as using a dishtowel as a doll blanket, or it may be as complex as the creative contributions of Shakespeare or Einstein.

FREE PLAY   In the conventional depictions free play is exemplified by games of catch, running, and romping. Certainly this is the most basic type of free play. However, there are free-play forms which transcend the physical. Beyond the physical there are types of free play which are primarily characterized by cognition. A prototype is invention. Finally, there are free-play forms in which cognition alone is not enough, but must be blended or modulated by affective tone. Within this category lie most works of art, such as painting and sculpture, musical composition, and writing.

Of all the types, physical free play is the easiest for the child, and the most disturbing for the parent. Despite its simplicity, this form of free play plays a predominant role in the socialization process, for it is here that social ordering and even social roles develop, that the rules of social intercourse are shaped, and eventually, that the control of immediate demand and aggression is established. Unfortunately there is almost no free-play research with human children—and there is some question as to whether most of the information we do have represents data gathering or woolgathering. We cannot help but think that much of

79

FIGURE 4–4   *Rough-and-tumble play.*

the observational data are poisonous parodies of physical free play's better and best behaviors. In spite of the lack of human data, the social and psychological impact of free play is amply documented by meticulous macaque monkey studies. Fortunately there is also one effective human study modeled after this monkey material [Jones, 1967]. For indeed, the best way to find whether monkey behavior can be generalized to man is to discover that a parallel already exists.

No other single form of play is more important to basic socialization in the monkey than physical free play. Frequency and finesse of social interaction in such play determines social status. Such contact play also shapes and shifts social roles.

Roughhousing monkeys wrestle and roll and sham bite, but no one ever gets hurt and no one cries out in pain (see Fig. 4-4). While the participants energize, of course, the parents agonize. The development of contact or roughhouse play in rhesus monkeys is shown in Fig. 4-5. It is obvious that this form of free play increases in frequency and force until the age of one year and then remains at a plateau for a considerable period of time. Since the entire laboratory staff was unsophisticated concerning sex differences when these experiments were planned, the enormous difference between the male and female babies in rough-and-tumble play was totally unexpected. The data presented in Fig. 4-5 give strong presumptive evidence that males and females are innately different in their approaches to play. This significant difference between the sexes is doubtless the primary biological basis for the subsequent cultural shaping of appropriate sex roles.

In addition to rough-and-tumble play, experimenters have observed and recorded a form of noncontact play or approach-withdrawal play. In this play pattern the infant monkeys chase each other back and forth, up and down, and round and round. Frequently the role of the chaser and the chased alternates, and occasionally, but rarely, brief body contact is made. The social importance of this play cannot be denied. It appears, for example, that if young female monkeys are not chased early, they remain chaste forever. Noncontact play matures a little later than contact play, but typically the two play forms intertwine for a long developmental period. Actually, there is now a considerable body of

80

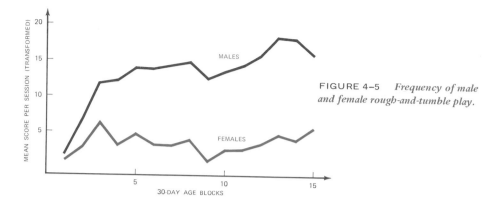

FIGURE 4-5 *Frequency of male and female rough-and-tumble play.*

data showing that noncontact chasing play is probably predominantly feminine. It certainly would not be surprising to discover innate sexual differentiation in play patterns. Such differences may uncover a secret to sexual segregation. They would be one of the unconditioned responses that are basic to learned social and cultural behaviors.

The British child psychologist Jones [1967], who trained with Tinbergen as an ethologist, tested the Harlow model of monkey rough-and-tumble play on human infants through free observation of infants five years of age and under in three nursery schools. Jones found that these children spent most of their time with age mates, and the teacher was relegated to the role of a distant agent disbursing basic comfort, care, and trust as a positive reinforcing mechanism for the expression of free play. Jones has concluded that "almost identical patterns [to the monkey pattern] of play occur, and are clearly definable, in human children." As an ethologist he describes this kind of free play in children and, with objective propriety, outlines the components of human responses as differing from those in the monkey, which, of course, they do; man is more than a monkey captured by culture. Human components include jumping up and down, open-handed lashing, laughing, and making mischievous faces; these are obviously human fixed-action-patterns evoked by social stimulation.

Human rough-and-tumble play looks hostile to the outsider, adult or peer, and it is agonizing to mothers, but it is an activity of gaiety and charm for the participants. Jones found rough-and-tumble play in human children as early as eighteen months and as late as three to five years. He points out that this primitive free play develops rather sharply into formalized games such as tag and cowboys and Indians, in which the same motor patterns apply but rules and verbal explanations have been added [Jones, 1967]. This is an obvious point at which monkey children and human children part company; monkeys do not play by verbalized rules.

Jones interprets the rough-and-tumble play in children as non-aggressive, although it is vigorous and must be basic to social-dominance role formation. Limited data suggest that human rough-and-tumble play, like monkey rough-and-tumble play, is much more masculine than

81

feminine, and that this difference is not culturally determined. Such sex differences in free play have wide implications for social and sexual development. As Jones points out, this infantile vigorous but joyous play pattern is "such conspicuous behavior that one could not have long disregarded it and its effects in an ethological study of children." It is quite obvious that rough-and-tumble play could lead to aggression, when aggression matures. However, it is unlikely that real concerted aggression has developed to any large extent in the four-year-old human child, reports from nursery schools notwithstanding. In retrospect, Jones' study serves as a clear reminder that human investigations, which are subject to bias, can overlook the obvious.

CREATIVE PLAY   Creative play begins when the child becomes the master, the creature becomes the creator, and all reality becomes subservient to the child's whimsical whirlwind of wishes. In creative play the child uses as raw materials things which to adults are finished products. He purifies and personalizes such objects to serve him on so unique a basis that neither trademark nor patent is necessary. This stage of creative play may be broadly defined as the use of objects for purposes other than their original ones. The child who constructs a staircase for dolls from blocks is enjoying creative play; so is the snow-soaked boy who builds a snow-packed dam in the gutter outside the house. Elements of mastery and self-actualization are seen in these creative constructions as the stairs ascend and the dam rises to the full limits of the impending gravity or turbulent torrent. What Piaget [1967] identifies as symbolic play and defines as the apogee of all children's play is, in this sense, an early aspect of creative play.

Unlike most free play, creative play is in no sense restricted to the activities of children. For example, an enormous amount of artistic effort—painting, sculpture, prose, and poetry—falls within this category. Of course motives other than pure entertainment might simultaneously be involved. Such motives might be economic, narcissistic, and even romantic. Attempts to identify and measure creativity [Roe, 1952; Taylor, 1964] have not been outstandingly successful, in spite of the fact that these attempts were made by people who are themselves recognized as creative. However, there seems to be relatively strong agreement on the characteristics of the creative individual. Less can be said of the available information regarding creative play. Psychologists have done virtually nothing to examine the effects of creative play. Is it a prerequisite for general creativity? Does it lead to withdrawal from reality or to a deeper involvement with reality? What accounts for the apparent decrease in creative-play activity during adolescence? How, when, and under what circumstances is it revived in adulthood? These are only a few of the questions which should concern the child psychologist and educational psychologist.

FORMAL PLAY   The moment a person surrenders his early creative-play position and possessions, he becomes a puppet. His moves are restricted and his movements restrained. Formal play is the dictatorship

82

of recreation. One is given rules, bylaws, and a credit system, and for each move or alternative the consequences are predetermined. This fatalistic fun is enjoyed by those who play ring around the rosie or drop the hankie, basketball or baseball, pinochle or poker. From a developmental standpoint there appears to be irony in this ritualistic recreation. As physical and mental independence increase, we tend to favor forms of play which have increased restrictions. Our recreational preoccupations are transformed from artistic adventures to scientific solutions.

While many of the important effects of free play are provided almost exclusively through animal research, no companionate body of information exists for formal play. Whether the human effects of formal play are restrictive or rejuvenating is a decision based at best on objective observation and at worst on sheer speculation. A problem of paramount importance in this connection is the influence of formal play on the apparently spontaneous efforts of the younger child. Does formal play stifle or stimulate, crush or create, integrate or segregate? These seem to be questions of concern for many but research topics for none. Even the parent-teacher associations recognize that creativity must not be stifled. They worry about the effect of classroom regimentation and formalization on spontaneity. Unfortunately educational researchers have failed to translate this clear concern into meaningful research. It may be that researchers are so preoccupied with work in a limited sense that they take pride in not being occupied with play. Whatever the reason, the child psychologist's contribution to the theory of human play warrants a modification of Churchill's eulogy to the British airmen: seldom have so few done so little for so many.

THE FUNCTIONS OF PEER PLAY

The various forms of presocial and social play may appear to defy their definitions, but this is a defiance in fashion rather than fact. Thus a child captured in a playpen experiences social constraint, but the awareness of an amused audience may make his play activity far more social than presocial. Similarly, the participant in an art contest may retreat into self-designed solitude and work unknown and unrecognized, but with the persisting presence of his imaginary audience as his primary motivation.

Exploration is not restricted to presocial play, although it originates at that stage. A lone child may visually examine and investigate a large culvert or tunnel but not dare to enter to culminate the acts of exploration. However, let him be joined by his gang of peers, and they will scurry to and fro through the tunnel without a tremor of fear. These examples of compounding and overlapping play forms not only give rise to complex play patterns, but also terminate in goals which are quite different from those achieved by any one single play form. For example, our monkey data show that presocial exploration is enormously

83

inhibited by the slightest fear, and this also appears to be the case with children. Social exploration, however, obliterates fear to a vast extent and encourages unrestrained exploration, which further reduces the fearsome aspect of the child's wondrous new world.

Friendship often begins in mutual exploration of some common object, task, or interest, but the fruit of such activities frequently includes subjective as well as objective discoveries. Thus the intertwining of presocial warp and social woof creates the color, complexity, and constructiveness of the child's play patterns. It is these complex patterns that facilitate the productivity, durability, and enrichment that characterize peer harmony. In this respect our classification of play forms fails to suggest the full fruitfulness of age-mate play functions. Classification is a hard task, and it forces us to digitalize that which in fact is a continuum. It is the haven of the professor and the hell of the student, who is forced to memorize as facts distinctions which at times are fiction. Nevertheless, classification does serve as a scanning device, permitting us to see some order in a situation otherwise bewildering in its perplexity.

By the same token, the paeans of peace which a mother sings for her child are achieved far less by her efforts than by the interactions of age mates. The primary basis of aggression control is the formation of strong, generalized bonds of peer love or affection. Fear may be thwarted by mothers, but aggression is controlled only by age mates. All primates, monkeys and men alike, are born with aggressive potential, but aggression itself is a relatively later-maturing variable. It is obvious that a one-year-old suffers from fear and is terrified by maternal separation, but the child neither knows nor can express aggression at this tender age. In fact he may long be hampered from expressing any aggression, for a child quickly learns that it is culturally unacceptable for him to be aggressive toward his parents, and frequently these are his only available associates.

This lack of aggression targets accounts in part for the fact that "evil emotion" culminates during the age-mate stage, long after peer affection and love have developed. It is the antecedent age-mate love that holds the fury of aggression within acceptable bounds for in-group associates. Thus one of the primary functions of peer play is the discovery and utilization of social and cultural patterns. Play acquaints the child with the existence of social rules and regulations and their positive as well as negative consequences. This may be looked upon as a rediscovery of the reality principle—not the individual-reality principle, which the infant discovers through interaction with its mother, but the social-reality principle discovered through interaction with his peers. Familiarity with the established social and cultural patterns offers the child the reward of social acceptance, the freedom to engage in play of challenging complexity, and guardianship against social failure and rejection.

With the discovery of this social-reality principle the child acquires new freedoms as well as new restrictions. For example, the fears and freedoms of a child newly initiated into a peer group are quite different from those he harbored prior to membership. The moral support supplied by the group diminishes the fear of real objective danger and intensifies

84

the fear of age-mate rejection. Thus it is not uncommon to find the child more self-conscious, although he gives the appearance of being far more overtly extroverted.

One of the primary socializing functions of age-mate or peer affection is the opportunity for the formation of personal love bonds. Most commonly these friendships are between members of the same sex because sexual differentiation of interests and availability has been established. However, friendship bonds are also established between opposite-sex members, and these friendships may be maintained for long periods of time at purely platonic levels. At the baboon level friendship may persist between males that are the dominant members of the troop. Neither age nor physical strength is a major variable in the establishment of these bonds. In fact friendship can be so overpowering that these, as well as such variables as physical attractiveness, intellectual ability, and even sex, may be subservient to the mysterious, unique, unidentifiable force that forms a friendship. This is one of the powers of peer passion— it cuts across age-mate relations to prepare the individual for adjustment to the inevitable.

HETEROSEXUAL LOVE

While the path to passion is paved with play, the heterosexual passion play is physically, behaviorally, and culturally distinct from the adolescent and adult forms of peer friendships. The heterosexual affectional system typically emerges at puberty, reaches full expression by late adolescence, and operates throughout most of adult life. We are not particularly concerned about the function of this system, since this is a matter of common—often extremely common—knowledge. Our interest in the heterosexual system centers on its developmental analysis—the variables which facilitate the development of this system into its culturally standardized form, and the variables which distort, disrupt, and destroy it.

Heterosexual affectional relations develop in all primates through three relatively separable subsystems—a sequence of postural potentialities, elicited by external stimuli and leading to the complex interbody positioning which adult coital behavior requires; a flow of gonadal gifts which indirectly and directly facilitate heterosexual interactions beginning at puberty; and an affective model built during the infant and age-mate love systems and applied, sometimes forever, after puberty. In other words, the heterosexual system appears with the development of mechanical sex, secretory sex, and romantic sex.

The postural problems in the development of the mechanical subsystem range from the relatively discrete reflexes, such as penile and clitoral erection and pelvic thrusting, to the complete coital combinations performed by adults. These responses are determined in part by anatomical structure, in part by basic sex-differentiating responses, and in part by environmental conditioning which shapes our destinies.

85

A great maturational gulf separates the appearance of mechanical sex from secretory sex. Components of mechanical sex appear from birth on, while secretory sex is the signal of puberty. Secretory sex operates through the action of gonadal hormones upon discrete sensory and motor elements of sexual behavior. The appearance of this subsystem in the female is marked by menarche and follows the cyclic pattern of hormonal fluctuations during the monthly menstrual periods. Secretory sex is acyclic in the male and is marked by the appearance of the ejaculatory reflex. The delayed timing of gonadal glory allows the two other heterosexual subsystems, the mechanical and the romantic, which emerge more gradually, to reach the development necessary for complete heterosexual relationships. Another difference between mechanical and secretory sex is the path through which each makes its influence felt. Mechanical sex is elicited by external stimulation, while gonadal hormones exert an internal influence on sexual behavior.

A third difference between these two subsystems is that the advent of mechanical sex is influenced by cultural variables, since its open expression can be either delayed or advanced by cultural disapproval or acceptance, or any other form of learned inhibition or reinforcement which individuals experience. Secretory sex is resistant to these influences since it operates in secret through internal physiological mechanisms which are insulated against cultural condoning or condemning. These two subsystems also differ in that social isolation early in life exerts profound negative influences on sexual mechanical expression, but learning leaves hormonal maturation and sexual excitement undisturbed. Nevertheless the failure to develop affectional bonds early in life has a profound impact on the naked realities of sexual performance. The power of love to mask love's labors is most evident in the emotional depression which may result when strong affectional bonds are disrupted. Sex secretions may create sex sensations, but it is social sensitivity that produces sensational sex.

Neither postural potentials nor gonadal glory are totally adequate to express the full range of heterosexual relationships in primates. They are particularly unproductive in providing the variables underlying romantic or idyllic ecstasies in humans. Beyond these two subsystems, there is a third one, which we commonly refer to in humans as romantic love and in monkeys as transient heterosexual attachments or preferences. This subsystem includes an emotional component of affection and the behavioral patterns defining masculine and feminine sociosexual roles. The affective component goes beyond the emotions of mechanical-secretory sex, and identifies the basic nature of the entire system. However, even this affection does not operate in a vacuum, and the context of male and female gender roles is required before romantic love can have any content or consequences. Masculine and feminine gender roles transcend postural differences during coital conquest and pervade courtship, companionship, child care, and community commitments.

Like the mechanical heterosexual subsystem, romantic love has innate and developmental roots in the preceding infant-love and peer-love systems. The basic trust gained from maternal love, the elaboration of contact acceptability, and the pleasures of propinquity acquired in age-mate play operate in the transition of peer affection to heterosexual love. The sex-differentiating behavioral patterns comprising adult male and female roles and social status also develop gradually from infancy onward. Like mechanical sex, the arousal of the affective component and the display of sex-appropriate behavior are elicited at times by external stimulation. For example, Paul Newman and Natalie Wood have acquired fame and fortune through their celluloidal capacity to create affective arousal which leaves females gasping and males groping. Similarly, exaggerated sex-role behavior prevails predominantly among the impressionable.

The third heterosexual subsystem is crucial for the future production of both monkeys and humans. However, it is vastly more complex in man than in monkeys because of the influence of a wide range of cultural variables. Through the increased capacity for abstract conceptual thought provided by language, human social life has complicated tremendously the basic primate patterns of social organization, and these cultural variables exert a pervasive influence on romantic attachments through children's learning about the culture's model for heterosexual relations. This model varies widely in different cultures, from promiscuity to monotony. Whatever the model, however, children accept it and expect to achieve it long before it acquires any functional significance for them. Romantic sex is also far more vulnerable than mechanical sex to early social isolation, since primates, especially male primates, who have not experienced love early will never learn to love, and social behavioral development cannot occur at a distance.

The romantic affectional subsystem also shares some of the basic features of the secretory subsystem. While it has early developmental origins, it is elaborated by maturational factors and by heterosexual learning throughout the growth period for secretory sex and reaches peak development at middle to late adolescence in those who are fortunate and not too foolish. This adolescent period of yearning and learning results in the assumption of adult roles in social groups of monkeys and men. It begins when promotion to puberty necessitates a redefinition of roles. Thus adolescents face the task of becoming familiar, through specific learning, with new modes of interaction with individual members of the opposite sex. Unchaperoned adolescents are almost universally successful in this learning. Parents of females in many cultures forget their own learning period and worry that their children are not facing the future cheek to cheek, that their learning is far too specific, or that practice sessions may not be limited to a single individual. Psychologists can assure such parents that their children are employing sound learning principles, including the partial reinforcement of unprepared parentage as a consequence of lack of precaution. Romantic love involves internal factors as well as external factors, and like secretory sex, these are mediated by the brain, although it is to be hoped,

87

by less primitive centers of the brain. These internal factors take the form of strong motives to be loved, and to be loved by a member of the opposite sex, acting as that sex should act. The need for close social bonds, the formation of gender identification as male or female, along with acceptance and adoption of sex roles and of the cultural reproductive model, are relatively permanent characteristics of human adolescents which operate with the strength of basic moral obligations.

Each of these three subsystems of the heterosexual affectional system provides independent contributions and can even operate to a limited degree in the complete absence of the others. Nevertheless, they normally operate together in adult male-female relationships. While there are doubtless many complex interactions among the three subsystems, our knowledge is relatively certain for only a few of these. For example, it is well-known that gonadal hormones act to lower sexual sensory thresholds, intensify sexual stimulation, and decrease the period of sexual arousal required to satiate coital responses, especially in males. A powerful interaction of the third subsystem of romantic love on the first is the total elimination of mechanical sexual responses when the capacity for male-female affection has been destroyed or distorted by inadequate or abnormal affectional opportunities early in life. This is not a regular occurrence in modern child-oriented cultures. It is, however, by no means unknown in humans who have been raised in institutions under impoverished social stimulation, or who have been raised by adults with little maternal merit. The total and often irreversible social crippling displayed by these few affectionless individuals provides striking evidence of the overwhelming importance of the affectional subsystem in normal heterosexual relationships. The importance of affection to sexual relationships is also revealed in the ease with which problems in the mechanical and secretory subsystems can be solved in the context of warm, intimate affection between a heterosexual pair. Problems such as premature ejaculation in the male, and vaginismus (vaginal contractions which totally prevent penile intromission) can be corrected within weeks by means of informed sexual procedures and a generous supply of remedial romance [Masters and Johnson, 1970].

This outline of the nature and variables of the heterosexual subsystems, their developmental trends, and their interactions, characterizes this affectional system in man and in monkey. The empirical basis for the outline comes in large part from experimental studies of heterosexual behavior in monkeys under controlled rearing conditions. These findings are described below to illustrate the bare facts of life. Similar studies of humans are, and in some cases must remain, nonexistent. Where partial human data exist, they in no case change this basic outline, although the human behavior is vastly more complex and these complexities will be considered. Abnormal heterosexual behavior often exists more in the minds of the created than the creator. Nevertheless, a separate section on this topic is included in order to reach the larger and more affluent of these two audiences.

88

The monkey neonate and the maturationally equivalent human infant possess two innate components of mechanical sex, even though their likeness to love is purely coincidental. These are penile erections, which are more prominent than clitoral erections in the female, and pelvic thrusting, which is more common but no more prominent in infant males. The normal and natural stimulus for infantile pelvic thrusting is a warm, soft body. The mother first provides these conditions, and any human mother who disclaims knowledge of this pelvic thrusting is either repressed or a bad maternal bet. Monkey research and competent psychiatric research leave little doubt that sexual reflexes involved in adult sexual behavior are present as soon as physical maturation will permit their display.

The next steps in the development of monkey mechanical sex achieve approximations to the essential components in adult male-female connubial combinations (see Fig. 4-6). One of the essential components of this adult pattern is the anatomical requirement for ventral-dorsal positioning of the male against the female. Another essential feature is that the female must support the male, at least in monkey societies, by standing on all fours and rigidly elevating the hindquarters. A third requirement is that the male must achieve genital propinquity by mounting and grasping the female's hindquarters with hands and feet and must achieve genital interaction by repetitive pelvic thrusting. These three features exhaust the postural possibilities for monkeys, although sex can be more stimulating to simple simians if the female's forelimbs are flexed, and if the female frequently reaches behind and looks toward the male, possibly in awe and admiration.

The first two components for this species-specific pattern, ventral-dorsal positioning and rigidly elevated hindquarters, grow out of three discrete responses—threat, passivity, and rigidity—during infant play. These three responses appear with regular frequency in monkeys by sixty days of age, soon after play begins—and they occur with statistically significant difference in frequency in males and females. As the data

FIGURE 4-6   *Basic adult sexual postures.*

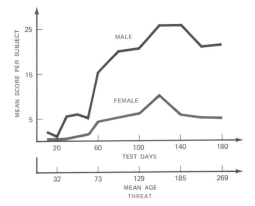

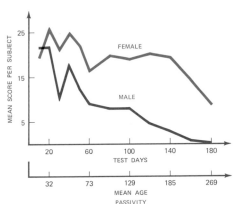

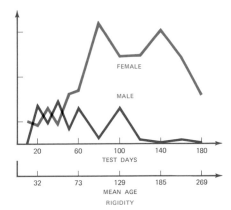

FIGURE 4-7   *Development of sexual postural responses.*

plotted in Fig. 4-7 demonstrate, threatening is a masculine prerogative, while passivity and rigidity are female prerogatives. Rigidity is the infantile precursor of the adult female sexual-presentation and sexual-support postures. When it is displayed by the female infant, after the male infant threatens and the female withdraws, stops, and waits (passivity), the ventral-dorsal situation is created by an assertive male approaching his diminutive playmate. But, while females presexually play by standing steadfastly, males presexually play by gripping and grasping. Figure 4-8 reveals that the male presexual pattern of hindquarter grasping, later followed by thrusting against a new, soft, and warm surface, is soon added as the third basic sexual component growing out of peer play. With all three components present, the approximation to the adult pattern is achieved with complete innocence (Fig. 4-9). At this point the sexual positioning pattern of adults is only one learning step away. Grasping and thrusting increases with age, as shown in Fig. 4-10, and a similar increase occurs in the complementary female rigidity reaction. This natural developmental sequence ensures that males and females will be at the right place at the right time when organismic opportunity occurs at puberty.

The appearance as early as sixty days of responses basic to adult patterns suggests that these are innate responses to specific external stimuli. Furthermore, their increase and refinement with age occur in the absence of reinforcement by sexual satisfaction or cultural comment.

90

FIGURE 4-8   *Basic presexual position.*   FIGURE 4-9   *The first presexual step.*

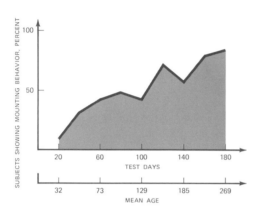

FIGURE 4-10   *Development of mounting behavior by males.*

The data on overt total-body sexuality in human infants are hidden in horror. It is reputed that such behaviors are seen in some more relaxed cultural communities, such as Indonesia and Appalachia, but we can describe no systematic developmental data. Obviously the particular postural potentialities would be different in form and related to the time and type of human play. The data collected by researchers in our society using survey questionnaires loaded for lust are devoid of broader developmental patterns and are both disappointing and depressing [Ramsey, 1943; Elias and Gebhard, 1969] . Data collected in this manner measure the end product of a hopelessly confused complex array of biological potentials, environmental and cultural conditioning, and the sex differences along these dimensions. However this complex array of variables operates, we discover that infantile self-exploration is present in humans, that limited and basically aimless sex play occurs in childhood, and that human males not only display more of everything than females, but also meander to maturity through masturbatory marvels. Males in our society have obviously written their own sexual developmental script by hand.

The details described for the development of mechanical sex in monkeys do not imply that mechanical sex is critical to the development of heterosexual affection. These responses do, however, illustrate that relatively complex behaviors can have a biological basis and emerge through mechanisms other than cultural ones. Moreover, there is no dis-

91

continuity from unlearned to learned behaviors, and complex capacities may well depend on a less than fortuitous combination of both. These responses also establish that there are innate sex differentiation mechanisms related to natural and normal social behaviors in primates, which undoubtedly operate in many aspects of social development in man as well.

THE SECRETORY SUBSYSTEM

Human females experience first menstrual bleeding at an average age of thirteen, which is the maturational equivalent of thirty months in rhesus monkey females. Using years when comparable data were available, McCammon [1965] reports that the age at menarche in humans did not change from 1930 to 1965, and anecdotal accounts of ancient China also placed menarche at thirteen years. Cultural variations and associated environmental changes apparently exert little or no influence on this subsystem in females. Data on equivalent pubertal age in human males is unavailable, but nonsexual measures of pubescence suggest that, like rhesus males, they lag significantly behind females.

Gonadal hormones in adulthood could conceivably influence the heterosexual affectional system directly or indirectly. A direct influence, for example, might affect the intensity or patterning of motives comprising the heterosexual systems in males or females. Direct and total control of human sexuality by secretory factors was a commonly accepted belief before the twentieth century—that is, before Freud and before the scientific study of sexual behavior. People then believed that deprivation of sexual activity in adult males created an irrepressible physical urge which could be relieved only through overt sexual expression. This belief functioned well for the management of guilt in men with unmanageable sexual appetites, but it did not survive empirical scientific digestion.

Gonadal hormones are not necessary for adult sexual expression in higher primates. The amazing amorous achievements of human and monkey males who are denied endocrine excitement, either by design or by disaster, demonstrate that the primary motivation for heterosexual relationships originates above the shoulders. Similarly, confessions of conjugal complicity by regularly menstruating and sexually active females reveal no systematic relationships between their secretory fluctuations and their sexual fantasies, frequencies, or fulfillments. However, female activity is so confounded by fear of conception that we may be at least two generations away from the necessary contraceptive calm. A more likely role for sex hormones in human sexuality is their influence in enhancing the affective impact of erotic stimulation. In this way hormonal action would contribute to learning that overt sexual responses produce positive affect, which could lead to the establishment of a pleasure seeking sexual motive. Once established, this hedonistic principle could operate alone even if hormonal support were withdrawn.

Whatever the direct contributions of the secretory subsystem to heterosexual behavior may be, it probably has far more important indirect effects in humans through the cultural and personal significance of the secondary sexual characteristics, which develop rapidly at puberty. The mediation of these effects through cultural influences can be demonstrated with a simple example of the significance of early and late maturation for boys in our society. The physical signs of puberty are taken as the mark of a dramatic leap toward emotional, cognitive, and social maturity. Consequently physically accelerated boys are treated as more mature by both adults and peers. They are rated as more popular and socially desirable and are given increased social status. Late-maturing boys, who do not receive this enhanced respect, become anxious about their status and adopt compensatory attention-seeking behavior, which in turn adds to their adjustment problems [Jones, 1954]. Cultural influence in mediating the transition from preadolescence to adolescence is often exerted through the rituals and badges which symbolize cultural recognition of new reproductive status and new social roles. The use of adolescent badges is probably culturally universal, although it is unknown in primates other than man. Beauty, however, is culturally arbitrary, and cultural conditioning determines whether unbelievable feminity and beauty are to be achieved with lipstick or labial lacerations.

Physical maturation and cultural recognition typically operate together to usher in the period of heterosexual potential, and their effects cannot ordinarily be separated for scientific study. However, the extraordinary confusion which occurred in the culture of Pukapuka demonstrates that cultural conditioning plays a powerful role in terminating the prepubertal period of sexual latency.

The island of Pukapuka is a tiny coral enclosure in the balmy paradise of the near South Pacific. For countless years fish teemed in the enclosing coral arms and the palm trees proudly presented their carbohydrate complements. The inhabitants were healthy and happy and such dominant hierarchy as there was existed in fashion and fiction only. In Pukapuka it was customary and conventional for the children to wear no clothes, since clothing had a special significance for postpubertal preparation. On warm tropical nights, when the full moon climbed heavenward over the bright blue waves, the adolescent boys would gather together and walk aimlessly eastward, and the adolescent girls, with their beauty for the first time clothed in bikinis, would gather together and walk aimlessly westward. By some unbelievable coincidence the two groups would meet and then disband as heterosexual couples. This was known as postpubertal preparation in Pukapuka.

All continued contentedly until the British missionaries arrived and were shocked to see unclad prepubertal children. They quickly resolved the problem by edict. All prepubertal boys and girls henceforth wore clothing. To the simple Pukapukan mind this had but one meaning— on warm tropical nights, when the full moon climbed heavenward over the bright blue waves, the prepubertal boys would gather together and walk aimlessly eastward, and the prepubertal girls would gather together and walk aimlessly westward. . . .

93

The essential characteristic of the romantic subsystem is an affectional bond between the two members of the heterosexual dyad. This affectional bond probably operates in some degree in every consenting heterosexual relationship which primates form. Anthropomorphic and cultural bias teaches us to identify this romantic subsystem with the ecstatic happiness of a cherished monogamous relationship. This same cultural bias categorizes deviations from this model as being devoid of romance, views cultures with less restrictive arrangements as primitive or semicivilized, and considers heterosexual behavior in nonhuman primates as mildly amusing examples of sexual depravity. However, comparative heterosexual analysis suggests that there may be less significance in the heterosexual variation among primates than in the variation between primates and more primitive mammals and vertebrates [Beach, 1969].

In most primitive animals heterosexual and other social behavior is under strict control of environmental variables such as temperature, hormonal variables, and external stimuli, such as the plumage of birds, which does no more than identify species and sex. These variables alone produce fortuitous and indiscriminate heterosexual dyads in primitive mammals and vertebrates for the period required for fertilization. A few species of birds are capable of individual recognition and form longer lasting relationships. These relationships, however, usually last no longer than the breeding season. They entail little behavioral variation in individual pairs from the species-specific pattern and are governed by the principle of impersonal, affectionless sex.

In contrast, all primates which have been systematically studied depart significantly from indiscriminate promiscuity. Their relationships are characterized by selectivity in pair formation, determined by affectional compatibility of individual pairs. This new principle of affectionate sex sets primates apart from more primitive animals and is a common element in all primate heterosexual behavior. Of course one rodent, the American beaver, some of the carnivores, most notably wolves, and at least one species of deer also display this selectivity, and some even form monogamous relationships for life. The scarcity of data on monogamous mammals does not imply that monogamy is the misfortune solely of primates. In fact, with the exception of the darling deer, our stereotypes of some animals are questionable; not all rodents are rats, and the wolf whistle is, in the wolf, a welcome only to faithfulness forever.

These comparative data suggest that the variations in human, ape, and monkey heterosexual relationships may be viewed as differences in the degree of affectional influence on the time and behavioral content devoted to the courtship phase, the conquest phase, and the consequence phase of the heterosexual bond. From this standpoint we can see similarities between the 15-minute march to conquest and the prolonged courtship and conquest involved in matrimonial morality. Thorough or limited selectivity is professed in both cases, and the affectional bridge leads to both bedrooms. In monkeys and apes, under natural conditions hetero-

94

sexual attachments are usually limited to consort pairs which last for hours or days. Such sexual arrangements might be described as brittle monogamy. The presence of a basic primate pattern for pair formation does not imply that there are not vast species and cultural gaps underlying heterosexual variations. However, affection as the foundation for heterosexual relationships in primates fosters the interpersonal propinquity in which learning, especially learned cultural complexities in man, may produce almost limitless variation.

Research has shown that humans and monkeys possess the same behavioral mechanisms which provide the transition from the preceding infant-love and peer-love systems to the romantic subsystem of the heterosexual affectional system. These transitional mechanisms lead to the basic requirements for the formation and functioning of the heterosexual affectional system. These basic requirements are heterosexual trust, acceptance of heterosexual contact, behavioral sex-role differentiation, and social motivation for sheer physical proximity. Although these four ingredients are necessary for all the major features of heterosexual relationships to appear, basic trust and acceptance of heterosexual contact are an absolute requirement for coital captivity. These four factors can also create the opportunity for additional learning at puberty, which may complement and elaborate heterosexual relationships. For example, as we have discussed, hedonistically motivated sexuality may develop as mechanical and secretory sex become fully functional.

While these four requirements adequately describe the common elements in all primate heterosexual behavior, in humans additional transitional mechanisms, as yet unknown, are required to explain the enormous cultural and individual complexities which the learning and language capabilities of humans provide. These learned variables probably operate through the exceedingly complex gender roles which human males and females acquire. Gender-role development in humans involves cognitive identification, acceptance, and adoption of the appropriate role. These roles are determined by anatomic variables, innate behavioral variables, and a host of cultural variables defining the prescribed heterosexual model for adults.

Unmistakable developmental reflections of all four transition mechanisms are seen in the peer-love system, and their extension to the heterosexual system requires only brief description here. Heterosexual trust is seen as the management of fear during male-female interactions. This fear potential is different from earlier fear, since it is created by a physical and emotional intimacy which is more intense than that of any preceding contact. Fear in the heterosexual relationship can be a monumental factor, especially in males, because of the sheer physical exposure. The most vulnerable surfaces of the body are openly exposed in the compromising postures required in adult sexual relations. In addition, sex occurs with an adult, and sometimes around other adults, in whom aggression is fully developed, along with the physical size and strength to inflict deadly damage. Fear generated by the need for physical safety is far more important in monkeys than in man, since human

95

culture usually provides for physical privacy in such situations. On the other hand, emotional vulnerability, which arises from open emotional intimacy, is probably more characteristic of human than monkey heterosexual relationships when the cultural model includes strong affective involvement. Greater emotional intimacy enriches human affection; it also covers psychiatric couches with exploited victims of love's betrayal. An analogous deep depression in chimpanzees—and in a few cases in monkeys—is produced only by total physical separation of pairs which had initially became partners in love through artificial long-term propinquity in captivity.

Acceptance of heterosexual contact is merely the sequel to the acceptance of nonspecific contact, an early mechanism in the transition from infant love to peer love. Humans and monkeys are similar in their capacity to develop an abundant amount of heterosexual contact acceptance from their earlier presexual play parties. This foundation of posterior knowledge will lead easily and naturally to learning the adult sexual knowledge necessary for creating babies or committing adultery. Monkeys in all social groups achieve this knowledge as infants and as adults without the aid of instruction or culture. Humans in less restrictive cultures also achieve this knowledge playfully. In restrictive cultures, where this path of presexual play to adult sexuality is prohibited, children must rely solely on their distinctly human capabilities to conceptualize and imagine heterosexual content, and they typically reach adulthood with a pattern of marginal expertise and expectations based on myth. Humans also differ from monkeys in their capacity to conceptualize their creator and their conceptions, which may add a dimension of guilt and fear to sex that is unknown in monkeys. However, conceptual and cultural variables seldom substitute completely for the absence of peer presexuality, with the result that human adolescents are typically faced with the task of developing acceptance and knowledge of heterosexual contact in the face of total ignorance or crippling inhibitions. Fortunately, through the remedial wonders which an intimate affectional bond can create, such knowledge and acceptance can be discovered and developed by human adults.

The behavioral sex-role component of the romantic subsystem includes the development of all those characteristics which we associate with masculinity and femininity. Development of gender roles is a vastly complicated developmental task, and we can do no more than make the broad outlines of gender-role development here. More than any other aspect of the heterosexual affectional system, gender-role development creates the greatest gaps between humans and other primates, both in the processes involved and in the sex-role contents. Nevertheless, there are some parallels in the sex-role development of all primates, as illustrated by the sex-differentiating behaviors in the age-mate system.

In monkeys the earliest sex differences appear in the patterns of penile erection and thrusting, and threat, rigidity, and passivity. These sexual precursors are early reflections of broader behavioral tendencies which separate male primates from female primates, although bisexual

96

potential is never completely eliminated. Male infants display an increasing preference for high-intensity total-body responses. High-intensity responses lead first to high frequencies of rough-and-tumble play, and as the nipping and wrestling becomes more intense aggression emerges as one of its components. In contrast females display decreasing preferences for rough-and-tumble play and engage increasingly in the moderate-intensity titillating play of chase and be chased. While male monkeys are learning about rank and assertive social roles through aggression episodes, females learn to passively communicate their recognition and acceptance of the brutish potentials of males.

In adults the sex-differentiating patterns of behavior in the peer group lead to the male role of provider and protector and the female role of specialist in nurturance and family, with special focus on child rearing. Monkey social groups are well organized and relatively peaceful, with males selecting the foraging and sleeping locations and protecting the group against destructive intragroup conflicts as well as unwelcome intruders. Unrestrained or frequent aggression, however, does not create tranquility, and a major task of all male primates is learning to manage aggression. The influence of the peer-group affectional bonds, along with the stabilizing influence of social ranks, accomplishes this goal, so that aggression is inhibited among in-group members and is displayed as concerted social action against outside threats.

The role of affectional bonds in socializing aggression is convincingly demonstrated by a study in which male and female monkeys were deprived of affection by raising them in individual wire cages during the ages when infant love and peer love normally develop [Harlow et al., 1966]. As adults these deprived monkeys were tested repeatedly in heterosexual dyads composed of a socially deprived monkey and a normal feral-raised test partner. Threat as a normal heterosexual behavior was used to communicate status and to settle disputes peacefully. Deprived males, however, not only displayed more threatening approaches, but also carried these threats through to damaging physical attacks (Fig. 4-11). These deprived males were totally unable to establish any affectional relationships with normal females because they had developed no aggression control through earlier affectional development.

Females in primate groups are apparently concerned with only the instrumental value of social status as it allows them to select their friends and lovers and provides the other concrete rewards of life. They

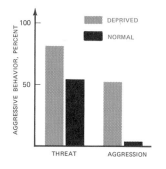

FIGURE 4-11   *Threat and aggression by normal and deprived males.*

typically do not engage in physical confrontations for status. The deprived females in this social-deprivation study did aggress initially against males. Negative feedback, however, quickly suppressed this aggression. Females win their way into male hearts and minds through passive resistance and social sophistication. In our society females usually attempt to combine love and marriage with social security.

In humans these gender-role landmarks are no less important or prominent. Young males prefer action and young females prefer active attention. Males in all cultures studied show greater preoccupation with and display of aggression, and management of aggression could clearly stand some improvement in modern societies. Social psychologists also recognize that social conformity can be more easily created and studied in the laboratory when female subjects are used. Even though child-rearing practices vary from culture to culture, early maternal care in some form is a cultural universal.

Countless studies on sex differences and gender-role development have been conducted on humans. The theories of sex differences and gender-role development, presented with thoroughness by Maccoby [1966], all focus on parental influences in shaping gender roles and claim that gender-role development is the exclusive domain of learning by the child. While learning variables must be heavily emphasized in the ultimate psychosexual outcome, it should be clear that biological behavioral potentials exist as basic primate characteristics. The richness of these potentials merely provides more innate response tendencies which can be shaped into more complex and flexible forms. An interesting theory by Kohlberg [in Maccoby, 1966] concerns the possibility that cognitive maturation provides a biological path to parental influence on children. Parental influences also play a greater role on sex-role development in humans than in monkeys. The advent of a child-oriented society places children under the direct constraint and instruction of adults for most of the daily learning period, and children partially develop the cognitive capabilities for sex-role learning well before their activities are predominantly centered in peer groups. Nevertheless, the peer group does eventually exert powerful forces in shaping behavior unless the capacity for peer love is destroyed. Parental influences on gender-role development should be traced through these age-mate experiences.

The social-motivation component of the romantic subsystem of heterosexual affection consists of the need for sheer and simple social proximity, as this finds a unique expression in heterosexual relationships. This motive for social affiliation has been measured and manipulated in human studies. In humans it appears more readily in females, possibly as a result of pressure toward independence in males. Need for affiliation is always present in greater or lesser degree, although it may be temporarily enhanced by threat or anxiety and temporarily satiated by prolonged propinquity. Affiliation begins at birth in primates in the arms of the mother, and in natural conditions it becomes strengthened through the learned associations in the social group. Deprivation of affectional development in infant monkeys also damages this motive (see Fig. 4-12).

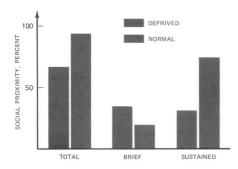

FIGURE 4-12 *Social proximity by normal and deprived females.*

In the monkey isolation study described above, the socially deprived females displayed the usual frequency of brief proximity with normal males, although these proximities were almost totally initiated by their heterosexual partner. However, they avoided any proximity that endured longer than 1 minute. Evidently the failure to experience affection early in life rules out the possibility of later reproductive heterosexual relations.

ABNORMAL SEXUAL PATTERNS

In an absolute sense there are no abnormal heterosexual behaviors. Any heterosexual behavior measured in an adequate sample of any primate, including humans, yields an approximation to a normal distribution. When the heterosexual behavior is sex differentiating we obtain two partially overlapping distributions, one for males and one for females. This overlap indicates bisexual potential, the sexual characteristics present to any and all degrees in the members of both sexes. Bisexual potential is a fact in humans and monkeys, and judgment of any sex-role behavior as normal or abnormal is only in relation to some manmade standard, real or fictitious.

As we saw in Chapter 1, behavioral normality must really be defined in terms of relative frequency of occurrence in any culture. A sexual response is thus normal if it occurs with sufficient frequency in other individuals with the same sexual and social status. Abnormal sexual responses are defined as responses which rarely or never occur in individuals with the same sex classification. On this basis, for example, masturbation is exceptionally normal in male primates and is subnormal, but not abnormal, in female primates. Evidently male primates, by reason of construction and constitution, have a better grasp on this aspect of reality than female primates.

However, statistical normality is not the only standard of heterosexual behavior, and in primates the standard of a male-female affectional bond takes priority. Thus relatively frequent masturbation, in either the bathroom or the bedroom, may be a little bizarre but it represents no intrinsic threat to heterosexual relationships provided that a heterosexual affectional bond has been well established.

99

The greater importance of the romantic subsystem in relation to the mechanical and secretory subsystems is often unrecognized by individuals concerned with the adequacy of their heterosexual adjustments. A prime example is one of the sexual-adjustment problems arising out of the new morality, or the orgasm revolution [Bernard, 1968]. According to recent studies, the current generation of parents has about the same pattern and frequency of premarital, marital, and extramarital sexual responses as yesterday's parents, but they are enjoying it far more than their own parents ever imagined possible—especially the females—as revealed by several measures, including orgasm [Bell, 1966]. Apparently the modern generation has escaped the clutches of guilt associated with orgasmic pleasure. However, cultural fear and guilt are in relation to the prevailing cultural standard, and the present standard is a high level of orgasm. As a result, the previous guilt over experiencing occasional orgasm has been replaced by apprehension over occasional failure to experience orgasm. Thus a perfectly normally functioning heterosexual affectional system can be subverted by application of an arbitrary and isolated standard for secretory sex. Alleged experts on love who equate coital captivity with heterosexual love do not understand the principle of relative frequency, nor have they imagined what life would be without affectional bonds.

We shall not detail here the wide variety of human heterosexual responses which have received value judgments ranging from outright perversion to mere personality problems. The variables operating to produce abnormal heterosexual behavior in humans are almost impossible to sort out from the data presently available since the individuals displaying these behaviors are usually adults when they are first studied, and by this time the bewildering array of variables which have operated simultaneously throughout life are hopelessly confounded. Theories in this area typically ascribe all romantic anomalies to learned variables, and particularly to parental influences on sex roles. Learning, and in part parental influence, clearly does play a significant role. We must assume, however, that learning always acts on some form of biological potential, and that whatever the environmental influence, it operates by interfering with the normal expression and shaping of biological potential in peer-group relations. Let us therefore consider some of the factors involved in abnormal sexual patterns.

Most modern theories of abnormal heterosexual behavior are in agreement that the most severe and irreversible sexual damage occurs when the romantic sex subsystem is destroyed or distorted. The overwhelming importance of this subsystem is borne out by the additional results of partial social deprivation in monkeys. As noted above, in this study male and female monkeys were denied the opportunity to develop infant love and peer love by being reared in individual wire-mesh cages. The heterosexual tests conducted when these monkeys reached reproductive maturity revealed that the secretory subsystem was undamaged by partial social deprivation. Deprived males achieved penile erection and masturbated, sometimes to ejaculation, with normal frequency. Females masturbated with normal low frequency, although orgasm is not presently a measurable response in female monkeys, if it occurs at all. The romantic subsystem, however, was severely affected by partial social deprivation. The need for sheer social proximity was depressed below normal levels, as noted above, and the component of sex-role behavior in the romantic subsystem was also damaged, particularly in males. Although deprived females quickly learned to suppress threat and aggression against feral males, deprived males never developed inhibition of their brutal aggression. The deprived males were sexually aroused by their feral partners, but even when they succeeded in recognizing the female's sex-role postures and solicitations, their only response was puzzlement or aimless groping, sometimes of their own bodies.

The mechanical sex subsystem was damaged but not totally destroyed in deprived females, who displayed the sexual-presentation posture with normal frequency but were unable to support the male adequately when he mounted. Although limited, the partial mechanical support led to the discovery that a major deficit in the romantic subsystem of deprived females was their nonacceptance of heterosexual contact and their basic mistrust of heterosexual contact when it did occur. Deprived females regularly fled when males attempted to mount, and even when mounting was managed on the sly, genital contact was a sufficient threat to convince these females never to leave their flanks exposed. The mechanical subsystem in deprived males was displayed rarely, and only in infantile forms resembling the fragmentary, disoriented presexual postures displayed by young infants during play. Since heterosexual trust and acceptance of heterosexual contact cannot occur at a distance, these components of romantic love could never play a role in the lives of the deprived males.

Figure 4-13 summarizes the coital consequences of partial social isolation in male and female monkeys. These results show that while social deprivation produced subnormal frequencies of mechanical sex in both males and females, the effects were far more severe in the deprived male. This pattern of greater heterosexual crippling in the male than in the female was found in virtually all heterosexual responses measured.

The greater effect of experiential factors in males than in females has been confirmed in a variety of test situations with many different species, ranging from rodents to carnivores to primates [Beach, 1947]. The human male has also been described as more susceptible than the

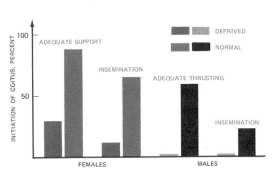

FIGURE 4–13   *Sex differences and partial social deprivation.*

human female to sexual developmental experiences, although the data used to support this sex difference in humans is based on biased samples and to some extent it undoubtedly measures differences in bias. It would not be surprising, however, to discover that human males are more sensitive to the operation of early social experiences than human females. As Money [1970] points out, the basic theme of nature is to produce a female, beginning prenatally and extending throughout the period of reproductive immaturity. Prenatally, a fetus develops with bisexual potential until the gestation period for sexual differentiation. At this time a female fetus develops unless specific hormones appear to create embryological differentiation into a male. Specific hormones must be added—and in "genetic" males they almost invariably are—to create a male fetus. The presence or absence of these hormones determines whether the individual will have the anatomical and physiological characteristics of a male or female. In monkeys the presence or absence of these hormones also influences whether the early sex-differentiating behaviors, such as threat responses and play-initiation responses, will be masculine or feminine in form. In humans the influence of prenatal hormones on postnatal differences in sex behavior is certainly less prominent, if it occurs at all.

A second developmental shift for males occurs at the stage when the male child must loosen the infant-mother bond and begin the development of male-appropriate behaviors of assertiveness and independence. The female child at this stage can maintain the infant-mother bond to a greater extent without cultural criticism or threat to her subsequent femininity. A third developmental difference between males and females may occur at adolescence, when the male's total devotion for intense athletic activities with boys alone must be tempered by tender loving manipulations with the allegedly frailer sex. Adolescent girls, in contrast, probably experience few problems in transferring their play with other girls to the nurturance and management of heterosexual affection.

Whether these basic development differences between males and females will shed any light on sex differences in heterosexual difficulties is a topic which must await the revisions of this text. However, other sex differences have been uncovered in the adult which may contribute to our understanding of the different heterosexual adjustments required by males and females. Males are apparently more capable of sexual arousal through the distance receptors than are females. Males, more than females, report sexual arousal when they are presented pictures and narrative material with sexual content. If this effect proves to be a reliable and biologically based sex difference, it will have implications for heterosexual behavior ranging from abnormal sexual fixations to panty raids. The most basic sex difference, the difference in anatomical location of the genitalia, may also create different adjustment problems for males and females. Bernard [1968] reminds us that the incompletely aroused male has no choice about disclosure of detumescence, whereas the female can and often does fake arousal and orgasm, usually to protect the male

102

against any feelings of inadequacy he might experience about his inability to bring her sexual fulfillment. The incompletely aroused male must hide his sexual performance in shame, while the incompletely aroused female can hide her sexual performance in love.

The paternal affectional system, tenderly illustrated in Fig. 4-14, is the affectional relationship of an adult male for an infant. The infant may be either a male or a female, and the infant may reciprocate with a greater or lesser degree of infant-adult male affection. Biological kinship between the adult male and the infant is not a defining characteristic of paternal love, since substitute fathers are not infrequent—and may even be a great deal more frequent than they think.

The paternal affectional system and the variables which affect it have been far less adequately studied in both monkeys and in humans than the other affectional systems we have discussed. While the data are limited, they nonetheless suggest that innate biological variables are minimal in paternal affection, and experiential variables are maximal, along with a great degree of cultural determination of human paternal love. The relative absence of innate biological paternal potential would imply, of course, that the paternal affectional system was not designed to serve an essential biological function. In nonhuman primates, when it occurs, it does often serve as a secondary protective system for infants. Paternal love occurs so irregularly in monkeys and apes, however, that this function appears to be little more than a coincidental consequence of learning to love and protect a baby through frequent contact with the baby's mother. Mitchell [1969] has summarized the studies of paternal affection in nonhuman primates, and the variables suggested by field studies strengthen the view that factors which create painless propinquity between an adult male and an infant create favorable conditions for learning a protective paternal passion. Adams [1960] suggests that the non-biological paternal affectional system results from the conditions created when the two essential biological dyads, the maternal dyad and the heterosexual dyad, function together. This model was designed for the

FIGURE 4–14   *Paternal love.*

human paternal system, but it also works well in organizing the variables which influence the paternal affectional system in monkeys and apes.

The paternal affectional system in monkeys has never been found with the length or strength in which it occurs in some cultures, such as our own. Adams thus maintains that the paternal dyad in humans, as in monkeys, is neither required nor designed to serve biological functions. In some primitive societies the maternal dyad and sexual dyad operate apart from the nuclear family arrangement of father-mother-children to provide the characteristic societal functions. In other societies, where there are different patterns of economic, educational, and socialization concerns, the nuclear family arrangement, or some other, may be an essential factor in carrying out these concerns. However, analysis of the functions and the variables underlying paternal love in primates probably should not be oriented toward a search for the biological variables and the biological roles of paternal love. Perhaps the paternal affectional system is unique in that it is learned along different dimensions to serve different functions in different societies.

Love, more than any other emotion, is characterized by the properties of both the devil and the divine. Since love encompasses such diverse facts and faces, it carries with it unlimited possibilities for frustration as well as fruition. Torn between love's potentials and penalties, we harbor thoughts and feelings about it which we often find difficult or impossible to express, let alone examine objectively. Although we look upon our own love as a gift, the framework of the laboratory setting enables us to view the multitudinous aspects of primate love in general with a greater measure of objectivity.

SUMMARY

It is primarily through the age-mate affectional system, expressed in peer play, that social and cultural patterns are learned, control of aggression is accomplished, and the foundations are layed for later sex-appropriate behavior. The stage of presocial play, characterized by exploration, parallel play, and instigative play, provides progressive preparation for interaction with peers. The stage of social play takes three forms—free play, creative play, and formal play. Free play, clearly the most important socializing influence, is typified by rough-and-tumble play and various forms of approach-withdrawal play which provide learning in social ordering, development of later sexual posturing, and the formation of specific affectional relationships. Creative play, typified by the use of objects for purposes other than their original or primary ones, extends to the creative efforts of adulthood. Formal play, characterized by the fixed rules of formalized recreational activities, also extends to adulthood.

The heterosexual affectional system develops in all primates through three discrete subsystems. The subsystem of mechanical sex begins in infancy with reflexes of penile erection and pelvic thrusting and develops through the gender differentiation and presexual posturing of the age-mate period into the complete behavioral pattern of adult coitus. The secretory subsystem develops with the maturation of hormonal influences on secondary sex characteristics and behavior. The romantic subsystem, which is based on an affectional bond between two members of the heterosexual dyad, is an outgrowth of the preceding affectional systems by transitional mechanisms that lead to the four basic requirements for normal heterosexual functioning—heterosexual trust, acceptance of contact, behavioral gender differentiation, and motivation for social proximity. The romantic subsystem occurs in all primates and in some other animals, but in man additional transitional mechanisms are probably required to provide for the enormous cultural, cognitive, and individual complexities engendered by man's capacity for thought and language. Abnormal sexual patterns are generally a result of improper development of the romantic subsystem. Although secretory sex is not affected, the failure or destruction of antecedent affectional systems, especially the peer system, damages not only the romantic subsystem, but the mechanical subsystem as well, with more severe effects in males than in females.

The paternal affectional system often serves as a secondary protective system for infants, but it varies widely with species and culture, and its roots seem to lie in experiential rather than biological variables.

CHAPTER FIVE

AVOIDANCE AND AGGRESSION

Human beings are born with the face of the devil as well as the face of the divine. We have already discussed love in its five aspects. The twofold face of the devil appears with the advent and development of the evil emotions, fear and anger. In a strict operational sense fear and anger are emotions, not behaviors. However, associated with these emotions are sets of behaviors which can be defined and delineated by observation. A major consequence of the emotion of fear is the expression of fear-elicited behavior. The emotion of anger has a similarly clear behavioral expression. In general fear is expressed in avoidance of the fear-eliciting person, object, or situation, while anger takes the form of approach behavior directed toward the infliction of psychological or bodily harm—aggression.

It is paradoxical that social integration is determined in large part by the antisocial motives of fear and anger. However, there are two reasons for this phenomenon. First, the emotions of love are ordinarily prepotent over anxiety, anger, and even pain. Therefore the positive, integrating forces of love can operate effectively to shape the individual and his society, regardless of the behavioral consequences of the evil

106

FEAR AND ANGER

emotions. Second, love matures before the evil emotions mature and operates to ameliorate or channel the evil emotions. Unrestrained aggression might well endanger the survival of any species with well-developed social structures, but controlled or socialized aggression in these species is essential to the development of cohesive groups which work together against outside enemies. Thus aggression operating through the channels provided by antecedent love increases the probability of survival for the species.

There can be little question that with respect to species which exhibit complex social behavior, particularly primates, the potential for fear-elicited and aggressive behavior is inherited. It is inevitable that any social organism will exhibit these responses throughout its existence, regardless of the environment in which it is raised. However, the form and frequency of such behaviors are shaped by environmental influences, social and nonsocial. Both the certainty of occurrence and the flexibility of expression are readily observable in maturation studies of human and nonhuman primates. The natural history of aggression and the neural mechanisms that produce it are considered further in the context of motivation (Chapter 10).

Data from a series of long-term experiments with rhesus monkeys

107

lead us to believe that the nature and operation of social learning depend in large part on the orderly maturation of the three basic social-emotional patterns of affection, fear, and aggression. Some form of affection—positive adient response toward members of the species—precedes widespread fear responses toward specific external stimuli of less than catastrophic physical intensity, and specific fears in turn precede severe and physically damaging intraspecies' aggressive responses. In the rhesus monkey these patterns mature in orderly sequence. Affection is normally well established by two months, signs of fear emerge at approximately three months, and signs of aggression are nonexistent before the age of six months. Furthermore, the normal progression of this sequence is essential to all later stages of development. Any environmental manipulation that distorts, disturbs, or otherwise denies this orderly sequence leads to maladjustment in later social-sexual development. In other words, the antisocial responses of fear and aggression are socially constructive for the individual, and ultimately for the species, only when they are preceded by the normal maturation and development of love.

FEAR AND ANXIETY

Like all basic emotions, fear arises from both unlearned and learned variables. Even though we know that all such emotions are primordially unlearned, it is sometimes difficult to show when they first arise in newborns of any species and also to define the stimuli that elicit them. The newborn human has little voluntary control over his musculature, and the few gross responses he can make are doubtless inadequate to express his full emotional repertoire. After extensive observation of many infants Bridges [1932] proposed that there were definite stages in the differentiation of emotions. She ascribed to the newborn only excitement, which differentiated at three months into delight and distress. Even before six months of age, distress differentiated into disgust, fear, and anger, and a short time later delight differentiated into elation and affection—affection first for adults and later for other children. There is reason to believe that the newborn child differentiates and responds to pain and pleasure long before three months and probably differentiates fear and anger before six months, but the pattern of differentiation is essentially the same for all infants.

Although the role of learning in the acquisition of specific fears and targets for anger is obvious, this evidence of a specific sequence of emerging emotional states enables us to reinterpret certain early theories concerning the hereditary basis of emotions. An infant does not, as was once believed, inherit the specific behavioral expressions of emotions that were exhibited by his ancestors. Rather, the capacity for certain emotional states emerges through maturation, and through learning the number and nature of stimuli that elicit reactions in the individual expand. Similarly, emotional behaviors are acquired not during embryonic life, but through learning based on antecedent maturation processes. A joyful mother may well produce a joyful child. However, this is more likely to be a result of imitation as the growing child constructs his picture of reality than the mother's joyful state during pregnancy. The mother's emotional state does, of course, influence the fetus. Emotional states in the mother are accompanied by changes in the autonomic nervous system, which affects hormonal secretions from various glands and influences the chemical composition of her bloodstream; these chemical factors are transmitted through the placenta to the fetus' circulatory system. Thus, although there is no direct connection between the nervous systems of mother and fetus, the mother's emotional state during pregnancy may clearly affect the general overall development of the fetus. Specific emotional reactions, however, are not transmitted from mother to fetus.

The first psychologist to investigate the fundamental stimuli that elicit emotional responses was Watson, who postulated that the basic emotions of fear, anger, and love were innate, and that each could be elicited separately at birth by a specific stimulus category [Watson and Rayner, 1920]. He contended that fear was elicited by loud sounds and loss of support (falling), anger by physical restraint, and love by stimulation of the erogenous zones—a kiss full blown to Freud. Although the foundations for these three emotions may well be innate, they are not discernible independently at birth. Watson's classification of eliciting stimuli has proved to be basically accurate. However, his theory does not include the possibility that the emotional differentiation that develops at later stages may be a result of maturation as well as learning.

ANXIETY-ELICITED BEHAVIORS

Two very prominent examples of emotional-response patterns which emerge through maturation at different ages are stranger anxiety and separation anxiety. Some time during the infant's sixth month a stranger's face elicits a reaction termed *stranger anxiety*, which is evidenced by tightening of the infant's face and the initiation of crying. The reaction ceases as soon as the stranger moves out of the infant's line of vision and is elicited again when he reappears. Fortunately for harassed parents, by the twelfth to fifteenth month this reaction has usually disappeared [Schaffer and Emerson, 1964a]. However, what is it in this situation that elicits anxiety? Anxiety is the typical emotional response to a situation which is perceived as novel or unfamiliar. By six months the child has sufficiently developed a schema or mental image of his mother's face that he is readily able to detect discrepancies from it. Hence at this age a feeling of anxiety follows awareness of a new or unfamiliar face. Undoubtedly the infant's schemata later expand to permit a greater tolerance for unfamiliar faces. Eventually the unfamiliar even offers delight and intrigue.

109

Another situation which often elicits anxiety in the six-month-old is a feeling of helplessness. When the normal flow of events as perceived by the infant is disrupted there is little he can do to alter the situation and his only available response is anxiety. This emotional reaction has been summarized by Mandler [1964], who has emphasized the fact that the inability to complete a sequence of activities and the lack of alternate completion sequences results in helplessness. Furthermore, he believes that helplessness is, by definition, anxiety.

In specific reference to stranger anxiety, the six-month-old is clearly limited in his ability to manipulate and control his environment. Stranger anxiety may subside during the following months and be totally absent by the age of two. At this age a stranger may indeed pose potential threat, but the two-year-old is more capable of alternative responses in order to control circumstances. Not only can he run to his mother, but he can also ask questions about the situation, which may include information about the stranger.

Another anxiety, termed *separation anxiety*, emerges at approximately ten months. This is evidenced by an increased tendency for the infant to cry whenever his mother leaves him. This protest reaction to temporary separation from the mother is not exclusive to human infants. Monkey infants exhibit similar reactions, characterized by marked increases in infant vocalization and agitation. As we saw in Chapter 3, an infant monkey placed alone in a strange situation will typically clutch himself, huddle, and scream with fright. However, in the safe presence of his mother, real or surrogate, the same situation fails to elicit any fear at all. In time the infant will actually search out and explore the novel environment, using the mother as a base for security. The object of separation need not be a mother. When a six-month-old monkey raised with only a cloth diaper as a companion is separated from his diaper, the same protest reaction is elicited. Protest reactions to separation and separation anxiety thus appear to be innate mechanisms which develop after the infant has formed an attachment to an object—any object—to which he has been exposed for a substantial period of time [Cairns, 1966].

THE LEARNING OF SPECIFIC FEARS

Doubtless most of our adult fears are learned, but the type of learning that produces fears also changes with age. Early in life most fears are probably learned by a conditioning process—the association of a new stimulus with an unlearned stimulus and generalization of the new stimulus to objects physically similar. The acquisition of fears by conditioning was first demonstrated by Watson [1920]. He began by showing a young infant, Albert, a toy white rat, which initially evoked no fear responses. Next, every time he presented the rat he also presented a loud sound, a stimulus he knew would evoke a fear response in young infants. It took only six or seven trials for Albert to exhibit fear toward the toy rat as well as the loud sound. Furthermore, Albert's fears gradually generalized to similar objects such as a cotton ball and a white beard, and the more similar the object to the rat, the more fear it evoked. Thus fears may be learned very early in life, certainly during the first year, and may persist long after memory of the event that caused the fear is lost. In addition, as indicated by Albert's behavior, fears tend to generalize very broadly, especially when they are formed early in life.

As soon as the child forms social attachments to his mother and father, and subsequently to playmates, he learns fears through social imitation, and there is a relatively high correlation between the nature and number of fears of mother and child. For example, during thunderstorms the tense and perturbed parent may unwittingly serve as a model for the growing child, who imitates the behavior of those closest to him. At later ages children may acquire a large number of fears as a result of language techniques and by sheer fantasy and imagination. Once formed, fears are very persistent. Many fears formed at the age of five persist past fifty. Even adults who are generally described as brave frequently have one or more persistent, disparate fears or phobias. Furthermore, fears are often formed without the desire or effort to learn them and are frequently acquired against the conscious or unconscious wishes of the victim.

As children mature their emotions become more specific and often deeper in their expression. Moreover, the stimuli that arouse specific fears are different at different stages of development. Before the age of two noises may account for as much as 25 percent of the fear-eliciting stimuli, whereas by age twelve only 3 percent of the child's fears can be attributed solely to agents of noise. There is a similar decline with age in fear of strange situations and strange persons. Imaginary creatures play an increasing role in the arousal of fear as the child grows older. For the young child, ghosts and goblins lie lurking in the darkness. An astonishing 20 percent of the fears held by young children deal with such imaginary creatures [Jersild et al., 1933].

Many childhood fears are just outgrown, especially if the environment offers a feeling of security and nonadaptive fears are actively discouraged. Intense fears, however, do not dissipate with time, and the customary techniques employed to eliminate them are by no means equally effective. Jersild and Holmes [1935] found that ridiculing or ignoring a child's fear was essentially ineffective in eliminating it. More drastic action such as physical punishment was found to be equally ineffective. Demonstration, explanation, and reassurance are substantially ᵦter, but not entirely successful. However, if a pleasurable association ᵦth the feared object can be established, the original fear may be overᵦme by _counterconditioning_. Watson found that Albert's fear of the toy ᵦhite rat was gradually removed by presenting something pleasurable, ᵦuch as candy, with the toy. An outgrowth of this technique is the ᵦehavior-therapy method of desensitization discussed in Chapter 1.

Many fears, of course, are healthy and adaptive in that they serve to protect the individual. Parents have every hope of instilling realistic fears of ocean undertows, busy intersections, and loaded guns. However, fears instilled to the point of obsession may limit the horizons of the growing child, who for maximal personal development should be in the process of exploring his environment. An obsessive fear toward one situation may gradually be generalized to other situations in which no fear is warranted and may even lead to a general state of apprehension or anxiety under all circumstances. In extreme cases anxiety can be totally disabling and result in the eventual elimination of all environmental and social interaction.

Perhaps the most frequent consequence of nonadaptive fear reactions is their generalization to a stage of *free-floating anxiety*. Here the emotional reaction is not in response to specific objects or situations. Instead the individual is burdened with feelings of apprehensiveness, uneasiness, and finds himself full of foreboding fears. Although there are exceptions, the emergence of anxiety in the child can often be traced to either direct or indirect parental factors and forces. In addition to the simple imitation of apprehensions in one or both parents, parental attitudes and child-rearing practices themselves may initiate feelings of anxiety. After extensive research Saranson [1960] has suggested that one antecedent condition leading to anxiety is the particular parent-child interaction in which there is a constant parental threat of negative evaluation of the child's performance. The one ready reaction to this negative evaluation is aggression. However, since the child is dependent on adults, the conflict that arises between his dependency needs and this aggression reaction may lead to anxiety. Saranson also reported that mothers of highly anxious children tended to evaluate their child's behavior in terms of unrealistic standards of his capabilities. As anxiety affects the adult, so it affects the child.

Anxiety is an uncomfortable experience, and the individual often puts forth considerable energy to avoid or alleviate this distressful state. In the sense that defense mechanisms provide protection against painful experience, they serve an adaptive function. However, in cases of more extreme anxiety the rigid and inappropriate behavior adopted as a defense can be self-defeating in that it becomes a source of further anxiety and eventually interferes with adaptive function. Thus in situations where initiative, creativity, or utilization of complex cognitive processes are required, anxiety takes its toll by inhibiting effective performance and fruitful pursuits.

Since fear and anger both are socially disrupting emotions, all primate social groups have evolved adaptive mechanisms of emotional control. Fears, particularly early fears, are held in check primarily by the antecedent formation of infant love, the formation of basic security and trust by the infant for the mother. In the mother's absence the infant monkey fears everything; it is a baby in terrible terror. Although the primary security safeguard is the mother, this function is extended by age mates and adults with chronologic development.

112

In the human infant anger becomes a distinct emotion when, along with fear and disgust, it is differentiated from the more general emotional state of distress. The human infant is allotted less than six months in his new world before he begins to experience this emotion many times, for many reasons, and he will express it in many ways all his life. The initial manifestations of anger, however, become modified very early in life. Goodenough [1931] noted that expression of anger changed from temper tantrums and outbursts of uncontrolled motor activity of the infant less than one year of age, to the directed motor and language responses of the child by the age of two. These latter responses had accounted for a mere 14 percent of the outbursts of the younger infant.

ANGER AND AGGRESSION

Although the antecedent conditions of anger in the adult usually involve psychological or social limitations or frustrations, the conditions leading to the arousal of anger in the very young are primarily physical. Restrictive clothing, confinement, and denial of desirable play activities are all situations which can give rise to anger in the child. Obviously some restrictions are necessary for the survival of the child and the sanity of the parent. However, many such restrictions are all too often based primarily on arbitrary rules or ungrounded parental fears. Arbitrary and inconsistent parental demands may present the child with an unsolvable, and hence frustrating, discrimination problem. Such feelings of frustration may be vented through aggressive behavior. Aggression, however, may be directed either inward, toward the self, or outward, either toward the members of one's own group or toward members of other groups.

Self-aggression can be observed in rhesus monkeys raised in social isolation. This behavior becomes prominent after three years of age and is frequently exhibited when strangers are present in the colony room. These angry monkeys chew on their own hands, arms, feet, or legs, sometimes to the point of tearing the flesh (Fig. 5-1). It is somewhat similar, in the anthropomorphic sense, to the self-destructive behavior displayed by some autistic children. Self-aggression in humans is often reflected in psychological disturbances, with the most extreme form being suicide. This violent form of self-aggression is a complicated aspect

FIGURE 5–1 *Self-aggression.*

113

of human life, and no simple variable can account for its various manifestations. For example, suicide rates are not constant across the United States. Urban-dwelling persons commit suicide more frequently than do rural-dwelling persons, with the greatest incidence in the most densely populated areas. Single, widowed, or divorced people have more suicidal tendencies than married people, and although more females attempt to take their lives, males have a higher rate of success. Also, the suicide rate increases with age.

Innate aggressive tendencies emerge through maturation at different ages, depending on species, sex, and individual differences. There is little disagreement among comparative psychologists that aggression is part of the biological heritage of primates. However, some social psychologists who limit their studies to the human animal still believe that aggression is basically a learned behavior, and that the differences which occur between the sexes or among individuals within their sex group are accountable solely on the basis of experience. No doubt the late appearance of aggression in the developmental sequence has led some observers to underestimate its biological basis. It is customary to accept maturation as a factor in the development of locomotor behavior, language, intelligence, and sex. However, with respect to human social behavior, which has a large and obvious learning component, there is apparently reluctance even to conduct the research that might demonstrate a maturational variable, and studies have focused on the variables that alter the expression of aggression after the behavior has already developed.

As we saw in Chapter 4, aggression not only has clear precursors in both monkey and human play long before it matures as a behavioral expression, but in the monkey there are innate gender differences which play a vital role in later heterosexual development and behavior. Although the specific patterns of behavior are different in the human being, these monkey data lead to the speculation that the sex differences observed in human aggressive expression result not from learning alone, but from learning superimposed on similar innate differences in aggressive tendencies. Learning undoubtedly exerts considerable influence in our culture, where young males are often actively encouraged by both maternal and psychological rewards to behave aggressively and young females are usually reprimanded for action which is aggressive. Given these conditions of reward and punishment, it is not surprising that the two sexes quickly develop exaggerated differences in the display of aggressive behavior. Increasing age produces not only greater sex differentiation, but also qualitative changes in aggressive behavior. Screaming, weeping, and physical attacks, evident in the very young child, decline with age as verbal aggression increases.

The emerging sex differences are also reflected in terms of the stability and continuity of aggressive behavior. Data from a longitudinal study indicate that aggression is much more stable in males than females [Kagan and Moss, 1962]. It was found that the rage and temper tan-

114

trums displayed by the male preschooler were more predictive of his later aggressive behavior and the ease with which he expressed anger in adulthood than was similar behavior in the female preschooler. Presumably the lack of punishment for aggression encourages the perpetuation of such behavior in the male, whereas aggressive young females soon learn through social pressures to inhibit overt expressions of aggression.

THE SOCIALIZATION OF AGGRESSION

Because the emotion of anger develops in all infants, and one outlet for this emotion is aggression, the socialization of aggression is a primary concern for any social group. Socialization of aggression does not mean the total inhibition of aggression, even in females. The aggressiveness of any male could not surpass maternal aggression when the life or safety of her young is threatened. Such behavior is adaptive for the survival of both the individual and the species. However, harmful aggression between members of a species must be controlled if the species is to survive. The techniques of control vary, of course, with the species.

In the rhesus monkey the maturation of positive affective feelings precedes aggression and operates to channel aggressive behavior. Thus when aggressive behavior does appear, usually at approximately eight months, it is ameliorated primarily through age-mate play behaviors. In the second year aggression becomes a commonplace social behavior for males. Not only is there direct aggression but displaced aggression as well, with clear-cut scapegoating. A common observation, both in laboratory and field situations, is that an animal intermediate in the dominance hierarchy of a social group, when attacked by a more dominant group member, will subsequently attack a less dominant member of the group with no apparent provocation; this is also a commonplace human phenomenon.

Part of socialization entails the learning of appropriate targets for aggressive tendencies, and the monkey must be reared in a group during the period when aggression matures in order to learn such targets. Monkeys reared only with their mothers for the first eight months of life are hyperaggressive when subsequently exposed to peers. Monkeys reared in total social isolation subsequently exhibit aggressive behavior, but it is exceedingly ill-directed. Such an animal may attack an infant, something a socially sophisticated monkey would never do, or attempt to attack a dominant male, something few socially reared animals are stupid enough to try. Whereas social isolates will often aggress against themselves, self-aggression is exceptional behavior for a socially sophisticated monkey, even under unusually stressful environmental conditions. Although aggressive behavior is inevitable for maturing and adult monkeys, it is obvious that its occurrence and direction are derived from social experience.

By the time anger has developed into a powerful social or anti-

115

FIGURE 5–2   *Monkeys collaborating against a crocodile.*

social force the mother-infant bonds have long since weakened. For this reason age mates become the primary social source of aggression control. Through peer play a new affectional bond develops which tends to hold aggression at a controlled, nonlethal level. The age mates with whom we play, in fact or in imagination, become our in-group, and all others serve as out-groups. Aggression against out-group members is strong and can be augmented by a host of environmental variables to the point of lethality.

Aggression control and cooperation by in-group members of a monkey clan are illustrated in Fig. 5-2. The monkeys on the island are a cohesive in-group, and those who play together slay together—not each other, but the out-group members, who in this case are innocent crocodiles, given that crocodiles are ever innocent. Working in happy cooperation, the monkeys are preparing to pull the crocodile against the cement wall of the moat in order to chew on its soft underbelly.

Although aggression control is achieved primarily through age-mate affection, there is no question that parental training exerts powerful influences, usually for the better and occasionally for the worse. In human socialization, of course, the young often learn to control their parents' behavior instead of their own. The child whose parent succumbs to temper tantrums quickly learns that aggressive behavior can be an effective operating procedure and continues to employ it as a means of gaining his own ends.

MODELING OF AGGRESSIVE BEHAVIOR

Human parents exert considerable influence on the child's containment and acquisition of aggressive behavior. This influence is often exerted as a conscious attempt to control undesired behavior, but probably just as

116

often they are unaware of their influence as available models for imitation. There is evidence that spanking, slapping, harsh verbal reprimand, and other methods of punishment lead to an inhibition of overt aggression in the home and places similar to the home. Studies by Sears et al. [1953] of aggressive behavior in nursery school children indicate that the overall effect of parental punishment is actually fairly complex. Those children who had mildly punitive mothers exhibited a relatively high number of aggressive responses, while those children who had either severely punitive mothers or nonpunitive mothers showed relatively few aggressive responses.

Although both the latter groups of children did not exhibit overt aggression, Sears argued that only the children of nonpunitive mothers were relatively free of aggressive feelings. He suggested that if aggressive reactions were inhibited by parental restrictions, the child would be more likely to express them in a fantasy situation that differed from the structured nursery school setting, which in many ways resembled or was associated with his home environment. In a permissive doll-play session the children of severely punitive mothers exhibited a relatively high number of aggressive responses. The investigators concluded that these children were actually highly frustrated and experienced aggressive feelings which they inhibited both at home and in other places similar to the home.

Although parental punishment may inhibit aggressive behavior at home, it also plays a much more complex role. Parental punishment, particularly physical punishment, provides the child with an excellent demonstration of how powerful an influence aggression can be (Fig. 5-3). Since it is effective in his case, he may very well apply it to others. Although the eventual results may be unfortunate, the discrimination problem is not a difficult one: inhibition of aggressive behavior at home avoids punishment and aggressive behavior away from home brings success—at least for a while.

The profound influence of an aggressive model on subsequent behavior has been demonstrated in a variety of experimental settings [Bandura and Walters, 1963]. Aggressive tendencies in children were observed after exposure to aggressive and nonaggressive models. The aggressive model engaged in highly novel aggression to ensure that the

FIGURE 5–3   *Monkey infant at the hands of a punitive mother.*

117

FIGURE 5-4 *Imitative aggressive behavior.*

modeled behavior could be clearly differentiated from previously exhibited aggressive behaviors (see Fig. 5-4). The findings overwhelmingly indicated that children who watched aggressive behavior in a model engaged not only in more imitative aggressive behavior, but also in more total aggressive behavior. In other words, an aggressive model may serve both as a transmitter of new patterns of behavior and as a stimulus to elicit previously learned aggressive behavior. Furthermore, those children who viewed a nonaggressive model performed fewer aggressive acts than did those in a control group who viewed neither model. Apparently an appropriate model, parental or otherwise, can also serve as an inhibiting agent for aggression.

Live models were used in the original study. However, in a subsequent study live models, filmed human models, and cartoon models were used to test for differential effects. Although the live model elicited more subsequent imitative aggression, there was no appreciable difference in the total aggression elicited by models of different forms. This finding has some bearing on the current controversy over the possible effects of violence on television. The question of whether violence begets violence, or whether viewing violence in others has a purgative effect on aggressive tendencies has long provided a battleground for proponents of Freudian theory and those who attach major importance to the influence of modeling. According to the Freudian position of *catharsis*, the individual possesses a limited amount of "aggressive energy," and if he views aggressive behavior in a model, he will "use up" some of this limited supply and hence will be less likely to engage in aggressive behavior than one whose supply of aggressive energy is still untapped. Many social learning theorists argue that the converse is true—observation of aggression is likely to increase rather than decrease the probability of aggressive behavior. The practical questions arising from these theoretical differences of opinion are of great import to our media-oriented society. Do television and movie scenes of destruction provide us with a "safe" way of venting our own destructive tendencies? Bandura's model study clearly shows that film models are extremely capable of eliciting substantial aggressive behavior from children viewing the film.

Additional data on college students strongly support the contention that viewing aggression begets aggression in the observer [Berkowitz, 1968]. It has been found that merely viewing objects such as guns associated with violent acts can serve as effective stimuli for triggering im-

118

pulsive aggressive acts. In one experiment half the subjects were first subjected to a condition of humiliation and physical discomfort by a confederate of the experimenter posing as a naïve subject. This condition was designed to create feelings of anger in the subject. The remainder of the students, who were not subjected to this condition, constituted the nonangry group. Subjects in both groups were then given an opportunity to express aggressive feelings. Each subject was to indicate any rejection of an idea suggested by his partner by administering an electric shock. Of course the "partner ideas" were prearranged and were the same for all subjects. Half the students in each group were exposed to weapons, guns, and rifles, which simply lay in the experimental room; tennis racquets were present for the other students. The mere presence of guns apparently triggered the release of aggression for those persons in the angry group. These subjects administered significantly greater numbers of electric shocks to their partners than did angry subjects exposed to the tennis racquets.

To test whether aggressive tendencies may be vented through a safe avenue simply by viewing another's aggressive acts, the experiment was repeated, but with a slight change. This time half the subjects were shown a violent film and the other half were shown a nonviolent film, after which all were subjected to a humiliating and uncomfortable condition. The results generally showed that subjects exposed to the violent film administered a greater number of electric shocks to their partners than did subjects exposed to the nonviolent film. Clearly the subject's feelings were not purged through viewing aggressive acts; on the contrary, such scenes seemed to justify the release of his own aggressive feelings.

Numerous other experiments have similarly failed to disclose any evidence of a cathartic effect. Rather, the overwhelming majority of these studies have demonstrated that in fact the opposite effect is likely. The catharsis hypothesis has compelling intuitive plausibility, but it serves as a frightening example of discrepancy between social ideals and social reality.

DISPLACEMENT OF AGGRESSION

Sometimes the target for aggression is not known or is repressed, or a direct attack would engender undesirable consequences. In such cases aggression may be *displaced*, often toward those not capable of effective retaliation. Once a "safe" target for aggression is found, it often becomes a scapegoat for any and all feelings of frustration. Displacement of aggression, or scapegoating, may be on an individual level—as when a man berated by his employer goes home and berates his wife—or it may take place on a social scale—as when one cultural or ethnic subgroup becomes the target for a large segment of society. However, displacement of aggression is not exclusively a human trait. Monkeys and mice displace displeasure as readily as men. Although displaced aggression in monkeys

119

is often viewed with tongue in cheek by man, human prejudice and scapegoating are seldom so humorous.

In spite of the fact that social-emotional control is determined in large part by learning, and in man by culture, the efficacy of this learning is made possible by maturational forces. Infant-mother love develops before external fears become overwhelming, and age-mate affection is firm and fast before aggression has become a powerfully pervasive force. There is a wealth of data supporting the position that both fear and anger have fundamental innate components and develop over a considerable period of time, probably throughout puberty. Although the potential for fear and anger is inherited, most specific fears and angers are learned--in man, monkey, or mongrel. In man emotional learning is so pervasive that the existence of basic unlearned variables may be obscured, even such important variables as those associated with gender differences. It is in the laboratory that the true role of these unlearned components has been unmasked.

SUMMARY

The behavioral expression of the emotion of fear is generally avoidance of the feared object. Anger is usually evidenced by some form of aggression. The potential for fear is innate in any species that exhibits complex social behavior, but specific fears and specific targets for aggression are determined by learning. Despite the fact that fear and anger are fundamentally antisocial emotions, they are channeled by the prior maturation of affectional feelings, and play an important role in social integration.

Fear and anger follow a basic developmental sequence. The first emotion displayed by the infant seems to be a general excitement, which differentiates at about three months into delight and distress; by six months distress has differentiated further into disgust, fear, and anger. A short time afterward delight differentiates into elation and affection, which is directed first toward adults and later other children. There are reasons to believe that the newborn child also responds differentially to pain and pleasure before three months and can probably differentiate fear and anger well before six months. Emotional reactions in the newborn are elicited almost as reflexes by a limited number of stimuli. With maturation other stimuli become signals for emotional reactions, as in the development of stranger anxiety and the later appearance of separation anxiety. Anxiety is also provoked in the infant by feelings of helplessness.

Children acquire early fears largely by conditioning. Later social imitation, imagination, and other more complex learning processes contribute to the formation of specific fears. Many childhood fears are outgrown, but intense fears do not always dissipate with time, and they may be generalized into free-floating anxiety. Sometimes intense non-

120

adaptive fears or phobias can be overcome by counterconditioning. Although fear is a socially disrupting emotion, it is held in check by the basic security and trust formed during the infant-love period and extended during the age-mate period.

Anger is elicited in the infant by physical restraint and later by various social limitations. Where there is no outlet for the resulting aggression, it may be turned inward, as in the self-aggression that characterizes autistic behavior and suicide. Aggression that is turned outward may be directed against either the individual's own group or against other groups. Although aggression within the social group usually has unfortunate consequences, to the extent that aggression against outgroups serves to protect the in-group it has an adaptive function.

All social groups have evolved mechanisms for the control of aggression. The mother and infant affectional systems serve initially to curtail aggressive tendencies. However, peer play is the primary means of aggression control, for it is in the interaction with peers that the appropriate targets for aggression are learned and misplaced aggressive responses are punished. Aggressive patterns are also learned from parental and other models. In some cases aggression is displaced, generally to those less capable of retaliation.

CHAPTER SIX

NATURE
AND NURTURE

For thousands of years man has had a general understanding of heredity. It takes no great insight to see that dogs give birth to dogs and cats give birth to cats. Nor is it difficult to see that the offspring of big dogs tend to be big, while the offspring of little dogs tend to be little. At a very general level the facts of heredity are obvious: like begets like. Our ancestors utilized these obvious facts to develop breeds of cattle, sheep, dogs, and cats long before there was any understanding of the underlying genetic principles. As early as the sixth century B.C. the Greek scholar Theognis noted that while great care was exercised in selecting rams, sheep, and horses for breeding, men and women readily marry an unworthy partner simply for money.

It is important to note that by selecting animals for breeding our ancestors were able to influence their behavior, as well as physical characteristics. The domestication of dogs, for example, required the selection of behavioral tendencies such as docility and the reduction of tendencies such as aggressiveness and excessive fear of man. A dog is not just a tame wolf. The dog has been domesticated through countless generations of

HEREDITY

selective breeding. Clearly, heredity influences behavior as well as physical structure. This is true for man as well as the other animals. Although we may not all have an explicit understanding of the exact nature of hereditary influences, we all have some general understanding that behavior is influenced by heredity. Intelligent parents expect to have intelligent children. Musicians expect to have musically talented children. Whenever a child is not a "chip off the old block," it is because of "something that came from *your* side of the family." However, expectations based on common-sense knowledge of heredity are not always fulfilled. Bright parents often have dull-witted children, and musically talented parents can have tone-deaf offspring.

The question of how heredity influences behavior is admittedly rather baffling on first consideration. Behavior seems to be so insubstantial. How can a pattern of thought or a personality trait be subject to the same forces of inheritance as those that influence body height or shape of the nose? The first scientific investigation of the hereditary basis of behavior was undertaken in the nineteenth century. It was not until this time that the sciences of biology and psychology had developed sufficiently to support systematic studies in this area.

123

EARLY FAMILY STUDIES

Studies of genetic influences on human behavior grew out of observations of family resemblances in behavior. Early thinking on the matter was necessarily based on folklore and anecdote. Particular cases of "like father, like son" were obvious. It was widely accepted that behavioral as well as physical characteristics tended to "run in families." Some families had many smart members. Others had had problems with alcohol for generations. Some families were blessed with good singers and others with strong backs. Less fortunate families were burdened with "queerness."

GALTON'S STUDY OF EMINENCE   The first systematic attempt to study family resemblances in psychological characteristics was conducted in 1865 by Francis Galton, who was a cousin of Charles Darwin. Since "greatness" obviously ran in his own family, Galton wanted to know whether this was generally true for other families. To investigate this problem he studied the relatives of selected men renowned for their accomplishments in a variety of fields, including science, law, literature, military service, politics, and the ministry. When Galton tabulated the number of eminent relatives of these selected men and arranged them according to distance of relationship, two facts became apparent. First, the number of eminent people in these families vastly exceeded the number to be expected on the basis of pure chance—that is, if everyone in the population were equally likely, or more accurately, equally *unlikely*, to become eminent. In short, eminence definitely did run in families. Second, those relatives closest to the most renowned member of the family (brothers, sons, fathers) were more likely to be eminent than were the more distant relatives such as cousins and uncles. The greater the proportion of genetic material shared with an eminent man, the greater the chances for eminence. Thus the evidence, viewed in this way, indicated that eminence is biologically based.

It is obvious, of course, that environmental influences are also involved. Close relatives share similar environmental influences as well as heredity. The privileged relatives of illustrious people have many educational and social advantages not available to relatives of the less illustrious. Such benefits might well be the critical factors in the development of eminence. Galton noted, however, that men had sometimes risen from low social rank to high positions. Moreover, although education was universally available in the United States, the proportion of eminent scholars was no greater than in Great Britain, where education was at that time a function of social class. Consequently Galton concluded that social advantage did not explain eminence. Subsequent studies by others attempted to show that musical talent was an inherited trait in the Bach family, and that such traits as obstinacy and love of scholastic pursuits were transmitted through heredity in the royal families of Great Britain. However, these studies did not resolve the problem of distinguishing the contributions of heredity from those of privilege.

The next important family studies dealt with the opposite side of the coin—immorality, criminality, and pauperism. These studies were so dramatic and became so widely known that the fictitious names of the families, the Jukes and Kallikaks, have come to represent the essence of dereliction and vice. The Jukes were a New York family who in a period of 130 years had contributed slightly more than 2000 citizens to the state. Over half the members of the Jukes family were committed to state institutions, either for feeble-mindedness or because of conviction for various criminal acts. The advocates of the view that behavior is influenced by "nature" interpreted this sordid family history to be proof of a "morbid inheritance." The patrons of "nurture" maintained that the high incidence of these undesirable characteristics in the family demonstrated the unwholesome effects of the miserable environmental circumstances in which the family had found itself. The study of the Jukes posed a problem but failed to solve it.

The Kallikak family had two branches. One was allegedly begun by a young Revolutionary War soldier, Martin Kallikak, who had an affair with a tavern girl who was reportedly feeble-minded. The members of this branch of the family were much like those of the Jukes family. They excelled only in dereliction and stupidity. After his return from military service Martin Kallikak married a girl from a "good family." The second branch of the Kallikak family, which resulted from this legal union, comprised people of good reputation and solid accomplishment.

These early family studies had a number of shortcomings. Of particular importance is that the standards of evidence were lower than we would require today. Galton based his judgment of eminence on biographical accounts and similar sources which are subject to bias in reporting. The paternity of the tavern girl's son was attributed to Martin Kallikak solely on the basis of the girl's testimony. Furthermore, the girl's condition of mental retardation was diagnosed after the fact on the basis of hearsay evidence. The evaluation of Kallikak family members, living or dead, was based largely on interviews by a field worker. The reports make lively reading, as can be seen in the following example [Goddard, 1914, pp. 28–29]:

> The field worker accosts an old farmer—"Do you remember an old man, Martin Kallikak (Jr.), who lived on the mountain-edge yonder?" "Do I? Well, I guess! Nobody'd forget him. Simple, not quite right here (tapping his head) but inoffensive and kind. All the family was that. Old Moll, simple as she was, would do anything for a neighbor. She finally died— burned to death in the chimney corner. She had come in drunk and sat down there. Whether she fell over in a fit or her clothes caught fire, nobody knows. She was burned to a crisp when they found her. That was the worst of them, they would drink. Poverty was their best friend in this respect, or they would have been drunk all the time. Old Martin could never stop as long as he had a drop. Many's the time he's rolled

off of Billy Parson's porch. Billy always had a barrel of cider handy. He'd just chuckle to see old Martin drink and drink until finally he'd lose his balance and over he'd go!"

However interesting they may be, such reports are of very limited scientific value. The findings do not lend themselves well to quantification or objective replication, and so there is no way to be certain that the reports are reliable. The fundamental weakness of the family approach to the study of hereditary influences on behavior is that the influences of heredity cannot be disentangled from environmental influences. Although the Kallikak family was considered by some as a neatly balanced natural experiment, since the two branches derived from a single male ancestor and two very different female ancestors, it was subjected to the same important criticism we have noted in the case of the Jukes—the families differed in environmental circumstances as well as in hereditary background.

Although the Jukes and Kallikak family studies must be judged deficient by current standards, it is well to keep in mind the context in which this work was done. At the time of Galton's study and the early investigations of the Jukes family the basic facts of genetics were not yet known. Moreover, there were no standardized objective tests for measuring behavioral characteristics. When the Kallikak study was under way the first discoveries of modern genetics had been published, but their implications and generality were not understood, and at this time only the very earliest, primitive devices for assessing intelligence had been developed. These classic studies must now be regarded as providing very little information of value to modern behavioral genetics. However, they played an important role in stimulating debate, in motivating further research, and in providing the background for contemporary research on the problem of hereditary influences on behavior.

TWIN STUDIES

One of the most widely used methods in studies of hereditary influences on behavior is the *twin study*. This method was introduced by Galton 20 years after his study on the inheritance of eminence. Since that time it has been modified and refined, and it is now an important approach to the problem of inheritance of behavior in human beings. The method is based on the fact that identical (monozygotic) twins develop from a single fertilized egg and thus are *exactly alike* in hereditary endowment, whereas fraternal (dizygotic) twins develop from separate eggs and are no more alike in heredity than are ordinary siblings. In both cases twins share the same basic enrivonment. They share a uterus in prenatal development, they are the same age at the same time in their families (unlike ordinary single-born siblings), and they tend to be treated alike by parents, teachers, and other children.

126

Thus the two kinds of twins appear to provide a naturally occurring simple experiment. One influence (genetic similarity) varies, while the effects of others (environmental influences) are held fairly constant.

Of course the situation is not quite this simple. For example, it is possible that individuals who are identical twins may be treated more alike than individuals who are fraternal twins. If this is so, then it becomes difficult to tell whether the differences between fraternal twins, in comparison with the differences between identical twins, are caused by heredity or environment. When both factors vary, the results cannot be easily interpreted. Although this is an interesting problem, it is not a serious one. Many studies of twins have provided results which are quite clear cut.

HERITABLE TRAITS

PHYSICAL CHARACTERISTICS   The basic twin method is illustrated by a study of body height [Newman et al., 1937] of 50 pairs of identical twins and 52 pairs of fraternal twins. The standing height was measured. The individuals of each identical-twin pair were not exactly alike in height; on the average, the members of a pair differed by 1.7 centimeters. This difference cannot be hereditary in origin, since the members of an identical-twin pair have identical heredity. The only possible source is environment. Although twins do receive very similar treatment, their environments cannot be exactly equivalent. There is evidence, for example, that different positions in the uterus can have detectable effects on body size. Differences in eating habits, diseases, or accidents suffered can also contribute to size difference.

Fraternal twins are, of course, subject to the same kinds of environmental forces, in addition to the fact that they differ from each other in heredity. Although they have the same parents, each received a different sample of hereditary material from their parents. If heredity also influences body height, we would expect the average height difference of fraternal-twin pairs to be larger than 1.7 centimeters. In fact it is over twice as large—4.4 centimeters. Thus it is clear that heredity does play a role in body size. We might further enquire if the relative similarity of environments of a pair of fraternal twins makes them more alike than ordinary siblings, who are comparable in hereditary similarity but somewhat different in environmental circumstances. The average intrapair difference for ordinary siblings, measured at the same age, is 4.5 centimeters—almost exactly that found with fraternal twins. Thus the differences between the environments of ordinary siblings and the environments of fraternal twins do not seem to be important in influencing body height.

INTELLIGENCE   The twin-study method shows that the same principles hold for intelligence as for physical characteristics such as height. The twins just described were also given the Stanford-Binet IQ test; the results of this assessment are shown along with those for height in

127

Table 6-1. Because different scales are employed, the greater intrapair difference for IQ is not significant (for example, if height were expressed in millimeters rather than centimeters, the height difference would have been 17 rather than 1.7). The IQ test is not a perfectly reliable test; a difference of about six IQ points is to be expected if a single individual is given the test twice. However, the average difference in IQ of identical-twin pairs is 5.9; in other words, identical twins are as much like each other in IQ as a person is like himself. For fraternal twins the average difference in IQ is 9.9. This difference is almost twice as great as that of identical twins, but it is about the same as the difference in siblings.

Since the results for IQ are very similar to those for height, we might conclude, at least provisionally, that IQ is as subject to hereditary influence as is body height. However, detailed studies of mental functioning indicate that some aspects of intelligence are more influenced by heredity than are others. For example, in one study traits labeled "verbal reasoning," "clerical speed and accuracy," and "language use" all showed evidence of substantial hereditary determination, whereas "numerical ability," "abstract reasoning," and "mechanical reasoning" showed little or no hereditary component [Vandenberg, 1968a]. These results clearly illustrate the important fact that some characteristics are more heritable than others. This is true, of course, for physical traits as well; body weight, for example, is somewhat more influenced by environment than is body height.

PERSONALITY TRAITS   Twin studies show that different aspects of personality are also differentially subject to hereditary influences. The evidence from twin studies of personality suggests that traits referred to as "active," "vigorous," "impulsive," and "sociable" are heritable, whereas "dominant," "stable," and "reflective" are not, or at least are much less so [Vandenberg, 1967]. Similarly, the different types of neuroses seem to be subject to different degrees of hereditary influence. One study indicates that neuroses characterized by anxiety, depression, obsession and schizoid withdrawal have substantial hereditary bases, but that those with features of hypochondriasis and hysteria are mostly environmental in origin [Gottesman, 1962].

Perhaps the most dramatic findings of twin studies concern psychoses, particularly schizophrenia. There is a strong indication that heredity plays a role in this disorder. The procedure is as follows: schizophrenic individuals who are twins are identified, and then the other member of each twin pair is studied to see if he or she is also schizophrenic. If the other twin is also affected the pair is termed *concordant*; if only the one twin is affected the pair is termed *discordant*. The results shown in Table 6-2 are typical. The higher incidence of concordance in identical twins indicates that heredity is an important variable in the development of schizophrenia. However, the fact that the concordance in identical twins is only 42 percent, and not 100 percent, shows that heredity is not the only factor involved. There is plenty of room for influences other than heredity.

	HEIGHT	IQ
Identical twins	1.7	5.9
Fraternal twins	4.4	9.9
Ordinary siblings	4.5	9.8

TABLE 6–1 *Average intrapair differences for height (in centimeters) and intelligence (IQ).*

	TWIN PAIRS INVESTIGATED	CONCORDANCE, PERCENT
Identical twins	28	42
Fraternal twins	34	9

TABLE 6–2 *Concordance for schizophrenia in identical and fraternal twins [Gottesman and Shields, 1966].*

STUDIES OF TWINS REARED APART

Sometimes for various reasons, twins are separated and reared in different homes. Studies of identical twins reared apart provide another way of examining environmental influences on intelligence. Since they have identical heredity, any differences must be due to the effects of the different environments. The first major investigation of twins reared apart concerned 19 pairs of identical twins who had been separated and reared in different homes [Newman et al., 1937]. In some cases the twins did not even know of each other's existence until the study was performed. The average intrapair difference in height found in twins reared apart was 1.8 centimeters, almost exactly the same as that found with identical twins reared together (see Table 6-1). The average difference in IQ was 8.2 points. This finding suggests that environment influences IQ score, since a difference of only 5.9 points was found for identical twins reared together. The effect is rather small, however—only slightly greater than two IQ points.

More recently the same problem has been examined in greater detail. The results were reported in terms of an index of similarity called a *correlation coefficient*. The magnitude of this index ranges from .00 to 1.00. A correlation of .00 would mean that identical twin pairs are no more similar than are pairs of people picked at random from the population. A *perfect correlation* of 1.00 would mean that each identical twin had exactly the same score as his twin. For our present purposes we wish to know only whether the correlation for identical twins reared apart is lower than the correlation for identical twins reared together.

Results from several investigations are given in Table 6-3. The evidence is not entirely consistent. One study shows no effect whatsoever of separate rearing, but the other two show some lessened similarity in IQ for twins reared in different homes. However, the high correlation in IQ is still remarkable. Even with varied home and school

129

TABLE 6–3 *Correlations of intelligence measures of identical twins reared together or apart.*	BINET*	SPECIAL*	STANFORD BINET*
Identical twins reared together	.88	.76	.92
Identical twins reared apart	.77	.77	.86

*Newman et al., 1937; Shields, 1962; Burt, 1966

TABLE 6–4 *Correlation between IQ of children and their parents.*	FATHER	MOTHER
Foster children	.07	.19
Biological children	.45	.46

circumstances, the twins were highly similar in IQ score. Of course, there is no guarantee that the environments provided by the different homes were particularly different. If they were similar, then there is no reason to expect a different influence on IQ. The environment provided by one middle-class home is not *necessarily* much different from that of another home.

STUDIES OF ADOPTED CHILDREN

The question of the hereditary contribution to the observation "like father, like son" can be examined by studying adopted children. Are they similar to their real parents or to their adoptive parents? It is assumed that a resemblance in IQ found between an adopted child and his adoptive parents results from environmental sources, while a resemblance of an adopted child to its real parents indicates a hereditary influence on intelligence. This assumption is not completely warranted if the adoption agencies attempt to place children on the basis of a similarity of IQ between the child and the adoptive parents. In general the findings of several studies indicate that children resemble their biological parents much more closely than adopted children resemble their adoptive parents. The findings of one representative study are shown in Table 6-4. The resemblance of children to their adoptive parents in IQ is positive but small; the resemblance of children to their biological parents in IQ is substantial.

Comparable results were obtained in a recent study of schizophrenia [Heston, 1966]. Forty-seven children who were born to schizophrenic mothers but adopted within three days of birth were compared to control subjects who were also adopted early in life but were born to nonschizophrenic mothers. Early adoption is important, of course, because if the child had lived with its mother for an extended period, it might be argued that the mother's treatment of the child influenced its later susceptibility to schizophrenia. Five of the 47 children born to schizophrenic mothers subsequently became schizophrenic in later life. In addition to the outright cases of schizophrenia, there was also a significant excess of psychosocial disability of various kinds in about half of the children of schizophrenic mothers. There were no cases of schizophrenia in the control subjects.

Overall the findings of studies of family resemblance provide rather compelling evidence that behavior is influenced by heredity. They also show that family resemblances are to some degree based on environmental influences. Obviously nature and nurture interact in complex ways to produce behavior, and the evidence from these studies is quite general. The findings indicate little about the *nature* of the hereditary influences on behavior, but a discussion of the genetic factors which underlie these influences will shed some light on the reason that like can beget "unlike" as well as "like."

THE GENETIC BASES OF HEREDITY

So far we have presented the problem of hereditary bases of behavior in very broad terms: the general arguments can be comprehended without any detailed knowledge of genetics. In order to proceed, however, we must now briefly examine the nature and function of the genetic material which underlies physical characteristics and behavior. Modern genetics began with the work of Gregor Mendel, a monk in Brunn, Moravia (now Czechoslovakia), in 1865. Prior to Mendel's discoveries there was, of course, considerable information about the resemblance of offspring to parents. For centuries breeds of cattle, dogs, and other domestic animals had been developed with no knowledge of the genetic bases of differences among animals. However, there was no explanation of the diverse and seemingly contradictory observed facts of inheritance. The general assumption was that the hereditary materials of the mother and father were blended in the offspring. Mendel's central discovery was that the hereditary substance is composed of individual elements which exist in alternate forms. Furthermore, they do not blend with each other. We refer to these individual elements as *genes* and to their alternate forms as *alleles*. Genes are located on structures called *chromosomes*, which are found in every cell of the body. An understanding of the biochemical nature of genes is one of the most exciting achievements of modern biology. Although the details are beyond our present scope, in essence a gene can be considered as the unit of heredity. It was at this level of analysis that Mendel contributed to an understanding of the way that individual genes provide the basis for heredity.

The distinction between an individual's genetic composition, or *genotype*, and the observed trait, or *phenotype*, was perhaps Mendel's most ingenious insight. To illustrate, let us represent some particular gene by a circle, where a blue circle distinguishes the *dominant* allelic stage from the alternate *recessive state*. An individual receives one allele

131

from each parent, so that the following genotypes (pairs of alleles) can occur:

●● ●● ●●

Individuals with the pairs ●● or ●●, where the alleles are alike, are called *homozygotes*; those with the arrangement ●● are called *heterozygotes*. The phenotypic value of a heterozygote does not necessarily lie halfway between the phenotypic values of the two homozygotes. In some genes partial or incomplete dominance results in a phenotypic value which is closer to that of one of the homozygotes than the other. In cases of complete dominance, however, the phenotypic value, or appearance, may be exactly the same as that of one of the homozygotes, even though the genetic makeup is not the same. Thus the *appearance* of some trait in an individual gives only an indirect indication of his genetic makeup. The genotype itself can be determined only by appropriate genetic studies.

BEHAVIORAL PHENOTYPES

There are numerous cases of single genes which affect behavioral phenotypes. A dramatic example is the condition known as phenylketonuria. The normal allele is dominant. Thus individuals who are homozygous for the *dominant* allele, ●●, are normal. Heterozygotes are also behaviorally normal, since the normal allele dominates. However, recessive homozygotes, ●●, suffer from severe mental deficit unless this condition is offset by special dietary treatment. A more frequent and less serious condition, red-green color blindness, is also determined by a single gene. Because it is located on the X chromosome it is transmitted in a pattern known as sex linkage. One consequence of this mode of transmission is that although females can pass this condition on to their offspring, it actually *occurs* only in males. Some other examples have been found in research with animals. A number of neurological disorders in mice have been shown to be due to single genes. One single gene that affects skin pigmentation in mice also influences learning ability, emotionality, and activity level.

Single-gene determination of a phenotype is a restricted case in genetics. Many, if not most, of the traits with which the behavioral geneticist is concerned are influenced by many genes, not just one. For example, a number of years ago it was observed that bees in some colonies are able to control disease by uncapping the cells of diseased larvae and removing the larvae from the hive. It was later found that this highly adaptive behavior is markedly influenced by just two genes. Note that two responses, each of which is quite complex, are required; uncapping of the cells and removal of the larvae. We may depict this situation as follows. Uncapping behavior is carried out by bees that are homozygous for the recessive allele ●; removing is done by bees homo-

132

zygous for the recessive allele ■. Thus bees of the genotype ● ● ■ ■ display a complete sequence of hygienic behavior. Bees that have at least one dominant allele of each gene, ● ● ■ ■, are completely nonhygienic in behavior. Bees of genotype ● ● ■ ■ will uncap the cells but will leave the diseased larvae in place. ● ● ■ ■ bees will do nothing in the absence of assistance; however, if the experimenter does the uncapping for them, they will remove the larvae efficiently [Rothenbuhler, 1964]. Each component of hygienic behavior is discretely recognizable and can be categorized as being either present or not present. In this situation two separate behavioral units, each controlled by separate genes, must be performed in sequence to accomplish a particular end result. This research provides evidence of genetically based division of labor in social animals.

POLYGENIC INHERITANCE

Most behavior is not reducible to such neat all-or-none subdivisions, but is describable only in quantitative terms; that is, it occurs in a greater or lesser *degree*. Inheritance in such circumstances can be understood in terms of a *polygenic* system, in which each of a number of genes makes a small contribution to the level of expression of the behavior. Several important aspects of polygenic inheritance can be illustrated by means of a three-gene model. For example, a person who is a heterozygote for all three genes might be depicted as

● ●   ■ ■   ▲ ▲

When this individual generates *gametes*, or sex cells, half will receive an ● allele and half an ● allele. Alleles are not influenced in any way by association with other alleles, and in contrast to the old "blending" notions of heredity, the ● allele in the gamete of an ● ● individual is in no way different from the ● allele in the gamete of an ● ● individual.

With some restrictions in the case of genes on the same chromosomes, the chances of one gene are completely independent of the chances of other genes in the gamete. For example, of the gametes with ● (instead of ●), half will get a ■ and half a ■, half will get a ▲ and half a ▲, and so on. Thus if our hypothetical triple heterozygote is a male, he can provide eight kinds of sperm with respect to these three genes:

● ■ ▲   ● ■ ▲   ● ■ ▲   ● ■ ▲   ● ■ ▲   ● ■ ▲   ● ■ ▲   ● ■ ▲

If such a male were to mate with a female of the same genotype, who could, of course, generate eggs with the same eight gene arrangements, the situation would be as depicted in Fig. 6-1. Each of these 64 possible genotypes would be equally likely in each offspring from this union. Moreover, only eight of these 64 possibilities are the same as the genotypes of either parent. It is evident that the system by which genes are reshuffled in gamete formation is a powerful mechanism for generating variability.

133

Suppose the mode of gene action were such that a blue allele of any gene added 1 to the phenotypic value; then the phenotypic scores of all the genotypes derivable from this mating would be distributed as in Fig. 6-2. The parents, of course, would each have a phenotypic value of 3. It is obvious that as the number of genes determining a trait increases, the number of possible genotypes rapidly becomes enormous. One important principle emerges from this example. Aside from the obvious influences of environment, there is a regular and systematic biological system for creating individuality in all living organisms. Even if all environmental factors were completely uniform, there would still be a genetic basis for individuality in behavior. Some appreciation for the nearly boundless capacity to generate variability can be gained by noting that each human individual (except, of course, identical twins and other identical multiple births) is a genetically unique creature. For all practical purposes, we can say that no other individual with precisely the same overall genotype has ever lived or will ever live. Of course the genotype of any individual may differ only slightly from a large number of other individuals.

Another extremely important point that can be taken from Fig. 6-2 is that in a polygenic system there are many genotypic ways to arrive at a given phenotypic end result. For instance, there are six genotypes in our model that give phenotypic values of 4. What this means is that different people may achieve the same outcome for quite different genetic reasons.

FIGURE 6–1 *Possible genotypes of offspring of two triple heterozygotes.*

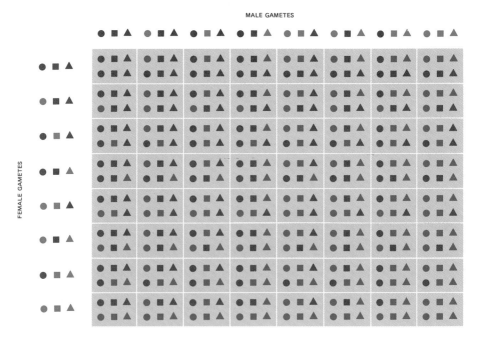

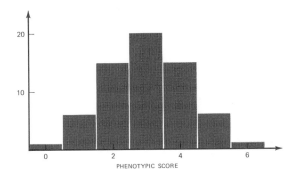

FIGURE 6–2   *Distribution of phenotypes of Fig. 6-1.*

Degree of genetic similarity among individuals can be experimentally controlled in studies with infrahumans. Through inbreeding it is possible to produce strains of animals in which the genetic variability is virtually eliminated. Such "pure" strains enable us to investigate a great many factors in genetic influences on behavior. In general *inbreeding* means the mating of individuals more closely related than would be members drawn at random from the population and assigned randomly in pairs. In laboratory animals, particularly mice, intensive inbreeding, usually the mating of brothers and sisters, is continued in successive generations to produce a progressive decrease in the amount of genetic heterogeneity. After about 20 generations of inbreeding each animal is very nearly homozygous for all genes and is virtually identical to each other animal of that strain. The chances that two such inbred strains with different origins will have the same genotype are vanishingly small; the exact degree and nature of the genetic difference between any two different inbred strains cannot be specified exactly, but it is certain that they will differ to some degree. Then, if different strains reared and tested under the same conditions exhibit any difference in behavior, the difference must be genetic in origin. Conversely, any variability found among members of the same inbred strain must be due to differences in the environment to which they have been exposed.

The first step in research with inbred strains is to show that the strains differ in behavior—in other words, that the differences in behavior are likely to be due to genetic differences. Mouse strains, for example, have been found to differ in a variety of behaviors such as learning ability in mazes, learning ability in shock avoidance situations, activity level, sexual behavior, food hoarding, susceptibility to sound-induced seizures, and alcohol preference. As an indication of the range of differences among inbred strains, Fig. 6-3 shows the distributions of locomotor activity in a novel situation for six mouse strains. The activity

135

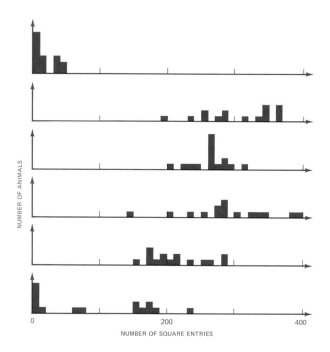

FIGURE 6-3   *Locomotor activity of six mouse strains.*

was measured by placing the animals on a chamber floor which was sectioned off into small squares by a series of rectangular barriers. An animal's activity score was the number of squares it traversed in a 5-minute period. The average differences among the strains on this measure are quite large. Animals from the more active strains cross squares nearly once a second, while animals from the least active strains cross barely four times a minute. However, strain differences in variability also are evident. Since all animals were reared under the same general laboratory conditions, this finding suggests that the strains differ in their susceptibility to environmental variation.

The simple fact of differences, of course, provides no information about the mode of inheritance. Once strain differences have been established, further genetic analysis entails measurement of the responses of the generations derived from the inbred strains. Some information about the average dominance of the genes involved can be obtained from the F_1 generation, the progeny of the two parent strains. However, much more valuable information can be obtained from study of the F_2 generation, which is derived by mating F_1 individuals with each other. Animals of the F_1 generation, like those of each of the parent strains, are alike genetically; each has received half its genes from one parent and half from the other. If two F_1 animals are mated, however, in their offspring the genetic material from either of the original strains may range from zero to 100 percent in any individual. Thus the F_2 generation should be more variable than the F_1. As with the twin studies, where fraternal-twin differences are compared to identical-twin differences, the amount

136

of this excess variability may be taken as a measure of the variability which is genetic in origin. For example, Fig. 6-4 shows the arena activity scores of two inbred strains, the F_1 generation and the F_2 generation. Because our interest here is comparison in variability, the square root of the original activity score was taken in order to provide a scale on which the parent strains are equally variable. As can be seen, the activity of the F_1 animals lies, on the average, between that of the two strains. However, the distribution of F_1 scores is displaced toward one parent, suggesting that, on the average, the genes for higher activity are dominant. The F_2 scores are distributed over a very broad range. In a sample as small as this we would not expect to obtain any animals whose genetic makeup is actually exactly the same as that of either parent strain. Thus it is not surprising that no F_2 animals are actually at the limits of the scale. The scores do, however, spread over a greater range than the F_1 scores. Without going into a detailed analysis, we can conclude from the amount by which the F_2 variability exceeds the F_1 variability that approximately two-thirds of the variability in the F_2 generation arises from genetic differences; the remaining one-third of the variability is attributable to environmental factors. Thus from careful analysis we are able to derive quantitative statements about genetic influences on behavior.

Similar analyses have been performed on a wide variety of mouse behaviors, including hoarding, alcohol preference, and learning. The results all support the general conclusion that in any population some of the variability in behavioral traits is of environmental origin and some is of genetic origin. In very general terms, the proportion of the total phenotypic variance that is due to genetic differences among members of the population is called the *heritability*. Heritability of a trait differs from population to population, depending on the amount of genetic variability present in the population. Within a single inbred strain there is no genetic variability, and hence no heritability. Note that when all animals are genetically identical, heritability is .00; all variation in behavior must be caused by environmental influences. If environmental effects could be made uniform for all members of a genetically *heterogeneous* population, then the remaining variability would be all genetic in origin, and the heritability would be 1.00. Theoretically the complete

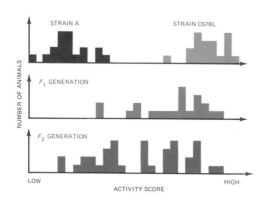

FIGURE 6–4   *Activity scores of two mouse strains and their F_1 and F_2 generations.*

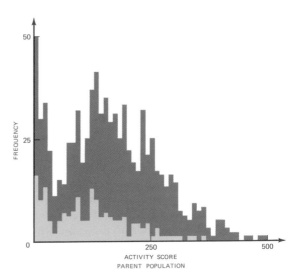

FIGURE 6-5 *Activity score distributed for a foundation stock of mice and for two generations of selected lines derived from that foundation stock.*

success of programs to provide equal education for all would result in a situation wherein all the differences among individuals would be due to heredity.

SELECTIVE BREEDING

Another major method in animal behavioral genetics research is that of selective breeding. To put it simply, animals who display extreme levels of some behavior are mated together. This procedure is continued over successive generations. If the behavior is genetically influenced, animals selected in the "high" direction will provide their offspring with alleles that make for high values of the behavior, and in successive generations the relative frequency of high alleles would be expected to increase in that line. Similarly, in a line selected for low values of the trait there would be an accumulation of alleles for low phenotypic value. A successful attempt to breed selectively thus demonstrates that the trait for which the selection was performed does indeed have a heritable basis, and the results also permit some estimates of mode of gene action. Animals have been selectively bred for a variety of behavioral tendencies, such as maze brightness and maze dullness in rats, high and low activity in rats, high and low morphine addictability in rats, aggressiveness and nonaggressiveness in mice, positive and negative geotaxis in fruit flies (*Drosophila*), and fast and slow mating speed in *Drosophila*.

Selective breeding is a powerful technique. Within limits, it enables an investigator to tailor-make his research subjects. A graphic example of the effects of selective breeding is given in Fig. 6-5. From a parental population of genetically heterogeneous mice the very active animals were mated together and the very inactive animals were mated together. In order to provide a continuing reference point some randomly selected animals also were mated. After six generations of such selective breeding

138

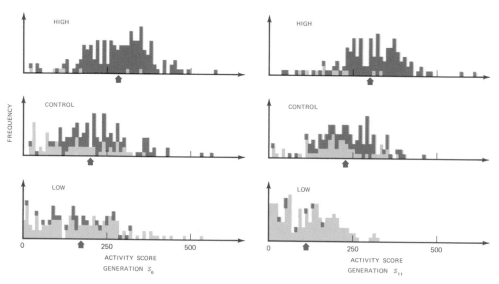

the activity-score distributions of these separate lines were as shown for generation S_6. The average score of each line is indicated by an arrow on the horizontal scale. It can easily be seen that the averages moved in the direction in which selection pressure was applied. There is still extensive overlap, however. After five further generations of selective breeding, in generation S_{11}, the averages are still farther apart, and by this time the most active of the low line is only about as active as the average mouse from the high line. In the control animals, where there has been no selection pressure, the average activity has remained quite stable over time; considerable overlap of the high- and low-line distributions is still evident in S_{11}. The extent to which the variability that results in this overlap is of genetic origin will be indicated by the eventual outcome of this experiment [DeFries et al., 1970]. These results are typical for a trait influenced by many genes.

This study also shows that recognizable single genes may participate in such a situation. In the foundation stock about 25 percent of the animals were albino, as indicated by the light squares in Fig. 6-5. By generation S_6 the albinos had become rare in the high line and the majority in the low line; by generation S_{11} the effect was even more pronounced. Obviously the albino gene has an effect on activity and is one of the genes being sorted out in the two lines by the selection pressure.

MECHANISMS OF GENE ACTION

The studies described above indicate that genes do indeed influence behavior and result in family resemblances in behavior. The basic question, of course, is *how* do genes influence behavior? Biochemical genetics and molecular biology have in recent years revealed the chemical nature of genes and the mechanisms through which they operate. Although we do not yet understand all the details, there is nothing mystical about the

139

way genes operate. Genes influence behavior by affecting all the body systems which are involved in behavior—the central nervous system, the autonomic nervous system, the endocrine glands, the receptors, the muscles, and the digestive system. The genetic material is known to be *deoxyribonucleic acid* (DNA). Genetic information is coded by a sequence of chemical substances, or *bases*, along the DNA molecule. From this molecule, which remains within the cell nucleus, *ribonucleic acid* (RNA) is copied and goes out into the cytoplasm of the cell, where the genetic "message" it transmits is used in establishing the specificity of proteins called *enzymes*, the organic catalysts which are essential to development and functioning of the body.

Although we know that this general description is accurate, we know little about the details of the biochemical path from DNA to behavior. For most behavioral traits little or no concrete information is available. In an increasing number of cases, however, parts of the pathway are being subjected to analysis, and our knowledge is increasing rapidly. Perhaps the best understood mechanism is that involved in the condition of phenylketonuria. The key biochemical deficiency in this disorder is an inability to metabolize phenylalanine, which is an essential amino acid found in normal diet. This inability is related in turn to a deficiency of the enzyme phenylalanine hydroxylase. The failure to convert phenylalanine to tyrosine results in an accumulation of phenylalanine, and also of a number of derivatives of phenylalanine, such as phenylpyruvic acid and phenylacetic acid. It appears that the presence of one of these substances in excess quantities inhibits normal development of the nervous system. The partial understanding of the biochemical basis of the condition has given rise to a rational therapy. A special diet, free of phenylalanine, was developed for afflicted children in 1959. Extensive testing programs of newborn children are now in operation in most of the United States to identify those for whom the dietary treatment should be begun. Although this therapy appears to effect considerable improvement in children afflicted with phenylketonuria, it seems that their development still may not be completely normal.

The success in establishing the nature of genetic determination in phenylketonuria, the discovery of the biochemical defects, and the development of effective therapy has encouraged extensive research on other conditions which involve defects in amino acid metabolism. A number of such conditions have been identified, and mental retardation is usually found to be a feature of the condition. Although none has been shown as clearly to be the consequence of a single gene, we are beginning to learn much about the nature of metabolic defects, and therapeutic diets have been initiated for many of the defects.

In studies using experimental animals there are active research efforts to relate genetically influenced neurochemical differences to learning ability, memory, and aggressiveness; endocrine differences to emotionality, activity, and social and sexual behavior; and enzyme differences to alcohol preference. This is a rapidly developing area of research which holds much promise.

140

The genes are located in series along the chromosomes in each cell nucleus. In man this genetic material is arranged in 23 *pairs* of chromosomes. One member of each of these pairs is derived from each parent. In the formation of gametes (eggs and sperm) one member of each pair is included, so that each egg or sperm ordinarily contains 23 single chromosomes. When a sperm and an egg unite, the normal situation of 23 pairs is restored. Occasionally, however, an accident occurs during this process, with the result that some particular sperm or egg has an abnormal number of chromosomes. The precise cause of these accidents is unknown, but in some cases we know that maternal age is a factor; chromosome mistakes occur more often in older women. When a gamete with an abnormal number of chromosomes is involved in fertilization, the resulting organism will also have an abnormal chromosome complement. Many of these abnormalities result in early death and account for a substantial percentage of spontaneously occurring abortions. However, some abnormalities are compatible with continued life, and of these conditions, a number have interesting though unfortunate behavioral features.

One of the first conditions shown to be the result of a chromosome abnormality was *Down's syndrome*, more generally known as mongolism. This condition, which is characterized by superficially oriental features, was singled out early for special investigation and had been the focus of active research efforts for a long time. The cause of the condition remained obscure, however, until it was found that affected individuals had 47 instead of 46 chromosomes. Detailed analysis revealed that the extra chromosome is a small one, and according to the classification scheme generally employed by workers in this area, it was designated as number 21. The condition of having three chromosomes instead of a pair is *trisomy*. Not all of the extra genetic material on chromosome 21 is required to cause this condition. Besides the anomaly which results from a complete trisomy for chromosome 21, there is another anomaly in which the extra chromosome 21 is attached instead to the somewhat larger chromosome pair 15—that is, there is a normal pair of chromosome 21 plus an extra fragment. In this case the prospect that a subsequent child of the same parents will also be affected is many times greater than it is for the standard trisomy condition.

Just as extra amounts of chromosome material can produce severe abnormalities, a deficiency of genetic material can also have serious consequences. It appears that the complete absence of a particular chromosome is usually (but not always) fatal. In one situation loss of an end of a certain chromosome is known to produce a condition of severe mental retardation, called the *cat-cry syndrome* because of the distinctive cry of the affected children.

The exception to the generalization that complete chromosomal loss is not compatible with life involves the sex chromosomes. With respect to 22 pairs of chromosomes, the complements of males and females

CHROMOSOME ANOMALIES

141

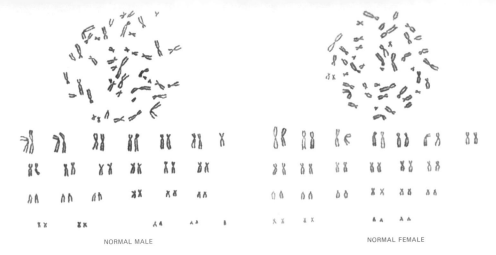

NORMAL MALE   NORMAL FEMALE

FIGURE 6-6   *Human karyotypes. The top section of each karyo-*
type is a photomicrograph of the chromosomal material of a single
cell of the individual. Below this the chromosomes are arranged in
pairs in order of decreasing size. The sex chromosomes are shown in
the right-hand column adjacent to other chromosomes of about the
same size. In the abnormal karyotypes an arrow indicates the anom-
aly. [Robinson, University of Colorado Medical Center]

are the same; each has chromosome pairs containing the same genetic loci,
with one member of each pair from each of the parents. With respect to
the sex chromosomes, it is also the case that one is provided by each
parent. However, the sex chromosomes come in two forms—the *X*
chromosome, which is relatively large, and a smaller *Y* chromosome. An
XX pair results in a normal female and an *XY* pair results in a normal
male. A condition called *Turner's syndrome* is frequently found in
females who have only a single *X* chromosome. These individuals are
sterile and have a variety of physical anomalies. They are not mentally
retarded in the usual sense—in fact, some evidence suggests that their
verbal abilities are somewhat higher than average. However, they appear
to be deficient in other kinds of cognitive functioning. The defect can
best be described as space-form blindness and difficulty in numerical
manipulations. In some respects these symptoms are similar to those
caused by certain kinds of damage to the parietal lobe of the brain.

Another anomaly of sex-chromosome number in females is the
triplow-*X* situation. This condition has not yet been found to be consistently related to any particular kind of behavioral deficiency. One
trisomy of the sex chromosomes in males involves the presence of two
*X*s and a *Y*. *XXY* individuals suffer from *Klinefelter's syndrome*, characterized by retarded sexual development and mental deficiency.

Another male trisomy, *XYY*, has been the subject of intensive
research efforts. A constellation of typical characteristics includes large
body size, moderate intellectual dullness, and strong aggressive tendencies. There is strong evidence that *XYY* males appear in institutions for
the criminally insane much more often than would be expected on the
basis of their frequency in the general population [Court-Brown et al.,
1968] . However, a comparison of close relatives of *XYY* males and nor-

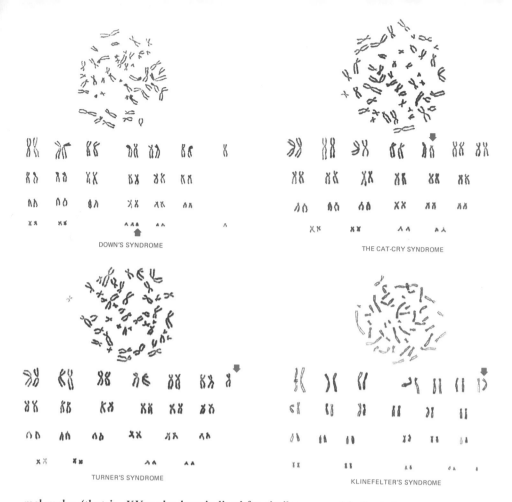

DOWN'S SYNDROME

THE CAT-CRY SYNDROME

TURNER'S SYNDROME

KLINEFELTER'S SYNDROME

mal males (that is, XY males hospitalized for similar reasons) indicated that the relatives of the XYY males were far *less* likely to have been convicted of a crime. In the control group many more of the relatives had a criminal record. This finding suggests that in an individual whose relatives are not known to be involved in crimes of violence the possession of the extra Y chromosome in some way significantly increases the probability of an individual's becoming involved in such crimes [Hirsch, 1970]. The principal unanswered question, of course, is the actual frequency of normal XYY individuals in the population at large. The chief problem, of course, is determining their actual frequency in the population at large. Estimates thus far have depended largely on extrapolations from other chromosome anomalies. It is extremely difficult to perform the large-scale population surveys for extra Y chromosomes that would be required to make a confident judgment that this syndrome is a reliable consequence of the XYY chromosomal constitution. Hence it is too early to say with certainty that there is a genetic basis for criminal behavior.

These cases of chromosome anomalies concern the abnormal presence or absence of whole blocks of genes. Such data do not provide much information about the mode of gene action. For example, we

143

know little about the particular pathways through which extra genes on chromosome 21 lead to mental retardation and the associated symptoms. It is clear, however, that genetic influence on behavior is relevant to the whole array of the social and behavioral sciences, both in terms of our thinking about the causes of behavior and as a powerful research technique for determining specific ways of altering behavior.

As man's biotechnological capacity advances, we come increasingly nearer to the time when we can intervene directly and deliberately to alter the genetic code of given individuals. Furthermore, the crushing population pressures that are foretold will eventuate in a change in our gene pool. Whether we take active steps to curb population growth or just let it happen, the result is certain to be a breeding pattern that is different from what it is now. To even predict the consequences of changed reproductive patterns, let alone influence them in any way, we will need a higher order of knowledge than we presently have. The behavioral sciences in general need more information. One of the critical needs is an understanding of the mechanisms that underlie hereditary influences on behavior.

SUMMARY

Even in the ancient times man employed the general principles of heredity to domesticate dogs and cattle. Interest in the hereditary basis of human behavior led to early family studies such as Galton's classical study of eminence and the famous Jukes and Kallikaks study. These studies demonstrated that certain behavioral traits do run in families, but they did not resolve the question of whether the resemblance was hereditary or due to environmental similarity.

A more recent approach to the study of heredity is based on the fact that identical twins have identical hereditary endowment and fraternal twins are no more alike than ordinary siblings. Comparison of these different types of twins on a number of behavioral and physical traits indicates that such intelligence measures as *verbal reasoning*, *clerical speed* and *accuracy*, *language use*, and *composite IQ* show substantial hereditary influences, while *numerical ability*, *abstract reasoning*, and *mechanical reasoning* show little or no hereditary component. Personality traits such as *active*, *vigorous*, *sociable*, and *impulsive* are heritable, while *dominant*, *stable* and *reflective* are not. In addition, neuroses characterized by anxiety, depression, obsession, and schizoid withdrawal all have substantial hereditary bases, but those with features of hypochondriasis and hysteria are not substantially influenced by heredity. Comparison of identical twins raised together with those raised apart indicates that schizophrenia is strongly influenced by heredity. If one member of a pair of identical twins is schizophrenic, the probability is greater than chance that the other twin will also be schizophrenic.

Modern genetics began with the work of Gregor Mendel, who observed that the elementary genetic units, the genes, exist in pairs of alleles, which may be dominant or recessive. Since the dominant allele governs the outward appearance of a trait, an individual's genetic composition or genotype must be distinguished from the observed trait, or phenotype. Some traits are determined by a single gene, such as the recessive condition of phenylketonuria or the sex-linked characteristic of red-green color blindness. Most behavioral traits, however, are determined polygenetically. The number of genotypes possible from a mating of two triple heterozygotes, for example, provides an important genetic mechanism for actually generating behavioral variability.

Inbred strains and the study of derived generations of experimental animals enable us to relate similarities and differences in genetic composition to differences in behavioral and physical characteristics. Subsequent generations of the inbred strains indicate which traits are heritable, and by selective breeding for particular traits the heritable variability can be distinguished from the variability due to environmental influence.

Genetic information is coded by the chemical constitution of DNA (deoxyribonucleic acid) and a "carbon copy" is transmitted from the nucleus of each cell by RNA (ribonucleic acid). The details of the biochemical path from DNA to behavior are not yet known; however, certain defects in this pathway lead to such defects as phenylketonuria, which, like most of the biochemically based defects, results in mental retardation.

The genetic material in man is carried by 46 chromosomes arranged in 23 pairs, with one member of each pair contributed by each parent. Sometimes an individual will receive more than the required number of chromosomes, which causes a condition of trisomy in one of the chromosome pairs. This anomaly often leads to such behavioral deficiencies as mongolism. The absence of a chromosome is generally fatal, except in the case of the sex chromosomes. There is some evidence that an extra Y chromosome in males may be related to criminal behavior. Further understanding of the genetic bases is important both for the treatment of abnormal behavior and the prediction of genetic makeup in future generations.

CHAPTER SEVEN

THE NEUROLOGICAL
BASIS OF BEHAVIOR

Neurobiology is the study of the neural basis of behavior, which comes down to the study of the brain and how it functions to control behavior. The human brain is the most complex structure in the known universe. An average human brain has on the order of 12 billion nerve cells, and the possible number of interconnections and pathways among them in a single brain is greater than the total number of atomic particles making up the universe. The physical basis of everything that we are and do, both as members of the species Homo sapiens and as individuals, is to be found in the brain. All our response and behavioral patterns, everything that we have learned and experienced throughout our entire lifetimes, are in some way coded in the brain. Indeed, our actions and subjective experiences are but outward reflections of the patterns of physical activity in the brain. If we could understand the brain we would understand the reasons for all aspects of human behavior.

Although the human brain is an enormously complex mechanism, there are certain principles of organization, in terms of both its structure

NEUROBIOLOGY

and its functions, that permit us to gain a relatively simple overview of what the brain is and how it actually works. The entire field of neurobiology has undergone a major revolution—a knowledge "explosion"—in the past few years, and in the process a great many fundamental and extremely important discoveries have been made about the brain. We shall touch only on some of the highlights of this exciting and many-faceted story.

We are rapidly approaching a level of knowledge and understanding of the brain that will permit us for the first time to determine more about what a person is experiencing by recording the activity from his brain than he is able to describe to us himself, at least in some situations. For example, a wire may be glued to the surface of a person's scalp to pick up the electrical activity, or voltage, that is generated by the underlying brain. Of course these electrical signals are very weak; they are in the microvolt (millionths of a volt) range. The signals are led through an amplifier and are displayed on a polygraph, usually an ink record made on moving paper. This record is termed an *electroencephalogram* (EEG). A simplified version of such a recording device is shown in schematic form in Fig. 7-1.

147

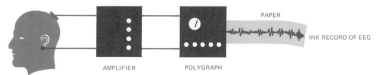

PAPER

INK RECORD OF EEG

AMPLIFIER POLYGRAPH

FIGURE 7–1   *General method of recording brain activity in man.*
Activity is picked up by a wire on the scalp, amplified, and written out
on moving paper by a polygraph. The paper record is thus a graph
of the changing voltage generated by the brain (on the ordinate) over
time (abscissa). The wire on the ear serves as a neutral reference
point.

Examples of EEG tracings are shown in Fig. 7-2. These are simply tracings of the voltages generated by the brain over time. The upper tracing is typical for a person who is alert and attentive; there are few obvious waves, but in general the activity (voltage change) is small, irregular, and fast. The next tracing is typical of a subject who is resting quietly but is awake. A regular rhythmic wave pattern, the *alpha rhythm*, becomes quite clear. The alpha wave occurs at a frequency of about 8 to 12 per second and waxes and wanes. When the subject is asleep and not dreaming the waves tend to be slower than alpha and of large amplitude (this condition is called *slow-wave sleep*). In the last tracing the subject has started to dream. The pattern has become much more like that characteristic of the alert awake state, but the subject is still asleep. If we were to awaken him at this point, he would report that he was dreaming. If we were to wait until he awakened naturally, he would probably be unable to tell us whether he had been dreaming or not, but we could tell with a good degree of accuracy simply by looking at the EEG.

The EEG is a record of the ongoing or spontaneous electrical activity of the brain, measured, of course, at some distance from the brain on the surface of the scalp. It is a kind of overall average of what many thousands or millions of nerve cells in the brain are doing. With the same simple arrangement of a wire glued to the scalp we can also record electrical activity evoked by a stimulus. In the recording setup shown in Fig. 7-1 the recording wire is at the back of the head overlying the visual area of the brain, where visual information is processed. If we suddenly flash a light or a visual pattern in the eye, a relatively clear electrical response will be picked up by the wire on the scalp. The activity is generated by many thousands of neurons in the visual area of the brain. These responses are actually averaged by a computer; individual responses are hard to see because there is so much brain "noise."

A striking example of the information conveyed by the averaged brain response is shown in Fig. 7-3. Simply by noting the characteristics of the responses, we can determine whether the subject is viewing a square or a diamond, regardless of what he chooses to tell us, and regardless of the size of the object. However, if the subject for some reason mistakes the two objects, the brain response seems to correspond to what the subject *thinks* he sees, not what is presented to him. Even more remarkably, if the subject is asked to imagine one of the stimuli,

NEUROBIOLOGY

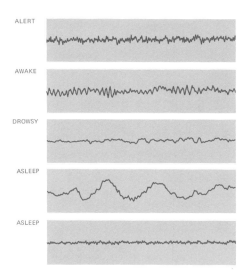

ALERT

AWAKE

DROWSY

ASLEEP

ASLEEP

FIGURE 7–2   *Typical human EEGs taken from subjects in different states, ranging from alert wakefulness to deep sleep [Brazier, 1968].*

FIGURE 7–3   *Human averaged evoked potentials. Stimulus forms are shown on the left, and the brain response evoked by each stimulus is shown on the right. Both the square and the diamond evoke the same first wave, but the diamond also evokes a later wave, independent of the size of the diamond. [John et al., 1967]*

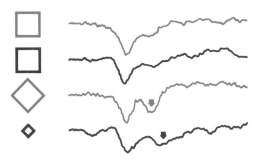

the brain response may correspond to the stimulus he is thinking about even when no stimulus is present. This type of averaged brain response may provide us, for the first time, with a way inside the mind—an objective method of measuring mental events.

THE BRAIN AND NERVOUS SYSTEM

We shall discuss here only a brief overview of the structural organization of the brain. Each of the regions described will be considered in detail later in connection with the important psychological processes to which they relate, particularly sleep and waking, motivation, sensation and perception, learning, memory, thought, and language. It is perhaps useful at this point to review a few simple definitions. The *brain* refers to the enlarged collection of cells and fibers inside the skull at the head end of an animal; it becomes the *spinal cord* as it leaves the skull (see Fig. 7-4). The *central nervous system* (CNS) includes both the brain and the spinal cord and is composed of nerve-cell bodies and their characteristic fiber processes, glial cells, and a variety of other types of cells making up blood vessels, membranes, etc. A complete nerve cell with its cell body and fibers is called a *neuron*. The functional connection from one neuron

149

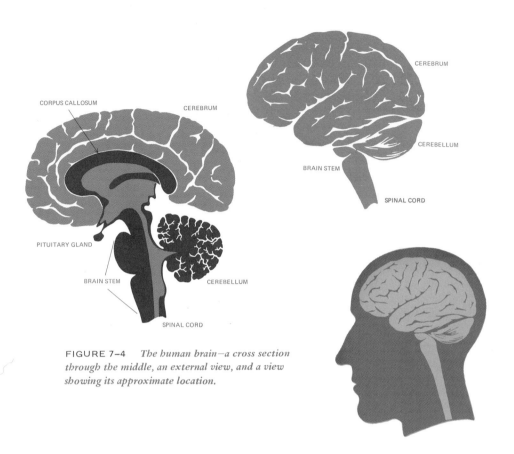

FIGURE 7–4   *The human brain—a cross section through the middle, an external view, and a view showing its approximate location.*

CORPUS CALLOSUM

CEREBRUM

CEREBRUM

CEREBELLUM

BRAIN STEM

SPINAL CORD

PITUITARY GLAND

BRAIN STEM

CEREBELLUM

SPINAL CORD

to another is called a *synapse*. The word *nerve* refers to a collection of nerve fibers (not including the cell bodies) outside the CNS; inside the CNS it is called a *tract*. Collections of nerve cell bodies are called *nuclei* if they are inside the CNS and *ganglia* outside.

COMPARATIVE AND DEVELOPMENTAL ASPECTS OF THE BRAIN

Most of what you see when you look at the brain in Fig. 7-4 is actually a surface structure of the forebrain, the *cerebral cortex*. In man and other higher vertebrates the cerebral cortex has enlarged enormously. In fact it has pushed out over all the rest of the brain, so that the basic tubular arrangement of the nervous system cannot be seen at all in the human brain, even at birth. However, we can get a clearer view of how the brain is formed by comparing the brains of simpler animals with man, and by comparing the adult human brain with the developing brain of the human embryo from early stages after conception to birth.

The basic organization of the vertebrate brain and spinal cord is perhaps most easily seen in certain invertebrates, particularly worms. A series of brains ranging from the flatworm (planaria) and earthworm to

150

man are shown in simplified form in Fig. 7-5. The fundamental plan is that of a segmented tube. This is evident in the earthworm, where each body segment has nerves going into and out from the corresponding segment of the tubular nervous system. Even in the worm there is an enlargement of the "head" end in relation to specialized receptors. The human brain maintains the basic tubular organization from spinal cord up to about the middle of the brain (midbrain). However, the front end of the tube is enormously expanded and laid back over the core tube to form most of what we usually refer to as the brain.

The hindbrain and midbrain of the human are a continuation of the tubular organization of the spinal cord and resemble the worm nervous system. In mammals the tubular portion of the nervous system is, of course, only relatively tubular. There is a very small central canal filled with *cerebrospinal fluid*. The tube is thus mostly wall, composed of nerve cell bodies and fibers, glial cells, blood vessels, and so on. However, the forebrain of the higher mammals is, as we noted earlier, so enlarged that it becomes most of the brain. It is worth emphasizing that the forebrain differs embryologically from the hindbrain in that they come from different types of primitive tissues. It is this relative enlargement of the forebrain, particularly the cerebral cortex, that distinguishes men from monkeys and monkeys from lower mammals. This is "where the action is" in the control of complex behavior.

FIGURE 7-5   *The general appearance of a series of brains ranging from worm to man. The drawings are not shown in scale. In actual relative size the flatworm (planaria) brain would be a dot too small to see on the human brain, and the frog brain would be about the size of the "O" in the label "frog". [Truex and Carpenter, 1964]*

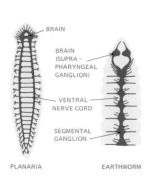

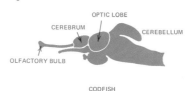

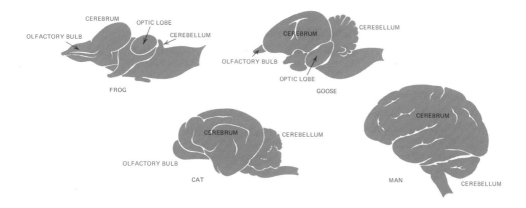

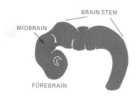
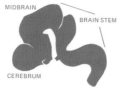
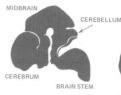
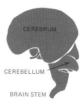

MIDBRAIN

BRAIN STEM

FOREBRAIN

MIDBRAIN

BRAIN STEM

CEREBRUM

MIDBRAIN

CEREBELLUM

CEREBRUM

BRAIN STEM

CEREBRUM

CEREBELLUM

BRAIN STEM

FIGURE 7–6   *Embryological development of the human brain (not to scale) at 4 weeks, 6 weeks, 7 weeks, and 12 weeks after conception. The brain at 12 weeks is actually 10 times larger than it is at 4 weeks.* [Peele, 1954]

It is a fundamental biological principle that "ontogeny recapitulates phylogeny"—that is, in embryological development the individual organism passes through many of the forms that comprise its evolutionary history. As the novelist Aldous Huxley [1928] put it:

. . . something that has been a single cell, a cluster of cells, a little sac of tissue, a kind of worm, a potential fish with gills . . . [will] one day become a man.

This principle is clearly illustrated by the developing human nervous system. Some of the embryological stages of the human brain are shown in Fig. 7-6. The brain of the 5-millimeter embryo is basically similar to the primitive vertebrate adult brain. However, there is already a sharp bend in the midbrain. By the time the embryo is 11 millimeters long the brain shows several subdivisions and is beginning to fold back on itself. At 15 millimeters the cerebrum is beginning to grow out, as is the cerebellum. Finally, the brain of the 53-millimeter embryo shows a marked similarity to the adult brain, although the cerebrum has not yet grown out to cover the midbrain.

ANATOMY OF THE NERVOUS SYSTEM

THE PERIPHERAL NERVOUS SYSTEM   The *peripheral nerves* are the nerves lying outside the central nervous system which connect to skin, muscles, and glands. There are in fact *two* peripheral nervous systems, the somatic system and the autonomic system. Each contains both sensory and motor nerves, but their functions are quite different. The *somatic nervous system* controls all the striated muscles—the muscles that we contract when we walk, write, talk, make all types of voluntary motions, and make involuntary adjustments in posture and other reflex functions. The somatic motor nerves thus control most of what we normally call behavior. The *autonomic nervous system*, in contrast, controls glands, smooth muscles and the heart, and what might be called the emotional aspects of behavior. Crying, laughing, fear, anger, and love involve the autonomic nervous system. Sensory input to the somatic nervous system is from skin, joint, and muscle receptors and includes touch, pressure, temperature, and pain. Sensory input to the auto-

152

nomic nervous system is from glands and smooth muscle and is generally much more diffuse, conveying a vague sense of feeling, pain, and organic sensations.

To add to the confusion there are two subdivisions of the autonomic nervous system, the *sympathetic* and *parasympathetic*, which have their ganglia in different locations. Often the functions of the two systems are opposite. Activation of the sympathetic system causes contraction of arteries, acceleration of the heart, inhibition of stomach contractions and secretion, and dilation of pupils, whereas activation of the parasympathetic system causes dilation of arteries, inhibition of the heart, stomach contractions and secretions, and constriction of pupils. It appears that the sympathetic system functions to mobilize the resources of the body for emergencies, whereas the parasympathetic system tends to conserve and store bodily resources. Thus in a sudden emergency a person will experience increased heart beat, inhibition of stomach activity, widening of pupils, and energy mobilization as a result of the sympathetic system. Such conservative functions as digestion, basal heart rate, and bladder control are carried on in periods between stresses by means of the parasympathetic system.

THE SPINAL CORD   Two general categories of activity are handled by the spinal cord. *Spinal reflexes* are muscular and autonomic responses to bodily stimuli which occur even after the spinal cord is severed from the brain, as in a paraplegic accident victim. In addition, a wide variety of *supraspinal* activity is channeled through the spinal cord. The cerebral cortex and other brain structures controlling movement of the body convey activity down the spinal cord to motoneurons, which in turn control the muscles, and all bodily sensations are conveyed up the spinal cord to the brain. Analogous sensory and motor relations for the head are handled directly by the cranial nerves, which are like peripheral nerves but go directly to the brain rather than to the spinal cord.

THE BRAIN STEM   The *brain stem* refers to the structures of the midbrain and hindbrain, which are overlain by the cerebral hemispheres as indicated in Fig. 7-4. The hindbrain represents the continuation and expansion of the spinal cord in the brain and contains all the ascending and descending fiber tracts interconnecting brain and spinal cord, together with a number of important nerve-cell nuclei. The vital autonomic control nuclei concerned with respiration, heart action, and gastrointestinal function are located in the lower brain stem.

The brain stem *reticular formation* has extremely important functions which have only recently been appreciated. Anatomically it is a complex mixture of cell bodies, fibers, and nuclei extending from the spinal cord to the cerebrum, generally located in a somewhat ventral (lower) position in the brain stem (see Fig. 7-7). The two major aspects of reticular function concern descending influences on spinal and cranial motoneurons and ascending influences on the cerebral cortex and other brain structures. Stimulation of descending portions of the reticular system

153

FIGURE 7-7 *The ascending reticular system, shown as a large central arrow that acts upward and outward on the brain [Magoun, 1954].*

may cause either decreases (inhibition) or increases (facilitation) in the activity of the motoneurons controlling the skeletal musculature. In a classic paper Moruzzi and Magoun [1949] demonstrated that stimulation of the ascending reticular formation, or the ascending reticular activating system, resulted in an arousal response on the EEG, a pattern of low-voltage fast cortical activity characteristic of the waking state (see Fig. 7-2). Destruction of the midbrain reticular formation tends to yield a sleeping or stuporous animal [Lindsley et al., 1949].

The ascending reticular formation thus appears to be critically involved in the control of sleeping and waking. It also seems to play a fundamental role in behavioral alerting and possibly in attention as well [Lindsley, 1958]. The reticular formation receives input from all sensory systems and is in fact the major ascending system for the pathways mediating pain. Still another very old brain stem system that has acquired a new significance is the *raphé nuclei*. These are groups of cells lying in the midline and extending throughout the brain stem. There are relatively few neurons in the raphé system, but they seem to play a significant role in regulation of sleeping and waking and form a very important chemical circuit in the brain.

The brain stem developed early in the course of evolution and is surprisingly uniform in structure and organization from fish to man. There are, of course, some variations among species. A general principle of neural organization is that the size and complexity of a structure is related to the behavioral importance of that structure. In fish, which have no cerebral cortices, the midbrain region contains the important centers of seeing and hearing and is relatively large. Among mammals, the bat, for example, has a much enlarged midbrain auditory nucleus, corresponding to its extensive use of auditory information. As you probably know, the bat employs a system much like sonar. It emits very-high-frequency sound pulses and determines the location of objects in space by the echo sounds of the reflected pulses. The relationship of size of structure to behavioral importance provides a number of clues about possible functions of the various brain structures.

In summary, the brain stem contains all the fiber systems interconnecting the higher brain structures and the spinal cord; it also con-

154

tains the cranial nerves and their nuclei (except for the olfactory and optic nerves), nuclei subserving vital functions, emotional expression, and many higher-order nuclei concerned with various sensory modalities. When all brain tissue above the midbrain is removed in a cat, for example, the animal is still capable of an amazing variety of behaviors. It will live for long periods, can walk, vocalize, eat, sleep, exhibit some components of emotional expression, and may even be capable of very limited learning [Bard and Macht, 1958]. Humans, on the other hand, rarely survive if all tissue above the midbrain is absent or destroyed, and if they do, they exhibit only primitive reflex responses.

THE CEREBELLUM AND BASAL GANGLIA   The cerebellum is in evolutionary terms a very old structure and was probably the first to be specialized for sensory-motor coordination. It overlies the brain stem (see Fig. 7-4) and is typically very much convoluted in appearance, with a large number of lobules separated by fissures. The cerebellum is basically similar from snake and fish to man. Although it may be involved in a number of other functions as well, the cerebellum is primarily concerned with the regulation of motor coordination. Damage to the cerebellum produces characteristically jerky, uncoordinated movement.

The *basal ganglia* are a group of large nuclei (ganglia is really a misnomer) lying in the central regions of the cerebral hemispheres. These nuclei appear to play an important but as yet poorly understood role in the control of movement. Although their specific functions remain a mystery, we are beginning to learn something about a most interesting and important chemical circuit involving the basal ganglia.

THE HYPOTHALAMUS AND LIMBIC SYSTEM   The hypothalamus encompasses a group of small nuclei that lie generally at the base of the cerebrum close to the pituitary gland, or *hypophysis*. The pituitary gland, the "master gland" of the endocrine glands, is actually controlled by neurons from the hypothalamus. In recent years it has been found that the interrelationships between these two structures are critical in the neural regulation of endocrine gland function. The very small nuclei that comprise the hypothalamus are of fundamental importance to the entire organism. They are critically involved in eating, sexual behavior, drinking, sleeping, temperature regulation, and emotional behavior in general. The hypothalamus is the major central brain structure concerned with the functions of the autonomic nervous system, particularly with its sympathetic division.

The hypothalamus interconnects with many regions of the brain. A number of these structures, including old regions of the cerebral cortex (the cingulate gyrus), the hippocampus, the septal area, the amygdala, portions of the reticular formation, and the hypothalamus itself, are viewed by many anatomists as an integrated network of structures called the *limbic system* (see Fig. 7-8). Many of these structures seem to be involved in aspects of behavior such as emotion, motivation, and reinforcement.

155

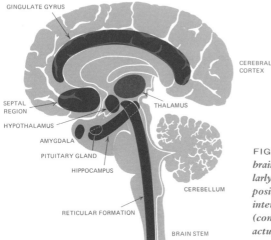

GINGULATE GYRUS

CEREBRAL
CORTEX

SEPTAL
REGION

THALAMUS

HYPOTHALAMUS

AMYGDALA

PITUITARY GLAND

HIPPOCAMPUS

CEREBELLUM

RETICULAR FORMATION

BRAIN STEM

FIGURE 7–8   *The limbic system of the human brain. These older structures are involved particularly in activation, motivation, and emotion. The position of the thalamus, a newer structure with interrelations to the limbic system, is also shown (compare with Fig. 7-4). The limbic structures are actually within the hemisphere, not on the midline.*

THE THALAMUS   The thalamus is a large grouping of nuclei located just above the midbrain. Its general shape is somewhat like that of small footballs, one in each cerebral hemisphere (see Fig. 7-8). One region of the thalamus, the lateral or sensory thalamus, is concerned with relaying sensory information to the cerebral cortex from specific sensory pathways for vision, hearing, touch, taste, and perhaps pain. Another region of the thalamus, the diffuse thalamic system, does not seem to be involved in relaying specific sensory information, but it plays an important role in the control of such processes as sleep and wakefulness and is considered a part of the limbic system.

THE CEREBRAL CORTEX   Psychologists have long been particularly fascinated by the structure and functions of the cerebral cortex. A number of considerations justify viewing this structure as the major system for the more complex and modifiable aspects of behavior. The cerebral cortex represents the most recent evolutionary development of the vertebrate nervous system. Fish and amphibians have no cerebral cortices, and reptiles and birds have only a rudimentary indication of one. More primitive mammals such as the rat have a relatively small, smooth cortex. As the phylogenetic scale is ascended, the amount of cortex relative to the total amount of brain tissue increases accordingly. In more advanced primates such as the rhesus monkey, the chimpanzee, and man the amount of cerebral cortex is enormous and disproportionately large. Of the approximately 12 billion neurons in the human brain, 9 billion are found in the cerebral cortex. There is a general correlation between the cortical development in a species, its phylogenetic position, and the degree of complexity and modifiability characteristic of its behavior.

All incoming sensory systems project to the cortex, each to a specific region. Motor systems controlling the activity of muscles and glands arise in other regions of the cortex. Interestingly enough, the basic organization of the cortical sensory and motor areas does not appear to differ markedly from rat to man. However, with ascending position

156

on the evolutionary scale there is a striking increase in the relative amount
of *association* cortex—areas that are neither sensory nor motor and have
often been assumed to be involved in higher or more complex behavioral
functions. Studies done on monkeys indicate that the different association areas of the cortex may play rather different roles in the mediation
of complex intellectual processes. In particular, the frontal areas (frontal
lobes) may be concerned more with short-term memory and the temporal areas with processing of complex sensory information [Harlow,
1952] . Rough-scale drawings of the cerebral cortex in rat, cat, monkey,
and man are shown in Fig. 7-9. Note the remarkable increase in absolute
brain size, the increase in the number of indentations or fissures, and the
increase in relative amount of association cortex. The depths of the
fissures are also covered by cerebral cortex. In fact the development of
fissures permits a vast expansion of the amount and total area of the
cerebral cortex; the human brain has more cortex in the fissures than on
the outer surface.

Man, incidentally, does not have the largest brain. The porpoise,
the whale, and the elephant all have larger brain masses, although the
packing density of cells may be less. The cortex is a multiple layer of
nerve cells about 2-millimeters thick which overlies the cerebrum. An
actual photomicrograph of a cross section of the visual area of the cerebral cortex in a human brain is shown in Fig. 7-10.

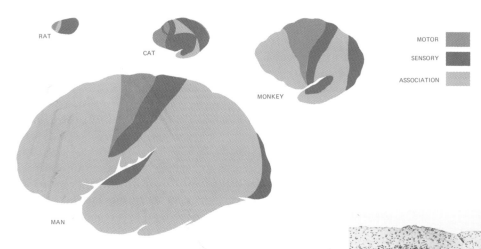

RAT

CAT

MONKEY

MAN

MOTOR

SENSORY

ASSOCIATION

FIGURE 7–9   *Rough scale drawings of the cerebral
hemispheres of four mammals. Note the increase both
in size and in the relative amount of association
cortex. [Thompson, 1967]*

FIGURE 7–10   *Photomicrograph of a
cross section through the visual area of
the human cerebral cortex. The surface
of the cortex is at the top. Each small
dot is a neuron. [Sholl, 1956]*

The cerebral cortex is the last or highest region in the brain where sensory information from the eye, the ear, the skin, and other senses is represented. If the visual region of a man's cerebral cortex is destroyed, he will be blind. If the auditory region is removed, he will be deaf. Similarly, if the motor region is destroyed, he will be very awkward and clumsy in his movements. However, the cortex is much more complex than this. A relatively small lesion in one region of the dominant hemisphere makes it impossible to speak (aphasia). Complete destruction of the cerebral cortex transforms a complex human being into a primitive reflex machine. The cerebral cortex is the neural substrate of all higher and more complex behavior in man and is essential to such phenomena as learning, language, and thinking. Not only does it distinguish man from other animals, but it marks the difference between one man and another.

THE BIOLOGY OF THE NEURON

The basic processes of the brain occur at the level of the individual neuron, the fundamental functional element of the nervous system. Various ways of studying the neuron have become artificially separated into different fields. Neuroanatomy is concerned with the fine structure of the neuron, neurochemistry deals with the chemistry of the neuron, and neurophysiology is concerned with the function of the neuron, particularly in terms of electrical or electrophysiological activity. Actually, it makes a good deal more sense to view the neuron and its synapses from all these points of view together.

The individual nerve cell, the *neuron*, resembles most other types of living cells. It has a cell membrane, a nucleus, various structural elements within the cell body, and is a single isolated or individual entity—that is, it is not structurally continuous with other cells. The neuron is specialized, of course, to conduct and transmit information. This is reflected in the fact that neurons have long fibers to conduct information to other neurons or to muscles and glands and the fact that they form *synapses*, the functional connections between neurons.

A typical nerve cell has several characteristic features. The cell shown in Fig. 7-11 is a common type called a *pyramidal cell*, which has a relatively long axon fiber. There are, of course, many specialized forms and shapes of neurons. However, the general features shown here are common to many types of neurons. The main cell body contains the cell nucleus and is referred to as the *soma*. It has many short fibers extending out from it, called *dendrites*, which serve to receive activity from adjacent cells. Synapses form on these dendrites and conduct this activity to the cell body. The long fiber which transmits activity to other neurons is called the *axon*. Actually, the axon will conduct in both directions, but impulses can cross the synapses between nerve cells in only one direction, from the axon of one cell to the cell body or fibers of another. The

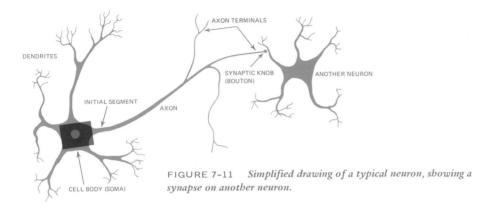

FIGURE 7-11   *Simplified drawing of a typical neuron, showing a synapse on another neuron.*

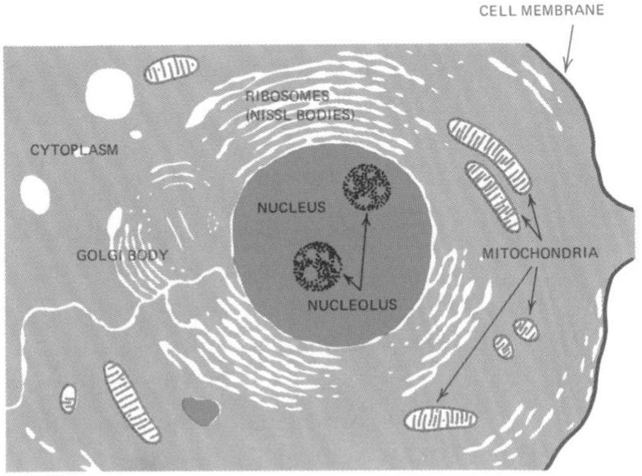

FIGURE 7-12   *Enlargement of the area marked off by a square in Fig. 7-11, showing the characteristic small organelles within the cell body.*

initial portion of the axon is called the *initial segment*. The presynaptic axon terminals are typically very fine as they branch out to end in knobs or *boutons*, in close apposition to other neurons to form the synapses.

The cell body or soma region marked off by the square in Fig. 7-11 is enlarged in Fig. 7-12. Several quite specialized structures called *organelles* ("little organs") are found within the cell body. Recent basic work in cellular biology on the organization and functions of these organelles, which are found in most living cells, has led to something of a revolution in our thinking about how cells function. In particular, we now know that such fundamental processes as the use of food energy (metabolism), use of oxygen (respiration), the synthesis of new chemicals and tissues, and of course reproduction of new cells do not occur uniformly throughout tissue or protoplasm, but occur instead in the specialized organelles within the cell.

Some of these organelles are indicated in Fig. 7-12. The *cell membrane*, which covers the entire nerve cell and all its fibers, is specialized to perform a very remarkable task—to conduct information. This process takes place only along the nerve-cell membrane, and not in tissue inside the neuron. The *nucleus* of the neuron contains the genetic material, the deoxyribonucleic acid (DNA), which is present as many

159

thousands of genes which make up the chromosomes. There is another structure within the cell nucleus, the *nucleolus*, that is made up of ribonucleic acid (RNA). This is the system involved in the synthesis of protein and is therefore of fundamental importance. In fact there are several theories that attempt to link RNA to learning and memory. After it is formed in the nucleus, RNA moves out into the cytoplasm of the cell, where it exists as particles called *ribosomes*. In nerve cells the ribosomes are very numerous and are called *Nissl bodies*. The *Golgi bodies* are found in neurons and other cells that are specialized to secrete substances (for example, cells in the pancreas that secrete insulin). It is believed that the Golgi bodies are involved in the manufacture and/or storage of the substances secreted. This is of particular significance for neurons, since it now appears that synaptic transmission, the transfer of information from one neuron to another, is accomplished through the manufacture and secretion of chemical transmitter substances. The last major type of organelle in the neuron is the fairly large football-shaped *mitochondrion*. The interior of the mitochondrion is literally a metabolic factory. It is here that the cell converts foodstuffs and oxygen into biological energy to run the machinery of the body.

Metabolism is a general term which refers to all the chemical processes in the body related to the production and utilization of energy. Considerable amounts of energy are used continuously by all living organisms, even under conditions of minimal activity. This energy is available to the organism only in the form of chemical energy, obtained from foods. When foods are ingested, they are broken down into component substances by the processes of digestion and transported to all cells via the bloodstream. The most common food substance carried by the blood is glucose, a sugar derived from natural carbohydrates. The processes of metabolism whereby glucose and other compounds are broken down to form energy occur separately in all individual cells of the body. Each cell contains a number of mitochondria. The major form of this biological energy is the substance adenosine triphosphate (ATP), produced in the mitochondria. Thus when muscles contract or nerves are active, they use ATP as a direct source of energy.

The brain uses only glucose as the food supply from which to make the energy substance ATP. This process requires oxygen, which means, of course, that the brain must be well supplied with blood. Although the human brain constitutes only about 2.5 percent of the total weight of the body, it receives 15 percent of the total blood supply and uses 25 percent of all the oxygen used by the body. The brain literally lives off the body. Interestingly enough, the energy requirements of the human brain are remarkably steady and constant. The amount of energy used in sitting quietly and not thinking about anything in particular for an hour and the amount of energy used in sitting and solving a problem or studying for an exam for an hour would differ by the equivalent of about half a peanut—and most of the half peanut would be used not for the intense mental effort, but for the increased muscle tension that usually accompanies intense mental effort.

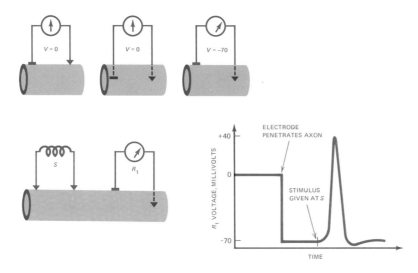

FIGURE 7-13 *Recording the membrane potential from a single nerve fiber axon. Above, the resting membrane voltage (−70 millivolts) is generated only across the axon membrane and does not occur if both electrodes are outside or inside the axon. Below, the conducted nerve action (spike) potential. When the electrode from R_1 penetrates the axon, the resting membrane potential of −70 millivolts is recorded. An electrical stimulus is then given at S, which induces a spike action potential that travels down the axon and is recorded at R_1.*

THE AXON AND THE NERVE ACTION POTENTIAL

All the stimuli impinging on us, all our sensations, thoughts, feelings, and actions, must be coded into the "language" of the neuron. Every neuron uses two quite different sorts of language to transmit information. Activity is initiated in a given neuron by the process of synaptic transmission. Once the nerve cell has been activated, the nerve action potential, or spike, develops in the initial segment of the axon and is conducted down the axon to the axon terminal boutons to induce activity at synapses on other neurons. Thus information has to be translated into two codes—synaptic *transmission* when it passes from one neuron to another and action potential *conduction* when it is conducted out along the nerve cell axon from the neuron cell body to the next neuron in the system. Our understanding of the two basic neural processes of transmission and conduction has been due in large part to the work of Hodgkin [1964] and Huxley [1964] in England (nerve action potential) and Eccles [1964] in Australia (synaptic transmission). These studies, for which all three shared the Nobel prize in medicine in 1963, rank among the great intellectual achievements of the twentieth century.

The basic kind of experiment used by Hodgkin and Huxley to study the nerve action potential is shown in Fig. 7-13. They used the giant axon from the squid, which is a single nerve fiber many times larger than axons in mammals and will live for some time after it is removed. In their early

161

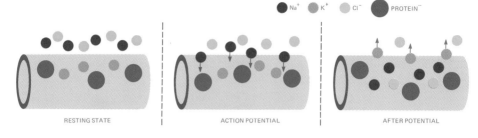

Na⁺ K⁺ Cl⁻ PROTEIN⁻

RESTING STATE   ACTION POTENTIAL   AFTER POTENTIAL

FIGURE 7-14   *The distribution of ions inside and outside the axon. In the normal resting state, when the axon is not conducting an action potential, protein and potassium ions are more concentrated inside and sodium and chloride ions*

experiments they tried recording from this axon without removing it from the squid. However, when the fiber was stimulated, the squid gave a powerful flip that smashed their recording electrode. It is easy to see from the figure that the electrical activity of the axon occurs entirely at the nerve membrane. If both electrodes to R_1 are outside the axon there is no voltage; if both are inside the axon there is no voltage. However, if one is outside and one is inside the axon, as shown, a steady voltage will be recorded regardless of where the internal electrode is, as long as it is inside. The graph portion of the figure shows what happens when the internal electrode is inserted through the membrane. The voltage, or potential, shifts from 0 to −70 millivolt (nearly 1/10 volt). This is called the *nerve resting membrane potential*. It is present at about the same value in all neurons, even the very tiny neurons in the human brain. Although the amount of voltage may seem small (it is about one-fifteenth the voltage in an ordinary flashlight battery), it is actually quite substantial in view of the tiny size of most neurons. Cells in the electric eel, using the same basic mechanisms, can develop several hundred volts, enough to stun a man.

The actual mechanisms that produce the resting membrane potential (which, incidentally, occurs in most types of cells, not just in neurons) are beyond the scope of our present discussion [see Thompson, 1967]. However, the essence of the situation is indicated in Fig. 7-14. The nerve membrane is semipermeable; in effect, it has small holes that allow some ions to cross, but not others. In the resting state the nerve membrane allows chloride ions (Cl^-) and potassium ions (K^+) to cross rather freely in both directions. However, it will not allow the protein ions, which are mostly inside neurons, to pass out, and it also has a specific barrier that keeps sodium ions (Na^+) from passing in. The actual level of the nerve resting potential, −70 millivolts, is determined entirely by the relative concentrations of potassium ions inside and outside the cell.

As we saw in Fig. 7-13, when the axon is stimulated at S, some distance away from the recording electrodes, an action potential develops and travels down the axon. The actual speed of the action potential

162

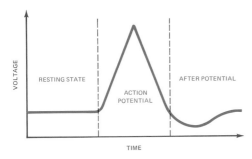

VOLTAGE

RESTING STATE

ACTION
POTENTIAL

AFTER POTENTIAL

TIME

are more concentrated outside. As the initial large spike of the action
potential develops, sodium ions rush into the axon. During the later
afterpotential phase of the action potential, potassium ions move out.
The drawings indicate the movements of ions at the same location
on the axon during different periods of the action potential.

is relatively slow—from a few feet to several hundred feet per second, depending on the size and other characteristics of the axon. The action potential is constant in amplitude; it does not decay as it travels down the
axon, but always stays at the same height, which is about 100 millivolts.
It is best viewed as a localized and temporary disturbance of the membrane which moves along the axon much as a wave moves across the
surface of water.

The actual mechanisms that yield the action potential, although
complex [see Thompson, 1967], are not difficult to describe. When the
action potential begins to develop, the membrane barrier to sodium ions
breaks down very briefly, and sodium ions rush in (see Fig. 7-14). This
creates the 100-millivolt shift in the positive direction (depolarization)
that is the major component of the action potential. After this there is a
somewhat longer period when the membrane becomes more negative
than usual (hyperpolarization, or afterpotential). This is due to a later
outward movement of potassium ions. The membrane then returns to its
resting level of −70 millivolts and is ready to respond again. The spike
action potential is *all-or-none*; it either does not fire at all, or it discharges to its full height and travels down the axon.

When the activity induced in a neuron by synaptic transmission
causes the membrane potential of the cell body and initial segment of
the axon to depolarize about 10 millivolts, to the spike discharge threshold of about −60 millivolts, the spike develops in the initial segment (see
Fig. 7-11) and travels down the axon. It had generally been assumed,
incidentally, that when a spike travels down the axon it activates all the
small axon terminal branches, but recent evidence suggests that this may
not always be the case. Under some conditions not all axon terminals
may be activated. When the action potential reaches a branching point,
where the axon branches into two smaller axons, the spike may or may
not continue in both branches. It is as though there might be some basic
element of uncertainty, chance, or "free will" in the system. In any
event, the action potential travels down the axon to many of the axon
terminals, where it initiates the process of synaptic transmission to activate the next neuron in the system.

163

SYNAPTIC
TRANSMISSION

The most important process in the human brain is synaptic transmission. As far as we know, the only way that a neuron can communicate with other neurons is through the synapses. The synapse is not an actual connection, but a close approximation to one. The distance between the axon terminal bouton of one neuron and the cell body of the other neuron is about 200 angstroms (approximately 1/50,000 millimeter). The presynaptic terminal contains a number of circular structures called *synaptic vesicles*, each of which is believed to contain the chemical synaptic transmitter substance which is released across the synapse to act on the postsynaptic membrane of the other cell. The presence of synaptic vesicles is characteristic, indeed even diagnostic, of the appearance of a synapse. The presumed transmitter chemical may be manufactured in the cell body, perhaps by the Golgi bodies, and then transported down the axon by some means and stored in the synaptic vesicles. Alternatively, the chemical may be formed in the terminal itself, where the vesicles are found.

Synapses are localized primarily on dendrites and cell bodies. The dendrites are the region of the cell where incoming information is summed and, in a very real sense, evaluated. Recent work indicates that there are important specialized structures on the dendrites called *dendritic spines*

FIGURE 7–15   *Synapses. In a typical neuron of the cerebral cortex, the dendrites are covered by many thousands of dendritic spines. Each spine is a synapse. The type 1 dendritic knob synapse (drawn from electron-microscope pictures) is characteristically excitatory. The presynaptic axon terminal knob is filled with small vesicles, presumably containing the chemical synaptic transmitter substance, and the postsynaptic membrane has a dark thickened region, presumably containing chemical receptors for the transmitter substance. On the type 2 synapse, which occurs on the cell body of the neuron, there is no spine or thickening of the postsynaptic membrane. This type of synapse is characteristically inhibitory.*

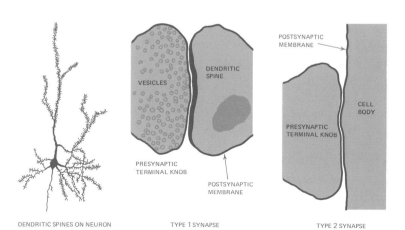

DENDRITIC SPINES ON NEURON   TYPE 1 SYNAPSE   TYPE 2 SYNAPSE (see Fig. 7-15). These very small knobs or spines cover all parts of the dendrites but are not found on cell bodies or axons. They are particularly numerous on the pyramidal type of neuron found throughout the cerebral cortex and certain other regions of the brain. The enlargements in the figure show the nature of the spine synapse in greater detail. Each spine is a place where an axon terminal from another neuron forms a synapse with the neuron dendrite. The many thousands of spines that appear on the dendrite are all terminations of other neuron processes. Thus each dendritic spine provides the means by which a fiber from another neuron can increase this neuron's excitability or tendency to be active. A different type of synapse, however, is found on the *cell body* of a neuron (see also Fig. 7-11). These synapses have no spines. Recent evidence indicates that there is also a fundamental difference in their function—the dendritic spine synapses (type 1) excite the neuron and cell body synapses (type 2) inhibit it.

There are several aspects of the dendritic spines that are of great significance. First, in higher mammals they seem for the most part to develop after birth. In the cat, for example, spines first become apparent about seven days after birth, a time when the infant kitten is just beginning to explore and learn about his world. They are not fully elaborated until the kitten is several months old. Equally important is the fact that if activity on the spines is decreased by damaging the input fibers to the spines, they do not develop normally. Even such a simple procedure as keeping an animal in the dark for a month leads to changes in the spines of cortical cells in the visual region. From this it is a relatively small step to the enormously important hypothesis that the dendritic spines are the fundamental structural locus of memory in the adult brain. Very recent evidence provides some support for this idea. It appears that if rats are raised in an "enriched" environment, with many more types of objects and stimuli than are usual in a rat cage, they develop more than the normal number of dendritic spines in cortical cells [Schapiro and Vukovich, 1970]. This finding opens up a most exciting possibility in the search for the memory _engram_—the physical basis of memory. It is also possible that the dendritic spines, if they reflect the structural development of synapses, may have a more general function than simply the coding of memory. They may reflect all the patterns of interconnections established among neurons in the brain during the growth and development of the organism.

In terms of structure, neurons, with their many thousands of dendritic spines, are far and away the most highly specialized cells in the body. All behavioral patterns—indeed, all the countless billions of elements of information and experience that we acquire in a lifetime—appear to be coded in the structural-functional relations among the neurons. Neurons are the only cells in the body that do not reproduce after birth. We are born with all the neurons we will ever have. As we grow up and grow older, we simply lose neurons. It has been estimated that on the order of several hundred neurons die each day in the adult human brain. If all memory is in fact coded in part by structural features of neurons such as the spines, then it would not be feasible for neurons to reproduce. If they did, the structural relationships would change, and the very fabric of memory would shift and dissipate. Although it is difficult to imagine an information-storage system in a higher organism in which the elements reproduce themselves, speculation on the kinds of psychological processes that might occur has resulted in some classic science fiction [van Vogt, 1940].

EXCITATION OF NEURONS

The operation of synaptic transmission is shown in Fig. 7-16. The presynaptic axon terminal contains vesicles of the transmitter chemical. The particular chemical transmitter shown here, acetylcholine (ACh), is in fact the chemical transmitter at the neuromuscular junction (where the motoneuron axon ends on the muscle fiber and induces muscle contraction), in certain synapses in the peripheral autonomic system, and in

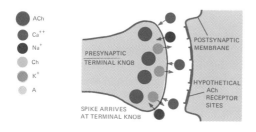

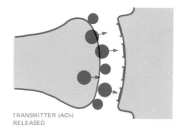

FIGURE 7–16   *Chemical actions that occur during synaptic transmission. The action potential arrives at the presynaptic terminal, causing sodium ions (Na⁺) to move in (and potassium ions out), which in turn causes calcium ions (Ca⁺⁺) to move onto the membrane. This produces release of the transmitter, in this case acetylcholine (ACh). When acetylcholine arrives at the "receptor" sites on the postsynaptic membrane, the postsynaptic electrical response is generated. The transmitter, acetylcholine, is broken down at the receptor sites into acetyl (A) and choline (Ch), which can then be reabsorbed by the presynaptic terminal and reformed into acetylcholine.*

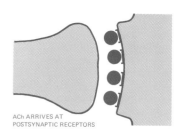

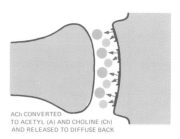

NEUROBIOLOGY

some brain synapses as well. When the action potential reaches the terminal, as shown, a reaction is started which leads to release of the transmitter. Recent work indicates that the important process here is an action of calcium ions (Ca^{++}) on the membrane. The influx of calcium is apparently started by the arrival of the action potential and the associated inward flow of sodium ions and outward flow of potassium ions. When the calcium ions move onto the membrane, the transmitter substance ACh is released into the synaptic space. The ACh molecules diffuse across the synapse, attach to receptor sites on the postsynaptic membrane, and induce an electrical response in the postsynaptic membrane. Since the excitatory synapse is on a dendritic spine, the electrical response occurs in the dendrite and cell body of the neuron.

The receptor sites on the postsynaptic membrane are not fully understood. They may actually be an enzyme that breaks down ACh into its components, acetyl and choline. This enzyme, acetylcholine esterase, is in fact present in all acetylcholine synapses. Such a receptor mechanism would indeed be a great convenience. The same process that inactivates the transmitter by breaking it down also induces activity in the postsynaptic membrane. The chemical receptor functions as both a receptor and an inactivator for ACh. If the ACh were not inactivated, the cell would respond for a long time instead of briefly. The components of the acetylcholine are then taken up, perhaps into the presynaptic terminal, to be reformed into ACh and used again.

If a recording electrode were placed inside the postsynaptic neuron, it would indicate a change in the membrane potential when the ACh arrived at the postsynaptic membrane. As shown in Fig. 7-17, the resting potential of the neuron is –70 millivolts, and the spike discharge threshold is –60 millivolts, the same as in the axon. The electrical change in the postsynaptic cell membrane during synaptic excitation is a very brief decrease in the membrane potential—a depolarization. If only a single synapse on a cell is activated, there will be only a small depolarization. If we activate a few synapses on the cell together, the depolarization will be larger. When enough synapses are activated to cause the membrane potential to reach the spike threshold level of the cell, then a spike develops at the initial segment of the axon and travels down the axon to act on other neurons. This kind of synaptic depolarization, which seems to occur particularly on the dendritic spine synapses (type 1), is called an *excitatory postsynaptic potential* (EPSP).

The actual mechanism that yields the EPSP is very similar to that producing the spike. When the cell membrane potential reaches the spike threshold point, the irreversible chemical reaction that generates the spike—the breakdown of the sodium barrier and the inward rush of sodium ions—occurs. The EPSP itself results from a brief, limited breakdown of the barriers to sodium and other ions on the postsynaptic membrane at the synapse. Since this occurs only at the synapse, the effect for one synapse will be small. The size of the EPSP, however, depends on the number of synapses activated. Hence it is a graded response; that is,

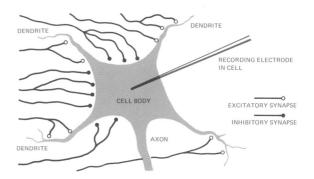

FIGURE 7–17 *Synaptic transmission. Schematic of a neuron with excitatory synaptic terminals (light) on the dendrites and inhibitory synaptic terminals (dark) on the cell body. A recording electrode has been inserted into the cell to measure the changes in the cell membrane potential during synaptic excitation and inhibition. During synaptic excitation the electrical response of the membrane to a weak excitation from only 1 or 2 synapses is a brief deplorization*

it can vary continuously in amplitude. This is in sharp contrast to the all-or-none action potential. The fact that the EPSP is graded is of fundamental importance. The neuron is continuously being bombarded by the actions from many synapses. It averages or integrates all this input activity into an overall graded level of membrane potential. When this level reaches the spike threshold, the neuron fires the action potential, thus converting the continuous graded synaptic activity or information into a discrete, fixed-amplitude, all-or-none spike discharge. For readers familiar with computers, every neuron is like a complex hybrid computer, the graded synaptic activity is comparable to an analog computer, and the all-or-none spike is comparable to a digital computer. People say that the brain is like a computer; it is in fact like 12 billion complex computers, each interacting with many others.

INHIBITION OF NEURONS

If the brain were composed entirely of excitatory synapses of the type we have been discussing, any stimulus that induced neural activity would immediately cause a runaway buildup of excitation to the point where the brain would be in a permanent state of massive continuous discharging, as in an epileptic seizure. Indeed, certain drugs that block inhibition, such as strychnine, produce just this effect—massive epileptic-like discharges of neurons. It is therefore necessary to consider processes of inhibition in order to account for the neural functioning of the brain.

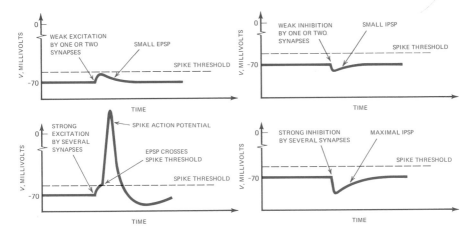

(EPSP) that does not reach spike threshold (upper response). Strong excitation from several synapses produces an EPSP large enough to cross the spike threshold level of the cell, which results in a spike developing at the initial segment of the axon and traveling down the axon (lower response). During synaptic inhibition the postsynaptic cell-membrane potential becomes greater in the negative direction (hyperpolarized) during inhibition. This response is called the inhibitory postsynaptic potential (IPSP). Weak inhibition from only 1 or 2 synapses (upper response) produces a small increase in negativity of the membrane and strong inhibition (lower response) produces a maximal negativity. The IPSP inhibits synaptic excitation by preventing the cell from developing an EPSP to excitatory input.

Perhaps the simplest possible way that an inhibitory synapse could act would be to do just the opposite of what an excitatory synapse does and *increase* the negativity of the membrane potential beyond that of its resting level. As noted above, the resting membrane is normally about –70 millivolts and an excitatory change of about 10 millivolts to the threshold level of –60 millivolts initiates spike discharge. If the membrane potential could be shifted in the opposite direction to a value of, say, –75 millivolts, then an EPSP of 10 millivolts that had previously caused discharge of the cell would just shift the membrane potential back to –65 millivolts, still 5 millivolts below the spike discharge threshold. This is essentially what does take place during inhibition; there is a brief *increase* in the negativity of the membrane potential.

Examples of inhibitory synapses are also shown in Fig. 7-17. These are the type 2 synapses on the cell bodies, which have no spines. Stimulation of an input fiber that exerts an inhibitory effect on the postsynaptic neuron causes release of a chemical inhibitory substance that diffuses across the synaptic space to act on the postsynaptic membrane of the cell body. However, the cell membrane potential is shifted toward a greater degree of polarization—that is, the cell membrane becomes hyperpolarized. The actual membrane potential may shift from –70 to –75 millivolts. This is termed the *inhibitory postsynaptic potential* (IPSP). When an IPSP occurs an excitatory action that previously depolarized the cell to firing threshold will no longer produce a depolarization sufficient to reach spike threshold. The ionic mechanism of the IPSP is different from that of the EPSP. The sodium barrier does not break down,

169

but is instead made stronger by small increases in the movement of potassium and chloride ions across the membrane. Examples of IPSPs produced in a neuron by weak and strong actions from inhibitory nerve fibers are shown in Fig. 7-17. The IPSP appears to be roughly a mirror image of the EPSP. Note that it grows in a *graded* fashion with increasing stimulus strength, just as does the EPSP. However, it moves the membrane potential level of the cell farther away from the spike threshold, and so, of course, no action potential is developed.

Postsynaptic excitation (EPSP) and postsynaptic inhibition (IPSP) are the major types of synaptic processes that occur in the brain. Remember that the spike action potential begins at the initial segment, where the axon leaves the cell body. Excitation occurs on the dendrites, some distance from the initial segment. However, the development of the spike at the initial segment is entirely due to synaptic excitation. Inhibition, in contrast, occurs on the cell body adjacent to the initial segment. Thus inhibition has a much more immediate and potent controlling effect than excitation on the tendency of the cell to fire spikes and hence influence other cells.

In the mammalian nervous system, where the basic mechanism of synaptic transmission is chemical, essentially all interactions among neurons take place through the processes of excitation (EPSP) and inhibition (IPSP). Virtually every nerve cell body and dendrite has an essentially continuous covering of synaptic terminal knobs (see Fig. 7-18), and in the normal state the cell is continuously being bombarded with thousands of excitatory and inhibitory synaptic influences. The extent to which the cell is or is not firing all-or-none spike potentials down the axon is determined by the dynamic balance among these classes of synaptic events. This complexity of organization makes it very clear that the usual simple diagrams and neural models, which show each neuron synapsing on only one or two other neurons and all synapses as excitatory, must inevitably fail to predict the complexity of behavior of the real nervous system.

The EEGs we discussed at the beginning of the chapter are averaged records of the electrical activity generated by literally millions of neurons. A basic question in the study of brain activity has been the nature of the processes in the neurons that produce the EEG. If all the neurons were acting differently, we would see nothing but noise in the record.

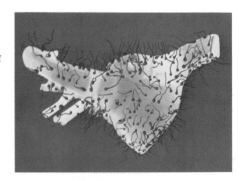

FIGURE 7-18   *A realistic drawing showing only the largest synapses in the cell body of a neuron [Haggar and Barr, 1950].*

Instead, under many conditions we can record clear wave patterns (see Fig. 7-2). The processes that act together to produce synchronous wave patterns are primarily the graded synaptic potentials we have been discussing. The brain activity that is shown in an EEG is the summed graded synaptic potential, both excitatory and inhibitory, generated on the dendrites and cell bodies of millions of neurons in the brain.

SYNAPTIC TRANSMITTER SUBSTANCES

The fact that synaptic transmission in the human nervous system is a chemical process means that chemical substances must play a fundamental role in learning, thinking, and other complex aspects of behavior. We can make very good guesses about the nature of some chemical substances that may serve as transmitters in the brain. However, there is a great deal more to be learned about this fundamental and important field than we know today.

ACETYLCHOLINE   As we noted earlier, acetylcholine is the transmitter at the neuromuscular junction, certain peripheral autonomic synapses, and in certain regions of the brain. It appears that ACh is substantially present in a large ascending system of neurons tentatively identified with the ascending reticular activating system. This system, which originates in the brain stem and projects anteriorly to the hypothalamus, the thalamus, the limbic system, and other regions, plays a fundamental role in the regulation of sleep, waking, and arousal. Thus ACh might have a very specific and important function in the control of sleep and waking, of behavioral arousal, and possibly attention as well.

NOREPINEPHRINE, DOPAMINE, AND SEROTONIN   There is considerable evidence that norepinephrine and two closely related compounds, dopamine and serotonin, may be synaptic transmitter substances in the brain. These three *biogenic amines*—amines which have biological activity or effects—are derived from naturally occurring amino acids, the major components of meat and other proteins. Norepinephrine is in fact formed from dopamine, which in turn is formed from the amino acid tyrosine. Serotonin (5-hydroxytryptamine, also referred to as 5-HT) is simply derived from the naturally occurring amino acid tryptophan.

Norepinephrine is a transmitter in portions of the peripheral autonomic system. Recently a group of scientists in Sweden developed a technique for identifying the presence of biogenic amines in the brain by converting them to highly fluorescent substances [Hillarp et al., 1960]. Norepinephrine and dopamine fluoresce with a greenish color and serotonin fluoresces with a yellow color. They have been able to show that there appear to be biogenic amine systems in the brain. Thus there is a norepinephrine system with cell bodies in the brain stem that send axons via the medial forebrain bundle (a fiber pathway) to the hypothalamus, the hippocampus, the limbic system, and the cerebral

171

cortex. This system appears to be similar to the acetylcholine system described above and may also be related to the organization and functions of the ascending reticular activating system. There is a particularly high concentration of norepinephrine in the hypothalamus, the small region in the depths of the brain that is most directly concerned with the motivational and emotional aspects of behavior.

Although norepinephrine is formed from dopamine, dopamine appears to exist and function independently in the brain. Hillarp et al. have demonstrated that there is a dopamine system in the brain that is quite distinct from the norepinephrine system. The cell bodies of this system lie in the *substantia nigra*, a dark-staining group of neurons in the region of the midbrain. The axons from these cells go to the basal ganglia, large masses of cells in the cerebrum that appear to have functions related to the control of movement. It is of considerable significance that parkinsonism, which produces forced involuntary repetitive movements of the hand and arm, is generally associated with degeneration of cells in the *substantia nigra*. Furthermore, in this disease there is a pronounced decrease in the dopamine content of the basal ganglia. Parkinsonism has been treated by making lesions in the basal ganglia, the region of termination of the dopamine system whose cell bodies originate in the *substantia nigra*. Very recently dopamine has been used with apparent success in treating this disease. Interestingly, it also seems to be of great benefit in the treatment of depression.

Serotonin is found in many portions of the central nervous system. Essentially all the serotonin neurons in the brain have their cell bodies in the raphé nuclei of the brain stem. These cells project to wide areas of the forebrain, including the hypothalamus, the septal area, and other regions of the limbic system. It appears that the projections of these cells can account for all of the brain serotonin. In other words, it seems likely that all serotonin is manufactured in these cell groups of the raphé nuclei and is then distributed to various other brain regions by the axons of the cells. The raphé nuclei appear to be involved in regulation of sleep and wakefulness, and the regions to which they project, the hypothalamus and the limbic system, are involved in the motivational and emotional aspects of behavior. It is as though the raphé cells were a very ancient system with its own neural transmitter, serotonin, concerned with such primitive aspects of behavior as sleep and basic emotion.

Schildkraut and Kety [1967] have developed an interesting theory relating the biogenic amines to emotion. In surveying the effects on mood and emotions of a number of drugs that influence brain levels of the biogenic amines they found that drugs which tend to cause *decreases* in brain levels or activity of biogenic amines tend to produce depression or sedation, while drugs which *increase* or potentiate the brain levels or activity of biogenic amines are associated with behavioral *stimulation*, excitement, or even mania, and in general have a clear antidepressant effect in man. This leads to the very simple and intriguing theory that depression is due to a deficiency of brain biogenic amines and elation is

172

associated with an excess of such substances in the brain; in short, happiness is having lots of brain biogenic amines. This theory is, of course, only in the stage of speculation, but it could have enormously important implications for the understanding of mental illness.

OTHER TRANSMITTER SUBSTANCES   Although a good many other chemicals have been suggested as synaptic transmitters, current evidence is strong for only three substances—glutamic acid, glycine, and gamma-amino butyric acid (GABA). Interestingly enough, they are all simple amino acids. Glutamic acid appears to be a transmitter chemical at certain excitatory synapses, and glycine and GABA seem to be transmitters for certain inhibitory synapses. Glycine is the simplest amino acid and one of the simplest of all biologically active chemicals. The fact that the nervous system appears to have utilized the simplest and most commonly occurring natural biological chemicals as transmitters is strong testimony to the elegant simplicity of evolution. If we wanted to design a system with roughly a trillion functional connections, each requiring chemicals to work, the ideal solution would be to use chemicals that are simple and widely present in the system. The brain has done just this. The chemistry of synaptic transmission, literally the chemistry of the mind, is an exciting and fundamental area of research.

THE EFFECT OF DRUGS ON BEHAVIOR

Drugs can exert extremely potent and sometimes lethal influences on behavior. Indeed, among the major influences on behavior, drugs can be of overriding importance because of their capability to *control* it. *Drugs* are usually defined as chemicals that have effects on animals. In this sense almost every substance might serve as a drug. The study of drugs that influence experience and behavior is termed *psychopharmacology*.

Since the interactions among neurons occur at synapses, and synaptic transmission is chemical, we might expect that many different drugs would have an effect on brain function and behavior. Such is indeed the case; many drugs do alter brain activity by acting on the chemical mechanisms involved in synaptic transmission. In some invertebrate animals certain synapses are electrical (the presynaptic spike directly induces an electrical response in the postsynaptic neuron). Because electrical synapses are not subject to chemical influences, it is very difficult to modify their actions in any way. However, there are no electrical synapses in the human brain; in fact in higher mammals all brain synapses are chemical. This is a great advantage in terms of flexibility. Chemical synapses can be modified very easily, not just by drugs, but by normal chemical and structural factors. It is probable that the great plasticity, or modifiability, inherent in the human brain—our capacity

173

to learn so much so well—is due to the fact that our brain synapses work by chemical rather than electrical processes.

Although psychopharmacology has existed as a field for only about 20 years, references to drugs that affect experience are as old as history. According to Homer, Helen of Troy was an opium addict; alcohol is at least as old as Western society; Herodotus described how the ancient Scythians heated hemp seeds on hot stones, inhaled the vapors (marijuana), and "shouted for joy." It is probably a safe generalization that every primitive culture in the world has discovered and developed its own brand of "trip" from naturally occurring substances. The major categories of drugs that influence behavior, with examples and typical effects, are given in Table 7-1.

NARCOTIC ANALGESICS

Morphine, heroin, and the other opium alkaloids are among the most severely addictive of all drugs. They have been used for centuries to ease pain; in fact morphine is still one of the most widely used drugs in medicine. The modes of action of the narcotics are unknown. In moderate doses they produce a sense of euphoria (a feeling of well being), drowsiness, and most important, a marked analgesia (relief of pain). Even the most severe chronic pains, from toothache to terminal cancer,

TABLE 7–1   *Psychopharmacological drugs.*

DRUG CLASS	EXAMPLES	EFFECTS
Narcotic analgesics	Morphine, heroin	Relieves pain; produces sense of well-being; highly addictive
Stimulants	Amphetamines, caffeine	Increases alertness; can produce anxiety; moderately addictive
Psychotherapeutics Antipsychotics	Reserpine, chlorpromazine	Aids some forms of mental illness
Antianxiety drugs	Meprobamate, chlordiazepoxide	Reduces some forms of anxiety
Antidepressants	MAO inhibitors, imipramine	Reduces some forms of depression
Psychogenics	Lysergic acid diethylamide Mescaline Marijuana	Produces psychoticlike symptoms

are markedly and often completely relieved by morphine. It is important to note that although chronic pain is eliminated, awareness is not. The pain threshold and the feeling of unpleasantness from a pinprick seem relatively unchanged after analgesic doses of morphine. It is often said that morphine does not alter the immediate sensation of pain, but only the patient's reactions to that sensation. Although this may convey the essential character of the morphine syndrome, it is probably not a scientifically tenable distinction. Furthermore, under many conditions, narcotics may reduce the response to imposed pain in man and animals.

A wide variety of substances can be categorized as stimulants in terms of their general effects on behavior. *Strychnine*, *picrotoxin*, and *metrazol* (pentylenetetrazol) are potent stimulants of the central nervous system which lead in overdoses to convulsions and death. Strychnine and picrotoxin, incidentally, are among the very few drugs whose actions on nerve cells are to some degree understood; they block particular forms of neural inhibition, thus leading to "runaway" excitation and convulsions. These three drugs and related substances are of particular interest to physiological psychologists because of their effects in facilitating certain kinds of behaviors, particularly learning [McGaugh, 1969].

Widely used mild stimulants include *caffeine* (in coffee, tea, and cocoa) and *nicotine* (in tobacco). One cup of coffee, for example, contains about 200 milligrams (0.2 gram) of caffeine, a dose sufficiently high to produce stimulation of the central nervous system. The effects of these drugs as stimulants are relatively mild. Caffeine in particular appears to be an almost ideal stimulant. It seems to allay drowsiness and fatigue, increase the "flow of thought," and increase motor activity, and for most people it has few or no side effects. There has never been a death attributed to an overdose of caffeine.

Amphetamines and related drugs—dexedrine, benzedrine, "speed," methedrine—are perhaps the most widely used and abused of the potent stimulants. They lessen depression and fatigue, increase motor and verbal activity, and can lead to increased alertness, lessened need for sleep, and lessened appetite. Elevation of mood, however, is followed by a corresponding letdown which can increase severely with successively higher doses.

Amphetamines are most commonly prescribed to overcome lethargia during pregnancy and to decrease the appetite in overweight patients. The effect on appetite, however, is quite variable in humans. Although dogs given amphetamine an hour before feeding will refuse food, and will even starve to death under such conditions, amphetamines often have little or no effect on appetite in humans.

Amphetamines are strongly addictive; in fact amphetamine addiction has become a serious social problem in both Europe and the United

175

States. It is significant from both a practical and a theoretical standpoint that amphetamines are the only drugs known to produce a psychotic state that is clinically indistinguishable from a naturally occurring psychosis, paranoid schizophrenia. A fact of great interest in this context is that the chemical action of amphetamines leads to an increased activity of biogenic amines in the brain.

PSYCHOTHERAPEUTICS

Psychotherapeutic agents, drugs used in the treatment of psychological disorders, have led to a genuine revolution in the care and treatment of the mentally ill. Their advent has enabled many thousands of persons who just a few years ago would have spent their lives in the back wards of mental institutions to live and function in society.

Psychotherapeutics do not, of course, cure mental illness. They are effective in varying degrees with different patients in treating and controlling the symptoms, particularly in cases of depression. However, this does not mean that we understand the causes of mental illness or that we understand why these drugs have the effects they do. Much of the work has been on an entirely empirical and even accidental basis. The psychotherapeutic effects of reserpine, for example, came to light as a more or less unexpected side effect when it was being used to control hypertension, a form of high blood pressure.

ANTIPSYCHOTICS   There are two major categories of antipsychotic drugs—the phenothiazine derivatives such as chlorpromazene, and the rauwolfia alkaloids, such as reserpine. The phenothiazene derivatives grew out of biochemical work on antihistamines and related substances. Although there are a great many similar substances now available, chlorpromazene, synthesized in 1950, is still most widely used. The rauwolfia alkaloids are derived from a naturally occurring plant that grows in India. Ancient Hindu writings recommend the use of rauwolfia for both hypertension and insanity—its two modern applications. Reserpine is the purified synthetic form of rauwolfia in present use. Although the drugs are chemically unrelated, many of the general behavioral effects of chlorpromazene and reserpine are similar. One major difference is that reserpine produces marked depression of mood, whereas chlorpromazine does not. As is true for most drugs, the mechanisms and modes of actions of the antipsychotic drugs are essentially unknown. It is noteworthy, however, that reserpine also causes a significant decrease in biogenic amines in the brain.

TRANQUILIZERS   Antianxiety drugs, usually referred to as tranquilizers, produce a generally relaxed and anxiety-free state somewhat similar to that produced by alcohol and barbiturates, but without their marked sedative effects. Two common but chemically unrelated antianxiety drugs are meprobamate (Miltown) and chlordiazepoxide (Librium). Meprobamate was initially developed as a muscle relaxant, and its tranquilizing properties were discovered later. The usual clinical dose has no effect on tested performance but alters the EEG slightly in the direction of that seen during sleep. According to subjective reports, it reduces anxiety and induces a mild euphoria. The mechanisms by which antianxiety drugs produce these effects are as yet unknown.

ANTIDEPRESSANTS   The antidepressant agents are a particularly interesting group of drugs which provide rather dramatic relief from certain forms of severe depression. Although amphetamines might also be classified as antidepressants, their effect is of much shorter duration, and they are generally classed as a stimulant. However, the mode of action is in some ways similar. There are two general types of antidepressant drugs, *MAO inhibitors* and *imipramine*. They are chemically unrelated, but they both seem to act in such a way as to increase the brain level of norepinephrine, one of the biogenic amines.

It was observations such as this that led Schildkraut and Kety to the theory that biogenic amines are related to emotions. Tranquilizers such as reserpine decrease brain amines, and stimulants and antidepressants such as MAO inhibitors, imipramine, and amphetamines increase brain amines. Hence the general level of emotional state may be determined by the levels of biogenic amines, particularly norepinephrine, in regions of the brain such as the hypothalamus and limbic system, which are involved in emotional and motivational aspects of behavior.

PSYCHOGENICS

The most widely known psychogenic agents are lysergic acid diethylamide (LSD or "acid"), mescaline (from the peyote cactus), psilosibin (from mushrooms), and marijuana. These drugs have been variously described in terms of their effects as psychotomimetics (imitating psychosis), hallucinogenics (inducing hallucinations), and psychedelics. Psychogenic, perhaps the best term, simply refers to the fact that these drugs produce psychoticlike symptoms.

LYSERGIC ACID DIETHYLAMIDE   LSD is one of the most potent and dangerous drugs known; the effective dose is as low as 100 micrograms (1/10,000 gram). It produces a variety of bizarre subjective experiences and behaviors that in many ways resemble insanity, and for a while there was hope that it would provide a good model of psychosis for experimental study. However, there appear to be some fundamental differences. Hallucinations, subjective experiences of stimuli that are not physically present, are common to both situations, but the type of hallucination induced by LSD is primarily visual, whereas in naturally occurring psychosis they tend to be predominantly auditory (hearing voices that are

177

not there). Furthermore, a normal person who has taken LSD is aware that he is under the influence of LSD; a psychotic person does not believe that he is psychotic. Following is a description by a normal subject of his experience with LSD [Farrell, 1966, pp. 8–9] :

I'm a hard-headed, conservative, Midwestern, Republican businessman. Under no circumstances would I consider myself a person who goes around taking strange drugs.

But my wife took LSD at a friend's house, and in order to get her to agree to come home, I took the stuff myself.

We got in the car, and I had only driven about three blocks, when suddenly the pavement in front of me opened up. It was as though the pavement was flowing over Niagara Falls. The street lights expanded into fantastic globes of light that filled my entire vision. I didn't dare stop.

It was a nightmare. I came to traffic lights, but I couldn't tell what color they were. There were all sorts of colors around me anyway. I could detect other cars around me, so I stopped when they stopped, and went when they went.

At home I flopped in a chair. I wasn't afraid. My conscious mind was sort of sitting on my shoulder—watching everything I was doing. I found I could make the room expand—oh, maybe a thousand miles—or I could make it contract right in front of me. All over the ceiling there were geometric patterns of light. To say they were beautiful is too shallow a word.

My wife put on a violin concerto. I could make the music come out of the speaker like taffy, or a tube of toothpaste, surrounded by dancing lights of colors beyond description.

A friend showed up. He was talking to me, and I was answering, all in a perfectly normal way. Then, I saw his face change. He became an Arab, a Chinese, a Negro. I found I could take my finger and wipe away his face and then paint it back again.

I made a chocolate sundae and gave it to him for a head. A great truth appeared to me. The reason he had all those faces was this: he was a reflection of all mankind. So was I.

I asked myself, "What is God?" Then I knew that I was God. That really sounds ridiculous as I say it. But I knew that all life is one, and since God is Life, and I am Life, we are the same being.

Then I decided to examine my own fears, because I wasn't really afraid of anything. I went down into my stomach and it was like Dante's inferno—all steaming and bubbling and ghastly. I saw some hideous shapes in the distance. My mind floated to each one, and they were horrible, hideous.

They all got together in a mob and started to come up after me—a flood of bogeymen. But I knew I was stronger than all of them, and I took my hand and wiped them out.

Now, I think there lies the real danger with LSD. Anyone who motioned with his hand and couldn't wipe out those creatures. He has to stay down there with them, forever.

The danger of LSD lies not only in its immediate effects on subjective experience, but also in the extreme and bizarre behavior that may arise from this experience. People on "bad trips" have fatally injured themselves and others. Moreover, there have been reports that the symptoms recur at a later date in the absence of LSD.

LSD is known to be a potent inhibitor of brain serotonin. Although the exact mechanisms are not known, it seems to inhibit or decrease activity of cells in the raphé nuclei, which apparently influence such basic functions as sleep and emotion. Of course, it is a long step from this information to a clear understanding of what LSD actually does.

MARIJUANA   The most widely used psychogenic agent is marijuana, the dried flowers and leaves of the hemp plant. In its naturally occurring form the dosage of its effective ingredient, tetrahydrocannabinol, is relatively low. However, the highly concentrated form hashish has long been known to induce pronounced psychoticlike behavior. The word "assassin" derives from the Arabic "hashshāshīn," a Mohammedan sect addicted to hashish, whose terrorist activities were notorious during the time of the crusades. The most frequently reported effect of marijuana is a mild euphoria. There are also occasional reports of increased appetite, a heightened sense of taste and smell, and some alteration of time perception. The drug itself is not known to have any long-range biological effects. The fact that it tends to lower productive activity levels may, of course, have social, if not biological, consequences.

DRUG ADDICTION

Addiction is a complex phenomenon, but a very real and prevalent social problem. Psychogenic agents such as marijuana and LSD do not appear to be addictive, at least in the sense that they do not appear to produce a strong biological need for their continued use. Addiction to heroin, barbiturates, amphetamines, and alcohol produces an extreme biological need. Sudden withdrawal from such drugs causes severe and violent withdrawal symptoms which in some cases may even be fatal. In contrast, a regular user of marijuana experiences no particular biological effects from sudden withdrawal. He may continue use simply because he likes it. However, since we know that "likes" are fundamentally biological phenomena—indeed, they are the result of brain processes—the distinction between addiction and nonaddiction may in part be only a matter of degree.

Sharpless, Jaffe, and others have developed a most interesting *hypersensitivity* theory which explains many withdrawal effects in drug addiction [Jaffe, 1965]. It appears that whatever effects the drug produces will occur in opposite form during withdrawal. If stomach contractions are decreased by the drug, for example, they become abnormally strong and produce stomach cramps during withdrawal. Since amphetamines produce a sense of well-being, the patient becomes severely depressed during withdrawal. The explanation of these effects is that during drug use

179

the biological systems that are inhibited or depressed by the drug compensate by stepping up activity, so that their base levels of activity are much higher than normal. As a result, when the drug is withdrawn the biological systems which had been artifically depressed are left in a hyperactive state and produce the symptoms of withdrawal. The duration of withdrawal symptoms corresponds to the duration of action of the drugs themselves. Heroin is relatively short acting; the withdrawal symptoms are relatively brief and extremely severe. A new synthetic drug, methadone, has effects similar to those of heroin, but it is much longer acting. The patient can be shifted from heroin to methadone addiction without difficulty. If he is then taken off methadone, his withdrawal symptoms are of much longer duration but much less severe. This fact provides a basis for what appears to be a most promising approach to the treatment of heroin addiction.

This chapter is only a very brief review of how the human brain is organized, how information is coded into the language of the neuron, and how synaptic transmission, the communication between neurons, works. The human brain is the most complex structure in the universe. Neurobiology, the study of how the brain controls behavior, is the most fundamental aspect of psychology. We are at the forefronts of knowledge in this exciting and challenging field. What remains to be learned is much more than that which we already know.

SUMMARY

The vertebrate nervous system has developed from the segmented tube of the lowly flatworm to the enormously complex nervous system of man. The peripheral nervous system includes all sensory and motor nerves of both the somatic system, which controls bodily movement, and the autonomic system, which controls emotional and other involuntary reactions. The central nervous system includes all structures contained within the spinal column and skull. The autonomic part of the peripheral nervous system is further subdivided into the sympathetic system, responsible for energy mobilization, and the parasympathetic system, which controls the processes of the internal organs. The lower portion of the central nervous system, the spinal cord, is responsible for spinal reflexes and for channeling all sensory and motor information going to and from the brain.

The brain itself is divided broadly into three sections. The *hindbrain* includes the reticular formation, ascending and descending fiber tracts, and many important nuclei. The *midbrain*, which is important in motivation and emotion, includes the hypothalamus and pituitary gland and the sensory relay centers for the brain, the thalamus. Overlying the midbrain is the cerebellum, important in sensory-motor coordination. The *forebrain*, the most recent evolutionary development, appears to dis-

180

tinguish man from other animals; it is predominantly cerebral cortex, which is important in such higher mental processes as language, speech, and thought, as well as the higher-order control of movement and sensation.

The individual unit of the nervous system, the neuron, has all the general properties of other living cells, including the nucleus and other organelles that allow for the processes of metabolism, synthesis, and respiration. It is more specialized, however, in that its axon, dendrites, and synaptic connections with other neurons allow it to conduct and transmit information.

Synaptic transmission within the mammalian nervous system is a chemical process. The resting potential across the cell membrane is temporarily altered by a change in the permeability of the membrane to various species of ions, especially sodium. This alteration, an all-or-none spike discharge which results from stimulation of the cell above a critical threshold, propagates unchanged down the axon of the neuron until it reaches the axon terminals, where a transmitter substance is released to cross the synaptic cleft and excite or inhibit the neuron next in line. Synaptic connections may be on the dendritic spines or the cell body of another cell. Excitation takes place by depolarization of the cell body, causing an excitatory postsynaptic potential (IPSP). Excitatory transmitter substances include acetylcholine, which functions at the neuromuscular junction; the biogenic amines; and various other naturally occurring substances in the brain. The drug effects on behavior take place primarily by interaction with these important chemical determinants of neural activity and behavior.

A drug is any substance that affects behavior, and psychopharmacology is the study of these effects. The narcotic analgesics include heroin, morphine, and the opium alkaloids, which are highly addictive. Stimulants include the amphetamines, strychnine, and picrotoxin. Various psychotherapeutic drugs, such as antipsychotic agents, tranquilizers, and antidepressants, have been useful in the treatment of mental illness. The psychogenics, which produce psychoticlike symptoms, include peyote, LSD, and marijuana. Drug addiction has become a serious social problem, and its treatment is an area of active interest.

CHAPTER EIGHT

SENSATION AND PERCEPTION

Look up from your book for a minute. As you look around you experience a number of stimuli. You see a whole range of different colors; you see many different objects and forms. You also see depth; some objects are closer than others, and they all appear three-dimensional. How is it that we have these experiences? Why does blue look blue and not red? Why do some objects look round and others rectangular? More generally, why does the world look the way it does to us?

A superficial answer is that things look the way they do because that is the way they are. However, a little thought should disabuse us of this notion. Optical illusions do not look the way they "are." The figures in a moving picture do not really move. The objects we see in dreams are not "real." Furthermore, the physicist tells us that real objects, such as watches and tables, are actually empty space occupied by a few electrons and protons, no matter what they look like to us.

This whole question of why the world looks the way it does is actually fundamental to any knowledge we have of the world around us. Philosophers and scientists have argued the matter for centuries. We can

SENSORY-MOTOR INTEGRATION

take comfort in the fact that the question seems ultimately to come down to our own common experiences. A theoretical physicist who conceptualizes the real world as clouds of elementary particles distributed unevenly in an n-dimensional space must ultimately rely on his own and other people's simple subjective experiences of what color a chemical solution is, what a dial reads, and what numbers appear on a counter. The basic measurements in science are all this kind of simple observation. The entire edifice of modern scientific knowledge is in fact built on the rather shaky and uncertain foundation of subjective observations. Fortunately, so far as we can tell, there is a high degree of similarity in such simple experiences for different people. Moreover, we are beginning to understand the physiological bases of these experiences. We now have some clear idea why colors look the way they do, why we see objects as having shape and form, and why one tone sounds high and another low.

However, understanding why things look the way they do is not enough. People are not inanimate objects; they respond to stimuli. In order to understand the appearance of things, our perceptions of the world, we must also know something about how we respond to things. Indeed, the way we act on the world has some effect on the way the world looks to us. All you need do to convince yourself of this is to watch a baby exploring his world—a world full of strange, interesting, and sometimes frightening things which seem continually to change, particularly when he makes them move. In this chapter we will discuss what is known about the way things appear and how we respond to them, in other words the sensory and motor systems and how they function together to yield the smooth, integrated behavior of the perceiving and responding organism.

Look at the painting in Fig. 8-1. What is your reaction to it? Perhaps you consider it trivial, odd, interesting, or even ridiculous. You react to it in an overall, integrated manner; in fact you evaluate it. This is an example of a very complex perceptual process. Psychologists are fond of distinguishing between sensation and perception, the idea being that *sensation* is an immediate experience of stimuli—in this case the various forms of the painting—and that *perception* is a more complex response to it in terms of past experience. In other words, perception is an interpretation of sensation in the light of learning.

The distinction between sensation and perception is traditional, but it is probably more correct to refer instead to a greater or lesser *degree* of interpretation of stimuli. The sky at the top of the painting could be viewed simply as a horizontal stripe. However, even this statement would require a knowledge, based on past experience, of "horizontal stripe." In fact we cannot really translate pure sensation into words at all, since all words involve learning. The object in the left foreground could be described as an irregular shape with a border and symmetrical markings, but we immediately identify it as a watch—even though it may be unlike any watch we have seen before. We know from experience that watches are usually round and have dial markings and hands. We also know that watches are hard to the touch and rigid—not limp like soft-boiled eggs. This, of course, is what makes the painting unusual—the depiction of familiar objects as having properties that are different from those we normally experience.

An even more extreme example of interpretative perception of the stimuli in this painting is evidenced in the following description by an art critic [Canaday, 1961]:

... the symbolism is clear enough. At a glance the theme is concerned with time and decay. The most obvious symbols are the watches and the dead tree, and the jellyfish-like monster melting on the beach. Scavenger ants attack one of the watches, with no success. We deduce from this that the symbolism is also concerned with immortality, the triumph of something or other over the forces of decay. The watches are a symbol not only of time but of infinite time, eternity, impervious to the frustrated insects who would devour them. They are also limp; somebody has bent time to his will. Who? The artist, of course, since he painted them that way. Thus seen, the picture is a restatement in fantastic terms of an old idea, popular in antiquity and in the Renaissance: the idea that through creative works during his mortal life, the artist defeats time and achieves immortality.

FIGURE 8–1   *The persistence of memory, Salvador Dali,*
1931 [collection, The Museum of Modern Art, New York].

This is admittedly a complex "perception," since it is based on individual past experiences that have little connection with the immediate stimuli of the painting.

Some of the more spectacular advances in psychology to date have been in the study of sensory processes. This was one of the earliest branches of psychology to develop, undoubtedly because of the ease of specifying the physical characteristics of stimuli. Learning, motivation, and other inferred processes have no such obvious physical starting points. We have found out a great deal about sensory processes simply by presenting physical stimuli such as lights and tones and asking a subject to describe what he experiences.

The fundamental problem in sensory function concerns the manner in which stimuli are coded by the brain. Physical stimuli come in a variety of forms—light, sound, heat, pressure, soluble molecules, women—which can change continually, often in several ways. A light can change in intensity, in wavelength, in area, in complexity, and in duration. Since we can perceive literally millions of different physical stimuli, it is obvious that stimulus characteristics must somehow be coded by the sensory receptors and sensory nerves. In what manner do we identify and respond to a physical stimulus as red, cold, high or low in pitch, female, or fragrant?

In 1826 Johannes Muller published his formal theory of "specific nerve energies" concerning the way in which nerve fibers code sensory stimuli. From the time of the Greeks people had assumed that a given stimulus somehow impressed its characteristic directly on the "mind," or brain. Muller noted the now obvious fact that gross sensory quality depends on *which* nerve is stimulated, not on how it is stimulated. Visual receptors of the retina and the optic nerve can be stimulated by

185

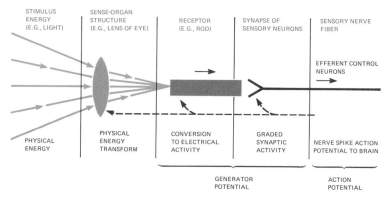

FIGURE 8–2   *The sensory coding process. Stimulus energy is focused or transformed be accessory sense-organ structures and then activates the receptors. Receptors develop graded electrical activity, the generator potential, which influences the sensory nerve fibers. This graded activity induces an all-or-none spike action in the sensory nerve fibers. Efferent pathways from the brain (dashed line) influence the coding process.*

anything—light to the eye, pressure on the eyeball, electric shock, mechanical irritation—and in all cases the subject reports *visual* sensations. It is not the stimulus that determines gross sensory quality, but the receptors and nerves that are activated by stimuli.

The sensory modality that is experienced, of course, depends on the portion of the brain to which the sensory nerve leads. Activation of the optic nerve produces visual sensations because this nerve projects to the visual system of the brain; similarly, activation of the auditory nerve produces auditory sensations because this nerve goes to the auditory pathways. The mechanisms underlying finer distinctions within a given sensory modality—distinctions between colors, frequencies of tone (pitch), or touch and pressure—are less obvious. Recent studies indicate that different stimulus characteristics activate different cells in the general brain area in question. For example, stimulation of the fingertip by either a very light touch or a strong pressure will activate the sensory cortex of the brain, but within this small region different nerve cells are stimulated by the light touch and the strong pressure.

The most direct and obvious type of coding process concerns the transformation of physical stimuli into nerve impulses by the various sensory receptors, a process referred to as *transduction*. Most receptors share a number of common features, schematized in Fig. 8-2. External energy in the form of light, sound, pressure, heat, or soluble molecules impinges on receptors, which in turn initiate spike discharges in sensory nerve cells. Some receptors have accessory structures, such as the lens of the eye or certain membranes in the ear, which serve to focus, alter, amplify, or localize the particular stimulus. The stimulus then activates receptor cells, such as the rods and cones in the retina of the eye or the hair cells in the cochlea of the ear. Activation of receptor cells produces a graded electrical activity, the *generator potential* (analogous to synaptic potentials in neurons). If this graded response is sufficiently large to cross the firing threshold, it initiates an all-or-none spike discharge in the sensory neuron, which is then conducted along the sensory nerve fiber into the central nervous system. Finally efferent neural pathways terminating on receptor systems permit the CNS to influence, or "gate," the activity of accessory structures, receptors, and sensory neurons.

THE BIOLOGICAL BASIS OF VISION

Light is a form of electromagnetic radiation, or radiant energy. Visible light is a very small region of the total electromagnetic spectrum, or range of wavelengths, which extends from radio waves (particularly AM waves, which have wavelengths of many miles) to visible light, which has wavelengths in the range of 380 (violet) to about 760 (red) millimicrons (1 millimicron is one-billionth of a meter). Cosmic rays are still shorter, with wavelengths of only 0.00005 millimicron.

As shown in Fig. 8-3, the wavelengths of visible light to which the human eye is most sensitive are green and yellow; we can see dimmer shades of these colors than of violet or red. Of course, light itself has no color; light simply has different wavelengths. Color is merely our *subjective experience* of these differences in wavelengths. Psychologists often use the term *hue* to refer to our experience of color.

Light also varies in intensity, the strength of the electromagnetic waves. The physicists tell us light itself consists of elementary particles called photons; the intensity of light could be expressed in terms of the

FIGURE 8-3   *The visible colors of light and their wavelengths. The graph shows the relative sensitivity of the human eye to color (we are most sensitive to greenish-yellow). The dots on the curve indicate relative absorption of light energy by chemicals in the cones of the eye. Our sensitivity to color is thus determined entirely by the chemical properties of the cones.*

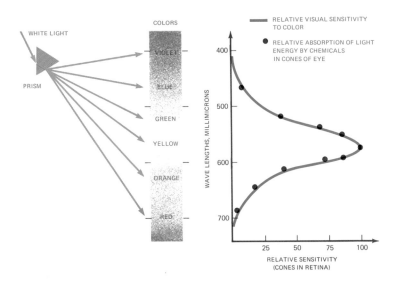

density of photons. The physical intensity of light, its *luminance*, is not the same as the degree of intensity we see or experience, its *brightness*. As shown in Fig. 8-3, violet and green lights that have the same luminance—that is, the same amount of physical energy—will not look equally bright; the green light will look brighter. The human eye, incidentally, is amazingly sensitive; we can see as few as seven photons. No physical measuring instrument developed is this sensitive to light.

A third aspect of light that we perceive is its "purity," the extent to which only one wavelength or a narrow band of wavelengths is present. Psychologists refer to our experience of this as *saturation*. Red, for example, may look very red (saturated), or it may look weak and faded (unsaturated). A weak red looks weak not because it has fewer red wavelengths, but because it contains many other wavelengths in addition to the red ones. In contrast, the light from a laser looks very saturated because it has almost no other conflicting wavelengths.

THE STRUCTURE OF THE EYE

Most organisms, even single-celled animals, can respond to light energy. However, the vertebrate eye is designed to do much more than simply signal the presence or absence of light. A detailed image of the external world is projected on the *retina*, the layers of receptors and nerve cells at the back of the eye. This structure transforms and codes the image into nerve impulses which carry a representation of the external visual world to the brain. The precision of detail vision is surprising. The image of the full moon on the retina has a radius of only about 0.1 millimeter, and considerable detail can be seen within this image. Lines that are much narrower than the single receptor cells of the retina can easily be seen. The vertebrate visual system is also particularly sensitive to movement of objects in the visual world. Most predators, animals that hunt to live, have eyes that point forward and focus together to give a clear, three-dimensional image of the object or prey being perceived and pursued. Most prey animals, such as rabbits and deer, have eyes far apart on the sides of the head, so that they can see better to the sides and behind to detect the predator. The faster a predator normally moves, and the faster its prey moves, the more acute the movement vision of each must be to ensure survival. Man has the eyes of a predator.

In general the retina functions more like a television camera than like a photographic camera. According to Rushton [1962, p. 13]:

Its purpose is not to fix a picture upon the retina, but rather to transmit in a code of nerve impulses the more dramatic features of the ever changing retinal scene. Our rods and cones are 100 million reporters seeking "copy." That which continues unchanging is not "news" and nothing will induce them to report it.

It has been demonstrated that if an image is stabilized on the retina it fades away. Normally the images are continually shifting back and forth

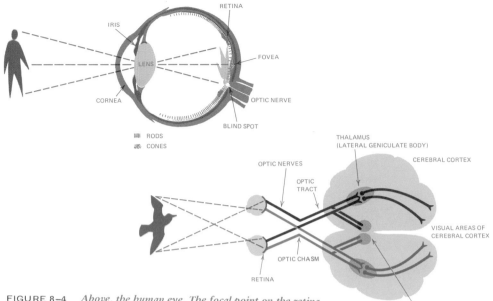

FIGURE 8–4   *Above, the human eye. The focal point on the retina,*
the fovea, is the region of best detail vision. The fovea has no rods and
has the greatest density of cones. The rods are most dense about
20 degrees away from the fovea. At right, the visual pathway in
primates (top view). The right half of the visual field projects to the
left side of each eye. These two left sides project to the left hemisphere
of the brain, to the relay in the thalamus, and thence to the visual
area of the left cerebral cortex. Similarly, the right half of each eye
projects to the right cerebral cortex. The optic tracts also give off
pathways to the visual midbrain (superior colliculus).

on the retina because the eye is always making small, rapid movements
or oscillations. Riggs et al. [1953] devised an optical system in which
the visual object was reflected to a viewing screen from a small mirror
attached to the side of a contact lens on the cornea of the eye. The
image moved with the eyeball and thus was always projected on the
same retinal elements. Under these conditions most objects tend to fade
out in a few seconds. This rather striking adaptation does not generally
occur because the image is always being shifted to different receptor
cells by rapid eye movements.

As indicated in Fig. 8-4, the rods and cones, the two basic types
of light-sensitive receptor cells in the eye, are in close approximation to
neurons. There are several types of neurons in the retina. The retina is
actually a very complex neural system and is perhaps best thought of as
a "little brain" lying between the photoreceptors and the brain. Embryologically, the retina is an outgrowth of the brain rather than a
peripheral formation.

Rods and cones serve different functions. The rods are sensitive
to very dim illumination (*scotopic* vision), whereas the cones require
greater intensities of light and are more involved in acuity and color
aspects of visual function (*photopic* vision). Rods and cones are easily
differentiable in terms of structure in mammals. This differentiation of

structure and function in rods and cones is of fundamental importance. The center of the visual field, the region we see most clearly when we look at an object, projects on the *fovea*, which is composed entirely of cones. The foveal cones have an almost one-to-one relation to outgoing nerve fibers. The rods have their greatest density at about 20 degrees of visual angle; this is the angle between the direct line of sight projecting to the fovea and the projection of any other position in the visual field away from the fovea (see Fig. 8-4). Thus you can see a dim star best if you look about 20 degrees away from it. There are about 125 million rods and 6 million cones in the human retina, but only about 1 million optic nerve fibers. Hence many receptors will activate each nerve fiber, particularly in the peripheral regions of the retina, where rods are predominant.

There are at least two visual pigments (chemicals responsive to light) in receptor cells of the mammalian retina, *rhodopsin* in the rods and *iodopsin* in cones. When light falls on a rod, the rhodopsin immediately breaks down into two chemicals, *retinene* and *opsin*. Retinene has a relatively simple chemical structure closely related to vitamin A (thus the necessity of vitamin A for adequate night vision), and opsin is a complex protein. The visual pigment of the cones, iodopsin, breaks down on exposure to light into two substances—retinene, in the same form as that from rhodopsin, and a different protein, *photopsin*. In other words, the visual pigments of the rods and cones are both made up of retinene and a protein, with only the protein differing; the chemical reactions of both are comparable. Actually human cones appear to have three iodopsins, made up of retinene and three different opsins.

A number of aspects of visual sensation, particularly those relating to brightness and color, can be deduced very accurately from the biochemical properties of rhodopsin and the iodopsins. Foremost among these is the virtually perfect correspondence between spectral sensitivities (sensitivity to different wavelengths of light) and the chemical-absorption spectra of the rod and cone pigments (see Fig. 8-3). Another striking correspondence concerns the time required for rod and cone *dark adaptation*. After exposure to a bright light it takes up to 30 minutes in the dark for the rods to dark adapt—that is, reestablish maximum sensitivity to dim light. The spontaneous rate of synthesis of rhodopsin in solution follows virtually the same curve as does the rate of rod dark adaptation. Cone dark adaptation is much more rapid; it requires only about 6 minutes. The rate of synthesis of iodopsin in solution is also about 6 minutes.

THE CODING OF VISUAL STIMULI

Our eyes receive a continual and everchanging barrage of light energy. The characteristics of visual stimuli are many and complex; however, in discussing the ways in which the visual system responds to light it is convenient to distinguish three different categories—response to the presence of light; response to the form, pattern, or spatial distribution of light energy, and response to wavelength (color). To understand how the visual system operates we must, at the very least, understand something about these basic coding processes.

In lower vertebrates such as the frog the eyes function as two independent visual systems; the nerve fibers from the right eye all go to the left side of the brain, and the nerves from the left eye go to the right side of the brain. However, in higher mammals there is *bilateral projection*; a part of each eye goes to each side of the brain. This tendency is most developed in primates, particularly man. As shown in Fig. 8-4, the left half of each retina goes to the left side of the brain, and the right side of each retina goes to the right side of the brain. This makes possible binocular vision with depth perception. The optic nerves carry the nerve fibers from cells in the retina to a visual relay nucleus in the thalamus called the *lateral geniculate body*. Here the fibers from the two eyes come together on each side of the brain and synapse on neurons that go to the visual areas of the cerebral cortex.

There are thus three major stations along the way from eye to cortex—the retina sending out the optic nerve, the lateral geniculate body of the thalamus, and the visual area of the cerebral cortex. Some fibers from the optic nerves also go other places, particularly to serve as the visual input for certain reflex functions such as control of pupil diameter. In lower vertebrates that have no cerebral cortex, a midbrain visual region called the superior colliculus serves as the visual brain and receives the optic nerve fibers. This system is also present in higher vertebrates, but its functions are not well known. In birds there is also a pathway from optic nerve fibers to the hypothalamus that plays a major role in reproduction and migrating behavior. Thus the critical stimulus that starts them on their migratory flight seems to be the relative length of day and night. In man the major visual path is from retina to lateral geniculate body to visual cortex.

THE PERCEPTION OF FORM

When we look at an object, it is projected onto the retina by the lens of the eye, as in a camera. This visual image on the retina activates the receptors, the rods and cones, and hence the appropriate neurons of the retina, to produce an accurate spatial layout of the visual world. Neurons in the visual cortex are then activated in such a way that a representation or spatial layout of the image is formed over the visual area of the cerebral cortex. This is termed *retinotopic projection*. A similar fundamental spatial coding mechanism exists in all sensory systems. The sensory receptor surface is laid out spatially over the sensory area of the cerebral cortex.

Some highly significant distortions take place in the visual image when it is projected to the visual cortex. If you look at someone's nose from a few feet away, the image of the entire person and his surroundings will be projected accurately on the retina of your eye. However, the

191

neural projection onto the visual cortex will be quite different; half the projected neural image will be nose, and the remainder will include the rest of the person and his surroundings. When we focus our eyes on an object, the line of sight projects to the fovea at the center of the retina. As we noted above, this region of densely packed cones is where our detail vision is best. We see small objects in good light best when we look directly at them. The fovea, which takes up only about 1 percent of the retinal area, projects to nearly 50 percent of the visual cortex. Half the visual area of the cerebral cortex is thus devoted to this very small central line-of-sight region of the retina. Our detail vision is so much better when we look directly at an object because a much greater relative area of the visual cortex is involved in the analysis of information that is focused on the central fovea of the retina. This fact is another illustration of the general principle, mentioned in Chapter 7, that the relative amount of brain tissue devoted to a particular region or function is proportional to the behavioral importance of that region. The center of vision is the region involved in detail vision; hence a great deal of the visual cortex is used to analyze the spatial pattern projected on the small foveal area of the retina. We see best in the line-of-sight gaze not because it is the center of the retina but because a relatively larger area of visual cortex is concerned with it.

Our experiential or perceptual visual world does not of course *look* distorted. It corresponds very closely to the real world. However the details are clearer at the point where we look. To convince yourself, close one eye and focus the other eye on one word in the center of this page. If you are very careful not to move your eye you will only be able to recognize three or four words in any direction around the word at which you are looking. The entire page is projected onto your retina, and hence to the visual cortex, but insufficient brain tissue is available for analysis of the rest of the page.

The retinotopic projection of the retina to the visual cortex can explain detail vision and our general perception of the spatial layout of the visual world. For some time scientists have attempted to explain *form* perception—the fact that we see lines, angles, rectangles, circles—solely in terms of the retinotopic projection. However recent and very fundamental work suggests that quite different mechanisms may be involved. Hubel and Wiesel [1965] have found that form is coded by single cells in the visual cortex. The experiment involves using a microelectrode to record spike discharges from single neurons in the visual cortex. The spike discharges show up as spikes—vertical lines of fixed amplitude on the baseline. This record is essentially the same as the recordings of spike discharges we saw in Fig. 7-13, except that they are recorded from outside the cell. Whenever the neuron is activated by the appropriate visual stimulus presented to the eye, it will discharge spikes. Examples of form-coding cells are shown in Fig. 8-5. One neuron responds only to a horizontal bar. It fires only when the horizontal bar is present at the correct place on the retina but does not respond if the bar is tilted away from the horizontal. An even more complex example is

192

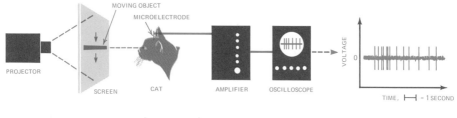

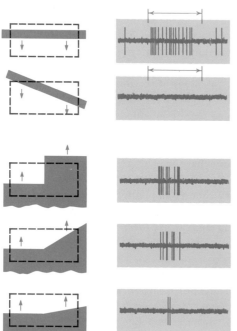

FIGURE 8–5 *Coding of visual form by single neurons in the visual area of the cerebral cortex. A small electrode is inserted in the visual cortex of the anesthetized animal and records the spike discharges of single neurons activated by stimuli presented to the eye. Center, a horizontal-bar-detector cell in the visual cortex. The bar stimulus induces spike discharges on the neuron as shown by the graph alongside. As the line above the spike discharges indicates, the cell does not respond when the bar is tilted away from the horizontal. At the bottom, a right-angle-detector cell in the visual cortex. The cell fires best (the most spikes) in the presence of a right angle.* [Hubel and Wiesel, 1962; 1965]

the right-angle-detector cell, which will respond only to an angle moving across the visual field and responds best to a right angle. This cell is an angle detector in the cerebral cortex; however, the story is a little more complicated in that there are several visual areas. In the primary visual area (area 17 on the striate cortex), cells respond best to simpler stimuli such as lines and edges, and in the higher-order visual areas 18 and 19, cells respond to angles, rectangles, and more complex forms. However, the overall picture is clear—forms are coded by single cells in the visual cortex. We see lines, angles, shapes, and forms as clearly as we do because the cells in the visual cortex are so wired that they respond selectively to these types of stimuli. We see the forms of the visual world the way we do because the neurons in our visual cortex are wired that way. We do not see forms simply because they are there; we see them because our visual cortex is put together in particular complex sets of networks connected together in very specific ways to code forms. Such a view provides a partial answer to the question of why we see the world the way we do. We see visual forms because that is the way our visual brain is wired.

193

Color is probably our most profound visual sensation. Young children can match colors to samples correctly long before they can learn the names for colors. Indeed, although we can denote a color by name, color is such an immediate given experience that we simply cannot describe it in words. Try to imagine how you would describe a color to someone who had never seen it. As we noted above, the physical basis of colors is the different wavelengths of light. The light itself, however, is not colored; color exists only in the eye of the beholder. It is in this way that color differs fundamentally from form. Form exists in the external world; color does not. Many of the greatest minds have attempted to solve this fundamental problem. Da Vinci, Newton, Helmholtz, and many others all developed theories of color vision. It is only in the past few years, however, that we have come to understand how it is that we see color.

Two differing theories have been held for some time in psychology about color vision, the Young-Helmholtz *three-receptor theory* and the *opponent theory*. It now appears that both theories are correct, at least up to a point. The Young-Helmholtz theory, first proposed by Thomas Young in 1802, assumed simply that there are three primary color receptors in the retina most sensitive to red, green, and blue. Any color attained its appearance from the relative degree it activated these three primary color receptors. Hering's opponent theory assumed, in contrast, that the receptor and neural processing of color in the retina was in the form of opponent functions. One process coded black-white and all shades of gray. This, of course, is now known to be the case—the rods code black-white vision. Another process coded red-green and intermediate colors, and still another process coded the range of colors included in yellow-blue.

Very important recent work by Rushton [1961] permitted determination of the colors selectively absorbed by the cones in the human retina. They found that there appear to be three cone pigments (iodopsins), one most sensitive to red, one to green, and one to blue. In short, they provided strong evidence in support of the Young-Helmholtz three-receptor theory. However, recordings of neural activity from the retina of the cat by Granit [1962] and from the lateral geniculate body of the monkey by DeValois [1965] gave quite a different picture of how color is coded. These investigators found two different general types of responses from different neurons. Some neurons responded to all wavelengths with varying sensitivity and in fact acted like rods; they coded the black-white dimension. In primates there are also two types of color-sensitive neurons. One type changed its activity when red and green lights were presented, and the other type changed its activity when blue and yellow lights were used. Furthermore, they responded in an "opponent" way. One red-green neuron might be excited by red and inhibited by green, whereas another would be excited by green and inhibited by red. Similarly, some blue-yellow neurons are excited by blue

194

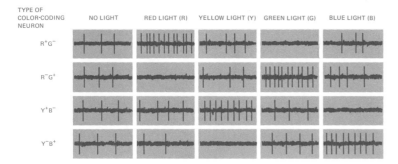

TYPE OF COLOR-CODING NEURON	NO LIGHT	RED LIGHT (R)	YELLOW LIGHT (Y)	GREEN LIGHT (G)	BLUE LIGHT (B)
R^+G^-					
R^-G^+					
Y^+B^-					
Y^-B^+					

FIGURE 8-6   *Patterns of response of the four types of color-coding neurons in the visual thalamus. The excitatory stimulus causes an increase in the number of spike discharges of the cell, and the inhibitory stimulus causes a decrease; for example, the green⁻-red⁺ cell has a given rate of spontaneous discharging which increases when red light is presented but decreases to no discharges when green is presented. [after DeValois, 1965]*

and inhibited by yellow, whereas others are excited by yellow and in-hibited by blue. In brief, these color-sensitive neurons respond in an opponent way to red-green and to yellow-blue, just as Hering had postu-lated. Examples of responses of opponent color neurons are shown in Fig. 8-6.

We seem faced with a direct contradiction. The chemicals in the cones of the eye respond to the three primary colors, but the neurons of the optic nerve and the lateral geniculate body code colors in terms of opponent function. Clearly there must be a conversion process in the retina that transforms responses from the three types of cones into op-ponent neural processes. Recent evidence from the work of Svaetichin et al. [1961], MacNichol [1964], and others may provide the missing link. Certain types of glial cellular elements in the retina respond to colors in the same way that neurons do—in an opponent manner. It may be that these glial elements somehow modulate the initial responses of the cone receptors so that responses to red, green, and blue interact on neurons to yield the four categories of opponent color neurons. Perhaps the most important point is that the information going into the brain about the color of lights is already coded into the opponent categories. The brain—that is, the visual cortex—can tell what color is being seen by noting what each of the four categories of opponent color neurons is doing. Thus if a pure green light is presented, the green⁺-red⁻ neurons will fire, the green⁻-red⁺ neurons will be inhibited (not fire), and the blue⁺-yellow⁻ and blue⁻-yellow⁺ neurons will not change markedly. Changes in color will be represented to the brain by changes in the rela-tive activity of these four types of color neurons.

In comparing the perception of form and color it is important to note the level of the nervous system where the coding process occurs. Color, as we have just seen, seems to be coded at the retina. The four categories of opponent color cells are present at the optic nerve. However, the coding of form and shape does not occur below the level of the cerebral cortex in mammals. Color is coded at a lower level of the

195

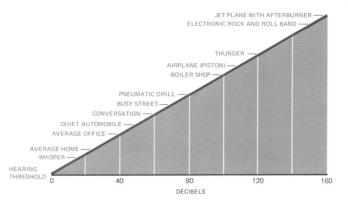

FIGURE 8–7 *The loudness of various common sounds as measured in decibels.*

nervous system than form and is a much more immediate subjective sensation in both man and monkeys. Perhaps the reason we cannot describe colors in words is that the coding is close to the stimulus, whereas shape is coded at the level of the cerebral cortex, where words are formed.

THE BIOLOGICAL
BASIS OF HEARING

We live in a world of sound. In fact it is rapidly becoming a world of unpleasant noise. Perhaps for the first time in history, ordinary noises in society have reached a level where they can cause permanent impairment of hearing. An electronic rock-and-roll band and a jet engine with an afterburner both produce significant hearing damage (see Fig. 8-7). A less obvious but perhaps more serious problem is the irritating and interfering effects of noise. If you live near an airport, conversation must stop every 2 minutes or so. Tempers flare much more readily in very noisy environments. Our hearing apparatus has evolved over millions of years to detect and analyze faint sounds; we are simply not biologically equipped to deal with loud noise.

Sound is, of course, more than noise. The daily activities of persons with normal hearing are determined by what they hear. Communication is largely verbal. The normal infant learns language in terms of sounds. Most of our responses to sounds are learned, but some are not. A very sudden loud sound produces the same innate startle response in man and mouse. The roll of thunder seems to induce very similar feelings of apprehension in man and other higher mammals. Faint sounds, in contrast, are often intrinsically pleasant [Buddenbrock, 1958, p. 93]:

When you feel an urge to get away from the burden of daily living, from the constant rush and noise of city life, the best escape is to return for a while to nature. Whether you retreat to the solitude of the lofty mountains, to the cool, green forest, or visit the sunlit fields and meadows, you will find everywhere in nature a tonic: the stillness which permits you to listen to the sound of your own breathing. If you are seated at the edge of a forest on a calm, windless summer evening, only now and then will the call of a pheasant, a noise made by a frightened roebuck, the raucous screech of a bird of prey, or the chirping of the crickets in the meadow break the silence.

The physical basis of sound is wave motion in the air. The way a loudspeaker or other sound source generates a sound is shown in Fig. 8-8. In this case a rigid membrane or diaphragm first pushes against the air to create a positive relative pressure and then pulls back to create a relative vacuum or negative pressure. This alternation of positive and negative pressure creates a pressure wave in the air that travels out from the sound source at a relatively slow speed of about 750 miles per hour. All waves have both frequency and amplitude. The frequency of a sound wave determines the tone, or pitch, of a sound—that is, how high or low it sounds to us—and the amplitude of the wave determines how loud the sound is.

Note that pitch and frequency are not the same thing. Frequency refers to a physical characteristic of the *stimulus*—the actual frequency of vibration of the sound waves in the air (commonly expressed in cycles per second or hertz). Pitch refers to the subjective sensation or response to the frequency of a sound—that is, how high or low a tone sounds to us. The relationship of pitch to frequency is not linear, or one-to-one. It tends instead to be logarithmic. For example, middle C on the piano is a tone of 256 hertz. The tone which has a frequency twice as high is C above middle C, 512 hertz. However, 512 hertz does not sound *twice* as high in pitch as 256 hertz; it sounds one octave higher, but much less than twice as high.

A similar difference exists between the physical and subjective scales in the case of sound intensity. The relationship between the amount of physical energy in a tone and the loudness we hear is also approximately logarithmic. This relationship was described a number of

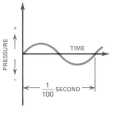

FIGURE 8–8 *Sound waves are pressure waves formed by compression and expansion of the molecules of the air. Below, representative sound waveforms varying in frequency and amplitude.*

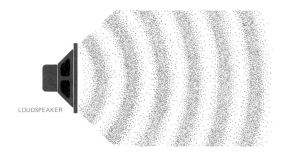

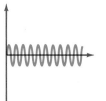

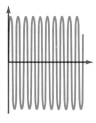

WEAK 100-HERTZ TONE   STRONG 100-HERTZ TONE   WEAK 1000-HERTZ TONE   STRONG 1000-HERTZ TONE

years ago in terms of the decibel scale for measuring sound intensity. The decibel scale is based on the logarithm of the sound energy level (actually 10 times the logarithm of the ratio of a given sound energy to the lowest threshold of sound energy). Consequently, the judged loudness of sounds corresponds in an approximately linear fashion with the decibel scale of sound intensity. The relationships between pitch and frequency and between loudness and intensity are examples of *psychophysical functions*, the relations between psychological or behavioral judgments of stimuli and physical characteristics of stimuli. We shall discuss some of the more general aspects of psychophysical relationships later in the chapter.

In contrast to the million or so fibers in the optic nerve of man, each auditory nerve has only about 28,000 fibers. Nevertheless, the total number of single tones discriminable on the basis of frequency and intensity is about 340,000. Curiously enough, this is approximately the same as the total number of single visual stimuli discernible on the basis of frequency (wavelength) and intensity of light. The nature of the mechanisms underlying the efficiency in the auditory system has puzzled investigators for many years. Historically there have been two major theories of auditory pitch discrimination—Helmholtz's *place theory*, which assumes that each tone frequency activates a different portion of the auditory receptor, and Rutherford's *frequency theory*, which proposes that the frequency of the tone is reflected in the frequency of auditory-nerve-fiber discharges. Recent developments in the field, particularly from the work of von Békésy, Davis, Tasaki, and Stevens, have shown that the more correct view lies somewhere in between these extremes.

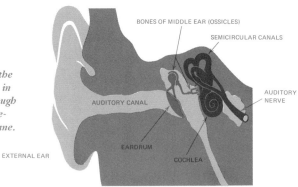

FIGURE 8-9 *General structure of the ear. The actual receptor mechanism is in the coiled cochlea. Below, a view through one coil of the cochlea, showing the receptor hair cells of the basilar membrane.*

BONES OF MIDDLE EAR (OSSICLES)

SEMICIRCULAR CANALS

AUDITORY NERVE

AUDITORY CANAL

EXTERNAL EAR

EARDRUM

COCHLEA

EUSTACHIAN TUBE

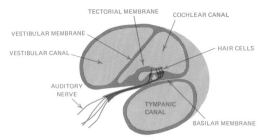

TECTORIAL MEMBRANE   COCHLEAR CANAL

VESTIBULAR MEMBRANE

VESTIBULAR CANAL

HAIR CELLS

AUDITORY NERVE

TYMPANIC CANAL

BASILAR MEMBRANE

The anatomy of the auditory receptor system is rather complicated. In brief, the external ear canal ends in the eardrum. This connects through three small bones (*ossicles*) of the middle ear to a membrane covering the end of the *cochlea*, which is a coiled tube shaped much like a snail shell. The tube is filled with fluid and contains within it a smaller tube, the *cochlear duct*, which in turn contains the sense organ proper. A cross section through the tube of the cochlea is shown in Fig. 8-9. Sound vibrations transmitted through the ossicles cause movement of fluid, which in turn produces vibrations of the *basilar membrane*. This rather stiff membrane bends relative to the *tectorial membrane*, thus bending and activating the *hair-cell* receptors lying between. These receptors are innervated by fibers of the auditory nerve, whose cell bodies lie in the *spiral ganglion* embedded in the skull. Axons of these fibers enter the central nervous system and synapse in the *cochlear nuclei* in the brain stem.

Identification of the particular aspects of receptor and neural processes that determine various aspects of sensory experience or behavior is one of the fundamental goals in the analysis of sensory processes. The absolute loudness threshold is a good case in point. In man the total range of audible frequencies is from 15 to 20,000 hertz. However, the ear is most sensitive to tones between 1000 and 4000 hertz. As frequency is increased or decreased away from this region of maximum sensitivity, increasingly greater sound energy is required to make the tone audible. The curve relating absolute threshold and frequency is shown in Fig. 8-10.

FIGURE 8–10   *Sensitivity curve for the human auditory threshold as a function of tone frequency. The approximate frequency and amplitude region of normal speech is indicated.*

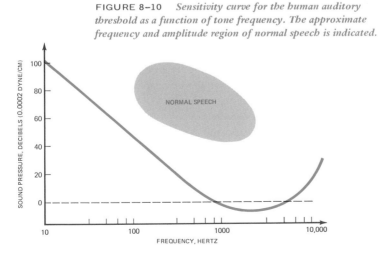

199

The acoustical and mechanical properties of the ear canal, eardrum, and the middle ear bones determine the efficiency with which sounds of various frequencies are converted to mechanical vibrations and transmitted to the cochlea. Because the absolute-threshold curve is determined by the physical properties of these accessory auditory structures, it might be expected that the size of an animal—that is, the size of its external and middle ear structures—would influence its threshold curve. In general this seems to be true. Among mammals elephants are sensitive to the lowest frequencies, and small animals such as rats and mice are sensitive to very much higher frequencies. Man, incidentally, has a relatively "middle"-frequency range. Cats can hear sounds ranging from about 30 to 70,000 hertz. There are some important exceptions to this general rule. Both bats and porpoises can hear sounds of up to about 100,000 hertz. However, these animals are exceptional in that they make use of a very specialized echo-location, or sonar, system; they emit very-high-frequency pulses of sound and determine the position of objects in space by the characteristics of the reflected sound pulses.

The degree of sensitivity of the human ear is quite remarkable, at least in the frequency region of best threshold (around 2000 hertz). A movement of the eardrum of less than one-tenth the diameter of a hydrogen atom can result in an auditory sensation. If the ear were more sensitive than this, the random brownian movements of air molecules would produce a constant roaring sound, which would tend to mask auditory stimuli. Thus, paradoxically, if the ear were more sensitive it would be less sensitive. As a matter of fact, persons with very good hearing are able to detect brownian noise under ideal listening conditions.

The movements of the basilar membrane of the cochlea in response to auditory stimuli were analyzed in a series of elegant experiments by von Békésy [1956], awarded the Nobel prize in 1962 for his work. In essence, he showed that if a tone of a given frequency is presented, a traveling wave of fluid is set up in the cochlea. The traveling wave causes a maximum displacement in a given region of the basilar membrane. The location of this maximum displacement on the membrane is related to the frequency of the tone (see Fig. 8-11). Some rather complex mechanical effects occur because of the differential stiffness of the membrane. The net result is that high-frequency tones selectively distort regions of the basilar membrane close to the base of the cochlea, intermediate tones distort a portion of the membrane in an intermediate region, and low-frequency tones tend to distort the entire membrane.

The findings of von Békésy actually seem to offer some support for each of the two major theories concerning pitch coding, place and frequency. There is a tendency for a given frequency of tone to produce greatest distortion at a given region of the basilar membrane. The original place theory proposed by Helmholtz assumed that the basilar membrane was a very large series of highly tuned elements, much like tuning forks or the strings on a harp. Von Békésy's data [1956], particularly for high frequencies, support this view with the modification that small differences in degree of distortion of the membrane can serve as "tuned

200

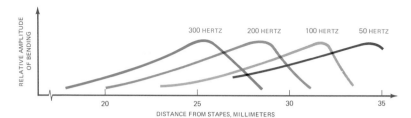

FIGURE 8-11   *The location and amount of distortion (amplitude of bending) of the basilar membrane produced by tones of different frequencies. Distance is from one end (the base or stapes) of the membrane. Note that low-frequency tones cause a broader region of distortion and that higher-frequency tones cause a narrower region of distortion closer to the base. [von Békésy, 1947]*

elements." In general the higher the frequency, the closer the distortion is to the base of the cochlea. However, low-frequency tones tend to activate the entire basilar membrane equivalently, and intermediate tones activate a substantial portion of the membrane. The differential distortion of the membrane does not seem great enough to provide for our very sensitive ability to discriminate pitch, and there is no differential distortion to code low-frequency tones.

If a recording electrode is placed on the cochlea near the auditory nerve, several types of signals can be recorded. The most noticeable of these is the *cochlear microphonic*, discovered by Wever and Bray [1930]. This is an electrical response that follows the frequency and intensity characteristics of the auditory stimulus *exactly*. If a Beethoven symphony is played into the ear of an anesthetized cat and the electrically recorded cochlear microphonic is amplified and connected to a speaker, you will hear the symphony with essentially no distortion. The cochlear microphonic is literally a microphone; sound waves are converted to electrical pulses in exactly the same manner as in a microphone.

The discovery of the cochlear microphonic seemed to provide very strong support for the frequency theory of pitch coding. It was initially believed that the electrical pulses of the cochlear microphonic were spike discharges of the auditory nerve. This would mean that the frequency of discharges in the auditory nerve exactly follows the input frequency of any sound. However, it soon became apparent that the cochlear microphonic can follow sound frequencies up to 70,000 hertz, which is a great deal faster than any nerve fiber can respond (2000 hertz is about the highest frequency recordable from a nerve fiber). It appears that the cochlear microphonic is produced by the hair cells in the cochlea and may represent a generator potential. The hair cells are bent with a frequency that follows the input sound frequency. The cochlear microphonic seems to result from a transducer action of the hair cells quite analogous to the conversion of mechanical vibrations into electrical pulses by the crystal in a phonograph cartridge. It has been suggested that the same kind of piezoelectric effect may be involved in both. Although the cochlear microphonic has been considered by some as merely an accidental electromechanical byproduct resulting from bending of the hair cells, many other authorities [Davis, 1959; Tasaki and Davis,

201

1955] favor the view that the terminals of the auditory nerve fibers are directly activated by the flows of current associated with the cochlear microphonic—that is, it acts as a generator potential.

Individual nerve fibers in the auditory nerve can follow low-frequency sounds up to about 1000 hertz. Each nerve fiber fires a spike each time the sound pressure wave activates the cochlea—that is, 1000 times per second. When the sound frequency exceeds 1000 hertz an interesting "volley" effect occurs. Different groups of fibers fire out of step. If a 2000-hertz tone is given, for example, one group of fibers may discharge 1000 times per second and another group 1000 times per second, out of phase with the first group; thus if we look at the activity of the entire auditory nerve, it is firing 2000 times per second, the same frequency as the tone, even though no individual fiber is firing more than 1000 times per second. This is another remarkable example of the adaptability of the nervous system. Consequently low frequencies of sound can be coded by the frequency of discharge of auditory nerve fibers.

It appears that both the place of excitation on the basilar membrane and the frequency of nerve responses are important in coding tone frequency. For high frequencies place is most important, but for lower frequencies (below 4000 hertz) synchronous discharges in nerve fibers also play a role. Intensity may be coded both by total number of fibers activated and by activation of high threshold fibers (nerve fibers that require considerable bending of the hair cells to be stimulated). The nerve fibers are stimulated by the bending of the hair cells, possibly as a direct result of the cochlear microphonic.

The auditory pathways from the cochlea to the auditory area of the cerebral cortex are rather complex, involving several relay stations. An important point to note is that the system is bilateral. Both ears

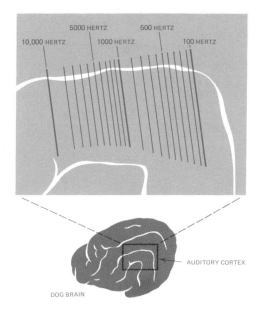

FIGURE 8–12 *Tonotopic representation on the auditory cortex of the dog (brain facing to the left). Low-frequency tones activate the most posterior region of the auditory cortex and higher-frequency tones activate progressively more anterior regions. Each line is a best-frequency line, indicating the region of auditory cortex most activated by a given frequency. [after Tunturi, 1952]*

5000 HERTZ   500 HERTZ
10,000 HERTZ   1000 HERTZ   100 HERTZ

AUDITORY CORTEX

DOG BRAIN

SENSORY-MOTOR INTEGRATION

contribute input to the auditory system on each side, although at the level of the cerebral cortex the ear from the opposite side contributes more. At the cerebral cortex, the auditory receptor surface, the basilar membrane, is sorted out again. In fact, a complete representation of the basilar membrane is laid out along the auditory cortex. Remember that high-frequency tones bend one end of the basilar membrane and lower tones bend the membrane farther toward the other end (see Fig. 8-12), but low tones bend the entire membrane. At the cortex, these effects have been converted into *place* representation along the auditory area. This is termed *tonotopic representation* [Tunturi, 1944]. As indicated in Fig. 8-12, a high-frequency tone activates neurons at one end of the cortex, and progressively lower tones activate a progressively more distant region of the cortex. Thus tone frequency is mapped out along the cortex. In addition to this general mapping of tone frequency, individual cells in the auditory cortex code frequency. For any given neuron there is a best frequency, a tone frequency that produces greatest activation of the cell. Many neurons in the auditory cortex also have best intensities; for a given frequency range a particular intensity of tone will cause the cell to fire more than will either a weaker or a stronger tone.

In summary, at the level of the auditory cortex, tone frequency is coded both in terms of a spatial representation on the cortex and by single neurons, and tone intensity is also coded by single neurons. It is likely that our perception of complex sounds is mediated by the auditory cortex. Of course, understanding the *meaning* of sounds, as in language, entails far more than merely perceiving sounds. This process involves other higher functions and association areas of the cerebral cortex.

THE SOMATIC SENSORY SYSTEM

The somatic sensory system, particularly the skin senses, provides one of the most important avenues of social interaction. In many higher mammals, nuzzling and mutual grooming are common social expressions; monkeys are often seen picking imaginary fleas from a fellow. In man skin stimulation provides some of the most pleasurable sensations. Even more to the point, it is essential to the fundamental process of sexual interaction.

The opposite sensation, pain, is also a part of the somatic sensory system. The sensation produced by damage to skin and deep tissues is one of the most compelling and intense of our subjective experiences. The immediacy of this sensation is such that, like color, pain is impossible to describe in words. The best the early introspectionist psychologists were able to do was to distinguish between fast, sharp, "bright" pain and slow, dull, aching pain. Society has long exploited the fact that avoidance of pain is among the most primary drives or motives. Torture or the threat of it has been used since time immemorial to shape and control human behavior.

203

The major types of somatic sensory sensation are light touch, deep pressure, awareness of limb position (where your legs, arms, and fingers are in space or in approximation to other body parts), heat, cold, and pain. It has often been assumed that there are specific receptors for each type of sensation, but this does not seem to be the case. There are special pressure receptors close to the surface of the skin that could provide some information about light touch, there are well-known special deep-pressure receptors (the pacinian corpuscles), and there are pressure receptors in the joints that provide us with information about the position of our limbs in relation to the body. The muscles themselves provide us with a complete array of information, via muscle-stretch receptors, about the degree of stretch and rate of contraction of every muscle in the body. This input serves to regulate such reflex activities as standing and moving, but it plays no role at all in our awareness of where our limbs are; this is provided entirely by pressure receptors in the joints. However, it has also been shown that light touch, warm, cold, and pain can all be experienced in the absence of specialized receptors other than free nerve endings [Lele and Weddell, 1956]. Although the cornea of the eye has only free nerve endings and contains no specialized pressure or other receptors, with careful and appropriate stimulation of the cornea, subjects can be made to experience light touch, warm, cold, and pain.

THE CODING OF SOMATIC SENSORY STIMULI

The major differentiation in our somatic sensory experience seems to be between specific sensations of touch, pressure, and limb position on the one hand and pain and temperature sensation on the other. Sensory nerves from skin and deep tissues separate into two separate pathways when they enter the spinal cord. One of these, which we will call the *discrete system*, mediates touch, pressure, and limb position, and the other, which we will call the *nonspecific system*, mediates pain and temperature. A simplified schematic of these two pathways is shown in Fig. 8-13. The details of these pathways are not important here; the major difference between them is that the discrete system goes directly from the lower brain stem to the thalamus in a pathway called the *medial lemniscus*, and then is relayed to the primary somatic sensory area of the cerebral cortex. The nonspecific system does not have a direct pathway to the thalamus, but instead relays into and through the ascending reticular activating system.

The discrete somatic sensory system is a more recent development in the evolution of the nervous system. It provides us with precise and specific information about stimuli and allows us to analyze the nature of adaptively "neutral" stimuli. The nonspecific system is much older and more primitive. It provides feelings and sensations that are vague in

204

terms of our ability to analyze stimuli, but overriding in terms of adaptive survival value. Pain and temperature sensations, for example, are essential to survival. A higher animal that is deprived of these sensations has no awareness of, and hence no protection against, tissue damage and infection that may be fatal. There are certain types of neurological diseases that selectively destroy the pain and temperature pathways in man. Such patients constantly develop serious infections because they are unaware of minor cuts and bruises that the rest of us avoid.

The fact that two different sensory pathways are involved is apparent in the action of general anesthetics such as ether. If a general anesthetic is administered slowly, the patient passes through several stages of anesthesia. In the lightest stage, called *analgesia*, he is still conscious and can respond to questions and can report auditory and visual stimuli. He also responds to tactile stimuli—but he has no awareness of pain. It appears that general anesthetics act first on the ascending reticular activating system (see Fig. 7-7). This very ancient nonspecific system is activated or influenced by many types of stimuli and is the major relay system for the nonspecific sensory pathway mediating pain. It has many synaptic relays and seems to be particularly sensitive to anesthetics.

In summary, there are two separate somatic sensory pathways—a more recent precise discrete system that permits analysis of stimuli in terms of touch, pressure, and limb position and a much older and more

FIGURE 8–13   *Simplified schematic of the two major somatic sensory systems. In the discrete system, which mediates light touch, pressure, and limb-position sense, the sensory nerve fibers enter the spinal cord and ascend to the lower brain stem, where they synapse in relay nuclei which in turn project to the thalamus and on to the cerebral cortex. The nonspecific system, which mediates pain, temperature, and diffuse touch, synapses in the spinal cord and then ascends and relays through the brain stem reticular system to the thalamus and on to the cerebral cortex.*

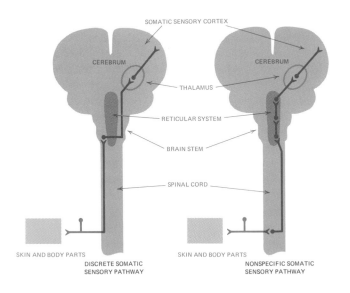

SOMATIC SENSORY CORTEX

CEREBRUM   CEREBRUM

THALAMUS

RETICULAR SYSTEM

BRAIN STEM

SPINAL CORD

SKIN AND BODY PARTS   SKIN AND BODY PARTS

DISCRETE SOMATIC   NONSPECIFIC SOMATIC
SENSORY PATHWAY   SENSORY PATHWAY

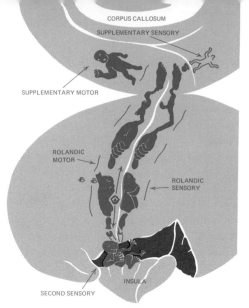

FIGURE 8-14 *Location and approximate representation of the somatic sensory and motor areas on the cerebral cortex of man. The drawings indicate the relative amount of cortex devoted to each region of the body. There are two major sensory areas, rolandic and second, and two motor areas, rolandic and supplementary. The brain is facing to the right, and a portion has been removed below to show the second sensory area. In the upper region, bounded at the top by the corpus callosum, the cortex in the middle of the hemisphere is shown folded up. The foot representation in the primary (rolandic) areas actually bends over the top of the hemisphere and down onto the middle side. [Penfield and Jasper, 1954]*

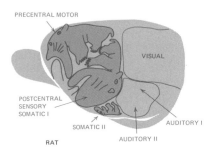

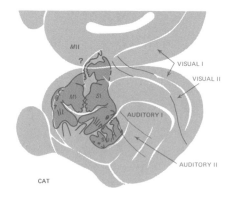

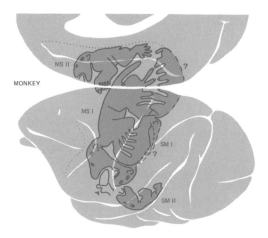

primitive system that is concerned with pain and temperature and is much more related to biological survival.

As with the visual and auditory systems, the somatic receptor surface is mapped out along the somatic sensory area of the cerebral cortex. In this case, of course, the receptor surface is the skin surface of the body. The entire body surface is laid out in representation along the somatic sensory cortex (see Fig. 8-14). The fact that the relative amount of cortex devoted to a particular receptor region is proportional to the behavioral importance of that region is nowhere more evident than in the somatic sensory system. The form of the representation on the cortex is termed a *homunculus*. In animals like the rat there is relatively less distortion of the homunculus on the cortex, although the nose area is somewhat enlarged. The cat has greater enlargement of forepaws and face, and monkeys have enormous enlargement of the hands and feet. Comparisons of somatic sensory homunculi on the cortex in these animals are shown in Fig. 8-15. The amount of cortex devoted to a given region of the body surface is directly proportional to the use and sensitivity of that region. In so far as the cerebral cortex is concerned, man is clearly a creature composed largely of hands, lips, and tongue.

Studies of the manner in which single neurons in the somatic sensory cortex code sensory stimuli indicate that this coding is extremely precise and detailed. A most important finding is the columnar organization of cells in the somatic sensory cortex [Werner and Mountcastle, 1968]. If a very small electrode is pushed down through the cortex at a right angle to the surface, so that it goes directly down through the cortex, it might first encounter a cell that responds only to light touch. As it moves down through the cortex it will encounter additional cells, all of which respond only to light touch. In other words, the light-touch cells form a minute functional *column* down through the cortex. If the electrode is removed, moved to the side a fraction of a millimeter, and pushed down into the cortex again, it might encounter cells that code joint position; all cells in that column will code joint position. Still another column will code deep pressure. Thus each different modality of the discrete system is coded by separate columns of cells. Each small region of skin representation on the somatic sensory cortex is filled with these small columns which code the different modalities. This is true, incidentally, only for the discrete, or lemniscal, system. The older non-

FIGURE 8–15   *Homunculi of the sensory and motor areas for monkey, cat, and rat. Note that on the rat cerebral cortex the sensory and motor representations look rather like the rat, except for the large nose and mouth. The cat has greatly enlarged forepaws and face. In the monkey the representation becomes grossly distorted and is mostly hands and feet (SM I, somatic sensory area I; SM II, somatic sensory area II; MS I, primary motor area; MS II, supplementary motor area). Note from Fig. 8-14 that in man a much greater amount of primary somatic and motor cortex is devoted to lips and tongue, and less is devoted to feet. [Woolsey, 1958; Schaltenbrand and Woolsey, 1964]*

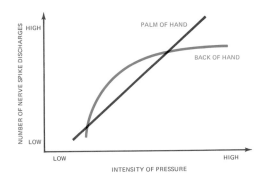

FIGURE 8-16   *Coding of tactile pressure by receptors on the palm and the back of the hand. The rate of spike discharge increases with pressure; on the palm this increase is linear, but on the back of the hand it is not. [data from Werner and Mountcastle, 1968]*

specific system does not have a separate or distinct representation on the cerebral cortex.

The neurons that respond to touch and pressure exhibit incredibly precise coding of the intensity of a stimulus; they discharge spikes in direct proportion to the intensity of pressure on the skin (see Fig. 8-16). In primates and man there is a most interesting difference in the way intensity of touch pressure is coded on the palm and back of the hand. For the palm or fingertips the number of spikes fired as a function of pressure on the skin is a direct linear (straight-line) relationship. For the back of the hand the relationship is direct, but it is not linear. As pressure increases, the proportional increase in number of spikes decreases toward a limit. What this means is that neurons activated by the fingertips and palm are more sensitive to differences in pressure at strong pressures, whereas neurons activated by the back of the hand cannot discriminate among strong pressures. This probably has adaptive significance in that higher primates must discriminate among relatively strong pressures when they grip objects.

COMMON FEATURES OF SENSORY SYSTEMS

In reviewing the major sensory systems we have noted several common principles of how the brain codes sensory stimuli. The first is the receptotopic organization of the cerebral cortex. The receptor surface—the retina of the eye, the basilar membrane of the inner ear, and the skin surface—is mapped out on the cortex in such a way that activation of different regions of the receptor surface leads to activation of differing groups of neurons in the cerebral cortex. This results in coding of location of objects in space for the visual system, tone frequency in the auditory system, and location of touch on the body surface for the somatic sensory system. Furthermore, that aspect of sensory experience that has the greatest functional importance for us,

208

such as center of gaze for vision and fingertips for touch, has relatively greater cortical representation.

A much more fine-grained analysis of sensory quality is provided by individual nerve-cell coding. Colors and forms are coded by various neurons in the visual system; tone pitch and loudness are distinguished by neurons in the auditory system; and type of tactile stimulus is differentiated by neurons in the discrete somatic sensory system.

Coding relationships such as those shown in Fig. 8-16 for pressure of stimulus versus number of nerve spike discharges are psychophysical functions. Psychophysical studies in which human subjects are asked to judge the relationship between stimulus pressure and their subjective experience of pressure yield identical results. Stevens [1961], who has analyzed such psychophysical relationships between physical stimuli and subjective experience in great detail for tactile, auditory, and visual stimuli, has shown that all these functions exhibit a particular kind of mathematical relationship between stimulus and response. It is called a *power function* and has the general form $\Psi = k\Phi^n$, where Ψ is the psychological response of the subject (his subjective judgment of how strong the stimulus is), Φ is the actual stimulus intensity, k is a numerical constant, and n is an exponent whose value depends on the type of stimulus used. In the curves of Fig. 8-16, for example, the palm stimulus yields a function with an exponent of 1, but the back-of-the-hand stimulus yields an exponent of about 0.3. Different forms of psychophysical curves are shown in Fig. 8-17.

It thus appears that for essentially all stimuli, the relationship between physical stimulus intensity and our subjective experience of stimulus intensity is a power function. A question of fundamental importance is where the transformation from the physical-stimulus scale to the

FIGURE 8–17   *Relationship between stimulus intensity (abscissa) and sensation of stimulus magnitude for three different types of stimuli. For length (of lines) the relationship is linear; perceived length corresponds exactly to stimulus length. For brightness, relatively large increases in actual stimulus intensity are perceived as small increases, permitting us to perceive a wide range of stimulus intensity. For electric shock it is just the opposite; above a certain point (about 30 on the scale) small increases in shock intensity are perceived as very large increases. This is at about the point where shock causes pain and tissue damage. [Stevens, 1961]*

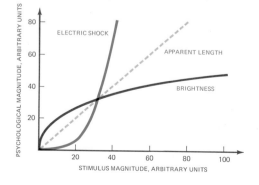

209

subjective-experience scale takes place. Detailed studies of various levels in the somatic sensory system indicate that this transformation is actually at the receptors [Werner and Mountcastle, 1968]. This means that we do not experience the world as it is; we experience it only as a power function of what it is. In other words, the entire sea of subjective experiences by which we guide our lives is not a direct reflection of the real world, but bears only a mathematical relationship to that world. Things are even less as they seem than you think.

In recent years it has been demonstrated that the brain itself can exert some control over incoming sensory information by means of certain descending neural systems. In the visual, auditory, and somatic sensory systems fibers project down from higher regions of the brain to sensory receptors or early central relay stations for sensory input to exert direct control over sensory input. For this reason electrical stimulation of a number of regions of the brain, particularly the reticular formation of the brain stem, will alter the nature of incoming sensory information.

The potential significance of these descending sensory control systems is considerable. The amount and kind of incoming sensory information can be controlled, or "gated," at the level of sensory input. Sensory information might even be prevented from reaching higher levels of the brain. Thus some aspects of selective attention, where we concentrate on one type of sensory input to the exclusion of others, may involve these systems. It is not yet clear just what role the descending control systems play in behavior; it is currently a research area of great interest.

MOTOR RESPONSE

Essentially all aspects of behavior that we can observe in other people and animals are muscle movements—walking, running, fighting, tightrope walking, ballet dancing, piano playing. All of these are simply sequences of skeletal-muscle contractions and relaxations. To the extent that psychology is the study of behavior, it is really the study of muscle movements. However, an understanding of the muscular actions themselves, and even the immediate neuronal mechanisms controlling the muscles, does not provide us with an understanding of behavior. A complete recording of all the finger-muscle actions made by a novelist as he types a novel will tell us nothing about the novel he has written; we would do far better to read it. To understand behavior we must learn about the higher-order systems involved in the control of movement.

The number and variety of brain structures that have something to do with the control of movement are large and somewhat bewildering, to say the least. The English neurologist Hughlings Jackson stated many years ago that the basic function of the nervous system is movement.

The motor systems of the central nervous system contain some of the most elegant and complex examples of feedback control systems known. In a sense the motor systems are a progressively more complex series of interlocking feedback systems, ranging from the exquisitely tuned gamma motor system of the spinal cord up through the basal ganglia and cerebellum to the pyramidal and extrapyramidal systems of the cerebral cortex. Most of these systems are concerned with the more immediate control mechanisms of movement, and the details are not of direct relevance [see Thompson, 1967].

The most complex aspects of movement control that we know about are mediated by the cerebral cortex. As we noted in Chapter 7, the cerebral cortex is essential for the most important movements we make—those of the tongue, lips, and throat associated with speech. Handwriting, typing, and even reading are really secondary to vocal movements. It is likely, in fact, that most thought processes have as an essential component some degree of movement of the vocal apparatus.

The role of the cerebral cortex in movement is graphically illustrated in the following protocol from a brain operation described by Penfield and Jasper. The patient was a right-handed woman of thirty-nine whose symptoms suggested a tumor in the left hemisphere of the brain. The motor region of the left hemisphere was exposed, and various points of the cerebral cortex were stimulated electrically to aid in locating the abnormal tissue. The patient was under only local anesthesia, so that she could respond and describe her sensations and feelings. The numbers at the left in the protocol are simply arbitrary designations for the specific points on the brain that are being stimulated [Penfield and Jasper, 1954, p. 97]:

> Stimulate 17   Patient made a vowel sound which was repeated rhythmically. After electrode withdrawn she explained that she thought she was starting to say something but "it" [the stimulation] had forced her to repeat.
>
> Stimulate 17   Repeated while patient was counting. Stimulation arrested speech completely. Patient added, "It [the stimulus] raised my right arm." The arm had actually raised itself.
>
> Stimulate 18   Patient counting. Stimulation caused her to vocalize in a continuous sound. She explained afterward that she was sorry she could not count. There was some movement in the right arm also.
>
> Stimulate 19   Patient counting. She made an exclamation and then was silent, but the whole body moved. This movement caused the head to turn a little to the right. There was not much movement of the arm. When asked whether she had felt as she did before one of her attacks, she said "Yes." When asked why, she replied "Because I repeated my speech."
>
> Stimulate 20   Patient counting backward. Stimulation caused the counting to stop. Two or three seconds after withdrawal she continued

counting backward. The observer noted no change during her silence except that she looked surprised.

Stimulate 19   Approximate repetition of 20. Vocalization was produced, somewhat rhythmical. There was some movement of both arms and both legs.

Stimulate 18   Repeated without warning. Stimulation produced vocalization which sounded like "da, da, da."

Stimulate 21   Stimulation while patient was counting. She hesitated and then continued. There was movement of right arm, the shoulder being drawn posteriorly. The right leg was extended and raised off the table. When asked what she had noticed, she said her right arm. When asked if she could prevent the movement, she said, "No."

Stimulate 22   Patient said, "Oh." There were generalized movements. When asked what she noticed, she said her body seemed to rise up but she did not seem to be doing it.

The motor area of the human cerebral cortex represents both muscles and movements. In fact it contains a complete mapping, or homunculus, of the body. Using the technique just described, Penfield et al. mapped out the representation of movement on the human cerebral cortex (see Fig. 8-14); this representation is essentially a mirror image of the somatic sensory projection that lies just posterior to it. Similar maps of the motor areas of a variety of mammals and particularly primates obtained by Woolsey [1958] have provided us with a comparative view of the development of the motor cortex (see Fig. 8-15). As in the somatic sensory cortex, man has become largely lips, tongue, and hands. Results of these studies indicate that the motor cortex is indeed a high-order control system. In both man and other higher mammals movements elicited by electrical stimulation of the motor cortex are not random twitches, but are well-integrated movements, even to the point of producing recognizable vocalizations in man. People seem to have no control over these electrically induced movements; in the example above the stimulus preempted the patient's voluntary control of her movements. Of equal importance is the fact that patients do not describe any experiences, memories, or even strong sensations other than the movements themselves that result from the stimulus. The motor cortex is the region that controls complex integrated movements.

Our discussion of motor cortex has thus far been concerned primarily with the kinds of movements elicited by electrical stimulation. Such a technique by itself will not necessarily tell us what the essential role of the motor cortex is in the control of movement. Removal of the primary motor cortex in man produces loss of the most delicate and skilled movements, particularly those of the fingers and hand. However, it has little or no permanent effect on the movements produced by electrical stimulation, which consist largely of flexion and extension of the arms and legs, opening and closing of the fist, and vocalizations. These movements have the same character in a child of eight, a man of sixty, a skilled pianist, and a manual laborer. This would seem to be a paradox. According to Penfield and Jasper [1954, p. 65]:

212

> The movements which are said to be "represented" in the precentral gyrus [motor cortex] because they are produced by stimulation of that gyrus are not abolished when the gyrus is removed and, on the other hand, the acquired skills of the contralateral extremities [hand and foot], which do not seem to be "represented" in the gyrus at all, are abolished forever by gyrectomy [removal of the motor cortex].

Apparently what happens is that electrical stimulation activates the cortex to play on subcortical motor systems already "wired up" at birth and under the ultimate control of the motor cortex. Thus the stimulus simply activates portions of this prewired system to produce certain types of unskilled and infantile movements. Movements such as closing the fist and vocalization are in no sense simple muscle contractions, but they fall far short of the complex skilled movements for which the motor cortex is essential. In normal development the motor cortex serves to coordinate highly complex and skilled movements resulting from complex actions on the motor cortex from other regions of the brain. The electrical stimulus cannot duplicate such complex patterns of activation. As Penfield and Jasper put it [1954, pp. 65–66]:

> The succession of motor units in the Rolandic (motor) cortex is like a keyboard. Each key is connected to a different peripheral resounding wire. Music results only when the keyboard is played upon according to a pattern that has its localization elsewhere in the central nervous system.

The crucial question is, of course, the nature and organization of the higher-order central control systems that play on the motor cortex. We cannot even begin to answer this question at present; essentially nothing is known about such systems.

SENSORY–MOTOR INTEGRATION

It is not necessary to tell you how the world looks to you; your perceptions of the world are your own immediate experience. We have considered how the major sensory systems code stimuli into sensations and at least simple perceptions such as form, color, pitch, and touch. Your own experience of the world is somehow compounded out of these sensations into a relatively integrated flow of awareness. We know very little about how this happens, but we are beginning to have some idea of how the complex perceptions of the adult human develop. Many aspects of perception, such as the ability to see form and depth, may be innate. As we saw in Chapter 2, primates raised in the dark from infancy have very poor vision. For a time it was believed that this was because the animal was unable to learn from visual experience and hence to develop the neural circuits to code pattern vision. However, more recent studies suggest quite a different interpretation. Hubel and Wiesel [1963] determined the characteristics of single neurons in the visual cortex of the newborn animal and found the same types of edge-, line-, and form-coding cells present at birth as in the adult animal.

213

Furthermore, they found that when an animal was raised for a period in the dark, or with one eye covered, cells in the cortex that were thus deprived of visual experience lost the ability to code complex forms. In other words, form perception may be present in the brain at birth, but if the system is not activated by form stimuli during growth and development after birth, form coding is lost.

These findings do not imply that there is no perceptual learning after birth, but they do demonstrate that significant aspects of perception may indeed be innate. In fact there is growing evidence that even complex visual perception is wired into the brain at birth.

We do not yet know the limits of predetermined sensory-perceptual experience. It may even be that certain types of complex perceptions or experiences are transmitted genetically. The Swiss psychoanalyst Karl Jung once proposed a theory of "archetypes," suggesting that certain types of symbolism, such as upright objects representing a penis, are inherited by man as a species and hence represent archetypical perception common to the human race. Of course there is no experimental evidence for this idea, but, at least in theory, it is possible. We do know that many aspects of perception are learned as a result of our responses to the perceptual world. This is particularly true in relation to the consequences of stimuli—that is, their significance in terms of reward or punishment. For a child the sight of candy means "candy to eat," and the sight of the strap means "run." The issue that concerns us here, however, is the extent to which the perceptual organization of our experiential world is influenced by learning. The studies by Held, Hein, and others reviewed in Chapter 2 show that actual behavioral responses are essential for plasticity of sensory-motor integration. Both the normal development of visual perception and visual adaptation apparently require an opportunity to make some motor response to visual stimuli. The fact that motor response is essential for visual "experience" indicates that "perceptual learning" may be fundamentally a motor plasticity rather than a literal reorganization of the sensory input.

The idea that learning in sensory-motor integration is more in the motor response than in the sensory input is entirely consistent with our general position concerning the predetermined coding of sensory stimuli by the sensory systems of the brain. Even very complex and abstract aspects of physical stimuli seem to be coded by preexisting, genetically determined neural circuits. What we normally learn during growth and development, then, is not how the world looks, but rather how to respond to it.

SUMMARY

Much of our understanding of sensation and perception, our sensory responses to stimuli, come from detailed analyses of the sensory systems. The particular sensory modality activated by a stimulus depends not on the nature of the stimulus, but on the sensory receptors that it activates and the sensory area of the brain to which these receptors are connected. The most direct type of stimulus coding is the transduction of stimulus energy into neural impulses by the rods and cones in the retina of the eye, the hair cells in the cochlea of the ear, and the specific and nonspecific nerve endings of the somatic sensory system.

One feature common to all sensory coding is that the receptor surface is mapped out on the corresponding area of the cerebral cortex, the retina on the visual cortex, the basilar membrane along the auditory cortex, the skin surface on the somatic sensory cortex. Single neurons in each of these areas code finer stimulus quality such as color, form, pitch, and type of touch. Stimulus intensity also appears to be coded by single neurons. For essentially all stimuli the relationship between actual stimulus intensity and our subjective experience of it is a power function of the general form $\Psi = k\,\Phi^n$. The brain itself may also exert some control over incoming sensory information through descending neural pathways, but this effect is not yet clearly understood.

The motor area of the human cerebral cortex is perhaps the most important of the various structures involved in the control and integration of movement. The results of electrical stimulation of motor cortex indicate that it represents both muscles and movements. Its removal in man causes a loss of delicate and skilled movements but does not affect the motor gross aspects of movement flexion and extension of limbs.

Sensory-motor integration appears to be innate in some simple organisms in the form of rigidly predetermined behavioral responses to specific sensory stimuli. Many aspects of perception may also be predetermined in higher organisms, including man. The single cells that code form are found in newborn animals. Evidence that motor response to visual stimuli is necessary for normal perceptual development indicates that the learned aspects of perception lie in the response to perception rather than in the perceptual processes.

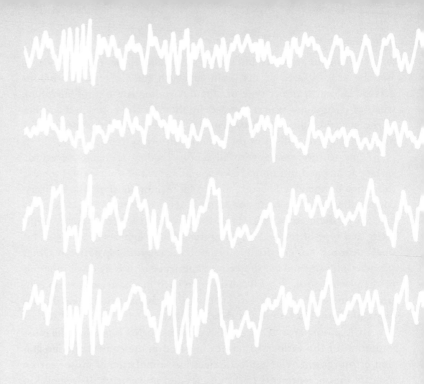

CHAPTER NINE

SLEEP AND WAKEFULNESS

Perhaps the most evident or pervasive experience which we have is the sense of our own existence, an awareness of our own consciousness. From a philosophic point of view man has long sought to understand the nature of his mental existence, and even to use it to "prove" his physical existence, as exemplified by the sixteenth-century philosopher Descartes: "I think, therefore I am." During the nineteenth century, as scientific psychology began to emerge as a discipline separate from philosophy, the problem of consciousness became the topic of "objective" methods of scientific analysis, principally the method of introspection. This consisted of "looking within" one's self and reporting the "contents" of one's own mind. It soon became evident that this method could never yield generally reliable data, for there was no way for one investigator to validate the contents of another's consciousness. Even the presentation of the same simple stimulus to several subjects simultaneously could result in widely different introspective reports of their various consciousnesses.

Although the contents of consciousness could not be agreed on, there was general agreement on the existence of different states of con-

SLEEP, DREAMING, AND ATTENTION

SLEEP, DREAMING, AND ATTENTION

sciousness, principally wakefulness and sleep. "Attention" was generally conceived to be a property of waking, but as we will see recent research suggests that we can also be attentive during sleep. In addition, intensive research into the state of sleep during the past 20 years has shown that sleep is not a unitary state, but consists of separate phases, and that dreaming may constitute, with waking and sleep, a third major state of consciousness. Interest in the "contents of consciousness" has not flagged, although this expression is no longer widely used. Developments in this area have relied on innovations in methods of behavioral measurement, to a large extent in the field of discrimination learning, in order to determine the stimuli or strategies which organisms use to solve particular problems.

One contemporary theory of the universe, the "big-bang" theory, holds that the universe which is now expanding eventually will start to contract until all matter comes together, at which time an unimaginable explosion will once again send matter hurtling outward until the next contraction begins. The time required for one complete pulsation, or cycle, has been estimated to be 80 billion years. This ultimate cycle is still a matter of speculation. The slow but unceasing rotation of our own pinwheel Milky Way galaxy is more firmly established; each cycle

217

of rotation requires 200 million years. Near our galaxy's rim a tiny star carries with it nine planets; they in turn circle this sun in periods ranging from 88 earth days to 247 earth years. Satellites periodically circumnavigate the planets (except Mercury, Venus, and Pluto), and each planet periodically rotates on its axis. We could continue to list cycles or periods of regularly repeating events down to those of the electrons, which spin around atomic nuclei, miniature mimics of star systems. It would be strange indeed if life forms were exempt from the periodicity which characterizes their universe. Life on earth is not. The alternation of sleeping and waking is a manifestation, in our lives and those of other animals, of this pervasive periodicity.

BIOLOGICAL RHYTHMS

The sleep-wakefulness cycle occurs daily, that is, it has a period of approximately 24 hours. Such biological rhythms are called circadian (after the Latin *circa* "about" and *dies* "a day"). However biological rhythms are by no means limited to periods of about 24 hours. They span a wide range, from yearly migrations, hibernations, and matings, to monthly menstrual cycles, to twice-a-day changes in the activity level of marine animals in coastal intertidal zones, down to heart beats on the order of several per second and wingbeats of several hundred per second in the locust.

What is the source of biological rhythm? It might seem that periodic behaviors such as sleeping and waking are controlled by the physical rhythms of the universe, in this case the daily rotation of the earth with its periodic day-night cycle. Indeed, there has been a great amount of controversy about whether such rhythms are controlled by external forces or are due to some process intrinsic to the organism. The truth seems to lie between these two extreme positions. For example, rats which have access to activity wheels will spontaneously enter the wheels and run enthusiastically for varying periods of time (this may be to compensate for limited opportunities for activity within their home cages, but the actual reasons are unknown). Daily activity records over a period of 47 days show one period of activity and one period of inactivity during each 24 hours, with the active period largely confined to the dark or night (Fig. 9-1). These findings support the notion of external control, presumably by changes in light as a result of the earth's rotation. However, this is not the entire story.

If illumination cues are eliminated by housing rats in constant light or darkness, the wheel-running behavior continues to exhibit periodicity. Furthermore, under such constant conditions the activity rhythm is still approximately 24 hours (circadian), with normal ranges from about 40 minutes shorter to 30 minutes longer than 24 hours. Because this "free running" cycle is not exactly 24 hours, it drifts with

218

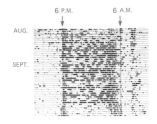

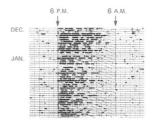

FIGURE 9–1   *Activity cycles for two normal rats over a 47-day period. Each horizontal line represents a 24-hour day, and each dark mark indicates spontaneous running activity. The rats were in total darkness each night from 6 P.M. to 6 A.M. [Richter, 1967]*

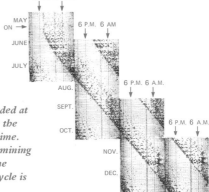

FIGURE 9–2   *Activity cycles for a rat blinded at ON (optic nerves were destroyed). Note that the period of activity drifts with respect to real time. In October this animal, with no way of determining whether it is light or dark, runs in the daytime rather than at night. However, this activity cycle is always nearly 24 hours. [Richter, 1967]*

respect to real time (Fig. 9-2) but it is still remarkably persistent and accurate over the long course of the experiment.

Since cyclic behavior continues in the absence of changes in light, it might be argued that some other physical phenomenon, such as humidity or atmospheric pressure, might be responsible. However, extensive studies by Richter [1967] have unearthed no evidence to support this "externalist" position. Rats housed next to each other may have rhythms that differ by almost 1 hour, so that after 12 days one animal is active while the other is not, although all external phenomena should be identical for both rats. Even more remarkably, Richter has found that the internal clock still runs even when the animal does not. For example, rats subjected to electric shock followed by nine days of inactivity resumed running at the predicted time. Also, the clock is impervious to almost every conceivable manipulation of internal environment, ranging from starvation to extensive brain lesions (Tables 9-1 and 9-2).

These and similar studies reveal that normal circadian rhythms are not controlled exclusively either by external stimulation, such as the day-

TABLE 9-1   *Endocrinological interferences that had no effect on clock.*

GLAND	MANNER PRODUCED	NO. OF RATS
Gonads	Gonadectomy	15
	Mating	17
	Pregnancy and lactation	15
Adrenals	Total removal	25
Hypophysis	Total removal	15
	Posterior lobectomy	8
Pineal	Total removal	26
Pancreas	Partial removal	4
	Alloxan injection	6
Thyroid	Thyroid powder in food	12
	Antithyroid compound	7
	Injection of I-131	4

TABLE 9-2   *Disturbances of the nervous system that had no effect on the clock.*

CONDITION	MANNER PRODUCED	NO. OF RATS
Anoxia	Nitrogen	8
Convulsions	Electroshock	18
	Caffeine—fourth ventricle	23
Tranquilization	Chlorpromazine	6
Poisoning	Lysergic acid diethylamide	11
	Serotonin	8
Anesthesia	Ether	20
	Pentobarbital	11
	Carbon dioxide	5
	Nitrous oxide	7
	Urethane	5
Intoxication	Alcohol	14
Deep sleep	Phenobarbital	5
	Barbital sodium	9
Acute stress	Forced swimming	32
	Restraint	5
	Electric shock	2
Hypo- and hyperactivity of autonomic nervous system	Atropine	7
	Acetylcholine	5
	Epinephrine	4
	Superior cervical ganglionectomy	16
Analgesia	Colchicine	8
Catalepsy	Bulbocapnine	7

220

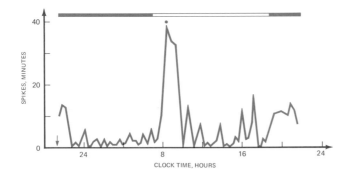

FIGURE 9-3   *Spike discharges generated by a circadian-rhythm neuron in the sea snail Aplysia. The animal had been conditioned previously to regular cycles of 12 hours light and 12 hours darkness, indicated by bar above. Note that although there was no light-dark cycle during the observation period, the cell's activity continued to follow the cycle to which it had been conditioned. [Strumwasser, 1965]*

night cycle, or by a "clock" located in the brain. It appears that each organism does indeed possess an internal clock which has a period of about 24 hours, but this clock is reset each day by external stimulation such as the day-night cycle. Thus the normal active period of a rat is during the dark, but the internal clock continues to cycle in the absence of light-dark cues (accomplished in the laboratory). In other words, circadian rhythms are the result of an interaction between an internal clock and external stimulation.

We know a great deal about the external forces which reset the biological clock, but where is this remarkable internal clock located? In extensive studies, Richter systematically destroyed various parts of the rat brain without affecting activity cycles. However, he did discover that lesions only in the hypothalamus, a tiny bit of tissue at the base of the brain (see Chapter 7), stopped the clock from running. Presumably some specialized group of nerve cells in this region comprise the clock. In fact even isolated single neurons possess the capability of exhibiting precise circadian rhythms. Strumwasser [1965] has found such cells in the marine snail *Aplysia californicus*. The intrinsic metabolic processes of such cells result in periodic changes in the rate of production of neuron firings (see Fig. 9-3). Such cells may act as "pacemakers," controlling the firing rates of large aggregates of other neurons so that their behavior mimics that of the pacemaker. A similar mechanism exists in heart tissue. Indeed, we owe our very lives to a relatively small number of cardiac pacemaker cells. Biological rhythms, then, have their origins in single cells, and circadian periodicities may be produced ultimately by pacemaker cells in the hypothalamus.

The most conspicuous of the circadian rhythms in man is the alternation between sleeping and waking. Many other circadian periodicities accompany this cycle. Body temperature drops to a low between 1 and 7 A.M.; oxygen consumption is highest during normal peak hours

221

of activity whether or not the activity actually occurs; the heartbeat is lowest between 10 P.M. and 7 A.M.; adrenal gland secretion is lower during sleep and rises prior to normal awakening; blood count, the number of red and white corpuscles, is minimal during the morning hours. These and other physiological rhythms exert a profound influence on behavior. The modern air traveler, who finds himself having to adjust to a time zone several hours different from that of his place of origin, may not only feel hungry at inappropriate local times, but he may also be somewhat sluggish and unable to perform well during waking hours even if he has had a good night's sleep. There has been real concern that pilots of intercontinental jets perform at less than peak efficiency in a new time zone and suitable precautions are now routinely employed. The physiological systems require a few days to adjust or be reset, and pilots may not fly again until the passage of two days.

It is apparently possible, although somewhat difficult, to alter the circadian period in man. Researchers have lived in caves for many days isolated from normal day-night cues. In one well-known study, two investigators attempted to live on a 28-hour day for a month. Richardson, the younger of the two, was able to reset his internal clock and adjust to the 28-hour day; Kleitman, 20 years his senior, had much more difficulty. Although the internal clock responsible for cyclic behaviors may be reset or entrained to some extent by external factors, this intrinsic mechanism acts autonomously in the absence of such factors. It is conceivable that in the early stages of evolution cyclic behavior was entirely governed by external forces such as the tides and day-night cycles and that these external rhythms were gradually internalized in the form of pacemaker cells. Whatever the origin of the biological clock, it is clear that the pervasive periodicity of the physical universe also characterizes the biological universe, and that behavior is inextricably intertwined with the periodicity of biological functions.

AROUSAL LEVEL

We generally think of sleeping and waking as distinct and separate states. However, at what point does a sleeping person become a waking person? Is drowsiness part of the waking or the sleeping state? There is now general agreement that a spectrum or continuum of arousal level spans the states of sleep and wakefulness, from a level of very high excitement or emotion down to the level of deep sleep. Thus there are various gradations of sleeping and waking. For example, a person who is poised to deal with an expected event, such as dashing across a busy street between onrushing cars, is far more than merely awake; he is highly aroused. If in crossing it appears that he may in fact be hit, arousal would increase to a state of intense emotional excitement.

Other gradations of arousal include alertness, relaxed wakefulness, drowsiness, light sleep, and deep sleep. We should bear in mind that

FIGURE 9–4   *Hypothetical relation between the degree of integrated behavior—the effective level of function—and the level of arousal. Note the characteristic inverted-U shape. [Hebb, 1966]*

these states of arousal are not distinct one from the other, like steps in a staircase, but rather, are adjacent positions along a ramp, with intense emotional excitement at one end and deep sleep at the other. We can easily move from one level to the next, as when we slip from relaxed wakefulness to drowsiness. Larger, sudden changes, as from quiet waking to deep sleep, do not occur except in unusual situations.

The relationship between arousal level and ability to perform in a well-integrated manner vis-à-vis the environment is not linear. Obviously our performance is poor when we are drowsy and much better when awake, but performance during the highest states of arousal or emotional excitement is not necessarily better than during quiet wakefulness. In fact there seems to be an optimum range of arousal for the performance of well-integrated behavior. This range consists of levels of moderate arousal during wakefulness. For example, on a task which requires the detection of a signal presented at unpredictable times performance is poor at both the low and high ends of the arousal continuum. This relationship is often referred to as the *inverted-U* function (see Fig. 9-4).

What is responsible for this odd relationship? The disorganizing effect of extreme arousal levels is apparently not a motor problem, for while it is true that the musculature of the sleeper is relaxed, that of an emotional person is well capable of particular discrete behaviors. We do not yet know to what extent the sensory systems are responsible, but physiological studies have indicated that sensory system processing of stimuli continues during sleep and, of course, high arousal. It is possible that sensory information processing is altered during extreme levels of arousal. However, there is more reason to believe that central integrative mechanisms in the brain which intercede between stimulus processing and motor behavior are responsible for the disorganizing effects of arousal-level extremes.

THE CEREBRAL CORTEX

The activity of the brain is reflected in actual minute electrical phenomena which are produced by the natural physiochemical processes that constitute brain functioning. The electroencephalogram (EEG) is one of these phenomena, and although its basis is still imperfectly under-

223

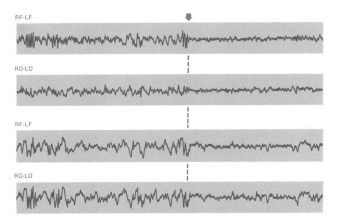

FIGURE 9-5   *EEG records showing the transition from sleep to wakeful-ness. The arrow indicates spontaneous awakening in the upper two tracings, and awakening caused by an imposed stimulus (sound) in the lower two tracings. RF-LF (right and left frontal) tracings were recorded over the frontal region of the brain; RO-LO (right and left orbital) tracings were taken over the posterior region.*

stood, it has proved to be a very valuable tool in the study of sleeping and waking (Chapter 7).

The EEG is recorded from the human cortex via scalp electrodes; in animals it can be recorded directly by electrodes placed on the cortex or in other brain regions. The EEG is characterized by somewhat rhythmic fluctuations in electrical waves which may range from very slow waves of a few tenths of a hertz (cycle per second) to faster waves in the range of 20 to 50 hertz. Biological periodicity is thus seen in the brain as well as in behavior. In general the slower brain waves are of greater amplitude than the fast waves, and the two types of EEG are described as *high-voltage slow* and *low-voltage fast*. However, the EEG is characterized by a single frequency only under restricted conditions; most records consist of a mixture of frequencies. The point is that there is a close relationship between the EEG and behavioral arousal level. Higher levels of behavioral arousal are accompanied by lower-voltage faster activity, while reduced arousal level, culminating in sleep, is associated with higher-voltage slower activity. This relationship between arousal and the EEG holds for mammals; less is known about nonmammals.

The human EEG differs from that of other animals, especially non-primates, in having a "richer" diversity. The alpha rhythm, characterized by a highly "pure" rhythm of 8 to 12 hertz, is a particularly interesting example. It occurs only during relaxed wakefulness, often only if the eyes are closed. It is easily blocked by an increase in arousal level produced simply by opening the eyes to admit visual stimuli, or by thinking about a simple addition problem, without any correlated overt behavior. When it is blocked, the alpha wave is replaced by lower-voltage faster waves, in accordance with the general principle that increased arousal is accompanied by low-voltage fast activity.

224

The transition from sleep to wakefulness is also accompanied by a shift from pronounced high-voltage slow activity to low-voltage fast activity, whether the awakening is caused by an imposed stimulus or is spontaneous (Fig. 9-5). This shift is often termed *cortical activation* or *desynchronization*. The transition from wakefulness to sleep occurs in stages which are characterized by differing EEG patterns. At stage 1, as waking merges into drowsiness, the alpha rhythm fades, and lower-voltage faster activity predominates. This stage is usually brief, and is an exception to the principle that low-voltage fast activity accompanies heightened arousal. At stage 2 short bursts of "spindles" invade the record. In stage 3 there are no spindles; the record is mainly slow waves in the range of 1 to 3 per second. Stage 4 has even larger and slower waves and constitutes a deep level of sleep. Body temperature and heart rate continue to decline, as they have since stage 1; respiration is slow and even, and wakening requires a fairly loud stimulus. The various sleep stages are summarized in Fig. 9-6.

The fact that the EEG of the cerebral cortex has a high correlation with behavioral arousal might indicate that the cortex itself is responsible for or constitutes the neural substrates of arousal level. One test of this hypothesis is to determine whether it is possible to dissociate the EEG and behavioral arousal. Can we demonstrate a "sleeping" animal with a "waking" EEG? As we shall see later, dreaming is an actual case in point; the EEG pattern is desynchronized, as is characteristic of the waking state. It has also proved possible to dissociate the EEG and arousal level by the use of drugs. The drug atropine, for example, produces a sleeplike

FIGURE 9-6   *The EEG record characteristic of the different stages of sleep in the human adult [Hartmann, 1967].*

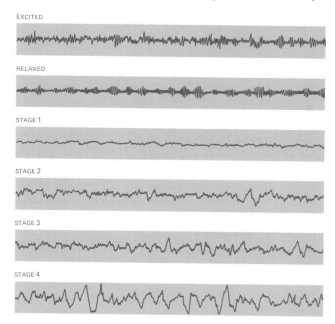

EXCITED

RELAXED

STAGE 1

STAGE 2

STAGE 3

STAGE 4

225

EEG dominated by slow waves while the animal is clearly awake and moving. Conversely, the drug eserine produces a behaviorally sleeping animal which has an activated or low-voltage fast EEG. These findings indicate that the cerebral cortex is not a likely candidate as the substrate of arousal level. One possibility is that the EEG of the cortex reflects the action of some subcortical arousal mechanism, and that the control of the cortical EEG by such a mechanism is disrupted by such pharmacological agents as atropine and scopolamine.

THE RETICULAR FORMATION OF THE BRAIN STEM

For many years the neural bases of sleep and wakefulness were considered to be controlled only by sensory stimulation received by the brain. This position seemed reasonable, for sensory stimulation is reduced during sleep because the eyes are closed and the body is reclining. It was thought that wakefulness was maintained by sensory "bombardment," which produced a sort of cerebral "tonus." This conception was changed overnight by a dramatic discovery.

Moruzzi and Magoun [1949] were investigating the action of subcortical mechanisms on spinal motor activity by stimulating the central core area of the brain stem, generally known as the *reticular formation* (see Chapter 8). They were also monitoring the cortical EEG of their subject, a lightly anesthetized cat. To their astonishment, stimulation of the reticular formation produced cortical desynchronization—that is, it changed the brain waves from high-voltage slow to low-voltage fast, mimicking the normal EEG changes from sleeping to waking. In a follow-up study Lindsley et al. [1949; 1950] found that lesions which destroyed portions of the reticular formation in cats caused them to remain asleep or in a coma, with accompanying sleeplike high-voltage slow cortical activity. Subsequent study indicated that the reticular stimulation and lesions had not impinged on the classical sensory systems, whose pathways lie in the lateral aspects of the brain stem. Here, then, was strong evidence for a subcortical arousal mechanism that was independent of the sensory systems.

However, since it is well established that sensory stimulation, such as a sudden noise, produces changes in arousal level, what about the role of the sensory systems? Lindsley found that when the sensory paths in the brain stem were destroyed without disturbing the reticular formation, this operation, which greatly reduced the amount of sensory input to the forebrain, did not produce sleep. Although such animals do not behave normally, their sleep-waking cycles are not grossly disrupted. Thus wakefulness does not depend on sensory input. Rather, it seems to depend on intrinsic brain mechanisms, including the reticular formation. How, then, does sensory stimulation normally cause arousal? The answer seems to be that while sensory information is processed in the sensory systems, if the sensory system analysis of the environment reveals a need

226

for arousal, signals are then sent to the reticular formation to trigger arousal. If there is no need for arousal—as with repeated unimportant sensory events such as the ticking of a clock—arousal signals are not sent to the reticular activating system.

Both extrinsic (sensory) and intrinsic (reticular formation) forces interact to produce arousal or determine arousal level, but like the internal biological clock, the intrinsic mechanisms can act in the absence of extrinsic control. This is to be expected if the reticular formation constitutes the neural substrate of arousal, whether arousal is indexed by wheel running, as in our rat studies above, or simply by observation of normal animal activity. At present, however, we still do not understand the relationships between the presumptive hypothalamic internal clock and the reticular formation. The evidence discussed above indicates that the reticular formation sustains the waking state; its stimulation causes awakening and its destruction produces coma or permanent sleep. Does this mean that sleep is produced by decreased activity of the reticular formation? In other words, is sleep simply the absence of waking, or, like waking, does it possess some neural substrates of its own? Extensive work during the past 20 years indicates that sleep is not at all a passive phenomenon, but has active neural substrates. One major finding has been that the reticular formation is not a unitary arousal system. Certain regions, principally the anterior portions, are especially important for increased arousal. Other, more posterior portions located just above the beginning of the spinal cord seem to be concerned with dearousal, or inducement of sleep. Electrical stimulation in this latter region can slow the cortical EEG from low-voltage fast to high-voltage slow and also produce behavioral sleep in cats. The same effects have been produced by stimulation of a region of the brain outside the reticular formation, just in front of the hypothalamus. Lesions of both these dearousing areas can produce insomnia or even complete inability to sleep, which culminates in death.

It has also been found that the onset of sleep can be conditioned. Wyrwicka et al. [1962] presented a tone followed by stimulation of the anterior hypothalamic "sleep" zone to waking cats. As expected, the brain stimulation produced sleep. However, after many pairings of the tone followed by stimulation, it was found that the tone alone, without brain stimulation, also produced sleep. However, this type of conditioning procedure is not necessary for sensory stimulation to produce sleep. The sleep-producing zones seem to be particularly sensitive to any rhythmic, periodic, or unchanging and highly predictable sensory events. Thus exposure to a monotonous environment to which we are not actively attending, such as a droning voice or the unchanging visual stimulation of a long drive on a superhighway, enhances sleep. So too does the steady rocking of a young child, which produces rhythmic vestibular input to the brain. Conversely, the arousal regions seem to detect surprising, unexpected, or suddenly changing aspects of the environment. Let the lecturer call a name or the mother suddenly stop rocking, and arousal is instantaneous.

227

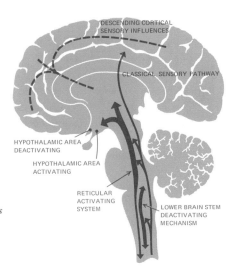

FIGURE 9–7   *Locations of the activating and deactivating regions in the hypothalamus and the reticular formation of the brain [Murray, 1965].*

Thus there are active sleep-producing regions in the brain as well as areas concerned with wakefulness. These occupy various regions of the primitive brain stem, from its lowest levels in the medulla to its highest levels in the hypothalamus, and appear to interact or balance each other in such a way as to determine arousal level from one moment to the next. If the higher region of the reticular system predominates then arousal level will increase and waking may be sustained; otherwise drowsiness and sleep may ensue. Both arousing and dearousing brain regions may be influenced by environmental stimuli, but in the absence of external stimulation they constitute wholly intrinsic mechanisms which regulate the degree of arousal at any given moment. These relationships are summarized in Fig. 9-7.

DREAMING

Dreams constitute vivid and intense experiences for many people. Other people believe that they never dream at all. Almost everyone is intrigued by the meanings of dreams, and dream interpretation has had a long and colorful, if somewhat varied, history. One of the most famous interpretations appears in the Old Testament, where Joseph took the king's dream of seven fat and seven lean cows as a sign that seven years of good harvest would be followed by seven years of famine. His premise was that dream content is symbolic, and that in this case cows symbolized years and the health of the cow symbolized the projected harvest. Freud also subscribed to the theory of symbolism. However, he considered dreams to be not a sign of future events, but an expression of wish fulfillment. According to his classical theory of dreams, we dream in symbolic terms in order to disguise a variety of anxiety-provoking wishes, ranging from minor discomforts to extremes,

228

such as the hope that a parent or sibling will suffer some misfortune [Freud, 1938, p. 211]:

> It is quite as simple a matter to discover the wish-fulfillment in several dreams which I have collected from healthy persons. A friend who was acquainted with my theory of dreams, and had explained it to his wife, said to me one day: "My wife asked me to tell you that she dreamt yesterday that she was having her menses. You will know what that means." Of course I know: if the young wife dreams that she is having her menses, the menses have stopped. I can well imagine that she would have liked to enjoy her freedom a little longer, before the discomforts of maternity began. It was a clever way of giving notice of her first pregnancy. Another friend writes that his wife had dreamt not long ago that she noticed milk-stains on the front of her blouse. This also is an indication of pregnancy, but not of the first one; the young mother hoped she would have more nourishment for the second child than she had for the first.

A series of controlled studies conducted by Hall [1959] showed little support for Freud's contention that dream symbols are disguises for anxiety-producing thoughts. However, Hall did conclude that dreams constitute thinking of a simplified nature, with symbols serving in place of words. Murray [1965] has suggested that complex mental activity cannot take place during sleep, and in his view Hall's conceptions are more likely correct. At the present time there is no general agreement on the approach to interpretation of dream content. However, there is considerable information on the dream state itself. In contrast to previous conceptions, we now know that dreaming is of biological importance and that everyone dreams every night.

THE REM SLEEP STATE

How can dreaming be studied objectively? As with studies of arousal level, the EEG has proved invaluable, particularly in conjunction with other measures such as eye movements and muscle tonus. It has long been known that the depth of sleep varies during the night. Aserinsky and Kleitman [1953] reported that during certain times, when the EEG has ascended to stage 1 (see Fig. 9-8), subjects often made many rapid movements of their eyes beneath closed lids, and that this activity occurred periodically throughout the night. Careful study revealed that the subjects were not briefly awake at these times, for among other indices these periods of rapid eye movement (REM) were accompanied by a complete loss of the slight muscle tonus which is ordinarily present during sleep and is always present during the waking state. When subjects were awakened during a REM period, in most cases they reported a dream. When they were awakened during other stages of sleep, in the absence of rapid eye movements, a significantly lower percentage of dreams were reported.

229

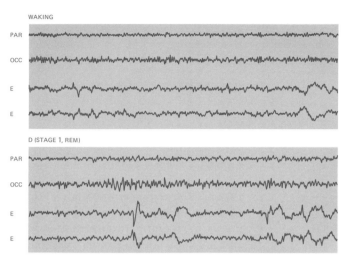

WAKING

PAR

OCC

E

E

D (STAGE 1, REM)

PAR

OCC

E

E

FIGURE 9–8   *Comparison of EEG activity and eye movements (E) during wakefulness and dreaming (REM sleep). The top two tracings of each set are EEG records from parietal (PAR) and occipital (OCC) locations on the scalp. Note in the lower two tracings of each set that the eyes move together (conjugate eye movements). [Hartmann, 1967]*

Further studies indicated that all subjects were in a REM state during sleep and that the REM periods occurred more than once. But what of the many people who apparently do not dream? Goodenough et al. [1959] compared people who considered themselves to be habitual dreamers with those who seldom if ever reported dreams. Both groups exhibited REM sleep periods. When awakened during REM periods the habitual dreamers reported dreams 93 percent of the time, and the non-dreamers 46 percent of the time. When awakened during non-REM periods the dreamers reported dreams on 53 percent of the occasions and the nondreamers on 17 percent. Thus, although there is a real difference in the amount of dreaming done by the two types of people, even "nondreamers" do dream. Why then, do some people believe that they do not dream? Apparently dreams may be forgotten during sleep, so that by the time they awaken the recollection may be gone. One significant point is that dreaming is much more likely to occur during the REM state. As it was also found to some extent during slow-wave sleep, it would seem that the REM state is not absolutely necessary for dreaming to occur. However, dream reports during non-REM periods may be due to the recall of dreams that occurred in preceding REM periods. This possibility needs to be explored.

The occurrence of the REM state during a night's sleep appears to follow a general sequence. Deep slow-wave sleep (stage 4) is usually reached soon after falling asleep, but about an hour later the progression of sleep from stage 1 to stage 4 is reversed; body movements are seen, and there is a short period of stage 1 sleep accompanied by rapid eye movements, lasting perhaps 10 minutes. This is generally followed by a progression back down to stage 4 sleep, but in an hour or so the cycle repeats itself. Generally the second and subsequent REM periods are longer than the first, lasting as long as 40 minutes. Stage 4 sleep may not occur again during the night, but stage 3 will be reached between REM periods. These events are summarized in Fig. 9-9. The long duration of REM periods strongly suggests, contrary to many popular beliefs, that dreaming does not occur in a mere instant of time.

Overall, adults spend about 20 percent of a night's sleep in the REM state; this amount decreases slightly after age fifty. Surprisingly, REM sleep is present in the newborn and is actually more prevalent during early childhood than during maturity. Infants spend up to 80 percent of their sleep in the REM state; young children up to the age of four are in REM sleep about 40 percent of the time; thereafter the adult pattern appears. If newborns spend most of their sleeping hours in the REM state, it follows that they must dream more than adults. But what do they dream about? Their cognitive capacity ought to be too unformed to sustain so much apparent visual imagery during sleep. We have no way of answering this question directly at present, but research with both human and nonhuman subjects has provided some clues about the function of dreaming and the REM state.

Asking whether animals dream is a bit like addressing the same question to the newborn; neither can verbalize his answer. Anyone who has closely observed a pet dog or cat during sleep has noticed occasional twitches of the limbs and vibrissae, as well as eye movements, perhaps accompanied by a few vocalizations. Studies, primarily with cats, have revealed that this behavior occurs during the REM state, which as in the human is accompanied by a complete loss of general muscle tonus and a change in the EEG from slow-wave sleep to a more desynchronized pattern. In fact the EEG in a sleeping cat appears identical to that when it is highly aroused during waking. Because of this odd conjunction of a "waking" EEG in a sleeping animal, it is termed *paradoxical sleep*. Paradoxical or REM sleep has been found in all mammals investigated, including apes, monkeys, sheep, dogs, and opossums; it has also been reported to appear for brief intervals, less than 1 minute, in birds.

Since the REM state is so prevalent in all mammals and manifests itself throughout life, it is bound to be of some biological significance.

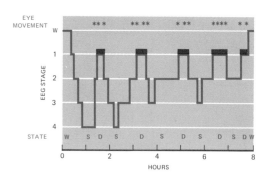

FIGURE 9-9 *A typical night of sleep— an average of many all-night recordings— in a young adult. Heavy lines indicate the dream (D) periods, characterized by a stage 1 EEG pattern and the presence of rapid conjugate eye movements.* [Hartmann, 1967]

SLEEP, DREAMING, AND ATTENTION

Studies of REM deprivation have indicated that it is in fact quite important. In both human and nonhuman studies subjects were selectively deprived of REM sleep by awakening them as soon as muscle tonus fell, which occurs just before the EEG changes (this is particularly easy to do in rabbits, because the only time that a rabbit's ears flop is during the REM state). Control subjects were awakened an equal number of times during slow-wave, non-REM sleep. This procedure was followed for several consecutive nights, and sleep patterns on subsequent recovery nights were then carefully analyzed. A universal finding was that REM deprivation resulted in a compensatory increase in the amount of time spent in REM sleep on subsequent nights. For example, Dement [1960] found an increase of about 60 percent in the amount of compensatory REM sleep. He also reported that many subjects deprived of REM sleep exhibited depression, anxiety, and other signs of disturbance, despite the fact that they had obtained 6 hours or so of normal slow-wave sleep per night. It is hoped that additional work will reveal possible relationships between some forms of behavioral pathology and sleep or disturbances in REM sleep.

THE REM AND SLOW-WAVE SLEEP STATES

It was earlier intimated that the state during which dreaming occurs might constitute a separate organismic state, quite distinct from the sleep state with which we are more familiar. The existence in animals of the REM state has permitted investigations of its neural bases and comparison with the substrates of slow-wave sleep. For example, the relative amount of time spent in REM and slow-wave sleep can be selectively altered by discrete brain stem lesions. Two separate areas appear to be involved—a portion of the central reticular formation and the raphé nuclei, which lie in the midline in the brain stem (see Chapter 8). Lesions of the central reticular region reduce or abolish REM sleep but not slow-wave sleep. Destruction of the raphé nuclei produces the opposite effect; it reduces slow-wave sleep without disturbing REM sleep. Electrical stimulation of the reticular region can produce the REM state if the animal is in slow-wave sleep. Thus the central reticular region seems to underlie the REM state, while the raphé nuclei are associated with slow-wave sleep.

Additional evidence comes from studies of brain amines and their manipulation by pharmacological agents. As mentioned in Chapter 8, discrete brain amine systems have been found by the use of elegant histochemical techniques. At this point we are particularly interested in two systems—a *catecholaminergic system* which originates in the central reticular region and contains large amounts of norepinephrine (noradrenaline) and a *serotonergic (5 HT) system* which originates in the raphé nuclei. Drugs which are known to increase the amount of available norepinephrine also increase the amount of time spent in the REM state. Thus injection of a precursor of norepinephrine, such as DOPA, produces more REM sleep. Conversely, drugs which increase the available serotonin also increase the amount of slow-wave sleep and reduce the amount spent in REM sleep. Thus injecting 5 HTP, a precursor of serotonin, produces an increase in the amount of slow-wave sleep. If both norepinephrine and serotonin are reduced by the injection of reserpine, which depletes reserves of all brain amines, then both the REM and slow-wave states are reduced resulting in a chronic waking state until the reserpine has been metabolized.

If REM differs from slow-wave sleep, is it "lighter" or "deeper" sleep? Animal studies have shown that the level of brain activity is much higher during REM than slow-wave sleep. In fact the number and rate of single-neuron activity approaches that seen during excited wakefulness. There are other indications that REM is a period of intense inner arousal; blood pressure rises, heart and respiratory rate increases, and in males of all ages penile erection occurs. This is not related to dreams having sexual content, but is part of a state of general high excitability. We have already noted that the EEG during the REM state tends to be desynchronized as in waking. From these indices it would seem that REM is "light" or "aroused" sleep, but in contrast to these indices of increased arousal, there are indications that the subject is quite deeply asleep. The threshold for awakening by auditory stimulation or direct stimulation of the reticular formation in cats is increased. Most strikingly, low arousal is suggested by the general reduction of muscle tonus, including depression of reflexes.

Actually, the REM state appears to be a condition of intense arousal in which the person is decoupled from his environment. Awakening by environmental stimulation is more difficult than during slow-wave sleep, and the absence of muscle tonus renders the dreamer unable to react to environmental contingencies. Some authorities consider the REM state to represent one of extreme attention or concentration to stored images, etc. Whether one calls the REM state "deep" sleep or "active" sleep, it is qualitatively different from both normal waking and slow-wave sleep.

The study of sleeping and dreaming presents more questions than answers, as is typical in any new field. Such simple questions as "Why do we sleep?" and "Why do we dream?" prove to be simple only in sentence construction. While we have no definitive answers to either of these questions, we have at least learned how to characterize the states to which they refer and how to investigate these states experimentally. It is clear that the understanding of behavior requires an understanding of all states of consciousness. The objective study of sleeping and dreaming promises to shed light on much of our behavior during the one-third of our lives we spend in the nonwaking state. From the general *states* of consciousness, we now turn to a finer level of awareness—attention.

233

ATTENTION

Like sleeping and waking, attention is a common part of our everyday lives. Any attempt to understand behavior must include a consideration of attention. We cannot attend to everything at once, and what we do attend to defines the scope of our behavior at any one moment. Although many people claim to be able to concentrate on several things simultaneously, full comprehension of all of them is extremely rare. There are limits to the amount of information we can process at any one time.

Scientific attempts to cope with attention date back to the middle of the nineteenth century, but they have much older roots in philosophy. The major issue for a long time was how sensory impressions reach consciousness. As we have noted, such introspective approaches proved unsatisfactory, and for many years there was little progress. An additional problem was the use of the term "attention" to refer to different phenomena. Whereas some investigators emphasized the clarity of sense objects in consciousness, others were more concerned about the selective aspects of attention. These differing concepts are evident in statements by the leading proponents of each view. According to Edward Titchener [1908]:

It seems to be beyond question that the problem of attention centres in the fact of sensible clearness . . .

and according to William James [1890]:

Millions of items of the outward order are present to my senses which never properly enter into my experience. Why: Because they have no *interest* for me. *My experience is what I agree to attend to.*

Clarity in consciousness was finally discarded as an important aspect of attention as psychology became more objectively oriented toward behavior. The selective aspects of attention did survive, perhaps because objective methods of determining stimulus selection were developed. Before we consider how attention is measured, however, let us consider the objects of this attention.

THE OBJECTS OF ATTENTION

In his classical consideration of attention William James distinguished two general types of things to which attention could be directed—objects of sense, or stimuli, and ideal or represented objects, our thoughts, ideas, and memories. An objective investigation of the stimulus properties that may be selected has proved to be a far easier task than that of studying ideational attention. This is because stimulus parameters, such as wavelength, shape, and tone frequency, can be directly manipulated by an experimenter; thoughts, ideas, and memories cannot at present be

234

systematically varied and measured as easily. Although objects of sense and objects of the intellect are both valid objects of attention and demand study, we shall restrict our consideration here largely to stimuli as objects of attention.

Any designated stimulus is of necessity somewhat complex. For example, suppose a person is trained simply to press a button whenever he hears a tone pip of 1000 hertz. The occurrence of the tone is made unpredictable, so that when the subject responds correctly we are fairly certain that it is not because of a lucky guess. If he does well—responds correctly most of the time—we may say that he paid attention to the 1000-hertz tone pip. Surprisingly, this interpretation may be incorrect. The subject may in fact have been responding to the change in the ambient stimulus environment rather than specifically to the auditory stimulus. Or even if he had been attending to the fact that the stimulus was auditory, he might not have paid attention to its pitch at all. The problem is that three different stimulus categories are involved in this situation. In the presentation of a 1000-hertz tone pip there is a change in the environment, a stimulus modality (auditory), and a *modality-specific attribute* (tone pitch). Attention to each of these would entail three responses—"Something happened"; "I heard something"; "I heard a 1000-hertz tone."

In addition, two other categories may be noted—locus or the place in the environment from which the stimulus emanated; stimulus pattern, such as shape or tune. Moreover, each of these five dimensions may vary in *intensity* and *duration*. In this case the tone pips must have had a locus in space, and they certainly possessed an intensity and duration. If a sequence of pips had been given, producing a pattern, then *all* of the stimulus categories would have been thoroughly confounded. Unless we untangle these various stimulus categories, we have no way to determine just what particular stimulus attribute constitutes the object of attention at a given time.

There is one last category which might serve as the basis of stimulus selection or attention, stimulus novelty. A novel stimulus may be regarded as one which is different from expected stimulation. Thus novelty is not properly a physical attribute of a stimulus, as are the dimensions above. Rather, novelty is a property of a stimulus in situations in which an organism makes some comparison between the actual stimulus and some memory or representation of other stimuli. Novelty thus involves both of James' categories of the objects of attention, sensory and ideational. As such, it may someday serve as an entrée into investigations of attention to memories, ideas, thoughts, and similar represented objects.

As an illustration of attention to novelty, consider the behavior of a dog placed in a strange environment, such as a new cage or yard. Intense exploration may ensue, indicated by locomotion, sniffing, looking about, and so forth. In this case we cannot be quite sure just what novel aspects are being attended, although we may infer these (perhaps incorrectly) from a casual observation of the animal's behavior.

235

A more systematic approach to novelty is illustrated by a now classical experiment performed by Sharpless and Jasper [1956]. Sleeping cats were presented with a 500-hertz tone, which promptly caused them to awaken. Both behavioral and EEG indices of arousal were measured. After the cats fell back to sleep, the same stimulus was presented again, and again it caused arousal, but of a shorter duration than on the first trial. As the procedure was continued, the cats stayed awake for progressively shorter periods, until after about 30 trials the stimulus produced no effect on either behavior or the EEG. When it was certain that this stimulus had lost its power to arouse, a new frequency, 100 hertz, was presented, and this caused prompt arousal. In this context the 100-hertz tone was considered novel not just by the experimenter, but also by the cats. Novelty was established by noting that the new tone produced arousal in a selective manner, for if the following trial consisted of the original 500-hertz tone, no arousal took place. The cats clearly regarded the 100-hertz stimulus as different from the oft-repeated and expected 500-hertz stimulus. Of course a stimulus that is initially novel will lose its novelty by repeated presentation—that is, through *habituation*. Thus continued presentation of the 100-hertz stimulus also resulted in an absence of response. However, a novel 1000-hertz stimulus could still cause arousal (Fig. 9-10). This procedure was repeated until the cats were not aroused by any tone stimulus and no longer responded to auditory stimulation. Arousal could be induced promptly, however, by lightly touching their fur. Although auditory stimulation was nonnovel, tactile stimulation was novel.

In this case responses to novelty served to determine which of the stimulus categories was being selected by the cats. Selective arousal to the 100-hertz stimulus showed that pitch had been selected. When no auditory stimulus caused arousal but tactile stimulation did, the animals were attending to the stimulus modality, to tactile versus auditory stimulation. Many other tests or measures of the objects of attention, some considerably more elaborate, have been devised.

THE MEASUREMENT OF ATTENTION

We generally believe that someone who "looks" attentive is attentive. By "looks" we are actually referring to general posture, facial expression, and head and eye orientation. Of course if this were an adequate index of attention, we would not be able to succeed in little social deceptions, as when we try to appear interested in the conversation of a bore at a party while thinking of something else (attending to ideational objects). As we all know, these deceptions do succeed. Even if it can be said that the attentive "look" is an index of attention, the object of this attention is clearly an unknown factor. Attempts to measure attention on the basis of the attentive "look" have had the same insufficient and uncertain results in laboratory studies of attention in animals. For example, in a classical study Hernández-Peón et al. [1956] attempted

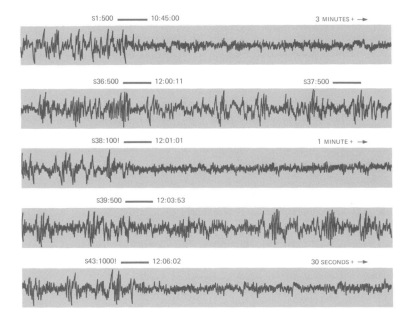

FIGURE 9-10   *EEG from the cerebral cortex of a normal cat showing typical habituation of the arousal reaction to a 500-hertz tone. In the first tracing the response to the first presentation of the 500-hertz tone is S1:500; the solid bar shows the occurrence of the stimulus in hours, minutes, and seconds (10:45:00). The second tracing shows the thirty-sixth (S36) and thirty-seventh (S37) trials and succeeding tracings show responses to a novel tone (!) of 100-hertz (S38:100!), a repetition of the habituated tone (S39:500), and another novel tone (S43:1000!). The duration of the activation in each trial is indicated at the right. [Sharpless and Jasper, 1956]*

to investigate brain processing of stimuli during attention and inattention by placing a jar of mice in front of a cat and noting its clear interest in the mice. They assumed that the cat was paying attention only to visual cues provided by the mice and was inattentive in all other sensory systems since the mice were in an enclosed vessel. However, they failed to consider that the cat may also have been listening intently for mouse noises and attempting to detect mouse odor simply because of the absence of these normal cues. Even in human studies it has been shown that posture and receptor orientation do not guarantee attention to a given stimulus. In studies of visual signal detection it has been demonstrated that even when the signal was clearly focused and fixated, there could be a failure to detect it. Although proper orientation of the eyes may be necessary for attention to a visual stimulus, it does not guarantee such attention; the subject may still daydream.

A more objective index of attention, since it reduces the need for inferences by the experimenter, entails having the subject perform a discrete response in order to be able to view a particular stimulus. These *observing responses* were first employed by Wyckoff [1952], who trained pigeons to press a treadle to produce one of two possible cues—a

237

red or a green light, each of which required different types of responses—in order to obtain a reward of grain. The cue produced by the observing response may also be one that is directly rewarding, as in the case of monkeys who learned to open a panel in order to view laboratory activities [Butler, 1953; Butler and Harlow, 1954]. The observing response can also be used to index stimulus *saliency*, the amount of interest a stimulus has for a particular species. The number of panel openings and duration of viewing on each occasion have been used as such a measure of interest in monkeys. In one study monkeys were found to prefer watching a movie to viewing a moving electric train [Harlow and Mc-Clearn, 1954].

Of course not all attentive behavior includes an overt observing response. For example, particular parts of a stimulus array which is presented for only a few milliseconds (in a device called a *tachistoscope*) can be attended even though the stimulus exposure is too brief to permit a discrete observing response or visual fixation of a given part of the display. Also, it is clearly possible to switch attention from one voice to another without moving one's head. Thus, while the occurrence of a discrete observing response does indicate that the subject is selecting some sensory stimulus, the absence of such a response does not guarantee that he is not appropriately attentive.

In so far as we need not exhibit gross or overt observing responses in order to be attentive, how is the psychologist able to determine the objects of attention? We discussed an appropriate method earlier, the task involving detection of a tone pip which is presented occasionally, on a schedule which precludes correct guessing. Recall that the subject was required to signify the occurrence of the signal by pressing a button—that is, by a discrete behavioral response. This widely used technique is referred to as a *vigilance task*. It requires the subject to monitor his environment continuously. Inattention is indexed by a failure to press the button when the signal occurs. Of course the task can be used with any modality. In one well-known study Mackworth [1950] required subjects to detect a double jump in the movement of the second hand of a clock. This jump of 2 seconds instead of 1 was programmed by the experimenter to occur infrequently, only about 24 times per hour. Mackworth found a performance decrement; there were fewer correct detections after the first half hour. This vigilance decrement has been found repeatedly in a variety of tasks and seems to represent a general loss of attention with time. The implications of these findings are of considerable practical significance, as many industrial and military jobs entail the continuous monitoring of displays and detection of unscheduled signals. In fact much experimental vigilance research grew out of concern about performance decrements exhibited by radar operators.

What causes the loss of vigilance? In a study of radar detection by military personnel it was found that vigilance decrement did not occur if a superior officer entered the radar room at unpredictable intervals. However, this finding does not indicate that vigilance decrements are caused by malingering. Rather, the loss of vigilance is probably due to a lowering of general arousal level during exposure to repetitive monotonous stimuli which have little significance. In the radar task these stimuli were the continuous sweeping of an illuminated beam; in the clock task they were the 1-second hand movements. Any significant change in the subject's environment, whether it is the entrance of an officer or a rest period every half hour, will produce an increase in the subject's general arousal level and a consequent improvement in his detection performance.

Up to this point we have been concerned with attention to relatively simple stimuli and have not asked about the limits of attention. How many things or stimulus dimensions can we attend to at the same time? What is the breadth of selection? One powerful and commonly used technique entails deliberately confounding two stimulus categories during initial training and later separating them to determine whether one, the other, or both were attended. For example, rats may be trained to discriminate between a white horizontal rectangle (rewarded) and a black vertical rectangle (not rewarded). In this situation, stimulus brightness (black or white) is mixed with stimulus orientation (vertical or horizontal). After training to some criterion of correct performance, which may require many sessions, the animal is given a second task in which brightness and orientation are separated; for example, the white horizontal rectangle (still rewarded) may be paired with a black horizontal rectangle. In this way the category of stimulus orientation is removed. If the animal continues to respond correctly to the white rectangle, this clearly indicates that he has been attending to stimulus brightness, not orientation. Should he perform poorly with the orientation cue removed, it would be taken to mean that he had been attending to stimulus orientation more than to brightness. Similarly, other animals trained on the original task could be tested for attention to brightness by pairing a white horizontal rectangle (still rewarded) with a white vertical rectangle. Animals which are tested under both conditions and exhibit a decrement on neither would have been attending to both dimensions (Fig. 9-11).

For this type of discrimination task rats do not attend to both dimensions. In fact it appears that the more an animal attends to one,

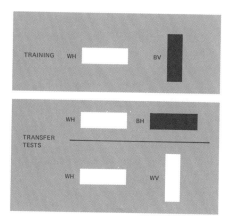

FIGURE 9-11 *Experiments used to determine which aspect of a stimulus is attended by an animal. After training on a horizontal white bar (WH) versus a vertical black bar (BV), the animals are tested on white versus black horizontal bars and horizontal versus vertical white bars. If the animal attends to stimulus orientation during training, he will respond equally to both stimuli in the first test but will respond to the horizontal bar in the second. If, however, he attends to color or brightness, he will respond to the white bar in the first test but equally to the two stimuli in the second.*

the less he attends to the other [Sutherland, 1968]. However, this particular finding does not imply that the rat or any other organism can attend to only one stimulus dimension at a time. The breadth of attention may vary with the situation. For example, Bruner et al. [1955] found that high levels of arousal, caused by extensive food deprivation, reduced the number of cues learned by rats in solving a spatial discrimination problem. Breadth of attention thus may depend on situational variables rather than the particular task and must be determined empirically. It cannot be stated unequivocally that attending to one stimulus dimension necessitates ignoring all others.

The general technique we have been discussing is often referred to as a *transfer test*, because it examines whether or not initial learning transfers to a later task. Complete or extensive transfer of a particular stimulus category is taken as evidence of attention to that stimulus attribute; failure to transfer indicates that the attribute in question was not attended. Note that transfer tests cannot indicate the actual object of attention during the subject's initial response; this information is acquired later during the second transfer task. There is one technique, however, that does provide an immediate index of the object of attention—that in which the subject tracks continuously a stimulus which is moving in space or time. An example of tracking in space might be holding a pointer in contact with a moving target. Tracking in time involves auditory stimulation, as in listening to a recorded message and repeating what is heard. In this case the tracking behavior is referred to as *shadowing*, because the repetition follows the stimulus message.

In research on the limits of human information-processing capacity dichotic selective listening experiments have been used, in which different messages are presented to the two ears simultaneously, and the subject is instructed to shadow the message to one ear. Attention to this message is indicated by success in shadowing. Extensive studies by Treisman [1964] and others have shown that very little, if any, of the unattended message is understood. In fact if the unattended message is given in a foreign language, the subject may not even be aware of this fact. This might suggest that sensory information to the unattended ear does not get processed in the unattended auditory system. However, if the foreign language is actually a translation of the message given to the attended ear, bilingual subjects come to realize this fact, even though subjects unfamiliar with this language will not even realize another language is being spoken. The realization by the bilingual subjects indicates that the unattended message must have been processed, not blocked in the auditory system. Further evidence of this is that words of importance, such as the subject's name or emotion-laden terms, given to the unattended ear in a known language will be recognized and reported. Simple stimuli such as tone pips interjected into the unattended message will also be reported. Moreover, if words appear in the unattended message which have a high probability of appearing in the attended message, they will be incorporated into the shadowed response, sometimes even without the awareness of the subject.

240

All these findings indicate that while information to the unattended ear seems to be blocked, in fact some analysis must take place. Simple or crude stimulus properties, such as tone frequency, are not blocked, and terms of relevance to the person or the attended message get through. It would seem that the meaning of the unattended message and its verbal components is analyzed and then rejected if found to be uninteresting. It is as if the unattended ear does in fact "listen" all of the time, so that interesting items can be attended to by the subject and not get lost. This is similar to the process that seems to be taking place during sleep. Thus it would appear that the sensory systems can continue to process information whether the total information load is low, as during sleep, or high, as during selective dichotic listening. Such a mechanism makes very good sense from an adaptive standpoint, in that it would enable the organism to attend to environmental events of significance even when it is not properly prepared for or expecting them.

We have seen that attention is measured in many ways. In all cases, however, stimulus selection is indexed by allowing the experimenter to determine what stimuli or stimulus aspects are selected by the subject. In other words, the techniques for assessing attention tell us more than the mere fact that a person or animal is attentive; they permit specification of just what he is attending to. For example, in the discrimination-learning experiment it was quite obvious that the rats were attending to some stimulus; the transfer tests revealed whether they were attending to, or selecting, stimulus brightness or stimulus orientation. When a rat selects brightness his behavior may be said to be controlled by that stimulus dimension. Attention to a stimulus, then, is evidenced by the behavior in which it results. In this respect stimulus *selection* is synonymous with stimulus *control*.

We have seen that it is possible to find out what aspects of the environment are selected or attended by an organism. Since an organism may be said to be at some level of arousal at any given moment, how are attention and arousal related? Common sense tells us that

ATTENTION AND AROUSAL

in order to be attentive, to behave quite selectively when presented with the barrage of stimuli which the environment offers, we must be awake, even moderately aroused. Is this actually the case? Does attention imply an existing background of wakefulness? One way to answer this question is to find out if attention is possible during sleep.

Several studies have indicated selective discrimination during sleep. Rowland [1957] conditioned cats to respond to one tone and to ignore a second tone while awake. These two stimuli were then presented while the cats were asleep, with some striking results; even during sleep the cats showed behavioral or EEG changes to the significant tone, but not to the ignored tone. Oswald et al. [1960] found that during sleep

241

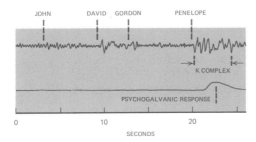

JOHN   DAVID   GORDON   PENELOPE

K COMPLEX

PSYCHOGALVANIC RESPONSE

0   10   20

SECONDS

FIGURE 9–12   *Arousal value of a significant stim-*
ulus. EEG activity is shown for a sleeping human
subject during a period in which names were called
out at irregular intervals of 4 to 8 seconds. The
names John!, David!, Gordon! have little effect on
the subject's EEG and provoke no psychogalvanic
responses, while the name of his beloved Penelope!
provokes a group of large waves forming a "K com-
plex" in the EEG and a surge of electric potential
at the palm. [Oswald, 1966]

people showed selective EEG responses to their own names versus other names (Fig. 9-12). Granda and Hammack [1961] trained people in the waking state to avoid shock following tone presentation by making some overt response. This behavior, including the pressing of a switch to avoid shock, also occurred during non-REM sleep. In addition, there is the study discussed earlier, in which sleeping cats exhibited selective arousal to novel stimuli. These and other findings support the idea that selective attention during sleep is possible. This is common knowledge to any mother, who may sleep soundly through a thunderstorm, but awakens promptly the minute her child whimpers.

Behavior during sleep is quite crude when compared to the waking state. The body musculature is quite relaxed in slow-wave sleep and actually inhibited during the REM state. Behavior is ordinarily restricted merely to awakening or to an EEG change which indicates a shift to a lighter stage of sleep. Continual integrated interaction with the environment is rare. Drowsiness and sleep, whether caused by boredom or prior sleep loss, invariably result in a performance decrement on vigilance and other tasks which require continuous scanning of the environment (performance during sleep in the Granda and Hammack study could be maintained only by the threat of shock). Learning during genuine sleep is rare, if it occurs at all; the exception is learning not to awaken to repeated stimuli which have no particular significance or urgency—that is, habituation of arousal.

The quality of sleep behavior is clearly lower than that of waking behavior. Nevertheless, the fact that selective attention does occur during sleep indicates that attention is not a property exclusive to one level of arousal, wakefulness. This distinction between arousal and attention implies that they may be served by different brain mechanisms.

242

The simplest encounter that an organism can have with its environment is to be presented with any environmental change—that is, with a single stimulus. If that stimulus is novel, a complex series of physiological reactions ensues. These constitute the *orienting reflex*, first identified and named by the great Russian physiologist Pavlov [1927]. Changes occur in several systems. The pupils dilate; the head turns toward the source of stimulation; ongoing behavior is temporarily arrested and general muscle tonus rises; there is vasoconstriction in the limbs and concomitant vasodilation in the head, which sends more blood to the brain; respiration and heartbeat are briefly interrupted; and the EEG exhibits activation (lower-voltage faster waves). These changes are illustrated in Fig. 9-13.

The orienting reflex constitutes a physiological syndrome which enhances preparedness on the part of the organsim to interact with its environment. It is not defensive in nature, but neutral. (In fact if the novel stimulus is noxious or too intense, a defensive syndrome will be elicited which differs from the orienting reflex in several ways, including vasoconstriction in both the limbs and head.) The form of the orienting reflex is constant, regardless of the particular nature of the stimulus which elicited it; thus this reflex constitutes a general reaction to un-

FIGURE 9–13 *The orienting reflex. When a sudden, novel, or significant stimulus is presented to a human subject (arrow), the pupil dilates, respiration is temporarily arrested, the heartbeat slows temporarily, muscle tone (EMG) increases, blood flow in the limbs decreases but blood flow in the head increases, the EEG shifts to a low-voltage fast aroused pattern, and the subject turns his head toward the source of stimulation. [after Sokolov, 1963]*

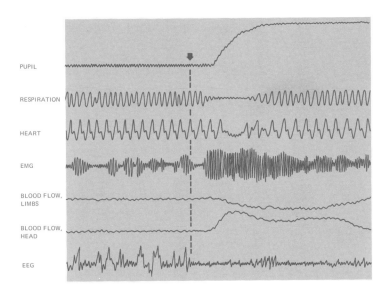

PUPIL

RESPIRATION

HEART

EMG

BLOOD FLOW, LIMBS

BLOOD FLOW, HEAD

EEG

expected or novel stimulation, and as such may serve as an objective index of attention.

We have discussed selective EEG desynchronization in cats in response to different tones. These EEG changes simply constituted one aspect of the orienting reflex. This reflex habituates with repeated presentation of stimuli which lack significance. Thus as an originally novel stimulus recurs, it loses its novelty and also its ability to elicit an orienting reflex. However, habituation does not take place if the stimulus in question bears some particular meaning for an individual: although you have heard your own name called thousands of times, its sight or sound still elicits an orienting reflex. The orienting reflex occurs during both sleeping and waking, and the changes, such as EEG activation, may be very subtle. You may not be aware of all the physiological changes taking place in your body during an orienting reflex, but they are there nevertheless.

In so far as the orienting reflex comprises a basic attentive "attitude" on the part of the body, its neural mechanisms are of particular interest. There is evidence that the part of the reticular formation which underlies increased arousal is responsible. Thus electrical stimulation of the anterior reticular formation produces the orienting reflex. This proposition seems reasonable because both increased arousal and the orienting reflex comprise general, rather than specific, reactions on the part of organisms.

The general sequence which begins with a novel stimulus and culminates in attention appears to be as follows. The stimulus is received and processed by the appropriate sensory system. After the nature of the stimulus is analyzed it is compared with memories of other stimuli in light of the present environment and state of the organism. If the stimulus is found to be either particularly significant or novel, signals are sent to the activating reticular formation, which produces both a general increase in arousal level (as evidenced by EEG changes) and the autonomic and somatic changes of the orienting reflex in preparation for environmental interaction. If the stimulus is found to lack significance, activating signals are not forthcoming. In fact signals may be sent to those parts of the brain stem which produce slow-wave sleep, actually making arousal less probable. This may explain why monotonous or repetitive stimulation often produces drowsiness and sleep.

It might seem from this sequence of events that attention, as indexed by the orienting reflex, and arousal have the same brain mechanisms. However, we have disregarded the selective aspects of attention, including the analysis and decision by sensory systems, which precede and may even initiate general arousal and the orienting reflex. Thus, while it is possible that the reticular formation is responsible for general aspects of attention, it is not the prime mover, but rather, an effector system. The discrete processes which permit us to discriminate among stimuli and attend selectively to particular aspects of our environment must have other brain substrates.

244

According to the schema outlined above, attention to a stimulus must involve sensory system analysis, but what of inattention or the ignoring of some stimuli? If a child fails to answer his mother's call to the dinner table while he is watching television, has he processed her voice and understood her words? His mother may think so, but some authorities believe otherwise. They hold the position that ignored stimuli can be blocked by inhibition in an unattended sensory modality, and that this blocking can take place at a peripheral level of the sensory system near the receptor, prior to any complex analysis of the stimulus. Evidence for this position comes from two types of studies.

Hernández-Peón et al. [1956] recorded evoked potentials in the cat auditory system which were produced by click stimulation. They found that when the cat viewed a mouse the amplitude of the evoked potentials decreased, and that when it lost interest in the mouse the amplitude was restored to its normal value. They concluded from these findings that when the cat looked at the mouse it was not listening, and was in fact blocking input to its auditory system, evidenced by smaller evoked potentials, and that after the cat lost interest in the mouse auditory function was restored. However, subsequent studies showed that evoked potential was reduced only when the cat *moved* while looking at the mouse, and not if it remained motionless [Dunlop et al., 1965]. Other studies showed that the reduction in evoked-potential amplitude was due to contraction of minute muscles located in the middle ear, rather than to inhibition of the auditory system. These tiny muscles contract during movement, reducing our ability to hear movements produced by our own bodies; they also slightly reduce the intensity of all acoustic stimuli. Since the auditory system evoked potentials were slightly reduced only when the cats moved, this reduction does not indicate that sensory inhibition occurs in one modality during attention to another modality.

The second type of study has concerned habituation of evoked potentials during the repetitive presentation of unimportant stimuli. Once again it was proposed that sensory inhibition occurs during inattention, in this case during inattention produced by monotonous stimulation [Hernández-Peón, 1960]. There has been an active controversy about whether sensory system potentials which are produced by repetitive stimulation do indeed show a systematic decline in amplitude—that is, habituation—and the issue is not yet completely settled. However, in several studies which included careful control of the effective intensity of the stimulus and careful measurement of evoked-potential amplitude, habituation of sensory system potentials has not been found [Worden and Marsh, 1963].

Most studies have not actually measured the attentive behavior of their subjects while evoked potentials were recorded. In one study,

245

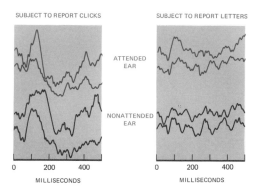

SUBJECT TO REPORT CLICKS

SUBJECT TO REPORT LETTERS

ATTENDED
EAR

NONATTENDED
EAR

0   200   400

0   200   400

MILLISECONDS

MILLISECONDS

FIGURE 9–14   *Average brain potentials evoked by sound (click)*
stimuli from the scalp of a human subject under various conditions
of attention. The subject was given both clicks and letters to each
ear and asked to attend to one ear and not the other. In all cases the
records show the brain responses to clicks, and each tracing is the
average of 50 individual responses. The brain responses to clicks are
large in both the attended and unattended ears. The brain responses
to clicks delivered to the two ears are much smaller when the sub-
ject is asked to report only the letters. [Smith et al., 1970]

however, auditory system evoked potentials showed no evidence of habituation, but the magnitude of eye movements elicited by auditory stimulation to one ear did show habituation [Weinberger et al., 1969]. Thus
there is no evidence in support of the proposal that sensory system habituation underlies behavioral habituation. Much further investigation
is needed, but at this point it seems unlikely that sensory system inhibition, particularly at primary sensory nuclei, is responsible for either
attending to or ignoring stimuli.

HUMAN EVOKED POTENTIALS

We saw in Chapter 7 that evoked potentials produced by stimuli can
be recorded from the human scalp. These differ from the evoked potentials discussed above in that they occur hundreds rather than tens
of milliseconds after the stimulus. In addition, these long-latency human
evoked potentials probably do not represent primary stimulus processing within one of the classical sensory systems, but are more likely
the result of some complex associational analyses. Whatever their neural
basis, they are of interest in the study of attention. Unlike the negative findings in nonhuman studies, human evoked potentials recorded
during attention have shown that these potentials definitely do change
in relation to selective perception or behavior. The human experiments generally employ some type of vigilance or detection task in
order to ascertain that the subject is or is not paying attention to a
particular stimulus, and evoked potentials are then compared under

246

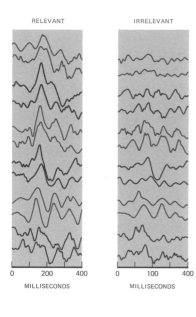

RELEVANT   IRRELEVANT

0   200   400   0   100   400
MILLISECONDS   MILLISECONDS

FIGURE 9–15   *Effects of attention on scalp-recorded brain potentials evoked by visual stimuli (light flash). Flashes are presented to the two eyes, but brain responses are recorded only for flashes given in the left visual field, and each tracing is the average of 100 individual responses. The evoked potentials in this left visual field are substantially larger if the subject is attending to the left flash—he is required to count to himself the number of left flashes to avoid an electric shock (relevant). When he is required to count to himself the number of flashes on the right in order to avoid shock, the brain potentials for the left flashes (irrelevant) are much smaller. [Eason et al., 1969]*

conditions of attention and inattention to that stimulus. The general results, which have been successfully repeated in many laboratories with different types of stimuli, indicate that the evoked potential produced by the stimulus is larger during attention. For example, Smith et al. [1970] studied the effect of attending to clicks in a selective-listening task by having subjects press a button when they heard a click. When they did so a particular wave in the evoked potential was enhanced, but when they failed to attend to the clicks no enhancement occurred (Fig. 9-14). Similar results have been found by Eason et al. [1969] in tasks based on visual stimulation. Some of these effects are shown in Fig. 9-15.

In summary, it appears that the neural substrates of attention include both general and specific components. The general aspects, which include elicitation of the orienting reflex and increased arousal, may be mediated by the activating part of the reticular formation. The specific components, which include analysis and decisions regarding the actual stimuli to be attended or ignored, involve sensory system processing, probably at all levels, from the receptor and peripheral relay nuclei up to and including the cerebral cortex. Evidence to date suggests that there are no significant changes in stimulus processing at peripheral levels of the sensory systems that could account for behavioral attention. However, experiments with human subjects definitely indicate that cortical events, related in some as yet unknown way to sensory system analysis, do change as a function of attention.

247

SUMMARY

The circadian rhythms which pervade the behavior and existence of all living things are determined by both internal factors, the pacemaker cells of the nervous system, and external factors, such as the ebb and flow of the tides and the variation in the light-dark cycle with the seasons. Perhaps the most obvious of the circadian rhythms that characterize man is the sleep-wakefulness cycle. The electroencephalograph (EEG) has been used to identify and classify levels of arousal, particularly the various stages of sleep. From the desynchronized, low-voltage fast activity during wakefulness, an individual might pass into relaxed wakefulness, characterized by the highly synchronized EEG pattern called the alpha rhythm. The onset of sleep stage 1 is signaled by a return to low-voltage fast activity; in stage 2 the EEG shows sleep spindles and higher-voltage lower activity; in stages 3 and 4 the EEG lacks spindles but shows progressively higher and lower voltage variations. Extreme values on the arousal continuum are accompanied by a disorganization in behavior which appears to be neither a motor nor sensory deficit, but a deficit in their integration.

Although there is good correlation between the characteristics of the cortical EEG and behavioral arousal, the cortical area apparently is not the neural basis of arousal, since the EEG and arousal level can be dissociated through the use of drugs and during the rapid-eye-movement (REM) state. The neural substrates of arousal seem to involve activity of the reticular formation and certain portions of the hypothalamus. The anterior portions of the reticular formation appear to be important in the production of behavioral and electrophysiological signs of arousal, while the more posterior portions of the reticular formation and an area near the hypothalamus appear to regulate the production of sleep. Thus neither sleep nor wakefulness is a passive process.

Dreaming occurs in cycles during the night, primarily during REM sleep periods, which is characterized not only by rapid eye movements, but by a loss of the slight muscle tonus normally maintained during sleep. REM sleep comprises about 20 percent of the normal adult's total sleep time. However, in infants it comprises 80 percent, indicating that they may dream much more than adults.

Whereas the raphé nuclei in the brain stem appear primarily responsible for the production of slow-wave sleep, a portion of the central reticular formation appears to control REM sleep—perhaps by means of the transmitter substances serotonin and norepinephrine, respectively. Although REM is a state of deep sleep, on the basis of the stimulus intensity required for wakening, it is characterized by an EEG similar to that for alert wakefulness.

Attention, which probably plays a role in arousal state, is measured in terms of specific stimulus dimensions. For example, a subject may attend to the mere presence or absence of a stimulus, its modality,

modality-specific attributes, its source, or its pattern, all of which may vary in intensity and in duration. Perhaps the most obvious, but least reliable, determinant of attention is whether an animal "looks" attentive. A more objective measure is provided by a behavioral response to a specific stimulus dimension; this is termed an observing response. Vigilance tasks, transfer tests, tracking, and monitoring some aspect of the environment are other ways of measuring stimulus selection.

Attention to some aspect of the environment elicits an orienting reflex, a complex series of physiological reactions which include dilation of the pupils, vasoconstriction of the limbs and vasodilation of the head, brief cardiac and respiratory arrest, and orientation of the receptors toward the stimulus source. The physiological consequences of inattention are not so clear, but it appears that sensory input is not impeded during inattention. The neural substrates of attention apparently have both general and specific components, and there seem to be no significant changes in stimulus processing at peripheral levels of the sensory system, although cortical events do appear to be involved.

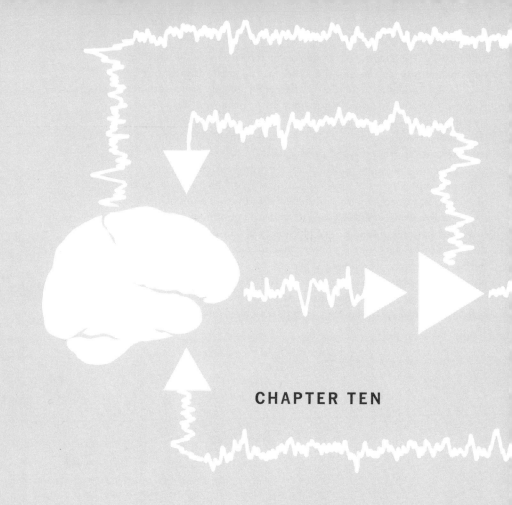

CHAPTER TEN

THE MOTIVATIONAL PROCESSES

Motivation is the fundamental driving thrust that generates behavior. There are many sources of motivation. Hunger and thirst are elemental forces compelling all animals to act—and in spite of the affluence of Western society, the majority of people in the world today are hungry. Sex, love, and affection—greed, aggressions, and war—exploration, achievement, and approval of our fellows—these are the sources and meaning of motivated behavior. The common definition of motivation as that which causes us to do what we do is true enough, but too broad for scientific purposes. We do not ask what "motivates" a person to give a knee-jerk reflex or why his pupils dilate in strong light.

Certain aspects of motivation may some day be expressed in terms of simple physiological reflexes. At this point, however, the term is generally reserved for particular classes of internal conditions which direct behavior. These background conditions are not directly responsible for the behavior, but they determine whether or not it will be emitted. An animal presented with food is at all times capable of feeding, but the

MOTIVATION

presence or absence of the motivational state of hunger determines whether or not it does so. However, saying that the study of motivation is the study of those states which direct behavior is still not satisfactory. Many would contend that emotion is an essential part of motivation, and that motivational states also have affective, or emotional, components. There have been many theories defining motivation according to scales of pleasantness or unpleasantness; others have insisted that such states "energize," or "drive," the animal, either in general or in specific directions.

Although the theoretical aspects of motivation are not entirely resolved, psychologists all agree on the facts of motivated behavior. Much is known about such primary aspects of motivation as hunger, thirst, aggression, and sex, partly because it is easy to observe and measure their behavioral expressions, feeding, fighting, and so forth. We shall examine aggression, hunger, and thirst as elemental forms of motivation, return to theoretical issues concerning the biology of motivation and emotion, and conclude with the more complex aspects of motivation in primates and man. Sex, a topic of particular interest for higher primates, was treated separately in Chapter 4.

251

It has been estimated that 59 million human beings were killed by other human beings between the years 1820 and 1945. This total, which is almost certainly an underestimate, provides a staggering indication of the extent of human aggression, but no indication of its character. The history of man is in large part a catalog of almost unbelievable cruelty, torture, and brutality. In fact we do other species a great injustice when we describe human actions as brutal or bestial, since we are evidently the only species that deliberately inflicts suffering on its own kind. William James [1890] described man as "the most formidable of all the beasts of prey, and indeed the only one that preys systematically on its own species." In view of contemporary man's unlimited capability for inflicting death, an increased understanding of aggression may well be essential for the survival of the species.

The development of anger and aggression from birth to adulthood in monkey and man has been discussed at length in earlier chapters. Here we are more concerned with the natural history of aggression and the neural mechanisms that produce it in the context of motivation. Aggressive behavior varies enormously among living forms, from species that rarely fight to animals that fight only their own kind, to animals that depend on killing for their survival. It is not surprising, therefore, that a single definition of aggression is likely to be unwieldy. In fact the term *agonistic* (fighting) is probably better in this context, because it has less implication about the origin or nature of the behavior to which it refers. In general there are three types of agonistic behavior—*flight*, in which an animal flees when encountered; *defense*, in which an animal protects itself against attack by fighting; and *attack*, in which an animal initiates fighting behavior.

It is important to distinguish between intraspecies and interspecies fighting behaviors. Most animals other than man do not kill their own kind for food, and it is apparent that intraspecies fighting is not normally related to food-seeking behavior. Intraspecies fighting often takes the form of "stylized" fights, and except in man, it rarely results in death. However, most, but not all, interspecies aggression is on a predator-prey basis and usually does conclude in death.

FACTORS IN AGONISTIC BEHAVIOR

Most theories of fighting behaviors have followed two approaches; one is concerned with the stimulus cues which elicit various agonistic responses, while the other emphasizes the learning history involved in these responses. Arguments have raged over which of these is the more important, although there is general agreement that both factors are involved. However, the relative proportion varies greatly according to the species and situation.

Few vertebrates are more aggressive than the fighting fish, *Betta*

252

FIGURE 10-1   *Intraspecies aggression in mammals. Both rats are receiving inescapable foot shock. Although the aversive stimulus is not produced by either rat, and a foreign stimulus (the doll) is also present, they attack each other. If only one rat is present he will attack the doll. [Miller, Rockefeller University]*

splendons, and it is therefore an excellent subject for analyzing the cues that elicit attack behaviors. On seeing another male the fighting fish goes through a series of complicated but stereotyped behaviors preparatory to attack. These include turning sideways to the intruder and extending the fins, and then turning toward the intruder; this is followed in turn by a sudden attack, culminating in savage biting. These attacks occur primarily when one fish is moving into the "territory" of another fish. What is it that "motivates" the fish to make this response? A sizable body of data suggests that innate responses to particular types of stimuli are involved. In a series of studies with models held outside the fish tank Thompson [1963] demonstrated that the color of the intruder as well as that of the defender fish was one critical variable in determining whether an attack was to be made. Red fish were found to be far more likely to attack green models than blue or red models, whereas blue fish were likely to attack red models and least likely to attack blue models. Other colors were intermediate in their ability to elicit attack behavior. A fighting fish may attack any male fish which appears to be entering its territory, but the probability of an attack apparently follows a strict color code.

Rodents also engage in considerable intraspecies agonistic behavior. When a strange male rat is introduced into the "home" cage of another male rat, the two animals will go through a series of postures which may or may not lead to a fight. The rat who has occupied the cage for some time makes a *threat posture*, in which it arches its back and presents its flank to the newcomer. If the newcomer makes a *submission response*, which usually consists in crawling under the other rat, he is left alone. However, if he adopts the threat posture himself, a fight usually ensues; both animals stand on their hind legs, box with their forepaws, and bite at each other (see Fig. 10-1). The fight stops only when one of the animals adopts the submission position.

Again we can ask what cues are directing these behaviors. Why, for example, does the male not attack female rats? Odors clearly play a

253

FIGURE 10–2 *Intraspecies aggression in man. Fighting occurs even though, as in Fig. 10-1, the underlying causes are often not produced by the fighters. [Los Angeles Times]*

major role, since rats with olfactory bulbs removed become considerably more aggressive. Probably more important, however, is the past history of the animal. This was illustrated in an experiment with mice, which engage in agonistic behaviors similar to those of rats [Lagerspetz, 1969]. The number of aggressive responses made by a male mouse when it was caged with randomly selected mice was recorded. The experimental mouse was then caged repeatedly with mice that other studies had established as being very aggressive and successful in their bouts. After several sessions in which the experimental mouse was usually defeated, it was found to be considerably less aggressive. It was then caged repeatedly with nonaggressive mice, and over time it not only returned to but surpassed its previous baseline aggressiveness. This experiment clearly demonstrates the extent to which previous successes and failures in fights—that is, learning—play a major role in aggression in male mice.

Other factors, which are apparently not related to learning, are also intimately involved in the control of aggression. The fact that rats can be bred for aggressiveness, for example, suggests that genetic factors may be related to the role of gonadal (sex) hormones in determining levels of aggressiveness. Environmental variables are also critical; the amount of cage space available to rats and mice directly affects the amount of fighting, as does the quantity of food. We have already seen that animals tend to regard their accustomed living areas as their own territories and will challenge any intruder who enters this space. The presence or absence of females also affects the probability of fighting among male rodents. Finally, the animal's position in the social hierarchy greatly influences his readiness to fight. In short, both the amount and the nature of fighting in rats and mice are determined by a complex interaction of environmental, genetic, and learning variables.

There is also great variation in primate agonistic behavior, both in individuals of the same species and from one species to another. Nearly all primates, however, have a ritualized pattern of behaviors that they follow when faced with conflict. These include facial gestures and radical arm movements, and significantly, vocalizations. Fights do not usually entail serious physical damage in primates (however, see Fig. 10-2). Environmental variables are an important factor in primate agonistic behavior. Southwick et al. [1965] found that decreasing the size of the animals' cages greatly increased the amount of fighting, but surprisingly enough, reducing the amount of food caused a reduction in the number of fights—the reverse of the effect on rodents. He also made the unexpected observation that captive rhesus monkeys were considerably more aggressive than animals found in forests. Again, this is the opposite of what has been reported for rats and nicely illustrates the danger of generalizing from one animal form to another. Factors within the group play a major role in determining primate aggression, but as always, variability is the rule. Thus adult male rhesus monkeys observed in the wild appeared to attack females and juveniles as frequently as other males, while fighting of caged males was usually directed at other males. The social hierarchies of primates are usually formed after an extended series of fights, and struggles to maintain this hierarchy are a major cause of agonistic primate aggression.

THE BRAIN SYSTEMS
THAT CONTROL AGGRESSION

The neural substrates of aggression have been the subject of investigation for some 40 years. Gradually three structures, all part of the limbic system (see Chapter 7) have become isolated as being critically important to the initiation and control of agonistic behaviors. These are the hypothalamus, the amygdala, and the septum (Fig. 10-3).

In the 1930s Bard investigated the effects of cutting the brain at various levels [Bard and Mountcastle, 1948]. A surgical instrument was lowered into the brain, and various amounts of the forebrain were "disconnected" from the remainder of the brain. He found that removal of the entire forebrain in front of the hypothalamus did not eliminate "rage" behavior; in fact it lowered the threshold for its elicitation. To be sure, this rage (attack) behavior was not smooth or well integrated, but there was no doubt that it was attack behavior. However, Bard was not sure that the affective components of rage were truly present in these animals and preferred to call this behavior "sham rage." When the hypothalamus itself was damaged, the rage response disappeared completely.

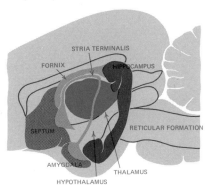

FIGURE 10-3   *Limbic system of the brain. Note the central position of the hypothalamus and the connections to it from the hippocampus and amygdala by way of fiber tracts (stria terminali and fornix). [Fernandez de Molina and Hunsperger, 1959]*

255

Bard's work demonstrated that much of the forebrain is not necessary for the production of attack behavior, and in fact appears to inhibit it, since removal of the forebrain lowers the threshold for the response. The hypothalamus, however, is critical for the generation of rage behavior.

Recent research has attempted to define the ways in which the hypothalamus is involved in the production of rage. Electrical stimulation of the hypothalamus has proved to be a technique of great value. The bare tip of an otherwise insulated wire is inserted into the target brain area (hypothalamus), and after the animal has fully recovered from anesthesia a tiny current is passed through the wire and the effects on its behavior are measured. This procedure elicits various types of agonistic behavior in cats. Most often the flight response is seen, but on other occasions defense or attack responses are elicited. The major factor in determining which kind of agonistic behavior is elicited seems to be the exact location of the electrode in the hypothalamus.

Flynn [1967] has described two very different kinds of attack elicited by stimulation of the hypothalamus in cats. One, *affective attack*, is sudden and resembles what most investigators have called rage (see Fig. 10-4). The cat strikes repeatedly but inefficiently at the attack object, with unusual amounts of accompanying vocalization, hissing, and other signs of rage. *Stalking attack*, the second type of aggression observed after hypothalamic stimulation, resembles the cat's normal mode of attack. The animal stalks the cage and approaches its target with caution. When the attack is made, it is sudden and very efficient. This type of attack behavior is sensitive to the environmental situation and will occur only with appropriate "targets," such as a mouse. In other words, it appears to relate in most details to normal predatory behavior.

FIGURE 10-4   *Two types of agonistic behavior elicited in a cat by stimulation of closely adjacent points in the hypothalamus. Above, rage and attack behavior. Below, quiet biting predation attack. [Flynn, 1967]*

These studies verify Bard's conclusion that the hypothalamus plays a critical role in organizing aggressive behavior. What, then, of his contention that the forebrain suppresses agonistic behavior? One answer to this comes from the functions of the *amygdala* in primates. The amygdala is a large nucleus in the forebrain that is a part of the limbic system (see Fig. 10-3). Primates form intricate social hierarchies, with each animal dominating the animal immediately below him in the social hierarchy. Pribram [1962] found that destruction of the amygdala produced dramatic changes in this hierarchy. When the amygdala was destroyed in a monkey who had been lowest on the social scale, he began to compete with his former superiors and was able to occupy a position at or near the top. When the dominant monkey was lesioned in the amygdala, the picture was reversed; he was no longer able to control the other monkeys and fell in social standing to the bottom of the hierarchy.

This report generated considerable interest and additional work on the role of the amygdala in controlling aggressive behavior, but the only clear finding that has emerged is that the amygdala is involved. It was soon found that electrical stimulation of the amygdala could either produce rage or block it. For example, a great deal more current to the hypothalamus is needed to produce attack behaviors when the amygdala is stimulated concurrently. However, stimulation of the amygdala alone often leads to attack. This suggests that the amygdala may have antagonistic subdivisions which inhibit or facilitate rage. Selective lesioning of the amygdala also suggests the presence of positive and negative systems. Since removal of the entire structure lowers the threshold for rage, it appears that the net effect of these subdivisions is inhibitory.

How does the amygdala control aggressive behavior? A logical approach would be to consider the brain areas to which it is tied. The major fiber connections of the amygdala are with the hypothalamus, which, as we have seen, is crucial for the appearance of rage behavior. Therefore it seems reasonable to hypothesize that the amygdala is working through the hypothalamus. However, this idea is not borne out by experimental evidence. When the hypothalamus is lesioned there are no aggressive responses to electrical stimulation of the amygdala. Lesioning of the amygdala, however, has no effect on hypothalamically induced rage behavior.

The experimental evidence linking the amygdala with aggression has generated considerable interest among neurologists, and there are now a number of reports showing that stimulation of the amygdala in humans can cause attack, while lesions have a calming effect. It is far too early for final evaluation, but it does appear that the amygdala plays a role in controlling aggression in a wide range of mammalian forms.

The third brain region which has been found to be involved in agonistic behavior is the septum. The septum is located between the amygdala and hypothalamus and has extensive fiber connections with both (see Fig. 10-3). The observation that the septal area might be involved in aggression came unexpectedly. During another experiment Brady and Nauta [1953] found that septal lesions caused laboratory rats, which are normally docile animals, to become so irritable and vicious that they would attack and bite animals many times their own size. This dramatic effect has since been obtained in several laboratories, but we do not yet understand the underlying mechanisms.

HUNGER AND FEEDING BEHAVIOR

Feeding behavior represents an area of interest to motivational scientists, whether they are working with behavior, brain, or body physiology. Analysis of feeding can be subdivided into four aspects or concerns—the behaviors which precede it; the feeding bout itself, the cues which start and stop it; the brain systems which initiate it; and the long-term consequences of feeding to body physiology. This sequence is illustrated in Fig. 10-5. Consideration of the long-term physiological consequences includes the question of what bodily variables are monitored by the brain—that is, how the brain "knows" when to initiate another search for food. It should be obvious by now that we cannot simply say that animals eat when they are hungry and stop when they are filled. Since hunger is a subjective experience we must approach it in terms of its observable behavior, feeding.

Let us start our analysis with the behaviors that animals exhibit prior to feeding. The first of these is an increase in motor activity level. In the natural environment this is not a random process but typically becomes directed toward locations in which the animal has found food previously. Here, as in all motivated behavior, we encounter the powerful influence of learning. The effect of learning on food-searching behavior is beautifully demonstrated in studies of the amount of time deer mice will spend digging for food [Hinde, 1966]. Deer mice have a strong taste preference for sawfly cocoons, which they sometimes encounter on or just beneath the surface of the ground. Normally they spend little time looking for this delicacy, but when the experimenter planted several cocoons in the cage, the mouse steadily increased the number of digs it made per day. In other words, as the mouse learned that this desirable food was available, it greatly increased its efforts to obtain it. This study also illustrates the importance of environmental factors in feeding behavior. It was found that the number of digs the mouse made per day was dependent on the other types of food it could obtain without digging. The mouse made fewer digs when the alternate food was sunflower seeds, which is a delicacy to deer mice, than when it was dog biscuits, which they do not especially like. Thus the animal's previous history of successes and failures in finding a particular food as well as what else was available determined its prefeeding behavior. It is important to keep this behavioral flexibility in mind when considering the feeding habits of animals.

The next step, feeding behavior, occurs when the animal encounters food. What determines whether or not he will eat it? The obvious

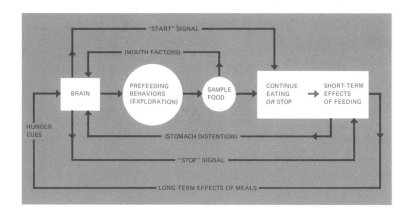

FIGURE 10-5   *Diagram of how the brain might interact with body factors to control feeding behavior. The brain senses bodily signals associated with hunger and organizes a behavioral search for food. When food is found, eating begins and continues until the brain receives sufficient signals to stop. The duration of eating is partly determined by the composition and taste of the food. The long-term consequences (hours) on bodily functions will determine when the brain next receives hunger signals.*

answer is taste, and to a large extent this is correct. The physiological and neurophysiological mechanisms of taste are beyond our present scope. Our main concern here is with the manner in which tastes interact with the underlying motivational states that lead to feeding.

Food preferences seem to have two origins, one learned and the other innate. It appears that animals can associate the long-term effects of a particular food type with its taste; taste serves as a cue that this food contains high concentrations of sugars and fats. This is something that an animal must learn; it does not represent a native ability. Experimental rats have been given a choice between two diets, one of which is low in some substance such as vitamin A. If the diets have the same flavor, the rats choose randomly between them and gradually become sick owing to an insufficiency of vitamin A. If one of the diets is given a distinctive flavor, so that the rats can tell the two diets apart, the rats will gradually eat only from the food supply that contains normal amounts of vitamin A. That is, they learn that a particular taste is associated with a poor diet and come to avoid that taste. This is a remarkable feat when we consider that the taste of food and its digestion and transmission to the blood supply and cells are separated in time by many minutes or even hours.

Many food preferences, however, are not learned. For example, neonatal rats prefer saccharin solutions (which have no nutritional value) to solutions of their mother's milk. This is an important point, because it demonstrates that taste can have motivational value independent of its nutritional value. Even more important, both adult and young, relatively inexperienced organisms tend to select a balanced diet over time if they are given a choice of foods. In one classical experiment human babies aged six months to one year were required to eat all their foods

259

from large trays containing 12 to 20 different foods in separate containers [Davis, 1928]. The experiment resulted in very messy babies, but also very healthy babies. At any one meal an infant might eat only one food, say, all butter, but over the long run each baby selected a well-balanced diet and grew as well as or better than a control group raised on a dietitian's formula. Pioneering cafeteria-type experiments with rats show similar results [Richter, 1942; 1943]. The exotic food cravings expressed by pregnant women provide still another illustration. It appears that specific nutritional needs are translated into rather specific taste preferences, which lead in the long run to a relatively well-balanced pattern of food intake.

PERIPHERAL VERSUS CENTRAL THEORIES OF FEEDING

When a food-deprived animal has found food, sampled it, and found it acceptable, he begins to eat. The next logical question is when does he stop? The intuitive answer to this question is that he stops when his stomach is filled, but this does not appear to be true. Animals, including humans, in which nerves connected to the stomach have been removed appear to be perfectly able to regulate their food intake. Since there is no nervous connection between stomach and brain, the organism has no way of knowing if its stomach is filled or not. Other studies have shown that simple distention of the stomach or loading it with nonnutritive substances does not reduce the hunger drive [Miller and Kessen, 1952]. These and many similar studies show that stomach distention is not the primary satiety cue

These negative conclusions force us to look beyond the stomach for the satiety cue and search for some postingestional consequence which the animal might be monitoring. Two theories which have obtained increasing recognition are Mayer's *glucostatic theory* [Mayer, 1955] and Brobeck's *thermostatic theory* [Brobeck, 1947; 1948]. As the names imply, both these theories are related to the concept of homeostatic functioning. Mayer contends that an animal eats to maintain its blood sugar at an optimal level for utilization. Brobeck is quite direct in stating the contrasting position that "animals eat to *keep warm* and stop eating to prevent hyperthermia." Each theory has in common the idea that a postingestional variable is monitored by the brain, and when certain values for this variable are exceeded or not obtained, the cessation or the initiation of feeding occurs.

According to the glucostatic hypothesis, the difference in blood-sugar concentration in brain arteries and veins provides the clues for the initiation and cessation of feeding. This difference, often called the *A-V difference*, is an indication of the rate of glucose utilization by the brain, so that low A-V values, which signal low utilization, serve as a satiety cue and high values, which signal high utilization, lead to eating.

260

Glucose is the only carbohydrate normally used by the brian, so the extent to which it is being utilized is an indicant of how active the brain is. The evidence for or against this theory has never proved entirely conclusive because of the difficulty in measuring A-V differences across the brain from moment to moment. Nevertheless, there is ample evidence that fluctuations in arterial and venous glucose concentrations are often accompanied by hunger in humans and increased feeding in animals. The most commonly cited evidence in favor of the glucostatic theory is the data obtained with the exotic compound gold thioglucose [Mayer and Marshall, 1956]. Mayer reasoned that if the brain really monitored glucose as its satiety signal, then destruction of these monitoring devices would cause animals to eat continuously. Gold is extremely toxic to living tissue. Consequently, if the hypothetical glucose receptors in the brain absorbed glucose and gold together, the gold would poison the glucoreceptors, leaving the animal no means of measuring glucose and hence no means of sensing satiety. When mice were injected with gold thioglucose, each of these predictions was fulfilled; damage was done to specific brain areas known to be associated with the measurement of satiety signals, and the animals ate ravenously to the point of becoming obese. Later experiments indicate that the brain damage is in fact fairly general and involves numerous regions of the brain which appear to have little to do with the regulation of food intake.

THE BRAIN SYSTEMS
THAT CONTROL FEEDING

The theories we have discussed have in common the idea that there are brain centers which monitor some blood variables—glucose, temperature, or circulating fats—and use these as cues for the starting or stopping of food intake. One of the major concerns of research has been to locate these receptive areas. For years it has been observed that brain damage in the area surrounding the pituitary glands often causes obesity in man. However, research conducted in the 1930s and 1940s showed that removal of the pituitary in experimental animals did not produce overeating obesity. This led to the thought that the critical areas were the brain regions immediately adjacent to the pituitary, the hypothalamus. Subsequent work showed that destruction of a nucleus in the medial region of the hypothalamus does produce chronic overeating, or *hyperphagia* (see Fig. 10-6). This suggested that the medial nucleus might normally suppress food intake, since its removal resulted in increased eating (see Fig. 10-7). However, it was not until the 1950s that satisfactory data were available on the brain areas which normally facilitate food intake. Anand and Brobeck [1951] reported that lesions in the lateral region of the hypothalamus, immediately adjacent to the medial hypothalamus, caused animals to stop eating (*aphagia*). It was later shown that electrical stimulation of the lateral hypothalamus region caused

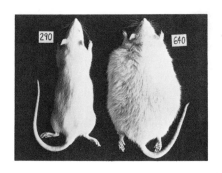

FIGURE 10–6   *Left, a normal rat. Right, a rat that has become fat by overeating (hyperphagia) after destruction of a small region in the medial hypothalamus of the brain. The same effect can be produced by feeding gold thioglucose. [Teitelbaum, 1964]*

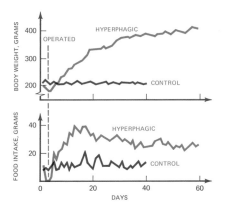

FIGURE 10-7   *Body weight and daily food intake of a hyperphagic animal with a lesion in the medial hypothalamus [Teitelbaum, 1961].*

previously satiated rats to begin eating voraciously and stimulation of the medial region caused starving rats to stop feeding. These results indicated that the hypothalamus contains antagonistic systems—one which causes animals to begin feeding and a second system which inhibits the first, thus producing cessation of feeding. This demonstration that the medial and lateral regions serve opposite functions in the regulation of food intake excited a great deal of interest and led to much additional experimental research.

One difficulty with the hypothesis that the medial region plays a role in the production of satiety is that experimental animals (usually rats) with medial hypothalamic lesions are finicky eaters. They will not eat bad-tasting foods but will overeat when foods that taste pleasant (to a rat) are available. At an intuitive level this does not make sense; if the medial region does produce the neural signals we interpret as satiation and thus makes animals rabidly hungry, we would expect such animals to be *less* selective in their diets. In fact, however, starved animals are more selective in their diets than normal ones, and in this sense the correlation between medial hypothalamic damage and hunger is very good.

Drinking behavior follows much the same sequence as feeding behavior. The brain recognizes some state which is perceived as thirst and initiates behavioral activity which continues until water is encountered; the animal then samples the water, drinks, and stops

drinking. Presumably some effect of the water eliminates the cues which the brain had originally sensed and acted on. Therefore the problem can be broken down into more manageable portions—the cues which initiate drinking, the cues which result in the cessation of drinking, and the brain regions which sense these cues. The general view is that a single mechanism produces both these cues—that is, an animal starts drinking when some physiological variable falls below a certain point and stops when the proper level is restored.

PERIPHERAL VERSUS CENTRAL THEORIES OF DRINKING

As with feeding behavior, there are two general theories about the origins of thirst. According to *peripheral theories*, prolonged water deprivation causes a physical change in bodily organs, such as dryness of mouth, and this change is recorded by the brain via the peripheral nervous system. The *central theories* are based on the contention that water deprivation changes blood factors, such as salt concentration, this change is recorded by the brain via the circulatory system, and the brain monitors the blood factors directly.

The strongest proponent of a peripheral interpretation of thirst was Cannon, who argued that thirst resulted from decreased saliva flow into the mouth causing the mouth dryness associated with thirst. The saliva, or *parotid*, glands dry out because of low water content of blood during prolonged water deprivation. In support of his idea that saliva flow is the cue for thirst, Cannon showed that saliva flow was inversely proportional to degree of thirst in man. From this model it could be argued that drinking is an attempt to substitute water for saliva. Other studies have cast serious doubt on the dry-mouth idea. Bernard had demonstrated years earlier that animals would show essentially normal cessation of drinking when water was placed directly into their stomachs (via an implanted tube called a fistula), without passing through the mouth and throat. Thus wetting a dry mouth cannot be the sole mechanism which controls drinking. Moreover, removal of the parotid glands does not eliminate or even drastically increase drinking. These findings pose severe difficulties for the dry-mouth theory. It is possible, of course, that mouth sensations interact with other factors in the control of thirst. However, they cannot be the only or necessary thirst cue.

Central theories have emphasized the obvious physiological effects of prolonged water deprivation on blood supply and body cells. The human body, for example, is about 75 percent water. Body water is

263

found both inside cells and outside cells (in the blood supply) as extracellular water. Since cell membranes are semipermeable, water moves back and forth across them according to relative concentrations. If water concentration is unusually low in the blood, water will tend to move from the cells out to the blood. Hence changes in extracellular water levels have a direct effect on the water content of cells—including neurons in the brain—and it is more likely that this serves as a direct cue for drinking behavior.

THE BRAIN SYSTEMS
THAT CONTROL DRINKING

The hypothalamus is also critically involved in the control of drinking. The central theories postulate that there are receptors somewhere in the body that monitor blood factors, and there is evidence that these receptors are to be found in the brain. Minute injections of hypertonic saline, high-salt-content water, into the carotid arteries, which lead directly to the brain, result in immediate drinking. Injections elsewhere in the body do not have this effect. This led to the idea that the brain had receptors for monitoring blood salinity—that is, cells responsive to a drop in salt concentrations below the level needed to influence normal cells [Grossman, 1967]. A major step in the development of a hypothalamic theory of thirst came with the work of Andersson [1953]. He carried the carotid injection experiments one step farther and showed that direct application of hypertonic saline to the hypothalamus produces prolonged drinking behavior. In fact he was able to isolate the anterior, or front, portion of the hypothalamus as the area in which the saline was effective; application elsewhere did not have the same effect. Andersson concluded that this area sensed the blood factor which was the physiological correlate of thirst and was thus involved in the behavioral response of drinking—an impressive example of the linking together of physiological, neurological, and behavioral variables to derive an explanation for a motivational phenomenon.

There is another aspect of the anterior hypothalamus that must be mentioned in the context of drinking. Located in this region is the *supraoptic nucleus*, which contains neurosecretory cells that synthesize and release the antidiuretic hormone (ADH). This hormone causes the kidneys to remove less water from the blood for excretion as urine. During conditions of water need ADH secretion is high, and the body conserves water. Moreover, the electrical activity of cells in this area is extremely sensitive to saline injections and they show a physical response to osmotic pressure. Thus this particular brain region contains cells that are responsive to blood factors related to imbalances in body water. Some of these cells organize a physiologically appropriate defense response, the secretion of ADH, while others produce an appropriate behavioral reaction. Additional evidence of hypothalamic involvement in drinking comes from lesion and electrical-stimulation studies. Briefly,

264

it has been shown that lesion of the lateral hypothalamus eliminates drinking. However, we are only beginning to differentiate contributions of the various parts of the hypothalamus to the control of drinking behavior.

There are only scattered reports on the roles of other brain structures in the control of drinking behavior. Not surprisingly, various parts of the limbic system have been shown to be involved, especially the septum. The most consistent model for limbic involvement in drinking comes from chemical-stimulation studies.

THE NEUROCHEMISTRY OF FEEDING AND DRINKING

It is obvious from our discussions of the neural substrates of feeding and drinking that there is a great overlap between the two systems throughout the limbic system. It is not possible to separate them with standard lesioning and electrical-stimulation techniques because these procedures are relatively nonspecific; they destroy or stimulate everything—axons, dendrites, synapses—at the tip of the electrode. However, since the synaptic transmission involved is a chemical process (see Chapter 7), it was reasoned that if the drinking and feeding circuits used different neurotransmitters, they could be selectively stimulated (or blocked) by drugs directly related to one or the other transmitter substance. To some extent this goal has been realized; it is in fact possible to produce eating or drinking from a particular brain locus by chemical stimulation.

The first successful application of this technique in motivational studies was injection of drugs into the lateral hypothalamus. Injections of norepinephrine caused rats to eat voraciously; injections of carbacol, a synthetic form of acetylcholine, produced prolonged drinking behavior. This is the pattern found throughout the limbic system. The sites at which carbacol produces drinking are more extensive than those at which norepinephrine-induced eating can be obtained, but much of the limbic system—the hypothalamus, septum, amygdala, and hippocampus—are involved in both. Not all regions are involved in the same fashion. The amygdala, for example, appears to modulate feeding and drinking behavior rather than to initiate it directly.

A similar and relatively simple overall picture emerges of feeding and drinking behavior. Deprivation leads to activation of certain neural receptor mechanisms—glucose receptors for hunger and fluid salt content for thirst—which in turn activate specific brain systems, particularly in the hypothalamus. Peripheral factors such as stomach contractions and dryness of mouth may enhance these effects but are not crucial for them. Increased activity in certain hypothalamic and related limbic regions of the brain leads to increased activity level and increased goal-directed activity—the seeking of food and water. Both innate and learned preferences and behavior patterns are important at this point. As the needed substance is ingested the balance of neural activity in the hypothalamus and related brain regions shifts toward a net pattern of satiation, and ingestion ceases.

The control of feeding and thinking, and their underlying motivations of hunger and thirst, are elegant examples of homeostatic systems designed to maintain the organism at a stable normal level of nutrition and water balance. The fact that higher animals seem to derive considerable enjoyment from these activities is both an added benefit and an essential aspect of feeding and drinking behavior.

MOTIVATION: THEORY AND BIOLOGY

Feeding and drinking are particularly easy aspects of motivated behavior to analyze in terms of their underlying mechanisms. These behaviors serve to maintain an optimum state of physiological stability and fit beautifully in the general framework of homeostatic-balance theories of motivation. During the middle of the nineteenth century physiologists became aware that the internal environment of the body exists in a remarkable state of balance. For every action or change there appears to be a response which restores the original equilibrium. The French physiologist Claude Bernard coined the phrase the *internal milieu* for the internal environment of the body and with great foresight suggested that much behavior might represent attempts to maintain the optimal balance for this system. This idea has had great appeal for behavioral scientists because it places behavior on the same continuum with physiological responses; for example, feeding occurs when internal defenses against low blood sugar are no longer adequate.

The value of the balance theories of behavior was apparent in the work of Richter and Cannon. Cannon's classical book *The Wisdom of the Body* [1932] elaborated the notion of homeostasis. According to this theory, the body senses changes from an optimal point for a given physiological process and then initiates physiological and behavioral responses appropriate to restoring the proper level. Building on Bernard's ideas, Cannon provided an explanation of specific physiological and, more important for our purposes, behavioral responses as defenses of internal balance. Thus for Cannon and many who followed him the study of motivation was a search for bodily imbalances and the physiological cues associated with them.

The most extensive behavioral formulation of motivation is the *drive theory*, developed by Clark Hull [1943] and subsequently expanded by Neil Miller [1963] and Judson Brown [1961]. According to this theory, which has its roots in the homeostasis approach, sources of motivation such as deprivation of food or water result in internal states that drive the animal to act. Appropriate actions such as eating and drinking reduce this drive. Since drive reduction is rewarding, the organism learns to respond to the stimulus cues present during reduction of drive. Sources of motivation have a dual function; they generate the

266

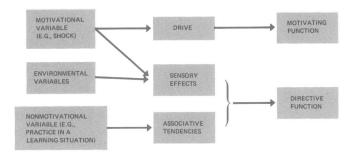

FIGURE 10-8 *Diagram of the hypothetical dual effects of a motivational variable such as food deprivation or painful electric shock. This results in an increased general drive level which is motivating, and also in sensory cues which interact with other stimuli in the environment and with innate and learned factors to produce directed behavior such as obtaining food or avoiding shock.* [Brown, 1961]

drive to act and they provide cues for appropriate action, as schematized in Fig. 10-8. Thus food deprivation leads to an increase in general drive state and also leads to a variety of internal cues which interact with other environmental stimuli and with learned behaviors to lead to food-seeking behavior. Drive itself is *nonspecific*; food deprivation and water deprivation together do not lead to a hunger drive and a thirst drive, but to a greater degree of general drive plus food-seeking and water-seeking behavior.

Drive theory is the most well-developed and consistent theoretical analysis of motivation, but other points of view have played important roles. Late in the nineteenth century William James and Herbert Lange developed an intriguing formulation that motivated states followed the occurrence of particular types of responses. This hypothesis, known since as the *James-Lange theory*, is best illustrated by the example of the man who encounters a bear and runs. A common-sense notion of the sequence of events is that sight of bear elicits the state of fear, which leads directly to the response of flight. The James-Lange model, however, suggests a less obvious sequence: sight of bear leads to the learned response of flight, which in turn results in the innate state of fear. This thesis has certainly not received the intense experimental interest generated by homeostasis and drive theories, but enough experimental data have been produced to suggest that the theory, or a near cousin of it, may contain a significant truth. The experiments by Sheffield are particularly relevant in this regard [Sheffield and Roby, 1950; Sheffield et al., 1951]. Sheffield's theory that rats will work to "induce" a particular central state is nearly a mirror image of the drive-reduction model. One of his more striking demonstrations was that male rats will continue to copulate almost indefinitely even if they are never allowed to ejaculate. It is difficult, though not impossible, to fit these results into a drive-reduction framework, since the behavior is continued despite the fact that it does nothing to reduce the presumed sexually derived drive state. The results are, however, explained by a hypothesis that the animal works to produce a state which, unlike that produced by flight from a bear, is pleasant.

267

The concept of arousal provides a unifying bridge between drive theory and other approaches to motivation. We have already noted that the behavior of a rat toward food is not the same when it is hungry as when it has recently fed, but how would a hungry animal behave if no food was present? Rats in this situation become very active; they explore their environments and become very sensitive to stimulus areas that they might previously have ignored. In short, they become very excited or *aroused*. A similar phenomenon is observed in the female rat in the estrous state, or heat; her activity becomes greatly heightened, and she will pace her cage incessantly. This excitability appears to accompany most, and possibly all, motivational states. It even finds expression in theories of human motivation; for example, in Freud's psychoanalytic theory this nonspecific activation is related to the libido. In short, behavioral arousal may be considered the outward reflection of internal drive state.

In our discussion of drive theory it was emphasized that motivational states may have two aspects, one leading to general drive and the other interacting with environmental cues to result in goal-directed activity. Campbell and Sheffield [1953] demonstrated that the amount of activity exhibited by rats during starvation was directly dependent on richness of the environment in which they were placed. Rats housed in sensory-isolation chambers showed little or no increase in activity during prolonged food deprivation, while those whose cages were located in more normal environments showed great increases in activity. Later experiments have further dissociated the specific motivational effects of need states from their nonspecific arousal changes. For example, it has been shown that destruction of the frontal cortex in rats greatly augments the generalized activity caused by hunger without increasing bar-pressing behavior for food, an indicant often used to measure drive state [Campbell and Lynch, 1969]. Thus we can see that a motivational state is accompanied by two types of behavioral change— an increase in activity and responses to the environment (arousal) and a set of specific responses appropriate to the motivational state.

The greatest theoretical interest in the significance of arousal in motivation has to do with its effect on performance. One view is that behavioral efficiency is dependent on arousal level, which in turn reflects level of motivational state. We explored this view at some length in Chapter 9. The relationship between level of arousal—that is, level of motivational state or drive—is an inverted U (see Fig. 9-4). Up to a point, as motivational level increases, behavioral performance increases. Beyond that point behavior becomes disrupted and the organism shows increasingly severe signs of emotional disturbance. For example, Malmo [1959] measured heart rate as an indicant of arousal level in rats and found that it increased steadily over 72 hours of water deprivation. Bar pressing for water, however, increased only for the first 36 hours and then de-

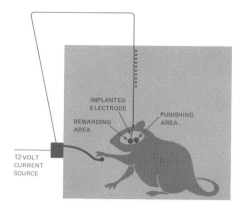

FIGURE 10-9 *Brain self-stimulation.*
An animal (including man) with an elec-
trode implanted in "rewarding" areas of
the brain, such as the lateral hypothalamus,
will learn to press a bar in a Skinner box to
turn on a mild electric current to that
brain area. [after Olds, 1955]

creased. Various controls established that this decrease was not due to physical weakness. Many other studies have demonstrated similar relationships in various species, including man, and across various types of performance tasks. A motivated, and hence aroused, animal performs better than a nonmotivated one.

We saw in Chapter 9 that one region in the hypothalamus activates or arouses behavior and the cortical EEG and another deactivates both cortical activity and behavior (see Fig. 9-7). Similarly, there is an activating system in the more anterior reticular formation and a deactivating system in the more posterior region. Recent work indicates that other regions of the limbic system, such as the hippocampus and frontal cortex, play critical roles in regulating these arousal effects. Finally, there is considerable evidence that the brain arousal system involves the action of a particular chemical synaptic transmitter substance, norepinephrine. This substance is found in high concentrations in the reticular formation and the limbic structures, and is particularly concentrated in the hypothalamus. Recall from Chapter 7 that drugs which increase brain levels of norepinephrine, such as amphetamines, tend to produce behavioral and EEG arousal.

Lindsley [1951] first suggested that the brain arousal system forms the neural basis of behavioral arousal, and Hebb [1955] proposed the specific hypothesis that the brain arousal system is the neural basis of generalized drive. This approach provides a unifying theme for much of the material we have considered, relating drive theory to the brain arousal system and to the mechanisms involved in such primary motivational behaviors as aggression, feeding, and drinking. The hypothalamus is a critical link. Motivated behavior has two aspects, a generalized drive or arousal component and a goal-directed component. Activation of the hypothalamus can elicit both aspects—arousal and specific activities such as stalking, eating, and drinking. Limbic forebrain structures *modulate* the actions of the hypothalamus (and reticular formation) in arousal and in specific activities such as agonistic behavior and food seeking.

If this general view is correct, then it ought to be possible to intervene directly in the brain motivational system. The discovery of Olds and Milner [1954] that rats will work very hard simply to receive an electrical stimulus to the brain motivational system seems to provide this evidence (see Fig. 10-9). By far the most critical region for self-

269

stimulation is the lateral region of the hypothalamus in the vicinity of the feeding center. Rats will press a lever hundreds of times per minute if they receive a weak electric shock in the lateral hypothalamus by doing so. The other effective brain areas are in the limbic system, particularly the septal area and hippocampus. Interestingly, electrical stimulation of these regions in conscious man has similar effects. Reported sensations include vague but intense feelings of well being and extreme euphoria.

COMPLEX MOTIVES

The monkey looking out at you in Fig. 10-10 has learned to push one of two panels from inside his prison cage for no other reward than to look out. Curiosity and its satisfaction seem almost as basic a motivation as hunger, aggression, and sex in higher animals, particularly primates. Theorists have argued at length about which aspects of motivation are primary and which are secondary. Primary motives are said to be "built in" to the organism without learning, and secondary motives are learned. One view limits primary motivation to tissue needs, such as the need for nutrition, water, and avoidance of tissue damage; all other motivation is held to be learned through associations rewarded by food, water, and avoidance of pain. However, there is considerable evidence that motivated behaviors ranging from activity, manipulation, and curiosity to affection and social behavior are not learned from eating, drinking, and avoidance of pain. In fact many of these more complex motivations have significant aspects that are not learned at all.

MANIPULATION AND CURIOSITY

Rats will learn to press a bar for no other reason than to turn the lights in their cages on or off. Kavanau [1963] showed further that rats will not run in an exercise wheel which is externally powered even if it is turning at a speed they normally select for themselves, but if they can turn the wheel themselves, they run for several hours a day. In both these instances the rats apparently are motivated merely to manipulate their environment. Experiments with primates are more dramatic. In order to prove that monkeys have basic motivation to manipulate or be curious it is necessary to show that they will work for long periods with the manipulatory behavior itself as the only reward, that the motivation to manipulate will produce learning in the same way as food reward, and that no motivation other than curiosity has a significant influence on the animal's behavior. A series of experiments by Butler and Harlow [1954], Harlow and McClearn [1954], and Butler [1954a; 1954b] have demonstrated all these points.

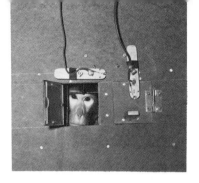

FIGURE 10–10 *A curious monkey peers out of his prison cage to watch the watchers watching him [Harlow, University of Wisconsin].*

FIGURE 10–11 *Monkeys will work on mechanical puzzles for no reward other than to work on the puzzle. This interest is apparent at a very early age. [Harlow, University of Wisconsin]*

The first issue, whether monkeys will manipulate for the sake of manipulation, was demonstrated in monkey puzzle experiments. A mechanical puzzle was devised that had three interlocking objects, a metal pin, a hook-and-eye, and a hasp. The three objects could be taken apart only in one order—by removing the pin, taking the hook out of the eye, and lifting the hasp (see Fig. 10-11). After a few sessions on this problem the monkey's score was nearly perfect. The puzzle was then made more difficult by adding other devices and was arranged to be reset every 6 minutes. Under these conditions the monkey kept on disassembling it for 10 hours. At this point the experiment was terminated because of experimenter fatigue; the monkey was still going strong.

Another set of manipulation experiments was designed to be analogous to ordinary visual discrimination learning, in which one of two different stimuli is rewarded with food when chosen. Here, however, no food was used; the only reward consisted in obtaining the object to play with. Ten screw eyes were mounted on a metal panel. Five were green and could not be removed; the other five were red and could be removed. They were arranged in a random order on the panel. The monkeys soon learned that the red screw eyes could be removed to play with and did not touch the green ones.

In an elegant series of experiments on play and manipulation of objects by chimpanzees Welker [1956] demonstrated that if a chimp is given a choice between a movable and a fixed object, he much prefers the movable object and will play with it for periods up to 30 minutes before losing interest. If series of different objects are given in succes-

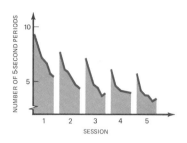

FIGURE 10–12 *Curiosity in chimpanzees as measured by the number of 5-second periods in a daily 6-minute session during which the chimpanzee made some response to a novel set of objects. "Boredom," or habituation, occurs each day (decrease in each curve) and from day to day (each successive curve starts at a lower point.) [Welker, 1956]*

sion, each for a few minutes, the animal will play with each for a decreasing period of time. As indicated in Fig. 10-12, the chimp plays most with the first object in the series and shows increasing boredom, both for each object and across objects. These results are particularly clear examples of habituation of curiosity behavior, both in response to each object and in response to the series. This phenomenon is familiar in young children with new toys. Whether the toy costs 10 cents or 10 dollars, the child will play with it happily for a short time and then lose interest.

The monkey peering out of Fig. 10-10 is an example of curiosity motivation. The animal learned to push the correct panel inside the cage for no other reward than being able to look out. Butler originally discovered this phenomenon by accident. He was testing a monkey on a food-reward learning problem and wanted to observe the monkey without being seen. Normally the monkey and experimenter are separated by a screen and cannot see one another. Butler drilled a small peephole through the screen to watch the monkey. Unfortunately the monkey soon found the hole and spent all his time peeking out at Butler. He then tried observing the monkey through a mirror, but the monkey outsmarted him again and kept an eye on him in the mirror.

These frustrating experiences led Butler and Harlow to the significant discovery that monkeys are strongly motivated to explore the world visually. In a typical experiment on visual curiosity animals are first familiarized with the box and are given an opportunity to peek out the open door. Then the doors of the box are closed; one door, identified with a yellow card on the inside, is locked, and the other, identified with a blue card on the inside, is left unlocked. If the monkey pushes against the blue card, the door will open for 30 seconds to allow the monkey to look out. In one experiment animals were tested 45 minutes per day for 57 days. Their curiosity was so persistent that they never tired of opening the door to look out.

These experiments indicate that motivation to manipulate and explore the world visually is fundamental and primary in monkeys and man. Under ordinary laboratory conditions visual curiosity is a much stronger motivation than food reward. In tests of visual curiosity where the door was closed each time 30 seconds after the monkeys had opened it, the animals worked continuously for up to 19 hours, far longer than they would work for a food reward.

The development of the infant's love and affection for his mother is considered by many psychologists to provide the initial foundation for more complex social motives. This early attachment can form the basis for the subsequent development of interpersonal relationships with other people. Love and affection were treated at length in Chapters 3 and 4, and as we saw there, the strong bond of affection the infant monkey develops for his cloth surrogate mother has nothing whatever to do with where he obtains his food. When the infants had two surrogate mothers, a nonnursing terrycloth mother and a nursing wire mother, their only source of food was the wire mother. According to the more extreme version of drive-reduction theory, the infants should have become attached to the wire mother; affection should have developed as a secondary or derived motive through hunger reduction associated with the wire mother. Freudian theory would also predict development of affection for the wire mother, on the basis of oral gratification associated with feeding. The results were quite different; the infant monkeys became attached to the cloth mother.

Another significant fact is that the infant monkey's attachment for his cloth mother develops only during the critical period of the first 30 to 90 days. Furthermore, if the infant does not form such an attachment, his later social behavior is markedly retarded and incompetent. These observations support the general view that social motivation is basic and innate and develops from an early critical experience of an affectional relationship.

COMPLEX HUMAN MOTIVATION

Let us consider a young man just entering college—full of bright hopes and great expectations. Why has he decided to spend four years of his life reading books, writing papers, and listening to lectures when he could get a job, get married, and provide for all of his physiological motives? Going to college cannot be explained on the basis of hunger, thirst, or even sex.

It is possible of course, that the student is motivated by an intrinsic curiosity motive—an unquenchable thirst for knowledge. This may be true for some, but most students have had this intrinsic motivation inhibited by years of dreary schooling or the general cultural antagonism to intellectual pursuits. Therefore, intrinsic curiosity cannot explain the intense, sometimes desperate, desire to go to college [Murray, 1964, pp. 83–84].

The reasons that we as moderately adult human beings behave as we do are obviously complex. A complete discussion of human motivation would be tantamount to a complete discussion of human behavior. Much that we have learned about the basic factors in human motivation comes from controlled laboratory experiments on infrahuman animals.

273

Everything we have said about primary motivation and its neurological foundations is approximately true for man. The human hypothalamus is not much different from the hypothalamus of the rat or cat. Hunger, thirst, aggression, sex, curiosity, and affection are powerful motives in rat, monkey, and man.

There are other potent aspects of human motivation that we may not be aware of in ourselves—*unconscious motivation*. A simple example is provided by the sexual symbolism in stories written by college students. Clark [1952] had groups of male students write stories as they viewed neutral pictures after having been shown pictures of attractive nude females. One group of students was tested in a classroom and another group was tested at a fraternity beer party. The stories written at the beer party, although they may have been somewhat less coherent, had more examples of overt sexual imagery than the classroom stories. However, imagery that the experimenters judged to be indirect or symbolic expression of sexual fantasies was more prevalent in the stories by the classroom group.

Basic biological factors can go a long way toward explaining certain aspects of human behavior. However, they fall short of providing an adequate account of normal human motivation, particularly in our affluent Western society. Hunger, thirst, aggression, curiosity, and probably even sex are not the dominant motives in our own ordinary daily life. Achievement of success in school or work, recognition and approval from peers, popularity, these are some of our more common motives and are *social*; they derive in part from our relations with other people.

A representative approach to the study of complex human social motivation is McClelland's work in achievement motivation. He uses the Thematic Apperception Test (TAT), a type of projective test in which the subject views neutral pictures of scenes involving people and writes stories about them. The stories are then scored by several raters in terms of the strength of the subject's desire to achieve success. Although this is a somewhat difficult procedure, good agreement among raters is usually obtained. The following is an example of a strong achievement story [Smith and Feld, 1958, p. 717]:

This young boy [in the picture] is dreaming of the day he will have completed his training and become a great and famous doctor. Perhaps this portrays someone already famous for research. He has been asked by his father or relative what he wants to do when he grows up and he is trying to tell them the mental picture that he has in his mind of himself in thirty years. The boy is thinking of the great thrill that must be experienced by a doctor when he performs a delicate operation saving someone's life. The boy will go on through college and eventually become a world-famous doctor.

McClelland et al. [1953] have studied the ways in which an individual's desire to achieve success affects speed of learning, performance efficiency, situational stress, and task complexity. The extent to which high and low achievers differ in these situations is truly remarkable; high

274

achievers are substantially better. To no one's surprise, it turns out that high achievers are ambitious, hard-working, and work toward personal standards of excellence rather than extrinsic rewards. Developmental studies have shown that the difference between high and low achievers in some part reflects parental attitudes, particularly maternal attitudes. Low achievers tended to come from homes where the parents insisted on dependence on the family, while those with high achievement motivation had backgrounds which encourage independence [Murray, 1964].

In addition to eating, reproducing, exploring, and socializing, we also think. In view of the fact that we spend much of our waking and sleeping time in thinking activity of one kind or another, it would be surprising if thought processes themselves did not provide a source of motivation. This cognitive approach to human motivation has been developed by Festinger [1957], with particular reference to the effects of contradictory thoughts or ideas. According to Festinger's theory of *cognitive dissonance*, if a person has two or more aspects of information or opinion that are inconsistent or mutually contradictory, a state of dissonance occurs which is uncomfortable and motivates an attempt to resolve it. Festinger's view is related to the old idea that people have logic-tight compartments, such as simultaneous beliefs in God and in science, but it goes one step farther and assumes that people do not *like* to have logic-tight compartments, a somewhat optimistic view of human nature.

Festinger cites cigarette smoking as an example [1957, p. 2]:

> ... the person who continues to smoke, knowing that it is bad for his health, may also feel (*a*) he enjoys smoking so much it is worth it; (*b*) the chances of his health suffering are not as serious as some would make out; (*c*) he can't always avoid every possible dangerous contingency and still live; and (*d*) perhaps even if he stopped smoking he would put on weight which is equally bad for his health. So, continuing to smoke is, after all, consistent with his ideas about smoking.

The data shown in Fig. 10-13 provide support; the more heavily a person smokes, the less convinced he is that smoking is linked to lung cancer.

Festinger et al. have attempted to isolate and define the various techniques people use to reduce dissonance. One of the most common is a *selective* search for information. The person seeks out material which supports one idea and ignores information that supports dissonant ideas. Our cigarette smoker might spend a great deal of time watch-

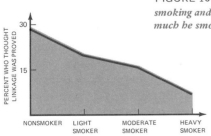

FIGURE 10–13　*The degree to which a person believes that smoking and lung cancer are linked is inversely related to how much he smokes [Festinger, 1957].*

MOTIVATION

ing television ads for cigarettes but avoid reading newspaper articles about lung cancer. In another commonly cited experiment purchasers of new cars were shown a series of ads for various makes of cars. The most commonly read ads were for the car the subject had just bought, while ads for competing models were relatively ignored.

Dissonance theory has obvious parallels with the drive-reduction theory of motivation we discussed earlier. Absence of cognitive dissonance is equivalent to maintenance of internal balance, cognitive dissonance serves the same purpose as drive, and reduction of dissonance is comparable to drive reduction. The dissonant person who learns to reduce dissonance through rationalization is like the hungry rat who learns to press a bar for food.

Our discussion of motivation has ranged from the brain mechanisms of hunger, thirst and aggression, through manipulation, curiosity, and the development of affection, to complex social and cognitive motives. Arousal was introduced as a behavioral and biological concept that can serve to unify various approaches to motivation, particularly for basic states that reflect innate tissue needs. What about the more complex aspects of motivation? Curiosity and manipulation, at least, have obvious parallels. Hunger provides tissue-need cues to the hypothalamus. The eyes, ears, and hands could provide analogous need cues to the central nervous system regarding exploration and manipulation. All these inputs can serve to modulate and regulate behavioral and neural arousal toward an optimal level. Social and cognitive factors can similarly influence arousal.

The distinction between primary and secondary sources of motivation may be more apparent than real. A case could be made that all major sources of motivated behavior are primary. Man is a social animal; he is one of a number of social species. Hence the ultimate source of his need for social approval may be found in the genes, just as is the tissue need for food. Perhaps what is learned is the behavioral expression of these needs. We need food, and even certain types of food, but we learn to like particular flavors. We need social interaction, and even certain types of it, but we learn to prefer particular forms of social interactions and activities.

SUMMARY

One important aspect of motivation that is observable in all species is aggressive, or agonistic, behavior, which takes the three general forms flight, defense, and attack. Intraspecies fighting is usually a pattern of threat and submission and rarely results in death. This is in contrast to interspecies fighting, as between predator and prey. In many species agonistic behavior is triggered by specific stimulus cues, such as color or shape. Fighting is further influenced, at least among rodents, by environmental factors, such as amount of living space available, amount of food, or presence of females. Genetic variables and the *history* of previous successes in fighting also play a role. Agonistic behavior appears to be controlled by the hypothalamus and the amygdala, which are critical in the appearance of rage and attack, and the septal area, which seems to suppress rage.

Hunger and thirst have been studied in terms of the behaviors that precede eating and drinking, the actual consumatory responses, the brain systems that control eating and drinking, and the long-term consequences to the internal environment. Peripheral effects of food or water deprivation, such as stomach contractions or dryness of the mouth and throat, are not sufficient to explain hunger and thirst. Actually, food deprivation leads to activation of hypothalamic glucose receptors and water deprivation to activation of hypothalamic osmoreceptors, which produce an increase in general activity or arousal, plus an increase in appropriate goal-directed behavior. Ingestion causes a cessation of neural activity, and hence cessation of the behavioral response, so that homeostatic balance is maintained.

The drive theory of motivation postulates that sources of motivation generate a drive to act and provide the cues for appropriate behavior. Drive reduction is presumed to be rewarding, and behavior which reduces drive is therefore learned. Another theory of motivation, the *James-Lange* formulation, proposes that motivated states *follow* the occurrence of particular behavioral responses rather than *precede* them. Both theoretical approaches have proved useful in the analysis of motivated behavior. Other types of motivation, such as manipulative needs and curiosity, do not appear to fit well into current theoretical frameworks.

There are also more complex aspects of motivation, particularly in primates, which biological analyses do not yet explain. The early infant-mother attachment may be the basis of later social motives for achievement, approval, etc. Formulations such as Festinger's theory of cognitive dissonance may be a first step toward understanding the substrates of complex motivation.

CHAPTER ELEVEN

LEARNING AND BEHAVIORAL ADAPTATION

As we know from our everyday observations, our behavior is profoundly influenced by our experiences. We have learned to talk, to read, to write, to plan, to hope, and to love. We have also learned to deceive, to fear, and perhaps to hate. Learning in its broadest sense makes human socialization possible. Society is based on the training provided by subtle as well as explicit experiences, such as formal education. Because of our enormous capacity for learning, human behavior can be and is extremely varied. For example, as humans we inherit molecules that program the neurobiological processes which make it possible for us to acquire and use language. However, the language each of us learns is the language spoken by those around us. So it is with all our skills, habits, aspirations, beliefs, and prejudices. For centuries scholars have wondered what human beings would be like if they were reared in isolation from other human beings. One speculation was that children reared in cultural isolation might speak some basic or "natural" human language. In all likelihood, however, they would acquire no language at all. They would in fact lack most of the characteristics that we regard as distinctively "human." We learn to be human beings.

LEARNING

Since it is learning that enables us to adapt to the complex requirements of our environments, it might be well to begin with a biological perspective of learning. The basis of evolution is adaptation. The survival of any species depends on its ability to adapt to the requirements of its own particular environment. There are, of course, many ways in which adaptation takes place. Through the slow process of genetic mutation and selection a species can acquire the necessary form and physiological machinery for almost any environmental condition. For example, many species, such as the polar bear, have evolved a coloration that serves as camouflage in their natural surroundings. The physiology of such arctic animals is also quite different from that of desert animals. Adaptation is particularly apparent in behavior. Lower animals can, without specific training, perform many complicated tasks, such as nest building, migrating, communicating, and mating. The development of such genetically influenced responses, commonly referred to as *instincts*, provides for rather complex behavioral adaptation to special environments. However, organisms sometimes become so specialized in form or function that they are unable to survive. In a complex environment the evolution of unique morphological, physiological, or even behavioral factors can prove fatal to the species.

Evolution of the ability to respond to *changes* in the environment clearly added a new dimension to the capacity of organisms to adapt. Specialized physiological responses such as the growth of plants toward light and hibernation of some mammals in cold weather provide for some adjustment to environmental changes. However, the most flexible basis of individual adaptation was provided by evolution of the capacity of the individual organism to vary its behavioral responses in terms of different environmental requirements—that is, to learn. Learning can do quickly what evolution can do only slowly. Whereas adaptation to a single environmental condition takes generations to achieve through evolution, an organism that can learn is able to tailor its own behavior to fit a variety of environmental conditions. Of course the ability to learn provides the basis for adaptation, but not all learning is adaptive. Just as effective behavior can be learned, so ineffective or neurotic behavior can also be learned.

For years psychologists and other biological scientists have attempted to develop a general definition of learning. Learning is most often defined as a more or less permanent change in behavior produced by experience. Although this is a useful working definition, it is admittedly imprecise. We will not have an adequate definition of learning until we know more about the varieties of behavioral plasticity that are considered examples of learning. For example, we use the phrase, "more or less permanent" as a hedge, because we do not yet know whether all the effects of experience are permanent. Certainly we and the other animals forget, and until we completely understand the nature of forgetting we cannot be certain whether, in the legendary words of William James, "nothing we ever do is, in strict scientific literalness, wiped out" [James, 1890, p. 127].

In analyzing behavior it is difficult to sort out the various influences which cause behavior to change. Learning does not take place in a vacuum, and the basic problem lies in distinguishing learning from other influences on behavior, such as fatigue, sensory adaptation, disease, injury, aging, and genetic contributions to the development of responses. For centuries man has trained animals of many species, including his own, by reward and punishment, or *instrumental conditioning*. A number of years ago two psychologists, Breland and Breland, developed a program of instrumental learning to train animal acts for county fairs and amusement parks. In general they were quite successful, but they encountered some interesting difficulties. For example, they trained a pig to pick up wooden coins and deposit them in a large "piggy bank" by rewarding it for successful responses [Breland and Breland, 1961, p. 683]:

At first the pig would eagerly pick up one dollar, carry it to the bank, run back, get another, . . . and so on. . . . Thereafter, over a period of weeks the behavior would become slower and slower. He might run over eagerly for each dollar, but on the way back, instead of carrying the dollar and depositing it simply and cleanly, he would repeatedly drop it, root it [that is, push it with his nose], drop it again, root it along the way, pick it up, toss it up in the air, drop it, [and] root it some more.

This pattern persisted even when the pig became extremely hungry because it worked too slowly to get enough to eat over the course of the day. Why did the learned behavior deteriorate? Breland and Breland suggested that the rooting behavior competed with the learned behavior because rooting is built into this species as part of the food-getting repertoire. On the basis of many similar observations with various other species, they reached the important conclusion that "the behavior of any species cannot be adequately understood, predicted, or controlled without knowledge of its institutional patterns, evolutionary history and ecological niche" [Breland and Breland, 1961, p. 684]. This point has bearing on many of the aspects of learning we shall discuss.

It is often assumed that only one or perhaps two forms of behavioral modification can properly be called learning. It is becoming increasingly apparent, however, that there are a number of types of behavioral modifications produced by experience. A complete understanding of learning must be based on an examination of each type. There is reason to believe that much of the variety simply reflects differences in the training procedures. However, there may well be actual differences in the neurobiological mechanisms of some types of learning.

One form of learning observed in all species, from the single-celled protozoan to man, is *habituation*, the decrease in response to a specific stimulus with repeated stimulation. When we hear an unexpected noise our attention is aroused and directed toward its

HABITUATION

source. If the noise is repeated, we habituate to it; we cease paying attention to it and eventually may not even be aware of it. For example, as we sit by a highway we often quickly come to ignore the sounds of passing automobiles. Responsiveness to repeated stimulation can decrease for other reasons which we must be careful to distinguish from habituation. In habituation the decrease in responsiveness is fairly specific to a particular stimulus. Following habituation of a response to a specific stimulus the response can still be elicited by stimuli other than the specific one to which it was habituated. This is in contrast to *sensory adaptation*, which affects sensitivity to all stimuli within a given sensory modality. Habituation must also be differentiated from *fatigue*, which decreases responsiveness to *all* stimulation. Under some circumstances repeated stimulation can also lead to increased responsiveness, or *sensitization*. However, the increased responsiveness is not necessarily

TABLE 11–1 *Average number of trials required for habituation in spirostomum to mechanical stimulation repeated at 5-minute intervals [Applewhite, 1968].*	AVERAGE NO. OF TRIALS
Whole naïve animals	9.0
Halves of habituated animals	
Anterior	3.1
Posterior	3.6
Halves of naïve animals	
Anterior	7.1
Posterior	9.6

stimulus specific. Habituation is often termed the simplest form of behavioral plasticity. It is obviously an adaptive function, and it is possible that the evolution of altered responsiveness in simple animals may have provided a basis of subsequent evolution of more complex learning processes.

Several examples will illustrate the pervasiveness of habituation. The protozoan *spirostomum* responds to stimulation by contracting. Applewhite [1968] found that when these single-celled animals were repeatedly stimulated by a mild jarring vibration every 5 seconds their response progressively decreased. In one experiment the animals ceased all contractions after only nine jarrings. After training the animals were cut in half, and the two sections (anterior and posterior) were given additional habituation training. Rehabituation of the severed halves took fewer than four trials (see Table 11-1). When naïve animals were cut in half the sections habituated in approximately the same number of trials as the intact animals (7 to 10 trials). Further tests showed that the decrease in responsiveness was not due either to fatigue or to local sensory adaptation. Clearly habituation in simple organisms does not require an organized nervous system.

Habituation of responses, including responses to socially significant stimuli, has been studied extensively in more complex species [Thorpe, 1963]. According to Lorenz [1969], wildfowl react to the approach of a furry animal such as a dog at the edge of their pond by escaping and "cautious mobbing" of the animal. However, birds that remain in the same region become habituated to specific dogs—that is, their responsiveness to them decreases. This habituation is highly stimulus specific; the birds respond readily when a strange dog wanders into the area. Some of the clearest evidence of habituation is seen in fish. The male three-spined stickleback will defend its newly constructed nest by attacking other males which intrude into its territory [Tinbergen, 1951]. Peeke [1969] studied the habituation of these aggressive responses by placing either a wooden model of a male fish or a live male stickleback (restrained in a clear plastic tube) directly into an aquarium each day for

10 days. Figure 11-1 shows the decrease with repeated exposure in attacks on the "intruder." The live fish elicited many more responses than the model. Note that the biting response decreased during each day but that some recovery occurred between each pair of days, although the responsiveness clearly decreased over a 10-day period. As is the case with other forms of behavioral plasticity, habituation is frequently short-lasting, as it is with the protozoan discussed above, and under other circumstances it can be quite persistent.

It is generally, and no doubt properly, assumed that in multi-cellular animals the plasticity underlying learning is due to changes in neural tissue. There is considerable controversy over whether learning can occur in restricted portions of the nervous systems of vertebrates, particularly in the spinal cord. Research by Thompson has provided conclusive affirmative evidence [Thompson, 1967; Thompson and Spencer, 1966; Groves and Thompson, 1970]. Habituation of a flexion response to repeated stimulation was obtained in laboratory animals in which the spinal cord had been surgically severed from the brain. The stimulus was a shock applied to the animal's skin and the response was a muscle contraction. The amplitude of the response decreased with stimulus repetition, recovered with time, and was then readily rehabituated. The electrical activity of nerve cells within the spinal cord, termed *interneurons*, was recorded by means of microelectrodes during habituation trials (see Fig. 11-2). Interestingly, three types of cells were found—cells which showed no changes in frequency of firing with repetition, cells which initially showed increased activity with repetition, and cells which showed decreased activity with repetition. The three types of cells are referred to as type *N* (nonplastic), type *H* (habituation), and type *S* (sensitization). In addition to differing in frequency of firing with repeated stimulation, the cells differ in their speed of response

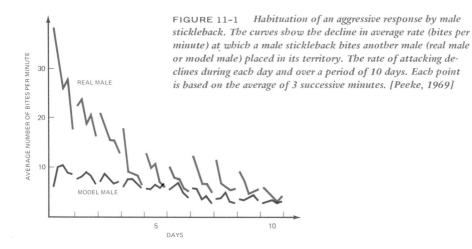

FIGURE 11-1   *Habituation of an aggressive response by male stickleback. The curves show the decline in average rate (bites per minute) at which a male stickleback bites another male (real male or model male) placed in its territory. The rate of attacking declines during each day and over a period of 10 days. Each point is based on the average of 3 successive minutes. [Peeke, 1969]*

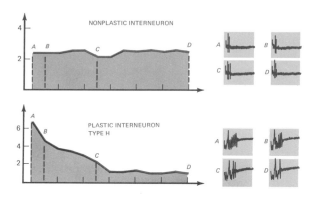

FIGURE 11–2 *Three types of spinal interneurons.*
The curves show responsiveness to sensory stimulation
(mean number of spikes per stimulus) with increasing
number of trials. A through D on the right of each
curve show the electrical response of a typical cell—
A before habituation, B on the first several trials,
C after a number of trials, and D at the end of the

following stimulation. Furthermore, the different types of cells are located in different regions of the spinal cord. Neurons in this phylogenetically old region of the nervous system appear to be specialized for different types of responses to stimulation.

These findings are not too surprising in view of the evidence that habituation can occur even in single-celled animals. Analysis of the features of single cells which make such plasticity possible may lead to an understanding of the neurobiological bases of more complex forms of learning—but again, this is a complex and controversial issue. Some of the reasons for the controversy will become clear as we consider other forms of learning which have been studied in man and the other animals.

CLASSICAL AND INSTRUMENTAL CONDITIONING

Although animal training has been practiced for many centuries and naturalistic observations of learning have been made by scholars since recorded history, experimental studies of learning began only in the latter part of the last century. Ebbinghaus' classical research on memory was published in 1885. The Russian physiologist Pavlov and the American psychologist Thorndike both began laboratory studies of learning in animals just at the turn of the century. For decades the research and writings of these pioneer investigators were dominant influences in the development of theories and experimental analyses of learning. Many contemporary techniques, problems, and theories stem directly from these influences.

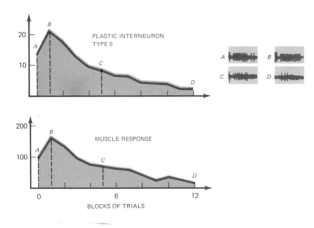

habituation session. In nonplastic interneurons responsiveness does not change with repeated stimulation. In plastic type-H interneurons responsiveness decreases with stimulation. In plastic type-S interneurons responsiveness first increases, and then habituates. [Groves and Thompson, 1970]

The methods used by Pavlov in his studies of conditioning in dogs were based on his earlier work on the physiology of digestion (for which he was awarded the Nobel prize in 1904). Some of his basic findings are common knowledge. When meat powder is placed on a dog's tongue, the dog salivates. If some other stimulus, such as a bell or sound of a ticking metronome, is presented along with the meat powder on several occasions, the other stimulus will eventually elicit salivation when presented without the food. The process of pairing the meat powder with the bell is termed *reinforcement*. The stimulus which elicits the response is termed the *unconditioned stimulus*, and the initial response is called the *unconditioned response*. The signal is referred to as the *conditioned stimulus* and the learned response is called the *conditioned response*. An essential feature of this *classical* conditioning procedure is that the conditioned stimulus and unconditioned stimulus are controlled by the experimenter; the dog has no control over the delivery of the meat powder. The speed of acquisition of the conditioned response in classical conditioning is influenced by many factors. One of the most important of these is the time at which the conditioned stimulus is presented. Optimal conditioning occurs when the conditioned stimulus terminates shortly (0.5 second) before the onset of the unconditioned stimulus. Conditioning probably does not occur when the unconditioned stimulus precedes the conditioned stimulus.

Pavlov also observed a number of other interesting phenomena, which are summarized in Fig. 11-3. After conditioning, if the conditioned stimulus is presented alone, the response will decrease, or *extinguish*. In

285

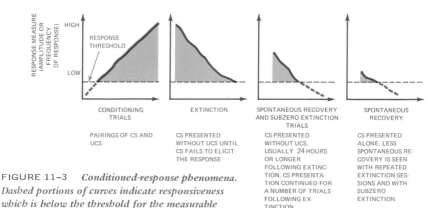

RESPONSE MEASURE (AMPLITUDE OR FREQUENCY OF RESPONSE)

HIGH

RESPONSE THRESHOLD

LOW

CONDITIONING TRIALS

PAIRINGS OF CS AND UCS

EXTINCTION

CS PRESENTED WITHOUT UCS UNTIL CS FAILS TO ELICIT THE RESPONSE

SPONTANEOUS RECOVERY AND SUBZERO EXTINCTION TRIALS

CS PRESENTED WITHOUT UCS. USUALLY 24 HOURS OR LONGER FOLLOWING EXTINC- TION. CS PRESENTA- TION CONTINUED FOR A NUMBER OF TRIALS FOLLOWING EX- TINCTION.

SPONTANEOUS RECOVERY

CS PRESENTED ALONE. LESS SPONTANEOUS RE- COVERY IS SEEN WITH REPEATED EXTINCTION SES- SIONS AND WITH SUBZERO EXTINCTION.

FIGURE 11–3   *Conditioned-response phenomena.*
Dashed portions of curves indicate responsiveness
which is below the threshold for the measurable
response.

the session following extinction the response recovers to a higher level, a phenomenon termed *spontaneous recovery.* Spontaneous recovery can be decreased by presenting the conditioned stimulus alone even after complete extinction has occurred; this is called *subzero extinction.* Following conditioning training with a conditioned stimulus such as a bell, *higher-order conditioning* can be obtained by pairing that conditioned stimulus with another conditioned stimulus such as a light, even though the food is no longer given. Higher-order conditioning is difficult to obtain, and without reinforcement with the unconditioned stimulus it is readily extinguished. Animals conditioned to respond to a specific unconditioned stimulus such as a 200-hertz tone will subsequently respond to other tones. This phenomenon is called *generalization.* Degree of generalization decreases as the difference between the conditioned stimulus and the test stimuli are increased.

These are some of the major phenomena studied by Pavlov. In numerous experiments, by Pavlov as well as other investigators, many stimuli have been used as conditioned stimuli, many responses other than salivation have been studied, and other stimuli, such as electric shock, have been used as unconditioned stimuli.

What conclusions can be drawn about classical conditioning? Pavlov regarded conditioning as the fundamental process of association and regarded the conditioning experiments as providing a means of investigating the mechanisms of brain functioning underlying complex behavior. According to Pavlov [1957, pp. 197–198] :

The conditioned reflex is a common and widespread phenomenon. It is, evidently, what we recognize in ourselves and in animals under such names as training, discipline, education, habits; these are nothing but connections established in the course of individual existence, connections between definite external stimuli and corresponding reactions. Thus the conditioned reflex opens to the physiologist the door to investigation of a considerable part, and possibly, even of the entire higher nervous activity.

Other investigators have regarded classical conditioning as one of two, or perhaps several, types of learning. However the facts of conditioning are interpreted, it is clear that classical conditioning is a specific method of training animals. In view of this, some of the phenomena obtained with classical conditioning may differ from those obtained with other methods. However, it seems likely that the neurobiological bases of classical conditioning do not differ fundamentally from those of other forms of learning. It is sometimes assumed that classical conditioning consists only of training an animal to make a specific conditioned response, say salivation, to a specific stimulus, say a 200-hertz tone, and that the conditioned response is identical to the unconditioned response [Pavlov, 1957]. If this were true, we would need only to understand how a conditioned stimulus can substitute for an unconditioned stimulus in order to explain conditioning. The facts of conditioning are somewhat different from this concept. Zener reported his experiments in using a bell as a conditioned stimulus and salivation as an unconditioned response [1937, p. 393]:

> Except for the component of salivary secretion the conditioned and unconditioned behavior is not identical. The *CR* [conditioned response] . . . is a different reaction from the *UCR* [unconditioned response] anthropomorphically describable as looking, expecting, the fall of food with a readiness to perform the eating behavior which will occur when the food falls. The effector pattern is not identical with the *UCR* [unconditioned response].

Another more complex and interesting observation was made by Liddell while he was working in Pavlov's laboratory. A dog which had been conditioned to salivate at the acceleration of the beat of a metronome was freed from its harness. As reported by Lorenz [1969, p. 47]:

> The dog at once ran to the machine, wagged its tail at it, tried to jump up to it, barked, and so on; in other words, it showed as clearly as possible the whole system of behavior patterns serving, in a number of *canidae*, to beg food. . . . It is, in fact, this whole system that is being conditioned in the classical experiment.

Obviously when animals are trained with classical conditioning procedures they learn much more than the specific response which is measured during the training. This is one of the basic facts of learning which has made it difficult to develop an adequate general theory of learning. It is relatively easy to control behavior through training. However, it is not easy to specify the nature of the changes produced by the training.

INSTRUMENTAL CONDITIONING

The learning obtained with reward-and-punishment training procedures, termed *instrumental conditioning*, was first studied by Thorndike during his graduate work under William James. These studies, like Pavlov's, were

287

begun just before the turn of the century. Thorndike placed laboratory animals, usually cats, in a small cage which could be opened, providing escape and a food reward, only if the cats made a specific response such as turning a latch or pulling a string. On the first few trials the animals made a variety of responses prior to making the "correct" one. As training continued, the irrelevant, or "incorrect," responses decreased, and the animals escaped within a short time after being placed in the problem box [Thorndike, 1932]. These procedures are, of course, the same as those we use to train our dog to "shake hands" or "roll over." In instrumental conditioning, in contrast to classical conditioning, the animal's behavior is "instrumental" in influencing the consequences of behavior; the reward is not given, or the punishment is not avoided, unless the animal makes the appropriate response. The environmental consequences—rewards and punishments—"select" adaptive responses, and the behavior of individual animals can thus become shaped to the requirements of the environment. From the animal's standpoint learning enables it to gain some degree of control over its environment.

In the artificial environment of the laboratory animals have been taught an enormous variety of responses. Instrumental-conditioning procedures have been successfully used to teach tricks to animals. Instrumental conditioning is also referred to as *operant conditioning*. This term was introduced by Skinner [1938], who also developed the well-known training apparatus—called the Skinner box—in which animals are given a small reward, or *reinforcement*, for pressing a lever. This technique enables us to study the effects of various rewards and other influences on the rate of response and has provided a means of investigating such things as sensory processes in animals. For example, an animal can be taught to press a lever only in the presence of a particular stimulus, and by varying the stimulus intensity, its sensory threshold for that stimulus can be measured. Studies of instrumental, or operant, conditioning have also revealed a number of interesting phenomena not observed in classical conditioning. For example, the pattern of responding is influenced by the frequency and pattern of rewards. Rewards can be given after each response, or they can be given only intermittently—that is, after either a fixed or random number of responses or after a fixed or random interval. Examples of the effects of different schedules of reward are shown in Fig. 11-4.

Operant conditioning in which response rate is the critical observation should be regarded as a special variety of instrumental conditioning. Most kinds of instrumental-learning tasks use measures of the time required for a response or of the number of errors made with repeated trials. A variety of other procedures are used in studies of instrumental learning. They all employ reward or punishment to induce animals to respond or stop responding (inhibitory avoidance). In some cases the response may produce a reward, and in others it may lead to the escape from or avoidance of a punishing stimulus. Each procedure produces a different type of behavioral modification—but all these procedures result in learning.

288

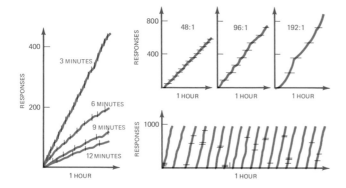

FIGURE 11-4 *Cumulative-response curves obtained with various schedules of rewards. Lines through the curves indicate delivery of reward. Left, fixed interval, the cumulative responses over a 1-hour period when rats are rewarded for the first lever pressing response made after 3, 6, 9, or 12 minutes. Center, fixed ratio, the cumulative responses of rats rewarded for every 48, 96, or 192 responses. Right, variable interval, the cumulative pecking responses of a pigeon rewarded at intervals ranging from 10 seconds to 21 minutes, with an average of five rewards per hour. Note that the rate of response varies with the type of reward schedule used. [Skinner, 1938; 1950]*

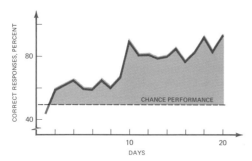

FIGURE 11-5 *Visual-discrimination learning by monkeys for visual exploration reward. Correct responses were rewarded only by an opportunity to look at a complex visual stimulus. [Butler, 1953]*

For some years researchers attempted to see whether events which are rewarding and punishing, termed *reinforcements*, might have a common basis. For example, Hull [1943] proposed that reinforcements act by decreasing biological drives such as hunger and thirst, and that such reinforcement was essential for learning to occur. One difficulty with this view is that an enormous variety of stimuli can act as reinforcers, that is, modify performance—and many appear to be unrelated to drives such as hunger and thirst. Animals will work for such rewards as variation in sensory stimulation. Neither beast nor man works for bread alone. Some examples of the reward effects of various visual stimuli are shown in Fig. 11-5.

The story is told of the researcher who, curious to find out what laboratory monkeys do when they are not being observed by psychologists, peeked through a laboratory door keyhole, only to see a monkey's eye peeking back at him. Harlow has shown that monkeys will press a lever for hours just for the opportunity to peek at an electric train, the laboratory room outside their chamber, or even the experimenter, and will solve problems when the only reward is the working of the problem or whatever satisfaction results from its solution [Harlow and McClearn, 1954; Butler, 1954b]. Humans, of course, engage in countless intellectual, athletic, and esthetic activities which are not rooted in the satisfaction of needs essential to life.

A number of years ago Olds and Milner [1954] discovered that laboratory rats could be trained to perform instrumental tasks such as pressing levers and even running mazes when the only reward was a small amount of electric current delivered directly to their brains. This remarkable discovery has been substantiated in extensive subsequent research, and demonstrations of the rewarding effects of intracranial stimulation are now commonplace. This finding also dramatically stimulated interest in the neural bases of motivation and learning.

Rewarding behavior by electrical stimulation of the brain has become a useful technique in examining possible differences between classical and instrumental learning. For example, it was long thought that responses controlled by the autonomic nervous system were modified only by classical conditioning, while skeletal responses controlled by the central nervous system were modified through instrumental conditioning. However, in a series of elegant studies Miller et al. have shown that such autonomic functions as heart rate and intestinal contractions can be modified by instrumental conditioning (see Fig. 11-6). After temporarily paralyzing rats with curare, which paralyzes the skeletal

FIGURE 11-6   *Instrumental conditioning of autonomic responses in rats. Left, effects on heart rate of rewarding increases or decreases in heart rate or in intestinal contraction. Right, effects on intestinal contraction of rewarding increases or decreases in intestinal contraction or in heart rate. Only the response specifically rewarded is modified by the reward. Intracranial electrical stimulation was used as the reward, with the animals paralyzed by curare in order to eliminate skeletal responses. [Miller and Banuazizi, 1968]*

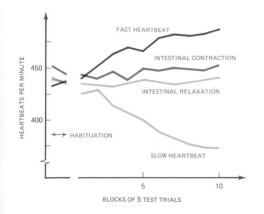
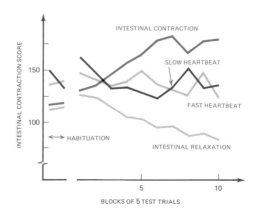

muscles without preventing autonomic responses, they placed electrodes into "rewarding" areas of the rats' brains and administered electrical stimulation whenever heart rate changed or degree of intestinal contractions altered. For some rats increases in autonomic responses were rewarded, while for others decreases were rewarded. The findings indicated that both responses were modified by the stimulation; the rates of autonomic responses could be either increased or decreased. Moreover, differential rewarding of one of the responses, such as heart rate, did not affect the other response, intestinal contraction. Comparable findings were obtained when the reward used was escape from mild electric shocks. Autonomically mediated responses are clearly influenced by instrumental conditioning procedures. Thus the contention that classical and instrumental conditioning have different neural bases is not borne out by the evidence.

In another interesting series of experiments Solomon et al. showed that a response learned through classical conditioning procedures can influence instrumental responses learned in the same situation [Maier et al., 1969; Rescorla and LoLordo, 1965]. In one study dogs were first trained to jump back and forth over a hurdle from one side of a shuttle-box to the other in order to avoid a foot shock. After the rate of response had stabilized at about six shuttles per minute, the dogs were given a series of classical conditioning trials in which one conditioned stimulus was followed by a foot shock and another conditioned stimulus was followed by no shock. The dogs were then tested in the shuttle box again. When the conditioned stimulus previously followed by a foot shock was presented, their shuttling rate increased dramatically; when the "safe" conditioned stimulus was presented, the rate of shuttling decreased. Clearly, the instrumentally conditioned behavior of the dogs was markedly influenced by the *meaning* of the two conditioned stimuli, which was acquired during the classical-conditioning training.

Studies of classical and instrumental conditioning have demonstrated that virtually any discriminable stimulus can acquire meaning through its association with another meaningful stimulus. Stimuli followed by rewards and punishments can come to produce behavioral changes. In instrumental conditioning the experimenter can specify the nature of the response by making the delivery of reward or punishment contingent on the response. In classical conditioning the animal responds to a previously neutral conditioned stimulus even though it has no control over the delivery of the rewarding or punishing unconditioned stimulus. In both cases environmental stimuli acquire meaning.

Because of the robustness of the phenomena of classical and instrumental conditioning, the effectiveness of conditioning in controlling behavior has sometimes been overestimated. Furthermore, it is widely believed that any arbitrarily selected stimulus can become a cue for any rewards or punishments which it precedes. Pavlov proposed, for example, that "any natural phenomena chosen at will may be converted into 'conditioned stimuli' " [Pavlov, 1927]. However, some interesting recent discoveries limit this generalization. It is well known that rats which have survived poisoning subsequently avoid the *food* that poisoned them, but not the *place* where the food was located [Barnett, 1963]. What is the basis of this selective and highly adaptive behavior? In a series of experiments Garcia et al. [1968] found that rats will associate a general illness with something they have eaten (as though they responded with, "It must have been something I ate"). However, if they are given a painful stimulus such as an electric shock, they selectively avoid visual and auditory stimuli which preceded the punishment.

Apparently rats cannot learn to associate general illness with sights and sounds or to associate pain with food taste. In another experiment hungry rats were given either large or small food pellets which were coated with either powdered sugar or flour. Several groups of rats were given a painful foot shock every time they selected a pellet of a particular size or flavor. Rats in other groups were made ill by an x-ray treatment given immediately after the 1-hour period of eating pellets of a particular size and flavor. Two days later each group was tested to see whether the rats had learned to associate flavor and size with the two types of punishments. As Fig. 11-7 indicates, the animals given foot shocks readily ate pellets of either *flavor*, but they selectively avoided pellets of the *size* associated with foot shock. Rats given x-ray treatments readily ate pellets of either *size*, but they selectively avoided pellets of the *flavor* associated with the x-ray treatment. Garcia et al. concluded from these findings that pairing a perceptible cue with an effective reinforcer does not necessarily result in associative learning and that for a cue to be effective it must be related to the consequences that ensue.

An added point of interest is that the x ray was effective as a reinforcer and led to selective avoidance of a stimulus even though the animals did not become ill for some time after x-ray treatment. Although rewards and punishments are generally effective only when they are given either immediately or shortly after a training experience, delayed punishment in the form of general malaise is readily associated with food eaten some time earlier. The adaptive consequences of this ability provide stomachaches and security for the rat and ulcers and headaches for the farmer. It seems likely that the selectivity of associations between cues and consequences may be a fairly general phenomenon. Apparently anything cannot be made to stand for anything else as is often assumed.

THE LEARNING AND PERFORMANCE OF RESPONSES

In one sense rewards and punishments are essential for instrumental learning; they clearly cause animals to perform, and they shape responses. Without rewards and punishments responses to stimuli usually extinguish or habituate. Rewards are essential to ensure the repetition of responses, but are they essential for learning to occur? According to Thorndike [1932], and later Hull [1943], rewards cause learning to occur. If this

292

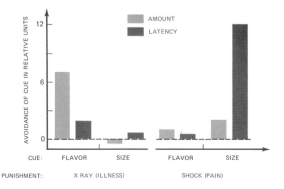

FIGURE 11–7   *Relative effectiveness of the size and flavor of food as cues when they are associated with either an electric shock or illness produced by x ray. When x ray is used as punishment the rats avoid foods with a particular flavor; the size of the food is not effective as a cue. When electric shock is used as punishment the rats avoid pellets of a particular size; flavor is not an effective cue. [Garcia et al., 1968]*

were true, of course, habituation and extinction, and perhaps even classical conditioning, could not be regarded as types of learning.

From another perspective, however, rewards and punishments control performance indirectly by influencing responses. According to this view, proposed by Tolman [1932], what is *learned* depends on the animal's sensory experiences, including the rewarding and punishing stimuli provided by the environment. What is *performed*, of course, depends not only on what has been learned, but also on the particular motivation of the animal when it is tested and the particular rewarding and punishing features of the environment. Thus a reinforced training trial provides an animal with the opportunity of learning about the environment—including, possibly, learning how to make a particular response. For example, if the reinforcement is irrelevant at the time, as when food is given to a satiated animal, the animal still may learn something about it even though there is no immediate behavioral response. A motivated animal may also have learned a great deal about its environment and not respond differentially in it until rewards are introduced to shape a specific response. Moreover, nearly all animals are capable at any given moment of performing any selection of an incredibly large number of previously learned responses, but what they do perform depends on the behaviors and motivations specific to their species.

There have been numerous studies of the effects of motivation on learning. Under some conditions performance varies with level of motivation, but this is not always the case, particularly when the response measure is errors rather than speed of response. In one interesting experiment Miles [1959] studied the effect of varying the length of food deprivation on discrimination learning in squirrel monkeys. In discrimination learning animals are taught to respond selectively to particular cues or objects. For example, an animal may be rewarded for choosing a black object presented along with objects which are white or grey. The monkeys were trained on both an easy and a difficult discrimination

293

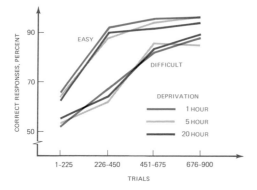

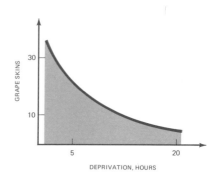

FIGURE 11-8 *Effects of degree of food deprivation and task difficulty on discrimination learning in monkeys. Deprivation did not affect performance on either the easy or the difficult task but did affect food motivation. Willingness to eat the grape skins increased with hours of food deprivation. [Miles, 1959]*

task. Each monkey was trained under three food-deprivation conditions— 1 hour, 5 hours, and 20 hours. As Fig. 11-8 shows, the deprivation conditions did not affect rate of learning, but they did produce differing degrees of motivation. Grapes were used as rewards. When the monkeys were deprived of food for 20 hours they ate the grapes skins and all. Under the 1-hour deprivation conditions they ate the meat of the grapes but spit the skins out on the floor, where they were counted.

Experimental studies of *latent*, or hidden, learning in rats have shown that performance and learning can and should be distinguished. In studies of latent learning animals are allowed to learn without rewards and are then given rewards to see whether their performance has been influenced by the nonrewarded training. For example, in one of the pioneering studies of latent learning Tolman and Honzik [1930] placed rats deprived of food and water in an alley maze once each day for 17 days. One group of rats was given a food reward each day when it reached the goal box, a second group was never rewarded, and a third group was not rewarded for the first 10 trials. On the eleventh trial and each subsequent trial this third group found food in the goal box. Figure 11-9 shows the average number of errors, the entrances into blind alleys in the maze, made by each group on each day. Over the 17 days the performance of the rewarded animals was clearly superior to that of the nonrewarded controls. This was to be expected, of course, since there was no particular reason for the animals to decrease their entrances into blind alleys, except as a result of habituation, or possibly, the mild punishing effect of being forced to turn around in a narrow alley. Clearly, however, the animals learned about the maze when they were not rewarded. On the last six days of the test the performance of

294

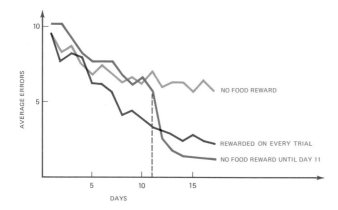

FIGURE 11–9   *Latent learning in rats. The rewarded group performed much better than the group that was never rewarded. The performance of a third group, not rewarded until the eleventh trial, was like that of the unrewarded group on the first 11 trials and like that of the consistently rewarded group (perhaps even better) on the last several trials; the latent learning was not apparent in performance until after the animals were given a rewarded trial. [Tolman and Honzik, 1930]*

the rats that had not found food in the goal box until trial 11 was even slightly superior to that of the animals that had been rewarded throughout the training.

This type of experiment has been successfully replicated many times. Although there is controversy over precise interpretation of the results, they strongly support the view that rewards do not directly influence learning. Furthermore these findings clearly indicate that learning must be distinguished from performance. Performance is influenced by many variables, and one important variable is what the animal has learned about its environment. The problem in defining learning, however, lies in distinguishing learning from the other variables that influence performance.

Thorpe [1963] has convincingly argued that latent learning is a basic capacity of many species, including insects. The digger wasp, for example, identifies its nest by the features peculiar to the terrain around it. As it leaves its nest the wasp may circle the area several times, suggesting that it is examining the terrain, and if salient landmarks are rearranged, it may subsequently be unable to locate the nest. Animals in their natural environments must be able to learn about the spatial relationships of important regions of their environments, such as food and water sources and the home or nest. If reward, such as the capture of prey, increases the probability that an animal will frequent a particular rotting log, brook, or meadow, the animal must be able to remember the location of that log, brook, or meadow. Laboratory training procedures provide highly useful data, but since the laboratory is an artificial environment, the findings must be interpreted in terms of the requirements of the animal's natural habitat.

295

Despite the customary emphasis on classical and instrumental conditioning, other forms, such as habituation and latent learning are at least equally pervasive and often equally efficient. It has been shown, for example, that cats and monkeys can learn from observing other animals [John, 1967]. Some years ago Herbert and Harsh [1944] placed cats in cages where they could watch other cats solve several instrumental-learning tasks. Some cats observed the entire training session on each task; other cats watched only the latter part of each session, by which time performance of the trained cats was rapid and skilled. When the observers were then trained on the tasks, both groups had benefited from their observations, but the best performance was obtained in the cats that had watched the entire training session. These cats had apparently profited from observing the errors as well as the correct responses made by the model cats. The extent of observational learning of the type outside of the laboratory is not known, but it seems reasonable to conclude that it plays an important role in the socialization of mammals.

We know from observing children, and from being observed by children, that observation learning provides a basis for imitation. This is one of the most extensively used techniques in teaching, particularly in teaching children. Most of the skills taught in school, as well as most of the habits and prejudices taught at home and in other social institutions, are based initially on observational learning and imitation. Instrumental learning provides the subsequent shaping of responses—that is, it determines what responses will be made and how well they will be made—but observational learning and imitation provide the opportunity for instrumental learning to occur. The learning of language by humans and the learning of songs by birds are perhaps the clearest examples. Many species of birds learn specific songs from the adults of their species by listening and imitating. White-crowned sparrows normally acquire the full song during their first two years of life. Young birds that are isolated from adults fail to develop the particular dialect of adults from the same region. In white-crowned sparrows reared in the laboratory several months elapse between the time that the song pattern is acquired through listening and the time that birds produce the full song; the learning remains latent for several months until the birds start to sing. If the birds are deafened either before or even shortly after they are exposed to the adult song, their subsequent singing is abnormal. Apparently in order to translate the song patterns they have learned (through listening) into the full song, the birds must be able to hear themselves sing. Once the full song is developed, however, deafening has virtually no effect on subsequent singing [Konishi, 1965].

Earlier we noted that in classical conditioning an animal learns more than is revealed by the particular behavioral response it exhibits. This is also true for the various forms of instrumental learning. Thus the question of what is learned in any learning task cannot be answered completely by examining the specific response which is rewarded or punished. As a matter of fact, restricting attention to the response can lead to quite erroneous conclusions about the nature of learning. A number of years ago Liddell [1942] trained a sheep to avoid a shock to its foot by flexing its foreleg at the onset of a signal. After the response was well learned the sheep was placed on its back and the signal was presented. Under these conditions the sheep did not flex its foreleg. Instead it stiffened all four legs and attempted to lift its head. This was not the response it had learned through instrumental conditioning, but a completely different one which was in fact much more appropriate to the altered circumstances.

This example illustrates an extremely important point in relation to interpretations of classical and instrumental learning in complex animals. Even though a training procedure may elicit or require a specific response, the learning does not consist solely of an altered tendency to contract a specific set of muscles in a precise sequence in the presence of specific stimuli. Typically, we do not even study the response of the animal in a literal sense. Rather we study the *outcome* of responses—frequencies of lever presses, or number of errors versus correct turns in a maze, or even speed or probability of response. Since responses are rarely, if ever, made more than once in precisely the same way, it is not surprising to find that even in any given restricted environment an animal may learn to make a variety of responses which are collectively regarded by the experimenter as "a response." Furthermore, as we have seen, an animal may learn about features of the task in ways that enable him to perform "the response," when necessary, in ways that he has never previously performed it.

The report of Liddell's sheep is only one of numerous examples of this phenomenon. For example, Tolman et al. [1946] showed that rats could learn to go to the same place in a maze for a reward even though they had to make different turning responses on successive trials. On the basis of these findings they argued that such learning is based on the acquisition of a disposition to go to a particular place rather than to make a specific response or set of responses. In one study animals did develop specific turning responses, tendencies to turn right or left, with extensive training [Ritchie et al., 1950]. When the highly trained turning response was then interrupted by introducing a 3-inch gap in the floor at the point where a turn was required, the animals hesitated and then went to the previously rewarded *place* in the maze. Thus interference with the response "habit" once again allowed the place "disposition" to determine alley choices. Even when an animal is well trained to make what the experimenter regards as a specific response, it is capable of making other responses, even novel ones, which indicates that it has learned more than a specific response.

One of the most dramatic examples of the plasticity of learned responses was reported a number of years ago by Lashley and McCarthy [1926]. Rats were first trained in a simple alley maze, and after they had learned the maze, the cerebellum of each animal was destroyed by surgery. Since the cerebellum plays an important role in controlling bodily movements, their locomotor behavior was seriously impaired. When the animals recovered from the acute effects of the surgery and were able to move about in some fashion, they were again tested in the maze. Although they had great difficulty in walking, retention of their maze training was virtually unaffected. One of the rats with the most severe impairment of locomotor activity made no errors at all on the retention test.

We do not know how the nervous system functions to provide for the phenomenal plasticity of learned responses. The adaptive advantages of this capacity are obvious. If learning consisted only of the acquisition of precise *movements* in the presence of specific stimuli, such a capacity would be of little adaptive value in a complex and changing environment.

IMPRINTING

The complex nature of learning is seen in the rather special form of learning termed *imprinting* [Lorenz, 1937]. Under natural conditions the young of many species develop strong attachments to their parents. The brood of ducklings following their mother is a familiar example. This kind of attachment, or imprinting, develops during an early period in the animal's life. In a sense it is only accidental that the young become attached to their mother, since they will readily imprint on any salient object available during the early critical period. Ordinarily the mother duck is the most salient object in the duckling's early environment. Thus imprinting serves the important adaptive function of assuring with some probability that the duckling will stay close by its mother.

Systematic observations of imprinting were first made by Spalding [1873], who noted that newly hatched chicks would follow *any* moving object and had no more tendency to follow a hen than to follow a duck or even a human figure.

Subsequent research clearly confirms Spalding's observations; young birds can be imprinted to a great variety of objects. For example, Hess [1957] exposed chicks to a moving colored disk for a brief period. When the chicks were tested the following day they tended to follow that particular disk in preference to other disks they had not previously seen. Hess also studied the effectiveness of various types of stimuli in producing imprinting and found that a round ball (with structures resembling wings and a tail attached) was more effective than various objects which resemble an adult chicken. Somewhat surprisingly, a stuffed leghorn rooster was the least effective stimulus of all those tested. Complex moving objects are typically used in laboratory studies of imprinting, but birds will apparently imprint to almost any salient perceptual stimulus [Sluckin, 1965]. In natural environments young birds are likely to be imprinted on stimuli that aid in their survival. There is evidence

298

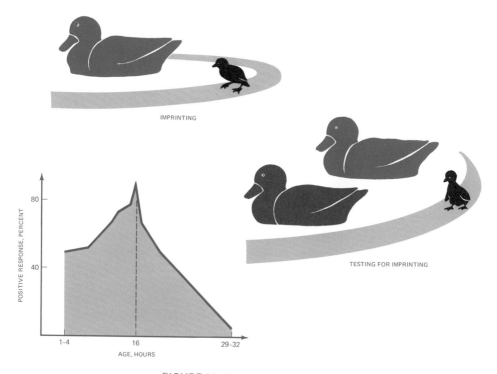

IMPRINTING

TESTING FOR IMPRINTING

FIGURE 11-10   *Imprinting in ducklings. In inducing imprinting the duckling is placed behind a model of a male duck which moves and makes sounds. The duckling is then placed between a female model and the male model used for imprinting, and the choice of the male is used as a measure of imprinting. The curve shows variation in effectiveness of imprinting as the duckling ages. Maximum effectiveness is found at 16 hours. [Hess, 1957]*

that naïve young chicks and ducklings have marked and stable preferences for the parental calls of their own species [Gottlieb, 1965]. These preferences increase the likelihood that the birds will imprint on members of their own species. Unfortunately it is also possible for birds to become imprinted on dangerous objects such as predators. Such birds are unlikely to become ancestors.

In chicks and ducklings the critical, or most sensitive, period for imprinting is the first day or after hatching (see Fig. 11-10). This sensitive period can be extended by restricting the visual environment for a day or two after hatching [Moltz and Stettner, 1961]; thus it is not determined completely by biological age. The sensitive period no doubt varies considerably in different species, probably in relation to the maturation rate of the particular species. There is some evidence that imprinting occurs in mammals including guinea pigs and sheep, although the evidence is much less convincing than that based on studies of chicks and ducklings.

Some of the most interesting effects of imprinting are seen in later social behavior, including courtship and mating. Numerous examples of

299

inappropriate or abnormal social behavior produced by imprinting have been described by Lorenz [1957, p. 146]:

A musk drake [*Cairina moschata*] hatched with four siblings by a pair of grey geese, and led by them for seven weeks, subsequently proved to be bound to his siblings, that is, to his own species, in all his social activities. But when his mating reactions awoke the following year, they were focussed on the species of the foster parents, to whom he had paid no attention for over ten months.

Frequently animals reared by scientists and zookeepers later court and attempt to mate with human beings rather than their own species. In the zoo in Basel, Switzerland, a tame emu regularly attempted to mate with its keeper during the mating season. Smaller animals may become attached to just the leg or shoe of the keeper [Hediger, 1950]. One of the strangest cases of mismating occurred at the Schönbrunn Zoo in Vienna, where a peacock was reared with giant Galápagos tortoises [Heinroth and Heinroth, 1959]. Clearly imprinting is not always adaptive.

In normally developed social attachments it is not always clear whether or not some sort of reward might have been a factor. In its purest form imprinting is not thought to be influenced by rewards or punishments. Nevertheless, a stimulus on which an animal has been imprinted can serve as a reward in instrumental learning [James, 1959; Campbell and Pickleman, 1961]. For example, in one study ducklings which were imprinted on a yellow cylinder were readily trained to peck at a disk which, when pressed, presented the yellow cylinder. Furthermore, the response did not extinguish even after the chicks made a large number of responses [Peterson, 1960].

Imprinting is clearly a form of learning and has a profound influence on later social life, including choice of a mate. The effects of the early imprinting experiences are thought to be lasting and at least partially irreversible. It is not yet clear, however, that imprinting is fundamentally different from other types of learning.

COMPLEX LEARNING

In the types of learning discussed so far—habituation, classical and instrumental conditioning, and imprinting—we have focused on procedures which are used in a restricted environment to teach animals to make responses to a fairly restricted range of stimuli. Let us briefly consider learning in tasks where the responses are less controlled by the particular features of the stimulation. Through the use of rewards and/or punishments animals can be trained to discriminate—that is, to respond differentially to different stimuli. For example, if a rat is repeatedly rewarded for entering the darker of two alleys, it will learn to discriminate between the two alleys. The rat can then be taught a discrimination reversal—that is, to choose the lighter of the two alleys. Initially, reversal learning will be a more difficult task. However, if the animal is taught a series of discrimination reversals, the rate of learning of each reversal increases, that is, it shows increasing profit from previous experiences (see Fig. 11-11). Under some conditions reversal learning can be improved by overtraining on the first discrimination. One interpretation of this effect is that through training with specific stimuli the animal comes to attend more readily to the particular stimuli involved rather than to other features of the training environment [Mackintosh, 1969].

Improvement in learning with training—learning to learn—has been extensively studied in primates by Harlow [1949a]. Monkeys subjected to prolonged discrimination training develop what has been termed *learning sets*—that is, they become increasingly skilled at solving discrimination learning tasks. They show improved learning not only of previously learned discriminations, but also of novel problems (see Fig. 11-12). Obviously the development of such learning sets frees them from the restrictions of the slow trial-and-error process of the original learning attempts. Through training experiences of this type monkeys can be taught highly complicated tasks, such as choosing the odd stimulus from an array of stimuli or choosing a stimulus which matches one displayed by the experimenter. Clearly much of the intellectual capacity of an individual animal depends on his previous learning experiences. The capacity for learning to learn provides even the monkey with a considerable degree of "intellectual freedom."

The most complex learning occurs in language development. The ability of the protozoan *spirostomum* to habituate to repeated stimulation seems trivial in comparison to the ability of the human child to learn to speak the language of its elders. Both phenomena, of course,

FIGURE 11-11   *Discrimination-reversal learning in monkeys. The monkeys are first taught to choose one object, and they are then rewarded for choosing the other object. The curve shows their performance on the second trial on successive block of 14 reversal problems. The animals have "learned to learn" to reverse their choices. [Harlow, 1949a]*

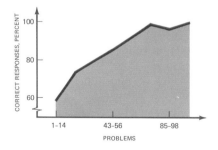

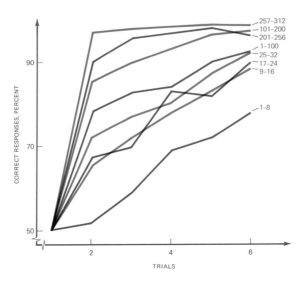

FIGURE 11–12   *Learning to learn how to discriminate objects. Monkeys were rewarded for choosing one object from a set. They were given six trials on each set, with a total of 312 problem sets. Each curve is the average performance on trials 1 through 6 for a block of problems. The rate of learning over the six trials improved steadily with experience. [Harlow, 1949a]*

must be considered in terms of their adaptive significance for the species in question. Man is unique in the degree of his capacity to acquire and use language. Infrahumans can communicate in many ways, and the higher primates have exhibited a capacity for acquiring some of the rudiments of language. However, the linguistic achievements of apes are primitive in comparison to those of man.

The learning of language consists not only in acquisition of a vocabulary, but in acquisition of syntax, the rules of language that govern the order of words in sentences. These rules are learned early in life, and as we know from listening to people whose first language is not English, the syntax of the first-learned language will influence the syntax used in other languages acquired later. How do we learn the programs for responding that we call language? Clearly language is not learned through the instrumental conditioning of words or sentences. The readiness with which different words can be used to express the same thought and the way in which the same words can be used in different orders in a sentence argue strongly against such a simplistic view [Miller et al., 1960].

We do not know how the programs, or structures, that we call language are learned; what is clear, however, is that it is necessary for us to understand the bases of the learning of language before we will be able to completely understand the neurobiological bases of behavior.

Lashley [1951] once pointed out that the various problems raised by the organization of language are characteristic of almost all other cerebral activity. There is, for example, a serial ordering of the vocal movements involved in pronouncing the words in a sentence, the sentences in a paragraph, and the paragraphs in a longer discourse. All skilled acts appear to involve similar problems of serial ordering, even down to the coordination of muscular contractions in movements such as those of reaching and grasping. Thus investigation of the neural organization of the more simple motor skills may well provide important clues which will lead to an understanding of the neurobiological bases of language.

Not all species have the capacity to learn a language. Different species obviously differ in learning capacity, and individuals within a species differ because of such factors as genetic makeup, age, and learning history. It seems fairly certain that one form of learning,

VARIATIONS IN LEARNING CAPACITY

habituation, can be obtained in single-celled animals, although it is less certain, and even doubtful, that they are capable of other forms of learning [Jensen, 1965]. It is still not clear whether conditioning can occur in higher invertebrates such as planarians. Rather convincing findings of conditioning in planarians have been reported by McConnell [1966], but little or no evidence of it has been obtained in other studies, and it is often difficult to rule out other effects of training, such as sensitization.

Conditioning, including instrumental conditioning, is readily obtained, however, in mollusks and arthropods. Maze learning has been studied in ants as well as rats, and observational, or latent, learning appears to be common in many insects.

There have been a number of studies of learning in the cockroach, particularly in relation to restricted parts of neural tissue. The purpose of such studies is to find out what type of tissue will sustain learning and, if possible, something about the neural changes that underlie the learning. Learning in restricted regions of the mammalian nervous system (the spinal cord) was discussed above. Horridge [1965] has shown that cockroaches can learn even if their heads are removed. A subsequent study showed that learning could occur even when the response was mediated by only one ganglion (the prothoracic ganglion) [Eisenstein and Cohen, 1965]. A cockroach was attached to a rod, with its leg resting in a dish of water. The water was in a series with a shock source, so that the leg was shocked every time it touched the water. The

303

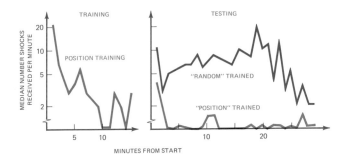

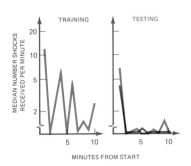

FIGURE 11–13 *Learning by a cockroach ganglion. Training and testing of position-trained and random-trained preparations. P leg received shock when a leg touched water. R leg received shock whenever P leg was shocked. Left curve shows decrease in shocks, with time, for P legs. Right curves show subsequent responses of P and R legs when both are given only P training. "Learning" by the R group was slower than original learning of P group. Below, training and testing of P and R legs in animals with ganglion removed. [Eisenstein and Cohen, 1965]*

learning consisted of holding the leg, designated the *P* leg, in a position that would keep it from touching the water. As a control the cockroach's other leg was given a shock whenever the *P* leg was shocked. Thus the *P* leg was shocked only when it was lowered into the water, while the control leg, termed *R* for random, was shocked in a variety of positions. Figure 11-13 shows the results. The *P* leg gradually learned to avoid the shock. When the *R* leg was subsequently trained, the earlier experience appeared to impair learning. Additional tests indicated that the learning did not consist merely in holding the leg in a fixed position. When the *P* leg was lowered slightly, so that the previously learned response would not avoid the shock, the animal (or ganglion) quickly relearned to avoid it even if a different type of response, extension rather than flexion, was required. Finally, as Fig. 11-13 shows, an avoidance response of some kind was also learned even if the leg was disconnected neurally from the ganglion, but such learning did not have the plasticity shown by the animals with an intact ganglion. Thus the plasticity of learning can be seen even in restricted portions of the nervous systems of infrahuman species of animals.

Vertebrate studies of learning have centered on the complexity of learning. As Fig. 11-14 shows, species differences in the formation of learning sets very roughly parallel evolutionary status. However, the bases of these differences are not yet known. In general it appears that species differ not simply in ability to learn, but in the complexity of the tasks they can learn to handle. Such differences are undoubtedly due to the evolution of neurobiological processes. Bitterman [1965] has reported that some types of learning tasks, such as discrimination reversal learning, reveal systematic species differences among vertebrates. He suggests that the evolution of learning is not continuous, but rather that the more complex tasks tap a capacity that is present in higher animals but poorly developed in the turtle and absent in the fish; such differences might result from the evolution of brain structures, particularly the cerebral cortex. Whether these conclusions can be accepted will depend on subsequent research findings. However, since species differ in many features, including sensory and motivational processes, it may well be that species differences in behavior seen in such tasks are due to differences in processes other than those underlying learning.

The same caution holds for analyses of other differences in learning that are related to differences in biological factors. Bovet et al. [1969] have reported evidence of strain differences in avoidance learning and maze learning in various inbred strains of mice (see Fig. 11-15). There is fairly convincing evidence that strains which learn well in one task also learn well in the other, and that some strains are poor in both tasks. There may be some general factor underlying the consistent strain differences in learning, and it is tempting to conclude that they are due to genetically based differences in neurobiological processes. However, until such processes are identified, this conclusion remains inferential.

It is obvious that the learning capabilities of the young of many species are different from those of adults, and it is a common complaint, not without supporting evidence, that learning efficiency is decreased in the aged. The results of numerous studies of aging effects in learning generally support casual observation. For example, Oliverio and Bovet [1966] studied age differences in maze learning and avoidance learning in mice. In both tasks learning was least efficient in 21-day-old and 360-day-old mice and most efficient in 60-day-old mice. These age differences in learning were particularly striking when many training trials were given on each session. Harlow [1959a] conducted extensive studies

FIGURE 11–14 *Learning-set formation in different mammals. Curves show improvement on second trial in a large number of discrimination problems. Rhesus monkeys improve rapidly, rats and squirrels improve very slowly, and the performance of cats, marmosets, and squirrel monkeys is intermediate. [Warren, 1965]*

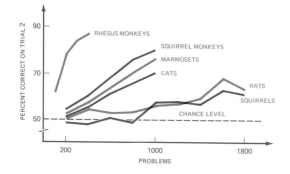

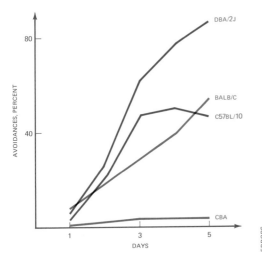

FIGURE 11–15 *Learning in four inbred strains of mice. Above, avoidance conditioning in a shuttle box. The animals were given 100 trials each day for five days. Right, maze learning. The animals were given one trial each day for 10 days. Note that strain CBA was worst on both tasks, while strain DBA/2J was superior on both tasks. [Bovet et al., 1969]*

FIGURE 11–16 *Improvement in discrimination learning with age in rhesus monkeys. Left, learning of a single discrimination problem as a function of age. Errors made in learning decrease with the age of the animals at the time that training began. Below, oddity learning. Monkeys learn to choose the object which differs from others in a set. Curves show performance on blocks of 64 problems, each 10 trials in length. Right, discrimination learning-set performance for training started at different ages compared to performance of an adult group. Curves show performance on trial 2 in a series of discrimination problems. [Harlow, 1959a]*

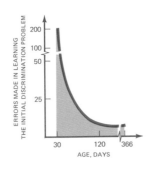

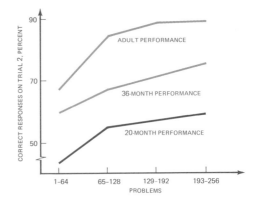

of age differences in learning in rhesus monkeys, with tasks which varied in complexity from a form of classical conditioning to learning-set formation. Simple classical conditioning was found even in neonatal monkeys. As Fig. 11-16 shows, the rate of learning of a simple discrimination problem increases with age up to about 150 days. However, in acquisition of learning sets 150-day-old monkeys are considerably inferior to year-old and adult monkeys. Finally, in oddity discrimination learning there are clear differences between twenty-month-old, three-year-old, and adult monkeys. No decline in performance was found with increasing age of the monkeys, but it was clear that the ability to learn tasks of varying complexity depends on the age of the animal [Harlow, 1959a, p. 478]:

> Early in life, new learning abilities appear rather suddenly within the space of a few days, but, from late infancy onward, the appearance of new learning powers is characterized by developmental stages during which particular performances progressively improve. There is a time at which increasingly difficult problems can first be solved, and a considerably delayed period before they can be solved with adult efficiency.

Although the effects of age in human learning have not been systematically studied, the available evidence is consistent with Harlow's findings on the effects in other primates. The general fact that at different ages humans are able to learn material of different complexity has considerable bearing on educational curricula. It is likely that the efficiency of the educational process could be dramatically improved if we knew more about the development of learning abilities in children. It is also well known that learning ability often declines in the aged. As yet, however, we know little about the neurobiology of either the development or the decline of learning ability.

We have discussed only a few of the important problems, concepts, and "facts" of learning. Since learning is a pervasive influence on behavior, it has dominated psychological research for the past century. The early ideas of pioneers such as Pavlov, Thorndike, and Tolman have stimulated research which has provided continuously increasing understanding of

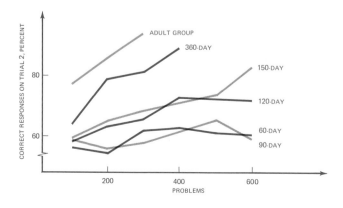

the way experiences shape our behavior. Nevertheless, there are still serious gaps in our knowledge of how experiences shape the behavior of man and other animals. We are only beginning to understand the highly complex processes of behavioral adaptation which we refer to collectively as learning, and as we acquire new information our understanding continues to change. As our understanding changes, so should our explicit use of the principles of learning in teaching and learning. As our knowledge increases we should become more effective in teaching our young to acquire the information and skills required by our society.

SUMMARY

The survival of any species depends on its ability to adapt to special conditions of its environment and evolution of the capacity to learn provides a means for adaptation even to changing environments. Learning, a more or less permanent change in behavior produced by experience, is difficult to isolate from the multitude of other influences on behavior. However, several types of processes may generally be described as learning phenomena.

Habituation, a decrease in response to a repeated stimulus, and sensitization, an increase in response to a repeated stimulus, are perhaps the simplest forms of learning. Habituation, which occurs even in the single-celled *spirostomum*, is specific to a single stimulus and is not generalized to other stimuli within a stimulus mode. In classical, or Pavlovian, conditioning if two stimuli are paired, one of the pair will later elicit the response initially provoked by the other. Instrumental conditioning is the familiar technique of reward and punishment to elicit the appropriate response.

Although these simpler forms of conditioning have been studied at length, they fall short of explaining many phenomena of learning. In latent, or "hidden" learning, for example, animals learn without any observable reward. Furthermore, although conditioning procedures are employed to produce a specific response or specific groups of responses, the animal actually learns much more than that. Thus behavioral performance must be distinguished from what is learned in any learning situation. Other varieties of learning include imprinting on some salient stimulus during a critical period after birth and observational, or imitation learning, which is an important influence on the behavior of children. There are perhaps other forms of learning which we have not yet untangled from the many other influences that affect the behavior of organisms.

In addition to these simple varieties of learning, higher animals are capable of extremely complex forms of learning. Through the use of rewards and punishments they can be taught to make complex sensory discriminations. They can learn to reverse their initial responses, and they can learn to learn, a phenomenon termed learning set. The most complex of all learning, the learning of language, appears to be unique to man.

A fruitful approach to the analysis of learning is represented by the comparative description and analysis of learning capacities and possible neural mechanisms underlying various types of learning. Habituation and sensitization have been analyzed in even the simplest of organisms and conditioning is readily obtained in mollusks and arthropods. Comparison of the complex learning in various vertebrate species has provided a great deal of insight into the evolutionary and psychobiological mechanisms by which these differences arise.

CHAPTER TWELVE

THE MEMORY
PROCESSES

Memory is quite clearly one of the most important capacities of man and the other animals. It is through memory that experiences of the past influence our present thoughts, plans, and actions. Without memory, of course, we would be unable to learn. It is difficult to imagine a human being lacking the ability to record experiences. Some signs of memory are usually seen even in the most severe cases of mental retardation. In the most general sense, memory refers to the lasting effect of stimulation—that is, the effect that remains after the stimulus is gone. As William James [1890] pointed out many years ago, "for a state of mind to survive in memory it must have endured for a certain length of time." We retain the influences of the experiences which occurred many years ago and we record the fleeting experiences of the moments just past. We remember our own telephone numbers and can report them at almost any time, but we remember a telephone number we have just looked up perhaps only long enough to dial it. What accounts for the wide variations in the lability or durability of memory?

Try to imagine what your life would be like if from this moment on you were unable to learn—unable to acquire any further information,

310

MEMORY

attitudes, or skills—even though you could remember most of what you have learned up to this point. Some of the consequences of this disability are obvious; others may not be.

A disability of just this kind sometimes results from brain damage produced by disease, injury, and chronic nutritional deficiencies or from surgical removal of portions of the temporal lobes. Examination of a classical case will illustrate the dramatic effect of such surgery on the patient's memory [Milner, 1966, pp. 112–115]:

> "This young man (H.M.) . . . had had no obvious memory disturbance before his operation, having, for example, passed his high school examinations without difficulty. [He sustained] a minor head injury at the age of seven. Minor [seizures] began one year later, and then, at the age of 16, he began to have generalized seizures which, despite heavy medication, increased in frequency and severity until, by the age of 27, he was no longer able to work . . . ; his prospects were by then so desperate that the radical bilateral medial temporal lobe [surgery] . . . was performed. The patient was drowsy for the first few post-operative days but then, as he became more alert, a severe memory impairment was apparent. He could no longer recognize the hospital staff, apart from [the surgeon], whom he had known for many years; he did not remember and could not relearn the way to the bathroom, and he seemed to

retain nothing of the day-to-day happenings in the hospital. His early memories were seemingly vivid and intact, his speech was normal, and his social behaviour and emotional responses were entirely appropriate."

There has been little change in this clinical picture during the years which have elapsed since the operation. . . . there [is no] evidence of general intellectual loss; in fact, his intelligence as measured by standard tests is actually a little higher now than before the operation. . . . Yet the remarkable memory defect persists, and it is clear that H.M. can remember little of the experiences of the last . . . years. . . .

Ten months after the operation the family moved to a new house which was situated only a few blocks away from their old one, on the same street. When examined . . . nearly a year later, H.M. had not yet learned the new address, nor could he be trusted to find his way home alone, because he would go to the old house. Six years ago the family moved again, and H.M. is still unsure of his present address, although he does seem to know that he has moved. [The patient] . . . will do the same jigsaw puzzles day after day without showing any practice effect, and read the same magazines over and over again without finding their contents familiar. . . .

Even such profound amnesias as this are, however, compatible with a normal attention span. . . . On one occasion, he was asked to remember the number "584" and was then allowed to sit quietly with no interruption for 15 minutes, at which point he was able to recall the number correctly without hesitation. When asked how he had been able to do this, he replied,

"It's easy. You just remember 8. You see, 5, 8, and 4 add to 17. You remember 8; subtract it from 17 and it leaves 9. Divide 9 in half and you get 5 and 4, and there you are: 584. Easy."

In spite of H.M.'s elaborate mnemonic scheme he was unable, a minute or so later, to remember either the number "584" or any of the associated complex train of thought; in fact, he did not know that he had been given a number to remember. . . .

One gets some idea of what such an amnesic state must be like from H.M.'s own comments. . . . Between tests, he would suddenly look up and say, rather anxiously,

"Right now, I'm wondering. Have I done or said anything amiss? You see, at this moment everything looks clear to me, but what happened just before? That's what worries me. It's like waking from a dream; I just don't remember."

Similar symptoms have been found in other patients with damaged brains [Whitty and Zangwill, 1966]. Patients with this type of memory disorder are forced to live only in the immediate present, and as time goes on in the distant past. Since they lack the capacity to learn, they rely heavily on memories acquired before their disability developed. Generally their stock of old memories remains fairly intact. Such patients remember their native language, as well as others they may have learned in their youth. They may readily recite poems and remember old songs. They are able to perform skills and play games they learned earlier. However, they are unable to learn a new game, even though it is similar to others that they know well. As Barbizet has noted [1963, p. 128]:

> Such patients therefore who no longer fix the present live constantly in a past which preceded the onset of their illness. Their disengagement from the present is, however, far from complete. Some are conscious of the disorder of memory, like [one patient], who said: "When I watch closely I know, but I soon forget. My brain feels like a sieve, I forget everything. Even in my tiny room, I keep losing things. It all fades away."

These findings clearly suggest that we must distinguish between recent memories and older memories, and that different processes underlie each type. Why is it that the recent experiences of such patients do not leave lasting effects? What processes are affected by the brain damage? Some possible answers to these questions have been provided by findings of experimental studies of memory in animals and men. It is often the case in science that discovering what happens when something goes wrong can lead to an understanding of how a system works. Our current thinking about normal memory processes is strongly influenced by the information from studies in which memory functions have been modified either by accident or by design.

Evidence from a variety of sources, including the clinical findings cited above, suggests there may be several kinds of memory processes [McGaugh, 1966; 1968a; Drachman and Arbit, 1966]. A distinction between at least two processes, *short-term memory* and *long-term memory*, was proposed some time ago [Hebb, 1949; Gerard, 1949]. Nevertheless, some researchers believe that there is only one type of memory [Melton, 1963]. We do not yet have enough evidence to be certain which of these views is correct. There is no doubt, however, that the characteristics of recent memory differ in many ways from those of long-term memory.

If you look at a picture for a brief period and then look away, perhaps at a blank wall, you may be able to remember a great deal of the details of the picture for a short time. Later you will have forgotten many of the details even though you retain the ability to recognize the picture. Immediately after you look at the picture, however, you may feel that you have an image of it, and that this image is rapidly decaying. Studies of memory have provided rather strong support for the view that memory for very recent experiences is in fact imagelike. Two types of imagelike memory, iconic memory and eidetic imagery, have been extensively studied.

MEMORY AND IMAGES

313

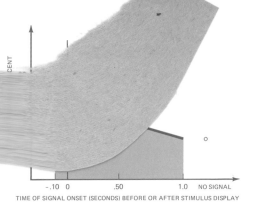

FIGURE 12-1   *Rapid decay of visual information. Twelve-item dis— numbers and figures (e)* ...

cates average performance when no signal was given. [Sperling, 1960]

-.10 0   .50   1.0   NO SIGNAL

TIME OF SIGNAL ONSET (SECONDS) BEFORE OR AFTER STIMULUS DISPLAY

ICONIC MEMORY

Iconic memory is the very short-term imagelike memory evidenced by humans. Human subjects have almost perfect memory for items exposed briefly in a display if they are tested immediately afterward. In one study combinations of letters and numbers arrayed in two or three rows were exposed to subjects for 50 milliseconds [Sperling, 1960]. If the subjects were simply asked to report what they saw, they typically reported about four items correctly (out of a display containing 8 to 12 items). This is referred to as the *span of apprehension* or *immediate memory span*. In other tests a tone was sounded at intervals varying from 50 milliseconds before onset to 1 second following offset of the display. The pitch of the tone signaled which row of items the subject was to report; the highest tone was a signal to report the upper row and the lowest tone signaled the bottom row. The important feature of this test is that when the tone was presented afterward the subject could not tell which row he was to report until after the display was gone. Figure 12-1 shows typical results obtained from this experiment. If the tone was presented either immediately before or immediately after the exposure, accuracy was better than 80 percent. If the tone was delayed for 1 second after exposure, the accuracy was the same as that when no signal was given.

The fact that the subjects were able to report any row requested with high accuracy when they were queried immediately after the exposure indicates that they must have had an accurate memory of nearly all the items in the display. Apparently they were able to use a visual image which was virtually perfect at first but which persisted for less than 1 second. Other studies, based on other testing procedures, show that under these general conditions iconic memory persists for approximately 250 milliseconds [Haber and Standing, 1969]. These highly labile images probably act to provide continuity in our visual experiences—that is, to prolong the otherwise fleeting effects of visual stimulation. Thus iconic memory aids the integration of information in skills such as those involved in reading [Haber, 1970]. Iconic memory is not, of course, limited to vision. Comparable findings have been obtained in studies in which complex information is presented by means of tactile stimulation [Bliss et al., 1966].

314

Another type of imagelike memory, *eidetic imagery*, is found only in certain people, particularly children. In this case the subject reports that *children mainly* after looking at a visual display he retains a detailed image which may last for minutes, or sometimes longer, under some conditions. This image is not simply a visual *afterimage*, since it is lost if the subject attempts to move it to another surface. In contrast, a visual afterimage can be projected onto any neutral surface (note that a visual afterimage is also a type of memory). In one study of eidetic imagery Haber and Haber [1964] showed a series of pictures to elementary school children. As each picture was removed, the children were asked to keep looking at the area where the pictures had been displayed and to describe in detail all features of the image. Some of the subjects (approximately 8 percent) were able to examine the images and give extremely detailed reports. For example, one subject was shown a picture from *Alice in Wonderland* showing Alice looking up at the Cheshire Cat in a tree. After the picture was removed the subject was able to give an accurate description of it, including the number of stripes on the cat's tail. Interestingly, the availability of an eidetic image did not necessarily result in better memory of the picture after the image faded. When they were asked to describe the picture from "memory," the performance of children with eidetic imagery was no better, or only slightly better, than that of noneidetic children.

Little is known about eidetic imagery. In particular, we do not know why it occurs primarily in children. There is no evidence that eidetic images are normally used by such children as a form of memory, but any complete understanding of memory will have to consider the role of eidetic imagery as a special form of memory.

SHORT-TERM AND LONG-TERM MEMORY

Most of us do not have eidetic imagery, and iconic memory is too labile to be the sole basis of our memory for recent events. Iconic memory may, however, be the first stage in a series of memory processes. Obviously we must have the capacity for "perfect memory," however brief, if we are to develop, with repetition, good retention over periods of time greater than 1 second. Memory lasting for several seconds or minutes after an experience is usually referred to as *short-term memory*. We have little difficulty remembering the last sentence we have heard or spoken. We can, with some effort, remember a telephone number long enough to dial it—that is, we can if it contains no more than seven digits (or if part of the number, such as the prefix or area code, is well learned in advance). Miller [1956] has pointed out that we are usually able to hold only seven (plus or minus two) items in short-term memory. If more items than this

315

are presented, accuracy generally does not improve unless the items are rehearsed or repeated.

We do not yet know what makes short-term memory "short term." There is some evidence that the rapid loss of retention following an experience may be due to a decay of the neurobiological trace of the experience. It is also clear, however, that short-term retention can be affected by interference from experiences that have occurred in the interval between the original experience and the retention test. This type of interference is termed *retroactive interference*. In one study Peterson and Peterson [1959] simply asked subjects to recall three letters at intervals ranging from 3 to 18 seconds after presentation. During the retention interval the subjects counted backward by threes or fours (to prevent rehearsal). As Fig. 12-2 shows, the percentage of letters recalled decreased directly with the retention interval. Only 10 percent correct recall was found after 18 seconds. Of course, this curve cannot be regarded as a "pure" short-term decay curve because of the possibility that the loss is caused by interference from the counting activity. We know that errors in dialing telephone numbers are increased simply by the requirement that a particular digit be dialed prior to the number [Conrad, 1958]. Apparently distraction of any kind can cause losses in short-term memory. Note, however, that similar distractions do not cause losses of retention of well-learned responses, such as your own telephone number.

Short-term memory is also affected by the acoustical *similarity* of the interfering information to material recently experienced [Broadbent, 1970]. Material which sounds like the original material is interfering. For example, if subjects are asked to remember the combination B C D and are then asked to copy the letters P T P V V T, the original letters are likely to be forgotten. However, copying the letters F L E M M L produces little interference [Wicklegren, 1965; Dale, 1964]. Also, in short-term memory similarity in meaning of the items does not appear to affect their recall. A sequence of words with similar meanings—broad, great, large, wide, big—is remembered as well as a sequence of words with different meanings—hot, old, strong, foul, deep [Baddeley, 1964]. Thus in short-term memory similarity of the sounds is much more important

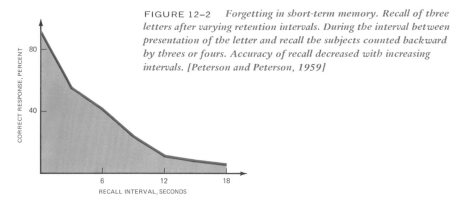

FIGURE 12-2   *Forgetting in short-term memory. Recall of three letters after varying retention intervals. During the interval between presentation of the letter and recall the subjects counted backward by threes or fours. Accuracy of recall decreased with increasing intervals. [Peterson and Peterson, 1959]*

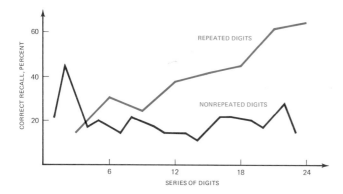

FIGURE 12–3   *Effect of repetition on recall of a series of 24 nine-digit numbers. Recall of each sequence was tested immediately after presentation. One nine-digit sequence was repeated in every third position in the series. Other points represent unrepeated nine-digit sequences. [Hebb, 1961]*

than similarity of the meaning. In contrast, similarity of meaning is very important in producing interference in long-term memory.

As we have just seen, we forget many of our experiences within a few seconds—and yet we know that experiences can leave fairly long-lasting memory. How do memories become permanent, or at least fairly long lasting? How is a recent experience stored in long-term memory? This question must be asked at two levels. We need to know the conditions which result in long-term memory, and ultimately we need to know the neurobiological (neuroanatomical, neurophysiological, and neuro-chemical) process underlying memory.

THE ROLE OF REPETITION

Many factors influence the development of long-term memory. Perhaps the most important influence is repetition. Although practice does not necessarily "make perfect," it does lead to good retention, as we know from our own experiences as well as extensive experimental research. In a simple but elegant study Hebb [1961] studied the effect of repetition on memory for a series of digits. College students were read a series of nine digits at the rate of one per second and were instructed to repeat the digits in the same order. This task is called the *digit-span* test. Twenty-four series of numbers were presented. In 16 of them the sequence of the digits was varied randomly. However, every third sequence was a repetition of the same nine digits in the same order. Even though the subjects were not aware that one sequence was being repeated they benefited from the repetition. While performance on the randomized series of digits remained fairly stable over the tests, performance on the repeated series improved with repetition (see Fig. 12-3). These findings suggest that each experience produced short-term memory which provided a basis for partial recall of the random series (as in

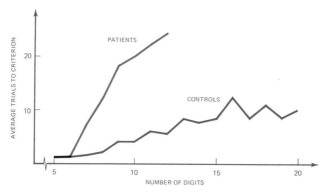

FIGURE 12–4   *Learning of series of digits by patients with temporal lobe brain damage and by college students. At all series larger than six digits the patients learned more slowly than did controls. For both groups the number of trials required to learn increased as the number of digits in the series was increased. [Drachman and Arbit, 1966]*

remembering a telephone number just looked up), as well as changes leading to the formation of more stable memory (as in *memorizing* a telephone number).

Under normal conditions repetition, through practice or rehearsal, is no doubt essential for memorizing, or "learning by heart." However, as we have seen, in some cases the capacity to memorize may be destroyed. Drachman and Arbit [1966] compared the performance of college students in digit-span learning tasks with that of patients with bilateral temporal lobe brain damage. All subjects were first given a digit-span test; the average scores of the two groups were not markedly different—seven digits for the patients and eight digits for the students. The subjects were then tested on successively longer series of digits, with each successive series repeated as necessary, up to 25 times. As Fig. 12-4 shows, for both groups the number of repetitions necessary for learning increased with the number of digits in the series. However, the patients were completely unable to learn a series of more than 11 digits, while the students were able to learn series as long as 20 digits after approximately 10 repetitions.

One of the subjects in this experiment was H.M., the patient discussed earlier in this chapter. H.M.'s digit span was six digits. He was completely unable to learn a series longer than this even with 24 repetitions. H.M. apparently lacked any capacity other than short-term memory for such material. This was also indicated by his performance on another memory task in which he was asked to say whether two stimuli, sounds and lights, presented in sequence were the same or different [Prisko, 1963]. Normal subjects are able to perform with no difficulty even if there is a 60-second interval between the two stimuli. H.M. made very few errors when less than 20 seconds elapsed between the two stimuli, but his performance was poor with a 60-second delay (see Fig. 12-5). On trials in which he was distracted during the interval his performance was no worse than on undistracted trials. Evidently his

318

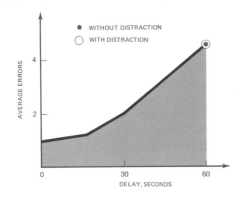

FIGURE 12–5   *Effect of temporal lobe surgery on short-term memory. Performance of the patient H.M. on a delayed-comparison memory task. The curve shows performance when the subject was distracted during the delay between the two stimuli to be compared. The open circle shows performance after a 60-second delay with no intervening distraction. [Prisco, 1963]*

short-term memory declined rapidly whether there was distraction or not.

Thus under certain abnormal conditions a person may have short-term memory but lack the ability to store experiences in a durable form. The Russian psychologist Luria [1968] has reported the extremely interesting case of the opposite difficulty. Apparently this person was unable to *avoid* storing his experiences, however trivial, in long-term memory. This "deficiency" caused interesting but unfortunate problems. Mr. S. was able to learn after only one presentation extremely complicated material, including numbers, nonsense passages, and passages in a foreign language. In one experiment he readily memorized a table of 52 digits (4 columns and 13 rows) within 3 minutes—a feat you might try yourself. He was able to report the numbers in any order requested, by columns, by rows, and even in diagonal zigzag patterns.

Not only was Mr. S. able to perform without error immediately after the material was presented, but he could also recall the material, still without error, when he was tested months later. This remarkable ability led him to become a professional memory expert, or "mnemonist." However, his major problem as a performer was that his memory was too perfect. He frequently gave several performances an evening, often in the same hall. In his recall of numbers written on a blackboard at one performance he had great difficulty ignoring his memory of the numbers written on the blackboard in earlier performances that evening or even previous evenings. He was plagued by an inability to forget. As Luria has asked [1968, p. 61]:

> How do we explain the tenacious hold these images had on his mind, his ability to retain them not only for years but for decades? . . . what explanation was there for the fact that . . . S could select at will any series ten, twelve, or even seventeen years after he had originally memorized it? How had he come by this capacity for indelible memory traces?

Mr. S.'s memory has been described, but it has not been explained. There is some indication that the ability may have been inherited; both of his parents and a nephew were also reported to have remarkable memory. However, we know nothing about the biological processes that would provide for such an ability. Clearly this "gift" is abnormal, and it is probably a good thing that we are not all afflicted with such talent. Mr. S.'s memory consisted of such detail that it limited his ability to function at an abstract level. The ability to forget is adaptive. The fact that normal memory is perfect, or near perfect, under two conditions— immediately after an experience and after repetition or rehearsal—makes it possible for us to remember best those events which are either recent or recurrent [Norman, 1969].

MEMORY CONSOLIDATION

The cases of H.M. and Mr. S. are obviously extreme examples of disorders of memory functioning. In one case memory was too "perfect" and in the other the patient apparently had completely lost the ability to memorize—that is, to form long-term memory. Ordinarily, an experience produces both short-lasting and long-lasting memory. We do not yet know what changes take place in the nervous system when memories are stored, but it is clear that memory-storage processes can be greatly modified by alterations in neural functioning. It seems likely that an understanding of the nature of the neural alternations which affect memory may provide important clues to an eventual understanding of the neurobiological bases of memory storage.

It is well known that people who have suffered head injuries are often unable to remember the events immediately preceding the injury. This selective loss of memory for recent experiences is termed *retrograde amnesia*. Generally the degree of amnesia varies directly with the severity of the injury, but in some cases there is permanent loss of all memory of events which occurred minutes, hours, or even days prior to the accident [Russell and Nathan, 1946]. These clinical findings show that long-term memory is not immediately fixed, or consolidated, at the time of an experience. Rather, it appears that memory consolidation involves processes which are time dependent. Thus development of long-term memory can be prevented or seriously impaired by conditions which disrupt neural functioning.

The strongest evidence that the consolidation of long-term memory involves time-dependent memory-storage processes has come from laboratory studies of retrograde amnesia, especially studies of the effects of *electroconvulsive shock* (ECS) on memory. This technique consists in passing an electric current through the brain for a brief period of time. ECS treatment produces brain seizures. Thus it can be used to produce short-lasting but gross alterations in neural activity in experimental animals. Duncan [1949] found that rats were unable to learn a simple task if they were given an ECS treatment each day immediately after training. However, they learned normally if the treatment was given several hours after the training. The treatments caused the animals to forget the immediately preceding experiences; retrograde amnesia was produced in the laboratory. Similar findings have been obtained in numerous other experiments [Glickman, 1961; McGaugh, 1966; Jarvik, 1968].

In studies of ECS-induced retrograde amnesia animals are typically given a single training trial, an ECS treatment, and then a single retention test. In one common test, inhibitory avoidance learning, mice are given a mild foot shock as they step from one compartment of an apparatus to another. When they are retested at a later time (usually 24 hours or longer) animals that are otherwise untreated usually remain in the first compartment; they remember the foot shock. Animals given ECS treatment shortly after the training trial will readily reenter the second compartment when they are retested; they seem *not* to remember that they were punished. Degree of retention varies directly with the interval between the training and the ECS treatment; Fig. 12-6 shows a "gradient" of retrograde amnesia typically obtained in such experiments.

Numerous other techniques are highly effective in producing retrograde amnesia in the laboratory. Amnesic treatments include anesthetics, convulsant drugs, and antibiotics [Cherkin, 1969; Barondes, 1968; Agranoff, 1968]. Retrograde amnesia is not an all-or-none effect. The degree of amnesia produced by an amnesic treatment depends on such factors as the strain of animal used, the intensity of the electrical stimulation or drug dosage, and the duration of treatment. The effect also varies with the region of the brain that is treated. The entire brain can be affected by ECS or drug treatments, but retrograde amnesia can also be produced by delivering small amounts of electrical stimulation to specific regions of the brain [Wyers et al., 1968; Zornetzer and McGaugh, 1970] as well as by damage to specific regions of the brain [Hudspeth and Wilsoncroft, 1970]. With all treatments the effects are

FIGURE 12–6   *Typical gradient of retrograde amnesia obtained in experimental studies of memory disruption. Degree of retention increases as the interval between the training and the posttraining treatment is lengthened. The slope of the "gradient" varies with a number of conditions.*

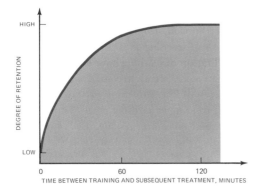

FIGURE 12–7 *Facilitation of learning with posttraining drug injections. Left, effects of different doses of pentylenetetrazol given daily immediately after training. Speed of learning varied directly with drug dose. Right, effects of time of drug injection (before or after daily training) on rate of learning. Marked facilitation of learning was found with injections given before training and up to 1 hour after training. Degree of facilitation decreased as the interval between training and drug injection was lengthened. [Krivanek and McGaugh, 1968; McGaugh and Krivanek, 1970]*

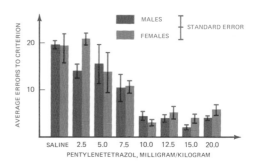

time dependent. Usually little or no effect is found if the treatments are administered several hours after training.

One interesting feature of experimentally induced retrograde amnesia is that it does not necessarily occur immediately after the amnesic treatment. Rather, it usually develops gradually over a period of hours or days. Geller and Jarvik [1968] found that mice given an ECS treatment after training remembered their training a few hours after the treatment but then gradually "forgot," or became amnesic, several hours later. This finding suggests that amnesic agents may act by directly interfering with the consolidation of long-term memory without destroying short-term memory processes [Barondes, 1968; Agranoff, 1968; McGaugh and Landfield, 1970].

The basis of this selective effect of amnesic agents on long-term memory is not yet understood. There is extensive evidence that retrograde amnesia can be produced by antibiotic drugs which interfere with the synthesis of protein, suggesting that protein synthesis may be involved in the consolidation of long-term memory. However, the amnesic effects of such drugs could also be due to some other general effect on neural functioning. The processes underlying long-term memory consolidation are highly labile, and it seems likely that consolidation can be impaired by any treatment which seriously disrupts neural functioning shortly after training. It may well be that interference with protein synthesis is the basis of amnesic effects, but a final conclusion must await further research.

Recent studies have shown that it is possible to *enhance* memory-storage processes with drugs or electrical stimulation administered shortly after training [McGaugh and Petrinovich, 1965]. That is, it is possible to produce *retrograde facilitation* of learning as well as retrograde amnesia. Most studies of drug facilitation of learning have employed drugs which stimulate the central nervous system. Krivanek and McGaugh [1968] gave mice different doses of the stimulant pentylenetetrazol each day immediately after brief training in a simple maze. Training was continued until each animal learned the maze. As Fig. 12-7 shows, the number of errors made in learning the maze was lowest in the groups given the highest drug doses. In another experiment McGaugh and

322

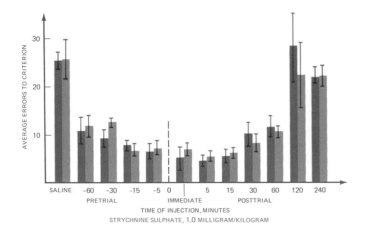

AVERAGE ERRORS TO CRITERION

SALINE   -60 -30 -15 -5 0   5   15   30   60   120 240
         PRETRIAL   IMMEDIATE   POSTTRIAL
              TIME OF INJECTION, MINUTES
         STRYCHNINE SULPHATE, 1.0 MILLIGRAM/KILOGRAM

Krivanek [1970] injected different groups of mice with the stimulant strychnine sulfate at different intervals either before or after daily maze training. The best learning was exhibited by mice injected either shortly before or shortly after training, but learning facilitation occurred with injections given as long as 1 hour after training. Similar results have been obtained with electrical stimulation of brain structures.

The graded effect of retrograde facilitation suggests that these stimulants enhance learning by influencing time-dependent memory-storage processes in the central nervous system. An understanding of the action of drugs which facilitate learning may help provide an understanding of the neurobiological bases of memory storage. It seems likely that the facilitating effects of posttraining drug and electrical stimulation of the brain may have a common basis of action at the neural level. Much of the evidence from these studies indicates that the drugs act on brain structures which are involved in controlling arousal level. For example, Alpern [1968] found that the rate at which rats learned a discrimination maze was facilitated by implanting strychnine sulfate directly into the midbrain reticular formation which is located in the brain stem (see Fig. 7-4). Denti et al. [1970] also found that learning was facilitated in rats by stimulation of the reticular formation with a small amount of electrical current each day immediately after training.

These studies of experimentally induced retrograde amnesia and retrograde facilitation of learning indicate that short-term memory and long-term memory are based on different processes, and that the processes of long-term memory remain labile for a fairly long time after training. We are only beginning to understand the nature of these time-dependent processes involved in memory storage.

The *consolidation hypothesis* of memory was originally proposed to explain the findings on learning and memory in humans. Mueller and Pilzecker [1900] reported that subjects forgot recently learned material if they were required to learn new material just after the original learning. Less forgetting resulted when a period of time elapsed between the two learning sessions. The second learning session was thought to interfere with the consolidation of neural processes initiated by the first session. Thus the hypothesis of consolidation was proposed as an

323

explanation of *retroactive interference*—the interference with retention produced by new learning.

Although the consolidation hypothesis cannot account for all forms of retroactive interference it does appear that, for both short-term memory and long-term memory, retention is best when there is a minimum amount of interfering activity after learning. Tulving [1969] asked subjects to remember a list of 15 common words, which were presented one at a time, and instructed them to be certain to remember the word in the list that was the name of a famous person; they were to recall that name before proceeding to recall the other words in the list. The subjects were tested with different lists, with the name in a different position each time. They remembered the names with little difficulty. However, they had great difficulty remembering the word that came just before the name; recall of items presented just after the name was not impaired. Apparently the activities involved in learning and remembering the special word caused a mild retrograde amnesia. This type of retrograde amnesia may well account for a great deal of forgetting of insignificant daily experiences.

It is a common belief that retention is better if the material is studied just before bedtime. There is some experimental support of this observation. Several studies have shown that retention is better if the subject sleeps during the interval between learning and a retention test than it is if he remains awake during this time [Jenkins and Dallenbach, 1924; Van Ormer, 1932]. One interpretation of these findings is that the sleep period merely delays the beginning of retroactive interference. Another view is that sleep provides an opportunity for consolidation of the newly learned material and thus protects it from retroactive interference [Heine, 1914]. To examine the effects of sleep and activity on retention McGaugh taught verbal material to four groups of college students. Two of the groups learned at night just before going to sleep and the other two learned in the morning about an hour after awaking. One of each of these two groups then relearned the material 8 hours later and one other relearned 24 hours later. The two groups that went to sleep shortly after the learning period relearned the material much faster than the two groups that remained awake (Fig. 12-8). Even 16 hours of waking activity produced little forgetting if the subjects had slept for 8 hours following the original learning. Sleep appears to aid retention at least in part because it provides conditions favorable for consolidation of long-term memory. It may be, as suggested above, that sleep simply decreases interference occurring during consolidation of long-term memory. Another possibility is that neural processes that occur during sleep enhance consolidation. Several experiments have shown that if mice are deprived of REM sleep (see Chapter 9), they tend to forget responses acquired just before the start of the deprivation period. Furthermore, retrograde amnesia can be produced by an ECS treatment given as long as two days after training if the animals are deprived of REM sleep during the interval between training and ECS treatment [Fishbein, 1970]. It is obvious that sleep has some influence on memory-storage processes, but we do not yet know why.

Since it is likely that memory-storage processes are active during sleep, is it possible to learn new material during sleep? Several investigators have reported some evidence of learning during sleep [Fox and Robbin, 1952], and on the basis of this evidence a number of manufacturers have marketed tape recorders for use in "sleep learning." Unfortunately, there is no real evidence that the subjects were actually asleep when the learning took place. As we know from our own experiences, we can be awakened for at least a short period of time by almost any abrupt change in stimulation—even *decreases* in stimulation. Weinberger and Lindsley [1964] found that cats were readily aroused from deep sleep (as measured by both behavior and EEG changes) by either an increase or a decrease in the intensity of a sound (see Chapter 8). You may have had the experience yourself of awakening when your clock stopped ticking.

It is evident that sleep does not cut us off from our sensory environment. If subjects are aroused from sleep when material is presented by an experimenter, then any learning that occurs may in fact occur while they are awake. To rule out this possibility Bruce et al. [1970] presented verbal material to subjects only when their EEG patterns showed a state of deep sleep. Under these conditions there was no evidence of learning during sleep. However, other research has shown that subjects can learn material presented while they are in deep sleep, as indicated by EEG patterns, if the presentation arouses them briefly. Koukkou and Lehmann [1968] read short sentences to subjects while they were in a state of slow-wave sleep (see Chapter 9). The duration of wakefulness induced by the sentences was indicated by the length of time over which the EEG patterns changed from slow-wave sleep to a pattern found in waking states. The subjects were asked to recall the sentences when they were awakened 15 minutes to 2 hours later. Accuracy

FIGURE 12–8 *Effects of sleep and waking activity on retention. Retention as reported in savings scores was better in the two groups which learned just before going to sleep. When waking activity followed learning, the effect of 16 hours was no greater than that found with 8 hours. [McGaugh, unpublished findings]*

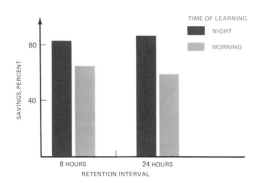

of recall varied directly with the length of the EEG wakefulness pattern elicited by the sentences. Of particular interest was the finding that they had no memory of sentences which elicited less than 30 seconds of wakefulness. Apparently material presented during sleep must cause at least 30 seconds of wakefulness if it is to be stored in long-term memory. Sleep machines may work, but if you plan to try one, be prepared to sacrifice your sleep.

RECOGNITION, RECALL, AND RELEARNING

Memory is evidenced in a variety of familiar ways. Perhaps the simplest measure of memory is *recognition*. We are able to respond appropriately in our own complex environments because we are able to recognize the people, places, and things that we have recently or frequently experienced. "Objective tests," such as true-false and multiple-choice tests, are based on the assumption that the correct answer will be recognized on the basis of previous study of the material. We can indicate recognition merely by answering yes or no, but as we all know from our own guesses on such tests, the answer is not necessarily reliable evidence of memory. We can make "false positive" responses, which indicate recognition of events not previously experienced. We can also make "false negative" responses, which indicate failure to recognize events previously experienced.

Accuracy of recognition depends on the complexity of the information presented at the time of learning as well as at the time of testing. Under some conditions memory assessed by a recognition test is extremely accurate. For example, Haber and Standing [1969] showed subjects over 2000 pictures, at the rate of one every 10 seconds. An hour later the subjects were shown 280 pairs of pictures and were asked to select the member of each pair that they had previously seen. Somewhat surprisingly, 85 to 95 percent of their recognition responses were correct. This does not mean that they remembered every detail in every picture, but only that they remembered sufficient detail to distinguish pictures which were previously presented from those which were new.

Recall is a more complicated process, and it is subject to greater forgetting. This is one reason that many students prefer true-false tests over essay tests. You may not be able to recall the name of your second-grade teacher; you might immediately recognize it if you heard it. You may feel that the name is on the "tip of your tongue"—that is, you know, but are unable to recall. This experience is described by William James [1890, p. 251]:

Suppose we try to recall a forgotten name. The state of our consciousness is peculiar. There is a gap therein; but no mere gap. It is a gap that is intensively active. A sort of wraith of the name is in it, beckoning us in a given direction, making us at moments tingle with the sense of our closeness and then letting us sink back without the longed-for term. If wrong names are proposed to us, this singularly definite gap acts immediately so as to negate them. They do not fit into its mould. And the gap of one word does not feel like the gap of another, all empty content as both might seem necessarily to be when described as gaps.

Recent studies of "tip-of-the-tongue" memory have provided some understanding of the features of words which are important in recall. For example, the first and last letters of a word are more important than the middle letters [Brown and McNeill, 1966]. However, why is it that we are able to reject incorrect words without being able to recall the correct ones? As yet, we know little about the nature and bases of this phenomenon. Recall appears to require both retrieval and recognition; once a sought-for word is retrieved, we must be able to recognize it as the particular word which was sought.

Although recall can be highly accurate under some circumstances, it is also subject to a considerable degree of "creative" forgetting. Bartlett [1932] pointed out that a remembering experience is subject to many influences. New information is readily assimilated into knowledge that we have built up on the basis of our first experiences. In a real sense we filter much of our experience. Thus when we are asked to remember, we report our experiences as they have been modified by assimilation into our own schemata. Answers to essay questions are sometimes highly creative. In some instances information may be so distorted by organizing influences that subsequent recognition is difficult. For example, Hunter [1957] reported that he had once met a male student whose Nordic features so impressed him that he frequently thought of the young man later and visualized him as a Viking at the helm of a ship crossing the North Sea. When he encountered the student a month after this first meeting he did not recognize him and had to be introduced. The difficulty was that the student's appearance did not match the distorted recollection; his hair was darker, his eyes less blue, his build was less muscular, and he was wearing glasses. What we store and recall as memory depends on how we classify our experiences. Memory is not a passive process.

The relearning, or *savings*, method of studying retention was introduced by Ebbinghaus in his classical book *Memory* [1885]. The rationale is simple. We may retain some effects of prior learning of material even though we are unable to recognize or recall correctly. If we do have some degree of retention, then we should be able to relearn the material with less effort—fewer trials or less time—than would be required for original learning. That is, there should be some savings. The general formula used to calculate savings is

$$100 \times \frac{OL - RL}{OL}$$

where OL is the measure of original learning and RL is the measure of relearning. If no relearning is required—that is, if retention is perfect—the savings score will be 100 percent. If relearning requires the same effort as original learning, savings will be zero. Strictly speaking, the savings method is used only when the material is learned to some specified criterion, such as one trial in which no errors are made. Thus its use is restricted; however, it is an extremely sensitive technique for measuring retention. The findings reported in Fig. 12-8 were based on this method of studying retention.

As we have seen retention is measured in many ways. There is no "true" measure of retention, and the evidence obtained depends on many conditions. It is well known that retention, by whatever measure, is best when the conditions at the time of the retention test are similar to those at the time of original learning. Examination grades for a course are generally higher if the examination is given in the room where the lectures were given. We often experience temporary difficulty remembering the names of friends or colleagues when we are on vacation, that is, when we are away from the environment where the names were learned and used. Part of our difficulty in remembering childhood experiences may be due to the absence of the environmental conditions under which the learning occurred. In other words, in some cases it is the environment that has changed, not the memory.

Reinstatement of the conditions under which the learning took place can aid recall. For example, you may have forgotten how you wrote when you were in the third grade, but you may be able to recall and write that way again just by writing very slowly. Try this yourself: write your name at the rate of approximately one letter each second or two, and then compare the result with your regular signature and, if you have a sample, your third-grade signature. There is some evidence that recall is better under hypnosis [Reiff and Scheerer, 1959]. The effects of hypnosis may be to reinstate some of the conditions, feelings, images, etc., of the original learning situation. The phenomenal Mr. S. was able to recall without error material he had learned years earlier, but before doing so he first recalled very carefully the details of the situation, including the room, in which the learning had occurred.

The most striking demonstration of the importance of reinstatement of similar conditions in retention of learning was reported by Overton [1964]. Rats readily learned two conflicting responses, a left-turn response and a right-turn response, in the same maze but under different drug states. One response was taught while the rats were in a normal state and the other was taught while they were heavily drugged with a barbiturate. Overton found that their learning under one state was dissociated from their learning under the other state; the response that was "recalled" depended completely on the rat's drug state at the time it was tested. This is an extreme case of reinstatement, or state-dependency, effects in retention, but it seems likely that much normal forgetting, particularly temporary forgetting, may be due to differences in both

328

internal states and environmental conditions from those during learning.

A favorite scene in "B" movies and television is the one in which a captured suspect or spy, or perhaps a kidnapped heroine, is given an injection of "truth serum." This drug is supposed to make the captive reveal the secret formula, the plot, or an important incident. Drugs are sometimes used in psychiatric interviews and "voluntary" interrogation. Subjects interviewed under the influence of drugs such as sodium amytal are often quite communicative, but there is no evidence that they tell only the "truth." Drugged subjects may confess crimes they have never committed, and they may deny having committed crimes that they obviously have committed. The drug undoubtedly affects memory processes, but the subject is just as likely to report his fantasies as his "real" experiences [Freedman, 1960]. There is no pharmacological "pipeline" to truth.

Surgical procedures have also shed some light on memory consolidation. As mentioned earlier, severe epilepsy is often treated by surgical removal of a region of brain tissue which is the focus of the abnormal electrical activity and generates the epileptic seizures. In the course of surgery, which is done under local anesthetic, so that the patient remains conscious throughout the operation, the surgeon removes the skull overlying the brain and then stimulates the cortex with weak electric current. This is done in order to map the regions surrounding the epileptic focus and localize the region of the seizure, and so that regions involved in the control of speech will not be removed during the surgery (the patient's speech is blocked when the speech areas are stimulated by the current). Most of the seizure foci are found in the temporal lobes of the brain. This is the region which appears to be involved in memory consolidation in humans.

Several decades ago the great neurosurgeon Penfield reported that electrical stimulation of the exposed temporal cortex of human patients sometimes produced dramatic results [Penfield and Perot, 1963, p. 596]:

> A past experience, which had occurred regularly as a part of the patient's seizure pattern, was reproduced by electrical stimulation of the cortex of the temporal lobe. And also, more surprising still, a previous happening which was not related to previous attacks, was recalled by the surgeon's electrode.

The electrical stimulation appeared directly to elicit a vivid memory. Over the years experiential responses to mild electrical stimulation were reported by approximately 8 percent of over 500 patients whose temporal regions were explored. Such responses have never been elicited by stimulating any other regions of the brain cortex (see Fig. 12-9).

Many types of experiential responses have been obtained. Some are primarily auditory sounds and sound sequences such as conversations and music—and others are primarily visual scenes of persons or objects. Sometimes the experiences are complex ones with both visual and auditory aspects. The patient is fully aware that what he is experiencing is not based on real events occurring at the moment, but the experience

329

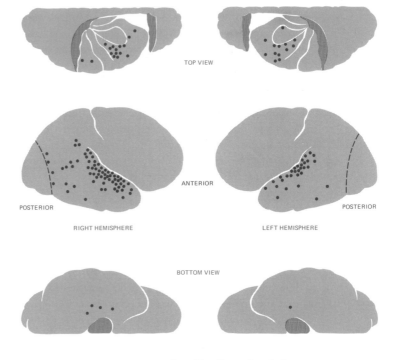

TOP VIEW

ANTERIOR

POSTERIOR

POSTERIOR

RIGHT HEMISPHERE

LEFT HEMISPHERE

BOTTOM VIEW

FIGURE 12-9   *Experiences produced by direct electrical
stimulation of the brain in human patients. Dots indicate
summary of all places in the two cerebral hemispheres
where experimental responses were produced in patients.
[Penfield and Perot, 1963]*

is more vivid than a recollection. For example, one patient responded in
the following way to a series of stimulations applied to various regions
of the temporal lobe [Penfield and Perot, 1963, pp. 640–641]:

During stimulation he said, "I am trying to find the name of a song."
The electrode was removed. "There was a piano there and someone was
playing. I could hear the song, you know. It is a song I have sung before
but I cannot find out quite what the title of the song is. That was what I
was trying to do when you finished stimulating!"

[The stimulation was then repeated without warning.] After removal of the electrode, he said, "Someone was speaking to another and
he mentioned a name but I could not understand it." When asked
whether he saw the person, he replied, "It was just like a *dream*." When
asked if the person was there he said, "Yes, sir, about where the nurse
with the eyeglasses is sitting over there."

[The stimulation was repeated] again without warning . . . and
without questioning him. "Yes, 'Oh Marie, Oh Marie'—someone is
singing it." He was then asked who it was and he replied, "I don't know,
Doctor, I cannot recognize the voice."

[The stimulation was repeated] again without warning. He observed, while the electrode was being held in place, "Again, 'Oh Marie, Oh Marie.' " He explained that he had heard this before. "It is a theme song," he said, "on a radio program. The program is called the 'Life of Luigi.' " The patient then discussed the identity of the song with [the surgeon] and he ended by singing the well-known refrain, "Oh Marie, Oh Marie." All in the operating room recognized the song.

In some cases the experimental responses seemed clearly to be vivid memories of past experiences, while in others they seemed to be more like fantasies or hallucinations. As Penfield and Perot interpret these effects [1963, p. 679]:

The conclusion is inescapable that some, if not all, of these evoked responses represent activation of a neural mechanism that keeps the record of current experience. There is activation too of the emotional experience. The responses have that basic element of reference to the past that one associates with memory. But their vividness or wealth of detail and the sense of immediacy that goes with them serve to set them apart from the ordinary process of recollection which rarely displays such qualities.

By what process memory is evoked by brain stimulation remains one of the exciting and challenging problems for future research.

FORGETTING OF LONG-TERM MEMORY

As we have seen, we forget for many reasons. The initial stages of memory, iconic and short-term memory, are highly labile. Forgetting can occur because of conditions which produce retrograde amnesia and interfere with consolidation of long-term memory. Forgetting can occur because of changes in external conditions and internal states which interfere with retrieval. In fact it almost seems that forgetting is the most salient phenomenon of memory. Even well-learned responses may be forgotten over time unless they are continually relearned or rehearsed. Although we usually do not think about it in this way, we maintain our skills, even our language skills, by constantly practicing them. At one point a colleague from a Spanish-speaking country spent several years in Italy, where he spoke only Italian. Upon his return to his native country he found he was unable to lecture in Spanish; his language was a strange combination of Italian and Spanish. Fortunately he completely recovered (relearned?) the ability to speak Spanish within a year following his return. Clearly he had forgotten.

What causes the forgetting of such well-learned responses? One possibility is that, with time, the neurobiological bases of memory decay or change, or that the memories simply fade. Another possibility is that two sets of well-learned responses compete with or obscure each other,

331

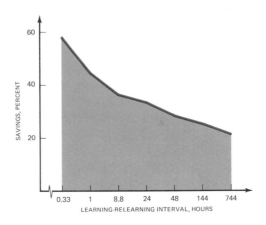

FIGURE 12-10 *Ebbinghaus' forgetting curve. Lists of nonsense syllables were learned at one period and relearned at one of several intervals. Curve shows percent savings score for each retention interval. Perfect retention would be 100 percent and complete forgetting would be 0 percent. Savings scores are computed as (original learning − relearning)/original learning. [Ebbinghaus, 1885]*

causing retroactive interference (if the later learning interferes with retention of earlier learning) or *proactive interference* (if older learning interferes with retention of more recently learned responses). Although these hypotheses are typically considered as alternative explanations, they need not be. In fact, forgetting of long-term memory may be caused by both interference and decay, as well as all the other influences mentioned. Ebbinghaus commented on forgetting as follows [1885, p. 62] :

All sorts of ideas, if left to themselves, are gradually forgotten. This fact is generally known. Groups or series of ideas which at first we could easily recollect or which recurred frequently of their own accord . . . gradually return more rarely, . . . and can be reproduced by voluntary effort only with difficulty and in part. After a longer period even this fails, except, to be sure, in rare instances.

Ebbinghaus conducted the first experimental studies of memory, and his approach, techniques, and findings provide a superb model of scientific investigation of a complex psychological problem. Over the course of several years he studied the effects of numerous conditions on learning and relearning of verbal material, using only himself as a subject. He developed the use of "nonsense syllables" and the savings method discussed above. He described many phenomena of memory, and for the most part, his conclusions have been substantiated by subsequent research. Among his major contributions was the first study of forgetting over time. In order to study forgetting, Ebbinghaus first learned eight series of lists, each consisting of 13 nonsense syllables. He then relearned one list at one of seven intervals—20 minutes, 1 hour, 9 hours, 2 days, 6 days, or 31 days—and repeated this complete procedure 163 times. Thus the measurements of learning and relearning were highly reliable. The forgetting curve obtained from these studies is shown in Fig. 12-10.

332

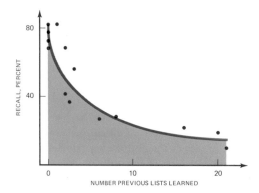

FIGURE 12–11   *Proactive interference effects on retention. Recall of lists of material 24 hours after learning decreases as a function of the number of lists learned earlier. Each point is based on the results of one experiment. The curve summarizes the results of 14 different experiments. [Underwood, 1957]*

As the figure shows, forgetting was rapid at first and then slowed; more forgetting occurred over the first 24 hours than between 24 hours and 31 days.

These findings and similar ones obtained from hundreds of other studies provide excellent descriptive evidence of forgetting over time. However, they do not explain why forgetting occurred. Some of it might be due to decay, but the procedures used also provided a great deal of both proactive and retroactive interference. Subsequent research has shown that in studies of this type forgetting over the first 24 hours depends largely on the number of lists that the subject has learned previously—that is, on proactive interference. Figure 12-11 summarizes a number of studies in which recall was measured 24 hours after learning. In spite of numerous differences in procedures, the results are surprisingly consistent. The degree of forgetting over a 24-hour period increases as a function of the number of lists previously learned. Subsequent research generally supports the view that a considerable amount of forgetting is due to interference, both retroactive and proactive. Learning does not always add to knowledge. It can make older memory difficult to retrieve, and it can interfere with both the learning and retention of subsequent information. The story is told that a university president who was an expert on fish set out to learn the names of all the students in the university; he gave up the effort when he discovered that he forgot the name of one fish for every student's name that he learned.

Is all forgetting over time caused by interference? In a series of experiments with rats Gleitman [1970] has found considerable evidence of forgetting which cannot be readily explained by interference or by changed stimulus conditions. He concludes that the interference hypothesis is attractive as an explanation of forgetting because it requires no

333

further physiological machinery beyond that required for learning, and it is equally possible that the underlying mechanism may be some decay process. We saw that there was rapid decay of short-term memory in the case of the patient H.M. It seems likely that long-term memory may also be subject to disintegration or decay with time. If so, the rate of disintegration should be subject to variations in biological states. Campbell [1967] has reported that weanling rats show much more forgetting over long intervals of time than adult rats. Gleitman [1970] has reported preliminary evidence that the rate of forgetting in goldfish varies with the temperature of the water in which the fish are kept during a retention interval of several weeks; forgetting was more rapid when the water was warm.

Deutsch [1969] has shown that in rats retention varies considerably with the amount of time between learning and testing. In one experiment Huppert and Deutsch [1969] trained rats in a Y-shaped discrimination maze. The rats were given 15 training trials in which they could escape from an electrified grid floor by entering the arm of the maze in which a light was on at the end of the alley. Rats in different groups were then given additional training to a criterion of 10 correct choices at one of 8 retention intervals. The best retention of the partially learned response was obtained in the groups trained either 7 or 10 days later. Performance at those times was clearly better than performance tested 30 minutes after the original learning. Furthermore retention was poor when the retraining occurred 17 days after the original training. In other words, retention first *improved* and then *declined* over time.

Deutsch has also shown that at the longer retention intervals, where considerable forgetting has occurred, memory can be improved by administering drugs which inhibit the enzyme acetylcholinesterase. This enzyme is responsible for hydrolyzing, or destroying, the molecules of the neurotransmitter acetylcholine (see Chapter 7). On the basis of this evidence he proposes that memory depends directly on the amount of acetylcholine available at synapses of the neurons which participate in the learning. The amount of acetylcholine is assumed first to increase with time after training and then to decrease. The rate of decrease is assumed to vary with the degree of original learning. Inhibiting the enzyme acetylcholinesterase with drugs should result in greater amounts of acetylcholine, and hence should improve memory if forgetting has occurred. This overall picture fits well with the hypothesis that changes in strength of memory with time are based on changes in neurotransmitter availability, but the evidence remains circumstantial. If this hypothesis is correct, the major question is what neurobiological processes underlie the alterations in transmitter levels? Nevertheless, Deutsch's findings do provide further evidence that changes in memory with time, including forgetting, are in part related to ongoing biological processes. There is reasonably clear evidence that memories do decay with time, even though we do not yet understand the biological processes which constitute decay.

As yet we do not know what neurobiological processes underlie memory. We do not know what changes in the nervous system must take place if experiences are to leave traces which affect subsequent behavior. If there is more than one type of memory trace, as

much of the evidence suggests, then the problem is enormously complicated. We need to know the neurobiological bases of each type of memory, as well as the possible interrelationships among the various memory processes. The questions of memory processes must be examined at several levels. We need to know how neurons are altered by experience and how different structures in the nervous system participate in the various aspects of memory processing. Finally, we need to relate these neurobiological findings to our understanding of memory gained from behavioral studies. A complete understanding of memory will require an integration of all levels.

Although we are quite far from an understanding of the neurobiological bases of memory, we are beginning to find neurobiological *correlates* of learning. That is, we are beginning to discover neurobiological changes which are associated with learning. The discovery of *correlates* is essential if *bases* are eventually to be understood. Our experiences produce a variety of anatomical, neurophysiological, and biochemical changes in our brains. Whether these changes are critical for memory storage or are merely byproducts of memory-storage processes remains to be seen.

STRUCTURAL CORRELATES

The search for an anatomical locus of memory has been almost completely fruitless. Extensive studies by Lashley [1960] of the effects of lesions in various regions of rats' brains have turned up no evidence that retention of specific responses could be eliminated by selective destruction of specific brain areas. Brain lesions quite clearly interfere with learning and retention, as well as with other processes, but the neurobiological processes that underlie memory, termed *engrams* by Lashley, do not appear to be precisely located in discrete regions of the brain. If they are, the lesioning approach has as yet failed to find them.

A number of years ago it was discovered that the two cerebral hemispheres in man as well as other animals are functionally connected by the *cerebral commissures*, particularly the *corpus callosum*. When the commissures are cut by surgery, each hemisphere can function independently; the brain is split functionally as well as physically. In human patients commissural surgery is sometimes performed to alleviate severe epilepsy. Sperry [1968], who has conducted extensive studies of such split-brain patients, notes that each hemisphere has a "mind of its own," its own sensations, perceptions, ideas, memories, and experiences, all of which are unrelated to the corresponding experiences of the other hemisphere.

335

Although the patient can learn with either hemisphere, the two hemispheres learn quite different types of material. The dominant hemisphere, usually the left, is the only one capable of speaking and writing. Such patients are thus able to report in detail, talk about, only that information which reaches the left hemisphere. For example, split-brain patients cannot name or describe objects flashed in the left visual field because this visual information projects to the right hemisphere of the brain (see Chapter 7). They are also unable to name objects held in the left hand because the sensory information from the left hand projects to the right hemisphere, which is unable to "talk." However, the right hemisphere functions better than the left hemisphere in memory for tactile experiences. In a study of short-term memory for tactile experiences split-brain patients were asked to grasp an unfamiliar and irregular wire form which was hidden from view and then select it by touch after a short delay from among several other forms. As Fig. 12-12 shows, they were almost completely unable to perform this simple task with their right hands (and left hemisphere). However, when they were tested with their left hands (their right hemispheres), most were able to respond correctly even after delays of longer than 2 minutes.

It appears that different regions of the human brain became specialized for processing and remembering different types of information. Thus memory processing is at least somewhat localized in the brain. It seems reasonable to anticipate additional evidence that different regions of the brain perform different functions in memory as we increase our knowledge of neuroanatomy and our ability to discover regions of the brain which are functionally connected.

If experiences produce changes in the neural processes which underlie memory, as we must certainly assume, then we should be able to observe the changes. The difficulty is that we are not yet sure what changes to look for, and it well may be that the critical changes are too

FIGURE 12–12   *Retention of a tactile experience in split-brain patients. Five of seven subjects were unable to perform correctly with the right hand. All could perform correctly with the left hand; four of the seven performed correctly even with a delay of 2 minutes. [Milner and Taylor, 1969]*

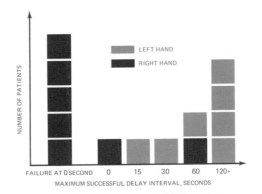

FIGURE 12-13   *Rats living in an enriched environment. "Toys" are changed frequently. [Rosenzweig, University of California, Berkeley]*

small to detect with current techniques. One possibility is that neural activity produced by training induces anatomical changes or growth in nerve cells and their processes. Evidence of alterations in the anatomy of neural tissue produced by specific training has eluded even the most imaginative researchers. However, as new techniques are developed for studying the fine structure of the nervous system, we may be able to detect more subtle differences than are presently discernible, and it is possible that these will indicate the effects of experience on brain anatomy.

We do know that gross alterations in brain tissue can be produced by experience. Bennett et al. [1964] compared the brains of rats reared in a complex environment with those of rats reared with restricted environmental stimulation (see Fig. 12-13) and found a number of important differences. The brain cortex tissue of the rats reared in the complex environment was heavier and thicker and activity of the enzyme acetylcholinesterase was higher than in rats deprived of such environmental stimulation. There was, of course, no difference in the number of neurons in the brain cortex; however, the increase in cortical thickness may have been due to an increase in number of glial cells (see Chapter 7). Control experiments indicated that the effects were not due to differences in stress or amount of exercise. It seems likely that the neural changes are produced by the different sensory experiences of the animals. However, as these researchers have pointed out [Bennett et al., 1964, p. 619]:

> . . . finding these changes in the brain consequent upon experience does not demonstrate that they have anything to do with the storage of memory. The demonstration of such changes merely helps to establish the fact that the brain is responsive to environmental pressure—a fact demanded by physiological theories of learning and memory.

As discussed in detail in Chapter 7, the living brain generates electrical activity which can be readily recorded. The dramatic technological advances in this method of investigation have led to numerous studies of the changes in electrophysiological responses during learning. In these "wire-tapping" procedures electrodes are temporarily or permanently implanted in the brain tissue, and the electrical activity is recorded from large regions of the brain, restricted structures, and even single cells.

Training has been found to produce changes in EEG patterns in different regions of the brain. Gross changes in brain wave patterns, such as desynchronization at the cortex and slow synchronous rhythms (theta waves) in the hippocampus, are commonly seen early in training but usually disappear with further training. John [1967] has found that under some conditions long-lasting changes in electrical activity can be produced by training. When an intermittent stimulus, such as a flashing light, is used as a signal for food for a hungry cat, rhythmic electrical activity of approximately the same frequency as the signal can be recorded from many structures in the animal's brain. These "labeled" responses may appear in different brain structures as training proceeds. If signals of different frequencies which have different consequences are used—say 10 hertz signals food and 6 hertz signals no food—the distributions of these labeled responses may become quite stable in various brain structures. Such changes are usually most marked in regions of the brain that are not involved in specific sensory processes. After animals are trained with such signals as flashing lights or particular frequencies, the responses can also be elicited by rhythmic electrical stimulation

FIGURE 12–14 *Average gross evoked responses to pattern of circles and squares. The evoked responses were recorded from human subjects stimulated by a weak flash which illuminated a visual field containing either a square or a circle. Each wave is based on 200 repetitions. The sequence of stimulation was large circle, large square, large circle, small square. Note the similarity of the evoked potential resulting from stimulation by large and small squares. [John, 1967]*

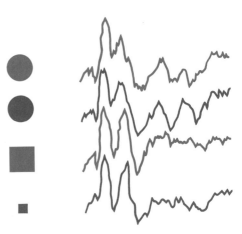

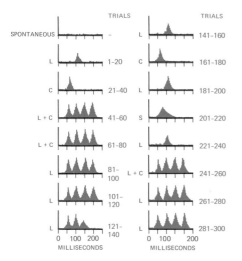

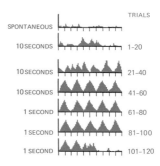

FIGURE 12–15   *Responses of single cells in a cat's visual cortex to various periods of sensory stimulation. Each line represents the distribution of responses summed over 20 stimulus presentations. At right, the response of a cell firing spontaneously followed by three series of 20 trials in which the cat was stimulated by a light flickering at 10 hertz. (The cell was in a region which was stimulated with anodal-surface positive current, but this is not a critical factor.) With the repeated stimulation the cell begins to respond at a rate of 10 hertz. It continues to respond at 10 hertz even when stimulation rate is changed to 1 hertz. The 10-hertz rate becomes weaker with repeated stimulation at 1 hertz. At left, the response of a cell (in another cat, not subjected to anodal cortical stimulation) following stimulation by a flash of light (L) and a click (C). When L and C are presented together, a new pattern of firing results. On trials 81 to 120 the L + C pattern is seen even though only L is presented. On trials 121 to 140 the response weakens, and by trials 141 to 200 the original L and C patterns return. The pattern of response to a shock (S) on trials 201 to 220 is different from the other patterns. After L and C are paired again on trials 241 to 260, L alone will elicit an L + C pattern. [Morrell, 1967, in John, 1967]*

applied directly to the regions of the brain from which the labeled responses were recorded.

In a very interesting series of experiments John demonstrated that the gross electrical responses of the brain evoked by sensory stimulation are modified by experience. In cats signals that have different consequences produce evoked potentials with different shapes [John, 1967]. Moreover, studies of evoked responses recorded from human subjects suggest that the wave shape of evoked potentials is related to the meaning of the stimulus. For example, brain response evoked by a square differs from that elicited by a circle (see Fig. 12-14).

Other studies have shown that the electrical responses of single neurons can be modified by experience. Morrell [1967] has recorded activity from single cells in the visual cortex of cats during stimulation with various patterns of lights and other stimuli. In one experiment anodal (positive) current was applied to the cat's cortex while the cat was stimulated with light flickering at the frequency of 10 hertz (see Fig. 12-15). After about 40 trials the cell began to respond at an average frequency of 10 bursts per second for about 50 trials. Morrell [1967]

339

also recorded the electrical activity of cells which were responsive to two or more types of sensory stimulation. Responses of one cell to a light and a click presented simultaneously were found to differ from responses to either stimulus presented alone. However, after presentation of the two stimuli together the same average pattern of firing was elicited by the light alone.

These findings indicate that patterns of neuronal activity can be markedly influenced by training. The EEG patterns appear to be correlates of learned responses. We do not yet know, however, whether they are *essential* components or merely *correlates* of memory-storage and retrieval processes.

CHEMICAL CORRELATES

There is considerable interest in the possibility that memory might have a chemical basis. The spectacular success of recent research in molecular genetics has spawned numerous investigations of the effects of training on macromolecular synthesis in the brain. Research on this problem is a recent venture; speculation is not. In the last century William James anticipated this interest in molecular bases of memory [1890, p. 127]:

Every smallest stroke of virtue or of vice leaves its never so little scar. The drunken Rip Van Winkle, in Jefferson's play, excuses himself for every fresh dereliction by saying, "I won't count this time." Well! he may not count it; but it is being counted none the less. Down among his nerve-cells and fibres the molecules are counting it, registering and storing it up to be used against him when the next temptation comes.

Experiments with antibiotics which interfere with macromolecular synthesis suggest that memory storage may require protein synthesis. Since protein synthesis is directed by ribonucleic acid (RNA), it seems reasonable to expect that RNA might be affected by training. Several recent studies have shown that it is [Glassman, 1969]. For example, Zemp et al. [1966] found that training enhances RNA synthesis in mice. The effect was measured as an increased incorporation of radioactive (H^3) uridine in trained animals compared with stimulated but otherwise untrained animals injected with radioactive (C^{14}) uridine. The effect of training was seen in brain tissue, but not in liver or kidney tissue. However, the changes lasted for less than an hour. Thus they cannot be regarded as correlates of long-term memory. They may be due to processes involved in memory storage, or they may simply reflect processes involved in the maintenance or repair of stimulated cells. It is particularly interesting to note that the changes are most evident in the region of the hippocampus [Adair et al., 1968].

Changes in RNA associated with learning have been obtained in several types of studies. Hyden [1967] has shown that training may alter both the amount as well as the composition of neuronal and glial RNA. For example, Shashoua [1968] attached a small polystyrene

340

float below the jaw of a goldfish. Within 3 to 4 hours the fish learned to adjust to this condition and swim fairly normally. Following the training the ratio of uracil to cytocine in the newly synthesized RNA was found to be markedly changed. In untrained fish the ratio was 3:1; in the trained fish it was 6:1. In several experiments with rats Hyden [1967] also found that various types of training produce changes in the base ratios of neuronal RNA. These findings also suggest that training alters protein, but it is not yet known whether such alterations are due to increased protein synthesis. Although there is substantial evidence that various kinds of experiences alter the synthesis of macromolecules, it is too early to conclude that such changes underlie memory consolidation. It would be important to know whether the time course of the development of these changes parallels the time course of consolidation measured in studies of retrograde amnesia produced by antibiotics.

Can memory be transferred from one individual to another? Is it possible to "transfer" memory by injecting an animal with an extract of the brain of another animal? This is probably the most dramatic, as well as controversial, question in current research on the neurobiological bases of memory. Evidence of "memory transfer" by such procedures would provide dramatic evidence that memory storage is based on chemical changes. Furthermore, the nature of the changes underlying memory could be discovered by determining the molecule responsible for the transfer. The hope of discovering "memory molecules" has stimulated a large number of memory-transfer experiments [Byrne, 1970]. The earliest experiments used planarians. Transfer was obtained by feeding trained planarians to naïve ones [McConnell, 1962]. Subsequent research has indicated, however, that equally effective transfer is obtained by feeding planarians other planarians that have been subjected to stimulation but are otherwise untrained [Hartry et al., 1964]. Thus the transfer effects do not appear to be due to transfer of any specific "memory molecule."

Most recent studies have used rats and mice [Golub et al., 1970]. The experiments have used a variety of behavioral and chemical procedures, as well as numerous criteria for "memory transfer." The findings have been extremely conflicting, and consequently it is impossible to draw any firm conclusions at this point. The bulk of the evidence indicates some sort of transfer effect, although no research has as yet been able to specify either optimal or reliable procedures for producing it. Moreover, it is not yet clear whether these effects, when they are obtained, are due to memory transfer or facilitation of learning [McGaugh, 1967]. The effects are most likely not due to RNA, but to some other molecule or molecules [Luttges et al., 1966; Ungar, 1970]. Should some of the experiments turn out to be reproducible, they may provide a clue to the molecular bases of memory storage. Such evidence would have interesting implications for education. Certainly the social, ethical, and scientific implications of "memory" transplants are even more far-reaching than those related to heart transplants. Nevertheless, we have not yet turned up a "memory molecule," and at least for the moment, you will have to continue to acquire information through the conventional neurobiological processes which underlie learning and memory. We have as yet developed no chemical substitute for study.

In this chapter we have briefly reviewed only an extremely limited selection of theories and research concerned with the nature and bases of memory. Obviously memory involves an incredibly complicated set of processes. When we are able to obtain a completely adequate understanding of memory processes, we shall be able to deal effectively with many of the disorders of memory, and perhaps even some types of mental retardation. The findings reported here indicate that progress is being made, but we will need to know a great deal more before we will understand the "machinery" of memory.

SUMMARY

Memory represents the lasting effect of stimulation. The inability to remember or the inability to forget are thus severe handicaps in our ability to adapt to the environment. There appear to be several forms of memory processes. One type of imagelike memory, iconic memory, is represented by the fleeting images that provide continuity to our sensory experience. In another type of imagelike memory, eidetic imagery, detailed images can be remembered for many minutes or longer under appropriate conditions.

In addition to these special forms of memory, the processes of short-term memory appear to have different characteristics from those of long-term memory. Short-term memory, recollection for several seconds or minutes of details such as a sequence of digits, may be disrupted by either retroactive or proactive interference. These effects are influenced by such factors as acoustical similarity rather than meaning similarity of the interfering information.

The consolidation of short-term memory into long-term memory depends particularly on repetition or practice. Evidence that long-term memory involves time-dependent processes comes partly from studies of retrograde amnesia which can be produced experimentally by ECS or drug treatments. The degree of retrograde amnesia produced depends on the intensity of the treatment, the time between original learning and amnesic treatment, the type of animal, and other factors. It has also been possible to enhance memory with drug treatments or with electrical stimulation of certain parts of the brain. In addition, the consolidation hypothesis has received experimental support from studies of the effects of retroactive interference, and sleep on learning and memory.

Two measures of information retention and retrieval from memory are recognition and recall. The accuracy of recognition depends on such factors as the complexity of the information learned and the time of testing. Recall of long-term memory, which is subject to greater forgetting, has been used, for example, to study the phenomenon called tip-of-the-tongue memory. Recall is subject to a great deal of distortion, since memories are modified by information previously acquired. A limited but extremely sensitive measure of retention is provided by the amount of savings in relearning.

The psychobiological bases of memory processes represent an active area of research interest. Physiological and environmental states profoundly influence the ability of animals and men to recall previously learned information. Studies of forgetting indicate that the apparent loss of information from long-term storage may be influenced not only by interference, but by an intrinsic decay process. A number of neurobiological correlates of memory have been observed. Although the search for a precise anatomical locus of the engram has been fruitless, research with split-brain subjects points to areas of the brain, particularly the cerebral cortex, that play an important role in memory processes. Electrical activity of various areas of the brain has been shown to change with learning, as have such biochemical processes as RNA and protein synthesis in the brain.

CHAPTER THIRTEEN

INTELLIGENCE AND INTELLIGENT BEHAVIOR

In a sense we all know what the word "intelligence" means. You may have concluded that some of your friends are more intelligent than others. You probably know some people who have achieved distinction because of their intelligence. You may know of some who have such low intelligence that they have to be kept in an institution for the mentally retarded. You may also share the generally accepted view that human beings are more intelligent than apes, who are more intelligent than cats and dogs, who in turn are more intelligent than slugs or sponges. On what basis do we make these judgments? It is "obvious" that some people are more intelligent than others, but exactly what is it that is obvious? Certainly intelligence is not an observable attribute, like body size and form. It is one thing to say that cats and dogs have more hair than sponges; it is another thing to say that they are more intelligent.

Since the word "intelligence" is a noun it is easy to fall into the trap of thinking of intelligence as some "thing" which causes individuals to behave intelligently. Intelligence is not a thing. Individual men and

INTELLIGENCE

beasts differ in the degree to which their *behavior* is intelligent, just as they differ in height and weight. However, height and weight do not *cause* stature; they merely describe it. In the same sense, intelligence is not the *cause* of intelligent behavior; it is merely a term we use to refer to certain features of an individual's behavior. Just as stature is determined by many influences, including genetics, nutrition, disease, and injury, so intelligent behavior is a result of many influences. We assume that intelligence is a function of the brain and that the various factors which determine intelligence do so through their influences on the development and functioning of the central nervous system. In this chapter we shall examine some of the bases of individual differences in intelligence in man and the other animals.

There are many definitions of intelligence, each emphasizing a different feature of behavior. The problem lies in specifying exactly what intelligent behavior is. Is it, as some definitions suggest, the capacity for abstract thinking, or is it simply the ability to learn? The most useful definition, as well as the least satisfactory from a theoretical standpoint, is that intelligence is what is tested by an intelligence test. However, you do not need to know the results of an intelligence test to make a

345

judgment about someone's intelligence. Furthermore, you may feel, perhaps with some justification, that the performance measured by an intelligence test is not what *you* mean by intelligence. This is the basic reason there is no universally accepted definition of intelligence. It is also why studies of the nature and bases of intelligence have not awaited a definition.

Until the publication of Darwin's influential book *The Origin of Species* [1859], we human beings regarded ourselves as quite different from the other animals. In fact, the term "animal" is still used interchangeably with "infrahuman." Until quite recently even the causes of behavior were thought to be different in humans and infrahumans. All lower animals were believed to be endowed with instincts, while man was endowed with reason. Acceptance of the idea that species, including man, evolved from other species required a rejection, or at least a reexamination, of this view. If evolution is a continual process, then man and other animals must be at least somewhat similar in behavior as well as in anatomy and physiology. In a subsequent, less well-known book *The Expression of the Emotions in Man and Animals* Darwin [1872] attempted to show that many of our emotional responses, such as facial expressions and blushing, are similar to those seen in lower animals. Darwin clearly needed some such evidence of continuity in some aspects of behavior. At the same time one of Darwin's friends, Romanes, collected evidence of humanlike behavior in lower animals, which he published in the book *Animal Intelligence* [1895]. Since animal behavior had not yet been subjected to extensive scientific investigation, Romanes was forced to rely on the reports of "reliable observers." Some of these reports may cause the reader to wonder about the intelligence, and even the sanity, of the "reliable observers." In some cases the observations appear to be more like hallucinations. The following is a typical example [Romanes, 1895, p. 364]:

Powelsen, a writer on Iceland, has related an account of the intelligence displayed by the mice of that country, which has given rise to a difference of competent opinion, and which perhaps can hardly yet be said to have been definitely settled. What Powelsen said is that the mice collect in parties of from six to ten, select a flat piece of dried cowdung, pile berries or other food upon it, then with united strength drag it to the edge of any stream they wish to cross, launch it, embark, and range themselves round the central heap of provisions with their heads joined over it, and their tails hanging in the water, perhaps serving as rudders. [Since this observation was met with considerable skepticism, one investigator] . . . therefore, determined on trying to arrive at the truth of the matter, with the following result:—"I made a point of inquiring of different individuals as to the reality of the account, and am happy in being able to say that it is now established as an important fact in natural history by the testimony of two eyewitnesses of unquestionable veracity, the clergyman of Briamslaek, and Madame Benedictson of Stickesholm, both of whom assured me that they had seen the expedition performed repeatedly. Madame Benedictson, in particular, recollected having spent a whole afternoon, in her younger days, at the margin of a small lake on which these skillful navigators had embarked, and amusing herself and her companions by driving them away from the sides of the lake as they approached them.

Although mice may not be capable of displaying intelligent behavior of this particular type, research conducted since the time of Romanes has provided extensive evidence that infrahumans are capable of quite complex behavior which involves problem solving, or reasoning.

Infrahumans are not mere bundles of instincts and man is not completely rational, but there is little doubt that in terms of intelligence man is at the top of the phylogenetic pile. We do not yet know the basis of this superior intelligence. We assume that our brains are "better" than those of infrahumans, but we do not yet know exactly what structures and neurobiological functions of our brains make us more intelligent. We assume that we are more intelligent because of our abilities to plan, invent, solve problems, use language, develop culture, and create and appreciate art. We do not differ from other animals simply because we can learn; this is a capacity we share with most, if not all, animals. Insects and even protozoa are quite capable of some types of learning. Higher animals appear to differ from lower ones in terms of the complexity of the tasks that they are able to learn. The ability to learn is essential for intelligent behavior, but learning is not synonymous with intelligence.

Of course, it is our own view of intelligence that places man at the top of the evolutionary pile. Intelligence is sometimes defined as the ability to adapt to the requirements of an environment. In this sense all processes that contribute to adaptation, such as the growing of white hair by arctic animals, are "intelligent." Of course this is tantamount to defining intelligence as the process of evolution. There is nothing inherently wrong with such a definition. However, in this chapter we are considering intelligence in a more restricted sense, as the nature of and the processes underlying intelligent behavior in individual animals.

By implicit general agreement *instincts*, the complex genetically influenced responses of species which develop without specific training, are excluded from the concept of intelligence as we are considering it here. Such responses are, of course, "intelligent" in an evolutionary sense, as the following example shows. In a series of brilliant experiments Von Frisch and other workers [Lindauer, 1961; Wenner, 1964] discovered how honeybees returning from a food source communicate the location of the food to other bees in the colony. When they return to the hive the bees perform an agitated "dance" on the face of the combs inside the hive. Some of the findings are shown in Fig. 13-1. The speed of dancing is closely correlated with the distance of the food source. The direction of the food source is indicated by the vertical direction of

347

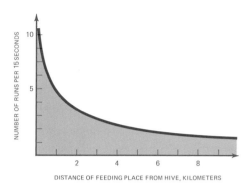

FIGURE 13-1   *Dance of honeybees.*
Honeybees returning from a food source
dance on the vertical surface of the honey-
comb inside the hive. Speed of the dance
decreases with the distance of the food
source. This is the round dance; the wag-
gle dance, indicated by the wavy lines,
communicates the direction of the food
source in relation to the sun. If the source
is in the direction of the sun, the dance is
vertical; if it is 60 degrees to the left of
the direction of the sun, the waggle dance
is 60 degrees to the left of vertical.
[Von Frisch, 1953]

a portion of the dance called the "waggle dance." The bees also emit different sounds during different phases of the dance. Thus they "show and tell" in a rather abstract language. Moreover, different species of bees speak different dialects. A species of Italian bees indicates direction of food with a form of dance entirely different from the one shown here.

There is much about this type of communication that we do not yet understand. What causes the bee to perform the intricate dance when it returns to the hive? How do other bees in the colony know what the signals mean? This highly interesting communication has been described, but we do not yet understand its bases. From the colony's perspective such communication is highly intelligent, but bee language is not like our language in that it consists only of very specific signals. The fact that different species of bees perform different dances suggests that the pattern of the dance is genetically controlled. In contrast, although our genetic endowment allows for the development of language, the particular language we speak is not genetically determined. We have the ability to acquire any language that is spoken around us, and we can communicate an almost infinite amount of information through language. Man's linguistic abilities must thus be regarded as one indication of greater intelligence.

MEASURES OF INTELLIGENCE

Since it has proved so difficult to develop an acceptable definition of intelligence, it seems that it would be even more difficult to measure intellectual performance. However, as you know from your own experience intelligence tests have become a standard part of the armamentarium of modern education. Before the turn of the century there were no intelligence tests. The first systematic attempts to measure mental functioning were made by Francis Galton, Darwin's cousin. During the 1880s Galton maintained a laboratory in London where, for a small fee, he measured visitors on a variety of simple psychological tests for color vision, reaction time, and hearing acuity. The differences

348

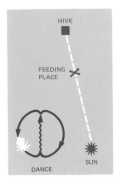
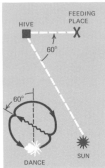
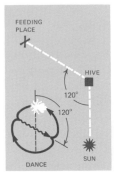
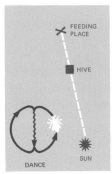

in individual performance even in these simple tasks was striking. Early tests developed by others, such as Cattell [1890], were also based on simple measures of perceptual judgment or speed of reaction.

The difficulty with these early attempts was that they provided highly reliable measures of highly uninteresting responses. Most of us would not regard speed of response as a measure of intellectual prowess. It was clear even then that tests of intelligence must measure more complex mental functioning. The first systematic efforts in this direction were made by the great French psychologist Alfred Binet. Binet and his associates attempted to develop tests of such complex abilities as memory, imagination, attention, comprehension, suggestibility, esthetic appreciation, persistence, moral sentiments, motor skill, and judgment of visual space. Binet also tried to determine which tests provided measures that showed improvement with age and related closely to school achievement. In other words, Binet attempted to see if his tests were *valid*—if they tested what they were supposed to test, intellectual performance. Obviously, even a test that is highly reliable—one that gives consistent results—should not be regarded as an intelligence test unless it measures responses which relate to other indices of intellectual functioning. Since there was no "Bureau of Standards" for intellectual measures, the best that Binet could do was to see how the test scores related to teachers' judgments of intelligence. As imperfect as this criterion of validity may seem, it turned out to be adequate for the purpose. Gradually Binet abandoned the attempt to develop tests which theoretically *should* measure intelligence in favor of tests providing measures which correlated with academic ability and in which children's performance improved with age.

In 1904 the French Minister of Public Education appointed a commission to recommend procedures for identifying children who would be unable to profit from regular schools. To aid the commission Binet and Simon developed a test which is the direct ancestor of most modern intelligence tests. It is important to note that the purpose of the test was practical, not theoretical. The sole function of this test was to identify children who were likely to fail in the current school system. Binet made quite clear [Tuddenham, 1962, p. 483] :

Our goal is not at all to study, to analyze and to disclose the aptitudes of those who are inferior in intelligence. That will be the object of future work. Here we confine ourselves to evaluating, to measuring their intelligence in general; we shall establish their intellectual level; and to give an idea of this level, we shall compare it to normal children of the same age or of an analogous level.

The Binet-Simon test consisted of a series of subtests, each with items of increasing difficulty. The items were so selected that the likelihood of giving a correct answer increased with age. Thus the performance of retarded children could be compared with normal children of the same age. Many types of tests were found useful—naming objects in a picture, repeating a series of digits (digit span), and defining words. Binet's contributions to the study of intelligence were, in a basic sense, both the first and the last. All subsequent intelligence tests were highly influenced by his work, and his tests became the standard against which all other tests were validated or compared.

The Binet tests were improved and revised by Binet as well as others. The Stanford-Binet test, developed by Terman at Stanford University [Terman, 1916; Terman and Merrill, 1937; 1960] yielded the *intelligence quotient*, or IQ, a term with which we are all familiar. The formula used to compute an IQ on this type of test is

$$\frac{\text{Mental age}}{\text{Chronological age}} \times 100$$

where mental age is computed on the basis of the overall test score. A mental age of 10, for example, indicates that overall performance is comparable to that of the average ten-year-old. If a child's mental age equals his chronological age, his IQ is 100. You might compute IQs for two ten-year-old children: one with a mental age of 12, and the other with a mental age of 8.

The original Stanford-Binet test was limited to children, since mental age, as measured from the particular test items used, does not continue to develop greatly after the age of sixteen or so. Since this is the case, the use of the IQ formula with individuals older than sixteen would produce a rapid and unappreciated decline in IQ with age; at age thirty-two the calculated IQ of a normal adult would be 50. To overcome this problem other tests were developed, such as the Wechsler scale [Wechsler, 1958], in which IQ is computed on the basis of how far an individual's test score is above or below the average for others of the same age. In general the two types of tests are based on similar items, and the resulting IQ scores tend to be highly similar.

The tests were so constructed that with 100 as an average IQ the distribution of IQs would approximate a normal curve. Figure 13-2 shows a theoretical IQ distribution that closely approximates actual test results. As you can see, 50 percent of all IQs range between 90 and 110; only 2.5 percent are above 130 and 2.5 percent are below 70. Note that IQ is not some absolute measure of a physical attribute; it is merely a

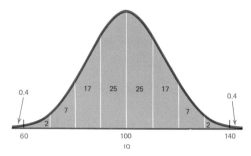

FIGURE 13-2 *A theoretical normal distribution of IQ scores. The percentages shown are the theoretical percentages of the IQ test scores in each 10-point IQ range. These values are very close to the actual percentages in the population except at the extremes (below 70 and above 130).*

measure of an individual's performance on a test in relation to the performances of others of the same age. Obviously an IQ of 100 does not mean that such a person is twice as intelligent as one with an IQ of 50. An IQ of 100 is a score that is equaled or exceeded by 50 percent of the individuals tested, while an IQ of 50 is equaled or exceeded by over 99 percent of the population.

Since most research on intelligence is based on data obtained with some kind of IQ test, it is extremely important to bear in mind how such tests were developed. Their original purpose was to predict academic failure, and the initial criterion of intelligence was teachers' evaluations of children's academic achievement. As a result, the tests include many items which depend on specific knowledge, such as vocabulary. The tests were developed strictly on an empirical basis, and not on the basis of theoretical concepts of intelligence.

In recent years the terms "IQ" and "intelligence" are often used almost interchangeably. This is an unfortunate practice. For example, most of the controversies concerning human "intelligence" are based *solely* on studies of IQ scores. This is legitimate only if it is agreed that intelligence is to be defined as IQ. Furthermore, many questions about the development of intelligence have been studied in infrahumans, but there is no standardized test of infrahuman intelligence. Generally such studies have used some measure of learning ability, but it is not at all clear that learning in infrahumans can be directly related to IQ in humans. An IQ test is not simply a test of learning ability, and tests of infrahuman learning ability do not provide any simple measure of "infrahuman IQ." Thus the evidence from animal studies should be considered with appropriate caution.

Since the first intelligence test was developed there have been several important and controversial questions about the nature of intelligence. Is it something that is learned, or is it inherited? Is the intelligence of an individual stable, or does it vary? Do intelligence tests measure some general ability, or do they measure more than one type of ability? Finally, what are the neurobiological bases of intelligent behavior? We do not yet have final answers to any of these questions.

351

BIOLOGICAL INFLUENCES

Since behavior, whether it is intelligent or stupid, is controlled by the brain, it stands to reason that intelligent behavior must require a good brain. Unfortunately we do not yet know what a "good brain" is. We do, however, know a great deal about bad brains—those that are diseased and injured—and we know a great deal about biological influences on brain function and on certain types of intelligent behavior.

BRAIN SIZE AND STRUCTURE

In comparison with the brains of most other animals, man's brain is rather large. The average human brain weighs approximately 1300 grams. There are, however, species with larger brains. A dolphin's brain, for example, weighs over 1400 grams [Ridgway, 1966]. Obviously brain size alone cannot account for the difference in intellect. A slightly more encouraging observation, at least from man's perspective, is that in man the ratio of brain weight to body weight is approximately 1:45; in the rhinoceros it is 1:3000 and in the whale approximately 1:10,000. However, even the ratio of brain to body weight does not explain man's intellect. As Tobias notes [1970, p. 7]:

. . . it is sobering to see that while Man's exalted brain constitutes just over 2% of his body weight, this percentage is surpassed by the lowly house mouse (2.5% or 1:40), the porpoise with 1:38, the marmoset with 1:19, and the attractive squirrel monkey of tropical America whose brain occupies 1/12 or 8.5% of its body weight.

Of course the human brain differs from those of other animals in structure and organization. One important difference is the amount of brain cortex that is not devoted to specific sensory and motor functions [Hebb, 1949]. Since association cortex is apparently not committed for sensory-motor coordination, it might be involved in higher-level cognitive processes such as learning, thinking, and problem solving. Association cortex constitutes a high proportion of the brain cortex of man. According to this view, for which there is some empirical support, the absolute size of the brain is less important than the ratio of association cortex to cortex with specific sensory-motor functions. It is too early to say whether this particular measure will differentiate the brain of man from brains of other animals in so far as intelligence is concerned. No doubt some distinguishing measure will eventually be found [Tobias, 1970, p. 7]:

Because man, the sapient, did not come out on top [in brain weight or ratio of brain to body weight] it is not surprising that man, the vainglorious and the arrogant, has been searching ever since for an index which would place him unequivocally and unassailably on the highest branch of the tree of life.

One final point about gross brain size deserves mention. Comparison of the brain weights of great men indicate that brain size alone is no key to greatness. While it is true that Oliver Cromwell and Lord Byron had large brains (about 2200 grams), the brain of the great French writer Anatole France weighed only a little over 1000 grams. In view of this, it appears extremely unlikely that variations in gross brain size among men can account for individual differences in intellectual functioning. This does not mean that the brains of great men do not differ from those of ordinary men; it only means that we do not yet know how they differ.

INBORN ERRORS OF METABOLISM

One of the most obvious facts of brain function is that intellectual functioning can be impaired by disease and injury which affect the brain. Severe impairment of intelligence often results, for example, from diseases such as encephalitis, in which brain cells are damaged by excessive body temperature. Intellectual impairment can also result from numerous hereditary disorders such as phenylketonuria, which is an inherited inability to metabolize phenylalanine (see Chapter 6). This disorder causes brain damage which results in mental retardation. Severe mental retardation can be prevented, at least reduced, in part, by decreasing the amount of phenylalanine in the diet, but the dietary changes must be introduced in infancy. If phenylketonuric infants are not diagnosed and put on a special diet early in life, permanent mental retardation is highly probable [Woolf et al., 1958].

Harlow found that monkeys reared from birth on a diet high in phenylalanine developed profound and lasting mental retardation [Waisman and Harlow, 1965]. The effects on monkeys given phenylalanine in adolescence were less severe. The excessive phenylalanine appears to produce mental retardation only during infancy, or perhaps early childhood. This finding is consistent with the evidence in children that the earlier the diagnosis and onset of treatment, the greater the likelihood that intellectual performance will not be severely impaired [Berman et al., 1961]. It is interesting to note that although hundreds of monkeys have been tested in the Primate Laboratories of the University of Wisconsin, there has never been an idiot monkey, except, of course, for the experimental animals just described [Harlow and Griffin, 1965]. Apparently, in Harlow's words, "we have to be human to be an inborn idiot." Phenylketonuria is but one of several inborn errors of metabolism known to affect mental functioning.

NUTRITIONAL FACTORS

There is growing evidence that mental retardation can be caused by inadequate nutrition in infancy. One of the most severe, persistent, and increasing problems of our planet is the inadequate production and unequal distribution of food among its inhabitants. In many areas of the

353

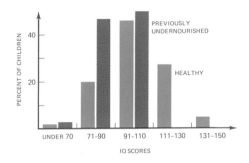

FIGURE 13-3   *Distributions of IQ test scores of normal children and 36 children at ages seven to fourteen who suffered from malnutrition at some time between the ages of four and twenty-four months. None of the malnourished children scored above 110. In comparison with the normal children, a greater percentage had scores of 90 or lower. [Cabak and Najdanovic, 1965]*

world human beings regularly starve to death, while millions of others, particularly children, barely subsist on diets that are inadequate in either calories or protein. The acute symptoms of starvation are, unfortunately, well known because of the publicity given to the relatively frequent outbreaks of famine in underdeveloped regions of the world. What has come to light only in recent years is that acute starvation, such as that seen in the illness *kwashiorkor*, has lasting effects on mental functioning [Eichenwald and Fry, 1969]. *Kwashiorkor* is commonly seen in children whose diet is grossly deficient in protein. Afflicted children become apathetic and sluggish, and without adequate treatment they may, and often do, die.

An even milder degree of malnutrition can cause mental retardation if it occurs in infancy or early childhood. Cabak and Najdanovic, [1965] studied the IQs of a group of seven- to fourteen-year-old Yugoslavian children who had been hospitalized for malnutrition when they were under two years of age. Although the children were underweight by at least 25 percent, the degree of malnutrition was less than that seen in cases of *kwashiorkor*. As Fig. 13-3 shows, the IQs of the undernourished children were clearly lower than those of normal children; none of them had IQs greater than 110. We do not yet have any clear understanding of how undernutrition produces mental retardation. Presumably it is because the lack of adequate protein interferes with normal brain development. However, these findings on the effects of nutrition level on IQ indicate that millions of children throughout the world are, at this moment, becoming mentally retarded simply because of insufficient food. Even worse, these same children are also more likely to suffer from diseases, injuries, and social-deprivation conditions which prevent normal mental development.

HEREDITARY FACTORS

There is very strong evidence that "normal" variations in intelligence, as well as the more severe disorders such as phenylketonuria, are subject to hereditary influences. Intelligence is not inherited like money from a rich uncle, but IQ scores are strongly influenced by heredity. There are close family resemblances in IQ scores, and in general the closer the relationship—that is, the greater the genetic similarity—the greater the

354

similarity in IQ scores. Figure 13-4 summarizes the results of a number of studies of this relationship. Each point in the figure represents a correlation coefficient obtained in a single study involving a number of pairs of individuals. A correlation coefficient expresses the degree of relationship between two sets of scores (see Chapter 6). In 14 studies of identical twins reared together the correlations ranged from approximately +.75 to +.93—that is, the IQs of each pair of twins were highly similar. By contrast, in four studies the correlations between pairs of unrelated individuals reared together were only about +.15 to +.32. In general, then, the correlation in IQ increases with the degree of genetic relationship. Note also, however, that for all degrees of genetic relationship the correlation is higher if the pairs of individuals are reared together—that is, if their environments are similar. Moreover, the specific correlation coefficients vary greatly from study to study.

What do these correlations indicate? The answer to this question is complex. To begin with IQ is not an attribute; it is a test score. In groups of individuals IQ test scores show a high degree of *heritability*. As we saw in Chapter 6, heritability is measured as the proportion of the *total* variation in a population (or group of individuals) which is due to genetic factors. If all the measured variation in IQ scores were due to genetic factors, heritability would be 1.00; if all the variation were due to nongenetic factors, heritability would be .00. Of course, since both genetic and environmental influences contribute to the variability of IQ scores, heritability of IQ falls between these two values.

On the basis of the kinds of results shown in Fig. 13-4 estimates of heritability of IQ have generally ranged around a value of 0.75. That is, for the groups studied, approximately 75 percent of the variation in

FIGURE 13-4   *Genetics, environment, and intelligence. A summary of correlation coefficients obtained in 52 studies of the relationship in IQ between pairs of individuals with varying degrees of genetic relationship. Each point represents the correlation coefficient obtained in a single study. The vertical lines indicate the average (median) coefficient for that particular condition. With the exception of the correlations for unrelated persons living apart, all conditions show positive relationships. The correlations increase with the similarity in genetic makeup and environmental experiences. [Erlenmeyer-Kimling and Jarvik, 1963]*

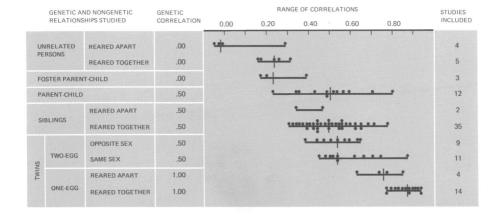

GENETIC AND NONGENETIC RELATIONSHIPS STUDIED		GENETIC CORRELATION	RANGE OF CORRELATIONS	STUDIES INCLUDED
UNRELATED PERSONS	REARED APART	.00		4
	REARED TOGETHER	.00		5
FOSTER PARENT-CHILD		.00		3
PARENT-CHILD		.50		12
SIBLINGS	REARED APART	.50		2
	REARED TOGETHER	.50		35
TWINS	TWO-EGG	OPPOSITE SEX	.50	9
		SAME SEX	.50	11
	ONE-EGG	REARED APART	1.00	4
		REARED TOGETHER	1.00	14

test scores is estimated to be due to genetic factors. This estimate does *not* mean that 75 percent of *any particular individual's* IQ is determined by genetic factors. Heritability refers to groups of individuals, not to single individuals. Moreover, conclusions about heritability are restricted to the particular conditions under which the estimates were obtained. There can be no "true" measure of heritability [Huntley, 1966, p. 201]:

We cannot measure *the* heritability of intelligence once and for all. All that can be offered is an estimate of the heritability of intelligence as measured from scores obtained on a particular test by a particular group of people living at a particular time in a particular area. If any one of these were different the heritability might be different too.

Heritability estimates are strongly influenced by nongenetic influences. In particular, heritability will be high when nongenetic influences are similar for all of the individuals tested. If all individuals in our society were subjected to *identical* nongenetic influences, such as nutrition, disease, injury, and environmental stimulation, then heritability of IQ would be 1.00—that is, all variations in IQ scores could be due only to genetic variation. However, all men are created unequal; genetics guarantees variability, and no society yet has had the ability to create equal nongenetic influences. Even if nongenetic factors were identical, their effects would depend on the genetic makeup of the particular group of individuals tested. Equal exposure to the sun does not produce the same effects on blondes as on brunettes, and normal amounts of phenylalanine in the diet do not have the same effects in normal children as in children who have inherited an inability to metabolize this amino acid. Similarly, the effects on IQ of such nongenetic factors as nutrition and environmental stimulation also vary with genetic makeup. Thus it should be clear that the IQ of an individual is not fixed, or completely determined, by genetic factors. As Hirsch [1970] has pointed out, the fact that heritability estimates of IQ tend to be fairly high does not mean that IQ scores cannot be altered by many nongenetic factors.

In some classical experiments Tryon [1942] demonstrated that rats could be selectively bred for maze-learning ability. Rats obtained from a number of laboratories were trained on a complex maze. Males which made low error scores were mated with comparable females and males which made high scores were mated with high scoring females. The offspring of these initially selected groups of "bright" and "dull" parents did not differ. However, there were clear effects when the selective-breeding procedures were continued for eight generations. Figure 13-5 shows the performance of the parental stock and of generations 1, 3, 6, and 8. Separation of the scores of the two groups was seen as early as the second generation, but complete, or at least almost complete, separation did not occur until the eighth generation. The same results have been obtained in subsequent studies.

The animals in these experiments were reared under fairly constant laboratory conditions. It would be interesting to know whether genetic selection for the maze learning would occur as readily if different

356

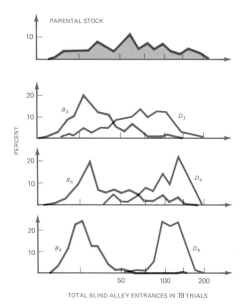

FIGURE 13-5   *Genetic selection for maze-learning performance in rats. The figures show the distribution error scores (blind-alley entrances) of the parental stock of 142 animals and the performances of the third, sixth, and eighth generations of strains selectively bred for maze brightness and maze dullness. The strains were almost completely separated by the eighth generation. [Tryon, 1942]*

animals in each generation were reared under different and changing nutritional and environmental conditions. In all probability selection would be difficult. Subsequent studies of the offspring of the two strains developed by Tryon have shown that the strains did not differ in general learning ability. The maze-bright strains were not uniformly superior to the maze-dull strains on other learning tasks. We do not know why the two genetically different groups of rats differed in maze learning. It could be because of genetic influences on neurobiological processes underlying learning, but the differences could also have resulted from other factors, such as motivation [Searle, 1949]. The same cautions apply to interpretations of the differences in learning of different inbred strains of rats and mice.

ENVIRONMENTAL INFLUENCES

Environmental influences begin, of course, long before birth. Factors in the intrauterine environment, such as nutrition of the developing organism, undoubtedly influence intelligence. There are many kinds of postnatal environmental influences on behavior. Over 50 years ago the German psychologist Köhler spent several years studying the behavior of chimpanzees on the Tenerife Islands, off the coast of Africa. In his book *The Mentality of Apes* [1925] he described in detail numerous examples of highly intelligent behavior that he witnessed. The apes were not only able to use sticks, but assembled several sticks into a long pole in order to reach bananas that were beyond their reach. Some of the apes were even able to stack boxes in order to reach bananas suspended above them. Köhler stressed that the problems were often solved extremely rapidly, as though the animals had flashes of "insight." The animals he studied were captured in the jungle. Conse-

357

quently we do not know the extent to which their rather amazing ability was influenced by previous learning. Subsequent studies of problem solving in monkeys, chimpanzees, and children have shown that this type of behavior is exhibited only after extensive problem-solving experience. Flashes of natural insight are not made by untutored brains.

In an extensive series of studies Harlow [1949*b*] has shown that, with training, monkeys can learn to learn. Their ability to solve complex discrimination problems can be dramatically improved by intensive training on simple and complex problems (see Chapter 11). Although the ability to solve complex problems is undoubtedly influenced by genetic factors, obviously such intelligent behavior in monkeys is also highly modifiable by experience. Learning to learn is no doubt an essential feature of the intellectual development of monkeys, apes, and children growing up in their natural environments.

Since the development of the first IQ test there has been considerable disagreement concerning the effect of experience on IQ [Jensen, 1969]. The extreme view that IQ scores provide a pure measure of inherited intelligence is not widely held by psychologists. In fact IQ tests are more often criticized because they do not measure intellectual ability which is independent of experience. Binet's position on this controversial issue was clear; he was convinced that intelligence, as measured by his test, could be improved by training [in Tuddenham, 1962, p. 488]:

Having on our hands children who did not know how to listen, to pay attention, to keep quiet we pictured our first duty as being not to teach them the facts that we thought would be most useful, but *to teach them how to learn.* We have therefore devised . . . what we call exercizes in mental orthopedics [practice in sitting still, carrying a full glass, etc.]. . . . In the same way that physical orthopedics straightens a crooked spine, mental orthopedics strengthens, cultivates, and fortifies attention, memory, perception, [and] judgment. . . . With practice . . . one can succeed in . . . becoming literally more intelligent than before.

Does IQ remain constant, or is it like the ability to learn to learn, influenced by experience? The evidence that intelligence is influenced by heredity does not require the assumption that it is unvarying. Height is highly influenced by heredity, but one's absolute height as well as one's height in relation to others changes with age. There is quite clear evidence that IQ scores of individuals may vary considerably over time. One reason is that the types of questions included in IQ tests are different for different ages. Obviously the questions that can be asked of two-year-old children are different from those that can be asked of older children, as well as from those which are appropriate for adults. IQ test scores can also be depressed by temporary conditions such as illness or emotional states. The intellectual abilities of individuals may be improved by experience.

Studies of IQ test scores of individuals tested several times over a period of years indicate that the greater the time interval between the

CHANGES IN IQ	NO. OF CHILDREN	PERCENT
Less than 9 points	33	15
More than 10 points	189	85
More than 15 points	129	58
More than 20 points	78	35
More than 30 points	20	9
More than 50 points	1	0.5

TABLE 13–1   *Changes in IQ from ages six to eighteen [Honzik et. al., 1948].*

tests, the less the similarity in the IQ scores. Table 13-1 shows the findings of a study of IQ changes in children tested eight times between the ages of six and eighteen. Only 15 percent of those tested showed changes of less than 9 points; over 35 percent of the differences in IQ score were greater than 20 points. In one case a child's IQ fluctuated from 128 to 113 to 163 to 111, depending on whether the tests were administered during stable periods of his life or during periods of disturbing home influences [Honzik et al., 1948]. Significant increases in IQ have been found in individuals who had moved to an environment that provided better education and increased social stimulation. The IQs of blacks reared in the South have been shown to increase when they move to northern cities. Studies of children brought up in a kibbutz in Israel, where they are given nursery school rearing for 22 hours a day for four years or more, suggest that this experience increases the children's IQ scores. The average IQs of kibbutz-reared children is 115, in comparison with IQs of 85 and 105, respectively, for mid-Eastern and European Jewish children brought up in individual homes [Bloom, 1969].

At least part of the differences in IQ scores obtained in different regions of the world are due to cultural differences in the responses to the questions on the test. Tests developed to measure the performance of urban European or American school children may or may not be appropriate for children in other cultural settings. One somewhat extreme example of the responses of a child from a rural area illustrates this problem [Pressey, in Klineberg, 1969, pp. 69–70]:

> [The tester] presented the familiar Binet problem: "If you went to the store and bought six cents worth of candy and gave the clerk ten cents, what change would you receive?" One youngster replied, "I never had ten cents and if I did I wouldn't spend it for candy, and anyway candy is what your mother makes." The examiner made a second attempt and reformulated his question as follows: "If you had taken ten cows to pasture for your father and six of them strayed away, how many would you have left to drive home?" The child replied, "We don't have ten cows but if we did, and I lost six, I wouldn't dare go home." The examiner made one last attempt: "If there were ten children in a school and six of them came out with the measles, how many would there be in school?" The answer came even more promptly: "None, because the rest would be afraid of catching it too."

This example also illustrates another general and important point about IQ tests. The tests require answers which can only have been learned. To be sure, they require *more* than retention of previously learned information, but the fact that such information is assumed should not be overlooked. An answer to the problem presented in the example above requires an elementary knowledge of arithmetic as well as the ability to reason. The vocabulary test, which is included in most intelligence tests, is an even better example. The answer to the question, "What is an apple?" is not supplied by one's genes. IQ tests are based on a general assumption that most individuals tested will have been exposed to the information requested. It is not certain that all children, even in the affluent United States, will know about apples. The answer to a question on one intelligence test requires the knowledge that moss grows on the north side of trees. Where does moss grow in the .deserts of Arizona, Nevada, and New Mexico? Television does not solve this problem for children reared in the deserts of Africa. A more obvious problem is the use of IQ tests in English with children from homes in which English is not spoken. This practice is still common in many parts of the United States, and no doubt provides empirical support for the view that certain ethnic groups tend to have low IQs.

A number of studies have reported slightly lower average IQs in groups of blacks than in groups of whites in the United States. Some investigators have inferred that these average differences in IQ are due to genetic differences. Several factors, however, render any such inference invalid. To begin with, blacks in the United States have not had, and do not have, environments which are similar to those of whites. As in any group isolated from the mainstream of society, there are many cultural, linguistic, and experiential differences. In addition, there are differences in the incidence of disease, the quality of nutrition, and the quality of education. When the environmental differences are decreased, the differences in tested IQs of blacks and whites tend to decrease. In a study of draftee scores on the Army Alpha test during World War I it was found that in all states the average scores of blacks were lower than those of whites. However, the average scores for blacks in several northern states were higher than those for whites in several southern states [Yerkes, 1921]. Furthermore, for both whites and blacks, the average IQ of the draftees from each state varied directly with the state's average expenditure for public education; for both blacks and whites the correlation between average IQ and average expenditure of the state for education was approximately +.70 [Spuhler and Lindzey, 1967].

Since expenditures for education have great bearing on the quality of education, it appears that IQ is influenced by educational experiences. Of course there is probably also a correlation between expenditures for public education and expenditures for public health. Thus the cause of the correlation between expenditures for education and IQ of the recruits from each state is not a simple matter. Regardless of the reasons, it is clear that the IQs of blacks and whites alike are influenced by environmental factors. In fact, as Washburn comments [1963, p. 529]:

I am sometimes surprised to hear it stated that if Negroes were given an equal opportunity, their I.Q. would be the same as the Whites. If one looks at the degree of social discrimination against Negroes and their lack of education, and also takes into account the tremendous amount of overlapping between I.Q.'s of both, one can make an equally good case that, given a comparable chance to that of Whites, their I.Q.'s would test out ahead. Of course, it would be absolutely unimportant in a democratic society if this were to be true, because the vast majority of individuals of both groups would be of comparable intelligence.

INTELLIGENCE AND ACHIEVEMENT

As we have seen, IQ test scores can be profoundly influenced by culture. Nevertheless, the biological contributions to intelligence, such as genetics, nutrition, and disease, indicate that some aspects of intelligence depend more on having a "good brain" than they do on cultural experiences. Recent studies by Cattell [1968] indicate that intelligence tests may well measure two different types of intelligence. *Fluid intelligence*, according to Cattell, is fairly free from cultural influence and appears to be fairly closely related to overall physiological efficiency. This type of intelligence increases up to the age of about twenty and then gradually declines. Fluid intelligence appears to be roughly a measure of judgment and reasoning. *Crystallized intelligence* is seen in skills that are influenced by experience, such as vocabulary, mechanical knowledge, and in general, knowledge of facts and skills. As might be expected, crystallized intelligence increases steadily with age because of increased opportunity for acquiring knowledge and skills. For example, Cattell reports that he has studied [1968, p. 58]:

> . . . deck hands and farmers who scored [quite high] in fluid ability but who acquired no comparable level of crystallized ability because they had not systematically applied their fluid intelligence to what is usually called culture. Such men will astonish you in a game of chess or by solving a wire puzzle with which you have struggled in vain, or in swift insights into men and their motives. But their vocabularies may be arrested at a colloquial level, their knowledge of history negligible, and they may never have encountered algebra or geometry.

It is too early to tell whether this simplified view of intelligence is valid. If it is, it should help clarify some of the controversial issues which surround the general problem of human intelligence. It may be possible, as Cattell has suggested, to develop tests that provide relatively pure measures of fluid intelligence, tests which are minimally influenced by cultural differences, but this possibility seems remote. As we have seen, intelligent behavior results from a large number of influences on brain development and function. Intelligence is not simply the functioning of the nervous system with culture "added on."

The complex way in which biological factors interact with experience in influencing later abilities is seen in studies of the effects of environmental stimulation on learning ability in rats. Several studies have shown that rats reared in a complex environment are better in maze learning than rats reared in a conventional laboratory cage. Studies by Bennett et al. [1964] show that the brains of environmentally "enriched" rats are different in a number of ways from those of either normal or environmentally deprived rats, indicating that the general environmental stimulation appears to have biological as well as psychological effects. Other research has shown that the maze-learning ability of rats reared in an enriched environment can be improved by giving the young rats daily injections of drugs which stimulate the central nervous system. Their learning ability is improved even if the drug and environmental stimulation treatments are administered only when the rats are young and the learning tests are not given until several weeks after the last drug treatment [LeBoeuf and Peeke, 1969; Shandro and Shaeffer, 1969]. These conditions suggest that the drug appears to produce rather permanent improvement in the ability to learn. We do not yet know the basis of the facilitation. We do not know whether the conditions of these experiments produce a general improvement in learning ability for tasks other than mazes. It is interesting to note that the same drug injections result in *impaired* learning ability if the rats are reared in an environment which offers little stimulation. The drug cannot offset the effects of impoverished environmental stimulation. It is obvious that biological and psychological factors interact in complex ways to produce what is measured either as IQ in human beings or learning ability in infrahumans.

THE IDIOT SAVANT:
AN UNSOLVED PROBLEM

We all vary in our special talents as well as in our intelligence, but in general our abilities in special areas are not grossly different from our general intellectual abilities. The *idiot savant* is a striking exception. This dramatic and puzzling phenomenon is best defined by example. Horwitz et al., [1965] described a pair of identical twins with IQs of approximately 60 to 70, well below normal, but with uncanny memories for dates. Furthermore, they were "calendar calculators"; they were able to give almost instantaneously the day of the week for any date over a range of centuries. One twin had a range of at least 6000 years. When asked the years in which a given date, such as April 21, would fall on a Sunday, both twins correctly answered 1968, 1957, 1946, etc. One twin, when encouraged, continued to give the correct years as far back as 1700. The twins were also able to reply that the fourth Monday in February, 1993, will be the twenty-second or that the third Monday in May, 1936, was the eighteenth. The ability to perform these calculations is all the more impressive in view of the fact that neither twin was able to add, subtract, multiply, or divide numbers, even single digits. Thus, although they were unable to add up to 30, when told a person's birth date, they were able to tell that it would be 30 weeks until the person's next birthday or 13 weeks since he last had a birthday.

An examination of the histories of these twins has revealed nothing that suggests an explanation. The only fact of any significance is that the twin who was best at calendar calculating discovered a perpetual calendar in an almanac when he was six and spent hours poring over it. The other twin developed an interest in the calendar several years later. However, the availability of the calendar and the expression of interest in it does not explain their ability to calculate. This is a very special, unique talent found in two otherwise mentally retarded boys. When the twins were asked how they were able to perform the calculations, they could only respond, "It's in my head." With our present knowledge we cannot actually do much better. As Holstein notes [1965, p. 1078]:

> The importance . . . of the Idiot-Savant lies in our inability to explain him; he stands as a landmark of our own ignorance and the phenomenon of the Idiot-Savant exists as a challenge to our capabilities.

The problem of the *idiot savant* is part of the much larger question of the psychobiological bases of intelligence. Since we do not yet understand the bases of normal variations in intelligence, the *idiot savant* presents no greater mystery. It merely serves to remind us of our present ignorance of how intelligent behavior is controlled by the machinery of the brain.

IQ AS A PREDICTOR OF ACHIEVEMENT

The *idiot savant* achieves "distinction" in one highly special area, but this talent, regardless of its degree, does not provide a basis for his adaptation to a complex environment. In the most fundamental sense intelligent behavior is adaptive. IQ tests were originally developed to predict the ability of children to perform in school—that is, their ability to adapt to the requirements of the classroom. To a great extent they have succeeded in this. All in all the IQ score remains the best predictor of scholastic success. In numerous studies of the relationship between IQ scores and college grade-point average, for example, the correlations have averaged slightly better than +.50. Clearly this is not perfect correlation. However, IQ could not be expected to provide a perfect prediction of scholastic success since so many factors contribute to academic performance—illness, emotional problems, distractions, motivation, study habits, and just plain hard work. Application, including application of the seat of the pants to the seat of the chair, is a necessary condition even though it is not a sufficient condition.

The IQ test, then, is an effective predictor of academic performance, but does it predict anything else? Do individuals with high IQ scores tend to do better outside of school? The answer is, quite clearly,

363

yes. Individuals with high IQs are often referred to as "gifted," and no doubt they are. They have received adequate nutrition and stimulating environments, and they have been protected from injury to their brains. In this sense they are indeed gifted—but the gift is not solely genetic, as has often been implied.

In 1921 Terman, who developed the Stanford-Binet intelligence test, began a long-term study of 1500 children with IQ scores of 140 or higher. At that time the children were eleven years old. The study examined in some detail the physical characteristics, behavior, and accomplishments of most of the subjects over half a century. These gifted individuals are still being studied by Terman's colleagues, and a complete report will not be forthcoming perhaps until after the turn of the century [Terman, 1925; Terman and Oden, 1947; 1959]. However, there have been a number of important and interesting findings thus far [Butcher, 1968].

The results of this study do not support the popular view that IQ compensates for deficiencies in physical ability, health, or personality. In comparison with average children, the gifted children were heavier at birth, learned to walk earlier, talked earlier, and matured physically at an earlier age. They did not differ significantly from average children in sociability, masculinity or femininity, popularity, or social maladjustment. Moreover, they performed well both inside and outside of school. Their school performance was highly accelerated (about 40 percent faster than average), and they performed, on the average, at a level of the top 10 percent in high school. More than 90 percent of the boys and 80 percent of the girls went to college. The average income of the group has been quite high, and the literary and scientific achievement has been most impressive. As of 1959 the group had to its credit 33 novels, many hundreds of shorter writings, 230 patents, and about 2000 scientific papers. Clearly these individuals are richly talented. It is worth noting, however, that the study did not reveal an Albert Einstein, a Leonardo da Vinci, a Thomas Edison, or a George Washington Carver. Such individuals appear much less frequently than 1 in 1500—even in 1500 gifted.

Overall, Terman's study has provided extensive evidence that the IQ test predicts more than performance in primary school. Of course intellectual ability is no guarantee of success, even in intellectual areas of achievement. Not all the gifted children achieved distinction—and, no doubt, equal or greater distinction has been achieved by many children who were not included in the studies because their IQ scores were below 140. High IQ is associated with high levels of achievement in a wide variety of tasks and occupations, but it does not account for all the variation in performance; at best, it accounts for only about half. There is plenty of room for such factors as motivation.

Terman's study of gifted individuals is only a descriptive study. It provides no additional specific clues to the bases of intelligence. Presumably the gifted have "good brains," but we do not yet know how to distinguish the brain of a gifted child from that of an *idiot savant*.

The nature and bases of intelligence are obviously extremely complex. Intelligent behavior is at least the outcome, and yet more than the outcome, of the efficient functioning of all the basic processes underlying sensory-motor integration, learning, and memory. We are only beginning to understand the factors that contribute to individual and species differences in intelligence. The problems of the bases of intelligence constitute some of the major unsolved problems of science.

SUMMARY

Intelligence is, in its most basic sense, synonymous with intelligent behavior. Thus intelligence is exhibited by many animals, and man's superior intelligence seems to be related to his position on the phylogenetic scale rather than to any qualitative difference between "reason" and "instinct." The basis of this superiority is not yet clear, but of the many factors that have been explored, such as gross brain size and ratio of brain weight to body weight, the most significant difference is in the relative amount of association area in the sensory cortex of the brain. The most outstanding contribution to the study of human intelligence was the first useful intelligence test, developed by Binet on a completely empirical basis as a predictor of academic ability. The later Stanford-Binet test yields the familiar IQ score, which unfortunately has come to be used interchangeably with "intelligence."

The development of intelligence is markedly affected by such factors as injury, disease, inborn errors of metabolism, and malnutrition. Genetic studies indicate that intelligence is also influenced to a great extent by heredity. There is considerable controversy over environmental influences, chiefly because all studies are based on comparison of IQ scores. It is clear, however, that cultural, educational, and social variables are important factors in measured IQ. The interaction of biological and environmental variables also plays a major role, especially in relation to learning ability in animals. For example, in rats an enriched environment apparently increases learning ability, causes discernible differences in neural anatomy, and determines the effect of drug injections on learning ability. However, we still know very little about the neural bases of intelligence. The classical case of the *idiot savant* is merely one of the unsolved problems, and although IQ is an effective predictor of future overall achievement, it tells us nothing about the actual nature of human intelligence.

CHAPTER FOURTEEN

THINKING
AND THE MIND

Thought and language are the most complex and important activities of man. They are the characteristics that set man apart from all other animals. Man is not the only animal that thinks. The higher mammals, particularly primates, think very well indeed; they can solve difficult problems and form very complex concepts. However, no species other than man has developed a genuine language. It is largely through the use of language that man has acquired culture and his knowledge of the world. Thought and language seem almost inextricably interwoven in man. Your ordinary thinking activity is invariably accompanied by the use of language, even if only to yourself. (Regrettably, the reverse is not always true.) In this chapter we will review thought and language, treating them as separate topics solely for convenience of discussion.

The study of human thinking is perhaps the most basic and also the most difficult area of psychology. Thought is largely a private activity. Your thoughts belong mostly to you and to no one else unless you choose to communicate them. Overt or behavioral signs of thinking are not easy to detect in normal adults, although young children, the men-

THOUGHT
AND LANGUAGE

tally retarded, and the mentally ill frequently do provide us with a running verbal and behavioral commentary on their thoughts—often in much greater detail than we might wish.

There is no specific or technical definition of thinking in psychology. Many aspects of thinking, particularly such problem-oriented behaviors as concept formation, problem solving, and creative thinking, which we term *directed thinking*, have been studied at length. However, thinking involves much more than simply working on problems. The common dictionary definition reflects what most of us mean by thinking: to have the mind occupied by some subject. It is very likely that we are always thinking when we are awake. You have no doubt had the experience of being asked what you were thinking about and replying "nothing," when a moment's reflection revealed that you actually had been thinking about something, usually something quite trivial.

This brings us to another undefined term—the *mind*. In fact thinking may really be said to be that which the mind does. Understanding the human mind is for many the fundamental goal of psychology. We cannot measure the mind's activity directly—only you know your own mind, and often even you do not know it very well—but we can study the behavioral expressions of this activity, the measurable indications

367

or signs of thought. In the seventeenth century the French mathematician René Descartes proposed a theory of the mind which has had enormous influence in psychology and philosophy and is still the view held by most laymen. The theory, which is very simple to describe but impossible to understand, retarded the development of psychology for at least 100 years and still causes great difficulties for many scientists. Descartes proposed that every human being has both a mind and a body, and that the body is material, made up of matter, but the mind is not. Furthermore, according to this theory, only men have minds; other animals are simply bodies or material machines. As flattering as this formulation may be to our sense of uniqueness, if mind is defined as nonmaterial, and not made up of the electrons, protons, and neutrons of matter—if it is not any conceivable "stuff," but some "nonstuff"—it would be impossible both in practice and in principle ever to measure, analyze, or study the mind by the methods and techniques of science. Thus, even if Descartes' theory is correct, we will never be able to study the mind scientifically. Consequently, the theory is either wrong or of no scientific value, since, by definition, it cannot be tested.

Rejection of Descartes' theory does not mean, of course, that we must also reject the concept of mind. Some psychologists have done this—most notably Watson, the founder of behaviorism, who championed the view that thinking consisted solely of small movements of the vocal apparatus, as when we talk to ourselves, and that this constituted the mind. Watson is claimed to have said, "I made up my windpipe this morning that there is no mind." Actually, the mind can be treated on the same basis as such concepts as learning, motivation, or intelligence. These are inferred phenomena, often termed *hypothetical constructs*. Just as we measure gravity, not directly, but in terms of its effect on objects, so we hypothesize or guess that a phenomenon or process occurs, describe its characteristics, and attempt to figure out ways that its operations will have some measurable effect that we can study. Thus learning is generally defined as an improvement in performance as a result of experience. We cannot measure learning directly—instead we measure performance, the responses of the organism. Learning is not a thing that you can hold in your hand. Gravity is perhaps a more familiar example. "Gravity" is a theoretical idea, a hypothetical construct—you cannot touch it or see it. However, from this theory physicists deduce certain measurable consequences—that objects exert gravitational forces on one another. If you doubt this, try jumping off the nearest building.

Mind, then, is no more mystical a concept than gravity. The major difference is that we think we know more about it from personal experience, whereas we actually know less about it in scientific terms. It is important to make a clear distinction between mind and conscious experience. Mind is a much more inclusive concept, referring to a wide variety of processes, both conscious and unconscious. The final arbiter of whether or not a construct or concept is of value is its utility or usefulness. Does it enable us to make meaningful and useful predictions

368

about behavior? Of course. Our daily activities are determined in large part by our inferences about what is going on in other people's minds. We infer from their behavior that they have certain thoughts, ideas, and reasons in mind, and we predict correctly on this basis. If your girl friend is taking the pill, you have a rather good idea of what she has in mind. A good chess player correctly infers what is going on in the mind of his opponent. This is equally true, incidentally, when his opponent is a computer. There is a very famous answer to the question "can a computer think?" In a classical study of simulation of thinking, Turing [1950] proposed a game in which an interrogator, a man, and a computer were each placed in a separate room, with communication conducted by means of typed questions and answers. The interrogator could ask any question at all (except, of course, questions of the type "are you the computer?") and had to decide on the basis of the answers which was the computer and which was the man. Turing proved that in general it is not possible for the interrogator to distinguish. Such theoretically possible computers are often referred to as *Turing machines*.

The American legal system is another case in point. In many respects guilt or innocence depends on what occurred in the mind of a person who has committed a crime. Had he thought about it ahead of time (premeditation), and was he able to distinguish in his own mind between right and wrong (legal insanity)? This is not necessarily a proper interpretation of the construct "mind," only an illustration of its widespread use. In fact, in view of all that we know about the innumerable factors, many of them "unconscious," that determine behavior, the legal interpretation is, at the very least, inadequate.

In summary "mind" is a perfectly respectable scientific construct or hypothesis. Your own mind, particularly the part that forms your immediate stream of conscious experience, is largely your own private affair—but not entirely. The psychologist can determine with rather good accuracy some aspects of your individual mental activity. More generally mind is a legitimate subject of scientific study, and as we shall see, much is known about some aspects of the human mind and the minds of higher animals.

NONDIRECTED THINKING

Psychology has emphasized the study of the directed aspects of thought—thinking about particular tasks such as the formation of concepts, the solving of problems, creative thinking, and discovery. This is, of course, only one part of thought. Idle thought, daydreaming and fantasy, conscious and unconscious processes, dreaming—these are the more general aspects of thinking and form the fabric of our everyday thinking activities. We think idly much of the time, particularly in ordinary conversation, and we solve problems only a small part of the time.

369

The terms "conscious" and "unconscious" seem to cause difficulties for some people, since like "mind," "learning," and "gravity" they are constructs that we cannot see or measure directly. Instead we rely on behavioral measures, the easiest and most reliable being verbal reports. A normal, cooperative adult can describe what it is that he is conscious of in considerable detail and with good reliability. The classic description of the stream of consciousness by William James is an example from a particularly intelligent and literate observer [James, 1890, p. 238]:

When Paul and Peter wake up in the same bed, and recognize that they have been asleep, each one of them mentally reaches back and makes connection with but *one* of the two streams of thought which were broken by the sleeping hours. As the current of an electrode buried in the ground unerringly finds its way to its own similarly buried mate, across no matter how much intervening earth; so Peter's present instantly finds out Peter's past, and never by mistake knits itself on to that of Paul. Paul's thought in turn is as little liable to go astray. The past thought of Peter is appropriated by the present Peter alone. He may have a *knowledge*, and a correct one too, of what Paul's last drowsy states of mind were as he sank into sleep, but it is an entirely different sort of knowledge from that which he has of his own last states. He *remembers* his own states, whilst he only *conceives* Paul's. Remembrance is like direct feeling; its object is suffused with a warmth and intimacy to which no object of mere conception ever attains. This quality of warmth and intimacy and immediacy is what Peter's *present* thought also possesses for itself. So sure as this present is me, is mine, it says, so sure is anything else that comes with the same warmth and intimacy and immediacy, me and mine. What the qualities called warmth and intimacy may in themselves be will have to be matter for future consideration. But whatever past feelings appear with those qualities must be admitted to receive the greeting of the present mental state, to be owned by it, and accepted as belonging together with it in a common self. This community of self is what the time-gap cannot break in twain, and is why a present thought, although not ignorant of the time-gap, can still regard itself as continuous with certain chosen portions of the past.

Consciousness, then, does not appear to itself chopped up in bits. Such words as "chain" or "train" do not describe it fitly as it presents itself in the first instance. It is nothing jointed; it flows. A "river" or a "stream" are the metaphors by which it is most naturally described. *In talking of it hereafter, let us call it the stream of thought, of consciousness, or of subjective life.*

Consciousness is measured as the sum total that you can describe about your own experience at any given point in time. What, then, is the *unconscious*? Very simply, it is everything else you might have been aware of, and hence might have said, but did not. More specifically, the unconscious is the totality of your past experience and current existence of which you are not aware at any particular time. There are many aspects to the unconscious, ranging from simple reflex phenomena, through memory, to complex unconscious motivation, all of which nevertheless have considerable bearing on many of our conscious activities.

Close your eyes and lift your arm part way. You can describe with considerable accuracy the position of your arm. There are several kinds of receptors that provide information to the brain about the position of a limb. In particular, pressure receptors in the joints signal the angle of bend of a limb, and stretch receptors in the muscles signal the degree of stretch of the various muscles involved. The activity of the sensory nerve fibers from both these sets of receptors provide adequate information about the position of the arm. We could, by recording the activity from either type of nerve fiber (the fibers differ in size), determine the position of your arm. However, only the joint receptors provide you with conscious information about the position of your arm. In experiments in which the joint receptors are temporarily blocked by a local anesthetic the subject cannot describe the position of his limb even though complete information is still provided to his central nervous system by the stretch receptors from the muscles. The subject is unconscious of this input. It plays a major role in the determination of limb position, particularly in relation to posture and such activities as walking and running, but it never enters into consciousness. There are many thousands of such reflex actions in the human organism, ranging from basic biochemical processes such as maintenance of proper acid-base balance to control of heart rate, blood pressure, and breathing, of which we are usually not conscious. This is a part of the unconscious.

The total amount of past experience and knowledge stored in the brain of a normal adult is almost inconceivable; it amounts to many billions of bits of information. Much of this information is available on demand. If, for example, you are asked for the numerical value of the mathematical constant pi, you immediately answer 3.14 (if you know, that is). The process involved in retrieving this information from among the billions of other bits of stored information was discussed in Chapter 12. The point here is simply that you were not conscious of "3.14" until you were asked. At any one point in time you are unconscious of most of your stored information and experience. This is another aspect of the unconscious.

These unconscious processes and knowledge are often referred to by psychoanalysts as the *preconscious*, to distinguish them from what is termed the *unconscious*. Freud developed a specific theory of the unconscious which is basically a theory of unconscious motivation. In simplified terms, a normal person is said to be unable to accept his own basic biological urgings or motivations, particularly those relating to sex and aggression, and relegates such matters to the unconscious, a murky and often evil territory of the mind filled with thoughts of sex and incest, rage, hatred, and the desire for death. Much of our behavior is said to be motivated and molded by unconscious forces. For some this view

371

has become reality rather than a theory; they make the unconscious a separate entity, much like Descartes' view of mind, but even less comprehensible.

More important than arguments over the merits of Freud's theory is the fact, established by Freud beyond question, that many aspects of human motivation are unconscious. A highly motivated person may be quite unable to tell you why he is so motivated. The case histories of clinical psychology and psychiatry are filled with examples illustrating the fact that people are quite commonly unaware and unable to describe the motives and reasons for their behavior, particularly when the behavior is abnormal or maladaptive.

DAYDREAMING AND FANTASY

How many times were you told as a child to stop daydreaming and pay attention, or get to work, or whatever? Daydreaming is often considered an idle or wasteful activity. However, it is clear that everyone daydreams. Daydreaming means approximately the same thing as fantasy, although fantasy may be more extreme. All creative literature is really well-executed fantasy.

Studies by Singer [1966; 1968] have provided interesting information about daydreaming and fantasy. It appears that most people enjoy their daydreams and make active use of them both for pleasure and for problem solving. Content ranges from simple possibilities to wild dreams of inheriting a million dollars, being the Messiah, and obtaining a variety of normal and abnormal sexual satisfactions. Singer feels that nothing human (or inhuman) is alien to the imaginative realm of the accomplished daydreamer. Daydreams of men and women differ markedly in content, but not in frequency. Women tend to have daydreams involving passivity, a need for personal contact, and physical attractiveness, whereas the daydreams of men usually are much more concerned with explicit sexual activities. Singer categorized daydreaming as follows [1968, p. 2]:

General daydreaming reflected a predisposition to fantasy with great variety in content and often showed curiosity about other people rather than about the natural world.

Self-recriminating daydreaming was characterized by a high frequency of somewhat obsessional, verbally expressive but negatively-toned emotional reactions such as guilt and depression.

Objective, controlled, thoughtful daydreaming displayed a reflective, rather scientific and philosophically inclined content, and was associated with masculinity, emotional stability and curiosity about nature rather than about the human aspects of environment.

Poorly controlled, kaleidoscopic daydreaming reflected scattered thought and lack of systematic "story lines" in fantasy, as well as distractibility, boredom and self-abasement.

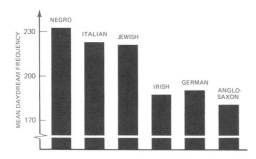

FIGURE 14-1   *Frequency of daydreaming for different groups in the New York area [Singer, 1968].*

Autistic daydreaming represented the breakthrough into consciousness of material associated with nocturnal dreaming. It reflected the kind of dreamy, poorly controlled quality of inner experience often reported clinically by schizoid individuals.

Neurotic, self-conscious daydreaming revealed one of the clearest patterns—the one most closely associated with measures of neuroticism and emotional instability. It involved repetitive, egocentric and body-centered fantasies.

The frequency of daydreaming appears related to relative social insecurity, at least in studies by Singer in the New York area. As indicated in Fig. 14-1, persons from Negro, Italian, or Jewish subcultures had much higher frequencies of daydreaming than those from Irish, German, and Anglo-Saxon subcultures. The content differed considerably for each group. The Irish showed a tendency toward religious, extremely fantastic, or heroic daydreams, while Negroes fantasized about sensual satisfactions, eating well, comfort, fine clothes, and cars. This would seem to fit rather well into a general view that unmet needs or motives, both biological and social, form the basis of much of our daydreaming. At a very simple level, you have probably noticed that when you are thirsty your own idle thoughts tend toward something cold to drink and when you are sexually frustrated your thoughts tend toward something not so cold.

Dreaming while asleep, which was discussed at length in Chapter 10, is a rather different and often far more vivid and compelling kind of fantasy than daydreaming.

DISORDERED OR AUTISTIC THINKING

Autistic thinking refers to the abnormal or disordered thought that is characteristic of schizophrenia. The thought processes of schizophrenics, particularly in idle thought and daydreaming, are markedly different from those of most people. The idle thoughts of normal people have a certain degree of logic or coherency. For example, if you ask a person what he would do with a million dollars, he will think about ways to spend it, invest it, or give it away. A schizophrenic might respond, "I have a million dollars and there are six white horses and the voice said I must . . ." White [1926] has recorded a characteristic example of autistic thought [in Morgan and Lovell, 1948, pp. 538-539]:

One patient was asked: "What did you say the other night to the students?" He replied: "Told them about locks and keys." "What else?" "Myriads of us keep growing in numbers, also in largeness; locks and keys, keys, keys, locks, locks, keys, keys, locks, locks, keys, keys, locks. Myriads of us quick-foot through, ev-er no mat-ter. Locks, keys, keys, locks, locks, keys, keys. Myriads of us ev-er full us as keep lives giant's growths, ev-er lives giant's keeper, ev-er no mat-ter. Locks, keys, keys, locks, locks, keys, keys, locks. Lives giant's wealth, health and pleasures, ev-er no mat-ter."

DIRECTED THINKING

Higher organisms, certainly from the level of the rat up to man, give behavioral signs of directed thinking. In a very general sense directed thought is thought related to the external environment—adequate responses to stimulation, solving problems, forming concepts, making discoveries. Hebb [1949] gave a good behavioral definition of directed thinking as "some sort of process that is not fully controlled by environmental stimulation yet cooperates closely with that stimulation . . . the [observance of a] delay between stimulation and response."

In addition to a delay, directed thinking entails transformations between stimulus input and response. A simple example is *clustering* of items in recall. Try the following experiment. Select four common names from each of four categories—four planets, four fruits, four animals, four first names—write each on a separate card, shuffle them into a random sequence, and have someone go through the 16 cards once. Then ask him to recall the 16 words. He will recall them, not in the order you presented, but by category. You might object that this is merely a simple learning task and does not involve thought. However, the occurrence of clustering reveals the transformational aspect of directed thought. Thought and learning are, of course, closely interrelated. The distinction between classical learning, as in Pavlov's conditioned reflex, and thinking, as in Einstein's development of the theory of relativity, may in part be a matter of degree. Learning is involved in both activities, but Einstein's efforts included considerably more thought. Between these extremes there is a wide range of behavior that entails some degree of directed thought.

In a classical experiment Hunter [1913] showed that animals as lowly as the rat could learn a *delayed reaction*. As indicated in Fig. 14-2,

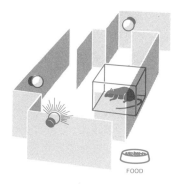

FIGURE 14–2   *Delayed-reaction experiment. One of the three lights goes on, indicating correct location of food, and then goes off. The animal is required to wait for varying periods of time after the light goes off before being released to go for the food.*

FOOD

FIGURE 14–3   *The* umweg *(roundabout) problem. The animal must go away from the food in order to go around the barrier and obtain the food.*

FOOD

the rat was placed in a start box from where it could see three light bulbs, one of which was lit and baited with food. After the light was turned off, the rat was kept in the start box for a period of time and then released. It had to "remember," or "keep symbolically in mind," which of the lights was on. In Hunter's original experiment rats could do this for 10 seconds, cats for 18 seconds, dogs for 3 minutes, a two-and-a-half-year-old child for 50 seconds, and a five-year-old child for at least 20 minutes. Actually the amount of delay time an animal can handle varies markedly with the particular conditions, but even rats can locate the right bulb after some delay. This might, of course, be termed only short-term memory. Nevertheless, it fits within Hebb's general definition of directed thought.

A somewhat more difficult problem is the *umweg* (roundabout) situation (see Fig. 14-3), in which the animal can see the food through the wire screen but must head away from it in order to reach it. Dogs can solve this problem, but rats cannot. At a still more complex level, if a food object is held above reach and a box is lying nearby, a chimpanzee will push the box over to the food, climb up, and get the food. A dog, although physically capable of doing this, will not. Such examples will be accepted by most people as evidence of simple thinking. We seem to be describing a kind of evolutionary or phylogenetic species-comparative intelligence test. This is not necessarily the case. It is difficult to find a task on which animal intelligence or ability to think can be compared directly across species. For example, the chimp uses the box in part because he is a climbing animal; the dog is not. Apart from the problem of comparison across species, however, there is ample evidence of simple directed thinking in nonhuman animals.

375

What do the terms in each of the following pairs have in common?

apple—orange
wheel—donut
fly—tree
Platonic ideal—categorical imperative
wood—song

The apple and the orange, of course, are both fruits. The wheel and the donut are both round. About the only thing "fly" and "tree" have in common is that they are both living things. "Categorical imperative" and "Platonic ideal" are both philosophical concepts of idealism (or both meaningless terms, depending on your point of view), "wood" and "song" do not seem to have anything in common, except that each has four letters. These are simple examples of concepts. A *concept* is a somewhat general category or term that includes several objects or terms within it. It is generally agreed in psychology that an organism has a *concept* if it has a disposition on the basis of which it can make nominal classificatory statements or responses ("this is X, that is not X") [Van de Greer and Jaspars, 1966]. This is a somewhat elaborate way of saying that concepts are categories of things or terms. Concepts are not correct or incorrect, or mutually exclusive. "Apple" and "orange" are both fruits; they are also both plants, both round, both sweet, and so on. Concepts need not have any reference to the real world—witness the two philosophical formulations.

Concepts can be developed by lower animals as well as man. Language is often involved in concept learning in man, but it does not appear to be essential. Hebb [1958] made the important observation that if different organisms are trained in the same kind of visual form discrimination, they may learn quite different things. For example, rats, chimpanzees, and two-year-old children were trained to choose a triangle form (1 in Fig. 14-4). The chimps took longer to learn this simple task than the rats. When the rats were tested with other triangle forms (2, 3, and 4), they had to start all over again; they had not formed a general concept of "triangle." However, the chimps did in fact form a

FIGURE 14–4   *Degree of concept learning of triangularity. Trained to respond to figure 1, the rat makes random responses to diagrams 2, 3, and 4; chimpanzees respond correctly to 2 and 3; and two-year-old human children respond correctly to 2, 3, and 4. [Hebb, 1958]*

somewhat general concept. They responded to forms 2 and 3, even though their initial training was to only one specific triangle. The children did even better, responding to forms 2, 3, and 4. This seems to be characteristic of children after infancy; they tend to *generalize* from one instance to another. It is almost as if the forming and use of concepts were a natural part of primate behavior.

It has often been noted that concept development seems to occur suddenly as *insight*, often referred to as the "aha" phenomenon. In his classical study of apes on Tenerife Island Köhler [1925] described a chimpanzee faced with the problem of retrieving a banana lying outside his cage. He had two sticks, one of which could fit inside the other, but neither of which was long enough to reach the banana. He tried for a while to reach the banana with each stick and gave up. Later, while he was playing with the sticks, he accidentally discovered they could be put together. He immediately did this, rushed to the edge of the cage, and pulled in the banana. Gestalt psychologists hold that such insights entail a spontaneous reordering of the organism's conceptual world—that they occur suddenly and *de novo*. In further studies on the chimp's use of sticks to obtain food Birch [1945] found that the more prior experience he had with the stick, the more easily he formed the concept of using the stick to obtain food. It seemed that once the chimp had learned to use the stick as an extension of his arm reach, he was able to generalize this use to a variety of situations. Birch concluded that the ability to reorganize previous experiences in accordance with the requirements of a new problem situation is the essence of problem solving.

Spence [1938], a reinforcement theorist and student of Clark Hull, held that learning, even learning of concepts, is the result of trial-and-error performance that is appropriately rewarded and punished. His analysis of the learning curves of chimpanzees on discrimination-learning tasks revealed that "sudden" learning with particular stimuli was closely correlated with the number of previous rewards and frustrations an animal had experienced with these stimuli. Spence concluded that the results failed to support the interpretation that sudden solutions are marked by the presence of insight independent of past reinforcement history.

Bertrand Russell once suggested that apes in American psychology laboratories form concepts by running blindly about using only trial-and-error methods, whereas apes in German laboratories sit quietly and evolve concepts out of their inner consciousness. The truth seems to be somewhere in between. Wisconsin monkeys utilize trial-and-error learning, but they learn more than the solutions to particular problems. As we saw in Chapter 13, they form *learning sets*—that is, they learn how to learn. In a comparison of learning-set performance by rhesus monkeys and human three- to five-year-old children on sets of discrimination-reversal problems it is clear that the children win. However, note that the discrimination-reversal data in Fig. 14-5 clearly illustrate set-formation and transfer-producing adaptable abilities, rather than specific bonds.

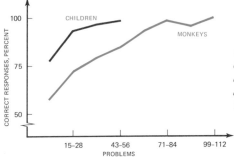

FIGURE 14–5   *Learning-set performance of rhesus monkeys and young children on discrimination reversal problems. The curves are based on trial 2 responses. [Harlow, 1949a]*

Without the monkey's learning curves we might be tempted to assume that the children's better performance indicates a gulf between human and subhuman learning. However, the extremely rapid learning by the children is not unlike the rapid learning by the monkeys, and an analysis of the error-producing factors shows that the same basic mechanisms are operating in both cases.

Reinforcement theorists such as Hull and Spence have constantly emphasized the need for a historical approach to learning, but their actual research on the influence of experience has been largely limited to the development of isolated habits and their generalization. Hence their failure to find any discontinuity in learning may stem from their study of individual rather than repetitive learning situations. Gestalt theorists (e.g., Köhler), unlike reinforcement theorists, have stressed insight and hypothesis in their description of learning, giving the impression that these phenomena are properties of the innate organization of the individual. However, if such phenomena do appear independently of a gradual learning history, they have not been found in the primate order.

There have been numerous studies of concept development in humans. The standard experimental situation employs objects that vary in form, color, and size (see Fig. 14-6). The concept the subject is to learn may consist of any one or more of these three dimensions. For example, suppose "blue square" is the concept; all the stimulus patterns which embody both blueness and squareness (there are three in the figure) are positive instances, and all which do not—24 in all—are negative instances. In an experiment the subject might be given each stimulus separately and instructed to guess whether or not it is "correct." He would then be told whether he was right or wrong.

Early studies by Hull and others investigated the relative difficulty of simple concepts. Heidbreder [1946], for example, had subjects learn nonsense terms for particular concepts; examples are shown in Fig. 14-7. The subject would then be tested on the next trial with a different picture of the same thing. The results of these studies indicated that simple concrete object concepts, such as face, building, or tree, were the easiest to learn, followed by spatial form and color, and then number.

In a careful analysis of conceptual behavior Bourne [1966] has distinguished between *stimulus attributes* and *conceptual rules*. The stimulus attributes are such things as shape, color, and size, each with numerous gradations, and the conceptual rules are rules for grouping stimuli on the basis of their attributes—that is, the rules are the general form of the concept. Bourne uses as a simplified example the development of the learning set for oddity in monkeys (Fig. 14-8). In this task the monkey is presented with a set of three stimulus objects, one of which is different from the other two. He is allowed to choose one of the objects. If he chooses the odd one—in this case the triangle—he is rewarded with food, candy, or some other incentive. If he chooses incorrectly, all the objects are removed and no reward is given. On the second trial the same objects are presented, but in different positions, and the monkey is again allowed to choose and is rewarded for a correct choice.

After several trials with these three objects three new objects are presented, with the oddity based on a different stimulus attribute—for example, this time one block may be larger than the other two. Once again, the odd object is associated with reward. This procedure is continued over a series of problems, each with different stimulus

FIGURE 14–6   *A set of geometric designs illustrating the kinds of stimuli and dimensions (shape, size, and color) used in many human concept-learning experiments [Moon and Harlow in Bourne, 1966].*

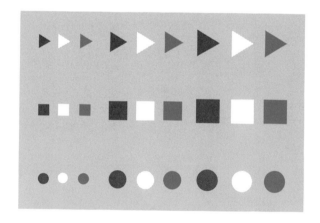

FIGURE 14–7   *Examples of stimuli and nonsense concept "words" used in studies comparing the difficulty of learning simple concepts in man [Heidbreder, 1946].*

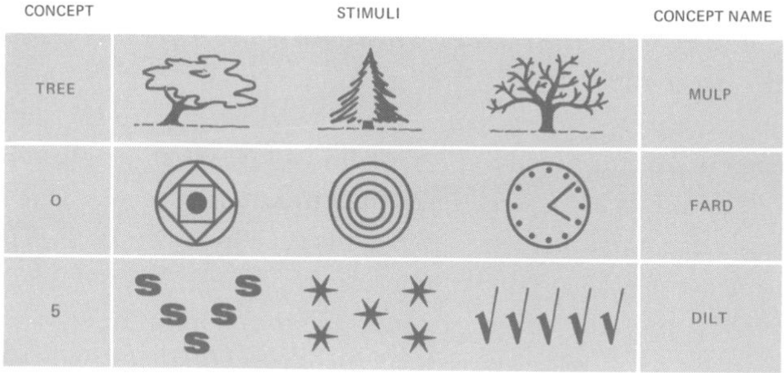

CONCEPT	STIMULI			CONCEPT NAME
TREE				MULP
O				FARD
5				DILT

FIGURE 14-8   *The oddity principle. Left, a monkey solving an oddity problem [Harlow, University of Wisconsin]. Below, three sample oddity problems. The subject is rewarded on each trial only if he chooses or responds to the odd member (marked +) of each stimulus set. The first graph shows performance changes over trials within single oddity problems. The learning function is elevated with successive problems until, after very many problems, performance is errorless. The second graph shows actual data from a study of oddity learning in monkeys [Moon and Harlow, 1955]. The score plotted on the ordinate is the percentage of responses to the odd stimulus on trial 1 of each problem. After 250 problems these subjects make about 90 percent correct trial 1 responses. [Bourne, 1966]*

EXAMPLE PROBLEMS

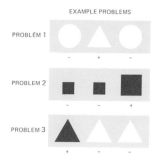

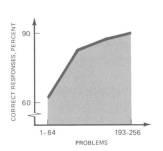

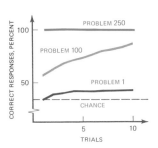

objects and a different cue or critical attribute, but the rule is always the same—reward is associated with the odd object of the group. Subjects improve both within problems (particular stimulus-attribute learning) and across problems (learning set). After a good deal of training the subject nearly always scores perfectly on new oddity problems. He has learned the concept of oddity. As Bourne notes, the oddity rule is a simple one, perhaps too obvious for most adults to appreciate fully. However, the data indicate that oddity is not a simple concept for a young or naïve subject; it is acquired only through extensive practice. Oddity, then, is a simple example of a general rule that is independent of particular stimulus qualities and refers only to the abstraction "same or different."

Bruner et al. [1956] introduced three types of rules in concept learning, conjunctive, disjunctive, and relational. A conjunctive rule requires that two stimulus attributes be present, such as red and square. A disjunctive rule requires that either one stimulus attribute or the other be present, such as red *or* square. A relational rule requires a comparison; in a simplified situation when two objects are compared each time, the larger of each pair is correct, independent of absolute attributes. In general it appears that disjunctive concepts are the most difficult to learn. An additional important finding was that people typically adopt certain kinds of strategies in trying to attain concepts. One example is *successive scanning*. The subject adopts a hypothesis, tries it until it is proved wrong, then adopts another, and so on, always attempting to remember and not reuse previous incorrect hypotheses. Another example is the more risky strategy of *focus gambling*, in which the subject changes more than one stimulus attribute at a time in an attempt to hit on the correct combination of attributes for the concept.

Still another formulation of the general features of concept strategy is the TOTE system of Miller et al. [1960]. Having formed a hypothesis, the subject *tests* (T) it against new problems or data. If it proves wrong, an *operate* (O) phase is instituted that generates a new hypothesis. This continues until *tests* (T) against new problems do not contradict the hypothesis, at which point the subject *exits* (E) from the problem situation. These strategy formulations are not restricted, of course, to particular experimental problems, but also apply to human behavior in complex real-life problem situations.

PROBLEM SOLVING

Concept formation and problem solving overlap considerably; both are types of problem situations. They are sometimes distinguished in terms of the "correctness" of a solution. A specific problem may have only one solution, but a concept solution can have several correct forms—for example, an apple and an orange are both fruit and are also both round. This difference is also reflected in the distinction between *inductive* and *deductive* logic. Inductive logic is the formulation of a general law or principle to explain or apply to many specific examples. A common use of inductive logic is in science—the general theories and laws of science are inductions or concepts. Inductive logic is the forming of concepts. In simple terms it consists of making educated guesses about the world.

In deductive logic, on the other hand, we are given a set of terms and a set of rules and asked to prove or disprove a particular hypothesis. Geometry is a familiar example. To prove the Pythagorean theorem which says that the sum of the squares of the two sides of a right triangle equals the square of the hypotenuse you must use the rules and terms of Euclidean geometry in a fixed and prescribed way. Indeed, all of formal mathematics is deductive logic—it can be deduced from basic rules of logic. In actual fact, it is unlikely that human beings solve deductive problems in a purely deductive manner. As we noted above, subjects quite typically adopt and test hypotheses in trying to solve problems. This is inductive rather than deductive thinking. A particularly clear example is provided by the famous Indian mathematician Srinivase Ramanujan. He had no formal education beyond high school, and yet, almost entirely on his own and with little knowledge of past work in mathematics, he discovered more than 6000 theorems in mathematics, some previously known and many quite new. He did not develop and prove the theorems deductively, but worked almost entirely by "intuition"—inductive thought. Subsequent efforts proved him correct in most instances. Newman [1956] has described Ramanujan's work as the "most prodigious feat ever accomplished in the history of thought." His thinking was almost purely inductive in mathematics, an area that is in formal terms a purely deductive field.

381

You have had considerable experience in solving problems and are quite familiar with the general features of problem-solving behavior. If you wish to do an observational study yourself, try working out the correct solution to the "missionaries and cannibals" problem and note down each step, both correct and incorrect, that you make:

Three missionaries and three cannibals wish to cross a river. All can row, but their boat will carry only two people. It must never happen that on any shore there are more cannibals than missionaries, for the missionaries would promptly be eaten. The task is to specify the schedule of boat loads back and forth across the river so that all six will eventually end up safely on the far side of the river.

An actual solution process for this problem is shown in Fig. 14-9. The subject's initial behavior consisted largely in trying out various alternatives, first more or less mechanically on a trial-and-error basis—the first six steps. As many of these proved incorrect, he tended to develop hypotheses, and finally developed a new concept—staying in the boat—which ultimately led to the correct solution of the problem.

Specific problem tasks such as this can be solved by computers as well as or better than by men. An excellent example of this is the General Problem Solver (GPS) computer program developed by Newell and Simon [1963]. They set the program to derive the theorems in *Principia Mathematica*, the classic work by Bertrand Russell and Alfred North Whitehead, in which all mathematics is deduced from the rules of logic.

FIGURE 14–9   *A typical solution to the missionaries and cannibals problem. The green square stands for missionary and the blue circle stands for cannibal. Locations of the six men and the boat are indicated before each step. A cross marks the spot where a missionary passed on to greater rewards. [after Newell, 1968]*

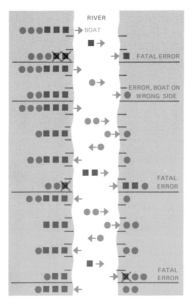
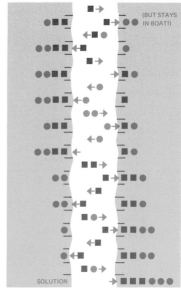

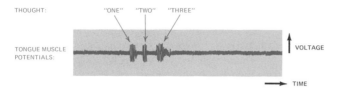

FIGURE 14–10   *Muscle potentials (voltage measurement) generated
by the tongue as a subject thinks of counting "one," "two," "three"
[after Jacobson, 1931].*

In at least one instance the computer produced a shorter proof than
had Russell and Whitehead. According to the story, the proof was sent
to Russell and he wired back congratulating the computer on developing
a more elegant proof.

The GPS was intended to do more than high-powered logical
deduction; it was an attempt to program a computer to solve problems in the same general way that people do. The program has been
remarkably successful in this respect and does in fact solve many problems of the missionaries-and-cannibals type in much the same way that
people do. The issue is the extent to which such programs can tell us
more about how people actually think. One might suppose that there
would be an endless variety of such programs. Actually, so far there are
only a few general types of programs possible that will solve problems
in this way. Perhaps as this approach is developed further the computer
may be able to tell us much about the general features of human thinking, at least at the problem-solving level.

THE NEURAL BASIS OF THOUGHT

Most of us take for granted that thinking
occurs in the brain. However, some brave
theorists have asserted that thinking is an
entirely peripheral activity done with the
muscles and involving the central nervous system only in so far as the formation of learned
connections is concerned. Watson, as we noted earlier, was perhaps the
first to propose such a theory. More recently Skinner [1957] developed
a somewhat similar view. In essence small movements of the vocal
apparatus—tongue, lips, throat, and chest—are assumed to occur whenever we think. These movements, the behavioral representation of non-
spoken words, are chained together through reinforcement learning. It
is quite possible to represent human thought with sufficiently complex
interchaining of sequences of such movements.

Early experiments in which the muscle activity of the tongue and
throat were recorded electrically during thinking gave considerable support to such a view. An example from the pioneering work of Jacobson
[1931] is shown in Fig. 14-10. A needle electrode was inserted in the
tongue, and each subject was told to think of counting "one," "two,"
"three." The three deflections on the electrical tracing occurred when
he thought of the three numbers. Whenever the subjects were asked to

383

engage in thinking activity, electrical potentials were recorded from the tongue. Even more remarkable are studies on deaf-mutes who had learned sign language [Max, 1935; Novikova, 1955]. Subjects deaf from birth and unable to speak showed electrical activity in their fingers but not their tongues during thought and when they were asleep and dreaming. Deaf children who had been taught to speak as well as use sign language showed activity in both tongue and hands. Although this type of research has not been actively pursued in recent years, it seems likely that with the sophisticated electronic technology available today it might well be possible to "read a person's mind" by recording the electrical activity of his tongue. Such evidence would seem to provide strong support for the peripheral theory of thinking.

It is important to distinguish between the extreme peripheralist position that thinking *is* small movements of the vocal apparatus and the more moderate view that such movements generally *accompany* thinking. The extremist theory was disproved in a heroic experiment in which an anesthesiologist was totally paralyzed by a form of the drug curare. As he became paralyzed, stimuli were repeatedly presented to him. He was kept totally paralyzed for a period of about 10 minutes. During that time he was conscious, mentally alert, and reported accurately the events that occurred. The protocol makes fascinating reading [Smith et al., 1947, pp. 4–8].

2:00   Electro-encephalographic and electrocardiographic continuous recording started. Control observations made on blood pressure, pulse rate and respiratory rate, neurologic signs, etc. . . .

2:11   *D*-tubocurarine chloride [the curare drug] injected intravenously at a slow constant rate so that 200 units were administered over a fifteen-minute period. Feels "a little bit dizzy and quite a 'glow.' " "A little hard to focus on anything." Weakness in jaw muscles noted. "Hard to talk." Difficulty in swallowing and keeping eyes open. "No unpleasant sensations, legs feel weak."

2:18   Upon subject's request, oxygen administration with face mask started. "Can hardly bring teeth together." Complains of residual odor from rebreathing bag. Alpha rhythm in electro-encephalogram prominent and inhibited by pattern vision. Total of 100 units *d*-tubocurarine chloride given. . . .

2:20   Speech no longer possible. Can hear distinctly. Still able to nod head and to move hands slightly, but can scarcely move fingers. . . .

2:24   Head movement impossible. Unable to open eyes. Can wrinkle forehead slightly and indicates in this manner, in response to inquiry, that he can see clearly when his eyelids are manually elevated.

2:26   Ability to comprehend and answer questions accurately is indicated by correctness of replies when the inquiries are restated in the negative or double negative. Indicates he desires the experiment to continue. Upon request, moves feet and hands slightly. Total of 200 units given. . . .

2:30   No further spontaneous respiratory movements. Ability to wrinkle forehead almost gone, but indicates he can hear, see, and feel touch and pain as well as ever. . . .

2:32   Can no longer move feet or hands upon request, and indicates by slight remaining movement of left eyebrow that he is trying to do so. . . .

2:37   Subject signals in answer to inquiries that sensorium is normal, airway is not troublesome, and painful stimuli are felt. Additional 100 units *d*-tubocurarine chloride given rapidly; total 400 units. . . .

2:42   Ability to signal by slight movement inner aspect left eyebrow almost gone. Indicates he desires the final 100 units, that he is perfectly conscious and that his sensorium is unimpaired.

2:44   Additional 100 units *d*-tubocurarine chloride given rapidly; total, 500 units. [*d*-tubocurarine discontinued at this point.]

2:45   Subject now unable to signal response to inquiries, due to complete skeletal muscular paralysis. . . .

2:48   Eyelids manually opened. Alpha rhythm of electroencephalogram inhibited by pattern vision (object held in line of gaze). Subject stated upon recovery that he was "clear as a bell" all this period. . . .

2:56   Subject can now contract muscles of medial aspect left eyebrow. Communication thus being reestablished, he signals that he can hear and see normally, and the painful stimuli are felt. . . .

3:06   Respiratory effort becoming more prominent. Extremities still completely paralyzed. Muscle of eyelids and forehead much more active. Can open eyes with difficulty. . . .

3:14   Subject indicates that he is uncomfortable when artificial respiration is even briefly discontinued. Can move his feet slightly, but not hands. Can move tongue but cannot speak. . . .

3:25   Spontaneous respirations improved. Speech is weak and slurred, but now intelligible. . . .

4:50   With assistance, subject is able to sit up on edge of bed. Complains of dizziness. Complete subjective report dictated. . . .

SUBJECTIVE REPORT   . . . The subject remained acutely conscious throughout the experiment and memory was unimpaired. At no time was there any evidence of lapse of consciousness or clouding of the sensorium. This statement is based particularly on the fact that at intervals of a minute or less, during the period when communication with the subject was impossible, various statements were made, questions asked, stimuli presented, objects placed in the line of gaze and so forth, on which the subject was requested to report when speech returned. In each instance, the report was accurate in all details and properly oriented as to temporal sequence. Indeed, several occurrences which were forgotten or unrecorded by the experimenters were recalled by the subject. Visual acuity and color sense were not affected. Vision was handicapped only by diplopia ["double vision"; since the muscles that control the eyes could not focus on a common point] and the inability to focus on anything that was not directly in line of gaze. The eyes remained passively shut most of the time. Hearing and smell were unimpaired. Indeed, it seemed to the subject that hearing was more acute than normal and remarks whispered at a distance of 20 feet were heard distinctly. Taste sensation was not examined.

This account is given at length not only because of its rather dramatic character, but because it conclusively disproves the extreme peripheralist position that thought consists in muscular movements. The subject was able to perceive and think in a relatively normal manner while his entire musculature was totally paralyzed.

We know relatively little about the neural basis of thought. It is clear that the cerebral cortex, the most recent neural structure to evolve, and the structure that has its greatest elaboration in higher primates, particularly man (see Chapter 8), is essential for the development of higher mental processes. More specifically, the *association areas* of the cerebral cortex, which are neither specifically sensory nor specifically motor, are critically involved. Extensive experiments in which specific regions of association cortex were removed in monkeys, together with careful evaluation of the behavioral effects, have given us fascinating glimpses of what comparable regions of the human brain might do. Accidental brain damage in humans from injury or disease also provides "experiments of nature" that have, in the hands of skilled clinicians, given further hints of cortical function in thought. Finally, work of neurosurgeons such as Penfield, who electrically stimulates the cerebral cortex of conscious patients, has offered tantalizing suggestions about the neurology of mind. We do know something from such work about the cortical areas involved in speech and language.

The sensory and motor areas of the brain are shown in Fig. 14-11, along with possible functions of the association areas. A general distinction can be made between frontal and posterior association areas. The frontal cortex seems more involved in the processes that involve "thought in time," and the posterior areas are involved more in complex perception. More specifically, damage to the frontal cortex in primates produces loss of the ability to perform delayed-response tasks of the sort shown in Fig. 14-2 [French and Harlow, 1962; Jacobsen, 1935]. Damage to the posterior association cortex, however, impairs complex visual and other sensory discriminations [Harlow, 1952; Pribram, 1954]. In particular, learning set is severely impaired after posterior lesions [Riopelle et al., 1953].

It is difficult to compare these studies on monkeys directly with effects of accidental damage in man. There do seem to be some consistencies. Pribram et al. [1964] have developed a general view, based on extensive studies with monkeys, that frontal damage results in the continued use of responses that were correct in the past, even though the same stimuli are no longer rewarded in the new situation. On the basis of extensive studies of humans with frontal damage Milner [1964] concludes that it results in a deficit in situations that require a constant shifting of response to meet changing environmental demands. Under

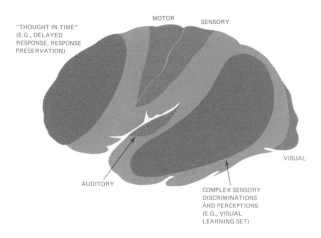

FIGURE 14–11   *Summary of the general types of higher functions mediated by the frontal and posterior association regions of the primate brain—a greatly oversimplified schema.*

such conditions the patient seems unable to suppress his ongoing response tendencies or to rid himself of interference from previous sensory events.

There is an analog between the effects of damage to posterior association cortex in monkey and man. As we noted, complex sensory discriminations and learning set are impaired in the monkey. In man damage to comparable regions in the nondominant hemisphere—usually the right, which is not essential for speech in right-handed people— produces loss of awareness of visual-sensory orientation; such persons are often unable to orient themselves in space. Penfield provides a clear example [1969, p. 151]:

> In one patient, this area on the nondominant side was removed completely. In the years that followed the operation, the patient's epileptic attacks stopped. He was able to earn his living, but he had a penalty to pay. With his eyes closed, he had no conception of his position in space. On leaving his house in the village where he lived, he seemed to be well oriented until he turned a street corner. After that he was lost. To get back home, it was necessary for him to ask the direction from a passerby.

In a brilliant book *The Organization of Behavior,* Hebb [1949] proposed a theory of how the brain might develop neural coding of perception and concepts. In essence he suggested that during development after birth the organism learns to perceive visual objects as a result of numerous experiences with simple forms. Lines and other simple stimuli are coded by complex interconnecting groups of neurons, which he termed *cell assemblies*, and these in turn interconnect with one another in still more complex ways to form *phase sequences*, which code squares, triangles, and other more complex forms. As learning continues these processes are elaborated into very complex coding of concepts in association cortex. A somewhat different view has been developed by Konorski [1967], Thompson [1969], and others. Konorski suggested

387

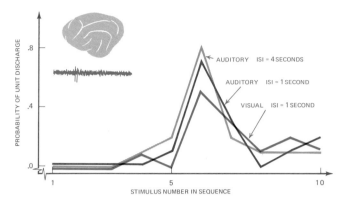

FIGURE 14-12   *A neuron in the association cortex of the cat that could serve to code the concept of number six. A series of 10 stimuli are given repeatedly, and the probability of spike discharge of the cell is plotted against stimulus number in the sequence. The cell tends to fire most on the sixth stimulus, regardless of whether the stimulus is auditory or visual and regardless of whether it is given at a rate of one every second or one every 4 seconds. ISI is the interstimulus interval, the time between successive stimuli. The location of this cell is shown by the dot in the association center of the cat brain, and the tracing is an example of the cell discharging to a "six" stimulus. [Thompson et al., 1970]*

that even very complex concepts could be represented by single neurons in the cerebral cortex which he termed *gnostic cells* (from the Greek *gnosis*, knowledge). Actually these two ideas are not contradictory. Gnostic cells could well develop through learning by means of the complex assemblages of neurons that Hebb envisaged.

The work of Hubel and Wiesel [1959] seems to support the idea that single neurons code concepts, at least in visual perception. As we saw in Chapter 8, single neurons in the visual cortex code angles and forms, and this coding is apparently present at birth. In a very real sense these visual form-coding cells are "concept," or "gnostic," cells; they respond to a category of stimuli in the same sense that human subjects learn to respond to a category such as triangle in simple concept-learning experiments (see Fig. 14-6). Even more complex types of concept-coding cells have been reported in recent times. For example, Gross et al. [1969] described a neuron in the posterior association cortex of the monkey that responded only to a form resembling a monkey's hand; the more the stimulus silhouette resembled a hand, the more the cell fired. This might be termed a "hand-concept" gnostic cell.

Thompson et al. [1970] have observed cells in the association cortex of the cat that could serve to code the concept of number. In the example shown in Fig. 14-12, series of stimuli were presented, one after the other, and the cell fired mostly on the sixth presentation. This was independent of the nature of the stimulus (sound or light), the intensity of the stimulus, and the time between successive stimuli. The response was only in terms of the number of stimuli. One cell of this number-coding type was even found in a very young kitten, suggesting that such cells may function as a result of an innate mechanism. As we saw in connection with human concept-learning experiments, color, shape, and number seem to form an increasingly difficult series of con-

388

cepts. Color is coded at the level of the eye (see Chapter 8), form is coded at the level of the visual cortex, and number may be coded in the association cortex. It is important to keep in mind that the evidence regarding such concept-coding or gnostic neurons is still preliminary and tentative. There are single neurons in the cerebral cortex that *could* serve to code angle, hand, and number, but it remains to be determined whether or not such neurons are in fact performing these functions. We stand at the very beginning in our knowledge of how the human brain, the most complex structure in the universe, can develop concepts and ideas.

LANGUAGE AND COMMUNICATION

Language is unique to man. Every human society possesses language. The development of all human culture has been possible only through the use of language. Language has provided the vehicle for an entirely new kind of evolution. Until the appearance of the language-using animal called man, animals adapted to their environments or they perished. With the development of the ability to transmit ideas and knowledge through language, man reversed evolution and began to adapt the environment to his own needs. In fact, in view of the present rate of increase in environmental pollution and ecological imbalance, man may gain the dubious distinction of being the only species to have adapted the environment to the point of engineering his own destruction.

We must make a fundamental distinction between language and communication. Only man possesses *language*, but many species of animals *communicate* and some, such as the parrot, can even emit clear speech sounds. However, the parrot can never learn to combine words in a meaningful way; it cannot develop syntax. Language has both grammar and syntax. *Grammar* refers to all the rules for correct use of a language, and *syntax* refers to that part of grammar concerned with the ordering of words, as in a sentence. Young children, who may possess a vocabulary smaller than that of a well-trained parrot, are able to generate meaningful *new* sentences, sentences they have not learned before as such, with appropriate use of syntax.

Communication among members of a species seems to be more a rule than an exception. At a very simple level *species-specific* communication involves the release of chemicals called *pheromones*, which serve as signals. The female Bombyx moth, when ready to mate, releases an odor that can be detected by the male as much as 7 miles away. This odor signals that she is ready and willing, and because of the way the male odor receptors function, it also provides information about where she is. The male receptors are extremely sensitive to very weak concentrations of the odor but respond differentially only to much higher concentrations. Since moths tend to fly against the wind, the male will approach the vicinity of the female simply by flying. When he is close the higher concentration of the odor provides differential cues that

389

guide him to the female. This, of course, is an extremely simple form of communication. Communication in the honeybee is a much more striking example; as noted in Chapter 13, when a foraging bee discovers nectar, he returns to the hive and performs a dance that communicates to the other bees the direction and distance to the food.

Communication is not necessarily species specific, particularly in higher animals. A baboon troop in search of food will often stay with a herd of zebras, and the alarm given by either species at the approach of a lion is correctly interpreted by both the zebras and the baboons. Some forms of communication seem to be shared among primates and are perhaps order specific. For example, the beckoning gesture with the hand and arm apparently means "come here" to wild chimpanzees as well as to men.

Examples of both intraspecies and interspecies communication are numberless. However, there are as yet no really convincing demonstrations that any species other than man has developed the specialized aspect of communication we call language. Chimpanzee tribes in the wild state show a wide variety of vocalizations that serve to communicate information, but the sounds appear to be species specific and not much dependent on learning. Human language is eminently learned. There are several hundred different human languages, many of them totally unrelated. They are not even limited to spoken word sounds. The bushmen in Africa developed a language consisting in large part of clicks, still other cultures developed whistle languages, and American Indians developed a sign language. The extent to which language is a result of the uniquely complex development of the human animal is a critical, and as yet unanswered, question. The fact that every human society or group, no matter how primitive, isolated, or culturally backward it may appear, has developed a complete and complex language suggests that language development is a necessary, perhaps even genetically determined, result of possessing a human brain.

One approach to this question is to attempt to teach language to nonhuman primates. Among the primates the gorilla has the largest brain next to man, but there are certain practical difficulties involved in raising a gorilla in the home. The chimpanzee has been most widely studied and seems a very good choice. He exhibits social behavior resembling that of man, he is our closest living relative in terms of biochemical criteria such as blood type and characteristics, and he is roughly similar in size. There have been several attempts to teach chimps to learn spoken language. The most notable was the effort of Hayes and Hayes, who raised a chimp named Vikki from birth to the age of six in their home. Vikki's social and emotional development were strikingly similar to that of a human child; indeed, the Hayes treated her as much in this manner as possible. They spent a great deal of time attempting to teach Vikki to speak, much more time than parents normally devote to such efforts. The results were conclusively negative. Vikki learned to speak only four words, and these were not clearly pronounced. Does this constitute complete failure to learn language? Actually Vikki's failure was in speaking, not necessarily in understanding. Vikki learned to communicate a good deal by gestures and expressions, and she evidently understood a great deal more than she could speak. Of course in terms of understanding and responding correctly to words, dogs can be trained to understand well over 100 separate verbal commands. Vikki used different gestures accompanying her few spoken words with sufficient consistency that outside observers watching movies of her performance could understand what she said equally well with and without the sound track. [Hayes, 1951; Hayes and Hayes, 1951].

The results of the Hayes' study, which showed clearly that chimpanzees cannot be taught to speak language, suggested that language as it is used by man is an exclusively human ability. This conclusion was widely accepted until very recently. There are several alternative explanations why chimpanzees cannot be taught to speak. Perhaps the most obvious is the possibility that their peripheral vocal apparatus is unsuited to speech. This is not clearly known. However, wild chimps produce a large variety of vocalizations, and humans with extensive throat surgery are able to speak intelligibly; thus chimps ought to be able to do so, even if pronunciation is imperfect. In any event, a proper vocal apparatus is clearly not a sufficient condition for language; parrots can speak words quite clearly, but they cannot learn language. This suggests a second possibility that chimpanzees simply do not have sufficient intellectual ability to learn language.

Such has been the general conclusion until the very recent and important work by Gardner and Gardner [1969; 1970]. They reasoned that perhaps chimpanzees did have the intellectual capacity for language, but not in terms of *vocal* behavior. Both wild chimps and chimps raised in captivity make very similar vocal sounds, suggesting that perhaps their "verbal" behavior is species specific—that is, genetically determined— and not much subject to influence or change; another way of putting it would be that the verbal behavior of chimps is not very plastic. The Gardners noted, however, that chimps use their hands with great skill—a chimp can do almost any manual task a man can do—and consequently it might be possible to teach a chimp sign language. The Gardners have succeeded in doing just this. Their report is fascinating reading. Their subject, Washoe, was less than ideal in that she was over a year old when they obtained her and had been captured wild. Instead of raising Washoe in their house, they set up a trailer-house apartment with a bedroom, kitchen, bathroom, living room, and a large outdoor play area. One of the experimenters was with Washoe from the time she got up in the morning until bedtime, but she spent the nights alone. From the beginning the experimenters refrained from using words and used only American Sign Language to "talk" to Washoe. They were not bound to any one type of training or learning-theory approach, but tried everything, including contingent reinforcement, shaping, demonstration (to provide opportunity for imitative learning), and directed training, whereby they simply held Washoe's hands and fingers in correct positions. Interestingly enough, the last approach, together with imitation, was the most

391

FIGURE 14–13   *Washoe "saying" words in American Sign Language. Left, Washoe fingerpainting. Above, Washoe making the sign for drink. Pictures taken in December 1967, when Washoe was two and one-half. [Gardner and Gardner, University of Nevada, Reno]*

successful, and reinforcement of spontaneous behavior was the least successful, which may surprise reinforcement-learning theorists but will come as no surprise to parents.

At the age of three Washoe had a vocabulary of nearly 100 words, including nouns, verbs, and pronouns. She used the signs spontaneously and appropriately, used them correctly in new situations, and generalized to similar objects and events. She spoke up to six-word sentences, and used subjects, verbs, objects, and pronouns in the correct sequences. In short, she has learned American Sign Language and apparently rather well when compared to a three-year-old human child deaf from birth. Linguists will no doubt argue for some time about the extent to which Washoe has actually developed language. The reader may judge for himself in the following excerpts from her language behavior [Gardner and Gardner, 1970]:

A listing of Washoe's phrases, together with the contexts in which they occurred, is striking because the phrases seem so apt. For play with her companions, she would sign *Roger you tickle*, *you Greg peekaboo*, or simply, *catch me* or *tickle me*. She indicated destinations with phrases such as *go in*, *go out*, or *in down bed*. Other phrases produced descriptions: *drink red* for her red cup, *my baby* for her dolls, *listen eat* or *listen drink* for the supper bell, and *dirty good* for the toilet chair. Asking for access to the many objects that were kept out of sight and out of reach by the various locked doors in her quarters, Washoe signed, *key open food* at the refrigerator, *open key clean* at the soap cupboard, and *key open please blanket* at the bedding cupboard. Combinations with *sorry* were frequent, and these were appropriate for apology and irresistible as appeasements: *please sorry*, *sorry dirty*, *sorry hurt*, *please sorry good*, and *come hug-love sorry sorry*.

These examples of apt phrases are by no means exceptional; there were hundreds of other such phrases, and particular phrases were observed repeatedly, as their appropriate situation recurred. Any participant in this project saw and responded to, *go out* and *tickle me* far more often than he would care to remember. Washoe also produced variants that left the key phrase unchanged while emphasizing her request. For example, sodapop, which Washoe referred to as *sweet drink* was requested by all of the following: *please sweet drink, more sweet drink, gimme sweet drink, hurry sweet drink, please hurry sweet drink, please gimme sweet drink*, and by variations in the order of these signs. . . .

About half of the longer combinations were formed by adding signs for demand to shorter combinations of the kind we have already discussed, as in *please tickle more, come Roger tickle*, and *out open please hurry*. In the remaining cases, the additional signs introduced new information and new relations among signs. Most of these added signs were proper names or pronouns. Sometimes the effect was to specify more than one actor, as in *you me in, you me out, you me Greg go*, or in *you Naomi peekaboo*, or *tickle Washoe me. You me drink go* and *you me out look* are examples of combinations which specify actors, action and a destination or object. There were also apologies, such as *hug-love me good*, which specified an actor, an attribute and an action. Finally, a number of Washoe's combinations specified both the subject and the object of an action, as in *Roger Washoe tickle*, and *you tickle me Washoe* and *you peekaboo me.*

An example of Washoe's "speech" is shown in Fig. 14-13.

Premack [1970] has also succeeded in teaching chimpanzees language, using a quite different approach. He employed little plastic cut-out forms to represent words. For example, a blue triangle is the sign for "apple." The chimp must place a blue triangle on a board in order to obtain an apple. His star pupil, a seven-year-old chimp named Sarah, now has a vocabulary of over 120 words, including common and proper nouns, abstract nouns for concepts, verbs, adjectives, adverbs, and uses them appropriately in sentences. The work of the Gardners and Premack would seem to settle the issue; chimpanzees can learn language.

PSYCHOLINGUISTICS

Of all human activities, language seems among the most obviously learned. A young child can learn any language with equal facility. There are well over 2000 different languages in use in the world today and many more that have disappeared completely. Linguistics, the formal study of language, has in part been an effort to bring order into this seeming chaos. Many languages, such as Portuguese and Spanish or Danish and Swedish, are clearly very closely related. Over and above these obvious similarities it appears that there are large families of related languages. The best known of these is Indo-European, which includes virtually all modern languages of the Western world—English, French, German, Spanish, Italian, Russian, the Scandanavian group, and so on. Interestingly, Sanskrit, the ancient literary and religious language of India, is also a member of the Indo-European group, but Finnish,

Hungarian, and Basque are not. Languages are grouped in families according to similarities in morphology and syntax. In the case of the Indo-European languages, rules have been developed which permit correct prediction of the form of the root word in virtually all Indo-European languages. By use of these rules linguists have constructed "Proto-Indo-European," the original "language" from which all other Indo-European languages developed. For example, English *wheel* and Russian *koleso* both trace to Indo-European *kwelos*, which in turn can be retraced to English *cycle* through Greek *kuklos*. *Beef* and *cow* come originally from Indo-European *gwous*, one through Latin *bōs, bovis*, and the other through Old English *cū*. All Indo-European languages have common words for natural phenomena—*night, star, dew, snow, wind, thunder,* and *fire*; for animals—*hound, goat, ewe, ox, steer,* and *sow*; for parts of a house—*door, timber,* and *thatch*; for primary family relationships—*father, mother, brother,* and *sister*; and for parts of the human body.

These common words evoke an interesting picture of the primitive common culture from which Western civilization may have developed [Potter, 1960]. Indo-European may never have existed as a single language, but dialects very like it apparently did. It was originally localized to a small region of southern Russia and spread throughout much of the Western world. Approximately half the world's population now speaks one or another of the Indo-European languages; the next largest language group is Sino-Tibetan.

Modern English has roughly 40 different elementary speech sounds, or *phonemes*. Most other modern languages also have about this number of basic sounds. The sounds may, of course, be quite different in different languages—so much so that it is impossible for most adults learning a second language to master pronunciation completely. The next largest unit of analysis of language is the *morpheme*, the smallest units of speech that have meaning. Words are made up of one or more morphemes. In English the 40 phonemes are combined into a vocabulary of approximately 1 million words. In spite of this enormous potential vocabulary, 60 percent of the average person's speech consists of 120 words. Indeed, language is extremely redundant and predictable. A great many common words can be omitted, particularly when they are used in certain sequences, without any loss of meaning or communication.

Our immediate concern here is the manner in which human beings acquire and use language, the field of *psycholinguistics*. The more traditional approach in psychology stems from reinforcement learning theory, most elaborately treated by Skinner [1957]. The basic idea is that as the young infant babbles random speech sounds his parents and others around him reinforce certain of these sounds that resemble the appropriate language words. Hence the infant develops a simple approximate vocabulary, and by the same principle comes to use simple sentences. Skinner notes that the earliest statements of the child are in the nature of commands or demands, which he terms *mands*. These are generally subject to rather immediate reinforcement; "bata" results in the child's

THOUGHT AND LANGUAGE

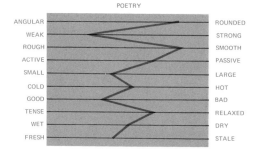

FIGURE 14-14   *The ratings made by a single subject for the meaning of the word "poetry" on a standard Semantic Differential Form [Deese, 1970].*

getting his bottle. At a somewhat later stage the child becomes more influenced by social approval, via reinforcement sequences, and learns responses that have a more subtle relationship to the world. These are termed *tacts*, from verbal contact with the world. The third and more complex class of utterances in Skinner's theory is the *intraverbal*—statements or terms that become conditioned to verbal stimuli. As an over-simplified example, "ball!" from a young child is a mand meaning "I want the ball"; "ball red" may be a simple tact describing a ball; and in "ball round," "round" might be an intraverbal. Skinner envisages the development of adult language from these elementary phenomena and the overriding influence of reinforcement—that is, reward and non-reward—first direct and later social. It is not possible to do justice to Skinner's interesting treatment here; he derives at least some features of the real complexity of adult language from these simple principles.

A somewhat different form of reinforcement-theory approach to one aspect of language, the nature of meaning, is Osgood's [1952] *mediation theory* of meaning, derived in part from Clark Hull's reinforcement theory of learning. It is not a general theory of language, but rather an analysis of connotative meaning—a way of measuring what words connote or signify to people. It is not fundamentally different from Skinner's view concerning reinforcement. However, Osgood assumes that some fraction of the learned verbal response to a specific object stimulus can later be made independently of the stimulus—that is, this fraction has abstract meaning. Large-scale rating studies of words led to the development of what Osgood calls the *semantic differential.* The meaning of words can be classified as *evaluative*—good-bad, beautiful-ugly, pleasant-unpleasant; *activity*—fast-slow, active-passive; and *potency*—strong-weak, masculine-feminine, hard-soft. The learned meaning of a word can be determined by its rating on each of these three dimensions. In actually rating a word, the subject judges it on a number of scales, as indicated in Fig. 14-14, and the three dimensions are then derived by statistical analysis. These three dimensions of meaning seem to occur in the major Indo-European languages and many Oriental tongues as well. The semantic differential is not only a useful device for analyzing how people evaluate words, but also appears to provide some insight into what it is that people mean by "meaning."

A quite different view of the genesis of language has been developed by some modern linguists, particularly Chomsky [1957; 1965;

395

1968]. According to this *generative theory*, characterized as *the* psycho-linguistics by some of its disciples, a universal language—or, more properly, a deep structure of universal syntax—exists in all men, and all specific languages are merely variations on this underlying theme or language structure. In essence, this view holds that we can learn much in general terms about the human mind by the study of the universal deep structure of language [Deese, 1970, pp. 10–11] :

Consider the hapless child trying to learn the sounds of his native language. How can he possibly learn to distinguish among speech sounds by their physical characteristics when carefully trained adults cannot do so under the best of laboratory conditions? In fact, the child does not simply discriminate among the speech sounds he hears. He invents a distinction and then, as a kind of hypothesis, applies that distinction to the signals he hears. If his hypothesis makes order among the signals he hears, he accepts that distinction as part of the language he is to "acquire."

From where do these invented distinctions arise? From a theory of language, or from a universal grammar? A child has as part of his native equipment a device embodying a linguistic theory of a high degree of complexity. That device enables him to perform analyses of the sounds that he hears. By applying the theory he possesses he can form an account of the language he hears in his particular culture. Eventually he learns how to interpret the language of his culture and to use it himself. It is clear that this process is not what we ordinarily mean by learning.

That children must have some inborn capacity for linguistic analysis is astounding, of course, and seems too radical for some psychologists to accept. At times this notion has been misinterpreted; it sometimes has been interpreted to suggest that each child has an inborn capacity for a particular language, or an inborn ability to speak a certain language. The capacity is aroused by the speech of adults, much as certain instinctive acts in young animals are aroused by stimuli provided by their parents. In fact, however, something much more abstract and difficult than language itself is innate. It is something that is best described as a universal grammar or as a device for producing language.

Because a universal grammar is innate, the study of grammar occupies a central position in modern psycholinguistic studies. While meaning, stylistic variations in use of language, and other matters are important, the basic concern of psycholinguistics is the nature of grammar, particularly those aspects of grammar that are universal. Some aspects of grammar are universal for superficial reasons. These are respects in which languages are alike simply as a matter of historical accident or for some other superficial reason. There are, in addition, deep reasons why all languages have basically the same structure, and these are of central importance to the psychology of language.

The generative theory of language does not mean to imply that there is or was some original universal language spoken by all primitive mankind, although scholars of a much earlier day did seriously consider this possibility. King James I of England proposed, with characteristic

THOUGHT AND LANGUAGE

directness, to settle the issue by having a group of newborn infants raised on an uninhabited island of the Hebrides with a deaf-and-dumb Scottish nanny. His own opinion was that the children would all grow up to speak Hebrew. What generative theory does imply is a kind of universal syntax, the deep grammatical structure which shapes all languages.

Much of the evidence for the generative theory comes from very complex linguistic analyses [Chomsky, 1968; Deese, 1970] ; there have been few experimental studies as yet. In one study Mehler and Carey [1967] compared the perception of sentences that differ in surface structure and those that differ in deep structure. For example, "John is easy to please" and "It is easy to please John" have the same deep grammatical structure, but differing surface structure, whereas "John is easy to please" and "John is eager to please" have the same surface structure but differ in deep structure. When subjects were given a series of sentences having the same deep structure and then one sentence having a different deep structure, the difference was more difficult to perceive than differences in surface structure. Experiments with children are perhaps more convincing. Deese [1970] has reviewed studies on linguistic performance of Japanese, English, and Russian children at comparable stages of language development and finds that although the adult languages differ markedly, children develop basically the same simplified deep structure in early language use. For example, English has a relatively fixed word order and Russian does not, but both English and Russian children develop initially the same simple fixed word order. In a careful observational analysis of the child's acquisition of grammar between the ages of one and three, Brown and Bellugi [1964] demonstrated that children develop the general rules for speaking English without training. An example familiar to all parents is the use of regular forms for irregular verbs, "I digged a hole!" Children know the rule for forming the past tense of words such as "dig" even though it has not been taught, and they persist in applying it even after numerous corrections. Brown and Bellugi conclude that "the very intricate simultaneous differentiation and integration that constitutes the evolution of the noun phrase is more reminiscent of the biological development of an embryo than it is of the acquisition of a conditioned reflex."

The generative theory of language, to the extent that it is true, has interesting implications for the neural basis of language; there must be an innate biological representation of the abstract structures of language wired into the brain. Lenneberg [1967] has discussed the biological foundations of language and develops some of the evidence for the view that there is no inherent variation in the basic characteristics of human language. Although particular sounds differ in different languages, each language has about 40 different sounds. The deep structure of all languages is the same. All children appear to develop

THE NEURAL BASIS OF LANGUAGE

397

the same initial universal deep grammar. In addition, there is no evidence of evolution or development of languages. All languages have the same degree of complexity; of course, they change over time, but they do not tend to become either more simple or more complex as a result of such changes.

A most important indirect kind of evidence concerns the plasticity of language development in children. A young child can learn a second language with no trace of an accent; an adult cannot. Even more important, if the dominant hemisphere for speech (the left hemisphere for the right-handed) is damaged in the young child, he will subsequently develop perfectly normal speech. However, if the damage occurs after about the age of twelve, he will have some degree of permanent speech defect.

Perhaps the most informative evidence about the biological basis of language comes from the study of *aphasia*, impairment of language behavior following brain damage. Although authorities disagree on the details of localization of the speech areas in the human cortex, the overall picture seems clear [Penfield, 1969]. A diagram of the dominant hemisphere of the human brain is shown in Fig. 14-15; it is damage on the dominant side that produces aphasia. Although this is always the left hemisphere in right-handed people, it may be either the left or the right hemisphere in left-handed persons. This is itself an intriguing fact, since the early signs of handedness and language development seem to occur at about the same time in infancy. However, there is not an invariable correspondence in the development of the individual. For example, if there is injury in early childhood to the left cortical hand area which controls the right hand, the child becomes left-handed, but the speech area remains in the left hemisphere. There may, however, be a correspondence between hand use and the development of language in evolutionary terms.

Of the three speech areas in the dominant hemisphere, the superior area is the least important. Aphasia following its removal does not continue for more than a few weeks. The anterior speech area, discovered by Broca, is next in importance and lies just anterior to and below the region of the motor cortex controlling tongue and throat (compare Fig. 14-15 and Fig. 8-14). Removal of this area results in severe aphasia, but it generally clears up over a period of months to years in the adult. Removal of the posterior speech cortex, *Warnicke's area*, which forms a large portion of the posterior association cortex in the dominant hemisphere, results in permanent aphasia in adults.

The effects of damage to these regions in young children are dramatically different. If the posterior speech area is destroyed before the age of twelve, the child who has already developed language will become completely aphasic, but after about a year he will begin to speak again and will in all likelihood learn language perfectly. After the age of twelve there is no relearning of speech. Note that this corresponds to the age limit for learning a second language without accent.

Electrical stimulation of the dominant-hemisphere speech areas in the conscious adult produces a temporary aphasia that lasts only as

398

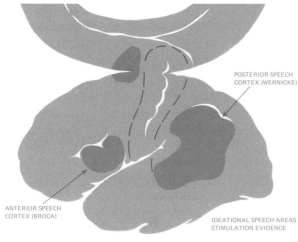

FIGURE 14-15   *Speech areas of the cerebral cortex in the dominant hemisphere of the human brain. Compare with locations of sensory and motor areas shown in Fig. 8-14. [Penfield and Roberts, 1959]*

POSTERIOR SPEECH
CORTEX (WERNICKE)

ANTERIOR SPEECH
CORTEX (BROCA)

IDEATIONAL SPEECH AREAS
STIMULATION EVIDENCE

long as the stimulus is applied. The electrical stimulus acts as an interference with normal function in these areas. This contrasts with the effects of stimulating the sensory cortex; if the visual area is so stimulated, the subject does not report interference with vision, but instead sees "lights." Localization of the speech areas mapped out by electrical-stimulation-produced aphasia agrees well with the evidence from the effects of brain damage.

The area in the *non*dominant hemisphere that corresponds to the posterior speech area is not normally involved in language behavior, but rather seems to be involved in awareness of spatial relations. As noted earlier (see Chapter 7), these areas in both monkey and man seem to subserve complex visual discriminations. Penfield [1969] discovered that when a young child learns to speak again after destruction of the speech area in the dominant hemisphere, the speech mechanism is found newly established in the speech area of the other hemisphere. It is as though in normal development the posterior association area in one hemisphere develops the neural substrate of language and the same area on the other side comes to code spatial relations. After these differing functions have been developed, they cannot be changed.

The fact that the essential speech area is limited to a particular region of association cortex in one hemisphere has significant implications concerning the neural basis of language. Many authorities believe complex learning involves the entire nervous system—at least the higher regions, including the cerebral cortex. However, the most important and complex learning man does, the learning of language, seems to be coded in a very specific area. Language learning may differ fundamentally from other forms of learning. The generative theory of language implies a genetically determined neuronal matrix which provides a universal grammar for all mankind. The structural basis of such a universal grammar may exist in the predetermined organization of the posterior speech area of the human cerebral cortex.

399

SUMMARY

Thought and language are, indeed, the most complex and important activities of man. The study of thinking includes two broad areas of research—nondirected thought and directed thought, such as problem solving and concept formation. The more general aspects of thinking include the distinction between conscious and unconscious thought processes. Daydreaming and fantasy, aspects of nondirected thought, can be categorized with regard to content as general, self-recriminating, objective, poorly controlled, autistic, and neurotic. Autistic thought, which characterizes schizophrenia, is typically disordered and illogical. Directed thinking occurs even in such lowly animals as the rat, as evidenced by the delayed-reaction task. However, more complex types of solutions, as in the *umweg* problem or *learning set*, occur only in higher animals. Concepts can be developed by lower animals as well as by man. They may develop extremely rapidly, as in insight learning, or only with much problem-solving practice, as in learning the concept of oddity.

Human conceptual behavior involves the use of strategies, or conceptual rules, in order to group or categorize objects or experiences on the basis of stimulus attributes. Examples include the conjunctive rule, in which two stimulus attributes define the correct concept; the disjunctive rule, which requires one or another attribute for the correct concept; and a relational rule, which requires a comparison of stimuli independent of absolute stimulus attributes. Another type of strategy is the TOTE system, in which incoming perceptual data are compared to existing hypotheses. The related phenomena of problem solving involve strategies such as deductive and inductive logic to arrive at the solutions to problems. Computer simulation of problem solving promises to provide interesting examples of the way in which human problem solving takes place.

Theories of thought emphasize peripheral or central processes. The extreme peripheral theory, suggesting that thought is nothing more than subvocal speech, has been discounted by the evidence that even a completely paralyzed person is capable of thinking. It appears that the association areas of the cerebral cortex are intimately involved in higher mental processes, with the frontal regions more involved in thought in time and the posterior regions involved in complex sensory discriminations and learning set. Simple concepts or perceptions may be coded by single cells in these areas, by groups of cells, or by both. Interwoven with the study of thought processes is the study of language and its development. Communication among members of a species may take the form of release of chemical pheromones, elaborate movements and gestures, or vocalizations. Many types of communication can be understood by more than a single species, although language as understood and used by humans cannot be learned by other animals, except perhaps in a nonvocal form such as sign language.

The formal study of language, linguistics, has revealed many similarities among the more than 2000 different languages in use today.

The largest and best known family of related languages, the Indo-European family, includes most of the modern languages of the Western world. The study of the way in which humans acquire and use language is called psycholinguistics. Reinforcement theorists have argued that the acquisition of patterns of communication is shaped and maintained by reinforcement from parents and others around the child. According to the mediation theory of meaning, the meanings of words (responses) are to some extent independent of the objects they might represent. The semantic differential analyzes these meanings into three broad categories—evaluative, activity, and potency. The generative theory of language development suggests that there is a universal deep grammatical structure in all human language.

The study of aphasia has provided evidence that specific areas of the brain control language. Damage to one of the three speech areas on the dominant side of the cerebral hemispheres causes aphasia, which may be permanent, as in the case of damage to the posterior speech area, or temporary, as in the case of damage to the superior speech area or the anterior speech area.

CHAPTER FIFTEEN

MAN: A SOCIAL ANIMAL

In the most general sense the study of man is the study of how we human beings relate, or fail to relate, to each other. Hermits are clearly in the minority in our society. Most of us, by necessity and by choice, have daily dealings with other human beings. In our daily activities we talk to and listen to others, we think about others, make plans to be with others or sometimes to avoid them. We love, we hate, and sometimes we kill other human beings. Even when we are alone our behavior is constantly guided by social factors. We eat socially acceptable foods, wear stylish clothes, and use socially proper drugs. What we mean by "acceptable," "stylish," and "socially proper," of course, varies. What is "groovy" or "cool" for a teenager is sometimes regarded as inappropriate by his parents—a fact that also guides much behavior. Thus, in one way or another, most of our behavior is influenced by what we think others will think about the way we behave. Our self-esteem depends on our appraisal of the reactions of others to us. Our feelings of security and accomplishment or of insecurity, inadequacy, and guilt

III

SOCIAL BEHAVIOR

all stem from our assessment of the approval or disapproval that we receive from others.

We live in a social environment and few, if any, of our experiences and activities lack social significance. It is perhaps not too surprising, then, that our major problems are social problems. While it is true that we form friendships, marry, and join social groups, it is also true that we discriminate against others, and participate in other forms of aggression such as riots and warfare.

We usually think of love, tenderness, and cooperation as human qualities and use the term "humane" to denote kind and considerate treatment, but human beings are equally capable of behaving inhumanely. The Nazi atrocities during World War II are cited as some kind of social insanity, but what of the "normal" atrocities of every war? Are the techniques of the Spanish Inquisition no longer in vogue? Although human cruelty and brutality are much easier to recognize at a distance—especially a distance in time—there is considerable evidence that many of us in all periods of history, including this one, have been specialists in inhumanity.

403

Unfortunately many "normal" human beings are perfectly capable of such behavior. In one study, for example, Milgram [1965] asked subjects to deliver electric shocks to others who were engaged in learning lists of nonsense syllables; they were to administer a shock every time an error was made. The person delivering the shock could not see the person receiving the shock, but saw only a red light indicating an error. There was in fact no other person learning nonsense syllables, but most of the subjects believed that there was, and they readily responded to the instructions to increase the shock level with each error. A dial indicated shock levels which ranged from "mild" through "painful" to "lethal." Almost one-third of the subjects administered shock levels which were at the lethal point on the dial. In a subsequent study the subjects were allowed to "hear" the responses of the punished subject. Of course, since there were no punished subjects, the responses were fake. As the level of the shock increased the subjects heard protests, followed by cries of pain and pounding on the wall, followed by screams, followed by silence (at "lethal" levels of shock). Even with these conditions a large percentage of the subjects complied with the experimenter's request to shock at the lethal level.

The experimenter who conducted these studies has been harshly criticized on ethical grounds. While concern for the well-being of individuals subjected to deceitful information and instruction is certainly justified, it is likely that much of the criticism stemmed from the nature of the findings. The degree of willingness of the subjects to comply with the requests made in these studies is not a particularly pleasant observation. The findings, however disturbing, may help us to understand why atrocities are so common. We need to know why it is that over 50 million human beings were killed by other human beings in the years between 1820 and 1945. We also need to know why we routinely subject each other to less lethal forms of punishment.

There are many approaches to the study of social behavior, and each contributes from a different perspective to our overall understanding. The Arab-Israeli conflict, for example, is rooted in history. It is maintained by cultural, economic, and political factors. However, the hatred and distrust that maintain it are expressed by *individual* Arabs and Jews and arise from individual attitudes and prejudices. Historical events have a bearing on behavior through their influences on the attitudes and resulting actions of individuals. The psychologist attempts to understand social interaction by examining the characteristics of individuals. From this perspective there are no special principles of social psychology. We assume that understanding what we are like as individual human beings will provide an understanding of the bases of social accord and social discord.

The social behavior of a cat is different from that of a dog, a horse, or a lion. In fact the social behavior of a species is as unique as its physical appearance. No amount of training can "socialize" a dog into behaving like a cat or a horse like a lion. So too is man's social behavior constrained by his biological characteristics. In fact much human social behavior makes sense only in terms of man's biological heritage [Cooper and McGaugh, 1963, p. 8] :

> The animal kingdom is composed of over a million species, of which man is but one. The underlying process common to all species is adaptation, and adaptation is accomplished in countless unique ways. In effecting adaptation, each species uses specialized processes and equipment, and the efficiency of its adaptation depends upon this interplay with the total environment. A truly comprehensive view of social man is possible only if we are willing to stand back and view him as part of this vast picture of adaptation struggle. While it is true that we cannot hope to understand man's social-psychological nature unless we study him in his own right and at his own level, it is also true that a healthy appreciation for the comparative perspective will assist immeasurably in this attempt.

Biological characteristics account both for man's similarities to other animals and for his differences from other animals. For example, human social behavior depends heavily on language and the use of abstract symbols. This is possible only because of the evolution of specialized neural processes. Because of this we differ greatly from most animals, including the great apes. In many ways, however, our social behavior is like that of other animals and is subject to the same influences. As we saw in Chapters 3 and 4, the development of love is similar in monkeys and men. Our motives are also similar in many ways to those of other animals. We want food, water, sex—and the fulfillment of these wants usually involves social behavior. In fact the parallels between infrahuman and human social behavior are sometimes striking. Although female chimpanzees ordinarily do not permit mating unless they are in the estrous period of their hormonal cycle, they have been observed to permit mating by male chimpanzees in order to get food away from the male. Apparently the "oldest profession" was practiced long before man appeared on the scene.

Since we are in constant danger of annihilating the human species through warfare, we have an urgent need to know why it is that we have such difficulty getting along with other residents of this planet. A number of theorists contend that the roots of human aggression also lie in man's biological heritage—that in order to survive man evolved the physiological processes which were essential for living under dangerous and hostile conditions. Thus, much of our physiological machinery is *atavistic*. Our emotional responses of fear and anger evolved under conditions in which living depended on the ability to flee or fight. With the advent of civilization there is less need for such emotional responses, but having evolved, they remain with us.

Some writers consider the changing social conditions brought about by the rapidly increasing population density particularly significant. In his book *The Territorial Imperative* Ardrey [1966] argues that man, like other animals, is a territorial animal, and that the biologically based imperative to acquire and defend territory accounts for much of man's aggressive behavior [Ardrey, 1966, p. 236] :

The territorial imperative is as blind as a cave fish, as consuming as a furnace, and it commands beyond logic, opposes all reason, suborns all moralities, strives for no goal more sublime than survival. [One must bear in mind] that the territorial principle motivates all of the human species . . . whether we approve or disapprove, whether we like it or we do not, it is a power as much an ally of our enemies as it is of ourselves and our friends. The principle cause of modern warfare arises from the failure of an intruding power correctly to estimate the defensive resources of their territorial defender.

A related view is expressed by Morris. In *The Human Zoo* [1969] , he argues that many of the problems of modern man are caused by his inability to adapt to the requirements of urban living. The conditions under which man evolved as a species differ dramatically from those under which he must now live; hence his predicament is much like that of animals in zoos [Morris, 1969, p. 8] :

Under normal conditions, in their natural habitats, wild animals do not mutilate themselves, masturbate, attack their offspring, develop stomach ulcers, become fetishes, suffer from obesity, form homosexual-paired bonds, or commit murder. Among human city dwellers, needless to say, all of these things occur. Does this, then, reveal the basic differences between the human species and other animals? At first glance it seems to do so. But this is deceptive. Other animals do behave in these ways under certain circumstances, namely when they are confined in the unnatural conditions of captivity. The zoo animal in a cage exhibits all these abnormalities that we know so well from our human companions. Clearly, then, the city is not a concrete jungle, it is a human zoo.

Although these speculations are perhaps somewhat simplistic, they are important points to bear in mind as we examine human social behavior. Such views were in fact presaged by Darwin's conviction that emotional reactions evolved in response to environmental requirements. In his book *The Expression of the Emotions in Man and Animals* [1872] he presented evidence that our emotional responses, as evidenced, for example, in facial expressions, are similar to those observed in lower animals (see Fig. 15-1). The circumstances which cause our hair to "stand on end" (piloerection) are not terribly different from those that cause hair erection in dogs and cats.

Our emotional states are accompanied by obvious physiological responses such as blushing, as well as by other, more subtle responses. We do not ordinarily reveal our social attitudes, especially our dislikes of others, by attacking behavior. However, we do respond emotionally to others, and these responses are accompanied by subtle physiological changes. Emotional responses are accompanied by a lowering of the resistance of the skin to a weak electric current. This change in resistance

FIGURE 15–1   *Facial expressions of animals, drawn from life by Mr. Wood [Darwin, 1872].*

is termed the *galvanic skin response* (*GSR*). Cooper [1959] has shown that social attitudes can be assessed by measuring the GSR. Prejudice is accompanied by emotional responses, and hence under some conditions the GSR can be used to measure prejudice. In one experiment subjects were read four brief statements, a derogatory and a complimentary statement about a group that they disliked and a derogatory and a complimentary statement about a group that they liked. For example, one of the derogatory statements was, "People can be divided into two groups, the good and the bad. Close to the bottom of the list are the. . . . They certainly can be said to have caused more trouble for humanity than they are worth." One of the complimentary statements was, "The world over, no single group of people has done as much for us, for our civilization, as the. . . . The world will undoubtedly come to recognize them as honest, wise and completely unselfish." As the statements were read, the subjects were instructed to think about them, but not to respond verbally to them. Similar statements were also made about groups toward which the subjects had neutral attitudes. The results were striking. In 19 of 20 subjects the GSR was greater for complimentary statements about the disliked groups than for complimentary statements about neutral groups. Moreover, in 14 out of 20 cases the GSR was greater for derogatory statements about liked groups than for derogatory statements about neutral groups. In another study Cooper used

407

comparable procedures to measure attitudes toward various ethnic groups. The GSRs were found to correlate highly with other measures of attitude obtained from conventional attitude tests—that is, tests which rely on the subject's verbal statements about his feelings regarding different ethnic groups.

Clearly our attitudes toward other individuals are accompanied by strong emotional responses. We do not merely think about others; we "feel" about them as well. Social behavior is laden with emotion. This knowledge can help us understand why it is that social interaction can be so complex. Apparently it is not possible for us to be unemotional about other human beings, or groups of human beings, that we like or dislike—and the biological aspects of prejudice are as real and important as the biological aspects of hunger and thirst.

Our emotional responses can also *influence* our attitudes toward social objects. For example, in an interesting study (Valins, 1966), male subjects viewed slides of attractive seminude females and were given evidence that they reacted emotionally to some of the slides. This was done by allowing the subjects to hear heartbeats which they thought were their own. It was found that the slides accompanied by (false) heart-rate increases were better liked than those where no change occurred. This preference was still evident on a second test a month later. This result indicates that our emotional reaction to something, even if extraneous, influences our evaluation of it. In a later experiment [Valins and Ray, 1967] it was shown that people could be made to respond less fearfully to a frightening object if they were led to believe (falsely) that they had *not* reacted emotionally to cues of it. These studies clearly show that emotional behavior is complex. We still do not know very much about the biological bases of social behavior, but what we do know indicates that a biological approach may be fruitful.

SOCIALIZATION

Socialization refers to all the processes which help to mold the individual so that his behavior is acceptable to the society in which he lives. Thus socialization is the process of making socially acceptable human beings— a process that starts on the day of birth and continues until the day of death. Socialization is continuous throughout life, because as we age the socializing influences change and the behavior and attitudes that are expected of us change. As Bugelski has commented [1956, p. 1]:

From infancy on, the to-be-civilized human being is subjected to a training process calculated to make him an acceptable member of society. He is taught where and when to sleep, eat, wash behind the ears, read, write, and calculate, to earn his living, and to grow old gracefully, or die nobly, depending upon how the great divisions of society are getting along with each other at the time.

Socializing influences are, of course, not always explicit. In fact most often they are not. The human mother is about as knowledgeable as the monkey mother concerning the way in which her treatment of an infant will influence the child's later behavior. Furthermore, explicit socialization techniques are not always effective. The parent knows much less than the animal trainer about how behavior can be shaped through rewards and punishments. Obviously socialization occurs. We are moderately—and only moderately—successful in developing the young of our society into effective members. Much of the success is clearly accidental. We do not yet know what makes good parents and teachers. Beyond that we exercise little formal control over major sources of socializing influences such as that provided by peers and by communications media. The television set constantly tells our children (and us) what they are to think, want, and expect and provides examples of behavior which can be used to obtain what is wanted. The young of our society have learned through television that, contrary to what parents may say, aggression is commonplace, accepted, and often rewarded and that killing is acceptable under some, if not most, circumstances. Furthermore, there is a great discrepancy between what we say we are like and what we actually appear to be, as reflected on the television screen. These messages, however subtle, are not lost in the young of our society (see Chapter 5).

Thus, although socialization may begin at home, where it is well under the control of parents, particularly the mother, it is not at all clear that influences from the home constitute the *major* socializing influence. One can become socialized into a society without conforming to the behavior expected by one's elders, a fact which constitutes a major source of anxiety for the adults in our society. Parents want their children to "turn out like us," and then become distressed when they do not. Changes in a society's values are most readily reflected in the young and in a rapidly and continually changing society discrepancies between the attitudes and values of parents and those of their children are likely to be great.

DEVELOPMENT OF ATTITUDES

It is at home that children first develop their attitudes toward different aspects of their worlds. However, as Krech and Crutchfield have pointed out [1948, pp. 181–182]:

> [To say that parents are important in shaping attitudes] is not equivalent to saying that the child will take over attitudes and beliefs ready made from the parents. The influence is possible, but whether the child will develop . . . the same beliefs as [those held by its parents] . . . depends upon the importance and meaning of that belief for the child. . . . In some instances the effect of the parents' influence can be seen to account for the rise of a belief or attitude that is in opposition to the parents' belief.

Studies of the attitudes of college students and their parents indicate a moderate but significant relationship; generally the correlation coefficients range from about +.30 to +.60, depending on the attitude being measured [Hirschberg and Gilliland, 1942]. There is evidence that the degree of similarity varies with the attitude of the child toward the parent. College students who have unfavorable attitudes toward their parents tend to have social ideologies which are quite dissimilar from those of their parents, while in students who have favorable attitudes toward their parents there tends to be less of a discrepancy [Cooper and Blair, 1959].

It seems clear that exposure to parental attitudes is not enough to ensure their adoption by children. If the attitudes of the parents are consistent with those of other segments of society, the likelihood of similarity in attitude is increased.

Some of our attitudes are based on firsthand information. This fact is so obvious that we may be led to believe that information provides the basis for all of our attitudes. We may like ice cream because we know how it tastes, and we may like certain sports because we find them exciting. Social attitudes, however, are often based on the prevailing attitudes of the society. The attitudes adopted are very likely to be those to which the child is exposed. For example, actual contact with minority-group members is unnecessary for the development of unfavorable attitudes toward such groups. Radke and Sutherland [1949] reported highly developed prejudices toward Jews and blacks in Midwestern children who had had little if any contact with members of either group. In fact Rosenblith [1949] found that in a region of South Dakota where there were no Jews or blacks at all, prejudice scores were higher than those in areas where there had been extensive contact with both.

Experience with minority-group members is not any guarantee of favorable attitudes toward them. In a classical study of the development of attitudes toward blacks Horowitz [1936] found that boys from New York City were about as prejudiced as were children from Southern states. On the basis of these findings Horowitz concluded [1936, pp. 34–35]:

It has been found necessary to contradict many of the oft-repeated cliches current in the discussion of the race problem. Young children [are] not devoid of prejudice; contact with a "nice" Negro is not a universal panacea; living as neighbors, going to a common school, were found to be insufficient; Northern children were found to differ very, very slightly from Southern children. It seems that attitudes toward Negroes are now chiefly determined not by contact with Negroes, but by contact with the prevalent attitude toward Negroes.

Of course much has happened in our society since 1936. Nevertheless the general conclusion is probably still valid. This finding clearly poses a formidable problem for our democratic society. Since most of our social problems grow out of our emotion-laden attitudes, it is highly unlikely that the problems can be dealt with adequately without changing the attitudes which have led to their development and continue to support them.

Most of our social conflicts grow out of dislike for other humans, but fortunately we also sometimes like our fellow man. What factors influence social attraction among individuals? What is it that attracts us to one person rather than another? It is only recently that social psychologists have begun systematically to search for variables affecting the social attraction of one individual to another.

SOCIAL ATTRACTION

For the young of many species affiliation with mature species members, especially the mother, is virtually a prerequisite for survival. Imprinting provides a mechanism by which chicks or ducklings are directed to exhibit affiliative behavior toward the imprinted object, and the clinging responses of infant monkeys help to ensure that they will remain within the protective grasp of their mothers for appropriate periods of time. There is strong evidence that for most species, including humans, unlearned response patterns account for much of the affiliative behavior exhibited in early postnatal development.

Through the processes of socialization affiliative responses, initially reflex in nature and directed toward the most readily available social agent, gradually come to be discriminatively directed toward specific members of the social group. In Chapter 3 and 4 we examined the processes by which the infant monkey's social behavioral repertoire expands beyond initial relationships with the mother to include the peer and subsequently the heterosexual affectional systems. By adulthood affiliative responses constitute only a fraction of an individual's social repertoire, and exhibition of such responses is, of course, no longer controlled by reflex activity alone. Animal research is enormously useful as a basic model of similar development in humans. However, the adult human organism leads an exceptionally complex social life. Although maternal love, for example, is undoubtedly a prerequisite, the basis of specific social preferences of the adult is not fully explicable in terms of such global concepts. We turn now to a consideration of some of the factors which influence the attraction of individuals to other individuals.

SIMILARITY

It is consistently found that the more similar individuals are in attitudes and interests, the more they are inclined to like each other. For example, in one study [Byrne, 1961] subjects were asked to fill out question-

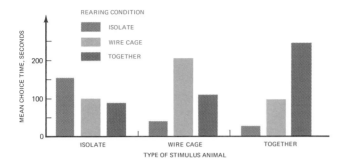

FIGURE 15-2   *Social preference and similarity of rearing condition for young rhesus monkeys [Pratt and Sackett, 1967].*

naires rating certain attitudes and interests, such as political positions and hobbies. At a later date the same subjects were asked to "score" similar questionnaires supposedly filled out by others. In reality the questionnaires had been prepared to be either very similar, slightly similar, or very dissimilar to the subjects' own ratings. The subjects were then asked to indicate how much they thought they would like the individual whose questionnaire they had scored. A surprisingly strong relationship between perceived similarity and expressed attraction was disclosed. Other studies of the attitudes and interests of good friends as opposed to casual acquaintances or people who were not friends have quite consistently shown that the more people like each other, the more similar they tend to be.

Highly similar results are found with rhesus monkeys. Pratt and Sackett [1967] found that when monkeys reared in social isolation, in individual cages, or in the presence of peers were allowed to choose among an isolate-reared, a cage-reared, or a peer-reared stimulus monkey, isolates tended to prefer isolates, cage-reared preferred cage-reared, and peer-reared preferred peer-reared stimulus animals (see Fig. 15-2). In this study similarity of rearing experience was clearly the primary factor in social preference. In another monkey study [Suomi et al., 1970] normal monkeys and monkeys with frontal lobectomies (with the frontal lobes of their brains surgically removed) were allowed to choose between normal and lobectomized monkeys either of their own or of the opposite sex (see Fig. 15-3). In choosing between animals of their own sex the lobectomized animals displayed no preference, while the controls preferred lobectomized animals. However, in choosing between animals of the opposite sex the lobectomized animals chose lobectomized partners, while the normal animals chose to be with normal animals. In their discussion of these findings Suomi et al. commented [1970, p. 452] :

[As the monkeys] . . . had not personally observed the operations performed on their peers we must assume that their choices were made on the basis of observed behavioral differences. . . . The specific nature of these differences . . . are known only to the monkey subjects themselves.

It is obvious that monkeys are quite capable of discriminating among monkeys that look the same to human observers and, moreover, they apparently have good reasons for making the choices they do. The suggestion is that in some way monkeys are probably more knowledgeable observers of behavior than are humans—which need not be taken as a blow to an experimenter's pride. After all, they have had a bit more experience than we.

The assumption that likes attract likes underlies the computer-dating industry. Of course, as even monkeys probably know, perceived similarity is not all there is to social attraction, particularly the attraction to someone of the opposite sex. This fact was made abundantly clear by the results of one study using computerized matching of chance partners. Walster et al. [1966] arranged a computerized-date dance with partners matched for varying degrees of similarity. Partner attraction was measured both during the dance and in several followup questioning periods over the succeeding three months. The experimenters found, perhaps to their surprise, that perceived similarity to one's date had very little effect on attraction. They did discover, perhaps to no one else's surprise, that physical attractiveness of one's date had a whopping effect on how much the date was liked.

Of course the factors that influence attraction to dance partners are likely to be different from those influencing social attraction under different conditions.

Often we want to associate with others who have shared or will share similar experiences. People who are generally happy may not wish to relate to those who are depressed, and people in a festive mood usually choose not to mingle with those who are not. There is experimental support for the adage that misery loves company. In one study, for example, Schachter [1959] told female college students either that they would be subjected to mildly painful electric shock or that they would engage in a nonstressful task. All subjects were then told that they would

FIGURE 15–3 *Social choices of normal monkeys and monkeys with frontal lobectomies [Suomi et al., 1970].*

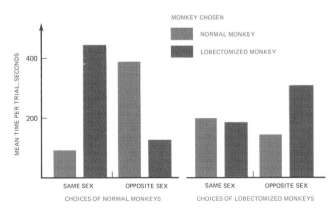

SOCIAL BEHAVIOR

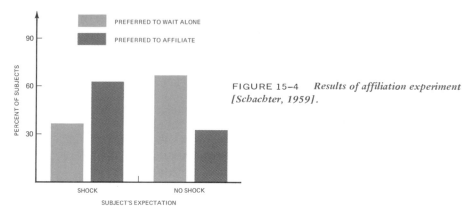

PREFERRED TO WAIT ALONE

PREFERRED TO AFFILIATE

FIGURE 15-4   *Results of affiliation experiment [Schachter, 1959].*

have to wait a few minutes before the experiment began and were asked to indicate whether they preferred to wait alone or in a room with other people. After the subjects had indicated their preferences the experiment was finished. Subjects who thought they were about to be shocked showed a greater tendency to wait with others than did subjects who did not anticipate shock (see Fig. 15-4).

In another study, also of female college students, all subjects were told that the experiment in which they were to participate involved electric shock, that they would have to wait before the experiment began, and that they had the choice of waiting either alone or in a room with others. If they chose to wait with others, they could elect to wait with other subjects who were waiting for the experiment to begin, with other subjects who had supposedly already been through the experiment, or with a group of people not involved in the experiment. Among those subjects who indicated a preference for waiting with others rather than alone, the overwhelming choice was to wait with people who were themselves about to be shocked. Apparently "miserable people seek out miserable company." In a third study Schachter found that if subjects were moderately anxious about the impending shock experiment, they preferred to affiliate with others who were also moderately anxious rather than those who were either extremely anxious or scarcely anxious at all. The adage can be further refined—"miserable people seek out miserable company who are about as miserable as themselves."

Why is it that people experiencing stress or anxiety tend to seek out others who share their predicament? To begin with, this finding is not limited to affiliation arising from emotive factors. Several studies have demonstrated that under appropriate conditions people will also choose to affiliate with others whose beliefs or abilities are similar. These observations have led to general theoretical interpretation termed *social comparison* [Festinger, 1954; Schachter, 1959; Latané, 1966]. According to this view, there exists in humans a tendency or need to evaluate one's abilities, opinions, and emotions, and in the absence of objective, nonsocial standards for comparison, people evaluate these elements by comparison with others. Hence a person who is unsure of his ability to perform a given task when objective standards are unavail-

414

able tends to affiliate with others who perform the same task. A person who is unsure of a belief or the validity of his emotional feelings will seek out others in a similar position in order to compare and evaluate his own beliefs and feelings.

According to social-comparison theory, people will select those whom they perceive to be relatively similar in the quality for which comparison is desired. For example, a moderately competent chess player will seek a partner who is neither a novice nor an expert, but rather someone in his own class. A member of the "silent majority" will tend to affiliate with politically moderate conservatives rather than with radicals or reactionaries. A patient awaiting minor surgery will prefer the company of others expecting an uncomplicated operation rather than the company of those merely taking a physical examination or those about to receive a heart transplant. Thus there is considerable evidence that birds of a feather do flock together.

Although perceived similarity is apparently a major factor in the way we choose to relate to others, another variable hypothesized to affect social attraction is *complementarity* of personality, or attraction of opposites. We might intuitively expect a sadist and a masochist to get along better together than either two sadists or two masochists, but there have been few studies of the variability of complementarity, probably because it is a difficult measure to define. There is some empirical support for the hypothesis. Married couples who are complementary in personality sometimes have stronger relationships than those who are not. However, the role of complementarity in influencing interpersonal relations has not yet been adequately studied.

PHYSICAL PROXIMITY

Common sense tells us that two people will rarely fall in love if they live 3000 miles apart and have never come into any sort of contact. However, the significance of functional proximity as a factor in determining the strength of social attraction is not so obvious. It may surprise some to learn that well over one-third of the urban marriages in this country are of couples who grew up less than six city blocks from each other.

One of the first empirical studies to emphasize the importance of proximity was a field experiment conducted by Festinger et al. [1950] in a newly constructed housing development, part of which consisted of two-story rectangular units with stairways at both ends. The experimenters collected data, by means of both questionnaires and personal interviews, from most families in the entire housing development when the development was first opened and over a period of many months afterward. On each of the surveys families were asked to name their best friends in the housing development. After an initial period of fluctuation, some consistent findings emerged. First, the nearer families lived to each other, the more likely they were to become close friends. Within each unit family 1 was more likely to be friends with

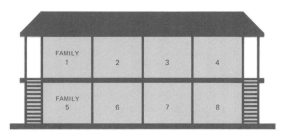

FIGURE 15-5   *Arrangement of apartments in two-story dwelling units [Festinger et al., 1963].*

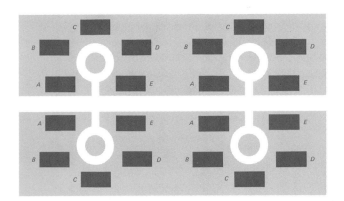

FIGURE 15-6   *Ground plan of housing units.*

family 2 than with family 3, and more likely to be friends with family 3 than with family 4 (see Fig. 15-5). Moreover, families living next to the staircase were significantly more popular (reported to be friends) than families living midway down the halls. Since all people on the second floor had to use the stairs to reach their doors, they would be more likely to meet people living next to the stairs than those living midway down the hall. The setup of apartment buildings is shown in Fig. 15-6. Families living in adjacent buildings were more likely to be friends than families living several buildings apart. Also, people living in units A and E tended to be more popular than those living in other units. Clearly functional proximity is an important determinant of social attraction. Similar findings were obtained in a study of the development of dormitory social relationships over a period of a year [Newcomb, 1961]. Proximity was positively related to degree of social attraction between individuals; roommates and floormates were more likely to be close friends than members of different dormitories.

Why should functional proximity affect social attraction? One possibility is that the closer two people are physically, the greater the opportunity for interaction. It is easier for people to become familiar with one another when they are physically close than when they are physically far apart. It is encouraging to know that people who live in relatively close proximity tend to like each other; it means that human relations are not altogether hopeless. However, whether familiarity will

416

lead to liking or breed contempt depends on many factors, including the nature of the people who come into contact with each other as well as the nature of the relationship. The ghetto resident who is constantly harassed by law-enforcement agencies will not necessarily come to like them. The high incidence of divorce also testifies to the fact that proximity and familiarity do not guarantee social attraction.

Another characteristic which influences social attraction is *rewardingness.* Simply put, people tend to like those who reward them with love or praise. Rewardingness is not an easy characteristic to assess, since what is rewarding to one person may be aversive to another. However, research has shown that people tend to like those who like them. Subjects report that it is usually reinforcing to be liked, and that they tend to prefer the pleasant company of those who like them rather than be with people who dislike them.

It has also been demonstrated that praise or criticism from an individual affects attraction to him. Subjects were placed in a group-discussion situation where they periodically received evaluations from group members concerning their contributions to the discussion [Aronson and Lindner, 1965]. The other members were paid confederates, and the evaluations were experimentally controlled. Some confederates consistently gave the subjects "positive feedback"; these people were generally liked by the subjects. Others consistently gave negative feedback, and not surprisingly, they were not as well liked. Other confederates played a traitor role; initially they gave the subject positive feedback and then switched and gave negative feedback. These people were the least liked of all. Finally, some confederates initially gave negative feedback and then switched to support of the subjects. These people were the most liked of all. Apparently being able to win over a dubious skeptic is more rewarding than receiving positive support from the outset.

Some cautions regarding the findings of the research on social attraction should be expressed at this point. First, most studies have attempted to hold all variables constant except the one in question. Thus we cannot conclude that rewardingness, for example, tends to enhance attraction; we can say only that all other variables being held constant, rewardingness tends to enhance attraction. This is an important distinction. Most of the research in this area has been on specific factors that may affect attraction. Relatively little work has been directed toward untying the complex interactions which certainly exist among the several variables. Second, much of the research is based on contrived and perhaps trivial social situations. We have much to learn about the bases of the formation and dissolution of attraction between people in real life situations.

417

CONFORMITY

Conformity is one of the most obvious and basic characteristics of social behavior. In the most general sense *conformity* refers to a person's tendency to behave like those around him. In a more specific sense it is the adherence to a norm of behavior set by a group [Jones and Gerard, 1967] —conformity to fashion tastes, conformity to styles of life, or even conformity to the act of being a nonconformist. The classical laboratory demonstration of conformity was performed by Asch [1951]. He presented a group of eight people with a slide of a line segment. He then flashed a second slide containing three line segments and asked each one to report verbally, in front of the rest, which of the three lines was most similar to the first line segment (see Fig. 15-7). After a specified number of the experimental trials each of the first seven people, who were in fact confederates rather than subjects, reported line *A* to be correct rather than the obviously correct line *B*. Asch was really interested in how the eighth person, the only real subject in the experiment, would respond. It is apparent from the figure that the subject was faced with an easy perceptual task. On earlier trials the consensus of the group had been in his favor, but suddenly everyone else was reporting the "wrong" answer. Asch found that in all such tests the subject showed a great deal of uneasiness, agitation, and hesitation before answering. Moreover, in approximately one-third of the cases the subject also reported the wrong answer as correct, in conformity to the answer given by the group.

This type of experiment has been replicated many times with exceptionally consistent findings. In some situations there appears to exist overwhelming pressure to conform to group norms, even when such conformity is clearly at odds with the subjects' own perceptions, attitudes, or beliefs. Further studies have isolated specific variables which tend to enhance or decrease the conformity behavior of subjects placed in the above situation. First, the size of the consensus group seems to be a factor. In the experiment above four confederates were needed to produce the maximum degree of subject conformity. With fewer than four the subjects were less likely to report conforming views, and more confederates than the "optimal four" did not result in sizable differences in either direction.

A second variable is status of the confederates. Subjects are more likely to conform when they perceive the group members to be equal to or higher than themselves in social status and less likely to conform when they view the group as below them in status. A related variable is "expertness" of the confederates. If, instead of line segments, the stimulus objects are mathematical equations, a subject is more likely to conform to the judgment of confederates purported to be math instructors than those introduced as art majors—that is, he is more likely to conform to the opinion of experts or authorities than to the opinion of novices.

A third variable found to affect tendency to conform is the difficulty of objective discrimination. For example, in the two situations

418

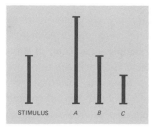

FIGURE 15-7   *Typical stimuli in Asch experimental paradigm.*

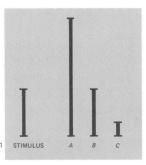

FIGURE 15-8   *Two Asch situations differing in difficulty of objective discrimination.*

SITUATION 1 STIMULUS   A   B   C

SITUATION 2 STIMULUS   A   B   C

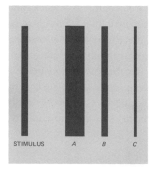

FIGURE 15-9   *Another typical Asch paradigm.*

shown in Fig. 15-8, segment *B* is the correct choice in both cases. However, subjects show a much greater rate of conformity to the group's choice of *A* in situation 2, where the distinction between *A* and *B* is much less extreme.

Other studies have focused on variables which decrease conformity in the Asch experimental situation. By far the greatest influence is the presence of other nonconforming members in the group. For example, when one of the seven confederates deviates from the group's decision, subject rate of conformity drops significantly. If two confederates deviate from the group's incorrect answer, virtually no subjects will go along with the incorrect evaluation. The presence of another nonconformer exerts a powerful effect even if he is dissenting to the correct answer to a problem. In Fig. 15-9, where the correct answer is obviously *B*, if all seven confederates choose *A*, then, as we have seen, the subject also tends to choose *A*. If one of the confederates chooses *B*, the subject is much more likely to make the correct choice of *B*. However, if one of the confederates chooses *C*, which is incorrect but also a nonconforming answer, the subject is less likely to agree with either the group or the dissenter and will tend to choose *B*.

419

It is interesting to note how the mere order of answering affects the manner in which subjects caught in an Asch situation evaluate the various confederates. For example, in a group of three confederates and one subject, where the subject is always the third person to answer and his judgment always differs from that of the three confederates, the subject consistently tends to evaluate the other members of his group as follows. The first confederate to choose a stimulus on each trial is seen as powerful but incompetent; he has the power to make the "right" choice and he invariably fails. The second person to answer is seen as a sniveling lackey, an insignificant yes-man who is too timid to disagree. The subject answers third. His evaluation of the fourth person, who follows him, is usually extremely negative. This person is a traitor who might have supported him but instead chose to lie and support the first two.

Some of the most extensive research on yielding to group pressure was conducted by Tuddenham. The stimuli were not restricted to simple line drawings, but dealt with various kinds of historical, geographic, economic, and social judgments. Many of the examples presented were sufficiently extreme or bizarre that there was relatively little subject conformity. Nevertheless, there were a few extreme yielders, individuals who made affirmative responses to extreme statements when they had to respond in the presence of others who had made affirmative responses. If they had yielded completely to all such statements, this is what they would have been agreeing to (I indicates an information item and O indicates an opinion item) [Tuddenham and MacBride, 1959, p. 260]:

[The United States] is largely populated by old people, 60 to 70% being over 65 years of age (I-1). These oldsters must almost all be women since male babies have a life expectancy of only 25 years (I-2). Though outlived by women, men tower over them in height, being 8 or 9 inches taller, on the average (I-4). This society is obviously preoccupied with eating, averaging six meals per day (I-5), this perhaps accounting for their agreement with the assertion, "I never seem to get hungry" (O-9). Americans waste little time on sleep, averaging only 4 to 5 hours a night (I-3), a pattern perhaps not unrelated to the statement that the average family includes 5 or 6 children (I-9). Nevertheless, there is no overpopulation problem, since the USA stretches 6,000 miles from San Francisco to New York (I-6). Although the economy is booming with an average wage of $5/hour (I-7), rather negative and dysphoric attitudes characterize the group, as expressed in their solidly rejecting the proposition, "any man who is able and willing to work hard has a good chance of succeeding" (O-3), and in agreeing with such statements as, "Most people would be better off if they never went to school at all" (O-5), "there is no use in doing things for such people, they don't appreciate it" (O-6), and "I cannot do anything well" (O-10). Such is the weird and wonderful picture of the world and of themselves allegedly entertained by the "others in the group."

Obviously some degree of conformity or compliance with the group is essential for adapting to a social environment. It is also probably useful in many circumstances, since the beliefs and opinions of one's peers are not always outrageous. Nevertheless, it is fortunate that most of us do not yield so readily to group pressure that we would share such extreme beliefs as those above.

GROUP PROCESSES AND LEADERSHIP

Loosely speaking, a *group* can be described as a collection of individuals. However, groups can have such an enormous range of size and purpose that it is difficult to make useful generalizations about group processes. Hence some sort of classification of groups is necessary. We can distinguish between *nominal groups*, collections of individuals who function relatively independently of each other, and *true groups*, collections of individuals who interact with each other. The activities of nominal groups are seldom analyzed in the same terms as those of true groups which have some express purpose or function. Among true groups, we can further differentiate between *task-oriented groups* and *process-oriented groups*, at least at a hypothetical level. The goals of task-oriented groups are generally expressed in terms of work output. Members of an assembly-line unit or a committee to prepare a report on a specific project would qualify as a task-oriented group. A typical example of a process-oriented group would be a collection of individuals engaged in sensitivity training. Here the expressed goal is not that of producing an objective output, but rather of achieving a certain level of interpersonal understanding. In many cases, of course, the distinction is arbitrary. It is easy to conceive of a collection of individuals who would qualify equally well as a task or process group.

There are numerous other ways of classifying groups—leaderless groups versus those with a designated leader, structured versus unstructured groups, permanent versus temporary groups, static versus dynamic groups. The primary reason for making such distinctions is that variables found to affect performance in one type of group may have very different effects on another type of group.

COMPETITIVE VERSUS COOPERATIVE GROUPS

Deutsch [1949] formed artificial groups of two types, each consisting of five subjects. Each group met for 3 hours per week for six weeks in order to fulfill the requirements for an introductory class in psychology. The cooperative groups were told that they were to function as a team, and that the course grade of each person in the group would depend on the merits of the group solution. The competitive groups were given the same tasks, but they were told that each of the five members would receive a different grade, depending on his relative contribution to the

421

group's solutions of the various problems. The cooperative groups were generally more productive. They solved simple tasks more rapidly than the competitive groups and produced more realistic recommendations for solution of complex tasks. There was more communication in the cooperative groups, and the members of these groups reported having fewer difficulties understanding each other. One could hardly paint a rosier picture for the spirit of cooperation.

Related experiments, termed the "bastard studies," indicate that the picture is less than rosy in cooperative groups if the subjects fail to cooperate [Hastorf, 1966]. Typically, subjects are assigned to groups and told they are to perform individually a menial task for which they will receive a numerical score. If each member of the group achieves a score greater than 100, the entire group will receive a substantial monetary reward; however, if even one member fails to achieve the criterion score, no one will be paid. After subjects perform the designated tasks, they are told that their scores came out as shown in Fig. 15-10. The subjects are then asked to rate how they feel about each of the other members of the group. Of course the scores are fictitious and subject D is a paid confederate, but the following results are consistently obtained. In condition 1 the typical attitude expressed toward D, the paid confederate who has failed, is one of sympathy. One would have to be really incompetent to perform so inadequately, and the poor fellow probably deserves pity rather than anything else. Condition 2 produces far different evaluations of D, the most typical being "that bastard!" (hence the study's nickname). Here D is usually seen as possessing the ability and having failed the rest of the group only through lack of motivation; thus he is perceived as the sole cause of the group's failure. Obviously the effectiveness of a cooperative group depends on the behavior of its individual members. Nevertheless, most studies indicate that individuals in cooperative groups have higher morale, discuss problems more freely, and report greater satisfaction than those in competitive groups.

GROUP ORGANIZATION

Groups can also differ in terms of the distribution of authority. For example, Lippitt [1940] studied five-person groups of fifth- and sixth-grade children with both democratic and authoritarian leaders. With the authoritarian leadership the children were restricted to group tasks and were allowed no individual goals. All assignments were doled out, and the decision of which children were to work together was arbitrarily decided. In the groups with democratic leadership the goals and purposes were explained, and the children were given a role in deciding the goals to be achieved. There were numerous differences between the two types of groups. In general the democratic situation created an atmosphere of easy communication and mutual help. The children produced better work, were less dominating and more friendly to each other, and showed fewer instances of aggressive behavior to each other.

FIGURE 15–10 *Fictitious scores given individual subjects in "cooperative" groups [based on Hastorf, 1966].*

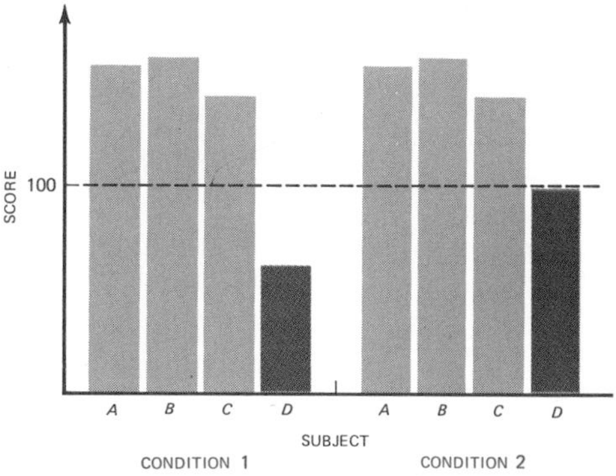

In a more elaborate study by Lewin et al. [1939] groups of boys were exposed not only to authoritarian and democratic types, but also to a laissez-faire situation in which the leader allowed virtually complete freedom, refrained from participating himself, and made few comments. As in Lippett's study, the children under authoritarian leadership were more aggressive or apathetic, and those who were apathetic tended to become aggressive when the leader left the room. It was also found that the children liked the leader better when he functioned in a democratic role than when he behaved autocratically. They even preferred laissez-faire leadership to authoritarian leadership.

Group processes are profoundly influenced by the type of leadership provided, but what differentiates an effective leader from an ineffective one? Are leaders born or made, or is this impossible to determine? Most of these questions have been asked for years, and we still do not have definitive answers. However, we do know quite a bit about leaders and leadership.

Leadership styles tend to fall into one of two classes—task oriented or process oriented—and the two types of leaders differ markedly in personality. A task-oriented leader, as the designation implies, is primarily concerned with pushing the group to create a finished product. He typically talks more than other members of the group, directs and issues orders, and executes rather than administrates. His concern is more with what is produced than with how it is produced. A process-oriented leader's *modus operandi* is almost the opposite; his primary concern lies in keeping the group intact, in maintaining group cohesiveness. He advises rather than issues orders, and listens more than he talks. He is more directed toward solving personal difficulties within the group than with meeting a production goal. Which type is better? Obviously this depends on the nature of the group being led and who is doing the evaluating. A process-oriented leader would probably not make an effective Marine Corps drill sergeant, while a task-oriented leader would be out of place in a sensitivity-training encounter group. A foreman who was a task leader might be praised by his contractor but loathed by his men; a process leader in the same position might claim the respect of his workers but not that of his employers. These two qualities are rarely found in the same individual. However, in spontaneously formed

423

groups it is often the case that two leaders will emerge, one of each type.

We know very little about how leadership is developed, but some recent studies suggest that its origins may be far from noble. In a classical experiment by Bavelas et al. [1965] spontaneously formed groups were given a variety of problems to discuss, ranging from the utility of free-trade legislation to whether the United States should recognize Red China. After each 20-minute discussion session all members were asked to indicate which person they thought was the leader. Within a few sessions a clear consensus usually emerged, with the leader typically being the person who talked the most. This is not a unique finding.

The group members were then told that their meetings would be monitored by "experts" who would evaluate each person's participation in the discussion. A set of lights was placed in front of each subject, hidden from the view of the other group members, and the subjects were told that every time they made a positive contribution the green light would go on and every time they detracted from the general train of the discussion the red light would go on. The goal was to make the person who had received the lowest leadership rating the leader of the group. Each time this person spoke, no matter what he said, he received a green light, while the other members consistently received red lights for their contributions to the discussions. Despite the fact that each group member would see only his own set of lights, eventually the previously low man was doing most of the talking, and when the next leadership pool was taken, he emerged as the group leader. Moreover, in the succeeding discussion, carried out in the absence of "experts" and lights, the new leader remained the chief, both in the amount he talked and in the postdiscussion opinion poll. Apparently it took only a green light to make a leader of a lackey.

Of course this experiment does not refute the possibility that there are born leaders. However, it does illustrate that many leaders can be made, quickly and relatively easily, out of virtual nobodies if conditions are proper. Anyone familiar with our national politics should view this finding with little surprise.

CHANGING SOCIAL BEHAVIOR

A person's attitudes reflect the way he perceives things in the world about him—other people, objects, opinions, beliefs. People are not born with the attitudes they hold. Rather, attitudes are learned, and as such are undoubtedly affected by subsequent experiences. Thus they may change with time, some more easily and more readily than others. The process of attitude acquisition and the mechanism of attitude change represent perhaps the most thoroughly investigated research topic within social psychology.

The practical implications of determining the mechanisms of attitude change are obvious. Selling a product, electing a political

424

candidate, reducing prejudice, accepting the need for population and pollution control, or educating parents and children on the effects of drugs all depend ultimately on the success of a communicator in shaping or changing the attitudes of his audience. The variables which affect the communicator's effectiveness are of interest both to those who seek a world of change and to those who would not "rock the boat."

Consider a political speaker trying to persuade an audience that the Republicans are correct on a particular issue and that the Democratic position is untenable. Will he be more successful if he presents only the Republican argument, or will he persuade more members of the audience if he includes some of the points made by the Democrats before presenting his position? Studies by Hovland et al. [1949] and Lumsdaine and Janis [1953] indicate that it depends on the political composition of the audience. The findings suggest that one-sided arguments are more effective in cementing existing attitudes, while two-sided arguments produce more change in a skeptical audience. Presentation of opposing views detracts from an argument supporting a position with which the audience agrees and may raise doubts among those who were initially in favor. However, where the audience is initially opposed a one-sided argument may be dismissed as unfair and unrealistic.

Another variable found to affect degree of attitude change is the speaker's credibility. Very simply, an audience is more receptive to arguments from a source they believe. This has been borne out both in numerous experimental situations and in public-opinion surveys indicating that a credibility gap accompanies a decrease in popularity of administrative policies. Credibility appears to be affected by both expertise of the source and coorientation of the source with the audience. Generally speaking, the greater the perceived expertise of the source, the more effective the persuasion. On the issue of a critical world food shortage people are more likely to believe the opinion of an eminent ecologist than that of an Indian mystic. A man interested in buying stocks is more likely to consult the *Wall Street Journal* than *The Militant* to determine the current economic conditions of the country. A jury will probably take the opinion of a court psychiatrist more seriously than the opinion of an eighty-year-old relative concerning the sanity of a defendent.

However, Hovland and Weiss [1951] have shown that the persuasive effects of expertise tend to diminish over time. More specifically, attitude change resulting from a source of high expertise diminishes over a period of weeks, while change resulting from a low-expertise source appears to increase (see Fig. 15-11). This *sleeper effect* has been explained on the basis that people forget the source of a persuasive communication more rapidly than they forget the content of the communication.

A second factor affecting credibility is the degree of coorientation of the source with the audience. The more a speaker appears to share the views and values of his audience, the more the audience will be influenced by what he has to say. Members of the John Birch Society are more likely to believe the arguments of Spiro T. Agnew than the arguments of Abbie Hoffman. The people of a ghetto are more likely to accept the argument

425

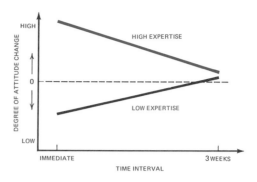

FIGURE 15-11 *The sleeper effect in the influence of communication source over time [Hovland and Weiss, 1951].*

that a black suspect was fleeing when he was shot by police than the police department's explanation that the officer shot in self-defense. Drug users respect the opinion that "speed kills" more when the source is an ex-addict than when the source is a narcotics detective. In short, the degree to which an audience can identify with the source of informa-
Y tion is an important factor in credibility. Being able to "tell it like it is" can be a powerful asset in bringing about attitude change.

Closely related to the credibility of the source is the plausibility of the argument. For example, fear-producing communication has been found to be a relatively useful technique in effecting attitude change particularly with respect to issues such as cigarette smoking, health, pollution, and the "threat" of Communist conspiracies. Generally speaking, the more disastrous the predicted consequences, the more likely the attitude change. However, this can be overdone. Janis and Feshback [1953] presented grade-school children with one of three lectures stressing the importance of oral hygiene and then measured the effectiveness of the lectures by surveying parents on any change in the children's dental-care habits. The lectures differed only in the amount of fear-arousing material; one discussed cavities and bad breath, the second showed some slides of minor cavities, and the third emphasized with gory illustrative slides the painful consequences of severe tooth decay and diseased gums. All lectures stressed that brushing teeth up and down rather than sideways would prevent dental problems.

The results indicated that the second condition was most effective, while the third produced a "boomerang" effect and promoted less attitude change than the mildest lecture (see Fig. 15-12). Two explanations have been offered. The first is that people avoid perception of intense fear-producing stimuli; by avoiding the message they avoid facing the problem. This has been termed *selective exposure*. A second explanation concerns the plausibility of the proposed cure; subjects are not likely to believe that brushing up and down rather than sideways will make a critical difference between healthy and diseased gums, but it might make a difference between cavities and no cavities.

The factors we have discussed concern the source and type of per-

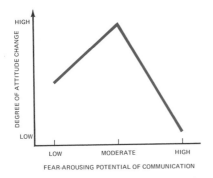

FIGURE 15–12   *The boomerang effect of fear-arousing material on attitude change [Janis and Feshback, 1953].*

suasive communication. However, another important factor is the nature of the attitude being subjected to change, especially its strength and saliency and the extent to which it is intimately tied to an entire value structure. These points are most likely to arise in matters that touch on racial prejudice or religious convictions. An attitude of this nature tends to be exceedingly resistant to change.

Obviously a complete understanding of the process of attitude change is far beyond the present state of knowledge. Despite current fears that ours is becoming a brainwashed society, controlled by those who control the media, in reality remarkably few advertising or political campaigns actually resulted in mass shifts of public opinion. It is a fortunate politician whose campaign sways more than 10 percent of the populace, and a rare new product that immediately captures the buying market from existing competitors.

We often hear the phrases "the battle for the minds of men" or "control of the mind." There is current concern in many circles that with the advance of technology we are gaining an increased ability to exercise control over the motivation and behavior of human beings. Most often the concerns are expressed as fears. There is considerable concern, for example, that manipulation of the mind through direct treatment of the brain can lead people to engage in behavior that is "against their will." Since it is possible to control the behavior of rats by delivering small electric currents to specific regions of the brain, is it also possible that such techniques will be used to control the behavior of human beings?

In some ways it is paradoxical that such questions should be asked, because from another point of view we are greatly concerned that we do not have enough control over the behavior of members of our society. Educational institutions of our society are specifically designed to help us socialize our children in specific and controlled ways. In a more forceful way, law-enforcement agencies and the armed forces are designed to exercise control over men.

The point is that the behavior of men can be rather effectively controlled by the agencies of our society, and in some cases the degree

427

of control is greater than that which could be expected by placing electrodes in the brains of humans. As a matter of fact, although that particular technique has been found to be effective in the control of severe emotional outbursts in severely disturbed individuals, it would be both dangerous and uneconomical for the control of social behavior in the "normal" individual.

The major question, then, is not whether human beings have the capability of exercising control over other human beings; clearly they do, as much of the evidence presented throughout this book testifies. The concern appears to center on the nature of the control and who is to be in control—the age-old question of *qui custodiat custodes*. We seem to be less concerned about controls that are exerted through normal communications processes than we are about controls which involve direct interference with brain function. Even here, however, we are selective. We object vigorously to the use of certain drugs, particularly those which are preferred by the youth of our culture, but we readily accept the use of other drugs, such as alcohol, nicotine, and caffeine, which are regularly used by the adults in our society. Drugs, of course, provide direct and effective control of behavior through their influence on brain function.

The most important problem and the greatest source of concern is that of who has the power to control the behavior of others. It seems as though most of us are worried about the possibility that others will gain too much control over our behavior. At the same time we seem to deplore the fact that we have too little control over the behavior of others. The effective means of control—that is, of influencing the behavior of other human beings—are available to us all. The most effective means are, of course, our ability to influence the behavior of others through our social relations with them. The fact is that we know more about how to influence behavior than we do about the bases of the influence. Adolf Hitler was able to exercise control over millions of people without a complete understanding of the nature of social influence. However, if we are to increase our ability to get along with other human beings with whom we share our planet, we need to make every effort to increase our understanding of human social behavior.

SUMMARY

Biological characteristics account for both the similarities and the differences in the social behavior of each species. Although human social interaction depends heavily on man's capacity for language, it is in many respects based on emotional states similar to those observed in many other animals. Emotional responses such as those which accompany prejudice can sometimes be measured by changes in galvanic skin response.

Socialization, the process of making socially acceptable human beings, begins at birth under the control of parents, but the home is not necessarily the major socializing force. Although attitudes and beliefs may be fashioned initially by parental example, they are altered and maintained by such other influences as the child's attitude toward his parents, the influences of peers, and the prevailing attitudes of society. Thus mere exposure to parental attitudes or to firsthand information does not ensure the adoption of particular attitudes. Through the process of socialization affiliative responses, which begin as reflexes, become directed toward specific members of the social group.

Particularly important in determining social attraction between individuals is the variable of perceived similarity. For example, the more similar two individuals are in attitudes and beliefs, the more likely they are to affiliate. This is true in many circumstances for nonhuman as well as human primates. Complementarity of personality has also been considered relevant in determining social attraction among individuals, although empirical support is not as strong for this influence. Proximity, familiarity, and rewardingness have all been found to affect social affiliation and attraction, but much is yet to be learned about social attraction outside the confines of the social-psychological laboratory.

Conformity is one of the most obvious and basic characteristics of social behavior. In extensive laboratory research it has been found that subjects will conform to an objectively incorrect group opinion, and that the degree of conformity is dependent on such factors as the size of the consensus group, the perceived expertness of the group, the presence of other nonconforming members in the group, and the difficulty of the objective judgment being made by the group. The mere order in which the members of the group express their judgments may have dramatic effects on the subject's rating of their personality and intellect.

Group processes comprise an important aspect of the study of social behavior. Groups have been classified in many ways. For example, nominal groups are collections of individuals working relatively independently, while true groups tend to work together for some common objective. True groups can be further differentiated as task oriented or process oriented, or as cooperative or competitive. In general cooperative groups tend to be more productive than competitive groups. Groups can differ in terms of distribution of authority, as in democratic leadership versus authoritarian leadership. Finally, leaders themselves may be task oriented or process oriented; their effectiveness for a particular type of group depends to some extent on the group goal. The qualities of leadership may well depend more on the circumstances than on any innate qualities of the leader.

Perhaps one of the most thoroughly investigated areas of social psychology is the process of attitude acquisition and change. Important influences on attitude change are the credibility of the source of a communication, the plausibility of the arguments employed, the degree of coorientation of audience and speaker. Other factors are the strength, complexity, and saliency of preexisting attitudes.

CHAPTER SIXTEEN

THE DISTURBED PERSONALITY

A young woman leaves college at midsemester and returns home. This is the third college she has attended in as many years, and despite her intelligence, she has not succeeded at any of them. She stays with her family only a short while and then, in the company of a young man, travels to a distant city. There she and her new friend "drop some acid," and she has a "bad trip." She begins to feel that she is the center of attention, that people are paying special heed to what she says or does not say. She is greatly concerned about her sexual conduct with the young man and feels guilty about having "used him," although they have actually had little to do with each other. She calls her state "paranoid," and in fact it does fit the professional definition of this term. She has definite feelings of unreality; it is difficult for her to distinguish what is in her mind from what exists outside her in the world. She is extremely frightened by what is happening to her and wonders if she is "going crazy." Her state of fear, withdrawal from people, and paranoia continue for some six months, long beyond the physiological effects of the LSD. The drug experience seems to have precipitated a more general psychological disturbance.

PERSONALITY AND ABNORMAL BEHAVIOR

A woman in her forties, who has apparently been doing well raising her children and working parttime as a teacher, suddenly becomes depressed. A series of colds forces her to stay home from work, but instead of returning when she is well, she begins to have trouble eating and sleeping. Her symptoms become worse; she cries, does not take care of herself, sleeps only fitfully, and requires a good deal of care from her husband and friends. Her two children are grown and living in distant cities, but her depression becomes so great, including a serious suicide attempt, that they too are forced to come to her aid.

A high school boy had always achieved excellent grades, owing in large part to the example and prodding of his father. The father, a successful physician, had hopes that his son would go into medicine, a plan with which the son agreed. Away from home at college, however, he begins to develop a curious set of symptoms. His premedical courses bring forth a special fear in him, although he has always done well in science. His mind is filled with thoughts of failure, and he feels driven to study extra hours on these subjects. However, when he tries to study his mind again becomes flooded with unrelated ideas. The harder he tries to concentrate, the more obsessed he becomes with other matters. He resorts to various rituals, for it seems to him that if the papers on

431

his desk are arranged in a certain way, or if he does things in a certain prescribed order, then he will be able to study. These rituals or compulsions are only temporarily effective, and overall they seem to increase his state of anxiety, conflict, and guilt over disappointing his father.

The paranoid young woman, the depressed mother, and the obsessive-compulsive student are all examples of abnormal or disturbed personality development. They all show disturbances in the emotions or feelings associated with core human relationships. Instead of love and trust in others, the young woman feels fear and anxiety. Unable to feel happiness over her own and her children's accomplishments, the mother is overwhelmed with unhappiness and depression at losing them. Outwardly wishing to please the father he admires, the young man is driven to disappoint him and punish himself in the process. What brings about these disturbances in emotion and relationships? Do such troubled people suffer from some disease, or are their abnormalities the extreme expression of tendencies that exist within all of us?

Emotions of fear, unhappiness, and guilt are not unique to abnormal psychological states. We are all familiar with these feelings from our own experiences, and many of us may even have experienced conflicts similar to those described in the examples above. Abnormality is not a separate world populated by people with some "mental illness" that sets them apart from the rest of us. Rather, disturbed people are struggling with the same emotions and conflicts that we all struggle with, although they may be doing so less successfully. Whereas the normal person has been able to solve certain of life's problems, the disturbed person gets stuck and does not develop beyond a certain point. To answer the question of what brings about psychological disturbance we must examine human emotions and social relations. This can best be done by describing their biological background and then by tracing the course of human personality development and noting how emotional disturbances can occur at various points along the way.

BIOLOGICAL BACKGROUND

Man is a primate and like the other primate species, he has evolved complex mechanisms for regulating his social life. All primate social life is regulated by behavior patterns which are accompanied by strong emotions. Anthropologists and psychologists have studied the behavior of the most social of the nonhuman primates—baboons and chimpanzees—living in their natural environments [Washburn and DeVore, 1961; Goodall, 1965]. These studies have revealed that primate social relations are regulated by bonds of affection and attachment, primarily between mothers and their offspring, and by dominance-submission hierarchies. The young baboon or chimp becomes socialized into the group as he establishes affectional ties, learns his place in the dominance hierarchy, and interacts socially with his peers.

432

FIGURE 16-1   *Mother monkey with her infant.*

The same is true for the young human. His first social relationship is the affectional tie with his mother, and he too must become socialized through experiences of emotional interaction as he grows up. The period of human development is much longer than that of the nonhuman primates; hence there is much more time for things to go wrong, for disturbances or abnormalities to develop. Before we discuss human personality development, however, let us briefly review the general areas of primate social-emotional development.

ATTACHMENT AND LOSS

As we saw in Chapters 3 and 4, love is a primary emotion in primate social relations. The infant's first attachment is to its mother who supplies him with warmth, care, and comfort and becomes a secure home base for his relations with the rest of the environment (see Fig. 16-1). Primates are a particularly inquisitive species. In fact a good deal of evidence from psychological studies shows that monkeys and humans are strongly motivated to explore out of sheer curiosity. Curiosity and exploration are at their peaks in the young, who of course have more to find out about the world. However, there is an important relationship between exploration and secure affectional attachments. As we have seen, infant monkeys will happily explore a new environment in the presence of even a surrogate mother but become terrified if the surrogate is not there. The same is true of human infants. In a strange situation the infant with his mother nearby will explore much more than the infant who is separated from his mother and is so anxious that all his efforts are spent on an attempt to reinstate attachment [Ainsworth and Bell, 1968].

When an infant monkey has become firmly attached to his mother, separation causes extreme anxiety [Harlow et al., 1970]. If the separation is prolonged, the infant stops acting overtly anxious and becomes depressed. Kaufman and Rosenblum [1967] found that infant monkeys separated from their mothers reacted in three phases. First, they protested, showing a high level of activity, anxiety, and rage. When this did not bring mother back, they passed into a period of despair in which

433

FIGURE 16-2   *An emotionally depressed infant monkey.*

they appeared depressed, weepy, and relatively inactive. When separation
was prolonged, despair passed into detachment, a phase in which the
infant was seemingly unresponsive to others (Fig. 16-2).

This exact sequence of protest, despair, and detachment has been
observed in human infants when they are separated from their mothers
[Bowlby, 1969]. Attachment works both ways, of course; mothers become anxious when separated from their babies and may react with
depression to loss. The evidence from both nonhuman primate and
human sources indicates that anxiety and depression are primary reactions to loss or disruption in a vital interpersonal (or intermonkey) relationship. In monkeys and young infants the loss that causes depression
is a literal one; the mother is physically absent. As humans grow older
and their ability to symbolize increases, the possible meaning of "loss"
expands. For example, the depressed mother described at the beginning
of the chapter did not really "lose" her children; but the fact that they
were no longer children represented a symbolic loss. By the same token
the loss of a job or status or youth may precipitate the same kind of
loss reaction.

PEER PLAY AND
CONTROL OF AGGRESSION

In addition to the bonds of affection, social order in primate groups is
built around dominance-submission hierarchies. In troops of baboons,
for example, the largest and strongest males lead the group to feeding
areas or away from danger [DeVore, 1965]. Perhaps more important,
the dominance hierarchy lets every troop member know how he is supposed to act toward every other member, whether it is with deference,
with a challenge, or as an equal. These interactions are evidenced by
aggression and attack on the one side and cowering or flight on the other.
Although dominance-submission interactions are the most frequent kind
of social contact, most encounters consist of feints and bluffs. As the
more dominant animal asserts himself, teeth are bared, noises are made,
hair is ruffled, and brief chases occur. The well-socialized baboon has
learned how to threaten and fight but also how to control his aggression
434   against members of his in-group.

FIGURE 16–3   *Young monkeys engaged in rough-and-tumble play.*

The control and redirection of aggression are a major part of socialization, and as we have seen, much of the practice for adult dominance-submission behavior occurs during periods of rough-and-tumble peer play (see Fig. 16-3). Control of aggression is, of course, a central problem in human society, and our long history of warfare suggests that we are not doing a very good job of it. As a species we seem to have special problems in controlling aggression, and this frequently becomes a central area of psychological disturbance.

UNIQUELY HUMAN CHARACTERISTICS

Attachment, exploration, aggression, and play are common to all primates. There are some social-emotional areas, however, that are unique to the human species. One such area is human sexuality. In all nonhuman primates—as well as in most other mammals—the female is sexually receptive only during periods of estrus, and sexual relations between adults are usually limited to these periods. Thus sex is an issue only at specific and infrequent intervals. Sex is always an issue with humans, since the female is potentially receptive at any time. Humans are thus a much sexier species than the other primates, and as a result human sexual relations are surrounded by more complex learning patterns and cultural rules, customs and taboos. As with aggression, the regulation of sexuality is frequently a critical source of psychological disturbance.

It is in the areas of language and thought that man parts company most radically from the other primates. However, the same capacity to symbolize that enables man to develop language, to think in abstract terms, to dream, and to create also enables him to develop neurotic fantasies and psychotic delusions. Nevertheless, the basic feelings of love and trust, of fear and anger, of curiosity and interest persist in human relationships even when these relationships involve the complexities of language and other symbolism. To understand disturbances in personality development we must bear in mind both the general characteristics of primate behavior and the specific characteristics of the human species.

Although socialization of aggression is one of the important functions of peer play, deprivation of peer experience can prove disastrous for other aspects of personality development as well. Monkeys reared in

435

social isolation never seem able to develop normal interaction with the other members of their species—sexually, aggressively, playfully, or in any way. They become as withdrawn as the most severe schizophrenic.

While the picture is more complicated with human beings, in general we can assume that peer play is extremely important in shaping later social and emotional patterns. The child who has ready access to other children may acquire much of the necessary social experience even if his family experiences are fraught with anxiety and loss. However, the child who misses out on peer experiences may have later difficulties in handling both love and aggression in interpersonal relationships, for which peer socialization is a preparation. At the extreme is the schizophrenic who withdraws from the world of peers into a world of private fantasy, like the isolation-reared monkey.

DEVELOPMENT OF HUMAN PERSONALITY

Man differs from the other primates in his greater capacity for learning—the flexibility to adapt to a more complex environment. In order to achieve this flexibility the human infant has a much longer period of both dependency and openness to new learning. Thus the very feature that provides for unique adaptation in the human species—long dependency and openness to learning—also provides greater opportunity for the development of abnormal behavior.

For purposes of discussion we can divide this long period of human development into four phases—infancy and early childhood, childhood, adolescence, and adulthood. In each of these phases certain core conflict areas—areas of strong emotion and intense human relationships—are worked and reworked. No one experience, in and of itself, causes abnormality in an adult. Rather, difficulties encountered during any phase form a basis or a direction set for what happens in the following phases. For example, repeated losses during infancy form a basis for anxiety in his relationships after infancy. However, later experiences can either reaffirm or change this basis. If a child continues to be abandoned and/or is so fearful of people that he prevents relationships from becoming established, he may be on his way to a lifetime of abnormal anxiety. Conversely, if he and his parents are able to overcome the early anxiety during the childhood phase, the direction of development may swing back to normal. Let us now look at the four phases and note those areas which may shape later abnormalities.

INFANCY AND EARLY CHILDHOOD

At birth the infant has no sense of himself or of other people. Over the course of the first year he begins to impose order on his world; he learns to distinguish objects, and at about six months he reacts to his mother (or caretaker) as a special object. When all goes well he becomes firmly attached to his mother in this first important emotional-social relationship. Erikson [1950] has described the healthy outcome of this attachment phase as a "sense of trust." The infant's sense of trust or security derives from the predictability of the care that he receives when his basic needs for food, warmth, stimulation, contact comfort, and love are met in a consistent and meaningful way. Separation, loss, or rejection, which disrupt the predictable flow of care, create the opposite state in the infant—a state of distrust, insecurity, and anxiety. Severe disruptions in these early attachments may result in a basic anxiety or interpersonal insecurity in all later relations.

With a secure base of attachment, after the first year the infant begins to explore the world around him. As he achieves new motor and intellectual skills, he progresses from a position of almost complete dependence to the discovery that he can do many things "by myself." As at many points in development, the young child tends to push the new direction to its limits, with an upsurge in willfulness and demandingness during "the terrible twos" when he is likely to say no to anything and everything. This overplayed independence, an expression of aggressive-dominant behavior, eventually requires social restraint, usually in the form of parental restrictions. This is the child's first major experience with a conflict between his own wishes and desires and the prohibitions of authority. Just as the earlier experience with attachment shapes later relations of love, so his experiences at this phase influence later emotional reactions and relations to authority. At one extreme his early surge toward independence may be so harshly opposed that he becomes overly fearful of his own healthy tendencies toward aggression, exploration, or independent action. At the other extreme his willfulness may be completely unchecked, creating the basis for an unrealistic, self-centered view of the world.

A common feature of the child's early battles with authority is *negativism*, an early, very primitive way in which a smaller or weaker person attempts to defeat larger, more powerful opponents. The persistence of negativism into adult forms of disturbance is seen in the passive-resistance nature of many neurotic behavior patterns. It reaches an extreme form in the catatonic schizophrenic, who literally will not do anything, even move his own body.

CHILDHOOD

The period of childhood involves a reworking of the core areas of interpersonal attachment, aggression and its control, and independence. First, the child becomes capable of increasingly complex modes of thought, and second, he moves farther out of the world of parents and siblings and into the world of peers and other adults. For example, in the infant phase love and attachment are based on certain forms of physical care. During this early phase the infant's concept of himself is primarily a sensory-motor one—he feels secure when he is securely cared for, bad

437

when his body hurts, and so on. With continued development the child's concept of himself encompasses greater complexities. By age four it encompasses not just his body, but his skills and accomplishments, his fantasies, and the way other people interact with him. An important new area of self comes about with the learning of socially appropriate sex roles. The young child ceases to be simply a baby and becomes a "boy" or "girl" who is expected to act in the appropriate ways and resents being treated either as a baby or as a member of the opposite sex.

As the child becomes aware of this new sex-role identity, the older relations of attachment must be reworked. A "big boy" cannot always be clinging to mama for support. In addition, society's taboo on incest may cause the child to feel guilty about the very attachment that had been his source of security. In Freud's view of this *oedipal period*, as he termed it, the young male begins to feel guilty about his love for his mother (and the young female about her love for her father) because such love is now both competitive with the same-sex parent and potentially incestuous. When these feelings are not adequately resolved, guilt may continue to color adult heterosexual relations.

Many maladjustments, such as impotence or frigidity, inhibition of love feelings, and self-punitive relationships can stem from the oedipal period. For example, a young boy may develop an especially close relationship with his mother—an intensified continuation of the infant-mother affectional tie. The mother may encourage this relationship, treating her son as a "special" child. As the childhood years progress both mother and son may sense that there is something wrong with the relationship. The mother may express her own guilt feelings by pushing her child away even as she attempts to keep him close. This behavior may take such forms as punishments and reprimands that are inappropriate to the child's transgressions, excessive concern about his sexual behavior, or not allowing him to play with peers, which also keeps him close to her. As mother and son play out this drama over a period of years their relationship becomes characterized by intense *ambivalence*—feelings of both love and anger toward the same person. The boy comes to associate this ambivalence, along with his anxiety and guilt, with the idea of intimacy with a woman. Thus as a young man, when he is expected to have close relations with women, he may find that the old guilt, anxiety, and ambivalence learned in this first relationship are experienced in a way that disturbs his later relationships. Phillip Roth's novel *Portnoy's Complaint* [1967] gives a funny-sad picture of this state of affairs.

In this simplified example of what Freud called an *unresolved oedipus complex* we see how an early disturbance in the area of love may form the basis for later disturbance in the same area. Disturbances in other areas, such as relationships with authority or sex-role behavior, may similarly set the stage for later difficulties.

Another aspect of the childhood years concerns the relative balance of achievement, competence, and successful play on the one hand and withdrawal, passivity, and fantasy on the other. Childhood ushers in an

438

important move away from parents and home and into the world of peers and school. This move like earlier separations, arouses anxiety; the child must give up familiar people and places for strange and frightening—but also new and interesting—situations. By this time, however, his play and fantasy skills permit him to deal with new situations in ways that were not available to him earlier. His ability to fantasy and dream allows him to experiment mentally with many aspects of his expanding world. Before starting school for the first time, for example, he can play out or fantasy about all the interesting-frightening things he anticipates there. In general childhood play and fantasy are preparations for social life and ways of experimenting with situations before acting.

The expanding sphere of childhood also presents opportunities for achievement and increased competence. New social skills acquired through peer interaction, new intellectual skills acquired in the classroom, and adaption to new situations in general all contribute to the child's mastery of his world, and as his competence increases, his self-esteem grows accordingly. It is the balance between fantasy and mastery that determines the next step in social development. When the balance is tipped too heavily in the direction of fantasy, the child may set a pattern of dealing with anxiety or conflict by an overreliance on fantasy and withdrawal from the social world. For example, the young child may deal with the anxiety of leaving home for school by fantasying himself a conquering hero on the playground. When the time actually comes he may conquer his own fears, have a good time, and actually achieve some social mastery, with its attendant growth in self-esteem, or he can stay home with a stomachache, which may be a real one from anxiety, and avoid the feared move into new social experience, substituting instead an overreliance on fantasy. No one point is fateful for later personality development, but a pattern of fantasy at the expense of actual achievement may lead to an arrest of personality development and form a basis for later disturbances.

ADOLESCENCE

Just as childhood involves a reworking of the central social-emotional areas of infancy, so adolescence involves a reworking of these same areas from the childhood phase. The child has achieved some stability in his identity in the areas of love and sex-role identity, independence from family, and channeling of aggression. This stability is challenged in adolescence by rapid physiological and intellectual changes. The final spurt in growth to adult size, the development of secondary sex characteristics, and the onset of puberty all represent a virtual transformation in the body that the child was accustomed to living in. In the intellectual sphere, the adolescent takes the final step to the capacity for abstract thinking, which provides him with new perspectives of the world and his place in it. These drastic changes are also accompanied by changes in social expectations. Other people increasingly expect the adolescent to behave as an adult.

439

Many of the seeds of disturbance sown during the earlier phases of infancy and childhood come to fruition in adolescence. One area of frequent difficulty concerns dependence-independence. The infant is totally dependent on adults. Childhood represents a large step in the direction of independence, but the child can still rely on the security of home and family. As adolescence progresses to young adulthood, the final push toward independence begins. The young adult is expected eventually to establish a life of his own, apart from his family. This final push toward independence may touch off disturbances that have lain more or less dormant during the years of childhood.

For example, a child with excessive anxiety may go through the motions of school and peer relations, but he may in fact have been relying heavily on passive fantasy and has achieved little actual mastery in the social world. Adolescence, with its sudden transformations and increased push toward independence, puts additional stress on such a tenuous adjustment. Although some kind of adjustment was possible while he was still a dependent child, as an adolescent he faces a crisis. He must either venture out into the anxiety-arousing world of peers and achieve some mastery or withdraw further into fantasy.

The end point of such withdrawal may be a schizophrenic breakdown. In fact the first occurrence of most schizophrenic episodes is in late adolescence and early childhood. The case of the paranoid young woman described at the beginning of the chapter is an example of a beginning schizophrenic breakdown resulting from the push toward independence of the late adolescent period.

Adolescence also brings with it new demands for sex-appropriate behavior. The childhood phase has sometimes been referred to as a period of *sexual latency*, since, at least in our culture, children are not expected to engage in heterosexual activities. During this period of sexual latency potential disturbances in sex-role behavior may easily remain hidden or dormant. Boys play with boys and girls play with girls, and no one is likely to notice that a child does not interact with members of the opposite sex. Adolescence, with the emergence of an adult body and sexual equipment and increased expectations for heterosexual performance, puts an end to the period of latency, and potential disturbances in heterosexual relations now become apparent. For example, the guilt, anxiety, and ambivalence created by an intensely ambivalent mother-son relationship may not arise until adolescence brings increased opportunity and pressure for heterosexual relations. Thus the adolescent is confronted with the problem of resolving his sexual anxieties in order to achieve a successful heterosexual relationship or of withdrawing into increasingly disabling defenses against his anxieties. Many of the classical neuroses, such as *hysterical paralysis* (disfunction of some part of the body for which no organic cause can be found), *phobias* (irrationally intense fears), and inhibitions, have this kind of origin. For example, the young woman who experiences intense anxiety at the thought of sexual relations may develop a neurotic fear of leaving the house, which, among other things, protects her from coming into contact with men.

440

There is no fixed point at which adolescence ends and adulthood begins. The central social-emotional areas of dependence-independence, attachment and separation, aggression and its control, relations with authority, and so forth continue throughout life. Some people achieve fairly stable identities in the early adult years. For others the conflicts and instabilities of the adolescent period persist much longer. Some, of course, are never able to overcome patterns of severe disturbance laid down in their earlier years. These are the people who retreat into the semipermanent fantasies of psychosis or who are never able to achieve relations of intimacy with others or who suffer from one or another form of neurotic symptomatology.

The adult phase brings its own stresses, and there are many people who make more or less adequate adjustments during the early adult years, only to break down later. The depressed mother described at the beginning of the chapter functioned relatively well during the years when her children were young. However, she had a special sensitivity to loss, and as she approached late middle age the loss of her own youth, coupled with the symbolic loss of her two children and the related loss of her well-ingrained role of mother, all came together to precipitate a severe depression. Related forms of depression associated with the stresses of old age, bodily deterioration, and especially the loss of established skills and social roles are common.

Life involves a succession of changes—changes in body, in mental capacity, and in social roles and expectations—and each change brings new challenges and new opportunities for growth and progress. At the same time each brings its own stresses, and the manner in which the

THE PERSON OR THE CIRCUMSTANCES

stresses of one phase are met determines the outcome of later phases. People meet stresses in different ways. However, some people have more stresses to cope with than others. There has been a good deal of controversy over which set of factors—those within the person, usually referred to as *hereditary* or *constitutional*, or those in the environment, such as seductive or rejecting mothers, a history of losses, and so on—is most important in causing later disturbances in personality. For example, there is evidence that schizophrenia has a genetic basis [Kallman, 1953]; other evidence indicates that schizophrenia results from circumstances within the family environment [Bateson et al., 1956; Lidz, 1963]. Both views are likely to be correct. Abnormal directions in personality result from an interaction of constitutional and environmental factors.

There is abundant evidence that both sets of factors influence personality development in important ways. A child comes into the world with certain predispositions. He may be active or inactive, relatively sensitive or insensitive to such traumas as loss, aggressive or unaggressive.

441

One study has even demonstrated innate difference in the desire of infants to be held and cuddled [Schaffer and Emerson, 1964b]. Environments obviously vary tremendously—from that of the only child of wealthy doting parents to that of the ghetto child with eleven siblings being raised by one working parent, from parents who encourage the child's healthy psychological development to parents who express their own frustrations and fears through their children, from a suburban area full of children to a rural area with no other family within miles. However, one type of person may be sensitive to environmental circumstances that would not affect another type in the same way.

No variable has been relied on more in explaining personality than the influence of family. Almost all general theories of personality assign a central role to the family, and most researchers and practitioners in psychopathology operate on the assumption that the patient's family experiences are primarily responsible for abnormal personality development. Although there is strong evidence to justify this assumption, there is much about family influence that remains to be demonstrated [Frank, 1965; Spiegel and Bell, 1959].

One of the difficulties is the enormous research problems in testing the actual influence of family experiences on a person's ultimate behavior. In our society a person is exposed to family influence for about 20 years, and we cannot give equal attention to what happens over this whole period. A volume entitled *One Boy's Day* [Barker and Wright, 1951] records the events which occurred during only one day in the life of one child. Corresponding observations on 20 children until age fifteen would fill $15 \times 365 \times 20 = 109,500$ volumes, enough for a moderate-sized library. Clearly we must restrict the inquiry to a particular period of observation. Although some periods of life are probably more important than others, unfortunately, if we choose one period, we may miss important events happening at some other stage of development.

Another problem is determining the sources of influence within the family. The usual family constellation in our society includes parents, siblings, and often others as well. All kinds of interactions take place between the child and members of his family, but what are the truly significant ones? A great many specific experiences have been examined, but there are many more that have not been studied and perhaps not even considered. Moreover, even if we could easily select the events responsible for influencing behavior, any person displays an enormous array of behaviors—some exceedingly simple and others very complex, some occasional and others quite frequent in occurrence. Which aspects of behavior should we consider? Of course some are obviously important and are more likely to be examined first.

In spite of these formidable research problems, the role of the family has been under study for a long time, and there is an accumulation of relevant evidence. For example, in a well-known and somewhat controversial study which focused on the mother, Spitz [1945; 1946b] measured numerous behavioral and physical characteristics of children living in two institutions somewhere in South America. The two institutions are described as comparable and as providing good food and care, with the only important difference between them the fact that in one the baby was cared for by his mother, while in the other this duty fell to nurses. The reported differences between the children in these two places are highly dramatic. Those without mothers scored above average on psychological tests two to three months after birth but failed to make further progress; by the age of one year they were well below average, and far below the children raised by their mothers. While the children raised by their mothers were healthy, those who did not have mothers were not, and over one-third of them died over a two-year period. The survivors were markedly retarded in all areas of functioning measured, such as walking and talking, as well as in physical development. The implications of these results are that family experiences are of paramount importance in shaping all development, and specifically that the mother is a crucial ingredient in these experiences. There are other studies, however, which indicate that the mother's role is not nearly so important [Sears et al., 1957].

While the mother has perhaps had the lion's share of attention, fathers have also been the subject of scrutiny, and to no great surprise, they also appear to influence the growing child. Suedfeld [1967], who studied Peace Corps volunteers classified as successful or unsuccessful on the basis of whether or not they completed their overseas assignments, found that a significantly higher proportion of the failures had been raised without a father for some period during their first fifteen years. It is interesting that no other variable examined, including absence of the mother, differentiated the groups. Possibly for the type of behavior examined the role of the father is even more important than that of the mother. Other research has shown that father absence interfered with the development of masculine role behaviors in boys [Hetherington, 1966]. However, this disruption was found only if the absence occurred during the child's first four years. This supports the widely held view that family influence is more critical during some periods than others. The particular period, of course, depends on the behavior. Many other personality characteristics, such as guilt development [Moulton et al., 1966], moral development [Hoffman and Saltzstein, 1967], and intellectual development [Hurley, 1967], have been shown to be related to parental behavior. Thus, in spite of the research problems and the work which remains to be done, there is good evidence that the family's role in personality development may be as important as the theorizing suggests.

In our society school is also an important influence on personality, particularly in the early years. Bühler [1952] asked adult subjects to recall all they could of their school experiences in an effort to determine how much these experiences had influenced them. In general the recollections were sufficiently vivid to indicate considerable impact. However, the experiences recalled were generally unhappy rather than happy ones. Many of the subjects felt that their existing insecurities over physical or socioeconomic problems had been increased by school experiences. Findings such as this, coupled with the high incidence of school aversion

443

reported by child-guidance clinics, suggest that school experiences can be quite traumatic. It is likely that the classroom teacher, who is in a position to be either supportive or nonsupportive, is the most important single influence on the child in school.

ANXIETY AND PRESERVATION OF SELF

We have all experienced anxiety—a general state of fear that may be accompanied by different physical sensations such as tension, upset stomach, headache, or general shakiness. Anxiety goes by different names—nervousness, fear, or even mental illness—and may range from mild states of apprehension to severe and incapacitating attacks. Anxiety, like physical pain, has an adaptive side; a state of wary uneasiness must have stood primitive man in good stead as general preparation against predators. This characteristic evolved because of its earlier adaptive value, and the fact that it causes trouble for us now may be in part because our biological evolution has not caught up with our cultural evolution. Man is no longer at the mercy of predators, and the major sources of anxiety now are changes in interpersonal cultural and social conditions. However, human beings evolved over the years to fit an environment which was probably similar to that of the present-day chimpanzee or baboon. Such an environment presented a number of situations in which anxiety reactions played an important role. A prime example is the *separation anxiety* that arises when the infant's attachment to his mother is disrupted. Unable to cling during the first year of life, and more helpless than the other primates, the human infant had to remain closely attached to his mother in order to survive. Thus over the course of evolution intense anxiety on separation, leading to crying and rage as cues to the mother to reinstate contact, became strongly established in the human species as a means of preserving the infant's life under primitive conditions. Anxiety probably plays a related role in binding together the members of those small human groups, such as the family, on which all culture and society are built.

Security, the absence of anxiety, may also be thought of in terms of attachment to the familiar. What the infant or child knows best early in life are his mother and the care she provides. There is also a certain amount of security that derives from well-known places and routines. Change is likely to be frightening—to arouse anxiety—and to send the infant scurrying for the security of the well-known person or place. Even as adults we may sometimes experience a slight uneasiness in trying to fall asleep in a strange bed.

As the infant progresses into early childhood, his own sense of himself—what Erikson [1969] has termed the *sense of identity*—becomes a source of security. For example, the infant derives security from sucking his thumb, the two-year-old from his negativistic self-assertion, the six-year-old from being a "big boy" who can manage school on his

444

own, and the adult from the successful performance of a social role. Transitions from infancy to the world of childhood or from childhood to adolescence arouse anxiety because they require the abandonment of a well-known identity. Just when the infant has figured out how to get what he needs and wants, his parents and his own drive toward competence force him to give it all up. When he finally has childhood, school, and the world of peers pretty well under his control, his body becomes that of an adult and people start expecting a whole different set of behaviors from him. All growth and development involve change, and all change means giving up the security of the familiar whether it is familiar people and places or a familiar and well-ingrained identity. Hence all development is potentially anxiety arousing.

The psychological experience of anxiety not only has important adaptive origins, but also accompanies the continual challenge to identity that is posed by all growth and development. Thus anxiety is clearly a normal part of everyone's experience. However, what of the role of anxiety in personality disturbances? To answer this question we must first examine what a person typically does when he is anxious—when his identity is threatened.

As we have discussed, mastery and fantasy are two available modes of dealing with developmental crises. This distinction points toward the two major ways in which people deal with threats to the security of their identity—*mastery* and *dissociation* [Breger, 1971; Klein, in press]. When a person is threatened he may face up to the threat in some fashion, master the problem, and acquire new competence and self-esteem in the process. Mastery is involved in all the progressive aspects of psychological development. If he is unable to face up to the threat, he may deal with it by turning to the fantasy of dissociation. He acts as if the threat is not happening to him; in other words, he attempts to dissociate it from his sense of self or identity. This mode of reaction which encompasses all *defense mechanisms*, or *ego defenses*, is involved in all those aspects of psychological development that form the basis for personality disturbance.

Some examples should help clarify this distinction. When a young child receives an injury—say a painful cut on the hand—it is not uncommon for him to act as if the injured hand is not a part of himself. Children can even be seen talking to parts of their bodies that cause them pain, as if they can influence them in this way. At a more complex level, a child may deal with a parent that causes him pain by pretending that the pain-producing parent is "not really" his. In both situations the child experiences something that is threatening and that he must deal with in some way—and in both instances there is little he can do to realistically affect the cause of his pain. Hence he does what must seem like the next best thing; he uses his fantasy skills to dissociate the source of pain from himself.

Except in situations that are completely overwhelming, there is usually a choice between the two modes of reaction. For example, adolescence ushers in new opportunities and demands for intimate relations

445

with members of the opposite sex, and specific anxieties over intimacy or sexuality may sometimes augment the general threat to identity that accompanies this period. As adolescence progresses the person makes a series of choices which add up to either mastery or dissociation. If he overcomes his anxiety and establishes relationships with members of the opposite sex, eventually his sense of self or identity undergoes a transformation. From a child living in a primarily nonsexual world, he becomes an adult who is competent and comfortable in intimate heterosexual relationships. If he is unable to master this new situation, he is likely to turn to some form of dissociation. He may pretend to his friends that he has many dates when he does not, or he may hide his fears behind a facade of bravado, or he may withdraw into intellectual pursuits on the pretext that sex is unimportant or that he is morally superior to those who engage in sexual relations. If a person consistently makes such dissociative choices throughout adolescence, they eventually determine his identity. That is, he becomes a sexually insecure individual who continues to affect the pretense or fantasy he has employed. Where mastery leads to an expansion of identity and a growth of self-esteem, dissociation produces an arrest in development.

Obviously everyone makes some choices in the direction of mastery and some in the direction of dissociation; what determines the outcome is the relative balance between the two modes. A preponderance of dissociative choices results in psychological disturbance.

Schizophrenia, the most commonly occurring psychosis, is the ultimate form of dissociation. This severe form of psychological disturbance is characterized by intense anxiety, withdrawal from reality, inability to function in normal social roles, and a curious split, or inappropriateness, between thought and feeling. The schizophrenic has found his life so fraught with anxiety that he abandons reality altogether. This withdrawal is so complete that the mind—the place where fantasies occur—is dissociated from the body—which exists in the world of painful reality. The schizophrenic becomes so identified with this fantasy world that it becomes more "real" than his body, which he then begins to experience as an alien or foreign "thing" [Laing, 1965]. We see here a much more extreme form of dissociation than the pretense of the child that the hand he has cut is not his own. The autobiographical novel *I Never Promised You a Rose Garden* [Green, 1964] gives a detailed account of the schizophrenic process.

Although they are less severe, the various ego defenses that characterize neuroses also exemplify dissociation at the expense of mastery. Hysterical neuroses for example, are typified by *repression*, the forgetting of important anxiety-related events, which in some cases reaches amnesic proportions. Repression employs the normal process of forgetting (see Chapter 10) for dissociative purposes. The person cannot remember certain anxiety-laden thoughts or acts, so that it is as if they had not happened to him.

Obsessive-compulsive behavior makes dissociative use of another normal process—the separation of thought and feeling. We are all faced with circumstances in which it is useful to think calmly about something without being overwhelmed by anger or fear. The obsessive-compulsive person carries this use of *intellectualization* to an extreme. He may talk without apparent feeling about the very things that cause him the most anxiety, as if they were of no concern to him. His excessive concern with details enables him to bury the important in a welter of trivia. The obsessive-compulsive symptoms themselves are clear illustrations of dissociation. The obsessive thoughts come unbidden into his mind, as if he himself had nothing to do with them. Compulsive acts are experienced as something he is made to do, as if by some external agent.

A defense commonly found in both neurosis and psychosis is *projection*, attributing one's own unacceptable feelings and acts to others. In its extreme form projection can assume paranoid proportions, in which the person actually experiences his feelings as having come from others. This is especially frequent with feelings of guilt. The person dissociates his guilt feelings from himself and struggles against them as if they had come from some outside source—others who are watching him or persecuting him, or some vague "they."

DISSOCIATION OR MASTERY

Dissociation and mastery are both modes of dealing with the anxiety created by threats and stresses. Given the same general stresses of development, why is it that one person relies heavily on dissociation, to the point of neurosis or psychosis, while another is able to master stresses and live a normal life? The answer lies in the function of dissociation in alleviating excessive anxiety. There are many situations which the child cannot master, either because he lacks the ability or because the environmental circumstances do not permit a solution. The two-year-old who is deserted by his mother cannot go out and find another, and he may be in a situation where no adequate substitute is provided. Or his despair and detachment over her loss may block the formation of a new attachment even when a substitute figure is available. In situations where mastery is not possible some form of dissociation is the only available means of dealing with anxiety.

Although constitutional and environmental factors interact, in any individual case one set of factors may play a greater role. Some children are probably more prone to anxiety, more sensitive to loss, or less able to adapt to new situations. A history of physical illness early in life often shapes special sensitivities. Various genetic factors and physiological weaknesses, such as deformities, are of obvious importance in this regard. On the environmental side, a history of losses and abandonments, particularly at critical ages, heightens anxiety. Moreover, some environments are not supportive of mastery—as when parents neglect or abandon their children or subject them to physical abuse or more subtle forms of psychological punishment.

447

The interaction of such internal and environmental factors may form the basis for dissociative reactions as the only means of relieving anxiety, the person is once again driven to dissociation even though his skills and circumstances might now make mastery possible. Thus from a temporary means of dealing with the stresses of development, dissociation can become a more or less fixed part of identity.

As we have seen, personality disturbance is essentially an arrest in development which arises from a pattern of dissociative responses to developmental stress. A person's self or identity evolves from his mode of dealing with the central social-emotional areas of his life. However, the fact that dissociated areas may be reworked and mastered at some later time means that personality disturbance need not be a permanent identity. A person whose life is disrupted by such disturbances is frequently troubled not only by his specific symptoms and anxieties, but also about the general meaning of his disturbance. If he needs professional help, is this a sign that he is intrinsically "abnormal" or "crazy"? Will he ever be able to lead a normal life? No one *is* a neurotic or a schizophrenic. We all have the potential for developing nonneurotic or nonpsychotic behavior. If the professional works with the person in such a way that he is able to master those areas that he has so far only been able to run away from, he may emerge a stronger person.

During the development of social-emotional relationships there are many points at which behavior can become "different," or "abnormal," or "disturbed." Abnormal behavior results from a complex interaction of biological and social factors. Because of this, there is no one simple remedy. To the extent that personality disturbances are biologically based, there may be "biological" remedies. Tranquilizers and antidepressants are used extensively (and effectively) in treating excessive anxiety and depression. Drugs are effective to a degree in the management of severe disturbances such as schizophrenia. The neurobiology of affective states is an active area of research. To the extent that behavioral disturbances are based on disturbed interpersonal relations or problems of identity, remedies require changes in experience and self-evaluation. Abnormal personality development occurs readily; it is not so readily corrected.

SUMMARY

Human beings, like other primates, have evolved complex social mechanisms for regulating social life, and these are invariably toned with emotion. The first social-emotional force centering on the infant is attachment for the mother, a love that is fundamental to all primate social relations. Probably the most frequent interaction among primates relates to the dominance-submission hierarchies. Thus the control of aggression and the display of nonlethal aggression where appropriate are important regulating forces in primate social behavior. Curiosity and exploration, important in socialization and development in young primates, depend on the development of security in the early attachment phase and age-mate relationship influences. In addition to the social-emotional areas shared by all primates, human emotional development is influenced by unique aspects of sexuality, language, and the ability to symbolize.

Human socialization and personality development may be divided for convenience into four major phases—infancy and early childhood, childhood, adolescence, and adulthood. At each stage certain core relationships must be worked and reworked. Difficulty in adjusting within each of these phases provides the potential for later disturbance. For example, in infancy and early childhood the important social-emotional infant-mother relationship provides a sense of trust or security in the infant, and improper development in this area may set the stage for later retarded peer interaction, a lack of social and environmental exploration, and potential pathology. The childhood period involves a reworking of interpersonal attachment, aggression and its control, and independence. The child must begin to achieve a new sex-role identity, develop some independence from the security of the maternal figure, and work with his new cognitive and social skills. Adolescence introduces major physiological changes and new social expectations, with a corresponding necessity to abandon a familiar self-concept, or identity. Thus the stresses of adolescence may bring to light many developmental problems that might have been unnoticed or dormant until this time. Inadequate development in the areas of independence and sex-role behavior are two common sources of disturbance occurring during adolescence. The adult is not relieved of the responsibility of dealing with the central emotional-social areas of dependence-independence, attachment and separation, control of aggressions, and relations with authority: these continue through life.

Abnormal directions of personality development result from an interaction of biological and environmental circumstances. The family, particularly the mother, has long been considered an important factor in the development of behavior; in spite of the research difficulties involved, an accumulation of evidence testifies to the profound influences of the family on psychological development.

Development itself entails a succession of changes, and although each change brings new opportunities, each also challenges identity and hence engenders its own anxieties and potential for psychological disturbance. Thus anxiety is a normal and necessary part of all development. It is the manner in which the individual meets these stresses that sets the pattern for normal development or personality disturbance. In a broad sense anxiety has an adaptive basis, but when an individual is unable to master anxiety-producing situations it becomes maladaptive and is an important factor in both neurosis and psychosis. A person who is unable to master a situation may react by dissociating it from his sense of self through such defense mechanisms as projection, repression, and other forms of neurotic and psychotic behavior. However, the concept that core social-emotional areas can be reworked and mastered at later stages implies that personality disturbance need not be a permanent identity.

BIBLIOGRAPHY

Adair, L., Wilson, J. E., Zemp, J., and Glassman, E. 1968. Brain function and macromolecules. III. Uridine incorporated into polysomes of mouse brain during short-term avoidance conditioning. *Proc. Nat. Acad. Sci.,* 61, 606–613.

Adams, R. N. 1960. An inquiry into the nature of the family. In G. E. Dole and R. L. Carneiro (Eds.), *Essays in the science of culture in honor of Leslie A. White.* New York: Crowell.

Agranoff, B. W. 1968. Biological effects of antimetabolites used in behavioral studies. In D. H. Efron et al. (Eds.), *Psychopharmacology: A review of progress.* PHS Publ. No. 1836, 909–917. Washington, D.C.: U.S. Government Printing Office.

Ainsworth, M.D.S., and Bell, S. M. 1968. Attachment, exploration and separation: A discussion illustrated by the behavior of one-year-olds in a strange situation. Paper presented at the meeting of the American Psychological Association, San Francisco.

Alexander, F. G., and Selesnick, S. T. 1966. *A history of psychiatry.* New York: Harper and Row.

Alpern, H. P. 1968. Facilitation of learning by implantation of strychnine sulphate in the central nervous system. (Doctoral dissertation, University of California) Irvine, Calif.

Anand, B. K., and Brobeck, J. R. 1951. Hypothalamic control of food intake in rats and cats. *Yale J. Biol. Med.,* 24, 123.

Andersson, B. 1953. The effect of injections of hypertonic NaCl-solutions into different parts of the hypothalamus of goats. *Acta Physiol. Scand.,* 28, 188–201.

Applewhite, P. B. 1968. Nonlocal nature of habituation in a rotifer and protozoan. *Nature,* 217, 287–288.

Ardrey, R. 1966. *The territorial imperative.* New York: Atheneum. (Copyright © 1966 by Robert Ardrey; reprinted by permission of the publisher.)

Aronson, E., and Lindner, D. 1965. Gain and loss of esteem as determinants of interpersonal attraction. *J. Exp. Soc. Psych.,* 1, 156–171.

Asch, S. E. 1951. Effects of group pressure on the modification and distortion of judgments. In H. Geutzkow (Ed.), *Groups, leadership, and men.* Pittsburg: Carnegie. (By permission.)

Aserinsky, E., and Kleitman, N. 1953. Regularly occurring periods of eye motility, and concomitant phenomena, during sleep. *Science,* 118, 273–274.

Baddeley, A. D. 1964. Semantic and acoustic similarity in short-term memory. *Nature,* 204, 1116–1117.

Bandura, A., and Walters, R. H. 1963. Aggression. In H. W. Stevenson (Ed.), *Child psychology.* Chicago: University of Chicago Press.

Barbizet, J. 1963. Defect of memorizing of hippocampal-mammillary origin: A review. *J. Neurol. Neurosur. Psych.,* 26, 127–135. (By permission of the Editor, *J. Neurol. Neurosur. Psych.*)

Bard, P., and Macht, M. B. 1958. The behavior of chronically decerebrate cats. *Ciba Foundation symposium, Neurological basis of behavior.* London: Churchill.

Bard, P., and Mountcastle, V. B. 1948. Some forebrain mechanisms involved in expression of rage with special reference to suppression of angry behavior. *Res. Publ. Assn. Res. Nerv. Ment. Dis.,* 27, 362–404.

Barker, R. G., and Wright, H. F. 1951. *One boy's day: A specimen record of behavior.* New York: Harper and Row.

Barnett, S. A. 1963. *A study in behavior.* London: Methuen.

Barondes, S. H. 1968. Effects of inhibitors of cerebral protein synthesis on "long-term" memory in mice. In D. H. Efron et al. (Eds.), *Psychopharmacology: A review of progress.*

PHS Publ. No. 1836, 905–908. Washington, D. C.: U.S. Government Printing Office.

Barron, F. 1969. *Creative person and creative process.* New York: Holt, Rinehart and Winston.

Bartlett, F. C. 1932. *Remembering.* London: Cambridge University Press.

Bateson, G., Jackson, D., Haley, J., and Weakland, J., 1956. Toward a theory of schizophrenia. *Behav. Sci.,* 1, 251–254.

Bavelas, A., Hastorf, A. H., Gross, A. E., and Kite, W. A. 1965. Experiments on the alteration of group structure. *Exp. Soc. Psychol.,* 1, 55–70.

Bayley, N. 1943. Mental growth during the first three years. In R. G. Barker, J. S. Kounin, and H. F. Wright (Eds.), *Child behavior and development.* New York: McGraw-Hill.

Bayley, N. 1968. *Bayley's scales of infant development.* New York: Psychological Corp.

Beach, F. A. 1947. Evolutionary changes in the physiological control of mating behavior of mammals. *Psychol. Rev.,* 54, 297–315.

Beach, F. A. 1969. Locks and beagles. *Amer. Psychol.,* 24, 921–949, 971–989.

Bell, R. R. 1966. *Premarital sex in a changing society.* Englewood Cliffs, N.J.: Prentice-Hall.

Belmont, L., and Birch, H. G. 1951. Re-individualizing the repression hypothesis. *J. Abnorm. Soc. Psychol.,* 46, 226–235.

Bennett, E. L., Diamond, M. C., Krech, D., and Rosenzweig, M. R. 1964. Chemical and anatomical plasticity of brain. *Science,* 146, 610–619. (Copyright 1964 by the American Association for the Advancement of Science, by permission.)

Berkowitz, L. 1968. Impulse aggression and the gun. *Psychol. Today,* 2, 18–23.

Berman, P. W., Graham, F. K., Eichman, P. L., and Waisman, H. A. 1961. Psychologic and neurologic status of diet-treated phenylketonuric children and their siblings. *Pediatrics,* 28, 924.

Bernard, J. 1968. *The sex game.* Englewood Cliffs, N.J.: Prentice-Hall.

Birch, H. G. 1945. The relation of previous experience to insightful problem solving. *J. Comp. Psychol.,* 38, 367–383.

Bitterman, E. R. 1965. The evolution of intelligence. *Scient. Amer.,* 212, 92–100.

Bliss, J. C., Crane, H. D., Mansfield, P. K., and Townsend, J. 1966. Information available in brief tactile presentations. *Perceptual Psychophysiol.,* 1, 273–283.

Bloom, B. S. 1969. Letter to the editor. *Harvard Educ. Rev.,* 39, 419–421.

Bourne, L. E., Jr. 1966. *Human conceptual behavior.* Boston: Allyn and Bacon. (By permission of the publisher.)

Bovet, D., Bovet-Nitti, F., and Oliverio, A. 1969. Genetic aspects of learning and memory in mice. *Science,* 163, 139–149. (Copyright 1969 by the American Association for the Advancement of Science, by permission.)

Bower, T.G.R. 1965. Stimulus variables determining space perception in infants. *Science,* 149, 88–89.

Bower, T.G.R. 1966. The visual world of infants. *Scient. Amer.,* 215, 80–92.

Bowlby, J. 1952. *Maternal care and mental health.* Geneva: World Health Organization.

Bowlby, J. 1969. *Attachment and loss,* Vol. I, *Attachment.* New York: Basic Books.

Bowles, G. T. 1932. *New types of old Americans at Harvard and at eastern women's colleges.* Cambridge: Harvard University Press.

Brady, J. V. 1958. Ulcers in "executive" monkeys. *Scient. Amer.,* 199, 3–6.

Brady, J. V., and Nauta, W.J.H. 1953. Subcortical mechanisms in emotional behavior. Affective changes following septal forebrain lesions in the albino rat. *J. Comp. Physiol. Psychol.,* 46, 339–346.

Brazier, M.A.B. 1968. *The electrical activity of the nervous system* (3rd ed. rev.). London:

Pitman Medical Publ. Co., also Baltimore: Williams and Wilkins, and Scientific Publ. Co. Ltd. (By permission.)

Breland, K., and Breland, M. 1961. The misbehavior of organisms. *Amer. Psychol.*, 16, 681–684. (Copyright 1961 by the American Psychological Association, reproduced by permission.)

Bridges, K.M.B. 1932. Emotional development in early infancy. *Child. Devel.*, 3, 324–341.

Broadbent, D. E. 1970. Recent analyses of short-term memory. In K. H. Pribram and D. E. Broadbent (Eds.), *Biology of memory*. New York: Academic Press.

Brobeck, J. R. 1947–48. Food intake as a mechanism of temperature regulation. *Yale J. Biol. Med.*, 20, 545–552.

Brown, J. S. 1961. *The motivation of behavior.* New York: McGraw-Hill. (By permission.)

Brown, R., and Bellugi, U. 1964. Three processes in the child's acquisition of syntax. *Harvard Educ. Rev.*, 34, 133–151.

Brown, R., and Fraser, C. 1964. The acquisition of syntax. *Monogr. Soc. Res. Child Devel.*, 29, 43–79.

Brown, R., and McNeill, D. 1966. The "tip of the tongue" phenomenon. *J. Verbal Learn. Verbal Behav.*, 5, 325–337.

Bruce, D. J., Evans, C. R., Fenwick, P. B., and Spencer, V. 1970. Effect of present novel verbal material during slow wave sleep. *Nature*, 225, 873–874.

Bruner, J. S. 1964. The course of cognitive growth. *Amer. Psychol.*, 19, 1–15.

Bruner, J. S., Goodnow, J. J., and Austin, G. A. 1956. *A study of thinking.* New York: Wiley.

Bruner, J. S., Matter, J., and Papanek, M. L. 1955. Breadth of learning as a function of drive level and mechanization. *Psychol. Rev.*, 62, 1–10.

Bugelski, B. R. 1956. *The psychology of learning.* New York: Henry Holt. (By permission.)

Bühler, C. 1952. School as a phase of human life. *Education*, 73, 219–222.

Burt, C. 1966. The genetic determination of differences in intelligence: A study of monozygotic twins reared together and apart. *Brit. J. Psychol.*, 57, 137–153.

Butcher, H. J. 1968. *Human intelligence: Its nature and assessment.* New York: Barnes and Noble. (By permission.)

Butler, R. A. 1953. Discrimination learning by rhesus monkeys to visual-exploration motivation. *J. Comp. Physiol. Psychol.*, 46, 95–98.

(Copyright 1953 by the American Psychological Association, reproduced by permission.)

Butler, R. A. 1954a. Incentive conditions which influence visual exploration. *J. Exp. Psychol.*, 48, 19–23. (By permission.)

Butler, R. A. 1954b. Curiosity in monkeys. *Scient. Amer.*, 190, 70–75.

Butler, R. A., and Harlow, H. F. 1954. Persistence of visual exploration in monkeys. *J. Comp. Physiol. Psychol.*, 47, 258–263.

Byrne, D. 1961. Interpersonal attraction and attitude similarity. *J. Abnorm. Soc. Psychol.*, 62, 713–715.

Byrne, W. L., (Ed.). 1970. *Molecular approaches to learning and memory.* New York: Academic Press.

Cabak, V., and Najdanovic, R. 1965. Effect of undernutrition in early life on physical and mental development. *Arch. Dis. in Child.*, 40, 532–534. (By permission of the authors and the Editor, *Arch. Dis. in Childhood*.)

Cairns, R. B. 1966. Attachment behavior of mammals. *Psychol. Rev.*, 73, 409–426.

Caldwell, B. 1962. The usefulness of the critical period hypothesis in the study of filiative behavior. *Merrill-Palmer Quart. Behav. Devel.*, 8, 229–242.

Caldwell, B. M. 1964. The effects of infant care. In L. W. Hoffman and M. L. Hoffman (Eds.), *Review of child development research.* Vol. I. New York: Russell Sage.

Campbell, B. A. 1967. Development studies of learning and motivation in infra-primate mammals. In H. W. Stevenson (Ed.), *Early behavior: Comparative and developmental approaches.* New York: Wiley.

Campbell, B. A., and Lynch, G. S. 1969. Cortical modulation of spontaneous activity during hunger and thirst. *J. Comp. Physiol. Psychol.*, 67, 15–22.

Campbell, B. A., and Pickleman, J. R. 1961. The imprinting object as a reinforcing stimulus. *J. Comp. Physiol. Psychol.*, 54, 592–596.

Campbell, B. A., and Sheffield, F. D. 1953. Relation of random activity to food deprivation. *J. Comp. Physiol. Psychol.*, 46, 320–322.

Canaday, J. 1961. *Main streams of modern art.* New York: Simon and Schuster. (By permission.)

Cannon, W. B. 1932. *The wisdom of the body.* New York: Norton.

Cattell, J. M. 1890. Mental tests and measurements. *Mind,* 15, 373–381.

Cattell, R. B. 1968. Are I.Q. tests intelligent? *Psychol. Today,* 2, 56–62. (By permission.)

Chamove, A., Harlow, H. F., and Mitchell, G. 1967. Sex differences in the infant-directed behavior of preadolescent rhesus monkeys. *Child Devel.,* 38, 329–335.

Cheng, N. Y. 1929. Retroactive effect and degree of similarity. *J. Exp. Psychol.,* 12, 444–458.

Cherkin, A. 1969. Kinetics of memory consolidation: Role of amnesic treatment parameters. *Proc. Natl. Acad. Sci.,* 63, 1094–1101.

Chomsky, N. 1957. *Syntactic Structures.* The Hague: Mouton.

Chomsky, N. 1965. *Aspects of the theory of syntax.* Cambridge: MIT Press.

Chomsky, N. 1968. *Language and the mind.* New York: Harcourt, Brace and World.

Chow, K. L., Riesen, A. H., and Newell, F. W. 1957. Degeneration of retinal ganglion cells in infant chimpanzees reared in darkness. *J. Comp. Neurol.,* 107, 27.

Clark, R. A. 1952. The projective measurement of experimentally induced levels of sexual motivation. *J. Exp. Psychol.,* 44, 391–399.

Cleland, J. 1950. *Memoirs of Fanny Hill.* Paris: Obelisk Press.

Conrad, R. 1958. Accuracy of recall using keyset and telephone dial and the effect of a prefix digit. *J. Appl. Psychol.,* 42, 285–288.

Cooper, J. B. 1959. Emotion and prejudice. *Science,* 130, 314–318.

Cooper, J. B., and Blair, M. A. 1959. Parent evaluation as a determiner of ideology. *J. Genetic Psychol.,* 94, 93–100.

Cooper, J. B., and McGaugh, J. L. 1963. *Integrating principles of social psychology.* Cambridge: Schenkman. (By permission.)

Court-Brown, W. M., Jacobs, P. A., and Price, W. H. 1968. Sex chromosome aneuploidy and criminal behaviour. In J. M. Thoday and A. S. Parkes (Eds.), *Genetic and environmental influences on behavior.* Edinburgh: Oliver and Boyd Ltd.

Crozier, W. J., and Hoagland, H. 1934. The study of living organisms. In C. Murchison (Ed.), *A handbook of general experimental psychology.* Worcester, Mass.: Clark University Press.

Dale, H.C.A. 1964. Retroactive interference in short-term memory. *Nature,* 203, 1408.

Darwin, C. 1859. *The origin of species.* New York: A. L. Fowle, International Science Library.

Darwin, C. 1872. *The expression of the emotions in man and animals.* New York: D. Appleton. Reprinted in 1965 by University of Chicago Press.

Darwin, C. A. 1877. A biographical sketch of an infant. *Mind,* 2, 285–294.

Davis, C. M. 1928. Self-selection of diet by newly weaned infants. *Amer. J. Dis. Child.,* 36, 651–679.

Davis, H. 1959. Excitation of auditory receptors. In J. Field, H. W. Magoun, and B. E. Hall (Eds.), *Handbook of physiology.* Vol. I, Sec. I, Neurophysiology. Washington, D.C.: American Physiological Society.

Deese, J. 1970. *Psycholinguistics.* Boston: Allyn and Bacon. (By permission of the publisher.)

Deets, A. C. 1969. The effects of twinship on the interactions between rhesus monkey mothers and infants. (Master's thesis, University of Wisconsin) Madison, Wisc.

DeFries, J. C., Wilson, J. R., and McClearn, G. E. 1970. Open-field behavior in mice: Selection response and situational generality. *Behav. Genetics,* 1.

Dement, W. 1960. The effect of dream deprivation. *Science,* 131, 1705–1707.

Denti, A., McGaugh, J. L., Landfield, P. W., and Shinkman, P. 1970. Further study of the effects of posttrial electrical stimulation of the mesencephalic reticular formation on avoidance learning in rats. *Physiol. Behav.,* 5, 659–662.

Deutsch, J. A. 1969. The physiological basis of memory. *Amer. Rev. Psychol.,* 20, 85–104.

Deutsch, M. 1949. An experimental study of the effects of cooperation and competition upon group processes. *Human Relations,* 2, 199–231.

DeValois, R. L. 1965. Analysis and coding of color vision in the primate visual system. *Sensory receptors.* Cold Spring Harbor, N. Y.: Laboratory of Quantitative Biology.

DeVore, I. 1963. Mother-infant relations in free-ranging baboons. In H. L. Rheingold (Ed.), *Maternal behavior in mammals.* New York: Wiley.

DeVore, I. (Ed.). 1965. *Primate behavior: Field studies of monkeys and apes.* New York: Holt, Rinehart and Winston.

Dewey, J. 1922. *Human nature and conduct.* New York: Henry Holt.

Drachman, D. A., and Arbit, J. 1966. Memory and the hippocampal complex. II. Is memory a multiple process? *Arch. Neurol.*, 15, 52–61. (By permission.)

Duffy, E. 1962. *Activation and behavior.* New York: Wiley.

Duncan, C. P. 1949. The retroactive effects of electroshock on learning. *J. Comp. Physiol. Psychol.*, 42, 32–34.

Dunlop, C. W., Webster, W. R., and Simons, L. A. 1965. Effect of attention on evoked responses in the classical auditory pathway. *Nature*, 206, 1048–1050.

Eason, R. G., Harter, M. R., and White, C. T. 1969. Effects of attention and arousal on visually evoked cortical potentials and reaction time in man. *Physiol. Behav.*, 4, 283–289. (By permission.)

Ebbinghaus, H. 1885. *Uber das gedachtniss.* Leipzig: Drucker and Humblat.

Ebbinghaus, H. 1964. *Memory.* New York: Dover.

Eccles, J. C. 1964. *The physiology of synapses.* New York: Academic Press.

Eichenwald, H. F., and Fry, P. C. 1969. Nutrition and learning. *Science*, 163, 644–648.

Eisenstein, E. M., and Cohen, M. J. 1965. Learning in an isolated prothoracic insect ganglion. *Animal Behav.*, 13, 104–108. (By permission.)

Elias, J., and Gebhard, P. 1969. Sexuality and sexual learning in children. *Phi Delta Kappan*, 50, 401–405.

Ellis, H. 1936. *Studies in the psychology of sex.* New York: Random House.

Erikson, E. H. 1950. *Childhood and society.* New York: Norton.

Erikson, E. H. 1969. *Identity, youth and crisis.* New York: Norton.

Erlenmeyer-Kimling, L., and Jarvik, L. F. 1963. Genetics and intelligence: A review. *Science*, 142, 1477–1479. (Copyright 1963 by the American Association for the Advancement of Science, by permission.)

Fantz, R. L. 1961. The origin of form perception. *Scient. Amer.*, 204, 66–72.

Fantz, R. L. 1965. Ontogeny of perception. In A. M. Schrier, H. F. Harlow, and F. Stollnitz (Eds.), *Behavior of nonhuman primates.* New York: Academic Press.

Farina, A., Holzberg, J. D., and Dies, R. R. 1969. Influence of the parents and verbal reinforcement on the performance of schizophrenic patients. *J. Abnorm. Psychol.*, 74, 9–15.

Farina, A., and Webb, W. W. 1956. Premorbid adjustment and subsequent discharge. *J. Nerv. Mental Dis.*, 124, 612–613.

Farrell, B. 1966. Scientists, theologians, mystics swept up in a psychic revolution. *Life*, March 25. Reprinted in Life Educational Reprint 22. New York: Time. (By permission.)

Fernandez de Molina, A., and Hunsperger, R. W. 1959. Central representation of affective reactions in forebrain and brain stem: Electrical stimulation of amygdala, stria terminalis, and adjacent structures. *J. Physiol.*, 145, 251–265. (By permission.)

Festinger, L. 1954. A theory of social comparison processes. *Human Relations*, 7, 117–140.

Festinger, L. 1957. *A theory of cognitive dissonance.* Stanford: Stanford University Press. (By permission.)

Festinger, L., Schachter, S., and Back, K. 1950. *Social pressures in informal groups: A study of human factors in housing.* New York: Harper. (By permission of the publisher.)

Festinger, L., Schachter, S., and Back, K. 1963. *Social pressures in informal groups.* Stanford: Stanford University Press.

Fishbein, W. 1970. Interference with conversion of memory from short-term to long-term storage by partial sleep deprivation. *Commun. Behav. Biol.*, 5, 171–175.

Flavell, J. H. 1963. *The developmental psychology of Jean Piaget.* Princeton: Van Nostrand.

Flynn, J. P. 1967. The neural basis of aggression in cats. In D. C. Glass (Ed.), *Neurophysiology and emotion.* New York: Rockefeller University Press and Russell Sage Foundation. (By permission.)

Fox, B. H., and Robbin, J. S. 1952. The retention of material presented during sleep. *J. Exp. Psychol.*, 43, 75–79.

Frank, G. H. 1965. The role of the family in the development of psychopathology. *Psychol. Bull.*, 64, 191–205.

Freedman, L. Z. 1960. Truth drugs. *Scient. Amer.*, 202, 145–157.

French, G. M., and Harlow, H. F. 1962. Variability of delayed-reaction performance in normal and brain-damaged rhesus monkeys. *J. Neurophysiol.*, 25, 585–599.

Freud, A. 1954. Psycho-analysis and education. *Psychoanalytic Study of the Child*, 9, 9–15.

Freud, S. 1938. *The basic writings of Sigmund Freud.* Translated and edited by A. A. Brill. New York: Modern Library.

Freud, S. 1949. *An outline of psychoanalysis.* New York: Norton.

Garcia, J., McGowan, B. K., Ervin, F. R., and Koelling, R. A. 1968. Cues: Their relative effectiveness as a function of the reinforcer. *Science,* 160, 794–795. (Copyright 1968 by the American Association for the Advancement of Science, by permission.)

Gardner, B. T., and Gardner, R. A. 1970. Two-way communication with an infant chimpanzee. In A. Schrier and F. Stollnitz (Eds.), *Behavior of nonhuman primates.* New York: Academic, in press. (By permission.)

Gardner, R. A., and Gardner, B. T. 1969. Teaching sign language to a chimpanzee. *Science,* 165, 664–672.

Gari, J. E., and Scheinfeld, A. 1968. Sex differences in mental and behavioral traits. *Genetic Psychol. Monog.,* 77, 169–299.

Geller, A., and Jarvik, M. E. 1968. The time relations of ECS induced amnesia. *Psychonomic Sci.,* 12, 169–170.

Gerard, R. W. 1949. Physiology and psychiatry. *Amer. J. Psych.,* 106, 161–173.

Gibson, E. J. 1942. Intra-list generalization as a factor in verbal learning. *J. Exp. Psychol.,* 30, 185–200.

Glassman, E. 1969. The biochemistry of learning: An evaluation of the role of RNA and protein. *Amer. Rev. Biochem.,* 38, 605–646.

Gleitman, H. 1970. Forgetting in animals: Phenomena and explanatory theories. In W. K. Honig and P.H.R. James (Eds.), *Animal memory.* New York: Academic Press, in press. (By permission.)

Glickman, S. E. 1961. Perseverative neural processes and consolidation of memory trace. *Psychol. Bull.,* 58, 218–233.

Goddard, H. H. 1914. *Feeblemindedness: Its causes and consequences.* New York: Macmillan. (By permission.)

Goldfarb, W. 1955. Emotional and intellectual consequences of psychologic deprivation in infancy: A reevaluation. In P. H. Hoch and J. Zubin (Eds.), *Psychopathology in childhood.* New York: Greene and Stratton.

Golub, A. M., Masiarz, F. R., Villars, T., and McConnell, J. V. 1970. Incubation effects in behavior induction in rats. *Science,* 168, 392–395.

Goodall, J. 1965. Chimpanzees of the Gombe Stream Reserve. In I. DeVore (Ed.), *Primate behavior: Field studies of monkeys and apes.* New York: Holt, Rinehart and Winston.

Goodenough, D. R., Shapiro, A., Holden, M., and Steinschriber, L. 1959. A comparison of "dreamers" and "non-dreamers" eye movements, electroencephalograms, and the recall of dreams. *J. Abnorm. Soc. Psychol.,* 59, 295–302.

Goodenough, F. L. 1931. *Anger in young children.* Minneapolis: University of Minnesota Press.

Gottesman, I. I. 1962. Differential inheritance of the psychoneuroses. *Eugenics Quart.,* 9, 223, 227.

Gottesman, I. I., and Shields, J. 1966. Schizophrenia in twins: 16 years, consecutive admissions to a psychiatric clinic. *Brit. J. Psych.,* 112, 809–818. (By permission.)

Gottlieb, G. 1965. Imprinting in relation to parental and species identification by avian neonates. *J. Comp. Physiol. Psychol.,* 59, 345–356.

Granda, A., and Hammack, J. 1961. Operant behavior during sleep. *Science,* 133, 1485–1486.

Granit, R. 1962. Neurophysiology of the retina. In H. Dawson (Ed.), *The eye.* Vol. 2. New York: Academic Press.

Gray, G. W. 1958. The great ravelled knot. *Scient. Amer.,* October.

Green, H. 1964. *I never promised you a rose garden.* New York: Signet.

Groos, K. 1901. *The play of man.* New York: D. Appleton-Century.

Gross, C. G., Bender, D. B., and Rocha-Miranda, C. E. 1969. Visual receptive fields of neurons in inferotemporal cortex of the monkey. *Science,* 166, 1303–1305.

Grossman, S. P. 1967. *A textbook of physiological psychology.* New York: Wiley.

Groves, P. M., and Thompson, R. F. 1970. Habituation: A dual-process theory. *Psychol. Rev.,* 77, 412–450. (Copyright 1970 by the American Psychological Association, reproduced by permission.)

Gubar, G. 1966. Recognition of human facial expressions judged live in the laboratory setting. *J. Personal. Soc. Psychol.,* 4, 108–111.

Gunther, M. 1961. Infant behaviour at the breast. In B. M. Foss (Ed.), *Determinants of infant behavior.* Vol. I. London: Methuen.

Haber, R. N. 1970. How we remember what we see. *Scient. Amer.,* 222, 104–112.

Haber, R. N., and Haber, R. B. 1964. Eidetic imagery. I. Frequency. *Perceptual Motor Skills,* 19, 131–138.

Haber, R. N., and Standing, L. G. 1969. Direct measures of short-term visual storage. *Quart. J. Exp. Psychol.*, 21, 43–54.

Haggar, R. A., and Barr, M. L. 1950. Quantitative data on the size of synaptic end-bulbs in the cat's spinal cord. *J. Comp. Neurol.*, 93, 17–35. (By permission.)

Hall, C. S. 1959. *The meaning of dreams.* New York: Dell.

Hall, G. S. 1920. *Youth.* New York: D. Appleton-Century.

Hamburg, D. A., and Lunde, D. T. 1966. Sex hormones in the development of sex differences in human behavior. In E. E. Maccoby (Ed.), *The development of sex differences.* Stanford: Stanford University Press.

Hansen, E. W. 1966. The development of maternal and infant behavior in the rhesus monkey. *Behaviour*, 27, 107–149.

Harlow, H. F. 1949a. The formation of learning sets. *Psychol. Rev.*, 56, 51–56. (Copyright 1949 by the American Psychological Association, reproduced by permission.)

Harlow, H. F. 1949b. The nature of learning sets. *Psychol. Rev.*, 56, 51–65.

Harlow, H. F. 1952. Functional organization of the brain in relation to mentation and behavior. In *The biology of mental health and diseases.* Ch. 16. New York: Paul B. Hoeber, Inc., Medical Book Dept. of Harper and Brothers.

Harlow, H. F. 1958. The nature of love. *Amer. Psychol.*, 13, 673–685.

Harlow, H. F. 1959a. The development of learning in the rhesus monkey. *Amer. Sci.*, 47, 459–479. (By permission.)

Harlow, H. F. 1959b. Love in infant monkeys. *Scient. Amer.*, 200, 68–74.

Harlow, H. F. 1969. Age-mate or peer affectional system. In D. S. Lehrman, R. A. Hinde, and E. Shaw (Eds.), *Advances in the study of behavior.* Vol. 2. New York: Academic Press.

Harlow, H. F., and Griffin, G. 1965. Induced mental and social deficits in rhesus monkeys. In S. F. Asler and R. E. Cooke (Eds.), *The biosocial basis of mental retardation.* Baltimore: Johns Hopkins Press.

Harlow, H. F., and Harlow, M. K. 1949. Learning to think. *Scient. Amer.*, 181, 36–39.

Harlow, H. F., and Harlow, M. K. 1962. Social deprivation in monkeys. *Scient. Amer.*, 207, 136–146.

Harlow, H. F., and Harlow, M. K. 1965. The affectional systems. In A. M. Schrier, H. F. Harlow, and F. Stollnitz (Eds.), *Behavior of nonhuman primates.* Vol. II. New York: Academic Press.

Harlow, H. F., Harlow, M. K., and Hansen, E. W. 1963. The maternal affectional system of rhesus monkeys. In H. L. Rheingold (Ed.), *Maternal behavior in mammals.* New York: Wiley.

Harlow, H. F., Joslyn, W. D., Senko, M. G., and Dopp, A. 1966. Behavioral aspects of reproduction in primates. *J. Animal Sci.*, 25, 49–67.

Harlow, H. F., and McClearn, G. E. 1954. Object discrimination learned by monkeys on the basis of manipulation motives. *J. Comp. Physiol. Psychol.*, 47, 73–76.

Harlow, H. F., Suomi, S. J., and McKinney, W. T. 1970. Experimental production of depression in monkeys. *Mainly Monkeys*, 1, 6–12.

Harlow, H. F., and Zimmermann, R. R. 1958. The development of affectional responses in infant monkeys. *Proc. Amer. Phil. Soc.*, 102, 501–509.

Harlow, H. F., and Zimmermann, R. R. 1959. Affectional responses in the infant monkey. *Science*, 130, 421–432.

Harlow, M. K., and Harlow, H. F. 1966. Affection in primates. *Discovery*, 27, 11–17.

Hartmann, E. 1967. *The biology of dreaming.* Springfield: Charles C. Thomas. (By permission of the publisher.)

Hartry, A. L., Keith-Lee, P., and Morton, W. D. 1964. Planaria: Memory transfer through cannibalism re-examined. *Science*, 146, 274–275.

Hastorf, A. H. 1966. Personal communication.

Hayes, C. 1951. *The ape in our house.* New York: Harper.

Hayes, K. J., and Hayes, C. 1951. The intellectual development of a home-raised chimpanzee. *Proc. Amer. Phil. Soc.*, 95, 105–109.

Hebb, D. O. 1949. *The organization of behavior.* New York: Wiley.

Hebb, D. O. 1955. Drives and the c.n.s. (conceptual nervous system). *Psychol. Rev.*, 62, 243–254.

Hebb, D. O. 1958. Alice in Wonderland or psychology among the biological sciences. In H. F. Harlow and C. N. Woolsey (Eds.), *Biological and biochemical bases of behavior.* Madison: University of Wisconsin Press. (Copyright © 1958 by the Regents of the University of Wisconsin, by permission.)

Hebb, D. O. 1961. Distinctive features of

learning in the higher animal. In J. F. Dela-fresnaye et al. (Eds.), *Brain mechanisms and learning.* Oxford, England: Blackwell Scientific Publ. (By permission.)

Hebb, D. O. 1966. *A textbook of psychology.* Philadelphia: W. B. Saunders. (By permission.)

Hediger, H. 1950. *Wild animals in captivity.* London: Butterworth.

Heidbreder, E. 1946. The attainment of concepts. I. Methodology and terminology. *J. Gen. Psychol.,* 35, 173–189. (By permission.)

Heine, R. 1914. Uber Wierdererkennen und ruckinirkinde Hemmung. *Z. Psychol.,* 68, 161–236.

Heinroth, O., and Heinroth, K. 1959. *The birds.* London: Faber and Faber.

Held, R. 1965. Plasticity in sensory-motor systems. *Scient. Amer.,* 213, 84–94.

Held, R., and Hein, A. 1963. Movement-produced stimulation in the development of visually guided behavior. *J. Comp. Physiol. Psychol.,* 56, 872–876. (By permission.)

Helfer, R. E., and Kempe, C. H. 1968. *Battered child.* Chicago: University of Chicago Press.

Herbert, M. J., and Harsh, C. M. 1944. Observational learning by cats. *J. Comp. Physiol. Psychol.,* 37, 81–95.

Hernández-Peón, R. 1960. Neurophysiological correlates of habituation and other manifestations of plastic inhibition (internal inhibition). In H. H. Jasper and G. D. Smirnov (Eds.), The Moscow colloquium on electroencephalography of higher nervous activity. *Electroenceph. Clin. Neurophysiol.,* Suppl. 13.

Hernández-Peón, R., Scherrer, H., and Jouvet, M. 1956. Modification of electric activity in cochlear nucleus during "attention" in unanesthetized cats. *Science,* 123, 331–332.

Herz, M. J., Spooner, C. E., and Cherkin, A. 1969. EEG and multiple unit correlates of retrograde amnestic treatment with flurothyl in chicks. *Proc. Western Pharmacol. Soc.*

Hess, E. H. 1956. Space perception in the chick. *Scient. Amer.,* 195, 71–80.

Hess, E. H. 1957. Effects of meprobamate on imprinting in waterfowl. *Ann. New York Acad. Sci.,* 67 (10), 724–733. (Copyright © 1957 by The New York Academy of Sciences, reprinted by permission.)

Hess, E. H. 1959. Imprinting. *Science,* 130, 133–141.

Hess, R. D., and Shipman, V. 1965. Early experience and the socialization of cognitive modes in children. *Child Devel.,* 36, 869–886.

Heston, L. L. 1966. Psychiatric disorders in foster home reared children of schizophrenic mothers. *Brit. J. Psych.,* 112, 819–825.

Hetherington, E. M. 1966. Effects of paternal absence on sex-typed behaviors in negro and white preadolescent males. *J. Personal. Soc. Psychol.,* 4, 87–91.

Hetherington, E. M. 1967. Family structure and sex role typing. In J. Hill (Ed.), *Symposium on child development.* Minneapolis: University of Minnesota Press.

Hillarp, N. A., Fuxe, K., and Dahlström, A. 1960. Demonstration and mapping of central neurons containing dopamine, noradrenaline, and 5-hydroxytryptamine and their reactions to psychopharmacia. *Pharmacol. Rev.,* 18, 727.

Hinde, R. A. 1966. *Animal behavior.* New York: McGraw-Hill.

Hirsch, J. 1970. Behavior genetic analysis and its biosocial consequences. *Seminars in Psych.,* 2, 89–105.

Hirschberg, G., and Gilliland, A. R. 1942. Parent-child relationships and attitudes. *J. Abnorm. Soc. Psychol.,* 37, 125–130.

Hodgkin, A. L. 1964. The ionic basis of nervous conduction. *Science,* 145, 1148–1154.

Hoffman, M. L., and Saltzstein, H. D. 1967. Parent discipline and the child's moral development. *J. Personal. Soc. Psychol.,* 5, 45–57.

Holstein, A. P. 1965. Discussion of "identical twins—'idiot savants'—calendar calculators." *Amer. J. Psych.,* 121, 1077–1078. (By permission.)

Honzik, M. P. 1938. The constancy of mental test performance during the preschool period. *J. Genetic Psychol.,* 52, 285–302.

Honzik, M. P., Macfarlane, J. W., and Allen, L. 1948. The stability of mental test performance between two and eighteen years. *J. Exp. Educ.,* 18, 309–324.

Horowitz, E. L. 1936. The development of attitude toward the negro. *Arch. Psychol.,* 28, 194. (By permission.)

Horridge, G. A. 1965. The electrophysiological approach to learning in the isolatable ganglia. *Animal Behav.,* Suppl. 1, 163–182.

Horwitz, W. A., Kestenbaum, C., Person, E., and Jarvik, L. 1965. Identical twin—"idiot savants"—calendar calculators. *Amer. J. Psych.,* 121, 1075–1079.

Hovland, C. I. 1940. Experimental studies in

rote-learning theory. VI. Comparison of retention following learning to some criterion by massed and distributed practice. *J. Exp. Psychol.*, 26, 568–587.

Hovland, C. I., and Weiss, W. 1951. The influence of source credibility on communication effectiveness. *Publ. Opin. Quart.*, 15, 635–650. (By permission.)

Hovland, C. I., Lumsdaine, A. A., and Sheffield, F. D. 1949. Experiments on mass communication. In *Studies in social psychology in world war II*. Vol. 3. Princeton: Princeton University Press.

Hubel, D. H., and Wiesel, T. N. 1959. Receptive fields of single neurons in the cat's striate cortex. *J. Physiol.*, 148, 574–591.

Hubel, D. H., and Wiesel, T. N. 1962. Receptive fields, binocular interaction and functional architecture in the cat's visual center. *J. Physiol.*, 160, 106–154. (By permission.)

Hubel, D. H., and Wiesel, T. N. 1963. Receptive fields of cells in striate cortex of very young, visually inexperienced kittens. *J. Neurophysiol.*, 26, 994–1002.

Hubel, D. H., and Wiesel, T. N. 1965. Receptive fields and functional architecture in two nonstriate visual areas (18 and 19) of the cat. *J. Neurophysiol.*, 28, 229–289. (By permission.)

Hudspeth, W. J., and Wilsoncroft, W. E. 1970. Retrograde amnesia time-dependent effects of rhinencephalic lesions. *J. Neurobiol.*, 1, 221–232.

Hulin, C. L., and Blood, M. R. 1968. Job enlargement, individual differences, and worker responses. *Psychol. Bull.*, 69, 41–55.

Hull, C. L. 1943. *Principles of behavior*. New York: Appleton-Century-Crofts.

Hunter, I. 1957. *Memory*. Baltimore: Penguin Books.

Hunter, W. S. 1913. The delayed reaction in animals and children. *Behav. Monogr.*, 2, 1–86.

Huntley, R.M.C. 1966. Heritability of intelligence. In J. E. Meade and A. S. Parkes (Eds.), *Genetic and environmental factors in human ability*. New York: Plenum Press. (By permission.)

Huppert, F. A., and Deutsch, J. A. 1969. Improvement in memory with time. *Quart. J. Exp. Psychol.*, 21, 267–271.

Hurley, J. R. 1967. Parental malevolence and children's intelligence. *J. Cons, Psychol.*, 31, 199–204.

Huxley, A. 1928. *Point counterpoint*. New York: Doubleday.

Huxley, A. F. 1964. Excitation and conduction in nerve: Quantitative analysis. *Science*, 145, 1154–1159.

Hyden, H. 1967. RNA in brain cells. In G. C. Quarton, T. Melnechuk, and F. O. Schmitt (Eds.), *The neurosciences*. New York: Rockefeller.

Jacobsen, C. F. 1935. Functions of the frontal association area in primates. *Arch. Neurol. Psych.*, 33, 558–569.

Jacobson, E. 1931. Electrical measurements of neuromuscular states during mental activities. VIII. Imagination, recollection and abstract thinking involving the speech musculature. *Amer. J. Physiol.*, 97, 200–209. (By permission.)

Jacobson, E. 1938. *Progressive relaxation*. Chicago: University of Chicago Press.

Jaffe, J. H. 1965. Drug addiction and drug abuse. In L. S. Goodman and A. Gilman (Eds.), *The pharmacological basis of therapeutics*. New York: Macmillan.

James, H. 1959. Flicker: An unconditioned stimulus for imprinting. *Can. J. Psychol.*, 13, 59–67.

James, W. 1890. *The principles of psychology*. New York: Henry Holt. Reprinted 1950, Vol. I. New York: Dover.

Janis, I. L., and Feshback, S. 1953. Effects of fear-arousing communications. *J. Abnorm. Soc. Psychol.*, 48, 78–92. (Copyright 1953 by the American Psychological Association, reproduced by permission.)

Jarvik, M. E. 1968. The significance of retrograde amnesia (RA) and forgetting in the problem of memory storage. In D. Bovet, F. Bovet-Nitti, and A. Oliverio (Eds.), *Recent advances on learning and retention*. Rome: Roma Accademia Nazionale dei Lincei.

Jenkins, J. G., and Dallenbach, K. M. 1924. Oblivescence during sleep and waking. *Amer. J. Psychol.*, 35, 605–612.

Jensen, A. R. 1969. How much can we boost I.Q. and scholastic achievement? *Harvard Educ. Rev.*, 39, 1–123.

Jensen, D. D. 1965. Paramecia, planaria and pseudo learning. *Animal Behav.*, Suppl. 1, 9–20.

Jensen, G. D. 1965. Mother-infant relationship in the monkey *Macaca nemestrina*: Development of specificity of maternal response to own infant. *J. Comp. Physiol. Psychol.*, 59, 305–308.

Jersild, A. T., and Holmes, F. B. 1935. Methods of overcoming children's fears. *J. Psychol.*, 1, 75–104.

Jersild, A. T., Mackey, F. V., and Jersild, C. L. 1933. Children's fears, dreams, wishes, day-dreams, likes, dislikes, pleasant and unpleasant memories. *Child. Devel. Monogr.*, No. 12.

John, E. R. 1967. *Mechanisms of memory.* New York: Academic Press. (By permission.)

John, E. R., Herrington, R. N., and Sutton, S. 1967. Effects of visual form on the evoked response. *Science*, 155, 1439–1442. (Copyright 1967 by the American Association for the Advancement of Science, by permission.)

Johnson, L. M. 1939. The relative effect of a time interval upon learning and retention. *J. Exp. Psychol.*, 24, 169–179.

Jones, E. E., and Gerard, H. B. 1967. *Foundations of social psychology.* New York: Wiley.

Jones, H. E. 1954. The environment and mental development. In R. Carmichael (Ed.), *Manual of child psychology.* New York: Wiley.

Jones, N.G.B. 1967. An ethological study of some aspects of social behaviour of children in nursery school. In D. Morris (Ed.), *Primate ethology.* Chicago: Aldine.

Kagan, J., and Moss, H. A. 1962. *Birth to maturity: A study in psychological development.* New York: Wiley.

Kagan, J., Rosman, B., Day, D., Albert, J., and Phillips, W. 1964. Information processing in the child: Significance of analytic and reflective attitudes. *Psychol. Monogr.*, 78(1, Whole No. 578).

Kallman, F. J. 1953. *Heredity in health and mental disorder.* New York: Norton.

Kaufman, I. C., and Rosenblum, L. A. 1967. Depression in infant monkeys separated from their mothers. *Science*, 155, 1030–1031.

Kaufman, I. C., and Rosenblum, L. A. 1969. The waning of the mother-infant bond in two species of macaque. In B. M. Foss (Ed.), *Determinants of infant behavior.* Vol. IV. London: Methuen.

Kavanau, J. L. 1963. Compulsory regime and control of environment in animal behavior. I. Wheel running. *Behaviour,* 20, 251–281.

Kelly, F. S., Farina, A., and Mosher, D. L. 1971. The ability of schizophrenic women to

create a favorable or unfavorable impression on an interview. *J. Cons. Clin. Psych.*, in press.

Kessen, W., and Mandler, G. 1961. Anxiety, pain and the inhibition of distress. *Psychol. Rev.*, 68, 396–404.

Keys, A., Brôzek, J., Henschel, A., Mickelsen, O., and Taylor, H. L. 1950. *The biology of human starvation.* Minneapolis: University of Minnesota Press.

Klein, G. S. 1971. *Psychoanalytic theory: An exploration of essentials.* New York: Knopf, in press.

Klineberg, O. 1969. *Characteristics of the american negro.* New York: Harper and Row.

Köhler, W. 1925. *The mentality of apes.* New York: Harcourt, Brace.

Konishi, M. 1965. The role of auditory feedback in the control of vocalization in the white-crowned sparrow. *Z. Tierpsychol.*, 22, 770–785.

Konorski, J. 1967. *Integrative activity of the brain.* Chicago: University of Chicago Press.

Koukkou, M., and Lehmann, D. 1968. EEG and memory storage in sleep experiments with humans. *Electroenceph. Clin. Neurophysiol.*, 25, 455–462.

Krech, D., and Crutchfield, R. S. 1948. *Theory and problems of social psychology.* New York: McGraw-Hill. (Used with permission of McGraw-Hill Book Company.)

Krivanek, J., and McGaugh, J. L. 1968. Effects of pentylenetetrazol on memory storage in mice. *Psychopharmacologia,* 12, 303–321. (By permission.)

Krueger, W.C.F. 1929. The effect of overlearning on retention. *J. Exp. Psychol.*, 12, 71–78.

Lagerspetz, K.M.J. 1969. Aggression and aggressiveness in laboratory mice. In S. Garattini and E. B. Sigg (Eds.), *Aggressive behaviour.* New York: Wiley.

Laing, R. D. 1965. *The divided self.* New York: Penguin.

Landers, A. 1963. *Ann Landers talks to teenagers about sex.* New York: Prentice-Hall.

Lashley, K. S. 1951. The problem of serial order in behavior. In L. A. Jeffress (Ed.), *Cerebral mechanisms of behavior.* New York: Wiley.

Lashley, K. S. 1960. In search of the engram. In F. A. Beach, D. O. Hebb, C. T. Morgan, and H. W. Nissen (Eds.), *The neuropsychology of Lashley.* New York: McGraw-Hill.

Lashley, K. S., and McCarthy, D. A. 1926. The

survival of the maze habit after cerebellar injuries. *J. Comp. Physiol. Psychol.*, 6, 423–433.

Latané, B. 1966. Studies in social comparison. *J. Exp. Soc. Psychol.*, Suppl. 1.

Laurendeau, M., and Pinnard, A. 1963. *Causal thinking in the child: A genetic and experimental approach.* New York: International Universities Press.

LeBoeuf, B. J., and Peeke, H.V.S. 1969. The effect of strychnine administration during development on adult maze learning in the rat. *Psychopharmacologia,* 16, 49–53.

Lele, P. P., and Weddell, G. 1956. The relationship between neurohistology and corneal sensibility. *Brain,* 19, 119-154.

Lenneberg, E. H. 1962. Understanding language without ability to speak: A case report. *J. Abnorm. Soc. Psychol.,* 65, 419–425.

Lenneberg, E. H. 1967. *The biological foundations of language.* New York: Wiley. (By permission.)

Lester, O. P. 1932. Mental set in relation to retroactive inhibition. *J. Exp. Psychol.,* 15, 681–699.

Levinson, D., and Gallagher, E. 1964. *Patienthood in the mental hospital.* Boston: Houghton-Mifflin.

Lewin, K., Lippitt, R., and White, R. K. 1939. Patterns of aggressive behavior in experimentally created social climates. *J. Soc. Psychol.,* 10, 271–301.

Liddell, H. S. 1942. The conditioned reflex. In F. A. Moss (Ed.), *Comparative psychology.* Englewood Cliffs, N. J.: Prentice-Hall.

Lidz, T. 1963. *The family and human adaptation.* New York: International Universities Press.

Lindauer, M. 1961. *Communication among social bees.* Cambridge: Harvard University Press.

Lindsley, D. B. 1951. Emotion. In S. S. Stevens (Ed.), *Handbook of experimental psychology.* New York: Wiley.

Lindsley, D. B. 1958. The reticular system and perceptual discrimination. In H. H. Jasper (Ed.), *Reticular formation of the brain.* Boston: Little, Brown.

Lindsley, D. B., Bowden, J., and Magoun, H. W. 1949. Effect upon EEG of acute injury to the brain stem activating system. *Electroenceph. Clin. Neurophysiol.,* 1, 475–486.

Lindsley, D. B., Schreiner, L. H., Knowles, W. B., and Magoun, H. W. 1950. Behavioral and EEG changes following chronic brain stem lesions in the cat. *Electroenceph. Clin. Neurophysiol.,* 2, 483–498.

Lippitt, R. 1940. An experimental study of the effect of democratic and authoritarian group atmospheres. *Univ. Iowa Stud.,* 16(3), 43–198.

Lorenz, K. 1937. The companion in the bird's world. *Auk,* 54, 245–273.

Lorenz, K. 1952. *King Solomon's ring.* London: Methuen.

Lorenz, K. 1957. The nature of instinct. In C. H. Schiller (Ed.), *Instinctive behavior.* New York: International Universities Press. (By permission.)

Lorenz, K. 1969. Innate bases of learning. In K. Pribram (Ed.), *On the biology of learning.* New York: Harcourt, Brace and World. (By permission.)

Louttet, C. M. 1927. Reproductive behavior of the guinea pig. *J. Comp. Psychol.,* 7, 247–263.

Lovell, K. 1961. *The growth of mathematical and scientific concepts in children.* London: University of London Press.

Luh, C. W. 1922. The conditions of retention. *Psychol. Monogr.,* 31(3, Whole No. 142).

Lumsdaine, A. A., and Janis, I. L. 1953. Resistance to "counterpropaganda" produced by one-sided and two-sided "propaganda" presentations. *Publ. Opin. Quart.,* 17, 311–318.

Luria, A. L. 1968. *The mind of a mnemonist.* New York: Basic Books. (By permission.)

Luttges, M., Johnson, T., Buck, C., Holland, J., and McGaugh, J. L. 1966. An examination of "transfer of learning" by nucleic acid. *Science,* 151, 834–837.

Maccoby, E. 1966. *The development of sex differences.* Stanford: Stanford University Press.

Mackintosh, N. J. 1969. Comparative studies of reversal and probability of learning: Rats, birds, and fish. In R. M. Gilbert and N. S. Sutherland (Eds.), *Animal discrimination learning.* London: Academic Press.

Mackworth, N. H. 1950. *Researches in the measurement of human performance.* MRC Spec. Rpt. 268, HMSO. Reprinted 1961 in H. W. Sinaiko (Ed.), *Selected papers on human factor in the design and use of control systems.* New York: Dover.

MacNichol, E. F. 1964. Retinal mechanisms of color vision. *Vision Res.,* 4, 119–133.

Magoun, H. W. 1954. The ascending reticular

system and wakefulness. In J. F. Delafresnaye (Ed.), *Brain mechanisms and consciousness*. Oxford: Blackwell Scientific Publ. (By permission.)

Maier, S. F., Seligman, M.E.P., and Solomon, R. L. 1969. Pavlovian fear conditioning and learned helplessness: Effects on escape and avoidance behavior of (a) the CS-US contingency and (b) the independence of the US and voluntary responding. In B. Campbell and R. M. Church (Eds.), *Punishment and aversive behavior*. New York: Appleton-Century-Crofts.

Malmo, R. B. 1959. Activation: A neurophysiological dimension. *Psychol. Rev.*, 66, 367–386.

Mandler, G. 1964. The interruption of behavior. In D. Levine (Ed.), *Nebraska symposium on motivation*. Lincoln: University of Nebraska Press.

Masters, W. H., and Johnson, V. E. 1966. *Human sexual response*. Boston: Little, Brown.

Masters, W. M., and Johnson, V. E. 1970. *Human sexual inadequacy*. Boston: Little, Brown.

Max, L. W. 1935. An experimental study of the motor theory of consciousness. III. Action-current responses in deaf-mutes during sleep, sensory stimulation and dreams. *J. Comp. Psychol.*, 19, 335–338.

Mayer, J. 1955. Regulation of energy intake and the body weight. The glucostatic theory and the lipostatic hypothesis. *Ann. New York Acad. Sci.*, 63.

Mayer, J., and Marshall, N. B. 1956. Specificity of gold thioglucose for ventromedial hypothalamic lesions and hyperphagia. *Nature* (London), 178, 1399–1400.

McCammon, R. W. 1965. Are boys and girls maturing at earlier ages? *Amer. J. Publ. Health*, 55, 103–106.

McClelland, D. C., Atkinson, J. W., Clark, R. A., and Lowell, E. L. 1953. *The achievement motive*. New York: Appleton-Century-Crofts.

McConnell, J. V. 1962. Memory transfer through cannibalism in planarians. *J. Neuropsych.*, 3, 42–48.

McConnell, J. V. 1966. Comparative physiology: Learning in invertebrates. *Ann. Rev. Psychol.*, 28, 107–136.

McGaugh, J. L. 1966. Time-dependent processes in memory storage. *Science*, 153, 1351–1358.

McGaugh, J. L. 1967. Analyses of memory transfer and enhancement. *Proc. Amer. Phil. Soc.*, 111, 347–351.

McGaugh, J. L. 1968a. A multi-trace view of memory storage. In D. Bovet, F. Bovet-Nitti, and A. Oliverio (Eds.), *Recent advances on learning and retention*. Rome: Accademia Nazionale dei Lincei.

McGaugh, J. L. 1968b. Drug facilitation of memory and learning. In D. H. Efron et al. (Eds.), *Psychopharmacology: A review of progress*. PHS Publ. No. 1836, 891–904. Washington, D.C.: U.S. Government Printing Office.

McGaugh, J. L. 1969. Facilitation of memory storage processes. In S. Bogoch (Ed.), *The future of the brain sciences*. New York: Plenum Press.

McGaugh, J. L. Unpublished findings.

McGaugh, J. L., and Krivanek, J. 1970. Strychnine effects on discrimination learning in mice: Effects of dose and time of administration. *Physiol. Behav.*, 5, 798–803.

McGaugh, J. L., and Landfield, P. W. 1970. Delayed development of amnesia following electroconvulsive shock. *Physiol. Behav.*, 5, 1109–1113.

McGaugh, J. L., and Petrinovich, L. F. 1965. Effects of drugs on learning and memory. *Intern. Rev. Neurobiol.*, 8, 139–191.

McGill, T. E. (Ed.). 1965. *Readings in animal behavior*. New York: Holt, Rinehart and Winston.

McGraw, M. B. 1935. *Growth: A study of Johnny and Jimmy*. New York: D. Appleton-Century.

Mehler, J., and Carey, P. 1967. Role of surface and base structure in perception of sentences. *J. Verbal Learn. Verbal Behav.*, 6, 335–338.

Melton, A. W. 1963. Implication of short-term memory for a general theory of memory. *J. Verbal Learn. Verbal Behav.*, 2, 1–21.

Miles, R. 1959. Discrimination in the squirrel monkey as a function of deprivation and problem difficulty. *J. Exp. Psychol.*, 57, 15–19. (Copyright 1959 by the American Psychological Association, reproduced by permission.)

Milgram, S. 1965. Some conditions of obedience and disobedience to authority. *Human Relations*, 18, 57–76.

Miller, G. A. 1956. The magic number seven plus or minus two: Some limits on our capacity for processing information. *Psychol. Rev.*, 63, 81–97.

Miller, G. A., Galanter, E. H., and Pribram, K. H. 1960. *Plans and the structure of behavior*. New York: Holt.

Miller, N. E. 1948. Theory and experiment relating psychoanalytic displacement to stimulus-response generalization. *J. Abnorm. Soc. Psychol.*, 43, 155–178. (By permission.)

Miller, N. E. 1963. Some reflections on the law of effect produce a new alternative to drive reduction. In M. Jones (Ed.), *Nebraska symposium on motivation.* Lincoln: University of Nebraska Press.

Miller, N. E., and Banuazizi, A. 1968. Instrumental learning by curarized rats of a specific visceral response, intestinal or cardiac. *J. Comp. Physiol. Psychol.*, 65, 1–7. (Copyright 1968 by the American Psychological Association, reproduced by permission.)

Miller, N. E., and DiCara, L. V. 1968. Changes in heart rate instrumentally learned by curarized rats as avoidance responses. *J. Comp. Physiol. Psychol.*, 65, 8–12.

Miller, N. E., and Kessen, M. L. 1952. Reward effects of food via stomach fistual compared with those of food via mouth. *J. Comp. Physiol. Psychol.*, 45, 555–564.

Milner, B. 1964. Some effects of frontal lobectomy in man. In J. M. Warren and K. Akert (Eds.), *The frontal granular cortex and behavior.* New York: McGraw-Hill.

Milner, B. 1966. Amnesia following operation on the temporal lobes. In C.W.M. Whitty and O. L. Zangwill (Eds.), *Amnesia.* London: Butterworths. (By permission.)

Milner, B., and Taylor, L. B. 1969. Differential specialization of man's cerebral hemispheres: Evidence from temporal lobectomy and from commissure section. *Symposium on Cerebral Dominance,* 9th International Neurological Congress. New York, September 26.

Mitchell, G. D. 1969. Paternalistic behavior in primates. *Psychol. Bull.*, 71, 399–417.

Moltz, H., and Stettner, L. J. 1961. The influence of patterned light deprivation on the critical period for imprinting. *J. Comp. Physiol. Psychol.*, 54, 279–283.

Money, J. 1970. Determinants of human sexual behavior. In A. M. Freedman, H. I. Kaplan, and H. S. Kaplan (Eds.), *Comprehensive textbook of psychiatry* (2nd ed.). Baltimore: Williams and Wilkins.

Moon, L. E., and Harlow, H. F. 1955. Analysis of oddity learning by rhesus monkeys. *J. Comp. Physiol. Psychol.*, 48, 188–194.

Morgan, J.J.B., and Lovell, G.D. 1948. *The psychology of abnormal people.* New York: Longmans, Green.

Morrell, F. 1967. Electrical signs of sensory coding. In G. C. Quarton, T. Melnechuk, and F. O. Schmitt (Eds.), *The neurosciences.* New York: Rockefeller.

Morris, D. 1969. *The human zoo.* New York: McGraw-Hill. (By permission.)

Moruzzi, G., and Magoun, H. W. 1949. Brain stem reticular formation and activation of the EEG. *Electroenceph. Clin. Neurophysiol.*, 1, 455–473.

Moulton, R. W., Liberty, P. G., Jr., Burnstein, E., and Altucher, N. 1966. Patterning of parental affection and disciplinary dominance as a determinant of guilt and sex typing. *J. Personal. Soc. Psychol.*, 4, 356–363.

Mowrer, O. H. 1960. *Learning theory and the symbolic processes.* New York: Wiley.

Mueller, G. E., and Pilzecker, A. 1900. Experimentalle Beitrage zur Lehre vom Gedachtnis. *Z. Psychol.*, Suppl. 1, 1–288.

Murray, E. J. 1964. *Motivation and emotion.* Englewood Cliffs, N.J.: Prentice-Hall. (By permission.)

Murray, E. J. 1965. *Sleep, dreams, and arousal.* New York: Appleton-Century-Crofts. (By permission.)

Newcomb, T. M. 1961. *The acquaintance process.* New York: Holt, Rinehart and Winston.

Newell, A. 1968. On the analysis of human problem solving protocols. In J. C. Gardin and B. Jaulin (Eds.), *Calcăl et formalisation dans les sciences de l'homme.* Paris: Centre National de la Recherche Scientifique. (By permission.)

Newell, A., and Simon, H. A. 1963. GPS, a program that simulates human thought. In E. A. Feigenbaum and J. Feldman (Eds.), *Computers and thought.* New York: McGraw-Hill.

Newman, H. H., Freeman, F. N., and Holzinger, K. J. 1937. *Twins: A study of heredity and environment.* Chicago: University of Chicago Press.

Newman, J. R. 1956. Srinivasa Ramanujan. In J. R. Newman (Ed.), *The world of mathematics.* Vol. 1, Ch. 13. New York: Simon and Schuster.

Norman, D. A. 1969. *Memory and attention.* New York: Wiley.

Novikova, L. A. 1955. Electrophysiological investigation of speech. In *Vsesoiuznoe Soveshchanie po Voprosan Psikhologii* (3rd ed.). Moscow: Acad. Paed. Sci. of RSFSR. Reprinted 1961 in N. O'Connor (Ed.), *Recent Soviet psychology.* Oxford: Pergamon.

Olds, J. 1955. Physiological mechanisms of reward. In M. R. Jones (Ed.), *Nebraska symposium on motivation.* Vol. 3. Lincoln: University of Nebraska Press. (By permission.)

Olds, J., and Milner, P. 1954. Positive reinforcement produced by electrical stimulation of septal area and other regions of rat brain. *J. Comp. Physiol. Psychol.,* 47, 419–427.

Oliverio, A., and Bovet, D. 1966. Effects of age on maze learning and avoidance conditioning of mice. *Life Sci.,* 5, 1317–1324.

Osgood, C. E. 1952. The nature and measurement of meaning. *Psychol. Bull.,* 49, 197–237.

Oswald, I. 1966. *Sleep.* Baltimore: Penguin Books. (By permission.)

Oswald, I., Taylor, A. M., and Treisman, M. 1960. Discriminative responses to stimulation during human sleep. *Brain,* 83, 440–453.

Overton, D. A. 1964. State-dependent or "dissociated" learning produced with pentobarbital. *J. Comp. Physiol. Psychol.,* 57, 3–12.

Pavlov, I. P. 1927. *Conditioned reflexes.* London: Oxford University Press.

Pavlov, I. P. 1957. *Experimental psychology and other essays.* New York: Philosophical Library. (By permission.)

Peeke, H.V.S. 1969. Habituation of conspecific aggression in the three-spined stickleback (*Gasterosteus Aculeatus L.*). *Behaviour,* 35, 137–156. (By permission.)

Peele, T. L. 1954. *Neuroanatomy.* New York: McGraw-Hill. (By permission.)

Penfield, W. 1969. Consciousness, memory, and man's conditioned reflexes. In K. H. Pribram (Ed.), *On the biology of learning.* New York: Harcourt, Brace and World. (By permission.)

Penfield, W., and Jasper, H. 1954. *Epilepsy and the functional anatomy of the human brain.* Boston: Little, Brown. (By permission.)

Penfield, W., and Perot, P., 1963. The brain's record of auditory and visual experience—a final summary and discussion. *Brain,* 86, 595–696. (By permission.)

Penfield, W., and Rasmussen, T. 1950. *The cerebral cortex of man.* New York: Macmillan.

Penfield, W., and Roberts, L. 1959. *Speech and brain-mechanisms.* Princeton: Princeton University Press. (By permission.)

Peterson, L. R., and Peterson, M. J. 1959. Short term retention of individual verbal items. *J. Exp. Psychol.,* 58, 193–198. (Copyright 1959 by the American Psychological Association, reproduced by permission.)

Peterson, N. 1960. Control of behavior by presentation of an imprinted stimulus. *Science,* 132, 1395–1396.

Phillips, L. 1953. Case history data and prognosis in schizophrenia. *J. Nerv. Ment. Dis.,* 117, 515–525.

Piaget, J. 1967. *Six psychological studies.* New York: Random House.

Potter, S. 1960. *Language in the modern world.* Baltimore: Penguin Books.

Pratt, C. L., and Sackett, G. P. 1967. Selection of social partners as a function of peer contact during rearing. *Science,* 155, 1133–1135. (Copyright 1967 by the American Association for the Advancement of Science, by permission.)

Premack, D. 1970. The education of Sarah. *Psychol. Today,* 4, 54–58.

Preyer, W. 1882. *Die seele des kindes.* Leipzig: Fernau.

Pribram, K. H. 1954. Toward a science of neuropsychology (method and data). In R. A. Patton (Ed.), *Current trends in psychology and the behavioral sciences.* Pittsburgh: University of Pittsburgh Press.

Pribram, K. H. 1962. Interrelations of psychology and the neurological disciplines. In S. Koch (Ed.), *Psychology: A study of a science.* Vol. 4. New York: McGraw-Hill.

Pribram, K. H., Ahumada, A., Hartog, J., and Roos, L. 1964. A progress report on the neurological processes disturbed by frontal lesions in primates. In J. M. Warren and K. Akert (Eds.), *The frontal granular cortex and behavior.* New York: McGraw-Hill.

Prisko, L. H. 1963. Short-term memory in focal cerebral damage. (Doctoral thesis, McGill University) Montreal, Canada. (By permission.)

Radke, M., and Sutherland, J. 1949. Children's concepts and attitudes about minority and majority American groups. *J. Educ. Psychol.,* 40, 449–468.

Ramsey, G. V. 1943. The sexual development of boys. *Amer. J. Psychol.,* 56, 217–233.

Rank, O. 1952. *The trauma of birth.* New York: Basic Books.

Reiff, R., and Scheerer, M. 1959. *Memory and hypnotic age regression.* New York: International Universities Press.

Rescorla, R. A., and LoLordo, V. M. 1965. Inhibition of avoidance behavior. *J. Comp. Physiol. Psychol.,* 59, 406–412.

Rheingold, H. L., and Eckerman, C. O. 1970.

The infant separates himself from his mother. *Science*, 168, 78–83.

Richter, C. P. 1942–43. Total self-regulatory functions in animals and human beings. *Harvey Lect.*, 38, 63–103.

Richter, C. P. 1967. Sleep and activity. Their relation to the 24-hour clock. In S. S. Kety, E. V. Evarts, and H. L. Williams (Eds.) *Sleep and altered states of consciousness.* Ch. 2. Baltimore: Williams and Wilkins. (By permission.)

Ridgway, S. H., Flanigan, N. J., and McCormick, J. G. 1966. Brain-spinal cord ratios in porpoises: Possible correlations with intelligence and ecology. *Psychon. Sci.*, 6, 491–492.

Riesen, A. 1950. Arrested vision. *Scient. Amer.*, 183, 16–19.

Riggs, L. A., Ratliff, F., Cornsweet, J. C., and Cornsweet, T. N. 1953. The disappearance of steadily fixated visual test objects. *J. Opt. Soc. Amer.*, 43, 495–501.

Riopelle, A. J., Alper, R. G., Strong, P. N., and Ades, H. W. 1953. Multiple discrimination and patterned string performance of normal and temporal-lobectomized monkeys. *J. Comp. Physiol. Psychol.*, 46, 145–149.

Ritchie, B. F., Aeschliman, B., and Pierce, P. 1950. Studies in spatial learning. VIII. Place performance and the acquisition of place disposition. *J. Comp. Physiol. Psychol.*, 43, 73–85.

Robson, K. S., and Moss, H. A. Bethesda, Maryland: Child Research Branch, National Institute of Mental Health. Unpublished findings.

Roe, A. 1952. *The making of a scientist.* New York: Dodd, Mead.

Romanes, G. J. 1895. *Animal intelligence.* New York: D. Appleton.

Rosenblith, J. F. 1949. A replication of "some roots of prejudice." *J. Abnorm. Soc. Psychol.*, 44, 470–489.

Roth, P. 1969. *Portnoy's complaint.* New York: Random House.

Rothenbuhler, W. C. 1964. Behavior genetics of nest cleaning in honey bees. IV. Responses of F_1 and backcross generations to disease-killed brook. *Amer. Zool.*, 4, 111–123.

Rowland, V. 1957. Differential electroencephalographic response to conditioned auditory stimuli in arousal from sleep. *Electroenceph. Clin. Neurophysiol.*, 9, 585–594.

Rushton, W.A.H. 1961. The cone pigments of the human fovea in colour blind and normal. In *Visual problem of color.* New York: Chemical Publ.

Rushton, W.A.H. 1962. The retinal organization of vision in vertebrates. *Biological receptor mechanisms.* Number XVI. Symposia Soc. Exp. Biol. Cambridge: Cambridge University Press. (By permission.)

Russell, W. R., and Nathan, P. W. 1946. Traumatic amnesia. *Brain*, 69, 280–300.

Sackett, G. P. 1966. Monkeys reared in visual isolation with pictures as visual input: Evidence for an innate releasing mechanism. *Science*, 154, 1468–1472.

Salk, L. 1960. Effects of the normal heartbeat sound on the behavior of the newborn infant: Implications for mental health. *World Mental Health*, 12, 168–175.

Saranson, S. B. 1960. *Anxiety in elementary school children: A report of research by Seymour B. Saranson and others.* New York: Wiley.

Schachter, S. 1959. *The psychology of affiliation.* Stanford: Stanford University Press. (By permission of the publisher. Copyright © 1959 by the Board of Trustees of the Leland Stanford Junior University.)

Schaffer, H. R., and Emerson, P. E. 1964a. The development of social attachments in infancy. *Monogr. Soc. Res. Child Devel.*, 29(3), 1–77.

Schaffer, H. R., and Emerson, P. E. 1964b. Patterns of response to physical contact in early human development. *J. Child Psychol. Psych.*, 5, 1–13.

Schaltenbrand, G., and Woolsey, C. N. (Eds.). 1964. *Cerebral localization and organization.* Madison: University of Wisconsin Press. (Copyright © 1964 by the Regents of the University of Wisconsin, by permission.)

Schapiro, S., and Vukovich, K. R. 1970. Early experience effects upon cortical dendrites. A proposed model for development. *Science*, 167, 292–294.

Scheff, T. J. 1966. *Being mentally ill: A sociological theory.* Chicago: Aldine.

Schildkraut, J. J., and Kety, S. S. 1967. Biogenic amines and emotion. *Science*, 156, 21–30.

Schlosberg, H. 1954. Three dimensions of emotion. *Psychol. Rev.*, 61, 81–88.

Scott, J. P. 1962. Critical periods in behavioral development. *Science*, 138, 949–958.

Searle, L. V. 1949. The organization of hereditary maze-brightness and maze-dullness. *Genetic Psychol. Monogr.*, 39, 279–325.

Sears, R. R., Maccoby, E. E., and Levin. H. 1957. *Patterns of child rearing.* Evenston, Ill.: Row, Peterson.

Sears, R. R., Whiting, J.W.M., Nowlis, V., and Sears, P. S. 1953. Some child rearing antecedents of aggression and dependency in young children. *Genetic Psychol. Monogr.,* 47, 135–234.

Shandro, N. E., and Schaeffer, B. 1969. Environment and strychnine: Effects on maze behavior. Paper presented at Western Psychol. Assn. Meeting, Vancouver, B.C.

Sharpless, S. K., and Jasper, H. 1956. Habituation of the arousal reaction. *Brain, 79,* 655–680. (By permission.)

Shashoua, V. 1968. RNA changes in goldfish brain during learning. *Nature,* 217, 238–240.

Sheffield, F. D., and Roby, T. B. 1950. Reward value of a non-nutritive sweet taste. *J. Comp. Physiol. Psychol.,* 43, 471–481.

Sheffield, F. D., Wulff, J. J., and Backer, R. 1951. Reward value of copulation without sex drive reduction. *J. Comp. Physiol. Psychol.,* 44, 3–8.

Shields, J. 1962. *Monozygotic twins.* London: Oxford University Press.

Sholl, D. A. 1956. *The organization of the cerebral cortex.* London: Methuen. (By permission.)

Singer, J. L. 1966. *Daydreaming.* New York: Random House.

Singer, J. L. 1968. The importance of daydreaming. *Psychology Today,* April 1, 18–27. (By permission.)

Skinner, B. F. 1938. *The behavior of organisms: An experimental analysis.* New York: Appleton-Century-Crofts. (Copyright 1938, 1966, reprinted by permission of the publisher.)

Skinner, B. F. 1950. Are theories of learning necessary? *Psychol. Rev.,* 57, 193–216. (Copyright 1950 by the American Psychological Assocation, reproduced by permission.)

Skinner, B. F. 1957. *Verbal behavior.* New York: Appleton-Century-Crofts.

Slobin, D. I. 1968. Imitation and grammatical development in children. In N. S. Endler, L. R. Boulter, and H. Osser (Eds.), *Contemporary issues—developmental psychology.* New York: Holt, Rinehart and Winston.

Sluckin, W. 1965. *Imprinting and early learning.* Chicago: Aldine.

Smith, C. P., and Feld, S. 1958. Appendix I. How to learn the method of content analysis for n achievement, n affiliation and n power. In J. W. Atkinson (Ed.), *Motives in fantasy, action, and society.* Princeton: Van Nostrand. (Copyright © 1958 by Litton Educational Publishing, Inc., by permission of the publisher.)

Smith, D.B.D., Donchin, E., Cohen, L., and Starr, A. 1970. Auditory averaged evoked potentials in man during selective binaural listening. *Electroenceph. Clin. Neurophysiol.,* 28, 146–152. (By permission.)

Smith, S. M., Brown, H. O., Toman, J.E.P., and Goodman, L. S. 1947. The lack of cerebral effects of *d*-tubocurarine. *Anesthesiology,* 8, 1–14. (By permission.)

Sokolov, Y. N. 1963. *Perception and the conditioned reflex.* New York: Pergamon.

Southwick, C. H., Beg, M. A., and Siddigi, M. R. 1965. Rhesus monkeys in north India. In I. DeVore (Ed.), *Primate behavior: Field studies of monkeys and apes.* New York: Holt, Rinehart and Winston.

Spalding, D. A. 1873. Instinct, with original observations on young animals. *Macmillan's Mag.,* 27, 282–293. Reprinted 1954 in *Brit. J. Animal Behav.,* 2, 2–11.

Spence, K. W. 1938. Gradual versus sudden solution of discrimination problems by chimpanzees. *J. Comp. Psychol.,* 25, 213–224.

Spencer, H. 1873. *The principles of psychology.* New York: D. Appleton-Century.

Sperling, G. 1960. The information available in brief visual presentations. *Psychol. Monogr.,* 74(11), 1–29. (Copyright 1960 by the American Psychological Associaton, reproduced by permission.)

Sperry, R. W. 1968. Psychobiology and vice versa. *Eng. Sci. Mag.,* 32, 53–61. (By permission.)

Spiegel, J. P., and Bell, N. W. 1959. The family of the psychiatric patient. In S. Arieti (Ed.), *American handbook of psychiatry.* New York: Basic Books.

Spitz, R. A. 1945. Hospitalism: An inquiry into the genesis of psychiatric conditions in early childhood. In *The psychoanalytic study of the child.* Vol. I. New York: International Universities Press.

Spitz, R. A. 1964a. Anaclitic depression. In *The psychoanalytic study of the child.* Vol. II. New York: International Universities Press.

Spitz, R. A. 1946b. Hospitalism: A follow-up report. In *The psychoanalytic study of the child.* Vol. II. New York: International Universities Press.

Spitz, R. A. 1950. Anxiety in infancy: A study of its manifestations in the first year of life. *Intern. J. Psycho-Anal.*, 31, 138–143.

Spuhler, J. N., and Lindzey, G. 1967. Racial differences in behavior. In J. Hirsch (Ed.), *Behavior genetic analysis.* New York: McGraw-Hill.

Stevens, S. S. 1961. The psychophysics of sensory function. In W. A. Rosenblith (Ed.), *Sensory communication.* Ch. 1. Cambridge: MIT Press. (By permission.)

Stevens, S. S., and Davis, H. 1938. *Hearing.* New York: Wiley.

Strumwasser, F. 1965. The demonstration and manipulation of a circadian rhythm in a single neuron. In J. Aschoff (Ed.), *Circadian clocks.* Amsterdam: North-Holland. (By permission.)

Suedfeld, P. 1967. Paternal absence and overseas success of Peace Corps volunteers. *J. Consult. Psychol.*, 31, 424–425.

Suomi, S. J. 1968. The effect of differential exposure on attraction toward individuals. (Undergraduate honors thesis, Stanford University) Stanford, Calif.

Suomi, S. J., Harlow, H. F., and Lewis, J. K. 1970. Effect of bilateral frontal lobectomy on social preferences of rhesus monkeys. *J. Comp. Physiol. Psychol.*, 70, 448–453. (Copyright 1970 by the American Psychological Association, reproduced by permission.)

Sutherland, N. S. 1968. Outlines of a theory of visual pattern recognition in animals and man. *Proc. Roy. Soc. B.*, 171, 297–317.

Svaetichin, G., Laufer, M., Mitarai, G., Fatehchand, R., Vallecalle, E., and Villegas, J. 1961. Glial control of neuronal networks and receptors. In R. Jung and H. Kornhuber (Eds.), *The visual system: Neurophysiology and psychophysics.* Berlin: Springer.

Tanner, J. M. 1962. *Growth at adolescence* (2nd ed.). Oxford: Blackwell Scientific Publ.

Tanner, J. M., Healy, M.J.R., Lockhart, R. D. MacKenzie, J. D., and Whitehouse, P. H. 1956. Aberdeen growth study. I. The prediction of adult body measurements from measurements taken each year from birth to five years. *Arch. Dis. in Child.*, 31, 372–381.

Tasaki, I., and Davis, H. 1955. Electric responses of individual nerve elements in cochlear nucleus to sound stimulation (guinea pig). *J. Neurophysiol.*, 18, 151–158.

Taylor, C. W. (Ed.). 1964. *Creativity: Progress and potential.* New York: McGraw-Hill.

Teitelbaum, P. 1961. Disturbances in feeding and drinking behavior after hypothalamic lesions. In M. R. Jones (Ed.), *Nebraska symposium on motivation.* Vol. 9. Lincoln: University of Nebraska Press. (By permission.)

Teitelbaum, P. 1964. Appetite. *Proc. Amer. Phil. Soc.*, 108, 464–472. (By permission.)

Terman, L. M. 1916. *The measurement of intelligence.* Boston: Houghton-Mifflin.

Terman, L. M. 1925. *Mental and physical traits of a thousand gifted children, genetic studies of genius.* I. Stanford: Stanford University Press.

Terman, L. M., and Merrill, M. A. 1937. *Measuring intelligence.* Boston: Houghton-Mifflin.

Terman, L. M., and Oden, M. H. 1947. *The gifted child grows up, genetic studies of genius.* IV. Stanford: Stanford University Press.

Terman, L. M., and Oden, M. H. 1959. *The gifted group at mid-life, genetic studies of genius.* V. Stanford: Stanford University Press.

Terman, L. M., and Merrill, M. A. 1960. *The Stanford-Binet intelligence scale.* Boston: Houghton-Mifflin.

Thompson, R. F. 1967. *Foundations of physiological psychology.* New York: Harper and Row. (By permission.)

Thompson, R. F. 1969. Neurophysiology and thought: The neural substrates of thinking. In J. F. Voss (Ed.), *Approaches to thought.* Columbus, Ohio: Charles E. Merrill.

Thompson, R. F., and Spencer, W. A. 1966. Habituation: A model phenomenon for the study of neuronal substrates of behavior. *Psychol. Rev.*, 173, 16–43.

Thompson, R. F., Mayers, K. S., Robertson, R. T., and Patterson, C. J. 1970. Number coding in association cortex of the cat. *Science*, 168, 271–273. (Copyright 1970 by the American Association for the Advancement of Science, by permission.)

Thompson, T. I. 1963. Visual reinforcement in Siamese fighting fish. *Science*, 141, 55–57.

Thorndike, E. L. 1932. *The fundamentals of learning.* New York: Teachers College.

Thrope, W. H. 1963. *Learning and instinct in animals.* London: Methuen.

Tinbergen, N. 1951. *The study of instinct.* Oxford: Clarendon Press.

Tichener, E. B. 1908. Lecture V. In *Lectures on the elementary psychology of feeling and attention.* New York: Macmillan.

Abridged 1966 as Ch. 2, Attention as sensory clearness. In P. Bakan (Ed.), *Attention.* Princeton: D. Van Nostrand.

Tobias, P. V. 1970. Brain-size, grey matter, and race—fact or fiction? *Amer. J. Physiol. Anthropol.,* 32, 3–26. (By permission.)

Tolman, E. C. 1932. *Purposive behavior in animals and men.* New York: Appleton-Century-Crofts.

Tolman, E. C., and Honzik, C. M. 1930. Introduction and removal of reward and maze performance in rats. *Univ. Calif. Publ. in Psychol.,* 4, 257–275. (Originally published by the University of California Press; reprinted by permission of the Regents of the University of California.)

Tolman, E. C., Ritchie, B. F., and Kalish, D. 1946. Studies in spatial learning. II. Place learning versus response learning. *J. Exp. Psychol.,* 36, 221–229.

Treisman, A. M. 1964. Selective attention in man. *Brit. Med. Bull.,* 20, 12–16.

Truex, R. C., and Carpenter, M. B. 1964. *Strong and Elwyn's human neuroanatomy* (5th ed.). Baltimore: Williams and Wilkins. (By permission.)

Tryon, R. C. 1940. Genetic differences in maze learning. *Yrbk. Nat. Soc. Study of Educ.,* 39, 36–37.

Tryon, R. C. 1942. Individual differences. In F. A. Moss (Ed.), *Comparative psychology.* New York: Prentice-Hall. (By permission.)

Tuddenham, R. D. 1962. The nature and measurement of intelligence. In L. Postman (Ed.), *Psychology in the making.* New York: Knopf. (Copyright 1962, reproduced by permission of the publisher.)

Tuddenham, R. D., and MacBride, P. D. 1959. The yielding experiment from the subject's point of view. *J. Personal.,* 27, 259–271. (By permission.)

Tulving, E. 1969. Retrograde amnesia in free recall. *Science,* 164, 88–90.

Tunturi, A. R. 1944. Audio-frequency localization in the acoustic cortex of the dog. *Amer. J. Physiol.,* 141, 397–403.

Tunturi, A. R. 1952. A difference in the representation of auditory signals for the left and right ears in the iso-frequency contours of the right middle ectosylvian cortex of the dog. *Amer. J. Physiol.,* 168, 712–727. (By permission.)

Turing, A. M. 1950. Computing machinery and intelligence. *Mind,* 59, 433–460.

Underwood, B. J. 1952. Studies of distributed practice. VII. Learning and retention of serial nonsense lists as a function of intralist similarity. *J. Exp. Psychol.,* 44, 80–87.

Underwood, B. J. 1953a. Studies of distributed practice. VIII. Learning and retention of paired nonsense syllables as a function of intralist similarity. *J. Exp. Psychol.,* 45, 133–142.

Underwood, B. J. 1953b. Studies of distributed practice. IX. Learning and retention of paired adjectives as a function of intralist similarity. *J. Exp. Psychol.,* 45, 143–149.

Underwood, B. J. 1953c. Studies of distributed practice. X. The influence of intralist similarity on learning and retention of serial adjective lists. *J. Exp. Psychol.,* 45, 253–259.

Underwood, B. J. 1957. Interference and forgetting. *Psychol. Rev.,* 64, 49–60. (Copyright 1957 by the American Psychological Association, reproduced by permission.)

Underwood, B. J., and Richardson, J. 1955. Studies of distributed practice. XIII. Interlist interference and the retention of serial nonsense lists. *J. Exp. Psychol.,* 50, 39–46.

Ungar, G. 1970. Chemical transfer of learned information. In W. L. Byrne (Ed.), *Molecular approaches to learning and memory.* New York: Academic Press.

Valins, S. 1966. Cognitive effects of false heart-rate feedback. *J. Personal. Soc. Psychol.,* 4, 400–408.

Valins, S., and Ray, A. A. 1967. Effects of cognitive desensitization on avoidance behavior. *J. Personal. Soc. Psychol.,* 7, 345–350.

Van de Greer, J. P., and Jaspars, J.M.F. 1966. Cognitive functions. *Ann. Rev. Psychol.,* 17, 145–176.

Vandenberg, S. G. 1967. Hereditary factors in normal personality traits (as measured by inventories). In J. Wortis (Ed.), *Recent advances in biological psychiatry.* Vol. 9. New York: Plenum Press.

Vandenberg, S. G. 1968a. Primary mental abilities or general intelligence? Evidence from twin studies. In J. M. Thoday and A. S. Parkes (Eds.), *Genetic and environmental influences on behavior.* Edinburgh: Oliver and Boyd.

Vandenberg, S. G. 1968b. The nature and nurture of intelligence. In D. C. Glass (Ed.), *Genetics.* New York: Rockefeller University Press and Russell Sage Foundation.

Van Lawick-Goodall, J. 1967. Motor-offspring relationships in free-ranging chimpanzees. In D. Morris (Ed.), *Primate ethology*. Chicago: Aldine.

Van Ormer, E. B. 1932. Retention after intervals of sleep and of waking. *Arch. Psychol.*, No. 137.

van Vogt, A. E. 1940. *Slan.* New York: Simon and Schuster.

Van Wagenen, G. 1950. The monkey. In E. J. Farris (Ed.), *The care and breeding of laboratory animals.* New York: Wiley.

von Békésy, G. 1947. The variation of phase along the basilar membrane with sinusoidal vibrations. *J. Acoust. Soc. Amer.*, 19, 452–460. (By permission.)

von Békésy, G. 1956. Current status of theories of hearing. *Science*, 123, 779–783.

von Buddenbrock, W. 1958. *The senses.* Ann Arbor: University of Michigan Press. (By permission.)

Von Frisch, K. 1953. *The dancing bees.* New York: Harcourt, Brace. (By permission of the publisher.)

Waisman, H. A., and Harlow, H. F. 1965. Experimental phenylketonuria in monkeys. *Science,* 147, 685–695.

Walk, R. D., and Gibson, E. J. 1961. A comparative and analytical study of visual depth perception. *Psychol. Monogr.*, 75, 44. (Copyright 1961 by the American Psychological Association, reproduced by permission.)

Walster, E., Aronson, V., Abrams, D., and Rottman, L. 1966. Importance of physical attractiveness in dating behavior. *J. Personal. Soc. Psychol.*, 4, 508–516.

Warren, J. M. 1965. Primate learning in comparative perspective. In A. M. Schrier, H. F. Harlow, and F. Stallnitz (Eds.), *Behavior of nonhuman primates.* Vol. 1. New York: Academic Press. (By permission.)

Washburn, S. L. 1963. The study of race. *Amer. Anthropol.*, 65, 521–531. (Reproduced by permission of the American Anthropological Association.)

Washburn, S. L., and DeVore, I. 1961. Social behavior of baboons and early man. In S. L. Washburn (Ed.), *Social life of early man.* Chicago: Aldine.

Watson, J. B., and Rayner, R. 1920. Conditioned emotional reactions. *J. Exp. Psychol.*, 3, 1–14.

Wechsler, D. 1958. *The measurement and appraisal of adult intelligence* (4th ed.). Baltimore: Williams and Wilkins.

Weinberger, N. M., Goodman, D. A., and Kitzes, L. M. 1969. Is behavioral habituation a function of peripheral auditory system blockade? *Commun. Behav. Biol.*, 3, 111–116.

Weinberger, N. M., and Lindsley, D. B. 1964. Behavioral and electroencephalic arousal to contrasting novel stimuli. *Science,* 144, 1355–1357.

Weiss, W., and Margolium, G. 1954. The effect of context stimuli on learning and retention. *J. Exp. Psychol.*, 48, 318–322.

Welker, W. I. 1956. Some determinants of play and exploration in chimpanzees. *J. Comp. Physiol. Psychol.*, 49, 84–89. (Copyright 1956 by the American Psychological Association, reproduced by permission.)

Wenner, A. M. 1964. Sound communication in honey bees. *Scient. Amer.*, 210, 116–124.

Werner, G., and Mountcastle, V. B. 1968. Quantitative relations between mechanical stimuli to the skin and neural responses evoked by them. In D. R. Kenshalo (Ed.), *The skin senses.* Ch. 6. Springfield, Ill.: Charles C. Thomas.

Wever, E. G., and Bray, C. W. 1930. The nature of acoustic response: The relation between sound frequency and frequency of impulses in the auditory nerve. *J. Exp. Psychol.*, 13, 373–387.

White, B. L., and Held, R. 1966. Plasticity of sensorimotor development in the human infant. In J. Rosenblith and W. Allinsmith (Eds.), *The causes of behavior.* II. Boston: Allyn and Bacon.

White, W. A. 1926. *Outlines of psychiatry.* New York: Nervous and Mental Disease Publ. Co.

Whitty, C.W.M., and Zangwill, O. L. (Eds.). 1966. *Amnesia.* London: Butterworths.

Wicklegren, W. A. 1965. Acoustic similarity and retroactive interference in short term memory. *J. Verbal Learn. Verbal Behav.*, 4, 53–61.

Williams, M. 1950. The effects of experimentally induced needs upon retention. *J. Exp. Psychol.*, 40, 139–151.

Wolpe, J., and Lazarus, A. A. 1968. *Behavior therapy techniques.* New York: Pergamon.

Woolf, L. I., Griffiths, R., Montcrieff, A., Coates, S., and Dillistone, F. 1958. Dietary treatment of phenylketonuria. *Arch. Dis. Child.*, 33, 31.

Woolsey, C. N. 1958. Organization of somatic

sensory and motor areas of the cerebral cortex. In H. F. Harlow and C. N. Woolsey (Eds.), *Biological and biochemical bases of behavior.* Madison: University of Wisconsin Press. (By permission.)

Worden, F. G., and Marsh, J. T. 1963. Amplitude changes of auditory potentials evoked at cochlear nucleus during acoustic habituation. *Electroenceph. Clin. Neurophysiol.,* 16, 866–881.

Wyckoff, L. B. 1952. The role of observing responses in discrimination learning. *Psychol. Rev.,* 59, 431–441.

Wyers, E. J., Peeke, H.V.S., Williston, J. S., and Herz, M. J. 1968. Retroactive impairment of passive avoidance learning by stimulation of the caudate nucleus. *Exp. Neurol.,* 22, 35–36.

Wyrwicka, W., Sterman, M. B., and Clemente, C. O. 1962. Conditioning of induced electroencephalographic sleep patterns in the cat. *Science,* 137, 616–618.

Yarrow, L. L., and Goodwin, M. S. 1960. Effects of change in mother-figure during infancy. Unpublished manuscript.

Yerkes, R. M. (Ed.). 1921. Psychological examining in the U.S. Army. *Memoirs of the Nat. Acad. Sci.,* No. 15.

Youtz, A. C. 1941. An experimental evaluation of Jost's laws. *Psychol. Monogr.,* 53(1, Whole No. 238).

Zemp, J. W., Willson, J. E., Schlesinger, K., Boggan, W. O., and Glassman, E. 1966. Brain function and macromolecules. I. Incorporation of uridine into mouse brain during short-term training experience. *Proc. Natl. Acad. Sci.,* 55, 1423–1431.

Zener, K. 1937. The significance of behavior accompanying conditioned salivary secretion for theories of the conditioned response. *Amer. J. Psychol.,* 50, 384–403. (By permission.)

Zornetzer, S., and McGaugh, J. L. 1970. Effects of frontal brain electroshock stimulation on EEG activity and memory in rats: Relationship to ECS-produced retrograde amnesia. *J. Neurobiol.,* 1, 379–394.

INDEX

NOTE   *Pages on which terms are defined are indicated in blue.*

physical, 22–23
principles of, 19–21
Developmental process, 19 (*see also* development)
DeVore, I., 52, 432, 434
Dewey, J., 74
DiCara, L., 8
Differentiation (*see also* development)
in development, 20
Digit span, 317–318, 350
Disattachment and environmental exploration, stage of, 68–69
Discrimination
and attention, 239–240
oddity, 307, 379–380
of depth, 30–31
of pitch, 198
of size, 30–31
visual, 289
Dissociation, 445, 447–448
Dopamine, 171–172 (*see also* biogenic amines)
Down's syndrome, 141 (*see also* mongolism)
Drachman, D., 313, 318
Dreaming, 228–233 (*see also* arousal, sleep)
Drinking (*see* thirst)
Drive theory, 266–268
Drugs, 173 (*see also* psychopharmacology, psychotherapeutics)
addiction to, 179–180
classes of, 174
effects on behavior, 173–180
Dunlop, C., 245
Ear, structure of, 199–208 (*see also* audition)
Eason, R., 247
Ebbinghaus, H., 284, 327, 332
Eccles, J., 111
Eckerman, C., 68–69
Ectoderm, 22
Ego defense, 445
Eidetic imagery, 315 (*see also* memory)
Eichenwald, H., 354
Einstein, A., 364, 374
Eisenstein, E., 303
Electroconvulsive shock, 320–321
Electroencephalogram (EEG), 147–149, 154, 170, 384
and arousal, 223–227
and habituation, 236–237
and memory, 338–340
and the orienting reflex, 244
and sleep, 222–226
Elias, J., 91
Embryo, 22
Emerson, P., 61, 68, 109, 442
Empiricist, 27
Emotions, differentiation of, 108, 113 (*see also* galvanic skin response)
Endoderm, 22

Engram, 165, 335
Epigenesis, 20 (*see also* development)
Erikson, E., 51, 75, 437, 444
Erlenmeyer-Kimling, L., 355
Evoked potentials
and attention, 245–247
and habituation, 245–247
and memory, 338–339
human, 246–247
Excitation, 154, 165 (*see also* neuron)
Excitatory postsynaptic potential (EPSP), 167–168, 170
Experimental method, 10, 12–14
Exploration, 83
Extinction, 286
Eye (*see also* vision)
retina of, 188–190
structure of, 190

Family constellation, 442
Fantz, R., 32
Farrell, B., 178
Fear, 84, 95, 106–107, 108–112, 432 (*see also* anxiety)
as adaptive, 112
counterconditioning of, 111
learned, 110–111
Feeding (*see* hunger)
Feld, S., 274
Fernandez de Molina, A., 255
Feshback, S., 426–427
Festinger, L., 275, 414–416
Fetus, 22
Field studies, 10
Fishbein, W., 325
Fixation, 44
Flavell, J., 38
Flight, 252
Flynn, J., 256
Forgetting, 331 (*see* memory)
Formal operations, stage of, 38
Fox, B., 325
France, A., 353
Frank, G., 442
Fraser, C., 40
Freedman, L., 328
French, G., 386
Freud, S., 14, 45, 51, 75, 109, 118, 228–229, 268, 371–372, 438
Fry, P., 354
Galen, 3
Galileo, 12–13
Galton, F., 124, 126, 348
Galvanic skin response (GSR), 407–408
Gametes, 133
Garcia, J., 292–293
Gardner, B., 391–393